Contents

Contributing Résumé Writers

Thank you to all of the writers who contributed to this edition. For complete contact information on any of these résumé writers, search by their last name at the website for the National Résumé Writers Association (www.thenrwa.com).

Marcia Baker	resumes@markofsuccess.net	Pages 118–119, 271
Dawn S. Bugni, CPRW	dawn@write-solution.com	Pages 50–51, 216–217, 240–241
Tawana Carter	tawana@tcbsolutions.net	Page 160
Beth Colley, CERW, CPRW, CSJFT	resume@chesres.com	Pages 126–127, 377–379
Betty Corrado, ACRW, CJSS	bacorrado@optonline.net	Pages 146–147
Jean Cummings, MAT, CPRW, CPBS, CEIP	jc@yesresumes.com	Pages 282–285
Norine Dagliano, NCRW, CFRW/CC, CPRW	norine@ekminspirations.com	Pages 60–61, 194, 246–247, 264–265
Kirsten Dixson, CJCTC, RCPBS	kirsten@kirstendixson.com	Pages 334–340, 342–343
M. J. Feld, MS, CPRW	mj@careersbychoice.com	Page 220
Cindy Funkhouser, CPRW	onlineeditor.biz@gmail.com	Page 130
Louise Garver, CPRW, JCTC, CCMC, CPBS	louisegarver@cox.net	Pages 140–141, 174, 212–213
Sharon Green	resource56@cox.net	Page 272
Ryon Harms	ryonharms@gmail.com	Page 349
Jennifer Hay	jhay@ITresumeservice.com	Pages 116–117, 228–229, 409
Phyllis Houston	phyllis_houston@msn.com	Pages 206–207, 372
Sandra Ingemansen, CPRW	singemansen@gmail.com	Pages 64–65, 100–101
Diane J. Irwin, CPRW, PHR	dynamicresumes@comcast.net	Pages 76–77, 187
Suzette Jolly, CPRW, MS, JCTC	jolly.suzette1@gmail.com	Page 272
Barbara Kanney	bkanney@abcdocuments.com	Page 387
Justin Keaton, CPRW	jkeaton@jfscolumbus.org	Pages 74–75
Jeanne Knight, JCTC, CCMC	jeanne@careerdesigns.biz	Pages 218–219
Myriam-Rose Kohn, CBPS, CCM, CPRW, CJSS	myriam-rose@jedaenterprises.com	Pages 136–137, 290–292, 380–382, 407
Ginger Korljan, M.Ed., NCRW, CCMC	ginger@takechargecoaching.com	Pages 150–151, 154–155, 238–239, 405
Lorie Lebert, CPRW, IJCTC, CCMC	lorie@resumeroi.com	Page 260
Violet Nikolici Lowrey, MBA, CPRW	violet@violetonresumes.com	Pages 286–287, 326
Jasmine Marchong	jmarchong@therightresume.biz	Pages 99, 192, 228–229, 403
Debra Mills, CPRW	dmills@pro-cv.co.uk	Pages 404, 408
Dr. Cheryl Minnick, NCRW, Ed.D.	cminnick@mso.umt.edu	Page 183
Kim Mohiuddin, NCRW	kim@movinonupresumes.com	Pages 252–253, 274–275
Laurie Mortenson, CCMC, M.Ed.	connect@legworkresumes.com	Pages 78–79, 86–87, 98–99
Melanie Noonan, CPS	peripro1@aol.com	Pages 167, 170, 195, 256–257, 327, 400
Debra O'Reilly, CPRW, JCTC, CEIP, CFRWC	debra@resumewriter.com	Pages 208–209
Jean Whalen Raymond, CPRW	jraymond@highland-training.com	Pages 262–263
Jared Redick	jredick@theresumestudio.com	Pages 204–205, 258, 278–279, 401–402
Michelle A. Riklan, CPRW, CEIC	michelle@riklanresources.com	Pages 304–305
Edie Rische, JCTC, ACCC, CPBS, CPBA	earische@suddenlink.net	Pages 386, 388
Alexia Scott, CPRW	resumes@alexiasdesktop.com	Pages 234–235, 250–251
Tammy K. Shoup, CPRW	awordpro@aol.com	Pages 330–331
Laura Smith-Proulx, CCMC, CPRW, CIC	laura@anexpertresume.com	Page 403
Marjorie Sussman, MRW, ACRW, CPRW	marjorie1130@aol.com	Pages 175, 276–277
Michelle P. Swanson, CPRW	michelle@resumeresultsonline.com	Pages 70–71
Donna Tucker, CPRW	jobsaz@att.net	Pages 41–42
Rosa E. Vargas, MRW, CERW, NCRW, ACRW	rvargas@creatingprints.com	Pages 350–352, 385
Charlotte Weeks, CCMC, NCRW, CPRW	charlotte@weekscareerservices.com	Pages 248–249

~~~~~~

Pat Criscito (author), CPRW
pat@protypeltd.com

Pages 48–49, 52–56, 62–63, 66–67, 72–73, 80–81, 84–85, 88, 94–95, 98–99, 102–103, 106, 109–111, 114–115, 120–121, 126, 130–134, 142–143, 145, 147, 150–156, 158–159, 162–165, 167, 170, 172–177, 180–181, 184–185, 188–189, 194–195, 198–201, 216–217, 222, 229, 234–238, 261, 266, 269–271, 274–286, 288–293, 296–297, 301–302, 359–364, 373, 384

RÉSUMÉS THAT POP!

FOURTH EDITION

by Pat Criscito, CPRW
President and Founder
ProType, Ltd.
Colorado Springs

Author of Barron's
e-Résumés, Interview Answers in a Flash,
How to Write Better Résumés and Cover Letters,
and *Guide to Distance Learning*

The résumés in this book are real résumés used by real people to get real jobs.
The names and contact information have been changed to protect their privacy.
Thank you to all the clients for their inspiration and permission to use their résumés.
Thank you to members of the National Résumé Writers Association (NRWA) for submitting résumés for this book.

All inquiries should be addressed to:
Barron's Educational Series, Inc.
250 Wireless Boulevard
Hauppauge, New York 11788
www.barronseduc.com

Library of Congress Control Number: 2010933867
ISBN-13: 978-0-7641-4350-2
ISBN-10: 0-7641-4350-6

PRINTED IN THE UNITED STATES OF AMERICA
9 8 7 6 5 4 3 2 1

Personal Branding

I've been writing résumés for 30 years, so I've seen everything in the career business come and go—from the typewritten résumés of the 1980s to the cram-it-all-on-one-page résumés of the 1990s and the Internet-driven resumes of the 21st century. So, I think it's hilarious that *personal branding* has become the latest buzz phrase. Résumés have always been advertisements for what you are selling, which is *you!* You have a personal brand, whether you realize it or not. The exciting thing about this new trend is that it forces us to look at ourselves as a product that requires marketing.

"By being your own career boss, you decide which positions you will take, how much effort you will invest in each job, and how you will handle the challenges you will inevitably encounter. You control how you present yourself and your intellectual and emotional assets," say Kirsten Dixson and William Arruda in their book, *Career Distinction: Stand Out by Building Your Brand (www.careerdistinction.com).* "Just doing your job, and even doing it well, is no longer enough…. Every day, in everything you do, you tell the world about yourself, your values, your goals, and your skills. In fact, you already have a brand—even if you don't know what it is and even if it isn't working for you the way you'd like it to. Clarify and create your personal brand in order to achieve career distinction. Then, communicate that brand unerringly to those around you."

That's exactly what this book will help you do. Remember, a résumé is just a way to get your foot in the door for an interview. It's a marketing tool—an advertisement for *Brand You!* Let's take a few minutes to visualize this concept.

Pretend that you are bottle of Coca-Cola. You know that you have lots of competition from products with exactly the same features and benefits that you have, i.e., Pepsi-Cola, Royal Crown Cola, Member's Mark Cola, and the list goes on. Your features include being brown, bubbly, cold, yummy, and sweet; in a bottle or can; with added caffeine; and valued at about the same price. Your benefits (your unique selling points) include being refreshing, thirst quenching, energizing, satisfying, convenient, and so on.

Because you are a commodity, it is difficult to differentiate yourself on the market. So, how does Coca-Cola entice more buyers than Pepsi? Advertising. The better the ad, the more people will buy the product—the same goes for *Brand You.*

There are more people in the job market than ever before, and somehow you need to stand out from your competition. To advertise your brand better than your competition and to build your reputation so you are more visible, you need an extraordinary résumé, cover letters, website/e-folio, blog, social networking profiles, elevator speech, and a network of supporters. You can make more people aware of *Brand You* by writing articles for the various media in your market or online, commenting on other people's blogs, sending press releases to local newspapers, attending community events, volunteering for nonprofits, sitting on boards of directors, mentoring others or being mentored by someone at a higher level in your industry, and the list continues. Use your imagination.

To be successful in this highly competitive personal branding game, you need to determine your unique features and benefits and reflect those consistently in every advertising piece. Luckily, you aren't a bottle of Coke with exactly the same features and benefits as your Pepsi competitor. You are more like the difference between Campbell's Chicken Noddle Soup and Campbell's Tomato Soup.

Your Features Might Include
- What you offer that other job seekers don't
- Your core values, passions, and talents
- What are you known for, your reputation
- Your special gifts/strengths
- Your unique selling points
- What you most proud of
- Something in your background that makes you better qualified
- Unique education and training
- Being a subject-matter expert

Your Benefits Might Include
- The valuable contacts you have in your network
- The kinds of problems you can solve for your new employer
- Your ability to control expenses or lower overhead
- The experience you bring from working for a competitor
- The vision or new direction you would bring to the company
- The ability to increase cooperation between team members, lower turnover, or improve morale
- The ability to attract customers or increase market share, profits, efficiency, quality, safety, or performance
- You get the idea

Your message must be clear, consistent, and authentic across all of your advertising media. You must have a Unique Value Proposition (UVP) that defines your personal brand. Your UVP defines your worth, the value you bring to an employer, which includes your knowledge, skills, abilities, core competencies, accomplishments, and marketable assets. It is a combination of your features (*who you are and what you have done*) and your benefits (*what you bring to the new employer*).

It is often difficult for my clients to come up with these values during our interviews. When that happens, I give my clients homework. They must ask at least three people what values or talents they see in them. A spouse, family, friend, or co-worker can often see us more clearly than we can see ourselves. The worksheets in Chapter 20 of this book can help you clarify these features and benefits as well.

Once you have these on paper, create a concise branding statement that will become a "tagline" for all of your career documents, from your résumé to your e-folio. Candidates with clear, strong brands will attract the interest of recruiters every time, and a tagline or slogan will make you more memorable.

Josh Hyatt, writing for *Fortune* in "Building Your Brand (and keeping your job)," emphasizes, "Today, at a time when jobs are scarce, successful employees working at large companies desperately need to create a brand within a brand, a professional passport that travels with them from place to place…. A personal brand must highlight your special strengths, yet at the same time it also must not be too self-promotional…. Employees who successfully build their own brands within companies are hyper-aware of workplace values … and make both sides look good."

CONTROLLING YOUR ONLINE BRAND

Now that you understand what personal branding is all about, let's talk about how to manage *Brand You*. The paper documents (résumé, cover letter) that are a part of your marketing strategy are similar to the advertisements you see in newspapers, magazines, brochures, proposals. However, just as in commercial brand management, a lot of advertising is being redirected from print media to online ads. To manage your online reputation, you can add an e-folio, blog, or other website to your portfolio. You should definitely join LinkedIn and maybe even Twitter, FaceBook, YouTube, or other social networking sites.

Jamie Varon, 23, had her heart set on working for Twitter. She did everything right but with no luck. Then she registered the domain name, *twittershouldhireme.com,* and put up a website with a blog, résumé, and recommendations. Within 24 hours, Twitter contacted her and two job offers from tech companies followed after noticing her site.

You never know when someone will "Google" you before an interview. (Do you Google someone before a first date? I thought so!) All a hiring manager needs to do nowadays is to enter your name in any major search engine and see what pops up . . . or what doesn't! Hopefully, what he or she finds is good. If you want to control what a hiring manager sees, then a well-designed and promoted e-folio and/or blog could be your answer. These Web tools allow you to have more control over your online image.

Research by ExecuNet shows that at least 77% of recruiters reported using search engines to find background data on candidates. Of that number, 35% eliminated a candidate because of what they found online. They are looking for the good, the bad, and the ugly on any site a search can turn up. That will include your e-folio, as well as your LinkedIn, Facebook, MySpace, Twitter, YouTube, Squidoo, and other social networking profiles.

The "good" includes anything positive about you—evidence of community service, volunteer activities, leadership roles, published articles, awards, recognitions, publicity, and media recognition of any kind. Positive information found online can improve your chances of getting hired by as much as 70%.

The "bad" and the "ugly" include inconsistent work histories and backgrounds, false academic or professional qualifications, ethics investigations, legal proceedings, suspended licenses, poor communication or technical skills, weird personal habits or hobbies, excessive alcohol use, health information, crimes you might have committed, illegal drug use, or religious, politically sensitive, or personal information that you would rather an employer not see. You might just be invisible, too, which is just as bad.

In addition to the above, a SHRM survey revealed that the following information on an applicant's social networking profiles could negatively affect a hiring decision:

- Revealing private or confidential information about former or current employers.
- Slanderous or otherwise negative discussion of former or current employers.
- Information on social sites that contradicts facts presented on an applicant's résumé or cover letter.
- Negative or slanderous discussion of the applicant's friends, peers, or coworkers.
- Personal views, values, and/or morals contradictory to the organization.
- Information or pictures concerning romantic exploits.

In light of this trend, you must learn how to manage your online identity. That means controlling every word you write on the Internet and in e-mails, and choosing Web tools that will enhance the position of information you choose to appear when your name is Googled.

If you were to conduct a Google search on your name today, what would you find? Would your career expertise pop up first? Or will you find digital dirt about yourself, like embarrassing photographs from college or something inappropriate that your children posted about you at their MySpace page? Don't limit your search to Google. You should also search *yahoo.com* and *bing.com,* among other search engines. Review, at a minimum, the first three to five pages of each search engine's results.

The most sound advice I can give is to simply avoid publishing potentially damaging or inappropriate content from the outset. If you think a statement will negatively impact your ability to land a job now or even ten years from now, don't blog it, don't put it in your Facebook or MySpace profiles, don't write about it anywhere.

You must build and manage your digital presence so your name appears on page one of a Google search. Buy your domain name. Add your website URL to everything you print or email. Publicize your site using social networking. Ask for links from your network contact. Submit your site to search engines and directories. And watch your brand flourish.

WHAT'S NEW IN THIS EDITION

This fourth edition has a new title (the book used to be called *Designing the Perfect Résumé*) and new résumés, all of which were written and designed by members of the National Résumé Writers Association (NRWA), including me. In the beginning of this book is a listing of NRWA résumé writers with their contributions. Feel free to contact any of the writers by navigating to *www.nrwa.com* and searching for them by name.

Even though content is extremely important in a résumé, many times well-qualified people aren't considered for positions because a poorly designed résumé didn't grab the reader's attention long enough to make sure the words were read, or the format of the résumé didn't make it through the company's electronic vetting process.

Just the opposite can be true as well. Even if your qualifications aren't the greatest, a well-designed résumé improves your chances of getting an interview because it stands out in a crowd of poorly designed ones. Using the correct electronic format for your résumé will help ensure it pops up in a keyword search of the electronic applicant tracking system where your résumé is stored.

Because I feel strongly that a résumé should reflect the personality of the person it represents, I respect my clients' wishes when it comes to the actual design of their résumés. This means that, even though my staff and I write and design nearly a thousand résumés every year for clients in 42 countries, no two are exactly alike. You won't like every résumé in this book, and you shouldn't. Each one is designed and written to reflect an individual's personal career goals, industry, and personality.

Even though Chapter 2 is devoted to writing the words in your résumé, the rest of the book is intended to help you express yourself visually in the design of your résumé. The choice of overall style, type font, graphics, and even paper color says something about your personality. If you consider yourself to be more conservative and if you are in a traditional job in senior management, banking, or accounting, you will probably be drawn to the conservative résumés in this book. Throughout the book, but especially in Chapters 10 and 15, you will find résumés for more creative types, like actors, graphic designers, artists, and advertising professionals. Electronic résumés, cover letters, and other supporting career documents will be addressed in Chapters 16–19.

If you remember only one thing from this book, it should be that everything in the résumé business "depends"! The length of your résumé depends on your relevant experience and education. It also depends on your industry—a CV for a doctor, college professor, or other professional can be as long as it needs to be (see Chapter 14).

Whether you choose to put your photograph on your résumé depends on whether your appearance is a bona fide occupational qualification in your industry (model, news anchor, actor). If you are sending your résumé overseas to an international company or you are a college student whose leadership is proven in your activities, then a list of personal interests might be an appropriate addition to your résumé (see Chapter 7).

Whether you can place a graphic design on your résumé or use creative lines depends on how creative your industry is and the expectations of hiring managers in that industry (see Chapters 10, 14, and 15).

Whether you choose to use a functional style instead of a pure reverse chronological style depends on your work history—do you have gaps in employment that you want to make less obvious, is every job repetitive, are you entering the job market for the first time and most of your experience is non-paid (see Chapter 12)?

Choose elements from various résumés in this book to create a personalized look just for you, but keep in mind where you will be sending your résumé. Today, many large companies and recruiters receive the majority of their résumés electronically through job boards, e-mail, or their own company databases. Because of this trend, certain design elements are not appropriate and you need to know what type of electronic format to choose to increase the chances of being selected for that all-important interview.

This book will show you how to create and use ASCII text files (for cutting and pasting into e-mails and e-forms), MS Word and PDF files (for uploading to websites and attaching to e-mails), and scannable résumés (there are still some large companies and government agencies using this technology) (see Chapter 16).

Although this book focuses on design, it doesn't mean you should neglect the words on your résumé. Chapter 2 will guide you through an award-winning twelve-step résumé writing process that will help you get your experience and accomplishments down on paper. Remember, once your résumé design has grabbed your reader's attention, the words must then keep that attention.

About half of the book is devoted to the various design elements of a résumé with full-page samples: name, address, headings, dates, geographic locations, fonts, bullets, graphic lines, and other graphic design elements. Chapter 11 will show you the visual difference between laying out your résumé with bulleted short lines and paragraphs. Chapter 12 will provide you with samples of functional résumés and functional/chronological combinations. Curricula vitae and executive/professional résumés have unique needs addressed in Chapters 13 and 14. Then we get to have some fun with creative résumés for artists, advertising professionals, actors, dancers, models, and other artistic people in Chapter 15. Brand new to this book are Chapters 16, 17, and 18 which cover electronic résumés, e-folios, blogs, and supporting documents (i.e., reference lists, LinkedIn profiles, Twitter résumés, KSAs, long-range plans, bios, proposals, and other résumé extenders). In Chapter 19, you will find sample cover letters on various letterhead styles and a discussion of paper color, type, and size.

You have a wealth of designs and job descriptions in this book from which to choose—more than in any other résumé book on the market today. If you find wording that works for you, please feel free to use it as a foundation for the words on your own résumé. The index at the end of this book will help you find specific job titles that might help you to describe your experience. Every job title from every résumé in the book has been pulled out in alphabetical order to make it easier for you to locate specific job descriptions. Now that you know what this book offers, let's get started writing your résumé!

12-Step Résumés

Writing your résumé is often one of the most difficult things you will ever do! Think about it . . . you must turn your life history into a one- or two-page advertisement that highlights a lifetime of experience, accomplishments, and education. Since we have been taught all of our lives not to blow our own horn, most people find this ultimate advertisement difficult to write.

Before you can begin to design your résumé on paper, you need to have the words. Use the following twelve-step writing process to help clarify your experience, accomplishments, skills, education, and other background information, which will make the job of condensing your life onto paper a little easier. I expanded this twelve-step process into an entire book for Barron's—*How to Write Better Résumés and Cover Letters*—which you can find at your local bookstore or online. If you want to download the Adobe Acrobat, MS Word, or Corel WordPerfect worksheets developed for that book, you can find them free at my website—*www.patcriscito.com*—by clicking on the *Pat's Book* link. You can also copy the same worksheets from Chapter 20 of this book.

STEP ONE—FOCUS

The first step in writing the perfect résumé is to know what kind of job you will be applying for. A résumé without a focus is never as effective as one that relates to a specific job. A recent survey found that the pet peeve of 23% of recruiters is a résumé that is not customized to their position. I recommend creating custom versions of your résumé for each job. Sometimes that means simply changing the first half of page one with a custom objective, profile, and areas of expertise. Occasionally, it requires a major reorganization of the various sections of the résumé. Rarely, it requires a major rewrite of your résumé.

Now, decide what type of job you will be applying for and then write it at the top of the Qualifications Profile you will find in Chapter 20 of this book. This can become your objective statement (should you decide to use one), the headline at the top of your résumé (just under your address), or the first line of the profile section to give your reader a general idea of your area(s) of expertise.

An objective is not required on a résumé, and often the cover letter is the best place to personalize your objective for each job opening. There is nothing wrong with using an objective statement on a résumé, however, provided it does not limit your job choices. As an alternative, you can alter individual résumés with personalized objectives that reflect the actual job title for which you are applying. Just make sure that the rest of your information is still relevant to the new objective.

Never write an objective statement that is not precise. You want to name the position so specifically that, if a janitor came by and knocked over the stacks of sorted résumés on a hiring manager's desk, he could put yours back in its right stack without even thinking about it. That means saying, "A marketing management position with an aggressive international consumer goods manufacturer" instead of "A position that utilizes my education and experience to mutual benefit."

STEP TWO—EDUCATION

The second step in writing your résumé is to think about your education. That means all of your training and not just formal education (college, university, or trade school). The education section of your résumé will include degrees, continuing education, professional development, seminars, workshops, and sometimes even self-study.

Turn to the forms in Chapter 20 of this book and list any education or training that you think might relate. If you participated in college activities or received any honors or completed notable projects that relate directly to your target job, then this is the place to list them. A business student might cite a marketing plan developed for a specific class, or a graphic designer might describe artwork created for a website and provide a link. A Ph.D. graduate would list a dissertation title, and under a master's degree would appear a thesis title. Think also about relevant course work, classroom projects, volunteering, internships, clubs, honor societies, fraternities, and sororities.

Showing high school education and associated activities on a résumé is only appropriate when you are under twenty and have no education or training beyond high school. Once you have completed either college courses or specialized technical training, drop your high school information altogether. The only exception to this rule is when applying for government jobs that specifically request your high school information (which is commonly required on an OF-612 application form).

When you attend a trade school, you receive either a diploma or certificate. This type of schooling can be listed under the "Education" heading or under a separate heading called "Training" or "Technical Training."

Continuing education shows that you care about lifelong learning and self-development, so think about any relevant training since your formal education was completed. *Relevant* is the key word here. Always look at your résumé from the perspective of a potential employer. Don't waste space by listing training that is not directly or indirectly related to your target job. This section can include in-services, workshops, seminars, corporate training programs, conferences, conventions, and other types of training.

Which sections go first? If you are a recent college graduate and have little relevant experience, your education section will be placed near the top of your résumé. As you gain more experience, your education almost always gravitates to the bottom. The same goes for information within each section. The most recent information is listed first and the oldest last.

There is an exception to every rule in the résumé business, however, so use your common sense. If you are trying to change careers and recently went back to school to obtain new credentials, your education section will appear at the top of the résumé even if you have years of experience. Think about your strongest qualifications and make certain they appear in the top half of page one of your résumé.

How you choose to list your school and degree can make a difference in how the reader perceives the importance of each item. For instance, in the following education section, the name of the university is prestigious, so I chose to list it first so the reader focused on the school. The job seeker had little real-life experience, so I provided valuable keywords by listing areas of study under each major. The GPA was relevant because he was competing for jobs through the school's career services center, which required GPAs on all résumés. As he gained more experience in the future, I removed some of the details.

SOUTHERN METHODIST UNIVERSITY, Cox School of Business, Dallas, Texas
Bachelor of Business Administration, May 2007
- *Major in Management Information Systems* (166 credit hours, GPA 3.9): Database Design and Administration, Business Computer Programming, Advanced Programming Techniques, Systems Analysis Design, Information Systems in Organizations, and Telecommunication Design and Policy.
- *Minor in International Business:* Introduction to World Cultures, International Politics, International Economics, and the Global Perspective.
- *Awards:* SMU Scholarship, Who's Who Among Students in American Universities and Colleges.
- Selected for a special *Electronic Commerce Honors Course* that provided in-depth, hands-on experience in the use of the Internet to help companies achieve competitive advantage, transform relationships with customers, suppliers, and business partners, and empower global business.
- Completed a *year-long mentoring program* with a senior executive at Southwestern Bell as part of the SMU Business Associates Program.
- *Honors:* Beta Gamma Sigma National Honor Society for Collegiate Schools of Business, Alpha Iota Delta honorary member of Decision Sciences Institute, Golden Key Honor Society, Financial Management Association National Honor Society, Alpha Chi National Honor Society.

When the degree is more important than the university where it was earned, list your education with the degree first. Prioritize your degrees in order of importance, like this:

Ph.D. IN AEROSPACE ENGINEERING (2007)
University of Maryland, College Park, Maryland
- Dissertation: The Optimization of Engine-Integrated Hypersonic Waveriders with Steady State Flight and Static Margin Constraints
- Received a four-year postgraduate research assistantship in the Hypersonic Research Group

MASTER OF BUSINESS ADMINISTRATION, FINANCE (2005)
The Pennsylvania State University, University Park, State College, Pennsylvania
- Graduated magna cum laude with a GPA of 3.93
- Graduate Student Association Representative for the MBA program (2001 – 2005)
- Awarded a Graduate Assistantship in the Real Estate Department during the final semester

BACHELOR OF SCIENCE IN NURSING (2003)
Beth-El College of Nursing, University of Colorado, Colorado Springs, Colorado
- Recipient of the Outstanding BSN Student Award for outstanding leadership, clinical, and academic achievement (May 2007)
- Hand picked by the university's nursing faculty to help teach Aging Simulations (February 2006)
- Beth-El College of Nursing nominee for the UCCS Student Achievement Award (May 2007)

If you are searching for a job that will utilize special language skills, cross-cultural experience, or international travel, the fact that you studied abroad or completed a foreign exchange program will be an important addition to your résumé. Study abroad falls under the "Education" category, while travel for recreation's sake could be included in a separate "International Experience" section on your résumé, if you are searching for a job that would make that experience valuable.

STUDIES ABROAD
Loyola University, Rome, Italy (Spring 2007)
Classroom study integrated with European field experiences

ITESM, Monterrey, Mexico (Summer 2006)
Intensive Spanish language and Mexican culture studies

When you did not complete a degree but have some college study, you can list the degree with the qualification that you have a certain number of credits left to finish (as in the first sample below) or classify the section as "Undergraduate Studies" (like the second sample). Whichever method you choose, just make sure it is quite clear that you didn't graduate. Falsifying education and training on a résumé is grounds for termination in many organizations.

BACHELOR OF SCIENCE, MARKETING (2004 – 2007)
Hawaii Pacific University, Honolulu, Hawaii
- Two credits short of completing an undergraduate degree
- Selected for the Dean's List
- Relevant course work completed: Marketing Management, Public Relations, Marketing Research, Consumer Analysis, Principles of Advertising, International Marketing, Principles of Retail, Industrial Marketing, Production Management, Principles of Marketing.

OR . . .

UNDERGRADUATE STUDIES
Pikes Peak Community College, Colorado Springs, Colorado
- Banking and Finance Program (2 semesters, full-time)
- Early Childhood Education (3 semesters, full-time)
- Course work included: Communications I and II, Minorities, American Indian, Human Relations

Northern Virginia Community College, Fairfax, Virginia
- Liberal Arts Program (1 semester, full-time)
- Course work included: English Composition, History/Western Civilization II

Colorado Mountain College, Glenwood Springs, Colorado
- Liberal Arts Program (1 semester, full-time)
- Course work included: Introduction to Psychology, Physical Science

The devil's in the details, and résumé details really do matter. Something as simple as a date in your education can affect your job search. For instance, writing from–to dates (1999 – 2001) implies that you did not graduate. If you graduated with a degree, list only the year you graduated (2001). Computerized applicant tracking systems and Internet résumé databases are programmed to show that you have college study but not a degree if they see from–to dates.

I am often asked whether or not to list GPAs on a résumé. My reply is, "If you have a GPA of 3.5 or above, it could help you. From 3.0 to 3.5 neither helps nor hurts you, in most cases.

Anything from 2.9 or below can actually hurt your chances of getting an interview." I recommend that you list your GPA if you are a recent graduate whose résumé will be competing against the résumés of fellow students in your college's electronic résumé database, provided it's a good GPA. Otherwise, leave it off.

As I've already mentioned, there is an exception to every rule in the résumé business, so use common sense. If nearly every résumé you see for your industry has GPAs listed, then you should list yours, too. For instance, in academic circles, a GPA is often important on a curriculum vitae.

One last cautionary note on your education. Many companies and all government organizations require that your degree come from a regionally accredited college or university. If you have a degree from a diploma mill, it will not be accepted and should not be listed on your résumé. To determine whether your school is regionally accredited, check with the Council for Higher Education Accreditation at *www.chea.org/directories/regional.asp.*

STEP THREE—JOB DESCRIPTIONS

What if it has been years since you worked at a job and you can't remember what you did? What if it was just yesterday and you can't remember what you did?! Don't worry. You're not getting old. Most of us forget that kind of detail, so now we need to come up with some strategies for finding ways to describe your work history.

First, get your hands on a written description of the job you wish to obtain and for any jobs you have held in the past, as well as for your current job. If you are presently employed, your human resource department is the first place to look. If not, then go to your local library and ask for a copy of *The Dictionary of Occupational Titles* or the *Occupational Outlook Handbook* (which can also be found on the Internet—see below). These industry standard reference guides offer volumes of occupational titles and job descriptions for everything from Abalone Divers to Zoo Veterinarians (and thousands in between).

Other places to look for job descriptions include:

- Your local government job service agencies
- Professional and technical organizations
- Recruiters
- Associates who work in the same field
- Newspaper advertisements for similar jobs
- Online job postings, which tend to have longer job descriptions than print ads

Here are some other sources for job descriptions on the Internet:

- Dictionary of Occupational Titles: *www.oalj.dol.gov/libdot.htm*
- Occupational Outlook Handbook: *www.bls.gov/oco/home.htm*
- Occupational Outlook Quarterly: *www.bls.gov/opub/ooq/ooqhome.htm*
- Career Guide to Industries: *www.bls.gov/oco/cg/*
- America's Career InfoNet: *www.acinet.org*
- JobProfiles.com: *www.jobprofiles.org*
- Exploring Occupations from the University of Manitoba: *www.umanitoba.ca/counselling/careers.html*

Performance evaluations, depending on how well they are written, generally list a description of your major responsibilities, a breakdown of individual tasks, and highlights of your accomplishments. You should *always* keep a folder at home of performance evaluations from every job you have ever held. If you haven't kept them up until now, please start.

Now, make copies of these performance evaluations so you can highlight them as you write your résumé. Use a different colored pen to highlight accomplishments—the things you did above and beyond the call of duty.

Also make copies of the job descriptions you discovered and mark the sentences that describe anything you have done in your past or present jobs. These job descriptions are important sources of keywords, so pay particular attention to nouns and phrases that you can incorporate into your own résumé. Now, set these papers aside until Steps Six and Seven when it will be time to begin writing the details.

STEP FOUR—KEYWORDS

In today's world of electronic résumés, make sure you know the buzzwords of your industry and incorporate them into the sentences you are about to write. Keywords are the nouns, adjectives, or short phrases that describe any experience and education that might be used to find your résumé in a keyword search of an electronic résumé database, either on the Internet or in a company's own system. They reflect the essential knowledge, skills, and abilities required to do your job. They are generally concrete descriptions such as:

- C++
- UNIX
- fiber optic cable
- network
- project management
- Spanish
- international
- business development
- Internet
- customer retention
- cost reduction
- long-range planning
- organizational design

Even well-known company names (AT&T, IBM, Hewlett-Packard) and universities (Harvard, Yale, Princeton, SMU, Stanford, Tulane, Columbia, etc.) are sometimes used as keywords, especially when it is necessary to narrow down an initial search that calls up hundreds of résumés from a résumé database.

Acronyms and abbreviations here can either hurt you or help you, depending on how you use them. One example given to me by an engineer at a software development company was the abbreviation IN. Think about it. IN could stand for intelligent networks, Indiana, or the word *in*. It is better to spell out the abbreviation if there could be any possible confusion.

However, if a series of initials is so well known that it would be recognized by nearly everyone in your industry and would not likely be confused with a real word, then the keyword search will probably use those initials (i.e., IBM, CPA, UNIX). When in doubt, always spell it out at least one time on your résumé. A computer only needs to see the combination one time for it to be considered a "hit" in a keyword search.

In my research over the years, I have been surprised to find soft skills included in most job requisitions, which are used to develop the criteria to search electronic résumé databases. Even though these soft skills are hard to prove and are often ignored by human readers, if they become keywords for a search of a résumé database and your résumé doesn't contain those words, then your résumé will not pop up. A recent survey by *CareerBuilder.com* listed the most frequently searched soft skills as *oral and written communication, problem solving, leadership, team building, performance, productivity, project management, customer retention,* and *strategic planning,* among others.

You will often find résumé advice that suggests you skip adding these words to your résumé and instead write bullets that describe the skill in detail. I agree that you should "prove" soft skills, but you also need to make sure the keywords themselves appear somewhere in your résumé. I often use soft skills as adjectives in a profile section and go on to "prove" the skill in the experience section. That way, all of my bases are covered.

The job descriptions and performance evaluations you found in Step Three are some of the most important sources for keywords. You can also be certain that nearly every noun, and some adjectives, in a job posting or advertisement will be keywords, so make sure you use those words somewhere in your résumé, using synonyms wherever you can. Just make sure you can justify every word on your résumé—don't exaggerate. If you don't have the experience or skill, don't use the keyword.

In the end of this chapter, you will find a more in-depth description of keywords and some examples of keywords for specific industries, although there is no such thing as a comprehensive listing of keywords for any single job. The computerized applicant tracking systems used by most companies allow the recruiter or hiring manager to personalize his or her list of keywords for each job opening, so it is an evolving process. You will never know whether you have listed absolutely every keyword possible, so focus instead on getting on paper as many related skills as possible, remembering to be absolutely honest and accurate.

The keyword forms in Chapter 20 will help you to make a list of the keywords you have determined are important for your particular job search. Also list common synonyms for those words when you can. As you incorporate these words into the sentences of your résumé, check them off.

One caution. Always tell the truth. The minute a hiring manager speaks with you on the telephone or begins an interview, any exaggeration of the truth will become immediately apparent.

It is a bad idea to say, "I don't have experience with MS Word computer software" just to get the words MS Word or computer software on paper so your résumé will pop up in a keyword search.

In a cover letter, it might be appropriate to say, "I don't have five years of experience in marketing but can add two years of university training in the subject to three years of in-depth experience as a marketing assistant with Hewlett-Packard." That is legitimate reasoning, but anything more manipulative can be hazardous to your job search.

According to *CareerJournal.com*, it is getting harder for job seekers to game the systems that recruiters use to identify potential candidates. Some candidates have tried to hide keywords so they can't be seen by the naked eye by using white text on a white background, typing so small that it looks like a solid horizontal line, and even inserting web coding in online résumés that's hidden from plain view. Newer applicant tracking and résumé database software are able to detect these tricks, discrediting the applicant. Some technology even penalizes job seekers who use keywords out of context by placing their résumé at the bottom of the search results.

STEP FIVE—YOUR JOBS

Now that you have the basic information for your résumé, you need to create a list of jobs and write basic sentences to describe your duties. Start by using a separate "Experience" form (you will find them in Chapter 20) for each job you have held for the past ten to fifteen years. You can generally stop there unless there is something in your previous work history that is particularly relevant to the new job you are seeking.

Starting with your present position, list the title of every job you have held, along with the name of the company, the city and state, and the years you worked there. You don't need to list full addresses and zip codes, although you will need to know that information when it comes time to fill out an application. You should use a separate page for each job title even if you worked for the same company in more than one capacity.

By the way, you can use a computer. I've had people assume that they had to write this all out in longhand simply because I suggest a separate piece of paper for each job. You can download MS Word and Corel WordPerfect files of all the forms in this book by going to my website at *www.patcriscito.com* and click on the *Pat's Books* button.

You can list years only (1996–present) or months and years (May 1996–present), depending on your personality. People who are more detail oriented are usually more comfortable with a full accounting of their time. Listing years alone covers some gaps if you have worked in a position for less than a full year while the time period spans more than one calendar year. For instance, if you worked from December 2000 through January 2001, saying 2000–2001 certainly looks better. If you are concerned about gaps in your work history, then listing years only is to your advantage.

From the perspective of recruiters and hiring managers, most don't care whether you list the months and years or list the years only. However, if you are writing a résumé for a U.S. government job, you will be required in almost every case to list the beginning and ending month and year for each job.

Regardless of which method you choose, be consistent throughout your résumé, especially within each section. Don't use months sometimes and years alone other times within the same section. Consistency of style is important on a résumé, since it is that consistency that makes your résumé neat, clean, and easy to read.

STEP SIX—DUTIES

Under each job on its separate page, make a list of your duties, incorporating phrases from the job description and keywords wherever they apply. You don't have to worry about making great sentences yet or narrowing down your list. Just get the information on paper.

This is the most time-consuming part of the résumé writing process. Depending on how quickly you write/type, it could take an entire day just for this step. Anything worth doing, however, is worth doing right, so you will want to take the time to do this step to the best of your ability.

Don't forget to list internships, practicums, and unpaid volunteer work in your experience section. Experience is experience, whether you are paid for it or not. If the position or the knowledge you gained is relevant to your current job search, then put it on your résumé. As little as five or ten hours a week of volunteer or internship experience can add meat to an entry-level résumé. If you are returning to work after a period of absence (time spent raising children, for example), adding PTA or other volunteer experience can cover gaps in employment.

You can either include unpaid experience along with your paid experience, or you can create a separate section just for your volunteer history.

STEP SEVEN—ACCOMPLISHMENTS

When you are finished with your work history, go back to each job and think about what you might have done above and beyond the call of duty. What did you contribute to each of your jobs? How did you measure your success? What were you most proud of? What made you feel good at the end of the day? Did you . . .

- Exceed sales quotas each month?
- Save the company money by developing a new procedure?
- Generate new product publicity in trade press?
- Control expenses or cut overhead?
- Increase the company's market share?
- Expand business or attract/retain customers?
- Restore lost accounts?
- Improve customer satisfaction ratings?
- Improve the company's image or build new relationships?
- Improve the quality of a product?
- Do something that made the company more competitive?
- Make money? Was it a record?
- Improve net profit?
- Save money or time without compromising the company's products or services?
- Introduce new and better policies, procedures, processes, or systems?
- Increase efficiency or make work easier?
- Lower the company's debt?
- Increase productivity?
- Improve workplace safety?
- Solve a problem?

- Create a business partnership?
- Improve recruiting systems?
- Train/mentor any personnel who were promoted?
- Lower employee turnover or improve morale?
- Bring new vision or direction to the company?
- Rate above average on performance evaluation?
- Get selected for a significant project(s)?
- Become recognized as a subject-matter expert?
- Get recruited especially to solve a major problem?
- Face significant competition in the market?

Go back to the experience forms in the last step and make a note of any accomplishments that show potential employers what you have done in the past, which translates into what you might be able to do for them in the future. This is not *bragging,* which is a prideful exaggeration. Instead, it is *advertising,* which is "to make known the positive features of a product (you)."

Quantify whenever possible. Numbers are always impressive. Be careful not to divulge confidential information about past and current employers, especially if they are privately held companies. Public companies have to reveal financial data anyway, so listing those numbers on your résumé isn't as much of a problem.

Don't duplicate wording throughout the résumé. If you use dollars in one case, use percentages in another. Overused words lose their effectiveness, like a song played on the radio again and again.

Remember, you are trying to motivate the potential employer to buy . . . you! Convince your reader that you will be able to generate a significant return on their investment in you. Try to focus on "before" and "after" examples. Identify a problem and explain how you corrected it using the CAR format—Challenge, Action, Result. For instance:

> **Challenge:** Evaluated the sensor that optimized combustion in a coal-fired power plant—determined that power levels were low and inconsistent.
>
> **Action:** Tuned the VCSEL-based laser that was at the heart of the process to optimize combustion.
>
> **Result:** Succeeded in making the controlled burning processes cleaner, greener, more consistent, and capable of operating at higher power levels. Improved manufacturability.

If you were part of a team, it is sometimes difficult to express accomplishments without claiming full credit for the work of the entire team. You should refer directly to the role you played: "Led a team of six engineers. . . ." or "Integral member of the team that . . . ." or "Part of the sales team that doubled sales in one year." Even though over-claiming credit in the case of team projects is somewhat expected, especially in today's tight job market, I would recommend being as accurate as possible on every word of your résumé.

Following are some real accomplishment statements used by real people on real résumés. They are extracted from many different résumés and industries, and each bullet is a separate accomplishment. They aren't used in a single résumé as they are listed here. For a full list of industries and sample accomplishment statements, check out my Barron's book, *How to Write Better Résumés and Cover Letters.*

- Successfully set the standard for safe operations throughout the organization.

- Reduced charge-offs from .2% to .1% and receivables turnover from 50 to 42 days during this period.

- Succeeded in delivering 25 complete systems to users, including the automation of a formerly paper-based order entry system that increased billing efficiency by 25%.

- Evaluated and changed the production schedule of the bakery department to introduce new products, which increased profits and better met customer needs.

- Increased assets from $60 million to $99.5 million in five years; led the city in annuity sales.

- Instrumental in the creation of the second-generation website offering an e-commerce component— the first in the textile converting industry *(www.tapetex.com).*

- Maintained computer network support levels despite a $1.2 million budget cut.

- Boosted customer retention rates from 85% to 99% by developing a Customer First program that was implemented in the field as well as in the call center.

- Created a safe, productive, caring, and positive school climate through effective leadership that included modeling, rewards, communication, increased visibility, and appreciation for diversity.

- Implemented an engineering approach to problem identification and achieved a defect density rating of 1.9 when the industry standard is 1.4 and perfection is 2.0.

- Successfully guided the company through a lengthy period of extreme financial distress.

- Solicited government, foundation, corporate, and individual contributions accounting for 32% of the $1.2 million operating budget.

- Part of the team responsible for the preparations that earned a score of 94 on the September 2010 JCAHO survey.

- Built the hotel into a strong competitor for the city's business market and ranked in the top 10% for customer service out of 1,140 Hampton hotels.

- Conceptualized, developed, and co-facilitated The Silent Retreat, an award-winning experiential weekend for students and staff.

- Improved productivity and morale by initiating systems for accountability, formalizing job duties, and instituting training programs.

- Re-engineered existing supply processes to save limited resources, recovering $26 million.

- Negotiated exclusive North American distribution agreements with two European mills, resulting in an annual sales increase of approximately $3 million.

- Changed the company's perception in the marketplace by creating innovative marketing materials and making it more visible.

- Managed the company's transition to a global marketing focus through targeted sales planning, re-engineering of operations, and sound financial management, leading to sales diversification and enhanced opportunities for future growth in a shrinking market.

- Enhanced domestic representation and diversified product lines, increasing sales by $36 million.

- Increased equipment availability from 78% to 94% within the first month by reducing down time through the implementation of a quality improvement strategy.

- Successfully managed the maintenance of automotive equipment returning from Desert Storm, taking on twice the normal workload with no additional assets.

- Designed and implemented a tool to identify victims of domestic violence who presented to the ER, which ensured proper care and follow-up.

- Served as a role model for county public health nurses and other providers.

- Investigated and resolved quality and service complaints, promoting repeat business and improving profitability.

- Honored for a commitment to 100% customer satisfaction and zero defects.

- Recognized by Lanier's Atlanta headquarters for generating the highest yearly sales volume in the Western Region during the first six months on the job; eight-time recipient of the monthly top production award.

- Increased gross sales from $1,500 to $80,000 per month in one year.

- Displayed a professional demeanor with a cheerful, positive attitude.

- Appointed to the Master Teacher Advisory Group for the U.S. Space Foundation.

- Selected for the national "Time Magazine Award" for developing and implementing a mock presidential election for all of the schools in the Cheraw District.

- Identified 180 leased communication circuits for removal, saving $2.1 million in annual leased line costs.

- Developed cross-training programs that improved the morale and the efficiency of operations and lowered turnover rates.

One last thought on accomplishments. You will notice in several of the accomplishment statements you have just read that I used an award's name but, more importantly, I described the purpose of the award. In a research study of corporate hiring practices sponsored by the Career Management Alliance *(www.careermanagementalliance.com)*, the researcher found that decision makers weren't much interested in awards even if they applied to the job they were trying to fill.

The study concluded, "Hiring managers don't know how to judge the value of awards. For example, a résumé that just mentions the name of the award might not provide enough information. However, readers would learn more if they knew this award went only to the top five performers in a sales force numbering more than five hundred."

The key, then, is to focus on the accomplishment more than the award itself. Naming the honor or award is secondary to the return on investment the hiring manager perceives from the sentence. Remember the rule that there is an exception to every rule in the résumé business? Well, here's another one. If the award is so self-explanatory in your industry that explaining it would be insulting to your reader, then list those awards or honors in a separate section at the bottom of your résumé, like this for a teacher:

- High Plains Educator Award (2009)
- Who's Who Among America's Teachers (2009, 2010)
- Outstanding Young Woman of America (2008)

STEP EIGHT—DELETE

Now that you have the words on paper, go back to each list and think about which items are relevant to your current job target. Cross out those things that don't relate, including entire jobs (like flipping hamburgers back in high school if you are now an electrical engineer with ten years of experience).

Remember, your résumé is just an enticer, a way to get your foot in the door. It isn't intended to be all-inclusive. You can choose to go back only as far as your jobs relate to your present objective. Be careful not to delete sentences that contain the most important keywords you identified in Step Four of this chapter.

You know the old saying, "The only constant is change." Perhaps you should make a copy of the pages before you begin marking them up. They are a great record of your work history, and you never know when you might want to change careers, which means you would need some of that information.

According to the U.S. Department of Labor, the average worker today will hold fifteen jobs in his or her career and change careers up to seven times. I have been writing résumés since 1980, and the biggest change I've seen since the early 1990s is the number of clients who have decided to, for example, leave computer programming for acting or to change from nursing to pharmaceutical sales.

Part of the reason for this transition is social and part is the result of the modern workplace. According to William Hine, Dean of the School of Adult and Continuing Education at Eastern Illinois University, "The half-life of a college degree is three to five years." There was a time when you could graduate from college and stay in the same job for thirty years and then retire with a gold watch. Not so today. You must be committed to lifelong learning or your career will leave you behind.

That means you can also make the choice to retool, get a new degree, and start a new career in mid-life. It's perfectly acceptable.

It also means that being a pack rat can pay off when you decide to change careers! So, store the original worksheets in the same file you created for your performance evaluations and job descriptions, and use the copies for this step.

Take the copies and decide which jobs are relevant to today's job search. You only need to use about ten to fifteen years of those jobs, unless there is something very powerful in your early career that will help you get a job. Now, set aside the jobs that are too old or irrelevant. Try to limit your list of final jobs to no more than six, although you can list more if they are truly relevant or contain valuable experience. Focus on the sentences in the relevant experience summaries.

- Which ones are the most powerful?
- Which ones summarize your experience the best?
- Which ones contain the keywords of your industry?
- Which ones highlight your accomplishments the best?

Next, do the same for your education and training worksheets. Copy them, file away the originals, and cross out anything that doesn't relate to your current job goal. That does not apply to your formal education, however. Even if you have a graduate degree in your career field and your undergraduate degree is unrelated, leave them both on your résumé. Your reader will need to see the progression of your formal education.

If you have a bachelor's degree and an associate degree, you don't need to list them both unless there is something about the major of your associate degree that you don't have in your bachelor's degree. Remember, it is okay to list almost anything on your résumé as long as it is relevant to your job search.

One last thing, if you have lied about (or exaggerated) anything on your résumé up to this point, delete it now! Did you know that it is against the law to lie on a résumé? You could be committing a felony. If you are caught and convicted, you could land in jail! And that's not all. If you claim to have a college degree you didn't earn and it leads to higher pay, you could be accused of criminal fraud by your employer, even if this is discovered years later.

According to a survey conducted by the Society for Human Resource Management (SHRM), among the 87% of hiring managers who check all references, 90% say they've caught job applicants making false claims and, of those liars, 35% fabricated a previous employer. Reuters reports that ADP Screening and Selection Services found that more than 50% of the people on whom it conducted employment and education checks had submitted false information, compared with about 40% a year earlier.

Anne Fisher, career columnist for *Fortune* magazine, says, "The vast majority of companies view lying on a résumé as grounds for firing or for putting a candidate right out of the running, so forget it." SHRM reports that 60% of employers said they automatically dismiss applicants caught making misstatements about their backgrounds, and that includes degrees you never earned or positions you never held.

Exaggerations might seem innocuous, but they have career-ending consequences every day. Former RadioShack chief executive David Edmondson was forced to resign after it became apparent that he had misrepresented his academic record on his résumé. The Food Network fired Robert Irvine, the star of *Dinner: Impossible,* for claiming on his résumé to have worked at the White House and for Princess Diana. He was later rehired when the show didn't fare as well under a different star, but his reputation will never be the same. Even if the embellishment seems tiny, once caught, people won't trust you for a very long time, if ever. Once that bond of trust is lost, it is very difficult to recover.

Another problem is that embellishments on your résumé have a much longer shelf life today because of social networking sites (LinkedIn, Facebook, Twitter, MySpace), web résumés, and e-mail. Even if you correct your résumé and upload the new version, old versions of your résumé can be archived on the web.

Companies are now conducting much more extensive due diligence to protect themselves, especially when hiring executives. They often hire outside agencies to conduct searches of media, professional licenses/credentials, college records, criminal and civil court records, lien/judgment filings, credit bureaus, bankruptcy filings, regulatory records (think SEC), driving records, military histories, sex offender repositories, the Internet, and the list is almost endless. Besides work references, some high-level positions and government agencies require interviews of spouses, friends, neighbors, colleagues, vendors, and customers, with your permission, of course.

It's time to do some serious writing now. You must make dynamic, attention-getting sentences of the duties and accomplishments you have listed under each job, combining related items to avoid short choppy phrases. Here are the secrets to great résumé sentences:

- Never use personal pronouns (I, my, me). Instead of saying: "*I planned, organized, and directed the timely and accurate production of code products with estimated annual revenues of $1 million*" you should say: "*Planned, organized, and directed . . .*" Writing in the first person makes your sentences more powerful and attention grabbing, but using personal pronouns throughout a résumé is awkward. Your reader will assume that you are referring to yourself, so the personal pronouns can be avoided.

- Make your sentences positive, brief, and accurate. Since your ultimate goal is to get a human being to read your résumé, remember to structure the sentences so they are interesting to read.

- Use verbs at the beginning of each sentence (designed, supervised, managed, developed, formulated, and so on) to make them more powerful (see the list at the end of this chapter).

- Incorporate keywords from the list you made in Step Four.

- Make certain each word means something and contributes to the quality of the sentence.

If it is difficult for you to write clear, concise sentences, take the information you have just listed to a professional writer who can help you turn it into a winning résumé. Choose someone who is a Nationally Certified Résumé Writer (NCRW), Master Résumé Writer (MRW), Certified Professional Résumé Writer (CPRW), Academy Certified Résumé Writer (ACRW), or Certified Master Résumé Writer (CMRW). That way you can be assured that the person has passed the strictest tests of résumé writing and design in the country.

Certification indicates that the writer is dedicated to providing you with the highest quality service and a superior product at the end of the process. The expense of a professional written résumé is a small investment when compared to the advantages it provides for your career. To find certified résumé writers, visit these websites:

- National Résumé Writers' Association, *www.thenrwa.com*
- Career Management Alliance, *www.careermanagementalliance.com*
- Professional Association of Résumé Writers and Career Coaches, *www.parw.com*
- Career Directors International, *www.careerdirectors.com*
- Resume Writing Academy, *www.resumewritingacademy.com*
- Certified Resume Writers, *www.certifiedresumewriters.com*

What are the benefits of partnering with a professional résumé writer? According to the NRWA, you will gain access to:

- Expert résumé writing, editing, and design skills.
- Needed objectivity and expertise to play up your strengths, downplay your weaknesses, and position yourself for interview success.

- The precise know-how to target your career and industry correctly.
- Winning résumé, job search, interviewing, and salary negotiation strategies from recognized experts.
- Experienced professionals who have passed rigorous résumé industry exams and demonstrated their commitment to the profession by obtaining ongoing training.
- Writers who are dedicated to providing the highest quality service and a superior finished product.

Résumé writers work in one of three ways:

1. They gather all of the information they need from you in a personal interview.
2. They require that you complete a long questionnaire before they begin working on your résumé.
3. They use a combination of both methods.

In any case, you have already done most of the data collection if you have followed Steps One through Six and Steps Ten and Eleven in this chapter. This preparation sometimes makes the résumé easier to write and many professional résumé writers will pass on that savings to you in the form of lower fees.

If you are going to proceed from here and finish the résumé on your own, let me show you how to rewrite sentences so they are more powerful. The original sentences in these examples were on real résumés. The rewrites are my fine-tuning based on interviews with each client, which gathered more information and clarified the original intent of the writer.

Original Sentence: Responsible for leading team of application engineers, delivery consultants, and technical trainers in pre-sales and post-sales activities.

Rewrite: Led a team of 20 application engineers, delivery consultants, and technical trainers in the development of customized enterprise software solutions.

Original Sentence: Generation of accurate and meaningful client proposals based on initial client needs and assessment.

Rewrite: Generated effective client proposals based on a comprehensive assessment of client requirements.

Original Sentence: Telecommunication sales associate who achieved quota each month after training phase.

Rewrite: Successfully sold telecommunication services, achieving sales goals each month and generated more than $1 million in annual revenue.

Original Sentence: Responsible to ensure that time is spent on being pro-active about the future financial needs of the district.

Rewrite: Proactive in ensuring that the future financial needs of the district were met.

Original Sentence: Helped the district make assessment and accountability that accompanies data not an event but rather a practice that we seek and value.

Rewrite: Assured that assessment and accountability became part of the district's culture and not a simple event.

Original Sentence: Marketing Coordinator; for all internal and external marketing for Club Sports six up-scale fitness clubs and a hotel and fitness resort.

Rewrite: Coordinated all of the internal and external marketing for six upscale fitness clubs and the Renaissance ClubSport hotel and fitness resort.

Original Sentence: Inside sale support responsible for aftermarket parts and equipment sales for over 200 municipalities as well as expediting and tracking purchase orders, sales generated yearly were approximately $100,000.

Rewrite: Provided inside sales support for aftermarket parts and equipment sales to 200+ municipalities, personally generating annual sales of more than $100,000.

STEP TEN—REARRANGE

You are almost done! Now, go back to the sentences you have written and think about their order of presentation. Put a number 1 by the most important description of what you did for each job. Then place a number 2 by the next most important duty or accomplishment, and so on until you have numbered each sentence.

Again, think logically and from the perspective of a potential employer. Keep related items together so the reader does not jump from one concept to another. Make the thoughts flow smoothly.

The first sentence in a job description is usually an overall statement of the position's major responsibilities. The rest of the sentences should begin with your most important duties and accomplishments and proceed to lesser ones.

Let me give you an example of a job description in rough draft format and one that has been rearranged, and I'm sure you will see what I mean.

JOHNSON UNIVERSITY HOSPITAL, New Brunswick, New Jersey (2000 – 2003)
Director, Pediatric Emergency Department
- Recently developed and implemented an expansion of the department into a new children's hospital.
- Hired and managed a staff of 40 employees, directed performance improvement initiatives, and implemented departmental standards of care.
- Analyzed trends for key indicators to improve subsequent code responses.
- Member of the Performance Improvement Committee.
- Analyzed 72-hour readmission trends to find problems with practice patterns.
- Selected for the Code Response Team: Developed a new performance improvement form.
- Redesigned resuscitation guidelines for residents and nursing staff.
- Directed clinical and administrative operations of a 12,000-visit-per-year pediatric emergency department.
- Developed and managed an operating budget of $1.3 million.
- Developed staffing standards and evaluated the qualifications/competence of department personnel to provide appropriate levels of patient care.
- Member of the Health Policy and Strategic Planning Committee responsible for preparing the hospital and staff for JCAHO accreditation reviews.
- Implemented a pain initiative.

After numbering and rearranging the sentences, the section reads much stronger and has a better flow.

JOHNSON UNIVERSITY HOSPITAL, New Brunswick, New Jersey (2000 – 2003)
Director, Pediatric Emergency Department
- Directed clinical and administrative operations of a 12,000-visit-per-year pediatric emergency department.
- Developed and managed an operating budget of $1.3 million.
- Hired and managed a staff of 40 employees, directed performance improvement initiatives, and implemented departmental standards of care.
- Developed staffing standards and evaluated the qualifications/competence of department personnel to provide appropriate levels of patient care.
- Member of the Health Policy and Strategic Planning Committee responsible for preparing the hospital and staff for JCAHO accreditation reviews.

Key Accomplishments:
- Recently developed and implemented an expansion of the department into a new children's hospital.
- Member of the Performance Improvement Committee: Analyzed 72-hour readmission trends to find problems with practice patterns. Implemented a pain initiative. Redesigned resuscitation guidelines for residents and nursing staff.
- Selected for the Code Response Team: Developed a new performance improvement form. Analyzed trends for key indicators to improve subsequent code responses.

Here is my reasoning for rearranging the sentences:

1. The first sentence was selected because it was a good overall statement of the job's major responsibility.

2. The second sentence added a further sense of scope by describing the size of the director's budget.

3. The third sentence also added a sense of scope by discussing the number of employees managed and other supervisory responsibilities.

4. The next two sentences are secondary job duties and special assignments.

5. In order to emphasize achievements, key accomplishments were pulled out into a separate section.

6. The first bullet was the most important accomplishment and the most recent.

7. All of the bullets that applied to the Performance Improvement Committee were listed together in a separate paragraph.

8. The last accomplishment was the least important.

STEP ELEVEN—RELATED QUALIFICATIONS

At the bottom of your résumé (or sometimes toward the top), you can add anything else that might qualify you for your job objective. This includes licenses, certifications, special skills, languages, credentials, publications, speeches, presentations, exhibits, grants, special projects, research, affiliations, volunteer activities, civic contributions, honors, awards, distinctions, professional recognitions, computer skills, international experience, and sometimes even interests if they truly relate. Here are some more specific examples:

- If you want a job in sports marketing, stating on your résumé that you play tennis or are a triathlete would be an asset.

- If you are a computer programmer or network administration, a technology section is a must.
- Résumés for a U.S. company doing business in certain foreign countries could benefit from an "Interests" section would show a prospective employer that your hobbies are compatible with the host country.
- Students, or those who have recently graduated, often have a difficult time coming up with enough paid experience to demonstrate their qualifications. But, if they have held leadership positions in campus organizations or have supervised groups of people and organized activities on a volunteer basis, then an "Activities" section could strengthen those qualifications.
- International résumés in almost all cases require date of birth, place of birth, citizenship, marital status, sex, and often a photograph.

And the list goes on. It is important to use your judgment, since only you know best what qualifications are important in your field. For instance, several of my clients are ministers. In their line of work, it is very important to list a great deal of personal information that most employers would not need to know or even be allowed by law to request. In their case, the information they provide relates directly to bona fide occupational qualifications for the jobs they are seeking.

STEP TWELVE—PROFILE

Last but not least, write four or five sentences that give an overview of your qualifications. This profile or qualifications summary should be placed at the beginning of your résumé. You can include some of your personal traits or special skills that might have been difficult to get across in your job descriptions. This section should reflect a clear target, a summary of your unique value propositions, and supporting keywords to emphasize your core competencies.

The profile section of your résumé must be relevant to the type of job for which you are applying, so customize it for each job application, if possible. It might be true that you are "compassionate," but will it help you get a job as a high-pressure salesperson? Write this profile from the perspective of a potential employer. What will convince this person to call you instead of someone else?

Some HR professionals might disagree with me. They say that they skip over descriptions of unverifiable claims about personal strengths, but there are just as many HR managers who read every word. Besides, you want to make sure you cover your soft skills for e-résumés where keywords defined in job requisitions often request such strengths.

Here is a sample profile section for a computer systems technician looking for a job with a military contractor:

- Experienced systems/network technician with significant communications and technical control experience in the military sector.
- Focused and hard working; willing to go the extra mile for the customer.
- Skilled in troubleshooting complex problems by thinking outside the box.
- Possesses a high degree of professionalism and dedication to exceptional quality.
- Current Top Secret security clearance with access to Sensitive Compartmented Information.

It is also acceptable to use a keyword summary like the one on the next page to give a "quick and dirty" look at your qualifications:

Certifications: CompTIA A+ Certified, Certified Work Group Manager.

Networks: Networking concepts and architecture, client/server and peer-to-peer local-area and wide-area networks (LAN/WAN), servers, routers, switches, hubs, cabling in Ethernet environments, command and control networks, secure SIPR nets, Windows NT, Windows 2000, Exchange, Proxy Server, Microsoft System Management Server (SMS), UNIX.

Equipment: Network interface cards, sound cards, SCSI cards, tape drives, hard drives, printers, and peripherals.

Software: MS Word, Excel, PowerPoint, Access, Outlook, Internet Explorer, Remedy, MS Exchange, SQL Server, Norton Antivirus, Ghost, MS Proxy, Sidewinder Firewall.

This type of laundry list isn't very interesting for a human being to read, but a few recruiters in high-tech industries like this list of terms because it gives them a quick overview of an applicant's skills. Don't use these keyword lists in place of the sentences of a profile section, though. Keywords used out of context do not have the same impact when processed by electronic résumé processing software. Newer applications use artificial intelligence to determine a keyword's credibility based on the surrounding text.

For human readers, however, it is okay to pull out a few key bullets that highlight your areas of expertise (see sample below). Just make sure you use the same words somewhere within the body of your résumé.

- Dedicated accountant with thirteen years of diverse experience that includes
  - Public accounting
  - Internal auditing
  - Nonprofit accounting
  - Compliance auditing
  - Tax preparation
  - Reporting
- Certified Public Accountant in California and Colorado; Certified Internal Auditor.
- Analytical professional with a track record of success managing the toughest assignments.
- Effective team player with exceptional communication, writing, and interpersonal skills.

In the keywords section of this chapter, I covered keywords that reflect soft skills in more detail. You can weave these "soft skills" and other adjectives into your profile: resourceful, team player, bilingual, confident, savvy, creative, positive, quick-thinking, reliable, dependable, effective, devoted, honest, loyal, tenacious, veteran, experienced, ambitious, inquisitive, accomplished, results-driven, proven, flexible, driven, analytical, self-motivated, dynamic, articulate, successful, tactful, certified, among many others.

When you get to the Executive Résumés chapter, you will find executive summaries, quotes that reflect your unique value proposition, keyword lists for areas of expertise, functional summaries, and other additions to the profile section that give your reader a head's up on what they will find in the body of your résumé. There is no reason that these tactics can't be used by anyone, especially if you want your résumé to stand out. Here's an example:

AREAS OF EXPERTISE

P&I Management • Strategic Planning
Transportation/Logistics • Budgeting
Supply Chain Management • Outsourcing
Technology Enhancements
Quality Management • Regulatory Affairs

"It's all about the people. The greatest reward of leadership is helping to develop people, which leads to exceptional organizational results."

EXECUTIVE SUMMARY

- Strong record of streamlining operations, reducing costs, and increasing profitability while facilitating quality and operations improvements for both large and small organizations.
- Definitive success in start-up and turnaround situations, as well as stable business environments.
- Domestic and international experience in a broad range of industries.
- Recent Executive MBA with a concentration in Finance, International Business, and Corporate Strategy.

A similar idea creates a section for quotes from performance evaluations, letters of reference, customer comments, and other positive comments that are difficult to weave into the body of a résumé. You can put the quotes in the margins of the résumé, in pull-out boxes, in a separate section, or worked individually at the end of a relevant bullet. You will find an example of such a résumé on pages 41–42, with another on page 73. Here is a sample of customer comments pulled out into a separate section:

CUSTOMER COMMENTS

"Allan has proven to be extremely knowledgeable and professional in executing my local Cable TV media campaigns. Having worked in cable advertising sales myself for six years, I can appreciate when a media salesperson does a great job from the initial schedule planning stage to the final invoice." – Mike Smith, Champion

"His thorough knowledge of his product and the sales process are evidence of his many years of success in media sales. I enthusiastically recommend Allen for any sales position and am confident that his competency and positive attitude would make him a valuable asset." – Christin Jones, Academy Agency & Advisors

"As a representative for Comcast, Allan was one of the few who understood the true meaning of the word 'service.'" – Robert Smith, Adams Advertising Agency

"Allan has the four traits that make him a great sales rep: friendly, responsible, efficient, and fun. If Allan is applying for a job with your company, I suggest hiring him immediately!" – Brian Jones, Hanson Marketing & Advertising

Busy recruiters spend as little as ten seconds deciding whether to read a résumé from top to bottom. You will be lucky if the first third of your résumé gets read on the first pass, so make sure whatever information is at the top entices the reader to read it all.

YOU'RE DONE—WELL, ALMOST!

Now it's time to put all of this information together into the perfect résumé. You have a qualifications summary, your education, experience, and other relevant information. The only thing you lack is your contact information.

For the contact information, you can use your full name, first and last name only, or shortened names (Pat Criscito instead of Patricia K. Criscito).

Do not use work telephone numbers or a work e-mail address on your résumé. Potential employers tend to consider that an abuse of company resources, which implies you might do the same if you are working for them. Listing a cellular telephone number on your résumé gives a hiring manager a way to reach you during working hours.

Avoid the use of "cutesy" e-mail addresses on a résumé. If you use *babycakes@ aol.com* for your personal e-mail, create a second e-mail address under your account that will be more professional. If your only access to the Internet is at work, then create a free-mail account at *hotmail.com, juno.com, usa.net, yahoo.com, gmail.com, aol.com, msn.com, mail.com, excite.com,* or *e-mail.com.* Try to get your name as your e-mail address *(patcriscito@yahoo. com)* and avoid underlines between words.

I highly recommend creating a special e-mail address just for your job search. That way, you can close it down after you get the job and you won't be inundated with junk e-mails that will inevitably follow posting your résumé online. Getting your own domain name *(www. patcriscito.com)* is the ideal way to create e-mail addresses *(pat@patcriscito.com)* since it helps you build your brand image and makes your name memorable.

Now it's time to typeset your information in a style that reflects your personality for your paper résumé. There is a science behind laying out a paper résumé, just like there is a science behind designing advertisements, and you need to feel comfortable with your word processing software before you even start. If you are not, then you should call in a professional typesetter, designer, or résumé writer for this part (see the list of résumé writing organizations on page 21). You have just finished the hardest part of a résumé—the writing of it—so you may be able to save some money by shopping around when getting it typeset. Make sure the designer/writer knows you need a résumé that will upload to websites and attach to e-mail messages, including MS Word, PDF, and ASCII text files.

An experienced résumé writer and designer can take the work you have done and enhance it with a wealth of seasoned knowledge, turning it into a finely tuned marketing instrument that truly reflects who you are. The finished résumé will attract a reader to learn more about you in an interview, which is the whole purpose of your résumé anyway.

Whether you typeset your résumé yourself or hire someone else to do it for you, the ultimate responsibility for the accuracy of your résumé is *yours*. Make sure every word is spelled correctly and that your grammar is perfect. Spelling and grammar errors are the pet peeve of 59% of recruiters, while 29% hate inaccurate information. Double proofread your dates, address, phone number, and any other numbers that might appear in your résumé. Make sure punctuation is consistent and that you haven't used the ampersand (&) in place of the word *and* (except in the case of a company name when the company uses it that way). When you are absolutely certain it is perfect, then have someone else read it again just to make sure!

Just because a computer will screen your résumé in the beginning and look for keywords is no excuse for poor writing. Your ultimate goal is to entice a human being to read your résumé, so keep the sentences interesting by using positive power verbs. Try to use a variety of these words. It is easy to choose the same one to begin every sentence, but there are synonyms buried within this list that will make your writing better.

A

abated
abbreviated
abolished
abridged
absolved
absorbed
accelerated
accentuated
accommodated
accompanied
accomplished
accounted for
accrued
accumulated
achieved
acquired
acted
activated
actuated
adapted
added
addressed
adhered to
adjusted
administered
adopted
advanced
advertised
advised
advocated
affirmed
aided
alerted
aligned
allayed
alleviated
allocated
allotted
altered
amassed
amended
amplified
analyzed
answered
anticipated
appeased
applied
appointed
appraised
approached
appropriated
approved
arbitrated
aroused
arranged
articulated
ascertained
aspired
assembled
assessed
assigned
assimilated
assisted
assumed
assured
attained
attended
attracted
audited
augmented
authored
authorized
automated
averted
avoided
awarded

B

balanced
bargained
began
benchmarked
benefitted
bid
billed
blended
blocked
bolstered
boosted
bought
branded
bridged
broadened
brought
budgeted
built

C

calculated
calibrated
canvassed
capitalized
captured
cared for
carried
carried out
carved
catalogued
categorized
caught
cautioned
cemented
centralized
conferred
configured
confirmed
confronted
connected
conserved
considered
consolidated
constructed
consulted
consummated
contacted
continued
contracted
contributed
controlled
converted
conveyed
convinced
cooperated
coordinated
copied
corrected
correlated
corresponded
counseled
counted
created
credited with
critiqued
cultivated
customized
cut

D

dealt
debated
debugged
decentralized
decided
decoded

decreased
dedicated
deferred
defined
delegated
deleted
delineated
delivered
demonstrated
deployed
depreciated
derived
described
designated
designed
detailed
detected
determined
developed
devised
devoted
diagnosed
diagramed
differentiated
diffused
directed
disbursed
disclosed
discounted
discovered
discussed
dispatched
dispensed
dispersed
displayed
disposed
disproved
dissected
disseminated
dissolved
distinguished
distributed
diversified
diverted
divested
divided
documented
doubled

drafted
dramatized
drew up
drove

E

earned
eased
economized
edited
educated
effected
elaborated
elected
elevated
elicited
eliminated
embraced
emphasized
employed
empowered
enabled
encountered
encouraged
ended
endorsed
enforced
engaged
engineered
enhanced
enlarged
enlisted
enriched
enrolled
ensured
entered
entertained
enticed
equipped
established
estimated
evaluated
examined
exceeded
exchanged
executed
exercised

exhibited
expanded
expedited
experienced
experimented
explained
explored
exposed
expressed
extended
extracted
extrapolated

F

fabricated
facilitated
factored
familiarized
fashioned
fielded
filed
filled
finalized
financed
fine-tuned
finished
fixed
focused
followed
forecasted
forged
formalized
formatted
formed
formulated
fortified
forwarded
fostered
fought
found
founded
framed
fulfilled
functioned as
funded
furnished
furthered

G

gained
garnered
gathered
gauged
gave
generated
governed
graded
graduated
granted
graphed
grasped
greeted
grew
grouped
guaranteed
guided

H

halted
halved
handled
headed
heightened
held
helped
hired
honed
hosted
hypnotized
hypothesized

I

identified
ignited
illuminated
illustrated
implemented
imported
improved
improvised
inaugurated
incited
included
incorporated
increased

incurred
indicated
individualized
indoctrinated
induced
influenced
informed
infused
initialized
initiated
innovated
inspected
inspired
installed
instigated
instilled
instituted
instructed
insured
integrated
intensified
interacted
interceded
interfaced
interpreted
intervened
interviewed
introduced
invented
inventoried
invested
investigated
invigorated
invited
involved
isolated
issued
itemized

joined
judged
justified

launched
learned

leased
lectured
led
lessened
leveraged
licensed
lifted
lightened
limited
linked
liquidated
listened
litigated
loaded
lobbied
localized
located
logged

made
maintained
managed
mandated
maneuvered
manipulated
manufactured
mapped
marked
marketed
mastered
maximized
measured
mediated
memorized
mentored
merchandised
merged
merited
met
minimized
mobilized
modeled
moderated
modernized
modified
molded
monitored

monopolized
motivated
mounted
moved
multiplied

named
narrated
navigated
negotiated
netted
networked
neutralized
nominated
normalized
noticed
notified
nurtured

O

observed
obtained
offered
officiated
offset
opened
operated
optimized
orchestrated
ordered
organized
oriented
originated
outdistanced
outlined
outperformed
overcame
overhauled
oversaw
owned

P

paced
packaged
packed

paid
pared
participated
partnered
passed
patterned
penalized
penetrated
perceived
perfected
performed
permitted
persuaded
phased out
photographed
piloted
pinpointed
pioneered
placed
planned
played
polled
posted
praised
predicted
prepared
prescribed
presented
preserved
presided
prevailed
prevented
priced
printed
prioritized
probed
processed
procured
produced
profiled
programmed
progressed
projected
promoted
prompted
proofread
proposed
protected

proved
provided
pruned
publicized
published
purchased
pursued

Q

quadrupled
qualified
quantified
queried
questioned
quoted

R

raised
rallied
ranked
rated
reached
reacted
read
realigned
realized
rearranged
reasoned
rebuilt
received
reclaimed
recognized
recommended
reconciled
reconstructed
recorded
recovered
recruited
rectified
redesigned
redirected
reduced
re-engineered
referred
refined
refocused

regained
registered
regulated
rehabilitated
reinforced
reinstated
reiterated
rejected
related
released
relied
relieved
remained
remediated
remodeled
rendered
renegotiated
renewed
reorganized
repaired
replaced
replicated
replied
reported
represented
reproduced
requested
required
requisitioned
researched
reserved
reshaped
resolved
responded
restored
restructured
retained
retooled
retrieved
returned
revamped
revealed
reversed
reviewed
revised
revitalized
revolutionized
rewarded

risked
rotated
routed

S

safeguarded
salvaged
saved
scanned
scheduled
screened
sculptured
searched
secured
segmented
seized
selected
sent
separated
sequenced
served as
serviced
settled
set up
shaped
shared
sharpened
shipped
shortened
superceded
supervised
supplied
supported
surpassed
surveyed
swayed
swept
symbolized
synchronized
synthesized
systemized

T

tabulated
tackled
tailored
talked

tallied
targeted
tasted
taught
teamed
tempered
tended
terminated
tested
testified
tied
tightened
took
topped
totaled
traced
tracked
traded
trained
transacted
transcribed
transferred
transformed
transitioned
translated
transmitted
transported
traveled
treated
trimmed
tripled
troubleshot
turned
tutored
typed

U

uncovered
underlined
underscored
undertook
underwrote
unearthed
unified
united
updated
upgraded

upheld	vaulted	**W** ▪ ▪	won
urged	verbalized		worked
used	verified	weathered	wove
utilized	viewed	weighed	wrote
	visited	welcomed	
V ▪ ▪	visualized	widened	**Y** ▪ ▪
validated	voiced	withstood	
valued	volunteered	witnessed	yielded

▪ ▪ ▪ ▪ **MORE ABOUT KEYWORDS**

Using the right keywords for your particular experience and education is critical to the success of your electronic résumé. Without the right keywords, your résumé will float in cyberspace forever waiting for a hiring manager to find it. If your résumé contains all the right keywords, then you will be among the first candidates whose résumés are reviewed. If you lack only one of the keywords, then your résumé will be next in line after résumés that have them all, and so on.

Remember, your keywords are the specific terminology used in your job that reflect your experience and skills. For instance, *operating room* and *ICU* immediately classify the experience of a nurse, but *pediatric ICU* narrows it down even further.

Don't try to limit your résumé by using fewer words. If your information is longer than one page, a reader looking at a computer screen won't be able to tell, but the computer doing a keyword search will know if a word is not there. Recall, however, that you only need to use a word one time for it to be considered a "hit" in a keyword search. Try to use synonyms wherever possible to broaden your chances of being selected.

You should also understand the difference between a simple keyword search and a concept search. When a recruiter brings an e-mailed résumé onto the screen and sends the computer on a search for a single word like marketing—which one can do in any word processing program with a few clicks of a mouse or function key—he or she is performing a keyword search.

You are also performing a keyword search when you type a word or combination of words into the command line of a search engine like Yahoo! or Google. In that case, sometimes the computer searches entire documents for matches and other times it looks only at headers or extracts from the files.

A concept search, on the other hand, can bridge the gap between words by reading entire phrases and then using sophisticated artificial intelligence to interpret what is being said, translating the phrase into a single word, like *network,* or a combination of words, like *project management.*

For example, in a simple keyword search on Manager of Product Sales, ordinary software would return a match on a candidate's résumé that reads "worked for a Manager of Product Sales." A concept search can distinguish between this résumé and another candidate's résumé that indicated "served as a Manager of Product Sales."

The various software packages that extract data from electronic résumés are incredibly sophisticated. They can read the grammar of noun, verb, and adjective combinations and extract the information for placement on the form that will become your entry in a résumé database. Expert system extraction engines use a complex knowledge base of more than 200,000 rules and over ten million résumé terms. They recognize grammatical structure variations, including synonyms and context within natural language text.

They even know the difference between words by their placement on the page and their relationship to the header that precedes it—Experience, Education, or Computer Skills.

Because of this complicated logic, and because each company and each hiring manager has the ability to personalize the search criteria for each job opening, it is impossible to give you a concrete list of the thousands of possible keywords that could be used to search for any one job.

For instance, Sun Systems graciously conducted a keyword search of their résumé database for me and brought up the following criteria from two different hiring managers for the same job title. These are keywords extracted from real job requisitions written by hiring managers.

FINANCIAL ANALYST/SENIOR ACCOUNTANT

REQUIRED:
- BS in finance or accounting with 4 years of experience or
- MBA in related field with 2 years of relevant experience
- certified public accountant
- forecasting

REQUIRED:
- BS in finance or accounting with 4 years of experience or
- MBA in related field with 2 years of relevant experience
- accounting
- financial reporting
- financial statement
- Excel

DESIRED:
- accounting
- financial
- trend analysis
- financial statement
- results analysis
- trends
- strategic planning
- develop trends
- financial modeling
- personal computer
- microcomputers
- DCF
- presentation skills
- team player

DESIRED:
- ability
- customer
- new business
- financial analysis
- financial
- forecasting
- process improvement
- policy development
- business policies
- PowerPoint
- Microsoft Word
- analytical ability

You can see why it is so difficult to give definitive lists of keywords and concepts. However, it is possible to give you samples of actual keyword searches used by the recruiters at Sun Systems to give you some ideas.

Let me emphasize again that you should list only experience you actually have gained. Do not include the keywords on the following pages in your résumé just because they are listed here.

ACCOUNT EXECUTIVE

REQUIRED:
- BS degree
- 3 years technical selling experience
- Fortune 500 account management experience
- sales
- storage industry
- solution selling

DESIRED:
- Siebel
- quota levels
- VAD
- VAR

ACCOUNTING ANALYST

REQUIRED:
- BA or MBA
- 2–4 years of experience
- asset management
- SAP
- accounting

DESIRED:
- fixed assets
- capital assets
- corporate tax
- US GAAP

BASE SALES REPRESENTATIVE

REQUIRED:
- 2–4 years of sales or contract management experience
- 2+ years of telemarketing or telesales experience

DESIRED:
- Siebel
- storage industry

BUSINESS MANAGER, CENTRAL ARCHIVE MANAGEMENT

REQUIRED:
- BS in engineering or computer science
- 10 years of related engineering and/or manufacturing experience
- strategic planning
- network
- product management
- program management

DESIRED:
- business plan
- line management
- pricing
- team player
- CAM
- marketing
- product strategy
- vendor
- general management
- OEM
- profit and loss

BUSINESS OPERATIONS SPECIALIST

REQUIRED:
- bachelor's degree
- 4 years of directly related experience
- production schedule
- project planning

DESIRED:
- ability to implement
- CList
- data analysis
- off-shift
- team player
- automation
- ability to plan
- customer interaction
- VM
- CMS
- JCL
- REXX
- MVS
- UNIX
- analytical ability
- customer interface
- network
- skills analysis
- automatic tools

DEVELOPMENT ENGINEER, ADVISORY

REQUIRED:
- BS/BA, Masters desired
- 5–10 years mechanical engineering experience
- 10+ years experience in hardware design
- EMC/EMI debug
- mechanical design
- tape drive

DESIRED:
- DFSS (Design for Six Sigma)
- ANSYS or Metlab
- mechanisms design
- shock
- vibration
- NARTE
- tape library
- data storage

FINANCIAL ANALYST, STAFF

REQUIRED:
- BS in Finance or Accounting
- 1–2 years related experience
- customer-focused experience
- excellent written communication skills
- collection
- financial forecast
- financial modeling
- financial reporting
- financial consolidation
- reconciliation

DESIRED:
- international finance
- hyperion consolidation software
- channel experience

ORDER SPECIALIST

REQUIRED:
- BS degree
- 1–3 years experience
- order administration
- order fulfillment
- invoice processing
- Microsoft Word
- Excel

DESIRED:
- database

PROJECT MANAGER, HUMAN RESOURCES

REQUIRED:
- bachelor's degree in human resources, business, or related field
- 6 years broad experience

DESIRED:
- communications
- project management
- milestone development
- time management
- credibility
- recruiting
- long-range planning
- sourcing

SECRETARY III

REQUIRED:
- high school education or equivalent
- 5 years of experience
- typing skill of 55–60 wpm
- interpersonal skills
- oral communication

DESIRED:
- administrative assistance
- clerical
- data analysis
- file maintenance
- material repair
- PowerPoint
- project planning
- reports
- screen calls
- troubleshoot
- answer phones
- communication skills
- document distribution
- mail sorting
- Microsoft Word
- presentation
- publication
- schedule calendar
- secretarial
- appointments
- confidential
- edit
- material
- policies and procedures
- problem solving

- records management
- schedule conference
- telephone interview

SOFTWARE ENGINEER—EMBEDDED, ADVISORY LEVEL

REQUIRED:
- BS or MS degree in one of the computer sciences or engineering
- 12–14 years of experience minimum
- controller architecture design experience
- disk controller
- fiber channel
- SCSI design
- embedded systems

DESIRED:
- open systems
- product development

SOFTWARE ENGINEER—EMBEDDED, STAFF

REQUIRED:
- BS or MS degree in one of the computer sciences or engineering
- 3–5 years of experience minimum
- C++
- embedded systems
- realtime

DESIRED:
- pSOS
- iCLinux

SOFTWARE ENGINEER, SENIOR

REQUIRED:
- BS/MS in engineering, computer science or closely related field
- 8 to 9 years of experience

DESIRED:
- C+
- customer
- hiring/firing
- prototype
- structured design
- code development
- DASD
- methodology
- real time
- supervision
- communication skills
- experiment design
- problem solving
- software design
- testing

SYSTEMS ENGINEER, SENIOR

REQUIRED:
- BS degree in related field
- 8–10 years of experience
- pre-sales
- systems engineering
- MVS
- data storage

DESIRED:
- systems configuration
- capacity planning
- DFHSM
- HSC
- presentation skills

GRETA FERGUSON

1212 W. Figeroa, Phoenix, AZ 85044

Cell: 602.555.5555   Greta.Ferguson@protypeltd.com

PHARMACEUTICAL / MEDICAL SALES

Drive brand awareness, sales, revenues, and market share in highly competitive medical markets.

Provide strong sales leadership with a focused and confident consultative approach throughout the sales cycle to identify new opportunities and consistently exceed performance goals. Combine well-developed technical knowledge and a commitment to service excellence with an earned reputation for innovative thinking, integrity, and professionalism.

Professional Strengths

Marketing Strategy ... Sales Planning ... New Business Development ... Market / Competitive Analysis
Territory Management ... Product Launches ... Market Penetration / Growth ... Negotiation / Closing
Relationship Management ... Regulatory Compliance ... Conversions ... Computer Proficiency
Presentation / Education ... Partnerships / Alliances ... Sales Mentoring ... Branding

---

EXPERIENCE

NaturCord, Inc., Tucson, Arizona   2007–2010
[Swedish-based umbilical cord stem cell banking organization]

TERRITORY MANAGER
- Pinal and Pima Counties
- Clients: OB/GYN physicians and hospital Labor & Delivery Departments as well as direct to consumer

> *"Greta's sincerity, commitment, and focus on company success were matched by her ability to drive out issues and risks of project activities, communicate clearly, and identify the right resources to tackle the problems."* – Amy Sulan, District Manager, NaturCord

Pioneered position to open new market / ramp-up in Southern Arizona, the first U.S. location, cultivating relationships and building brand to maximize visibility and enrollments.

- Developed a territory plan to achieve market presence, countering higher pricing with exceptional service. Recognized as #1 producer (of 6), generating most enrollments since first month in field.
- Galvanized sales force through "revolving door" of managers, sharing sales passion while guiding and training novice team to exude confidence and close first sales.
- Broke through barrier at Saddleback Hospital to create kit partnership and a potential 40% increase in sales. Identified and corrected quality issues, working collaboratively with materials management staff.

XYZ Medical Products, Pristine Valley, Arizona   2004–2007
[Leading provider of surgical and technical services / equipment]

TERRITORY MANAGER
- Phoenix Territory including Tucson and Flagstaff
- Clients: Urologists, cardiac surgeons, OB/GYNs, and ENT physicians in hospitals and private practice

> *"Greta was the driving force behind our success in the Phoenix market. She knows her product and her market better than anyone."* – Randolf Fisher, Regional Manager, XYZ Medical Products

Revitalized neglected territory, mending relationships strained by prior lack of follow-up and quality issues. Initiated focused quarterly and monthly territory plans characterized by targeted marketing strategies and personalized service to consistently achieve 115%+ of sales goal.

- Cultivated relationships with key hospital contacts—materials managers and operating room supervisors as well as physicians—applying persistence and consultative sales techniques.
    - Secured and sustained contracts / preferred vendor status, acquiring 20% more cases.
    - Gained back business from competitors at six major hospitals, converting 34 physicians for a total of 49 cases and 47% boost in revenues.
- Launched new surgical laser, scrubbing into OR to assist technicians with equipment set-up, talking doctors through initial usage, and obtaining feedback through procedures.
    - Increased usage 35% to earn second highest bonus payout for Q2 2008.

EXPERIENCE (continued)

Premier Oral Healthcare, Phoenix, Arizona   2000–2004
[Division of Bastian Electronics, one of world's largest electronics companies]

DENTAL FIELD SALES REPRESENTATIVE
- Phoenix and Tucson Territory
- Clients: Dental offices

Created daily call plan to access opportunities to build relationships within dental practices. Coordinated "lunch and learn" presentations to close new partnerships or convert dentists from competitor while cultivating future sales.

- Developed several marketing and sales tools to increase territory revenue that were successfully adopted by Premier nationwide.
- Earned numerous sales awards during tenure:
    - Ranked #1 (of 9) in region for dispensing unit sales, 4Q 2005.
    - Achieved #2 for most revenue generated 3Q 2006, 110.68% of goal.
    - Consistently outsold the competition, gaining 17 clients from largest competitor 3Q 2006.

> *"Greta turned it up by making her goal on every call to access the entire office looking for opportunities to brand each office with our product. In Q4 2003, Greta had 70% access!"* – Arlene Simington, Premier Oral Healthcare, Western Regional Manager

Living by Design, Inc., Phoenix, Arizona   1998–2000
[Nutraceutical company]

INTEGRATIVE MEDICAL CONSULTANT
- Northern Arizona Territory
- Clients: Nutritionists, naturopaths, primary care physicians and chiropractors as distributors

Promoted nurtraceutical products with a consultative sales approach, implementing protocols while building strong relationships, trust, and confidence. Increased monthly sales 285% within 6 months.

- Introduced private labeling opportunities to medical aesthetics company to win conversion from competitor.
- Developed customized protocols for seven-office physicians group, leading to long-term contracts and $10K additional annual sales.

> *"[Greta] is conscientious, hard working, and dedicated to the prime objective of keeping our patients and staff happy. She has been proactive in getting me educated about [the] products and how to integrate them into our practice."* – Arthur Drain, CEO, Western Aesthetics, Client

EDUCATION

Arizona State University, Tempe, Arizona
BACHELOR OF ARTS, COMMUNICATION (AS A PRE-NURSING PROGRAM)
- Course work included Anatomy, Physiology, Microbiology, and Chemistry
- Internships: Banner Thunderbird Hospital, ER Radiology and OB/GYN

Professional Development
- **Advanced Sales Training**, Premier Oral

VOLUNTEER SERVICE

- Mentor, Big Brothers / Big Sisters of Maricopa County
- Volunteer, Share and Share Alike (co-op food pantry)

Excellence is never an accident.

Résumé Design Rules

Rules, rules, rules . . . they're everywhere, including in advertising design and typesetting. You can't escape them, so let me simplify the rules for you. A good advertisement has a headline that grabs the reader's attention—in a résumé, the headline is your name. The next chapter will provide you with some ideas for creating letterheads around your name, which separates the "product name" visually from the text of the "ad," which is your résumé.

Next, the reader of your résumé needs to grasp its message quickly, which is why we use bulleted sentences on a résumé with short lines of text, power verbs, dynamic but concise sentences, and an opening (or profile) that summarizes the features of the "product," which is you.

When you typeset an advertisement, you want to draw your reader's eye naturally down the page from the upper, left-hand corner to the bottom, right-hand corner. You will accomplish that with strategic use of white space, graphic lines, paragraphs, all capital letters, bold, and italics. Consistency is key to the readability of any document. Use exactly the same space between all sections and less white space between items in a section. Thumb through the résumés in this book and you will immediately see the effects of these treatments.

In today's job market, résumés (whether electronic or paper) don't have to be limited to one page. Craig MacDonald, in a special report for the *Seattle Post-Intelligencer*, says, "The cold, hard truth is, writing a résumé is just like advertising. Effective advertising means capturing the audience's attention quickly, concisely describing why someone should want to buy the product (you), and then closing the sale by suggesting a means of rapidly making the purchase. This has nothing to do with length, but a lot to do with format, language, tone, and style."

With e-résumés in particular, the more keywords and synonyms you are able to use, the better your chances of being selected in a keyword search. Therefore, it is better to have a two-page résumé with all your skills and qualifications listed than to have a one-page résumé with information missing because you tried to conserve space. According to the 2010 Orange County Résumé Survey, only 35.3% of recruiters prefer one-page résumés. Here is the general rule for a résumé today.

- New graduates—one page
- Most people—one or two pages
- Senior executives—two or three pages

One caution, however. With e-mailed résumés, the reader sees only one screen at a time and may decide to stop reading after the first screen if something doesn't entice him or her to read on. With paper résumés, multiple-page resumes need to be structured so that the content is rich but quickly absorbable. Therefore, you should make certain that the meat of your résumé is on the first half of the first page.

SCANNABLE RÉSUMÉS

What happens when your beautiful paper résumé ends up being mailed or faxed to a company that scans résumés into a computerized database instead of forwarding it to a hiring manager for review? It ends up in cyberspace instead of on someone's desk. This automated process requires a few special design considerations in order to make your résumé scanner friendly, which is what this section addresses.

According to *U.S. News & World Report*, more than 10,000 unsolicited résumés arrive every week at most Fortune 500 companies, and before the days of computerized applicant tracking systems, 80% were thrown out after a quick review. In a recent conversation with a Chicago recruiter with access to Coca-Cola's résumé database, I learned that Coke receives as many as 100,000 résumés a month!

It was simply impossible to keep track of that much paper until now. Instead of opening and reading thousands of paper résumés, companies can either scan them or import them directly into their databases by e-mail or via online application forms on their websites. The resulting applicant database becomes an HR department's most valuable asset that contains the credentials of hundreds of thousands of potential employees.

Recent sources indicate that nearly all large companies with 1,000 employees or more are using computerized applicant tracking systems that scan paper résumés. Even though these numbers sound large, in actuality they represent only 24% of companies nationwide. According to a survey conducted by the Society of Human Resource Managers, 76% of companies do not scan résumés.

As more and more companies have established a presence on the Internet and opened up their computer databases to e-mailed résumés, the scannability of your résumé has become less of an issue. The majority of résumés are sent as attachments to e-mails or in the body of e-mail messages.

When you e-mail your résumé directly to a company, you have total control over whether or not your information is correct. You are not at the whim of a scanner's ability to read your font or formatting. However, Fortune 1000 companies that scan résumés will continue to use their investment in this technology as long as they receive enough paper résumés to make the process worthwhile.

The U.S. government has invested a great deal of money over the past five years creating their computerized applicant tracking system, so making your paper résumé scanner friendly will continue to be important when sending your paper résumé to government agencies. Actually, I recommend applying for government jobs through *www.usajobs.opm. gov* so the entire process is automated—no scanner worries! But for those rare occasions when the only way to apply for a government jobs is with a mailed or faxed résumé, you will need to know the secrets of scannability.

You will find all types of advice on the Internet about how to create a scannable résumé, but most of that advice is seriously out of date. The technology has improved to the point where there are only a few things that cause a résumé to scan poorly. These include choosing the right fonts, laying out the text of your résumé in such a way that it is scanner friendly, selecting the right paper color, and mailing it correctly.

Before I get into the specifics, let me help you understand the technology. When your paper résumé is scanned, a special kind of software examines the dots of ink on your printed page and determines by their shapes which letters they represent. This is called optical character recognition, or OCR for short. This software matches patterns with sets of characters stored in its memory, which is one of the reasons why it is important to choose a type style (or font) for your résumé that conforms to normal letter shapes. If you use a highly decorative type style, the OCR software will have difficulty making matches and will misinterpret letters. This means your words won't be spelled correctly, which of course means that a keyword search for the word *bookkeeping* will never turn up your résumé if the OCR thought you typed *bmkkeepmg*.

Once the scanner has passed its light over your pieces of paper and the software interprets the black dots of ink as letters of the alphabet, the computer then begins extracting information to fill in its electronic form, which will become part of your electronic résumé file.

The font you choose for the body of your résumé causes more scannability problems than any formatting choice. Use popular fonts that are not overly decorative in order to ensure optimum scannability. It doesn't make any difference whether you choose a serif or a sans serif font, but the font size should be no smaller than 9 points and no larger than 12 points for the text. I recommend Times New Roman, Bookman, Century Schoolbook, Garamond, Palatino, Utopia, Arial, Avant Garde, Myriad Roman, and Optima, among other fonts with standard shapes. Avoid italics or type faces where one letter touches another.

The key to choosing a font for a scannable résumé is that none of the letters touch one another at any time. This can be caused by poor font design, by adjusting the kerning (the spacing between letters) in your word processor, or by printing your résumé with a low-quality printer. Even some ink-jet printers can cause the ink to run together between letters with the wrong kind of paper. Any time one letter touches another, a scanner will have a difficult time distinguishing the shapes of the letters and you can end up with misspellings on your résumé. A keyword search looks for words that are spelled correctly, so a misspelled word is as good as no word.

Don't use underlining on your résumé for the same reason. Underlines touch the descenders on letters like g, j, p, q, and y and make it difficult for an OCR program to interpret their shapes. For example, g j p q y with underlines.

The size and boldness of the type of your name should be larger than the largest font used in your text. I generally choose 18 to 20 points for names. You may use all capital letters, a combination of upper and lower case, or capitals combined with small capitals (LIKE THIS). Following is an example of a Times New Roman Bold font in a few good point sizes for the name on a résumé:

- **14 POINT NAME**
- **16 POINT NAME**
- **18 POINT NAME**
- **20 POINT NAME**

Avoid using decorative fonts like these for either your name or headlines if you think your résumé will be scanned:

CRACK MAN

Broadway Engraved

Bard

Commercial Script

COTTONWOOD

Crazed

Freestyle Script

Lalique

Kaufmann

Linotext

Using reverse boxes to print white type on a black (or gray shaded) background is another mistake in a scannable résumé (see the nonscannable résumés on pages 48–51). Scanners can't read them and your name and other reversed information will be missing from your résumé.

Make certain your name is at the top of each page of your résumé. The clerks who scan résumés are often dealing with hundreds of pieces of paper every day. It is not a good idea to staple a scannable résumé, so it is very easy for the pages of your résumé to become separated from each other.

Next comes your contact information. It isn't always necessary to put your address at the top of your résumé. Today's sophisticated applicant tracking systems know by more than position on the résumé whether the text is an address or phone number. It doesn't matter whether you put your contact information at the top or bottom of your résumé. Always list your e-mail address, your home and cellular telephone numbers, postal mailing information, e-folio URL, as well as LinkedIn and Facebook addresses.

Related to fonts are bullets—special characters used at the beginning of indented short sentences to call attention to individual items on a résumé. These characters should be solid (•) for a scannable résumé. Scanners interpret hollow bullets (0) as the letter "o." Don't use any unusually shaped bullets that the scanner will try to interpret as letters, like hollow boxes.

While we are on the topic of special characters, the percent (%) and ampersand (&) signs used to cause problems for some OCR software, but that isn't a problem anymore. From the perspective of good writing, however, you should always spell out the word *and,* except in cases where the ampersand appears in the name of a company or in a heading.

Even though you have probably heard that italics are a no-no on a scannable résumé, today's more sophisticated optical character recognition software can read italics without difficulty, provided one letter does not touch another. I spoke with some of the engineers who design résumé scanning software, and all of them stated that their software has no problem reading italics, and my staff has confirmed that with tests. We have even scanned résumés typeset in all italics without a problem, although I don't recommend that simply from a readability standpoint. The key is to choose a font that is easy to read, is not overly decorative, and does not have one letter touching another. The italic typefaces of any of the résumé samples in this book would be fine to use as accents on your résumé.

Now, let's deal with paper. Print your résumé on a high-quality, light-colored paper (white, off-white, or *very* light gray). Never use papers with a background or watermarks (pictures, marble shades, or speckles). The scanner tries to interpret the patterns and dots as letters. This is a good rule to follow even for paper résumés that will never be scanned. Often, companies will photocopy your résumé to hand to a hiring manager, and dark colors or patterns will simply turn into dark masses that make your résumé difficult to read. If a company has multiple locations, the original résumé may even get faxed from one site to another and the same thing would happen.

Print your résumé on only one side of the page and use standard-size 8½" × 11" paper. The scanner cannot turn your page over, so the reverse side might be missed when the clerk puts your résumé into the automatic document feeder. That same process is the reason why you should not use 11" × 17" size paper. The pages would have to be cut into 8½" × 11" sheets and the printing on the reverse side would not get scanned.

Don't fold your résumé, since the creases make it harder to scan and to handle. It is much better to invest in flat 9" × 12" envelopes and an extra two bits of postage to make a good first impression. Laser print and copier toner tend to crack off the page when creased, making the letters on the fold line less than solid, which a scanner could easily misinterpret. Staple holes can cause the pages of a résumé to stick together, so never put a staple in a résumé you know will be scanned.

Now that you know all the secrets for designing a résumé that will pass the scannability test, let's look at some sample résumés that scanned well (pages 52–56) and two that would scan poorly (pages 48–51).

PROFILE

- Experienced principal, administrator, facilities manager, and instructor
- Demonstrated success in leadership and supervisory positions
- Outstanding communication, negotiation, and presentation skills
- Graduate degree in educational leadership, Type D certification
- Current Colorado Principal's License

EXPERIENCE

Assistant Principal
Mitchell High School

Colorado Springs
School District 11
Colorado Springs, CO
2008 – present

Interim Principal
11/09 – 1/10

- Assist in the management of an urban high school with 1,350 students from a wide range of socio-economic sub-communities.
- Provide leadership to 38 teachers in the Counseling, Special Education, Consumer and Family Studies, Industrial Technology, English, and Mathematics Departments.
- Supervise and evaluate instructional and educational support staff, and implement staff development programs.
- Manage the design and development of the annual master schedule.
- Supervise the Security Department; implemented a successful student ID pilot program to increase school safety.
- Facilitate community meetings and supervise the community liaison responsible for promoting community partnerships with businesses and helping families in need of local resources.
- Ensure that staff allocations and operating expenses stay within budget.

Key Accomplishments:

- Selected to provide instructional leadership and overall management of the high school program for two months during the principal's absence.
- Facilitated the implementation of the Response to Intervention Initiative and the Professional Learning Communities model to improve academic achievement.
- Increased collaboration between departments and enhanced course offerings to better meet the needs of a diverse student population.
- Collaborated with a private consultant (Change Agency, Inc.) to teach instructors in the English Department how to use achievement data to improve their instruction. The result was increased communication and collaboration within a core academic department and a curriculum that was more closely assigned with state standards.
- Refocused the advisement process of the Counseling Department, which resulted in higher enrollment in more rigorous courses and a dramatic increase in student meetings with college representatives.
- Selected to serve on the District 11 Technical Assistance Team. Audited underperforming schools and made recommendations for implementation of Baldrige performance indicators at the middle school and high school levels.

> This résumé will not scan well because of the reverse box for the name and the unique column format that is difficult for scanners to interpret.

Principal
West Valley High School

Pikes Peak BOCES
Alternative High School
Colorado Springs, CO
2002 – 2008

- Provided instructional leadership and overall management of the alternative high school program.
- Developed and managed a $500,000 program budget, and helped to write the $13 million BOCES operating budget.
- Responsible for financial planning for the school, including forecasting staff and resource needs, allocating resources for sustainability, and administering funds to minimize waste.
- Chaired the Pikes Peak Principals Group responsible for facilitating communication with area principals and providing solutions to issues common to the group.
- Conducted focus groups and assisted districts in long-range planning as a member of the BOCES Communications Team.

EXPERIENCE	**Principal** **West Valley High School** **(continued)**	• Supervised counseling and special education services, including 504 and IEP compliance. • Enforced attendance, discipline, and expulsion policies/procedures. • Implemented standards-based, integrated curriculum resulting in increased student achievement. • Improved attendance by 25% and doubled the number of credits earned per year when compared to the students' home high schools. • Wrote federal and state grants and secured funding that accounted for one-third of the total operating budget. • Built an extensive network of community partnerships to benefit BOCES. • Coordinated with BOCES superintendents, principals, and counselors for educational programming. • Developed and oversaw the Pikes Peak Region Expelled Student Program. • Served as a member of the School-to-Career Coordinating Council. • Awarded Pikes Peak BOCES Employee of the Year for 1998.
	Assistant Principal **Lewis-Palmer High School** **Monument, CO** **1999 – 2002**	• Supervised computerized school management database of student schedules, attendance, grades, and cumulative records. • Administrative supervisor of the special education SIED program. • Implemented and managed policies and procedures for student behavior, discipline, and attendance. • Conferred with teachers, students, and parents to resolve educational and behavioral problems. • Supervised teachers and head of the counseling department; assisted in hiring processes; evaluated performance. • Coordinated with counseling department to develop annual master schedule; projected staffing and resource needs. • Participated in the development of the Pikes Peak BOCES/School-to-Career partnership, leading to an $80,000 grant. • Co-authored a grant for the suspension and expulsion prevention program.
EDUCATION	**University of Colorado** **Colorado Springs, CO**	**Type D Educational Administration Program** (1999) **Master of Arts, Educational Leadership** (1998) • 1994 Outstanding Student Award in Educational Leadership
	University of Wyoming **Laramie, WY**	**Bachelor of Science, Science Education** (1989) • Phi Kappa Delta Education Honorary Society
	Colorado State University **Ft. Collins, CO**	**Bachelor of Science, Geology** (1984)
PROFESSIONAL DEVELOPMENT	**1999 – present** **2002 – present** **2004 – present** **2008 – present** **2009 – present** **2009**	• Colorado Association of School Executives Annual Convention—presented "At-Risk Students and Alternative High Schools" in 1999. • Pikes Peak BOCES Workshops on Standards and Assessments. • AVA National Conference on Career and Technical Education. • Professional Learning Communities Conferences. • Malcolm Baldrige Model of Continuous Quality Improvement. • Educational Trust Conference, Washington, DC.
AFFILIATIONS	**1999 – present** **2009 – present** **1999 – present** **2006 – 2007** **2005**	• Colorado Association of School Executives • Colorado Springs Association of School Executives • National Association of Secondary School Principals • Chair, Pikes Peak Principals Group • Board of Directors, Young Entrepreneurs Association

RANDALL K. LAURENT

12345 Main Street ♦ East Syracuse, NY 13057
315.555-1234 ♦ Laurent@protypeltd.com

EXPERTISE

♦ SENIOR MANAGEMENT

♦ OPERATIONS

♦ TECHNOLOGY ASSESSMENT

♦ SOLUTION DESIGN

♦ STRATEGIC AND ORGANIZATIONAL PLANNING

♦ BUSINESS AND SYSTEMS ANALYSIS

♦ PROCESS IMPROVEMENTS

♦ CLIENT AND USER SUPPORT

♦ PERFORMANCE ANALYSIS

♦ ARCHITECTURE INFRASTRUCTURE

♦ TRAINING AND EDUCATION

♦ PROPOSAL SUBMISSION

♦ TECHNICAL SUPPORT

♦ BEST PRACTICES

♦ TEAM BUILDING

♦ PLANNING

♦ IMPLEMENTATION

♦ LEADERSHIP

SENIOR IT MANAGEMENT

Accomplished professional with vast understanding of operational functions. Skilled in system analysis, implementation, and improvements. Able to galvanize teams and drive bottom-line success. Articulate communicator—able to garner user needs and convey complex concepts to technical and non-technical professionals. Proven ability to meet stringent timelines and build cohesive product teams. Competent in system configuration, network management, and strategic planning in a multi-technology environment.

Relocating to your area in the near future.

PROFESSIONAL EXPERIENCE

THE ERASER COMPANY

Controller / Manager of Information Systems, Syracuse, NY, 2005–Present
Accepted controller duties, in addition to retaining IS functions at owner's request when position was vacated. **Drove corporate profits from $.5 to $1.8 million in 2007** (most profitable year in the company's 95-year history). Re-focused business plan, structuring sales, profit, and quality goals. Established metrics to track progress and increase department accountability. Supervised four department heads and insured success by updating team regarding goals, plans, and benchmarks. Served on company board of directors from 2006–2009, molding long-range corporate vision and leadership.

ACCOUNTING:
♦ Revamped reporting methods and migrated data from dBaseIII and Excel spreadsheets to the more nimble SyteLine ERP system.
♦ Reduced accounts receivable by 53% using improved data access and account accuracy made possible with redesigned reporting system.
♦ Activated payroll system in existing management software, eliminated outside maintenance fee, and saved 90% of annual expenditure—$15,000 down to $1,500.

SALES AND MARKETING:
♦ Re-staffed sales and marketing department and focused on distribution network expansion. Increased distributor sales from 10% of all purchases to more than 40% after eliminating 75% of non-performers and ramping up support to remaining 100 locations.
♦ Introduced inventory control methods into material samples laboratory, accounting for materials and speeding up sampling process for customers.
♦ Implemented measurements for customer calls, split off product specialist from customer service function and raised closing rate to 50% on highly qualified samples.
♦ Analyzed advertising methods, incorporated an Internet presence, and eliminated more than $50,000 in printing costs annually.

INVENTORY CONTROL:
♦ Implemented a cycle count system, dispensing with need for annual physical inventory and resultant four-week facility shutdown.
♦ Narrowed product line SKUs, wrote-off non-moving inventory, reduced obsolete and scrap material, and saved $600,000 in carrying costs during a five-year period.

PROFESSIONAL EXPERIENCE, CONTINUED

THE ERASER COMPANY

Manager of Information Systems, 2002–2005

Took corporation through process to select and transition to new management operation system. Conducted initial needs assessment, and reviewed products from 10 vendors with the potential to meet required operating criteria. Narrowed field to four candidates. Headed planning committee for the $1.3 million purchase, selected product, and directed installation.

♦ Networked and connected the multi-building company campus, something not available with old system. Harmonized system to meet new software requirements. Centralized COBOL mainframe to a client-server environment, making real-time data available to the entire organization.

♦ Activated sales contact management system, customized controls for sales department, simplified outgoing communication, and improved sales department efficiencies, saving time and improving responsiveness.

♦ Provided ongoing support to a well-stabilized system after accepting expanded managerial roles.

R.K.L. BUSINESS SYSTEMS INC.

Senior IT Consultant / Owner, Syracuse, NY, 1993–2002

Identified niche and built a solopreneurship from zero to $250,000 annual gross income, generated by stellar service to a diverse, 60-client base within a 50-mile radius of Syracuse. Promoted services through community involvement and garnered 100% of clients through word of mouth after only two years of operation.

♦ Awarded Compaq dealership in a highly competitive marketplace, enabling improved service to client base with one-stop hardware, software and technical support.

♦ Listened to users, ascertained specific needs and challenges, and mapped out appropriate action to meet customer operational goals. Researched options and learned new software, if needed, to address issues.

ADVANCED MEDICAL PRODUCTS

Director of Operations, Syracuse, NY, and Columbia, SC, 1991–1993

Managed the operation, technical, and administrative efforts of up to 35 staff professionals in a medical equipment manufacturing facility. Orchestrated plant move from NY to SC with minimal disruption in customer shipping commitments. Upgraded from Manufacturing Resource Planning (MRP) to Enterprise Resource Planning (ERP) system. Spearheaded training and worked out challenges during 18-month move. Promoted after three years from operations manager, serving as director for seven years.

EDUCATION

SYRACUSE UNIVERSITY, Syracuse, NY
Master of Science, Information Resources Management

EMPIRE STATE COLLEGE (SUNY), Syracuse, NY
Bachelor of Science, Business Management and Economics

◆ ◆ ◆

Michael G. Preston

111 West Sheridan Drive • Colorado Springs, Colorado 80909
Cellular: (719) 555-8901 • Email: mpreston@protypeltd.com

PROFILE
- Accomplished Pastry Chef and Instructor with more than 25 years of experience in the culinary arts, including vocational training, resort hotels, conference centers, and a retail cake shop.
- Maintained high standards in the culinary arts educational program, receiving excellent evaluations from students and the AVP Department Chair.
- Won numerous gold, silver, and bronze medals in professional food shows and local competitions.

CREDENTIALS
- Certified Executive Pastry Chef
- American Culinary Federation (ACF) Practical Exams (2008–present)
- Evaluator for ACF Site Visits in Oregon, Missouri, Michigan, and Denver, Colorado (2009–present)
- Certified instructor/proctor for the National Restaurant Association and ServSafe (2009–present)

EXPERIENCE

CULINARY INSTRUCTOR / HEAD OF PASTRY DEPARTMENT (Aug 2006–present)
Pikes Peak Community College, Colorado Springs, Colorado
Manage the Pastry Department and teach students in both the college and Area Vocational Program (AVP). Teach six baking/pastry courses and a food service concept course. Prepare syllabi for seven courses. Create new courses for candies and confections. Assist with the AVP search and screen process. Advise more than 200 students in the baking curriculum for each semester. Procure ingredients and supplies for the Culinary Arts (CUA) program, including purchasing of products from specialty markets. Maintain inventory for the Pastry Shop. Assist with preparation of faculty and staff lunches, and create banquet dessert buffets for college programs. Assist Chef Hudson, Culinary Arts Department Chair, in managing the Pastry Department and coordinating associated academic programs. Collaborate with the Supplemental Services Administrator to help special-needs students become certified and succeed in an academic environment through OASIS. Serve as Culinary Arts Club Advisor and CUA Program Advisor.
- Designed and implemented the CUA-153 Candy and Confectionary Course, as well as the CUA-161 Advanced Baking Wedding Cake Course.
- Developed master training curriculum for the AAS baking and pastry degree program.
- Implemented Desire2Learn hybrid online content for all pastry courses.
- Helped fellow pastry instructors with development of baking syllabi and course curriculum.
- Mentored other culinary arts instructors as an advisor for the CUA program.
- Assisted in the development of program assessments and objectives for the Culinary Arts program.
- Advised the student who won the silver medal at an American Culinary Federation competition in Denver. Coached the Culinary Arts Team for two years.
- Selected equipment and helped with design and renovation of the Bake Shop.
- Participated in Hanover High School site visits to recruit students for Area Vocational Programs.
- Opened lines of communication with Family, Career, and Community Leaders of America (FCCLA).
- Selected as a member of the Advisory Board for the CUA program. Attended semi-annual Advisory Board meetings. Participated in the development of a five-year action plan for the CUA program.
- Creating a cooking show for the CUA program to showcase students' skills.
- Led students in preparing pastries and cookies for guests of the annual AVP Back-to-School Night.

PASTRY CHEF (Jan 1998–May 2006)
Cheyenne Mountain Resort, Colorado Springs, Colorado
Managed the bake shop and motivated a staff of seven. Helped customers with special requests, such as wedding cakes and specialty desserts. Purchased all products, supplies, and equipment. Planned menus and prepared production sheets.

EXPERIENCE

Cheyenne Mountain Resort (continued)
- Prepared desserts for 50 to 1,200 people (buffet and plated).
- Developed creative ideas for specialty cakes.
- Awarded first place in the Chef's Gala, sponsored by the Colorado Springs Chorale.
- Promoted from Lead Baker to Assistant Pastry Chef to Pastry Chef.

PASTRY CHEF (Mar 1989–Nov 1997)
Westfields Conference Center by Marriott, Chantilly, Virginia
Organized and supervised a bake shop with eight staff members. Developed menus and banquet packages. Prepared specialty desserts for groups from 50 to 1,500 guests. Consulted with and reported to the Executive Chef.
- Developed and implemented high standards of perfection for pastry specialties.
- Implemented cost-saving ideas.
- Promoted from Lead Baker to Assistant Pastry Chef to Pastry Chef based on exceptional performance.

EDUCATION

ASSOCIATE OF APPLIED SCIENCES, BAKING AND PASTRY ARTS (Anticipated Graduation Fall 2010)
Pikes Peak Community College, Colorado Springs, Colorado
- *A 1988 graduate of the American Culinary Federation Apprenticeship Program.*
- Completed teaching course work, including EDU-260 and EDU-250.
- Currently working toward a Bachelor of Arts in Organizational Management with an emphasis in Culinary Arts Management.
- Completed PSY-101 Psychology, CIS-105 Computer Literacy, EDU-263 Desire2Learn, BUS-115 Introduction to Business, and CUA-101 Sanitation. Finishing last two classes toward an associate degree, including ENG-121 and MAT-121.
- Observed lectures in CUA-190 Management with Chef Rob Hudson.

PROFESSIONAL DEVELOPMENT
- ACF Train the Trainer Seminar (annually, 2008–2010)
- ACF Western Regional Convention (2010)
- Completed course work and three exams for instructor/proctor certification, National Restaurant Association and ServSafe (2009)
- National ACF Convention (2008)
- Chocolate Show Piece Seminar (3 days, 2008)
- Sugar Décor Show Piece Seminar (3 days, 2007)

VOLUNTEER
- Secretary, American Culinary Federation, Pikes Peak Chapter (2010–2011)
- Seminar Instructor, Colorado Department of Education Secondary School Food Service Department Conference (2009)
- Manned the Pikes Peak Community College booth at the FCCLA competitions in Denver (2009)
- Examiner, Johnson and Wales Practical (2009)
- Prepared 300 desserts for Pikes Peak Christian School (2008, 2009)
- Created a 100-question written exam for ACF pastry certification (2009)
- Donated monthly birthday cakes for IN/OUT support group (2008–2009)
- Co-chair, ACF Food Show at Pikes Peak Community College (2008)
- Co-chair, Colorado ACF student team competitions (2008)
- Evaluator, Oregon ACF accreditation site visit (2008)
- Helped to prepare and serve Thanksgiving dinner for the Urban League (2008)
- ACF Fund-Raising Dinner (2008)

BRITT M. NISTOR

1234 South 56th Street • Lawrence, Kansas 66046 • (785) 555-1234 • bnistor@protypeltd.com

OBJECTIVE

A position as a Social Worker to complete requirements for the LSCSW designation. Will complete the boards for LMSW in May 2007.

PROFILE

- Compassionate, empathetic social worker who is able to put herself is the client's shoes.
- Able to use extensive experience and maturity to effectively counsel clients.
- Self-reflective professional with strong clinical skills and experience using the DSM-IVTR.
- Able to accept and appreciate differences in others; nonjudgmental and impartial.

EDUCATION

MASTER OF SOCIAL WORK (5/07)
University of Kansas, Lawrence, Kansas
- Social Work Courses: Clients with Alcohol and Drug Problems, Healthcare and Mental Health, Social Work Practice I/II, Cultural Diversity, Psychopathology, Research, Human Behavior in Social Environments, Social Policy and Program Analysis, Community and Organizational Practice, Social Welfare and U.S. Society.
- Psychology Courses: Psychology and the Law, Individual Differences, Abnormal Psychology, Sexuality Perspectives, Social Psychology, Child Psychology, Cognitive Psychology, Statistics and Psychology Research, Introduction to Child Behavior and Development.

BACHELOR OF ARTS, PSYCHOLOGY (2004)
University of Kansas, Lawrence, Kansas

NURSING UNDERGRADUATE STUDIES
University of Kansas, Medical Center, Kansas City, Kansas
- Nursing Courses: Nursing of Children, Nursing of Adults, Pharmacology, Alternatives in Physical Function I/II, Client Assessment, Fundamentals of Nursing: Clinical Lab, Fundamentals of Nursing and Health Problems, Computers and Information Management, Human Physiology, Human Anatomy, Microbiology, Biology, CPR.

RELEVANT EXPERIENCE

CAPS COUNSELING AND PSYCHOLOGICAL SERVICES, Lawrence, Kansas (8/06 – 5/07)
Second-Level MSW Practicum
- Manage 22 clients every two weeks for this counseling agency providing services to students on the University of Kansas campus.
- Perform initial assessments, make diagnoses, and present cases to a multidisciplinary team of psychiatrists, psychologists, social workers, drug and alcohol counselors, and dietitians.
- Co-lead a weekly psychotherapy group dealing with social anxiety, self-esteem, depression, eating disorders, ADHD, substance abuse, relationship issues, and academic problems.
- Serve as the outreach liaison to the Oliver Hall Dormitory, counseling students with problems who were referred for counseling by complex directors and resident assistants.
- Interface with outside community agencies, hospitals, government agencies, and the court system in planning patient care.
- Collaborate with medical and professional staff to help develop comprehensive patient therapy, evaluation, medication, and treatment programs.
- Meet with the supervising LSCSW weekly, both individually and in group sessions.
- Participate in professional seminars for two hours every Wednesday, including such subjects as disabilities, suicide risk, bipolar disorders, cognitive behavior therapy, and obsessive/compulsive disorders.

RELEVANT EXPERIENCE	**OPERATION BREAKTHROUGH,** Kansas City, Missouri (9/05 – 4/06) **First-Level MSW Practicum**

* Managed four cases with a collaborative team of doctors, nurses, dentists, occupational therapists, speech therapists, and other specialists.
* Made in-home visits to families with children from newborn to 18 years old.
* Co-led a counseling group for girls from 8 to 9 years old, as well as a book club group.
* Observed cases in the psychology clinic, occupational therapy sessions, music therapy groups, and drug/alcohol counseling.

COMMUNITY LIVING OPPORTUNITIES, Lawrence, Kansas (11/03 – 3/04)
Teacher / Counselor

* Taught and counseled mentally challenged adults in an independent living situation.
* Managed a case load of 3–5 clients per night, working 20 hours per week on weekends.
* Helped disabled residents with bathing, dressing, and other activities of daily living.
* Distributed rewards and explained to residents the rationale for earning rewards.
* Prepared residents for dinner and took them out into the community for special events.

LAWRENCE PRESBYTERIAN MANOR, Lawrence, Kansas (8/95 – 8/87)
Certified Nurse Assistant

* Earned Certified Nursing Assistant Certification (ID 091893) in the CNA training program.
* Maintained patient care standards and supported families, nurses, physicians, and administrators.
* Reviewed patient assessments and assisted in the planning of individualized patient care.
* Performed typical CNA responsibilities, including taking and record vital signs; observing, reporting, and documenting patient activities; providing physical, emotional and social needs to patients; and implementing appropriate emergency interventions.

OTHER EXPERIENCE	**MK CONSTRUCTION,** Lawrence, Kansas (10/6 – present) **Bookkeeper**

* Maintained bookkeeping records and reconciled bank accounts.
* Managed accounts payable, accounts receivable, payroll, depreciation schedules, billing, and collections.
* Prepared state and local tax reports and filed 940 and 941 employee tax forms.
* Supplied information to the accountant for federal and state tax returns.

AFFILIATIONS	Member, Asian-American Student Union (1994 – 1997); Treasurer (Fall Semester, 1995)

VOLUNTEER EXPERIENCE	**Douglas County AIDS Project,** Lawrence, Kansas (3/05 – 01/06) **Lawrence Memorial Hospital,** Lawrence, Kansas (10/03 – 3/04)

Charles M. Burleson III

1234 Bankhurst Court ► Monument, Colorado 80132 ► E-mail: cburleson@protypeltd.com
Phone: (719) 555-5555 ► Fax: (719) 132-1234

PROFILE

- Results-oriented sales and management professional with a proven track record of success in a wide variety of industries, including sporting goods, real estate, retail, fixtures, and plastic products.
- Strong background in building new territories and using creative marketing approaches.
- Respected for the ability to get to the decision maker and close the sale.
- Demonstrated ability to create client loyalty above and beyond the sales relationship.
- Dedicated to the highest standards of service with exceptional communication and interpersonal skills.
- Self-motivated and focused; comfortable working independently with little supervision.

EXPERIENCE

U.S. SALES AND MARKETING MANAGER (2001 – present)
CTA Fixtures, Inc., Ontario, California
Manage all sales efforts and develop new markets for retail display fixtures throughout the United States. Coordinate customer accounts from conception through manufacturing and installation. Create marketing strategies and collateral materials (brochures, website, flyers, etc.) to generate interest from key retail companies nationwide.

- Developed and delivered effective one-on-one and group sales presentations to prospective clients.
- Succeeded in winning a strong base of clients, including BassPro, Bag 'n Baggage, Del Sol, Dick's Sporting Goods, Guess, Hub Distributing, Maurices, Nordstrom, PetsMart, Postal Annex, Ross, Sean John, Target, Wet Seal, Whole Foods, Wilson Leather, and Windsor.
- In constant communication with more than 300 retail companies nationally, generating 20+ viable bid packages annually.

SALES ACCOUNT MANAGER, WESTERN REGION (1996 – 2001)
Excell Store Fixture Company, Toronto, Canada
Successfully sold store fixtures to local and national accounts in a territory that covers all of the states west of the Mississippi. Developed a targeted customer base of more than 200 accounts. Developed new business, evaluated customer needs, made product and value engineering assessments, and coordinated the design and development of custom fixtures.

- Built the territory from zero to more than $6 million in sales revenue in only three years.
- Succeeded in winning the Adidas account from competitors. Generated $2 million of annual revenue.
- Designed and developed a ten-store Computer City program worth more than $2 million.
- Developed the Leather Centers account, generating $1.5 million in its first year with potential annual revenue of $2.5+ million.
- Cold called on Great Indoors and captured a $300,000 contract with potential annual revenue of $15 million.
- Won a $200,000 program with Home Life Furniture Company with annual potential revenue of $1 million.
- Successfully developed a relationship with the Edison Brothers that created $500,000 per year.
- Collaborated with Gart Sport to develop a $350,000 display program.

OWNER / MANAGER (1994 – 1996)
All Maintenance, St. Cloud, Florida
Saw a need and developed a business to provide maintenance for more than 180 rental properties. Hired independent contractors and ensured the quality of their work. Accountable for strategic planning, profit and loss, payroll, marketing, and sales.

- Developed new accounts and doubled revenue every year.

FIRST ASSISTANT TO THE PGA PROFESSIONAL (1989 – 1994)
Kissimmee Golf Course, Kissimmee, Florida
Managed the pro shop, golf tournaments, youth programs, and other club-related events. Coordinated staff schedules and supervised subordinates.

- Opened the new pro shop and grew the business to $1.0 million of annual revenue.

Letterheads That Pop!

Chapter 4

Since your résumé is basically an advertisement for you and your skills, you should think about the design of your résumé from a marketing standpoint. When you see a well-designed ad, what is the first thing you notice (besides a picture of the product)? The product name, of course. Since *you* are the product, your name should be the first thing a reader sees and remembers. To accomplish that, there are really only two rules to remember: *Your name should be easy to read, and it should stand out above the rest of the text.* That can be done by using:

A Larger Font in Upper/Lower Case

ALL CAPS

First Letter Larger

A Creative Font

On the samples in this section, you will also notice the use of graphic elements and lines to help define the name and contact information to separate them from the rest of the text, creating a letterhead that can be used for your résumé, cover letters, references, and other documents. Even scanned clip art letters or a signature can be used to enhance a résumé, but the latter only works when you have great handwriting. Your name, however, should not distract the reader from the message. Make it part of the overall design of your résumé but separate it from the body text with lines or white space.

I am often asked whether to use a person's common name (Pat Criscito) or full name (Patricia K. Criscito) on a résumé, and the answer is, "It depends." If you have an uncommon name like mine, then it doesn't matter which you use. I might not like being called Patricia or if I want my reader to be in doubt about my sex (a unisex name), then I would choose Pat. If you have a common name, however, you need to think in terms of a Google search. How many John Smiths will turn up in a search? Then I would recommend John Q. Smith.

The most important thing is to make sure the style of your name reflects your personality, tempered by the expectations of your industry. If you are flamboyant and are looking for a job in the arts, then you have a license to be creative. Go for it! If, on the other hand, you work in a conservative industry or you feel uncomfortable with your name printed large, then it is important to tone it down.

CONTACT INFORMATION

Potential employers need to be able to locate you, but your address and other contact information are some of the least important marketing details on your résumé. Some managers spend only a few seconds perusing a résumé before making a decision whether to discard or keep a résumé for further review. They might get through the first third of your résumé, if you are lucky. The reader's eyes should be drawn immediately to the things that will motivate him or her to read all the way to the bottom.

However, you don't want to make the reader work too hard when it comes time to make that critical call for an interview. You should make the contact section part of the overall design of the résumé so it doesn't detract from the text, much as you did with your name, but keep it in an easy-to-find location. That can be done by placing the address either at the top or the bottom of page one of your résumé. You can also repeat it on the second page, if you want, but page one is critical.

Your contact information should include:

- Mailing address (permanent and temporary if you are a student)
- Mobile phone number and home number (if you still have one)
- E-mail address
- E-folio URL
- LinkedIn address
- Facebook, MySpace, Twitter address (provided they are appropriately professional)

My clients are sometimes worried about putting their mailing address on a résumé that will be posted on the Internet. I've never had a client experience identity theft from their online documents, but it can happen. If you are concerned, then it is okay to remove your mailing address from your online résumé. Otherwise, though, I recommend full contact information.

Why two addresses on a résumé? If you are a student who lives away from your permanent address or you are preparing to move soon, then it is appropriate to list both your current and permanent addresses on a résumé, along with dates to indicate when to use which address.

INTERNATIONAL LOCATIONS

With my international clients, the fact that they have worked, studied, lived, or traveled abroad strengthens their credentials for international jobs. Placing the geographic location of experience or schooling in a prominent location can be to their advantage. Other times, it is only part of the overall design of the information. However, making it prominent does give it more importance, whether that was the intention or not.

When you really want the geographic locations of your past experience—or anything else on your résumé—to stand out, the easiest way to accomplish that is to make them flush right or to place them in the left-hand column with the headings.

Michael Ellis

1234 17th Avenue North • St. Petersburg, FL 33710
ellis@protypeltd.com • 727-555-1234

STORE MANAGER

Store management professional focused on maintaining outstanding customer service and best practices in fast-paced environments. Exceptionally skilled in time management, visual merchandising, and training. History of success in mentoring staff to reach management positions, promoting products to achieve increased sales, and consistently exceeding weekly quotas.

AREAS OF EXPERTISE

- Budgeting
- Reports
- Marketing and Promotions

- Customer Service
- Employee Supervision
- Merchandising

- Inventory Management
- Team Building
- Training

EXPERIENCE

PUBLIX, St. Petersburg, FL, 2007 – present
Assistant Store Manager
Achieve corporate objectives through effective management of daily store operations. Track sales and relay profits to the district. Produce sales and inventory reports. Hire, train, and evaluate personnel. Administer schedules and timecards. Devise and implement methods and procedures to increase sales, expand markets, and promote business.

Achievements:
- Attained record revenues and profits through merchandising, marketing, and management proficiency.
- Mentored five employees to move successfully into management positions.

WINN DIXIE, St. Petersburg, FL, 2000 – 2007
Assistant Store Manager
Ensured the success of day-to-day operations for a store with more than 75 employees. Oversaw and directed department managers to meet quotas and expectations. Supervised customer service, marketing, advertising, sales, merchandising, and stock areas. Coordinated staff schedules.

Achievements:
- Conferred with other managers to implement corporate cost control programs.
- Collaborated to develop procedures to grow sales, expand markets, and promote business.

EDUCATION

University of South Florida, St. Petersburg, FL • Bachelor of Science in Business Administration

TECHNICAL SKILLS

MS Office (Excel, Word, Outlook) • Ordering, Inventory, and Payroll Systems • POS

Keith J. Mancuso

1234 Swallows Nest Road · Richmond, Virginia 23235

804.555.1357 · kjmancuso2@verizon.net

Professional Profile

I built my career around the culinary profession—as a corporate, fine dining and gourmet market chef...

And I discovered my passion in teaching ... wherever I go, it keeps calling me back.

Multi-skilled, talented, and knowledgeable professional with 20+ years of culinary experience. Trained on the job by some of Richmond's finest chefs and through formal instruction at The Culinary Institute of America. Demonstrate exceptional ability to balance diverse food preparation techniques with innate understanding and application of solid business management practices and principles. Possess strong public speaking and interpersonal skills—recognized for making learning fun while increasing student and employee confidence.

Business / Instructional / Culinary Expertise

- Employee Training and Cross-Training
- On-the-Spot Customer Education
- Curriculum Development and Adult Education
- Menu Planning and Recipe Development
- Purchasing and Vendor Relations

- Menu Pricing and Food Cost Control
- Culinary Math and Budgeting
- Business Marketing Techniques
- Food Preparation and Presentation
- Wine Selection and Pairing

Professional Experience

Richmond, Virginia

CENTER STREET FRESH SEAFOOD, INC.
Assistant Manager/Chef, 2008–Present

Recruited by this independently owned and operated retail fish business to help manage expansion of in-house operations, diversification of menu items, and transition to an upscale, gourmet market. Develop recipes and prepare multiple gourmet dishes for carry-out. Supervise a full-time cook and a kitchen assistant. Oversee inventory and food costs. Order all paper goods, packaging, and food prep supplies. Evaluate ways to increase market visibility and sales.

- Learned all aspects of retail seafood operations. Implemented costing of recipes to control food costs, and helped push fresh seafood sales to approximately 1,000 pounds per week.
- Promote sustainable farming practices and higher food quality by selecting and using locally grown produce for food preparation. Opened the door to selling fresh produce directly to customers.
- Developed prepared-foods side of the business and implemented various in-store tastings and sampling weekends—nearly tripled food sales.

TIMMONS MARKET
Executive Chef, 2001–2006

Maintained total creative license in developing recipes and preparing dishes for this gourmet grocery and catering business. Oversaw two assistant cooks. Heavily involved in inventory and ordering. Held full responsibility for all wine selection and ordering.

- Demonstrated personal approach to meeting customer needs. Recaptured lost customers and forged new business relationships.
- Turned around negative profits and produced 45% increase in gross annual sales over four-year period.

Culinary Instructor

UNIVERSITY OF RICHMOND
School of Continuing Studies | 2006–Present
- Teach core seafood and shellfish classes and several electives for the non-credit culinary arts program—6 to 8 classes per semester, average of 16 students per class.

SUR LA TABLE | 2003–Present
- As guest chef, provide hands-on cooking classes to groups of 16 to 20 adults. Help drive store business by promoting and nourishing appreciation for the culinary arts.

J. SERGEANT REYNOLDS COMMUNITY COLLEGE—P.A.V.E. Program | 2007 to 2008
- Taught students in the Program for Adults in Vocational Education. a vocational training program for adults with mental disabilities—two semesters; 9 hours per week.

Culinary Chef Instructor

RICHMOND GOURMET | 2001–2002
- Selected menu themes, developed recipes, identified techniques to demonstrate, and facilitated students' hands-on experience—Instructed 2 to 3 hands-on classes per month for as many as 16 students per class.

Letterheads That Pop!

Restaurant Experience

Richmond, Virginia

GG's RESTAURANT
Garde Manger Chef, 1999–2001

Expanded and diversified culinary experience and style by accepting position with Dale Reitzer, one of *Food and Wine Magazine's Top Ten New Chefs of 1999.* Developed and refined intricate presentation skills; learned creative dessert techniques.

BULLS AND BEARS BREWERY & CAFE
Sous Chef, 1997–1999

Studied with renowned local chef and learned innovative approaches to traditional cooking principles and importance of quality and freshness of ingredients. Supervised kitchen and menu preparations in Chef de Cuisine's absence. Maintained inventory, oversaw sanitation, and monitored costs.

- Managed B&B Café. Accepted full responsibility for menu development and planning, food preparation, presentation techniques, and quality standards. Prepared all Café lunches and banquets for 20–60 guests.

DUFFEY'S RESTAURANT AND DUFFEY'S STONY POINT CAFÉ
Regional Kitchen Manager/Kitchen Manager/Assistant Kitchen Manager/Line Cook, 1989–1996

Rapidly progressed through higher levels of responsibility in recognition of industry knowledge, demonstrated management skill, and work performance. Managed all HR functions for kitchen staff of 25 to 30 employees. Served as principal representative to owner, troubleshooting and resolving any operational and personnel issues.

> Trained and supervised kitchen staff. Demonstrated ability to lead by example. Promoted atmosphere of teamwork and instilled "can-do" attitude in employees.

- Maintained entire food and equipment inventory, implementing more efficient use of computerized spreadsheets. Tracked numbers and percentages to effectively control costs and maximize profits.
- Developed and implemented policies and standards of quality for off-site catering. Solicited and secured contracts. Planned and executed menus for catering events for up to 200 guests.
- Charged with responsibility for establishing new Farmville location, which included hiring, interviewing, and training kitchen staff and an on-site manager.
- Simultaneously oversaw day-to-day operation of Farmville and Richmond restaurants to establish and maintain quality standards for menu development, food preparation, plate presentation, service, and staff/customer satisfaction.

Education

CULINARY INSTITUTE OF AMERICA, *Hyde Park, New York*
Servsafe Food Protection Manager Certification, National Restaurant Association

VIRGINIA COMMONWEALTH UNIVERSITY, *Richmond, Virginia*
Bachelor of Arts—*magna cum laude*; Alfred Lund Award for Academic Excellence

Sharon T. Delaney

PROFILE
- Experienced staff developer, teacher, and grand administrator focused on helping educators.
- Skilled at understanding different perspectives and drawing out the best in others.
- Computers: Windows, MS Word, PowerPoint, Outlook, and Internet Explorer.
- Licensed Teacher (Colorado #0280073), Secondary Education, English Language Arts.

EDUCATION

MASTER OF ARTS, READING (2002)
University of Northern Colorado , Greeley, Colorado

BACHELOR OF ARTS, SECONDARY ENGLISH EDUCATION (1993)
University of Northern Colorado , Greeley, Colorado

PROFESSIONAL EXPERIENCE

STAFF DEVELOPER / CURRICULUM COORDINATOR (2005 – present)
East Central BOCES, Limon, Colorado
- Organize adults into learning communities by goals aligned with those of the school and district.
- Prepare educators to apply research to decision-making.
- Deepen educators' content knowledge, provide them with research-based instructional strategies to assist students in meeting rigorous academic standards, and prepare them to use various types of classroom assessments appropriately.
- Analyze disaggregated student data to determine adult learning priorities, monitor progress, and help sustain continuous improvement.
- Use multiple sources of information to guide improvement and demonstrate its impact.
- Manage resources to support adult learning and collaboration.
- Apply knowledge about human learning and change.

LITERACY COORDINATOR (2000 – 2005)
East Central BOCES, Limon, Colorado
- Coordinated literacy programs with 30 teachers in 17 districts.
- Planned and organized cluster meetings; co-developed differentiated staff development modules.
- Coached comprehensive school reform coaches in specific schools.
- Served as a Colorado Department of Education (CDE) Reading First Trainer, Denver (2003 – 2005).
- Coached and modeled literacy programs in teachers' classrooms.
- Planned and organized Step Up to Writing study groups.
- Designed Step Up to Writing and Six + One Trait Writing training workshops.
- Served as co-coordinator of the Alternative Licensure Program.

INSTRUCTOR (2001 – 2002)
Morgan Community College , Limon, Colorado

TEACHER (1994 – 2000)
Woodlin District R-104 , Woodrow, Colorado
- Taught Language Arts to 7th–12th grade students, including English, journalism, and drama.
- Prepared course objectives and integrated Colorado standards-based education and balanced literacy into the curriculum.
- Designed learning environments to meet the individual needs of students and created cooperative learning foundations.
- Counseled students with adjustment and academic problems, and communicated with parents
- Served as the National Honor Society advisor, drama coach, and speech coach.
- Successfully coached 11 out of 17 students to the state speech meet in 1997 and 10 out of 18 in 1998; placed second in the 1997 League Speech Meet.
- Sponsor of the class of 2001; helped the students to develop fund-raisers, including concessions, auctions, raffles, and special sales.
- Head volleyball coach from August 1996 through May 1999; organized practices, developed summer programs and money-making projects, and led the team during matches.

12345 CR 22 • Akron, Colorado 80720 • (970) 555-1234 • Email: sharontdelaney@protypeltd.com

PROFESSIONAL EXPERIENCE

Woodlin District R-104 (continued)
- Led the students to place first in the YWKC Volleyball League and fourth in the Colorado State Volleyball Tournament in 1996.
- Assistant Volleyball Coach from August 1994 through May 1996; coached practices and assigned duties during varsity and junior varsity matches.

Special Assignments:
- Project manager for the development of a Six-Trait Multimedia CD-ROM.
- Selected to manage a three-year, $330,000 literacy grant from the Technology Literacy Challenge Fund of the U.S. Department of Education.
- Implemented programs to improve the writing skills of K–12 students in 17 school districts throughout the East Central BOCES region.
- Developed and taught workshops for K–8 teachers in writing and technology integration; modeled six-trait writing in the classroom; trained teachers to implement the program in their schools.
- Integrated computers, smart-machines, and the Internet into standards-based curriculum to facilitate writing instruction.
- Hosted parent meetings to increase parental involvement in writing and technology usage.
- Organized accountability data for external evaluators; successfully managed a $330,000 budget.
- Member, Curriculum Committee responsible for reviewing curricula and aligning them with state standards (1994 – 1999).

PRESENTATIONS

- "Differentiated Staff Development," NSDC 37th Annual Conference (December 2005)
- "Education Under Renovation!," Colorado Association for School Boards (CASB) Convention (December 1, 2000)
- "It's All About Student Success!," 9th Annual Standards and Assessment Conference (June 16, 2000)
- "Improving Student Writing: Showing the Correlation Between Six-Trait Writing and the CSAP Rubrics," East Central BOCES (February 17, 2000)
- "Six-Trait Writing = Improved CSAP Scores," East Central BOCES (November 20, 2000)

PROFESSIONAL DEVELOPMENT

- Courageous Leadership for School Success (October 2007)
- Using Diagnostic Assessment to Guide Timely Intervention (October 2004)
- Closing the Achievement Gap (Fall 2003)
- Administrative Leadership Skills (Summer 2003)
- Classroom Management (Fall 2002)
- Improving Administrative Leadership Skills (Summer 2002)
- Improving Reading (May 2002)
- Language Essentials for Teachers of Reading and Spelling (LETRS) (September 2002 – 2004)
- Linking the Language Strands with Balanced Literacy (January 2002, 2003)
- Colorado Critical Friends Group Training (July 2002)
- Phun with Fonology (January 2002)
- Colorado Educators Consensus Institute 2000, Consensus Associates (2000 – 2002)
- Step Up to Writing, Sopris West, Maureen Auman (August 2000).
- Data Driven Instruction, Colorado Department of Education (October 2000)

HONORS AND AWARDS

- High Plains Educator Award (1998)
- Who's Who Among America's Teachers (1998, 1999)
- Outstanding Young Woman of America (1997)

AFFILIATIONS

- Colorado Staff Development Council (1999 – present)
- National Council of Teachers of English (1992 – present)
- International Reading Association (1999 – present)
- Colorado Association for School Executives (CASE) (2000 – present)
- National Staff Development Council (1999 – present)
- Colorado Council of the International Reading Association (1997 – present)
- Phi Lambda Theta (2001 – present)
- Association for Supervision and Curriculum Development (2000 – present)
- Professional Learning Communities (PLC) with Rick and Becky Dunfour (2003 – 2004)

Stephen L. Johnson

12345 Elizabeth Avenue, Pfafftown, NC 27040
Home: (336) 555-1234 • Cell: (336) 555-1234
Email: johnson@protypeltd.com

ACCOUNT EXECUTIVE / SALES MANAGER

PROFESSIONAL PROFILE

Tenacious, self-directed, and resourceful business development strategist and account manager with the ability to drive revenue missions via skillful sales techniques. Capable of harvesting speculative leads into highly lucrative deals through the establishment of a vast network of pivotal partnerships, astute marketing collaborations, and an eye on the operational bottom line. Notably accomplished in building and fortifying long-lasting client rapport through enduring trust, client service excellence as well as communicating supreme command of products and services with unrelenting reliability and precision. Inspire teams through enthusiasm and a wealth of expertise. Promote a culture of shared goals and success through training and hands-on guidance.

KEY QUALIFICATIONS

Negotiation and Closing Skills • Operational Leadership • Client Relations and Retention
Communication, Presentation and Interpersonal Skills • Marketing • Highest Level Customer Care
Process Analysis and Restructuring • Team Supervision and Training • Forecasting and Reporting
Business Development and Strategic Planning • Key Account Acquisition and Management

PROFESSIONAL SUMMARY

Account Executive, FLEXIBLE PAYROLL SOLUTIONS – Winston-Salem, NC   **2007–Present**

Full ownership for launch of entire range of service offerings, including payroll processing, tax filing, and payment services for a start-up business.

- Play an integral role in a 10-member team of Account Executives, ensuring superior client rapport when obtaining new and servicing existing key accounts.
- Liaise with clients to provide expert advice and guidance, promptly and efficiently responding to questions as well as offering quick and effectual solutions when troubleshooting.
- Take a diligent, diplomatic approach to cold calling and new contract acquisition in addition to spearheading peak business development and client partnership cultivation.

Key Achievements
- Received recognition for consistency in capturing **first ranking status in overall sales.**

Retail Planning Manager, HANESBRANDS, INC. – Winston-Salem, NC   **2006–2007**

*Instrumental in **controlling retail planning process for a multi-billion dollar company** stocking knit products from Hanesbrands until corporate downsizing and consequent closing in 2007.*

- Oversaw timely inventory flow and fill rates for renowned client to certify operational efficacy.
- Enforced accurate forecasting and succinct documentation into automated systems through collaborative efforts with the Forecasting, Customer Operations, and Marketing Departments.
- Focused on building superior working rapport with Retail Planner, influencing process and planning improvements for implementation.

Key Achievements
- **Spearheaded preparation and presentation of intricately compiled documentation** on quarterly bridges, plan explanations in addition to weekly and monthly reports emphasizing strategies, risks, and action plans.
- **Key contributor for divisional success in accountability for 30% of SLU increase over one year**.

SARA LEE – Winston-Salem, NC   **2001–2006**
Sales Service Manager, POLO / HANESBRANDS DIVISION   **2002–2006**
Business split into Hanesbrands Division from 2002 to 2006.

Overall accountability for management, training, and mentorship of a top-performing workforce of Sales Representatives and Sales Analysts.

Applied platinum-level customer service tenets while providing instantaneous response to concerns, proficiently managing hectic workloads, and identifying profitable new account opportunities.
- Emphasized personal face-to-face liaison with all principal accounts, providing superior product knowledge and advice on upcoming seasonal purchase strategies.

Sales Service Manager (continued)

- Continually interacted with internal departments to monitor superior service levels by Sales Representatives and overall assurance of client care.
- Inspected and compared current shipment statistics to operating plans from previous year for calculated alignment of bookings with tentative forecasts.
- Chaired seminal business management meetings with Sales Representatives to relay vital account information and client requirements awareness.

Key Achievements

- **Overhauled reporting systems to a simplified automated process**, facilitating noteworthy workload reductions within the Administrative Department as a consequence.
- Instituted plan to **incorporate new products into 83% of key accounts,** thereby **increasing existing product penetration from 6.9% to an impressive overall 10%** and effectually navigating team to outperform previously set targets.
- Presided over new Ultimate brand launch, **attaining notable sales results of $7.1 million**.
- **Initiated a ground-breaking defective allowance policy** for implementation throughout all department stores as a vehicle to annual cost savings of **$500,000** throughout all department stores.

Customer Compliance Manager, POLO / HANESBRANDS DIVISION   2001–2002

Proficiently managed principal customer account requirements with stringent adherence to routing and vendor guidelines. Continually liaised with interdepartmental personnel to advise on troubleshooting concerns with stringent compliance of established directives.

Key Achievements

- Negotiated well-planned deductions and **pioneered cost-effective solutions to facilitate zero chargebacks** and fines.
- Effectually surpassed set directives during first fiscal year with the **achievement of over $1.6 million in claim reversals.**

Business Development Manager, RANDSTAAD STAFFING AGENCY – Winston-Salem, NC   2000–2001

Enlisted to provide business development acumen and superior management for successful acquisition of key client base in accordance with set targets.

- Innovated and expanded new business strategies with a focus on garnering long-lasting partnerships.
- Expertly captured appointments through dogged cold calling techniques and skillful lead generation capabilities.
- Delivered skillfully-mastered sales presentations to attain principal new accounts.

Key Achievements

- Tactically exceeded sales objectives with the **acquisition of two new accounts** on a regular **weekly** basis.

EDUCATION AND TRAINING

Wake Forest University, Winston-Salem, NC
Bachelor of Science in Business Administration—Concentration in Marketing (1999)

Training—Workshops and Seminars
- **Outstanding Customer Service Skills**
- **Management / Supervisory Training**
- **Ethics of Selling**
- **Industry-specific Services and Products**

PROFESSIONAL AFFILIATIONS AND COMMUNITY ACTIVITIES

Professional Affiliations
- **Sales Leaders in North Carolina**—member and former President
- **Winston-Salem Chamber of Commerce**—volunteer work through company affiliations

Community Activities
- **St. Andrews Presbyterian Church**—active member
- **Choir Singer**
- **Boy Scout Leader of Troop 7219**
- **Volunteer,** Samaritan Soup Kitchen; local nursing homes for the elderly

QUALIFICATIONS

- Experienced customer service professional with a background in telephone support and direct customer assistance.
- Dedicated to helping others and ensuring complete customer satisfaction.
- Effective team player with exceptional interpersonal skills.
- Able to facilitate and develop good working relationships with cross-functional groups.
- Flexible professional who is open to new ideas and learns quickly.

EXPERIENCE

AUDITOR (2006 – 2010)
Wells Fargo Home Equity, Colorado Springs, Colorado
Audited loan files and ensured that the final document package was ready for booking or sale. Verified that applications met credit policies and would not result in either a moderate or material risk to the bank. Evaluated vesting, title, debt-to-income ratio, combined loan-to-value ratio, stipulations, income calculations, and whether the product and appraisal were correct for the parameters of the loan. Consistently gave clear, concise instructions for corrections to the issue resolution team. Answered the telephone queue weekly, providing support to loan officers and closing agents.

- Succeeded in significantly reducing risk to the bank by discovering errors before files were closed.
- Gained a reputation as one of the most accurate auditors in the office.
- Achieved 100% accuracy and 130% of productivity goals.

SUPERVISOR (2000 – 2006)
Wells Fargo Home Equity, Colorado Springs, Colorado
Supervised loan processing and customer service teams in multiple states, including Branch Retail Home Equity (BRHE) Processing, Customer Service, Centralized Retail Group (CRG), Sales Development Connection (SDC), Private Mortgage Bankers (PMB), Super Jumbo Processing Team, Purchase Money Seconds (PM2) Check and Wire Team, and the BRHE Rush and Escalation Team. Evaluated the performance of up to 32 team members. Coordinated phone queues, wore a telephone headset all day, and handled escalated processing problems. Ensured team's ability to provide exceptional customer service while answering customer phone questions and dealing with complaints. Accountable for processing loans in a timely manner, ordering titles and appraisals, preparing wire transfers and checks, and balancing general ledgers. Trained processors and mentored qualified team members to supervisor positions.

- Recognized as some of the highest producing and top quality teams in the company.
- Contributed to multiple reorganizations of the CRG, SDC, PMB, and Super Jumbo Teams.
- Met deadlines for escalated loans, often requiring processing times of less than an hour.
- Received the Rock Award for consistently being counted on to come through in a pinch.
- Maintained telephone customer service levels at 90% or more, jumping in to handle phone calls immediately when service levels began to fall.

LOAN PROCESSOR (1998 – 2000)
Norwest Direct, Colorado Springs, Colorado
Processed mortgage loans, handling a portfolio with as many as 200 files for purchase money seconds, refinances, home equity, and debt consolidation. Provided customer service to borrowers, loan officers, and closing agents. Ordered payoff statements and executed payoffs from such sources as mortgage lenders, banks, credit unions, attorneys, collection companies, private individuals, and IRS tax liens. Prepared releases for judgments and liens. Verified income, employment, residency, benefits, bank balances, and other assets. Ordered titles, surveys, appraisals, proof of income, and evidence of insurance. Performed initial data entry, reviewed applications for completeness and accuracy, and organized files for final closings.

1234 Brigantine Drive • Colorado Springs, CO 80920 • Phone: (719) 555-1234 • Email: lsutton@protypeltd.com

EXPERIENCE

LOAN PROCESSOR (continued)
- Served as a liaison between real estate agents, sellers, buyers, and lenders, building rapport and providing exceptional customer service.
- Used extensive knowledge of banking and lending processes to minimize processing errors.
- Achieved Certified Level I Title Processor; recognized as a top producer.

OFFICE MANAGER / BOOKKEEPER (1989 – 1997)
Pikes Peak Christian School, Colorado Springs, Colorado
- Managed the administrative functions of a private elementary/junior high school and served as school director for a five-month period during the director's absence.
- Managed the day care and after-school program, scheduled teachers and substitutes, and communicated with parents.
- Coordinated the school lunch program, including menus, money, scheduling, and overseeing the lunch room supervisor.
- Accountable for payroll, bookkeeping, general ledger, accounts payable, accounts receivable, and collections.
- Ensured that the building maintenance and custodial work was performed and met regulatory requirements.
- Supervised teacher's aides and taught classes as a substitute when needed.
- Trained school staff in clerical skills, registration, fund raising, telephone skills, child care, food service, and regulatory compliance.
- Developed themes, purchased prizes and t-shirts, and coordinated logistics and record keeping for annual fund raisers.
- Opened and closed the building, answered telephones, set the alarm system, and ensured that all exits were secured.
- Sourced and purchased school, office, and maintenance supplies.
- Coordinated fund raising events, including Gold C coupon books, incentive programs, etc.

BANKING SERVICES / LOAN OFFICER (early career)
Wells Fargo Bank, Davis and Sacramento, California
- Analyzed risk potential and made sound lending judgments as a loan officer for personal, auto, mortgage, and small commercial loans.
- Qualified borrowers, researched credit histories, set up merchant accounts, and maintained signature authority.
- Collected delinquent real estate and personal loans.
- Counted and balanced teller tills and acted as teller when needed.
- Assisted the operations officer with balancing the vault.
- Successfully maintained relations with unhappy customers whose loan applications were denied.

EDUCATION

BACHELOR OF SCIENCE
University of the Pacific, Stockton, California
- Major in History
- Elementary Teaching Credential

CONTINUING EDUCATION
- Advanced Leadership Seminar (2002)
- One year of Loan Officer training with Wells Fargo Bank (early career)

COMPUTERS

- Proficient in Windows, MS Word, Outlook, Internet Explorer, and banking software (ACAPS, LIS, LPS, First Mortgage, etc.)

FRANCIS J. KELLER

4538 South Canyon Court, Seattle, Washington 99344

805.555.2121 ■■■ Keller@protypeltd.com

CHANNEL AND BUSINESS MANAGER

OPPORTUNITY IDENTIFICATION | CONSULTATIVE STRATEGIES | PARTNER MANAGEMENT

Big-picture sales strategist credited with driving exceptional profits by transforming client relationships and introducing pivotal programs, products, and marketing plans. **Tenacious leader** who boosts demand and deal value by challenging established practices. Extensive manufacturing rep management, global sales presentation, C-suite rapport, and joint customer product success in high-energy roles. Basic abilities in Japanese and French.

Signature Revenue and Business Leadership Achievements:

— **New Product Introduction (NPI)**: Intensified account growth at Microsoft, gaining first approvals for new products through headquarters collaboration. Managed introduction processes.

— **Independent Rep Management:** Educated manufacturing/field reps on technology concepts to drive sales, supporting teams across 14-state territory at test equipment manufacturing firm JSK Inc.

— **Sales Leadership Recognition:** Won Newcomer of the Year, plus business unit sales achievement awards, including President's Advisory Council and Chairman's Summit Council distinctions.

— **Account Services Expansion:** Launched new professional service lines of business generating $500K+ revenue in first year and 350% product revenue increase.

— **OEM Relationships:** Widened revenue opportunities by connecting teams in remote territories as part of high-profile global OEM account program.

*"An incredible work ethic that is apparent to his **team, as he leads by example**."* — VP, 360 Profile Review
*"Stellar integrity that has **strengthened client perceptions**."* — Vice President Sales

CAREER PATH AND PERFORMANCE

ABC COMMUNICATIONS COMPANY, INC., Tacoma, Washington, 1989–present

Consistently handpicked for sales leadership roles based on revenue growth in new lines of business and major accounts, laying groundwork for high-ROI, long-term opportunities by maintaining account visibility and conveying product value. Drive multimillion-dollar improvement through product introductions, sole-source contracts, strategic client collaboration, and relationship-building, managing up to $50 million team revenue.

DIRECTOR, OEM SALES ■ 2007–present

- **Promoted information sharing critical to OEM sales growth,** establishing global account management processes. Identified/conferred with top account leads to produce actionable plans for leadership review.
  - Increased team connections with new SharePoint site and go-to market communications as vehicle for constant account updates.
  - Conserved project efforts by leveraging existing sales organization tool for global engagement plan.

- **Attained 192% revenue growth** in Cisco account with specialty product development, plus acceptance into account partner program.

- **Generated adjacent revenue,** securing ground-floor access to OEM customer needs by directing senior sales professionals to apply consultative methodologies—even with long sales cycles.

BUSINESS DEVELOPMENT MANAGER, OEM MARKETS ■ 2005–2007

- **Produced highest client-base margins with $2M Services** revenue at Cisco plus 320% revenue growth; prepared entire Services business unit to support new technology needs.
  - Commended by Cisco executives for gaining sweeping buy-in on new line of business.
  - Capitalized on team's Services knowledge with subsequent use in other accounts.
- **Earned new expertise in OEM market,** taking prominent role as advocate for unique client base.

BUSINESS DEVELOPMENT MANAGER, MICROSOFT ■ 2002–2005
ACCOUNT MANAGER, MICROSOFT ■ 1989–2001

- **Cut dedicated Account Manager volume nearly 50%,** transforming relationship to concentrate on strategic needs by pioneering self-service method/standardized configuration.
  - Laid foundation for continual growth with new-product introductions; built support for product approvals and managed launch processes.
- **Added multimillion-dollar revenue streams** with sole-source agreements that eliminated competition.

JSK, INC., Seattle, Washington, 1995–1998

Administered 3-year, sole-supplier contract with Microsoft, expanding product portfolio with new product approvals and in-depth sales training. Managed 4 manufacturing reps and 12 sales professionals.

REGIONAL SALES MANAGER

- **Produced 55% year-over-year sales increases**—plus subsequent revenue gains and growth—driving automatic ordering capability for field sales staff.

Worked closely with field reps to regularly identify and correct knowledge deficiencies.

EDUCATION AND SPECIALIZED TRAINING

BACHELOR OF ARTS IN BUSINESS AND ADMINISTRATIVE STUDIES
University of Wisconsin, Lacrosse

Targeted Account Selling: Siebel
Leading Innovation: ExecutiveWorks, Inc.
Developing Talent: Personnel Decisions International
Leading Change, Coaching for Improvement, Motivating Others, Essentials of Leadership:
Development Dimensions International

PROFESSIONAL AFFILIATIONS

GREATER SEATTLE AREA MINORITY EDUCATION ASSOCIATION
Golf Committee 1999–present | Co-Chair 2006–2007 | Board of Directors 1999–2003

Kelsey A. Mitchell

1234 Lake Drive • Granite City, IL 62040 • C 618.555.1234 • mitchell@protypeltd.com

MARKETING COMMUNICATIONS EXECUTIVE

> **Strategic Planning / Brand Management / Product Marketing**

Accomplished, innovative professional skilled in developing and directing strategic marketing initiatives to grow company visibility, generate revenue, reduce costs, and improve internal operations. Proven success in branding and positioning product lines for both B2B and B2C sales. Adept at establishing name recognition, brand identity, and positive image within multiple audiences. Advanced communicator and negotiator, able to gain buy-in from stakeholders with divergent priorities and interests.

Highlights of Expertise:

Marketing Strategy and Execution | Corporate Communications | Public and Media Relations
Social Media Strategy | Event Management / Planning | Team Building and Leadership
Competitive and Market Research | Press Releases | New Business Development | Branding and Messaging
New Product Launch | Collateral Development | Vendor Negotiations | Process Improvements

PROFESSIONAL EXPERIENCE

THOMASON CORPORATION, INC., Edwardsville, IL • 2009–Present
Director of Marketing

Hired as first member of marketing department. Tasked with developing company's first marketing plan, incorporating branding and messaging, logo and website redesign, advertising calendar, and collateral development. Administer $450K annual marketing budget and manage 5 freelance graphic designers. Define and drive tactics for customer acquisition and retention. Launch aggressive marketing and sales programs utilizing broad exposure media, high-touch media, and direct contact. Guide communications across all customer-facing teams for consistency across products, regions, and interactions.

- Increased leads 60% and enhanced brand awareness in new markets by creating marketing roadmap.
- Generated $75K in cost savings by focusing spending on targeted campaigns and negotiating with vendors to increase participation in co-branding opportunities.
- Saved $100K in costs by bringing previously outsourced design projects in house.

MACOMB TELECOM, Edwardsville, IL • 2006–2009
Marketing Communications Manager (2007–2009)

Promoted to management position to develop and execute global and regional B2B marketing plan. Administered $1 million budget and supervised three employees. Created marketing materials and collateral. Managed teams of up to 50 employees for special projects and events. Directed event management functions, such as pre-show planning, on-site management, and post-show ROI measurement. Led focused campaigns in market verticals, involving print and online ads, press releases, speaking engagements, website, tradeshows, and product placements.

- Saved $50K in outsourced design costs, achieved 300% growth in qualified leads, and expanded reach into previously untapped markets by redesigning communications and collateral for all product lines.
- Presented new law enforcement technology solution, earning product placement on CSI: Las Vegas.
- Organized annual customer conference for 1,000 attendees and achieved highest satisfaction levels in history while cutting costs $75K.
- Awarded prestigious Bravo Award (2008) for exceptional performance, awarded to only 25 employees annually. Earned Women's Business Council Networking Award.

…continued…

Professional Experience Continued...

Senior Marketing Communications Specialist (2006–2007)

Supported business unit's marketing campaigns and goals. Administered $250K budget. Researched and analyzed competitors' collateral and website and recommended new direction for business unit's communications. Developed marketing materials, such as product sheets, white papers, and customer case studies. Provided ongoing intelligence to product management and business development teams.

- Contributed to $7 million sales growth by producing interactive DVD showcasing launch of groundbreaking law enforcement technology. Managed $150K production budget, designed packaging, and hired actors.
- Increased positive media coverage 500% by producing webinars and media events.
- Developed business unit's first internal and external newsletters to build sense of community, drive website traffic, announce new products, and strengthen customer retention.
- Managed sales events for customers while staying $30K below annual budget. Organized and planned all aspects of tradeshows, conferences, and product demonstrations for existing and potential customers.

INTEGRATED MARKETING AGENCY, St. Louis, MO • 2004–2006
Brand Management Specialist

Directed execution of advertising campaigns for this provider of B2B and B2C integrated marketing services. Conducted market research and advised management on application of findings. Supported senior account managers with client tasks, such as researching web-based marketing tactics, evaluating competitors, and providing pricing information for PPC campaigns. Authored press releases for both agency and clients.

- Expanded college thesis project into major revenue-generating initiative. Facilitated 300% increase in web traffic and $4 million sales growth by analyzing competitive websites and presenting recommendations to senior management team.
- Doubled customer retention rate and increased satisfaction 20% by introducing social networking program. Led focus group to uncover needs of client's unique customer base, developed proposal, and established online community with product announcements and discussion boards.

PARKER CENTER ACADEMY, St. Louis, MO • 2001–2004
Supervisor

Supervised, trained, and developed team of 12 direct reports, ensuring resources were aligned with organizational goals. Led marketing and brand awareness efforts. Oversaw website and collateral development, and coordinated outreach efforts. Communicated with clients to address concerns and promote retention.

- Grew client enrollment 65% by designing new program offering.
- Participated in creating / editing copy for company website, which generated 40% growth in client base.
- Supported company growth by assisting in location selection, client acquisition, and relationship building.

EDUCATION AND CREDENTIALS

Master of Business Administration (MBA) in Marketing and Strategy
SAINT LOUIS UNIVERSITY, Saint Louis, MO

Bachelor of Arts in Communication / Bachelor of Arts in Psychology
SOUTHERN ILLINOIS UNIVERSITY EDWARDSVILLE (SIUE), Edwardsville, IL

Professional Development
Graphic Design Training (Adobe Illustrator and Photoshop) • Social Media Marketing
ROI Techniques • Search Engine Optimization and Marketing

Affiliations
Business Marketing Association (BMA) • American Marketing Association
Word of Mouth Marketing Association (WOMMA) • eMarketing Association (eMA)

Nanette Benitez

1234 Canyon Place • Peyton, Colorado 80831 • Email: nbenitez@protypeltd.com • Cellular: (719) 555-1234

PROFILE

- Dedicated teacher with the desire to instill in children a passion for art and life-long learning.
- Able to set and maintain high expectations with the belief that children will rise to them.
- Outgoing and patient instructor who enjoys working with children.
- Effective team player with strong communication and interpersonal skills.
- Certified Teacher in Colorado, Oklahoma, and Arkansas.

TEACHING PHILOSOPHY

Seeing a student succeed is my true reward! I believe that patience, understanding, and a lot of encouragement go a long way toward helping children succeed. Not all students can be coaxed to reach their full potential, but I am eager to exhaust all means to try. As a teacher, it is not just my job to pass on knowledge to my students but also to help them discover their own creativity. Just as we are all unique individuals with different talents and gifts, we all have different learning styles, and I believe we should accommodate them as much as possible to help students succeed.

EDUCATION

BACHELOR OF ARTS IN EDUCATION (2004)
Northeastern State University, Tahlequah, Oklahoma (2000 – 2004)
University of Arkansas, Fayetteville, Arkansas (2000 – 2001)

- Major in Art Education—graduated *magna cum laude*.
- Member of the NSU Art League—Treasurer.
- Awarded four honorable mentions in the NSU Juried Student Art Show (2003, 2004).
- *Teaching course work:* Elementary and Secondary Teaching Internships, Secondary Art Education, Teaching Methods and Practice, Elementary Art Education, Technology in Education, Clinical Teaching/Pre-Internship, Educational Psychology, Introduction to Human Behavior, Fundamentals of Oral Communication, Computer Information Systems.
- *Art course work:* Capstone Senior Exhibit, Silkscreen, Sculpture, Perspective, Native American Pottery, Native American Arts and Crafts, Art History Survey I/II, Watercolor, Painting, Design, Drawing, Color, Fundamentals of Art, Art in Life, Art Studio, Introduction to Arts/Aesthetics.

TEACHING EXPERIENCE

ART TEACHER (2004 – 2005)
Gentry Elementary School, Gentry, Arkansas

- Taught kindergarten through 5th grade art, providing a wide variety of activities for students.
- Developed a curriculum that emphasized the elements of art and design with hands-on experience using various mediums, tools, and techniques.
- Created an interactive learning environment designed to challenge students to do their best and to inspire them to be creative.
- Set learning goals and developed age-appropriate lesson plans in art history, appreciation, and production, adapting instruction to effectively target student learning styles.
- Established an authentic learning environment that was challenging and exciting.
- Integrated interdisciplinary units to connect art across core curriculums.
- Ensured that curriculum materials met lesson objectives and state standards.
- Helped students appreciate how people have used art to express ideas throughout history.
- Adapted teaching style to meet the unique needs of each student in various art mediums.
- Implemented effective classroom management strategies and ensured a safe learning environment.
- Instructed students from very diverse ethnic, socio-economic, and talent levels.
- Promoted the development of social skills by helping children learn to communicate their feelings and to listen to each other.
- Supervised children during activities and counseled them when social, academic, or adjustment problems arose. Established and maintained written and oral communication with parents.

TEACHING EXPERIENCE (continued)

TEACHING INTERNSHIP (2004)
Kansas High School, Kansas, Oklahoma / **Grove Elementary School**, Grove, Oklahoma
- Completed a full-time internship teaching art to 4th through 12th grade students.
- Prepared, administered, and corrected tests; maintained attendance records, daily notes, and student reports; created visual aids, bulletin boards, and other learning materials.

PRE-INTERNSHIPS I/II (2002 – 2003)
Central Elementary School, Tahlequah, Oklahoma / **Jay High School**, Jay, Oklahoma
- Helped to teach a wide range of subjects at the middle school and high school levels.
- Used a hands-on approach to teaching, incorporating cooperative learning and inquiry as often as possible.

TEACHER'S ASSISTANT (1997 – 2003)
Kansas Elementary School, Kansas, Oklahoma
- Helped to teach a 5th grade class; graded papers and created bulletin boards.

TUTOR (2002)
Kansas Elementary School, Kansas, Oklahoma
- Tutored elementary students in the after-school program.

SUBSTITUTE TEACHER (1995 – 1996)
Kansas Public School System / Moseley Public School System, Kansas, Oklahoma
- Taught kindergarten through 12th grade classes throughout two school districts.

OTHER EXPERIENCE

FIELD REPRESENTATIVE, Mega Health and Life, Denver, Colorado (2006 – 2010)
- Successfully sold health and life insurance to individual and business owners.
- Generated leads through cold calling, referrals from satisfied customers, and membership in Business Networking International (BNI).
- Planned and organized the territory to increase market share; created personal road maps to success and evaluated them monthly to gain momentum.
- Created strategic marketing plans for the target market, and built profitable relationships with clients that resulted in frequent referrals.
- Successfully penetrated new markets by cold calling, prospecting, and networking in community organizations.
- Analyzed the financial goals and desired lifestyles of clients and then tailored their insurance plans to accomplish both.
- Succeeded in a new industry by drawing on strong people skills and the ability to understand client needs.

COMPUTERS
- Proficient in MS Word, Excel, PowerPoint, Outlook, Internet Explorer, and Photoshop.
- Experienced in both Windows and Macintosh operating systems.

COMMENTS
- *Nanette possesses the maturity and self-assurance that allows me to confidently state that she would make an excellent art instructor at any institution.* —Bobby Martin, Northeastern State University
- *Mrs. Benitez has always demonstrated a very caring and willing attitude. She strives to go above and beyond any requirements when working on an assigned project. She readily accepts responsibility and demonstrates mature leadership ability.* —Carolyn Steele, Teacher, Kansas Elementary School

JACKELIN Smithe

6657 Anyhow Court • Anywhere, OH 43068
614-555-3456 • 614-555-4567 • jackelinsmithe@yahoo.com

Loss Control Manager

> "Jackelin, this past year has been a productive one for your department. Your department has been challenged in claims and fleet due to a hailstorm in October. You have handled this well, have given the proper direction for the rental branches and helped out during a difficult increase in business."
> – Brady Bonner, Regional VP of Enterprise Rent-A-Car

Dedicated and resourceful Loss Control Professional with over eight years of extensive management experience in claim subrogation, loss prevention, compliance and risk management. Proven track record of reducing operating costs and process improvement. Goal-oriented, dependable, and analytical leader with extensive knowledge of general liability claims, arbitration, litigation, Fair Debt Collection and claim policies; possesses strength in negotiation and a thorough understanding of accounting functions.

Areas of expertise include but are not limited to:

- Underwriting development
- Staff development and training
- Determination of loss trends
- Interpretation of state and federal laws
- Fiscal Management
- Subrogation

ACHIEVEMENTS

> "Jackelin continues to be very aggressive in her approach to her work and her desire to meet department and group goals. The recent month has seen her bring forward a number of ideas designed to improve the effectiveness of the department and move towards meeting goals..."
> – Robert Wantlin, Loss Control Manager, Enterprise Rent-A-Car

- Reduced claim cost by 10% in fiscal year 2005 resulting in being named as a finalist for the *Loss Control Exceptional Achievement Award*.

- Improved the exchange of information between the Loss Control Department and the Vehicle Repair Department resulting in a decrease in subrogation claims closed over 91 days by 3%.

- Initiated a quarterly participatory Safe Driving Contest for employees resulting in a decrease of employee related accidents by 4%, annually.

CAREER PROGRESSION

> "Jackelin, this past year, you have implemented many changes that have impacted our performance as it pertains to uninsured losses and undocumented damage. Good job with this! ...You have really taken it personal in terms of creating plans and putting systems in place that I believe will pay off down the road."
> – Brady Bonner, Regional VP, Enterprise Rent-A-Car

Enterprise Rent-A-Car, Company of Cincinnati – Hilliard, OH   **1995 – 2010**
Loss Control Department Head – Loss Control Department (2003 – 2010)

Managed Enterprise Rent-A-Car's Loss Control Department overseeing the areas of claims, human resources, risk management, training, underwriting compliance, and reporting. Supervised employees directly and expanded training and support to 175 daily rental employees at 30 locations throughout Columbus rental locations.

- Directed and resolved 400 subrogation claims while overseeing risk management.
- Led the successful recovery of subrogation claims.
- Implemented and oversaw underwriting of policies, analysis of losses to determine losses/trends, monitoring and tracking fraudulent/stolen/converted rental transactions.
- Reviewed all employees' Motor Vehicle Records to review risk/probationary issues/termination.
- Maintained awareness of all state and federal laws.
- Trained daily rental and Loss Control employees.
- Performed review of quarterly audits at rental locations and responded to all written subpoenas for the region.
- Testified in court regarding overall business operations related to any loss control matter.
- Implemented a regional underwriting compliance grid for all Columbus rental offices.

CAREER PROGRESSION (continued)

Subrogation Supervisor – Loss Control Department *(2000 – 2003)*

Led the daily functions of the Loss Control Department to ensure recovery. Enhanced underwriting compliance, the analysis of loss trends and file audits. Provided direction and training to administrators to assist in the effectiveness of subrogation/collection efforts.

- Created a process in which all uncollected subrogation files were reviewed by management prior to sending thereby lowering claim costs by 2%.
- Oversaw worker compensation monitoring and reporting.
- Implemented review of 90 day subrogation files which resulted in an increase of overall monies collected by 3% for fiscal year 2001.

Loss Control Specialist – Loss Control Department *(1999 – 2000)*

Investigated, analyzed, evaluated, and negotiated a large volume of claims files. Trained and developed other loss control team members. Traveled to rental branches to ensure underwriting compliance and conducted analysis of losses to determine trends to report to the Loss Control Department Head.

- Reduced file load from 185 to 120 files for subrogation claims.
- Increased the percentage of damages collected from 85% to 87%.
- Decreased closed claims over 90 days from 15% to 12%.

Senior Loss Control Administrator – Loss Control Department *(1997 – 1999)*

Managed investigation, evaluation, analyzing and negotiating a large volume of claims files. Simultaneously fulfilled day-to-day functions as a Loss Control Administrator while providing leadership and direction to the rental offices in an effort to lower costs and monitor underwriting compliance.

- Spearheaded a pilot that resulted in less salvage errors and an increase in total loss settlement amount by 2.5%.

Loss Control Administrator – Loss Control Department *(1996 – 1997)*

Handled claims, conducted investigation of claims, gained proficiency in internal accounting policies and negotiation. Reviewed monthly reports to check for accuracy and reconciled costs.

Management Trainee Program – Daily Rental Operations *(1995 – 1996)*

Oversaw the daily operations of rental branch to become familiar with the Enterprise philosophy. Provided high level of customer service, explained and executed rental contracts and sales. Expanded knowledge of company policies and procedures that connect to each area of Enterprise Rent-A-Car's business.

EDUCATION AND CERTIFICATIONS

"...All indications are that we are headed in the right direction and hopefully within the next few months we could be at $24/car range. You have really taken it personal in terms of creating plans and putting systems in place that I believe will pay off down the road... The loss control contest has been perceived well in the branches and I believe the results have also been positive...."
– Brady Bonner, Regional VP, Enterprise Rent-A-Car

Bachelor of Arts, Economics, Clark Atlanta University, Atlanta, Georgia

Certified in Auto Estimate Analysis for Examiners, Vale International

55 Main Avenue, Princeton, New Jersey 55555 ✧ (856) 555-1234 ✧ cills@protypeltd.com

DESIGN SALES ✧ HOME DÉCOR ✧ BUYER

Design is my Passion!

Ambitious, versatile designer with excellent abilities in design sales, merchandising, and buying. Warm, friendly ability to listen, relate well to customers, and understand their buying needs. Results-driven professional successful in generating leads and increasing business.

- Skilled in space planning, color stories, selection of fabrics, accessories, furniture, and more.
- Effectively develop collaborative relationships with vendors, designers, and furniture stores.
- Talent for orchestrating many different contractors and elements to ultimately please the client.
- Excellent ability to predict trends and select products and accessories that sell to a target market.
- Up to date with industry products and cutting-edge artistic painting techniques.
- Experienced with detailed order procedures and specification requirements for upholstery, case goods, window treatments, tiles, and more.
- Extensive knowledge of manufacturers and accessory lines, including Lorts, John Richard, Elden, Linrene, Murray Fiess, Dez Ryan, Scalamandré, Kravet, Robert Allen, and many more.

**CORE COMPETENCIES: Design Sales / Buying / Accessories / Merchandising / Space Planning
Trade Shows / Product Selection / Marketing / Artistic Painting**

CAREER ACCOMPLISHMENTS

DESIGNER / PRINCIPAL • Robin Cills Designs, LLC, Princeton, NJ   **2006 to present**
Residential and Commercial Design
Started up a full-service interior design company with emphasis on artistic painting, catering to high-end clientele and small businesses. Managed all aspects of business operations, marketing, sales, and design needs.

- **Effectively marketed services and generated referrals** through relationship development with key contacts, representatives, and designers at show houses and furniture stores.
- **Achieved highly aesthetic room designs** and merchandising creations for show houses, resulting in leads.
- **Highlighted in design publication**, "Design NJ" magazine, in a spread that showcased a painting project in a room for Ellen Exclusive furniture store.
- **Developed marketing programs** and materials; created a promotional brochure with photos and testimonials.
- **Kept abreast of industry products** and cutting edge techniques, with courses at Name Dropper Studios, Faux Best Studios, and Artists Plus Studios.
- **Experienced with environmentally friendly** products and their specific methods of application.

Accessory Designer / Online Sales • *www.YRU.com* , Princeton, NJ   **2008 to present**
Create and sell handmade accessories through *www.robincillsdesigns.YRU.com*, two-page spread in *Summerwood Studio* magazine.

(CAREER ACCOMPLISHMENTS, continued)

Design Associate / Sales • MASTER DESIGNS, INC., Princeton, NJ   2000 to 2006
Residential and Commercial Design
Handled all aspects of client sales, including design consulting, buying, promotional materials, and trade shows. Collaborated with vendors on purchase of products and accessories. Organized warehouse for efficiency.

- **Generated sales and business growth** by consistently achieving referrals from highly satisfied clients.
- **Guided clients in interior design needs** from space and color planning to fabric, furniture, flooring, and accessory choices. Able to show fabrics and textures in a way that helps clients visualize choices.
- **Assisted in buying at trade shows**. Keen ability to target vendors that would have strong appeal to specific clients as well as for stock inventory.
- **Maintained and updated a vast design library**, the largest in south Jersey. Developed extensive knowledge with all the lines that aided in creative recommendations.
- **Served as point person for trouble shooting and resolving problems** during all phases of design and implementation (damaged products, contractor issues, and more). Required ongoing follow-up and diplomacy with manufacturers, contractors, and customers.
- **Ensured quality through proficiency** with detailed, specific ordering procedures unique for each manufacturer.

Contract Design Assistant • JENNY STAR, Princeton, NJ   1997 to 2000
Assisted in faux finishes and painting for well known, high-end designer.

Sales / Office Support • ARTIST TREASURE, Princeton, NJ   1996 to 1999
Assisted in lead generation for this marketing firm, regularly meeting quotas for appointment bookings. Also handled administrative support needs.

Kiosk Sales / Face Painting Artist • SHERRI FAMOUS, Philadelphia Zoo, PA   1993 to 1998
Seasonal Work / Weekends—Painting Kiosk at the Major City Zoo
Independently ran the daily operations of a busy face-painting business. Entrusted to handle large amount of cash on a daily basis. Required excellent customer service skills and patience in working with crowd control.

EDUCATION AND TRAINING

Regularly attend training programs highlighting industry products and techniques
South County College • Certificate in Basic AutoCAD Drawing
Newark Academy of Fine Art • Color Theory, Life Drawing, and Painting
Trenton College of Art and Design, The University of the Arts • BFA Degree, Major in Illustration

PROFESSIONAL ASSOCIATION

International Decorative Artisans League (IDAL)

BRIAN I. GORDON

gordon@protypeltd.com
202.555.1212

Network Engineer | Network Administrator | Systems Analyst
Microsoft Certified Professional ♦ Certified Novell Administrator ♦ Certified NetWare Engineer

*Tenacious, High-Tech Achiever with 10 years IT experience
implementing office automation solutions including
network administration, system maintenance,
and technical troubleshooting.*

AREAS OF EXPERTISE

Backup and Disaster Recovery	Citrix Administration	IT Solutions
Server Patch Management	Client-Server Technology	Systems Integration
Multi-Platform Networking	Process Improvements	Technical Analysis

PROFESSIONAL EXPERIENCE

National Community Safety Administration (NCSA)
Department of Transportation agency improving safety practices through community planning.
Washington, DC (October 1999–present)

Recruited by NCSA's Director of Office of Technology and Information Management to oversee call center technology. Gained increasing responsibility and complexity in technology roles over 10 years.

Senior Systems Analyst	November 2008–present
Network Engineer	June 2005–October2008
PC/Network Support Specialist	October 1999-May 2005

SELECTED ACHIEVEMENTS

- Implemented remote access solution with Citrix Presentation Server and RSA integration.
- Recommended, installed, and configured patch management software program to scan servers, reducing time to execute patch processes by 60%.
- Piloted configuration and implementation of Systems Management Server (SMS) to upgrade software remotely, saving 300 hours of installation time.
- Rated *"Outstanding"* in client satisfaction category on 2009 annual review.

"Brian played a major role in upgrading and improving NHTSA's OCIO backup and recovery software and hardware systems. He also improved IT back end systems…."
~ J. Mitchell, Technical Project Manager, National Community Safety Administration

AREAS OF RESPONSIBILITY

Network Administration
- Administered and maintained mixed Windows 2000/2003 network for staff of 600 including computer hardware, systems software, applications software, and all configurations.

Remote Access
- Constructed Citrix system integrating Presentation Server, Citrix Secure Gateway, and RSA SecureID servers.
- Configured applications to operate in Citrix software for Windows web interface.

—Continued—

PROFESSIONAL EXPERIENCE

National Community Safety Administration (NCSA)

AREAS OF RESPONSIBILITY (continued)

System Backup and Recovery
- Planned, coordinated, and directed network-wide backup and recovery strategies.
- Upgraded backup software, technology, and strategies regularly to implement state-of-the-art processes.

Patch Management
- Developed and implemented patch management processes to ensure a secure server environment.
- Scheduled monthly and emergency security scans to identify missing patches and tested compatibility.
- Executed patching after office hours to prevent work interruptions.

Technical Support
- Consulted with network users at office headquarters and 10 regional sites regarding technology problems.
- Diagnosed and resolved networking and operating system software failures.
- Conferred with computer system personnel to troubleshoot and resolve problems.
- Trained call center staff in use of telephone and call center management software.

Network Engineering
- Monitored and fine-tuned network systems to ensure optimum level of performance. Tracked the health of 25 web servers and provided analysis to managers.
- Installed software and upgrades for network users resulting in greater productivity.

CERTIFICATIONS

Microsoft Certified Professional, July 2003
Certified Novell Administrator, April 2000
Certified NetWare Engineer, October 2000

TECHNICAL SKILLS

Systems: Windows 2000 and 2003, UNIX, Linux, Novell
Software: MS Office Suite, Symantec Backup Exec, Nagios, What's Up Gold, VM Ware
Networking: TCP/IP, DNS, DHCP, WINS, Ethernet
Hardware: Servers, Hubs, Routers, Switches, PC's

EDUCATION

Computer Learning Center, Springfield, VA
  Computer Programming Certificate
    3.9 GPA

Virginia Polytechnic Institute and State University, Blacksburg, VA
  BA in Theatre Arts
    Stage and Lighting Technology emphasis

Janine R. James

1234 Montezuma Avenue, NW
Albuquerque, New Mexico 87120
Cellular: (505) 555-1234
Email: jrjames@protypeltd.com

STRENGTHS

- Experienced administrative assistant with a diverse background that includes:
  - Sales support
  - Television ad traffic
  - Finance support
  - Office management
  - Automotive industry
  - Manufacturing
- Versatile, quick learner who enjoys the challenge of new opportunities.
- Personable team player with a proven track record of success in administration/coordination.
- Detail-oriented worker with excellent problem solving and communication skills.
- Able to build rapport and trust quickly with customers and co-workers.

AREAS OF EXPERTISE

- Logs and reporting
- Correspondence
- Customer relations
- Event planning
- Executive communication
- Accounts receivable/payable
- Accurate data entry
- Sales collateral material
- Purchasing
- Vendor management
- Client billing / invoices
- Market research

SUMMARY OF EXPERIENCE

TRAFFIC REPRESENTATIVE (2009–2010)
Comcast, Albuquerque, New Mexico
Coordinated the flow of advertising traffic on cable and satellite television networks. Reviewed and imported client advertising contracts. Accountable for spot listings, incomplete expired lines, preemptions, and make-goods. Monitored schedule exceptions, set availability types, locked in non-preemptable requirements, and monitored spot placement. Reconciled programming schedules and generated commercial play lists. Generated logs and processed daily verification reports, reconciling them against client advertising contracts. Entered data, maintained client master files, and ran reports for monitoring contract fulfillment. Processed and distributed daily notifications of missing copy instructions. Evaluated sold and scheduled inventory. Manually adjusted commercial placement daily. Communicated constantly with managers and sales executives regarding the status of advertising schedules and fallouts. Facilitated communication with clients, ad agencies, and account executives regarding missing content and video conflicts.

- Generated revenue by ensuring that advertising spots were run according to sales contracts.
- Used Novar and Strata software to monitor progress and make immediate corrections to maximize revenue.
- Rescheduled missed commercial spots to ensure that ads reached the intended markets and clients were satisfied.

OFFICE MANAGER (2007–2009)
Electric Edge Enterprises, Albuquerque, New Mexico
Managed the office of a busy electrical contractor. Supported commercial, industrial, and government electrical/mechanical construction projects valued at more than a million dollars per year. Managed employee records, filing, and customer service. Selected vendors and purchased equipment and supplies. Answered telephones and greeted guests.

- Managed accounts payable and generated timely payments to vendors. Procured discounts and built strong vendor relations.
- Maintained positive cash flow in accounts receivable through accurate invoicing, careful documentation, and follow-up on late payments.

PAID PROGRAM COORDINATOR / LOCAL–NATIONAL SALES ASSISTANT (2000–2007)
ACME Television of New Mexico, Albuquerque, New Mexico
Supported both national and local sales of television advertising for CW and MY50 television networks. Kept sales managers updated on all programming issues, including preemptions, overloaded breaks, missing copy, and conflicts with sales. Managed and entered orders daily to ensure that all paid programming contract inventory was correct. Checked all spots . . .

(continued)

SUMMARY OF EXPERIENCE

ACME Television of New Mexico (continued)
. . . before air time. Maintained the traffic library, program grids, and rate cards. Ran daily, weekly, and monthly reports, resolving any problems to ensure accurate customer billing. Generated management reports relating to pacing, client invoices, skims, and other issues. Updated weekly call reports and maintained trade files. Created printed sales pieces, such as program schedules, movie titles, sports packages, account lists, media kits, market overviews, sales brochures, and competitive analyses. Collaborated with account executives to produce client-specific marketing plans. Conducted market research using TV Scan, Scarborough Research, CMR, and Monitors. Trained account executives. Ordered business supplies and forms. Assisted with planning and coordinating special events. Prepared correspondence, faxes, and emails. Maintained expense reports, travel vouchers, budgets, and other financial records.
- Rapidly promoted from receptionist (first nine months) to the sales assistant and program coordinator positions (held simultaneously) with no prior industry experience.
- Generated sales leads, earning a commission and exceeding quarterly sales goals. Sold 30-minute infomercials. Cold called on media buyers and traveled to broadcasting association seminars to meet potential clients.
- Created perfect logs with correct program lengths and copy. Ensured there were no overloaded breaks and that all times were accurate.
- Maintained the security and confidentiality of all company processes, data, and information.

RECON POSTING CLERK (1999–2000)
ADT Automotive Auto Auction, Albuquerque, New Mexico
Entered accurate data into the computer system regarding the reconditioning of cars sold at auction to dealers. Tracked the cost of paint, body, and detail services, which was then used to set the sales price of fleet, used, and repossessed vehicles. Worked the auction lanes to facilitate the paperwork required for accurate sales transactions. Served as the liaison between management and clients. Coordinated meetings, appointments, travel, and visits by Ford and GM sales reps.

FINANCE SECRETARY (1997–1998)
Karl Malone Toyota, Albuquerque, New Mexico
Provided administrative support to two finance managers of this Toyota dealership. Served as the key point of contact for department executives. Prepared loan packages and submitted them for underwriting. Answered a multi-line telephone and greeted customers. Performed clerical tasks, including data entry, filing, faxing, emails, correspondence, among others.

ADMINISTRATIVE ASSISTANT / PRESS OPERATOR (1996–1997)
Plastech Corporation, Albuquerque, New Mexico
Operated equipment for the manufacture of custom plastic parts. Performed quality assurance on finished goods. Answered telephones and monitored security cameras.

LEAD CONTAMINATION CONTROL TECHNICIAN (1995–1996)
Intel Corporation, Albuquerque, New Mexico
Monitored air quality and calculated particles in a clean room for the manufacture of semiconductors. Had the authority to shut down the production line until particles could be lowered to acceptable levels. Directly supervised 6–10 contamination control tech crew members. Reported particle count levels to management daily.

TRAINING

- Mastering QuickBooks Seminar (2008)
- OSHA Safety Certification, Intel Protocol (1995)
- Hazardous Materials (1995)
- Intel Safety (1995)

COMPUTER SKILLS

- Proficient in Macintosh, Windows, MS Word, Excel, Outlook, Internet Explorer, QuickBooks, AS400, Novar, Strata, Marketron, Reynolds & Reynolds, Sales Analysis +, Wide Orbit.

HELEN WORTHINGTON

12345 Lafayette Way ♦ Boston, MA 23450
worthington@protypeltd.com
321.555.1234

♦♦♦♦♦♦♦♦♦

Senior Technical Writer ~ Communications Specialist

Eight years of technical writing experience with exceptional skills in
*transforming technical subject matter into clear, customer-oriented documentation,
analyzing and communicating complex business processes, and
coordinating individuals and teams across departments.*

--- VALUE OFFERED ---

♦ Technical Documentation	♦ Process Analysis	♦ Project Planning
♦ Content Development	♦ Systems Requirements	♦ Leadership and Supervision
♦ Document Editing	♦ Communications Planning	♦ Educational Materials Development
♦ Brand Development	♦ Cross-functional Team Coordination	♦ Staff Training

--- SELECTED HIGHLIGHTS OF KEY EXPERIENCE ---

Senior Technical Writer, Higher Achievements, Boston, MA (2007–present)
Contracted to develop internal communications program and policy library for nonprofit in process of 10-fold national expansion.

√ Spearheaded development of central, Intranet-based employee communications system, saving more than $100,000 from print communications budget.

√ Recognized by the Technology in Business Foundation for project accomplishments in article, *Higher Achievement: Nonprofits Investing in Technology Wisely.*

√ Built strong training infrastructure for employee development in expansion sites.

√ Wrote 500+ documents from concept to publication for non-technical audience.

- Collaborated with executives to define project scope and goals.
- Developed plan for documentation processes, established project time line, and determined external resource requirements.
- Coordinated documentation across all departments, ensuring alignment of materials.
- Coached lead trainer on implementing newly developed training program.
- Supervised vendor staff throughout the Intranet development process.

Senior Consultant, Ackerman Roberts, Boston, MA (2003–2007)
Hired by technology and management consulting firm to perform initial analysis of business processes, document system requirements, and identify technical communication and training needs for organizations ranging from 500 to 750,000 employees.

√ Expanded sole consultant role into leader of department, supervising eight technical writers.

√ Managed junior writers, overseeing 30–40 client documentation projects, in addition to own projects.

√ Chosen to lead re-branding initiative, including research coordination, vendor management, and rollout planning.

- Analyzed business processes through close collaboration with technical and non-technical clients.
- Documented system requirements, consulting technical staff throughout the development process.
- Designed communications plan for rollout, documenting policies and procedures, Intranet sites, employee communications, training courses, and marketing collateral.

HELEN WORTHINGTON

worthington@protypeltd.com

321.555.1234

◆◆◆◆◆◆◆◆

Technical Communications Consultant, IT Solutions Inc., Wesley, MA (2007–2008)
Contracted by owner to create core messaging and initial collateral suite for new technology consulting firm.
√ Mediated process of defining initial mission statement, with key role in resolving differences.
√ Created, in less than a month, corporate brochure, fact sheets, website content, and sales presentation content.

Communications Manager, Hayden & Associates, Boston, MA (2002–2003)

Writer/Editor, American Health Educators National Headquarters, Arlington, VA (2000–2001)
Hired to create internal communications and training materials for 15,000 employees nationwide.
√ Increased employee understanding of and compliance with IT policy by redesigning Intranet site structure and improving content clarity.
√ Created editorial style guides for information technology and biomedical departments.
- Collaborated with subject-matter experts to write information technology and biomedical departmental policies.
- Developed instructional materials to educate employees on policy standards.
- Taught mandatory policy and procedure writing courses to employees documenting policy.

—— EDUCATION ~ CERTIFICATION ——

BA in English, Business Communications emphasis
James Madison University. Harrisonburg, VA

Information Mapping Certification
Information Mapping Institute (IMI)

—— COMPUTER SKILLS ——

Microsoft Word, Excel, PowerPoint, Publisher, SharePoint, and Visio
Adobe InDesign, Photoshop, Illustrator, Acrobat, Captivate, and Fireworks
Quark XPress

Jon
Gonzalez

1234 La Costa Road
Colorado Springs, Colorado 80927
H: (719) 555-1234, C: (719) 123-5555
E-mail: jgonzalez@protypeltd.com

PROFILE
- Experienced manager with a strong background in the administration of elder services facilities.
- Proven leader who sets high standards for self and others while still being fair and consistent.
- Forward-thinking manager committed to creating a proactive environment that promotes humane, responsible care of resident populations in a highly competitive marketplace.
- Skilled at fostering relationships with people from diverse cultural and economic backgrounds.

EXPERIENCE SUMMARY

Administration
- Directed all administrative functions of seven long-term healthcare facilities (both assisted living and skilled nursing), including one start-up operation and two management turnarounds.
- Accountable for management of nursing services, staffing, budgeting, inventory, credentials verification, and policy/procedure development.
- Developed and implemented programs for facility maintenance, risk management, and safety.
- Created procedure manuals to meet OSHA regulations and community emergency/disaster plans.
- Planned, implemented, and evaluated the effectiveness of innovative marketing programs.
- Initiated community and media relationships to enhance the image of the company.
- Ensured the delivery of quality care based on each center's policies and procedures.

Fiscal Management
- Successfully developed and managed budgets as large as $2 million.
- Established financial controls and analyzed/projected fiscal performance.
- Oversaw the purchase and installation of a new computer system and software for financial and administrative applications.
- Implemented capital expenditures and purchasing systems to obtain skilled-unit medical supplies and equipment.

Personnel Management
- Hired, supervised, and motivated teams of up to 80 professional, technical, and support personnel.
- Created and revised personnel policies to ensure compliance with state and federal regulations.
- Conducted employee orientations and exit interviews, established performance appraisal systems, and supervised pension/benefit programs.
- Organized and implemented a well-rounded staff development program that was considered a model program for the system.

RELEVANT EXPERIENCE

EXECUTIVE DIRECTOR (1992–1993)
Canterbury Gardens, Aurora, Colorado
- Directed the operations of 200 independent-living apartments and 60 assisted-living units.
- Created and managed a $2.0 million budget. Hired and supervised 50 staff members.

EXECUTIVE DIRECTOR (1990–1991)
Vista de Santa Fe Retirement Community, Santa Fe, New Mexico
- Launched and managed the operations of a new, 84-unit retirement facility with a budget of $1.0 million and a staff of 20.
- Planned and developed all marketing efforts, and established team-based staffing patterns.

ADMINISTRATOR (1980–1989)
Evangelical Lutheran Good Samaritan Society, Spokane, Washington; Junction City, Kansas; Amarillo, Texas; La Crosse, Kansas; and Los Alamos, New Mexico
- Managed the operations of various Society facilities in four states.
- Filled one new operation to capacity within 12 months of opening.
- Made dramatic upgrades that raised state certification scores from "deficient" to "superior."

OTHER EXPERIENCE

HOUSING MANAGER (1994–2010)
Colorado Springs Housing Authority, Colorado Springs, Colorado
- Reviewed, evaluated/re-evaluated, and processed the applications of senior citizens desiring rental assistance from the Housing Authority, including Section 8 and other public housing.
- Interviewed applicants, determined eligibility, verified income, calculated rents, and scheduled inspections.
- Served as landlord or property manager for assigned housing units.
- Oversaw maintenance and repair of properties.
- Showed houses to prospective tenants and answered any questions.
- Resolved tenant concerns and issues.
- Evaluated damages when tenants were removed, and coordinated repayments.
- Prepared legal documents, lease agreements, reports, and related documents.
- Coordinated public-relations activities with city and outside agencies.
- Conducted public meetings and workshops to help promote elder self-sufficiency.
- Scheduled fire prevention education sessions and fire drills for senior citizens.
- Selected, trained, and supervised maintenance and clerical staff.
- Obtained certification as a Public Housing Manager from the National Association of Housing and Redevelopment Officials.

EDUCATION

MASTER OF SCIENCE CANDIDATE
Regis University, Colorado Springs, Colorado
Completed all but the professional project for a graduate degree in computer information systems.

BACHELOR OF ARTS IN SOCIOLOGY
University of Washington, Seattle, Washington

COMPUTERS

Windows, Microsoft Word, Excel, PowerPoint, Outlook, Internet Explorer, among others.

Rory Clarke

92 Anderson Lane · Worcester, MA 01601 · Mobile: 505.555.1234 · clarke@protypeltd.com

IT OPERATIONS EXECUTIVE

PERFORMANCE MILESTONES

➜ Recruited to a senior IT executive role at Gold Investments. Recognized as the only VP to manage two of the CIO's top five initiatives in 2002.

➜ Led consolidation of business impact solutions across three Gold operations groups to provide improved problem assessment and resolution.

➜ Grew project revenues from $3 million to $12 million in three years for an IT consulting firm serving premier clients (Bear Stearns, Unisys, AT&T).

EXECUTIVE SUMMARY

Senior-level IT Operations Manager with 17 years of experience including managing IT operations, driving product development and marketing, overseeing product management, and providing consulting services. Managed P&L of $20+ million and teams of 50.

Excel at driving global business operations by leveraging technology and positioning IT as strategic business partner. Skillfully communicate complex IT issues to all levels (talk strategy with C-levels and technology with engineers). MS in Computer Science.

CORE TECHNOLOGY AND BUSINESS STRENGTHS

Strategic Planning and Execution ... Project Management ... Networking ... Security ... Network Engineering
Operations ... Infrastructure Management ... Advanced and Emerging Technology Deployment ... Team Management

BOTTOM-LINE VALUE OFFERED

IT operations impact player who can be counted on to execute strategic IT plans in large enterprise environments and deliver rock-solid business results. With a unique blend of experience in a premier financial services enterprise, two IT product firms, and a consulting firm, bring value-added emerging technology, marketing, and entrepreneurial perspectives. Collaborative, team-based leadership style results in high employee satisfaction and low turnover. Bilingual with cross-cultural orientation. Passion for promoting IT/business success.

PROFESSIONAL EXPERIENCE

INFINITIE, INC., Worcester, MA   2005 — Present
Early-stage company specializing in software solutions for detection of application performance issues
Director of Product Management and Business Development

Drove growth across IT, product management, and business development functions. Currently lead business development functions, including corporate strategy, channel development, and account and sales management. Interface with global R&D operations and manage sales engineering staff.

▪ **Enabled on-time delivery to potential customers** by formalizing the product management process and aligning R&D with clients' IT operations.

▪ **Grew prospect base from two to thirteen in the first year** by developing a target list of beta users through personal contacts, setting up road shows, and collaborating with R&D on a sales demo. Signed up the first customer nine months prior to product release.

SANSAY COMMUNICATIONS, Worcester, MA   2002 — 2005
Manufacturer and market leader in IT performance management software ($170 million in annual revenue)
Product Manager

▪ Catalyst for business growth. Hired to manage development of Business Service Management (BSM) tools. Went on to oversee Voice Technology (VT) products and emerging technologies. Gathered customer requirements and conveyed data to engineers for product development.

SANSAY COMMUNICATIONS, Product Manager — Continued

- **Generated sales of $1.3 million from the first BSM product; garnered $8 million+ in pull-through sales of other products in first six months.** Led team to win **Product Innovation Award** in 2004 for the fastest product development in company history. Influenced and drove product direction of company by energizing the CTO/EVP of engineering with the creation of an initial product mock-up. Led a road show to gain input from key customers such as Unisys, Booz-Allen, AutoDesk, Commercial Insurance, and others.

- **Influential in refocusing product strategy on VoIP,** resulting in a software addition that rounded out product portfolio. Strengthened alliance with Cisco. Won buy-in for $100K expenditure to build out a Cisco VoIP lab, making Sansay one of the largest VP investor among Cisco's partners.

GOLD INVESTMENTS, Hartford, CT   2001 — 2002
One of the largest mutual fund companies in the U.S.
Vice President, Network Systems and Services

Accountable for all management and inventory applications for telecommunications and all internal Domain Name Service (DNS) and Dynamic Host Configuration Protocol (DHCP) environments serving 33,000 end users. Oversaw a team that expanded rapidly from two to five departments. Managed an annual budget of over $20 million.

- **Raised customer satisfaction levels and reduced operational inefficiencies** by leading a cross-functional team in a high-profile initiative. Replaced a silo model for identifying and resolving business problems with a unified solution across multiple operations groups.

- **Saved $60K monthly on call center application and 700 man hours** for volume changes in Hartford area. Executed global deployment of DHCP company-wide by developing project plans, overall architecture, and special solutions to integrate non-standard DHCP deployments.

- **Improved internal Gallop survey rating by 50% over prior year** by realigning IT organization to meet the needs of telecom, thus increasing team morale. Worked with management team to assess project loads across the organization and developed a three-year management strategy.

FUTURE SYSTEMS, New York, NY   1995 — 2000
National IT consulting firm
National Director for Network Engineering Practice

As founding member, brought in Finance-Invest's infrastructure project and grew the account by 29 consultants. Tested the firm's latest technology and served as key advisor for architecture group. Held full P&L responsibility for capital and operating budgets. Acquired and staffed new projects. Managed accounts. Served other industry giants including Unisys, AT&T, Pfizer, Allied Signal, DLJ, and Deutsche Bank.

- **Unified data center network using an elegant single-technology solution that reduced client's annual operating costs.** This was one of the largest data center consolidation projects ever completed regionally. Designed the network architecture plan, tested latest technologies, and created rollout plan.

- **Landed and executed the firm's largest project ever on-time and on-budget, reaping $6 million in revenues.** Developed a comprehensive Y2K mitigation plan for Finance-Invest's entire global infrastructure, put together a strong technical team, and created a reporting structure. Delivered the project despite limited staff.

- **Increased firm revenues by 400% in three years** and managed over 50% of project revenues for the New York region in 1999 and 2000. Developed key services for the firm, and forged strategic relationships.

EARLIER CAREER:
Bay Networks/Synoptics Communications, Staff Network Engineer, Eastern Region, 1993 — 1995
EJV Partners, LLP, Senior Engineer, Network Architecture and Planning Department, 1992 — 1993

EDUCATION

Master of Science in Computer Science, 1993
MASSACHUSETTS INSTITUTE OF TECHNOLOGY, Cambridge, MA

Bachelor of Science in Electrical Engineering, 1988
YALE UNIVERSITY, New Haven, CT

PROFILE

- Experienced educator with a practical background that includes:
  - Administration
  - School operations
  - Lesson planning
  - Team leadership
  - Staff development
  - Assessments and data analysis
- Astute educator who brings real-world experience to classroom and administrative settings.
- Dedicated team player with a personal commitment to excellence in education.
- Effective communicator with the proven ability to teach to the individual.

EDUCATION PHILOSOPHY

Our job is to prepare students for the future job market. Ultimately, we need individuals who will be flexible and able to transfer skills from one career to another, since changing technology will create ever new opportunities. As teachers and administrators, it is our goal to cultivate in students a passion for lifelong learning so they are prepared to maximize those opportunities as they present themselves. One way to accomplish that is to teach to the individual by maximizing each student's background. Few will not respond appropriately when their own interests are tied into a presentation. In addition, it is just as important to impart to students a balanced ability to critically examine current models and theories.

EDUCATION

COLORADO TEACHING (Type B, Secondary Science)
ADMINISTRATIVE (Type D, Professional Principal)
University of Colorado, Colorado Springs, Colorado

MASTER OF SCIENCE, ECOLOGY
Yale University, New Haven, Connecticut

BACHELOR OF SCIENCE, BIOLOGY
Rutger's University, New Brunswick, New Jersey

PROFESSIONAL EXPERIENCE

PRINCIPAL
Dayspring Christian High School, Greeley, Colorado (3 years)
Managed secondary unit of a small school with 300 students. Provided the leadership the school needed to improve administration, school climate, and academic achievement. Managed various operations, including staffing, resource allocation, financial planning, budgeting, staff development, and accreditation. Hired, supervised, mentored, and evaluated the performance of certified staff. Developed the master schedule and managed curriculum development. Organized and led annual programs, including graduations and honor presentations.

- Succeeded in revitalizing the staff, building consensus, and improving morale among teachers, the community, staff, parents, and students. Promoted a collaborative working environment.
- Established an emphasis on instruction and ensured that all students were academically challenged and individually successful.
- Initiated Knowledge Bowl and served as advisor when the team took third place in state competitions.
- Helped to create a secondary handbook for students and parents.
- Organized extracurricular activities, including sports (CHSAA), and other competitions.
- Participated in Colorado Association of School Executives (CASE) meetings and workshops.

HIGH SCHOOL SCIENCE TEACHER
Dayspring High School, Greeley, Colorado (7 years)
Coronado High School, El Paso, Texas (2 years)
Taught biology, chemistry, geology, and physical science in both small and large schools, setting high expectations for all levels of student achievement. Used creative instructional methods that bridged diverse learning styles. Set learning goals and developed lesson plans. Communicated progress with parents and encouraged active parental involvement in the educational process. Implemented effective discipline and classroom management strategies that promoted safe, rich learning environments.

- Successfully aligned curriculum to state standards.
- Created self-motivated learning environments that encouraged respect, responsibility, self-discipline, and organization.

Define Your Sections

Headings are one of the major design elements of a résumé. How you choose to divide sections determines the readability of your résumé. Graphic lines and/or white space help define groups of similar information and draw the reader's eyes down the page.

One of the keys to a readable résumé is the judicious use of white space, and consistent spacing is critical. You will notice throughout the samples in this book that more white space is used between major sections than within sections. This breaks the résumé into easily digested chunks of information. The white space between these sections should be identical throughout the résumé. Likewise, the smaller white space within sections should be the same throughout.

There are two basic positions for your headings. One is centered (pages 91–97, 104, 105) with or without lines, and the other is left justified (pages 98–103, 106). Which style you choose depends on what you find pleasing to your eye. There is no right or wrong way. If you like the design, then it is a good fit with your personality. Some of your options include:

- All caps (pages 102–106)
- First letter larger (pages 91–95)
- Upper/lower case (pages 96, 97, 100, 101)
- All lower case (page 98, 99)
- Very large fonts (pages 100, 101)
- Designer fonts (page 106)
- Reverse boxes with white lettering (pages 92, 93)

Since people read from the top to the bottom and from left to right, begin your résumé with the most important information. Then work your way down to less important information. The top half of your résumé's first page should be packed with your strongest qualifications.

So, which section goes first? Should it be education or experience? Start with the section that contains your strongest qualifications for your target job. If you have had little experience in your prospective field but have a degree that qualifies you for a starting position in the industry, then by all means list your education first. Most people eventually move their education below their experience as they get further from their school days. If you change your career and go back to school, then the education will move to the top again and begin to gravitate to the bottom as you gain relevant experience.

The same idea goes for information within each section. For instance, if you went to an Ivy League school, you would list the school before the degree. Look at the difference in emphasis between these two methods:

HARVARD, Cambridge, Massachusetts
Master of Business Administration

MASTER OF BUSINESS ADMINISTRATION
Little Known College, Backwoods, Idaho

The same principle applies to your experience. If your job title is more impressive than where you worked, then list it first.

VICE PRESIDENT OF MARKETING
Little Known Company, Boulder, Colorado

IBM CORPORATION, Boulder, Colorado
Assistant Export Coordinator

Avoid the use of underlining since it cuts into the descenders in lower case letters. For example, notice the "p" in

Assistant Export Coordinator

It is acceptable to use underlining when the letters are all capitalized since there are no descenders, but it is a bit of overkill in most cases.

ASSISTANT EXPORT COORDINATOR

Italics, bold, ALL CAPITALS, First Letter Larger, or any combination of the four are all good ways to make certain information stand out within the text. However, these styles can be overdone very easily. To make them more effective, use these type treatments sparingly.

MATTHEW B. FENTON

1234 Crimson Rd ▪ Clarksville, MI 28546 ▪ 125-444-5555 ▪ fentonmb@protypeltd.com

POWER GENERATION MECHANIC

Qualified professional providing expertise in the safeguard and maintenance of generation equipment under extreme conditions with minimal part and support availability. Coordinate and perform equipment inspection and maintenance. Supervise and train personnel. Awarded repeatedly for outstanding job performance. Qualified to drive in multiple foreign locations. Familiar with the German language. Areas of strengths include:

- Power Generators
- Troubleshooting
- Electrical Systems
- Control Equipment

- Combustion Engines
- AC/DC Motors
- Measuring and Diagnostic Equipment
- Switchboards and Control Panels

QUALIFICATION HIGHLIGHTS

- Trained in the principles of electrical and electronic circuitry and wire schematics.
- Supervised preventative maintenance and repair of 306 pieces of equipment worth more than $10 million.
- Awarded a driver's badge for the operation of heavy equipment vehicles such as Humvees and 2.5 ton trucks, often in hazardous conditions.
- Instructed personnel and provided hands-on training on repair, replacement, and troubleshooting techniques for essential equipment needed quickly in hostile environments.
- Coordinated training and high-level maintenance activities with various department supervisors.
- Ensured personnel complied with organization's policies, procedures, and industry safety standards.
- Cross-trained 18 vehicle mechanics on power generation equipment to increase company's efficiency.

EMPLOYMENT HISTORY

POWER GENERATION EQUIPMENT REPAIRER, KBR, Baharia Fallujah, Iraq, 2007–2010

GENERATOR MECHANIC, MOS 52D, US Army, Fort Campbell, KY, 1994–2006

EDUCATION AND TRAINING

Class A License, Swift Transportation, Millington, TN, 2007
Diploma, East High School, Rockford, IL, 1994
First Aid and CPR

AWARDS

- Driver's Badge
- Four Army Commendation Medals
- Three Army Achievement Medals
- Three Army Good Conduct Medals
- National Defense Service Medal
- Afghanistan Campaign Medal

- Global War on Terrorism Expeditionary Medal
- Global War on Terrorism Service Medal
- Korea Defense Service Medal
- Iraq Campaign Medal
- Army Service Ribbon
- Three Overseas Service Ribbons

RICHARD TUCKER

12345 North Main Street ▪ Salemburg, NC 28385 ▪ 910.555.1234 ▪ tucker@protypeltd.com

BUSINESS MANAGEMENT

BUDGET ADMINISTRATION · SUPERVISION · EDUCATION · PROJECT PLANNING · COMMUNITY SUPPORT · MENTOR
NON-PROFIT · GRANT APPLICATION AND ADMINISTRATION · STAFF AND VOLUNTEER TRAINING · PROGRAM QUALITY

Astute, tenacious professional with extensive experience planning, implementing, and managing business operations in diverse environments. Able to garner community support while rallying staff and volunteers to action. Strong ability to conceptualize new initiatives and sustain existing programs. Confident presenter, able to reach the unreachable and interact with individuals from all walks of life, garnering and galvanizing support for like-minded goals.

"Don't talk about it. Be about it."

PROFESSIONAL EXPERIENCE

SAMPSON COUNTY NORTH CAROLINA

Director of Sampson County Juvenile Restitution and Teen Court, Clinton, NC, 2000–Present
Charged to startup and drive success of both Juvenile Restitution and Teen Court programs in Sampson County. Spent three months researching community needs, establishing program objectives and operations, and devising volunteer and staff training. Hired "above-and-beyond" team members and took program from startup to success in first-year's operation. Managed $120,000—$140,000 annual budget while supervising 15 paid, full- and part-time staff members and 300+ program volunteers. Compiled grant information and wrote grant submission package. Applied for and awarded Juvenile Crime Prevention Council (JCPC) and Department of Juvenile Justice and Delinquency Prevention (DJJDP) grants for nine consecutive years. **Secured 80% of all funds allocated to county programs, based on result metrics and program success.**

- Touched lives of more than 150 juvenile offenders annually through court-ordered participation in either program.
    - ✓ **Realized 0% recidivism rate in first three years and never exceeded 5% any year with Teen Court initiative—acceptable state average is 50%.**
    - ✓ Established up to 200 hours of community service, providing meaningful services for the elderly, food banks, and area churches.
    - ✓ Adopted swix highways, reducing roadside trash problems and affording beneficial repercussions to juveniles.
    - ✓ Culminated program participation with visit to county jail, netting extremely low recidivism rate for the county. Reduced court backlogs by 30% with effective, real-life experience.

- Created and presented volunteer training manual. Ensured understanding and knowledge transfer, netting 98.7% passing rate.

- Spoke to countless regional organizations about the programs, area gang infiltration, and growing juvenile issues in the county. Became a sought-after speaker for supporters and other law enforcement offices hoping to duplicate program success in their region.

- Started with no volunteers and no program. **Offered training class in first school to 18 students, increasing class size to 80+ during the next four days through word-of-mouth excitement generated by program content.** Grew participation to an average of 300 volunteers for the Teen Court program from 15 public and 6 private schools along with 12 home-school groups.

- Presented public face for programs, frequently quoted in magazines, newspapers, and news reports. Wrote and contributed content. Approached by superintendent of county schools to give mandated training for all county after superintendent heard a presentation about the program.

> *Under Richard Tucker's Leadership*
>
> Juvenile Restitution and
> Teen Court Program
> Facts and Figures:
>
> - More than $5,000 in restitution paid to victims by youth offenders.
>
> - Delivered 7,100 community service hours, generating $100,000 in savings.
>
> - Success rate of 95% or better during nine-year program duration.
>
> - ROI = $88 for each $1 spent
>
> - Saved $3.24 million in court and service costs against a $98,000 investment.
>
> *Source: Report to the People*
> *Fiscal 2007–2008*

PROFESSIONAL EXPERIENCE, CONTINUED

- Networked with 12 third-party agencies to provide program participants with additional improvement opportunities, addressing topics like gang awareness, consulting, dropout prevention, and other teen issues.
- Acted as consultant for gang activity in the region and supported 12–15 officers behind the scenes with sign translation and gang intelligence gathered from informant relationships, continuing study, and extensive experience. Laid groundwork and wrote grant for Gang Resistant Education and Training (GREAT) for the county—realizing culmination of four-years of planning to bring program to Sampson County.

ONONDAGA COUNTY NEW YORK

Counselor / Correction Officer, Hillbrook Detention Center, 1990–2000
Provided security for one of two maximum-security holding facilities for juveniles in New York state. Oversaw block of 12–15 inmates, ranging in age from 10–18 (average age 16–18). Responded to violent and riotous actions while working to maintain order in a volatile environment. Attained certification with the Prisoner Extraction Response Team (PERT), an internal SWAT team.

- Nominated as lead counselor in 1997 after implementing effective suppression measures within the facility. Offered one-on-one counseling and introduced non-sanctioned gang prevention and anger management sessions for block residents.

ROSEWOOD HEIGHTS SKILLED NURSING FACILITY

Admissions Director / Social Worker, Syracuse, NY, 1995-1996 *(Concurrent with Hillbrook employment)*
Hired as the only non-MSW social worker in the facility managing a caseload of 80–100 short- and long-term care residents. Identified need and started an abused woman's class, meeting twice a week.

- Promoted to admissions director in 1996, taking occupancy rate from 80% to 98%+ in under four weeks. Connected daily with regional facilitators and hospital social workers to fill beds and boost census.
- Discovered untapped funds and assisted families with expenditures to improve patient care, personal goods, and amenities prior to expiration dates on funding.

EDUCATION

UNIVERSITY OF PHOENIX, Phoenix, AZ
Master of Science, Psychology, with honors (2009)
Bachelor of Science Criminal Justice, Psychology minor with honors (2003)
Member, Alpha Phi Sigma, Criminal Justice Honor Society

LEMOYNE COLLEGE, Dewitt, NY
Criminal Justice College Courses

ONONDAGA COMMUNITY COLLEGE, Syracuse, NY
Associate of Science, Criminal Justice, Juvenille Counseling minor with honors

NOTABLES

- Coached Sacred Hearts School, Syracuse, New York, basketball team (1992–1998). Inspired team-winning, back-to-back community championships. Started as a volunteer, offered a paid position. Awarded "Coach of the Year" (1998).
- Wrote outdoor column for the *Sampson Independent* weekly newspaper, circulation 12,000–15,000 (2000–Present).
- Contributed regular content to www.freeagentsportwriters.com (2009–Present).
- Certified to teach *"All Stars,"* a 16-step program helping children make better decisions (2006).
- Certified by American Red Cross in Disaster Shelter Operation.

■ ■ ■

RICHARD B. DENNISON

1234 Bethany Court • Colorado Springs, Colorado 80918
Home: (719) 555-1234 • Cell: (719) 123-4567 • Email: Rdennison@protypeltd.com

AREAS OF EXPERTISE

Sales • Sales Management
Strategic Planning • Customer Service
Business Development • Cold Calling
Lead Generation
Relationship Building
Flexibility • Communication
Team Leadership • Integrity
Thinking Outside the Box

SUMMARY OF QUALIFICATIONS

- Experienced Sales Representative with the proven ability to build markets and increase revenue.
- Able to meet and exceed sales performance targets and dedicated to delivering "Wow!" customer service.
- Committed to transparent communications and generating repeat business through relationship building.
- Intellectually and competitively equipped to excel in fast-paced, challenging environments.

DIRECT SALES EXPERIENCE

ACCOUNT EXECUTIVE
Town and Country
Colorado Springs, Colorado
(2006 – present)

Cold Calling
Sales Presentations
Lead Generation
Relationship Building

Key Accomplishments:

- Successfully sold three-year grocery contracts valued from $4,000 to $9,000, closing 85% of leads and building a strong customer base in the market.
- Made sales presentations that prospects understood, prevented overselling, and built relationships that generated referrals from satisfied customers.
- Suggested that the corporation implement a mass mailing program to high-income prospects who had recently moved into high-value homes.
- Participated in local networking groups (BNI) and MOPS groups to make contacts and generate new leads.

RETAIL MANAGEMENT EXPERIENCE

ASSISTANT MANAGER
Office Depot
Colorado Springs, Colorado
2001 – 2006

Daily Operations • Hiring
Team Training • Scheduling
Performance Evaluation
Opening/Closing the Store
Customer Service • Payroll
Merchandising • Inventory
Operational Reporting

Key Accomplishments:

- Promoted three times in the first year, ultimately achieving Assistant Manager responsible for managing the daily operations of this office supply store with a staff of 30 and $8 million in annual sales volume.
- Turned around an unprofitable store, taking it into the black for the first time in several years.
- Drove a 400% increase in computer sales, earning number one ranking in the region by raising staff morale, confidence, and product knowledge through effective product, customer service, and sales skills training,
- Earned a 94.45% FCSI (Fanatical Customer Service Index) score, ranking number one out of 19 stores for service-oriented culture.
- Consistently placed number one or two in the region for Kempers and market baskets by training customer service associates to upsell related products.
- Lowered turnover to 6% by implementing an open-door management policy and staff development and reward/recognition programs, propelling the store to 58th place out of 1,100 stores.
- Offered Store Manager positions three times, but wanted to stay in the Colorado Springs region.

RETAIL MANAGEMENT EXPERIENCE

ASSISTANT MANAGER
Office Depot
(continued)

Special Initiatives:
- Opened or remodeled seven stores on the Colorado Front Range, getting them up and running, hiring and training new staff, and turning them over to new General Managers.
- Initiated a recycling program for cardboard that was picked up nationwide, saving $2 million a year.
- Recommended a reduction in delivery from six trucks a week to four, significantly decreasing the cost of transportation for the entire company.
- Suggested that the company change payroll from weekly to biweekly, which reduced administrative costs and increased cash on hand.
- Significantly increased the sale of laptops by creating an end cap display for Gateway computers at all stores throughout the company.
- Automated light switches in restrooms, serving as a model for stores nationwide.
- Selected to lead a goals program for employees because of leadership and training skills. Won several contests and consistently exceeded district sales objectives.

ASSISTANT MANAGER
Albertson's
Houston, Texas
(1997 – 2001)

Operations Management
P&L • Customer Service
Sales Projections
Labor Forecasts
Inventory • Merchandising
Hiring • Coaching
Training and Development
Performance Evaluation

Key Accomplishments:
- Rapidly advanced from Sales Associate/Team Lead to Assistant Manager of Operations and then to Assistant Manager responsible for overseeing the Service Desk, Deli, Dairy, Butcher Block, Produce, and Front End departments of a $3 million store.
- Increased sales by 18%, earning number one ranking in sales, technology, market basket, and Kemper sales while gaining customer satisfaction and loyalty.
- Reduced inventory costs by effectively negotiating reduced prices with vendors, increasing profit by as much as 10%.
- Enhanced sales by initiating verbal announcements of sale items to shoppers and displaying prominent signs outside the store.
- Selected for Albertson's seven-week Career Advancement Program. Completed training in operations/P&L management, sales, scheduling, food safety, hiring, etc.

EDUCATION

ASSOCIATE OF ARTS, BUSINESS ADMINISTRATION
San Jacinto College, Houston, Texas (1998)

COMPUTER SKILLS

Windows, MS Word, Excel, PowerPoint, Access, Outlook, Internet Explorer, WordPerfect

JILL C. JOSEPH, JD, MBA

223 Oakland Drive, Bennett, CA 43210 ♦ jcjoseph@protypeltd.com ♦ 555.123.4567

───────── **Vice President ♦ Associate General Counsel** ─────────

Commercial Law | Contracts | Corporate Governance | Employment Law
Litigation Management | Intellectual Property

Highly accomplished attorney with more than five years of progressive legal experience demonstrating outstanding solution finding, client service, and team building skills, with a proven record of delivering high-quality work with quick turnaround time.

───────── **Professional Experience** ─────────

BANK OF CALIFORNIA, Santa Barbara, CA...May 2007–present
National venture bank providing financial services to entrepreneurs and venture capital firms. Recruited as sole attorney to build loan documentation department. Promoted twice in two years.

Associate General Counsel/ Vice President (July 2009–present)
Loan Documentation Attorney/Department Manager/Vice President (March 2008–June 2009)
Loan Documentation Attorney/Associate Vice President (May 2007–February 2008)

"You are a joy to work with, from your responsiveness to your attention to detail. I have made it clear to all that will listen how great a resource I believe you are for us here in McLean, but more importantly the bank." ~ Quentin Richardson, Venture Banker, Bank of California

Commercial Law and Contracts	▪ Drafted and negotiated commercial lending agreements, vendor agreements, commercial property leases, and all variety of contracts. ▪ Analyzed Uniform Commercial Code (UCC) and intellectual property lien search results to resolve identified issues.
Corporate Governance	▪ Counseled bank's executives and board of directors on corporate governance matters. ▪ Managed agendas and revised minutes for board meetings. ▪ Addressed structural issues relating to bank holding company and its subsidiaries. ▪ Advised bank executives on compliance and regulatory matters.
Employment Law	▪ Advised human resources department about employment law matters, including employee discipline, termination, stock option plan, and wage and hour issues. ▪ Collaborated with human resources staff and outside counsel to develop training program for bank managers to prevent and resolve legal employment risks.
Intellectual Property	▪ Coordinated pre-trial negotiations for trademark infringement suit. ▪ Developed procedures to monitor potential intellectual property infringements and assessed proper actions.
Risk Reduction	▪ Implemented systems to improve bank's monitoring of UCC lien filings, dramatically enhancing lien visibility and reducing the bank's risk. ▪ Created and led monthly meeting of risk managers and attorneys to generate process improvements, resulting in revision of loan documents and reduction in bank's risk.
Legal Management	▪ Built bank's loan documentation department into a thriving profit center, capturing nearly $1,000,000 of revenue per year from outside counsel. ▪ Achieved department profit of 330% in 2008 and 190% for January–June 2009. ▪ Led department in achieving 98.8% rate of error-free first draft of documents, while completing 98.6% of those documents within prompt turnaround time. ▪ Secured 90% market penetration for bank's new loan documentation service by building a reputation of trust and responsiveness among lenders. ▪ Supervised loan documentation staff and outside counsel; negotiated fee arrangements.

———————————— **Professional Experience** (continued) ————————————

BROWN, MORELAND, PHILLIPS & JONES, P.A., Santa Barbara, CA .... July 2004–May 2007
Attorney ... Full-service law firm with 76 years of providing legal services to individuals and businesses. Private practice attorney counseling clients in variety of legal disciplines.

"Jill is an outstanding attorney. She pays great attention to detail and communicates effectively with clients. I endorse her without reservation." ~ Betty Phillips, Partner, Brown, Moreland, Phillips, et al.

Commercial Law	▪ Drafted and negotiated wide variety of legal documents, including real estate leases and vendor, franchise, and confidentiality agreements.
	▪ Led acquisition of a construction company including successful resolution of numerous legal title issues and environmental complications at seven plant sites.
Corporate Law and Governance	▪ Counseled executives regarding corporate and governance issues.
	▪ Drafted and filed formation documents for corporate entities such as C-corporations, S-corporations, and limited liability companies.
	▪ Designed corporate structures for small and medium-sized businesses.
	▪ Prepared and filed required documents/applications with government agencies to include EEOC, IRS, NC Secretary of State, and NC Department of Revenue.
Employment Law	▪ Developed and implemented management training program focused on reducing employment-related litigation risks.
	▪ Represented employers in a variety of labor and employment suits, including wrongful termination, Title VII discrimination claims, and sexual harassment.
	▪ Successfully negotiated numerous employment-related, out-of-court settlements.
	▪ Drafted employment handbook for private business with more than 500 employees, employment contracts, and termination agreements.

NATIONAL HOTELS AND RESORTS, Arlington, VA...March 2003–July 2004
Senior Development Analyst ... Nation's largest independent hotel management company and leading hotel real estate investor. Analyzed and recommended strategies to competitively re-position hotel's assets.

SWISS CREDIT FINANCIAL SERVICES, New York, NY .... July 1997–July 1998
Investment Banking Analyst ... Leading global investment bank, advising clients in all aspects of finance. Selected through exceptionally competitive recruitment process to perform financial analysis of mergers and acquisitions and public offerings of stock and debt.

———————————— **Education | Certification** ————————————

UNIVERSITY OF NORTH CAROLINA AT CHAPEL HILL
Juris Doctor and Master of Business Administration, May 2002
Bachelor of Arts with Honors in Economics
  ▪ Second major: Political Science, Minor: History, May 1997
  ▪ Morehead Scholar. Highly selective scholarship, modeled after Rhodes Scholarship, providing all-expenses-paid undergraduate education and summer enrichment opportunities

CALIFORNIA SUPERIOR COURT MEDIATOR, certified by California Dispute Resolution Commission

———————————— **Licenses and Affiliations** ————————————

Licensed Attorney
  ▪ California, 2002 ~ District of Columbia, 2003 ~ U.S. District Court for the Middle District of CA, 2004
  ▪ U.S. Court of Appeals for the Fourth Circuit, 2004 ~ U.S. Supreme Court, 2006
California Bar Association, Member, Involvement: CA Lawyers for Entrepreneurs Assistance Program
Emerging Santa Barbara Leaders, Co-founder, Corporate Secretary, Board of Directors Member
  ▪ Successfully applied for IRS 501(c) (3) non-profit recognition and formed nonprofit corporation

Maria A. Kircher

profile

- Experienced Administrative Assistant who adapts quickly to changes in responsibilities.
- Proven problem solver who consistently takes responsibility for her own actions, proactively identifies problems, and creates innovative solutions.
- Effective communicator who shows a high degree of respect for the customer through courtesy and sensitivity. Very successful at resolving difficult or emotional customer situations.

experience

EXECUTIVE ADMINISTRATIVE ASSISTANT (2006 – present)
Peoples National Bank, Colorado Springs, Colorado
Provide administrative support to the bank's C-level executives, directors, and lenders (Chief Credit Officer, CEO, CFO, Chief Administrative Officer/House Counsel, Director of Business Banking, Business Development Officers, Director of Compliance), as well as the Board of Directors. Manage appointments and schedules; professionally screen telephone calls. Assemble and format reports, matrices, action logs, minutes, correspondence, and memorandums. Set up and maintain effective filing systems. Coordinate board meetings, including facilities, food, beverages, handouts, and presentations. Transcribe minutes for the Board, Executive Committee, Loan Committee, Executive Credit Committee, IT Steering Committee, and Criticized Asset Committee. Order appraisals for lenders and assure timely receipt. Prepare and submit corporate credit card applications. Evaluate and prepare expense reports for supported staff. Manage training room and board room schedules. Order and manage custom bank apparel, business cards, letterhead, envelopes, promotional items, supplies, and equipment, working closely with vendors to ensure accuracy and prompt delivery.

- Updated the bank's Intranet by posting policies, procedures, and forms for company use as needed.
- Improved the format of the appraisal order forms and ensured that the review process evolved smoothly.
- Planned and coordinated successful off-site meetings, including quarterly staff meetings, various corporate events, and the annual off-site board meeting. Set up hotel accommodations, airline reservations, ground travel, agendas, meeting amenities, and catering. Coordinate conference registrations.
- Developed new business at corporate-sponsored functions, including business expos, trade shows, and community events.
- Demonstrated an ownership attitude by completing tasks not specifically outlined but necessary for successful bank operations.

WORK DIRECTOR II (2005 – 2006)
Wells Fargo Home Equity, Colorado Springs, Colorado
Managed workflow for the loan documentation department, which is responsible for final reviews before documents are submitted to customers. Reviewed, prioritized, and distributed daily work to meet deadlines and goals. Ensured that state-specific requirements were met and that all documents were accurate and completed on time. Identified problems and escalated them to loan processors and managers. Interviewed, hired, supervised, and scheduled up to ten team members. Delegated work, coached/counseled employees, and helped with the performance evaluation process. Participated in daily production meetings to plan for excess capacity. Prepared daily reports of work completed. Led multiple special projects each year.

- Raised standards, reduced processing errors, and coached employees to achieve or exceed goals.
- Consistently achieved 100% of quality goals when the company standard is 95%.
- Contributed to the development of process improvements and procedures that impacted the organization at all levels.
- Created multiple quick reference guides and job aides to improve work flow.
- Developed a job certification program and cross-trained personnel to do the work of the audit and funding departments during slow times.
- Instituted a daily huddle meeting with the team to review goals, projected volume, and hot topics, which improved communication and team morale.

1234 Vaquero Circle South • Colorado Springs, Colorado 80918
Home: (719) 555-1234 • Email: mkircher@protypeltd.com

experience

OPERATIONS PROCESSOR III (2001 – 2005)
Wells Fargo Home Equity, Colorado Springs, Colorado
Served as senior loan funder and auditor responsible for reviewing all loan documents, entering transactions into the database, and delivering documents to closing agents. Initiated and researched wires and typed distribution checks. Coordinated the quality audit process, ensuring data integrity and minimizing risk. Audited loan documents in three channels of the business. Verified the accuracy of and balanced general ledger accounts. Developed training manuals for audit and funding procedures. Monitored the floor and workload volume, moving people between both processes and channels of business to increase productivity.

- Considered a "power funder," consistently booking more than 1,500 loans per month and producing at 100% to 190% levels throughout the year
- Served as an escalation point and subject matter expert for junior processors with complex transaction problems.
- Created quality checklists for multiple business channels, which decreased errors and improved efficiency.
- Implemented system macros to increase production, and trained team members how to create them on their own.
- Awarded multiple Legendary Service Points for exceptional internal and external customer service.

education

UNDERGRADUATE COLLEGE STUDIES (2003 – present)
Pikes Peak Community College, Colorado Springs, Colorado
- Working toward an Associate of Applied Science in Business Administration.
- Have completed more than 49 transferable credits.

PROFESSIONAL DEVELOPMENT
- Front-Line Leadership (2005 – 2006)
  - Knowing and Managing People: Personality Styles, Diversity, Individuals on the Team, Conflict Resolution, Team Building
  - Developing People: Situational Leadership, Feedback, Coaching, Motivation, Recognition, Continuous Learning, Delegation
  - Business Communications: Speaking with Influence, Write It for Clarity and Impact, Listen to Understand, Using Technology in Communication, Hidden Impacts of Nonverbal Communication
  - Organization and Analysis Skills: Organizing Work, Time Management, Problem Solving and Analysis, Meeting Management
  - Knowing the Business: NHEG Core, Product Knowledge, Systems Knowledge, Reporting Tools, Department or Site-Specific Systems and Reports
- Can We Talk: Interpersonal Communications (2005)
- Wells Fargo Code of Ethics and Business Conduct (2001 – 2006)
- Information Security, Privacy Policy, Bank Secrecy Act (2001 – 2006)
- Fair Lending, Fair Credit Reporting Act, Telephone Consumer Protection Act (2001 – 2006)
- Coaching for Peak Performance (2003)
- Magick Legendary Customer Service (2003)

computers

- Proficient in Windows, MS Word, Excel, PowerPoint, Access, STAR, ACAPS, Silverlake, Acculoan, and MS Publisher.

James Pitt
PRODUCTION MANAGER

Address: **12345 Park Way, Piedmont, CA 94611**
Phone: **(510) 555-1234**
E-mail: **pitt@protypeltd.com**

Professional Profile

Award-winning and self-directed web interactive production specialist with proven expertise working within high-tech environments across various platforms. An innovative over-achiever with a talent for quickly analyzing complex projects and formulating solutions to exceed expectations. Proven abilities to embrace ambiguities and, with responsiveness and flexibility, deliver a wide range of sophisticated usability design and improvement solutions for multiple and creatively challenging projects. Project management professional with a gift for transferring skills to any facet of a web-based landscape. Recognized by colleagues, clients, and stakeholders for constant dedication, versatility, passion for creativity, and relentless pursuit of perfection. Sought after for clear, strategic thinking, resourcefulness, and organizational intuitiveness.

Core Competencies

**Project Leadership • Production Management • Logistics • Sourcing • Resource Allocation
Cross-Functional Collaboration • Design and Usability • Time/Budget Management
Web and Video Production • Internet Research Techniques • Client Specialist**

KEY TECHNICAL PROFICIENCIES
**PC and Mac Platforms • MS Office • MS Project • XML • HTML • QuickBooks • ProSelect
Color Management • Lightroom • Capture One • Lumapix Fotofusion • Proshow Gold
InDesign • Illustrator • Photoshop**

Career Highlights

2002 – Present   JAMES PITT PHOTOGRAPHY (PHOTOPITT.COM)   Oakland, CA
High-end portrait business catering to children, family, and event photography for discerning clientele.

Owner/Principal
Business founder with full ownership of all operational aspects, including bookkeeping, expenditure control, vendor negotiations/relations, staff recruitment and management, sales, client relationships, as well as creative direction of all marketing and website initiatives.

- Provide creative expertise as lead artist and image editor to ensure utmost quality assurance for selective client requirements: color management, image enhancement, layout design, and album creation.
- Coordinate creative vision and maintenance of website, blog, and social networking sites. Drive web marketing and sales initiatives to include the design of HTML newsletters.
- Take on role of creative director in the innovation of marketing concepts by incorporating computer, print, personal networking, and referral processes.
- Perform extensive research and cost analysis when purchasing all supplementary photography products (albums, frames, and niche products) with a scrutinizing eye on operational bottom lines.
- Direct multiple assistants and flawless execution of photo shoots while evoking continuous client interaction.

Key Achievements:
- Devised and implemented an innovative archival work flow system to combat the documentation of approximately one million images through new software implementation.
- Concentrated on cost reduction strategies, resulting in **average annual cost of goods sold well under 35%.**
- Pursued artistic excellence while **driving sales in excess of $200K per year.**
- Expanded business to include fine art and travel images to both private collectors and stock photography agencies.

2000 – 2002   DRIVEBELT (DRIVEBELT.COM)   San Francisco, CA

Executive Producer/Director User Interface
Recruited and assembled an expert cross-functional team of staff and contractors for various projects with strict adherence to stakeholder requirements in successful project delivery for web-based software startup operation. Successfully led team tasked with front-end production and user interface of all remote file storage application interfaces with strict time and project objective guidelines.

(continued on page 2)

Executive Producer/Director User Interface (continued)

- Implemented production process for consumer site version 2.0 upgrade and redesign. Liaised with outside design vendor and piloted site technology conversion from straight JSP to XSL templates processing XML data.
- Took responsibility for rollout of new and enhancement features on consumer site including tips engine, categories, Laplink ActiveX control for synching, in addition to revenue projects including unique placement advertorial sections and premium partner opt-in registration capabilities.
- Progressed customer deployment process as well as development versions 1 and 1.5 for private label storage interface.
- Played pivotal role in heading initial interface design and coordination of version 1.5 redesign with outside interface design vendor for Drivebelt software platform.

Key Achievement:

- Gained post to project manage online redesign and concurrent construction of associated stand-alone application for Factor Design studio. Held key **primary control of project timeline and budget of over $400K** and efficiently directed the implementation team tasked with design-to-application translation.

1999 – 2000 *Senior Producer,* **THE INDUSTRY** San Francisco, CA

Assumed role to lead central web production group providing all online tasks for other business units in addition to coordinating with outside vendors, project managing in-house programs, and regular hands-on code wrangling in a high-pressure publishing framework. Grew production team from two to ten highly-skilled staff (producers and associate producers) during rapid company expansion period, delivering vital training on project-planning processes to staff with no previous experience of formal project management. Managed projects and all resources while reporting directly to group Executive Producer. Tasked with recruitment, program and project estimating, publishing process management, and resource allocation maintenance for a variety of supplementary web products.

- Actively directed widespread revamp and development of company website, theindustry.com, recording 10–15 million page views per month.
- Provided expertise as key source to internal groups (sales, commerce, business development, and editorial) for all web projects.
- Took leadership in overseeing version 1.0 of Intelligence Store, the company's online e-commerce venture through the sale of research reports.

1997 – 1999 *Executive Producer/Production Manager,* **INTUITIVE** Mt. View, CA

Served as lead and key contact for central web and multimedia production group of 25 personnel, holding overall budget responsibility in excess of $1 million. Instituted time tracking/management system to monitor web group production time, thereby ensuring accuracy for strict time/budgetary directives governing manpower hours while working for other internal business units. Influenced increase in traffic to Intuit.com from 2 million to 25 million page views per month through effective recruitment and people management, schedule coordination, budgeting, supervision of process and systems, troubleshooting, and website maintenance.

1996 – 1997	*Producer,* **EAGLE ROAD INTERACTIVE**	Mt. View, CA
1995 – 1996	*Associate Producer,* **WELDON OWEN**	San Francisco, CA
1995	*Production Artist,* **MORGAN INTERACTIVE**	San Francisco, CA
1989 – 1995	*Film/Television Camera Assistant,* **FREELANCE**	Los Angeles, CA

Credentials

Professional Training	**Multimedia Studies Program**—focus on multimedia, design, and web production (1994–1996) San Francisco State University
Bachelor of Arts	**Communication**—emphasis on visual arts, minor in studio art/photography (1988) Stanford University

Awards and Affiliations

- **Wedding and Portrait Photographers International**—Member in Good Standing
  Award of Excellence (2005, 2006, 2007)
- **Featured Photographer** (2007) "The International Registry of Children's Photographers" IROCP.com
- **Featured Artist** (2007) Amherst Media publication, *Professional Children's Portrait Photography* by Lou Jacobs, Jr.

MATTHEW HARRINGTON

1234 Prairie Road ♦ Colorado Springs, CO 80909
Email: harrington@protypeltd.com
Cell: (719) 555-1234

SUMMARY OF QUALIFICATIONS

- ♦ Experienced leader who is committed to achieving goals through hard work and dedication.
- ♦ Loyal team player with the ability to work with a broad range of people from diverse cultural and economic backgrounds.
- ♦ Energetic and self-motivated; able to handle multiple projects simultaneously and manage time efficiently.
- ♦ Proficient in Windows, MS Word, Excel, PowerPoint, Internet Explorer, Outlook, MS Publisher, and Macintosh.

EXPERIENCE

OUT-OF-STATE RECRUITER / ADMISSIONS COUNSELOR (2007 to present)
University of Colorado, Colorado Springs, Colorado
- ♦ Travel throughout the nation to establish relationships with high schools and to recruit students for UCCS.
- ♦ Set up, staff, and break down booths at national college fairs and high schools across the nation.
- ♦ Visit local high schools and meet with counselors and students to encourage enrollment at UCCS.
- ♦ Speak to families and prospective students who visit the UCCS campus. Answer questions about classes, costs, the application process, choosing a degree plan, becoming a student, etc.
- ♦ Provide tours of the campus for individuals and groups as large as 50 people.

DIRECTOR OF STUDENT ACTIVITIES (2007)
Colorado State University, Pueblo, Colorado
- ♦ Managed the operations of the Office of Student Activities, including the Student Activities Board, Special Events Committee, Nontraditional Student Services, Welcome Week, and Student Convocation.
- ♦ Developed and coordinated involvement activities and special events in order to expand students' educational experiences beyond the classroom and increase overall retention: performances, fairs, seminars, workshops, and other special programs.
- ♦ Managed event logistics, including hospitality, catering, venues, staffing, scheduling, transportation, ticket distribution, performance contracts, stage/equipment setup and takedown, and other infrastructure.
- ♦ Marketed and advertised programs to the university and community using radio, posters, flyers, print media, and television.
- ♦ Recruited, trained, supervised, and evaluated 12 students and volunteer staff.
- ♦ Prepared and managed department budgets and event budgets ($250,000+) and monitored expenditures.
- ♦ Developed relationships and collaborated with other university departments in goal setting, committees, and special projects.
- ♦ Developed and implemented social programming for a group of selected first-year resident students as the Resident Learning Community Programmer.

CO-PRESIDENT, OFFICE OF CAMPUS ACTIVITIES (2006 to 2007)
Office of Campus Activities, University of Colorado, Colorado Springs, Colorado
- ♦ Oversaw all programs of the Office of Campus Activities and set the organization's short- and long-term goals and objectives.
- ♦ Supervised and advised members through bimonthly meetings, and appointed assistants and/or committees as needed and approved by the board.
- ♦ Collaborated with the Program Coordinator and Graduate Assistant to create event proposals, balance a calendar of events, and evaluate the results.
- ♦ Planned, attended, and chaired weekly organization meetings, ensuring that the agenda was covered.
- ♦ Helped plan and attended all workshops, training sessions, retreats, and other meetings.
- ♦ Served as co-chair for DisOrientation Week and ROAR Daze (collegiate traditions) and form/lead committees.
- ♦ Developed the annual budget and ensured accountability for student fee expenditures totaling more than $225,000.

EXPERIENCE

GLOBAL ISSUES AND CURRENT EVENTS COORDINATOR (2005 to 2006)
Office of Campus Activities, **University of Colorado**, Colorado Springs, Colorado

♦ As the Global Issues and Current Events Coordinated, planned political events, Parade of Lights participation, and other meetings for the campus.

♦ Managed the events budget, and solicited and negotiated sponsorships from local businesses.

♦ Recruited, trained, and supervised volunteers for each event.

♦ Developed a panel discussion with students who had served in Iraq in order to raise awareness of war issues.

♦ Organized a nonpartisan debate over Colorado Referendums C and D, requiring two months of planning. Recruited the author of the referendums and an opposing speaker. Collaborated with various departments of the college to develop the format of the debate. Responsible for the venue, audio-visual equipment, catering, publicity, speakers, etc. The event was attended by 400+ participants and covered by all local television stations and newspapers.

SITE DIRECTOR (2002 to 2003)
YMCA of the Pikes Peak Region, **Downtown Center**, Colorado Springs, Colorado

♦ Managed two sites; hired three counselors; trained and supervised a staff of ten.

♦ Director of the 2003 summer day camp at Pinon Valley Elementary School, a five-day per week program with a different theme each week. Passed inspection by the American Camping Association with no deficiencies.

♦ Director of the before/after-school program at Foothills Elementary School for 5 to 10 year olds. Worked with state Health Department inspectors to achieve a 100% pass rate.

♦ Developed and implemented a variety of curriculums, ranging from the study of architecture, recycling, biology, and dinosaurs to space exploration and comic book heros.

♦ Managed two budgets and succeeded in being the first director in seven years who did not lose money.

♦ Successfully raised scholarship funds for the 2002 Partners Campaign.

RESEARCH ASSISTANT (2002)
Western State College, **Department of Behavioral Science**, Gunnison, Colorado

♦ Researched protests and riots for an article published by Dr. Daniel Harrison, PhD.

♦ Collected raw data, compiled a database of research findings, prepared the article's bibliography, and edited the final report.

♦ Cataloged the professor's personal library into a database.

EDUCATION

MASTER OF ARTS, **University of Colorado**, Colorado Springs, Colorado (May 2007)

♦ Major in Sociology with a major GPA of 3.75.

BACHELOR OF ARTS, **Western State College**, Gunnison, Colorado (2002)

♦ Major in Sociology with a major GPA of 3.9.

♦ Completed all but a few credits toward a double major in Business Administration.

♦ Awarded an academic scholarship in 2000 and achieved Dean's List status for multiple semesters.

♦ Selected for a social research project contracted by the State of Colorado. Surveyed Gunnison County residents to help determine distribution of lottery funds, which resulted in the addition of digital Internet services in the county.

CONTINUING EDUCATION

♦ Group Therapy and Psychodrama, Western State College (Spring 2003)

Joanna Madison

410-555-1234 ♦ E-mail jmadison46@protypeltd.com ♦ 590 New York Avenue NE, Washington, D.C. 20011

Trend-setter of Diversity and Inclusion Initiatives...

HUMAN RESOURCES EXECUTIVE

Senior-level Human Resources Professional possessing more than 15 years of experience. Proven track record of executing and delivering strategically solid human resources programs and initiatives, including diversity initiatives, organizational development and change management procedures, training and leadership development, succession planning, compensation, and labor relations. Highly valued for legal expertise and keen insight for building organizational structures that positively contribute to a company's bottom line.

...Change Management Strategist Who Achieves Performance Goals

EXECUTIVE LEADERSHIP ATTRIBUTES

Leading Change: Consistent high-level of performance in creating and directing strategic initiatives based on long-term and short-term corporate visions. Adept at building consensus and prioritizing communications in an effort to minimize the internal and external impact of organizational and cultural change.

Leading People: Foster open/inclusive team environment designed to promote workplace diversity and leverage inherent leadership strengths through leadership development training, professional education, and goal setting.

Business Acumen: Actively engage in regular discussions with CFO, Divisional President, and other senior leaders to analyze performance, organizational structure, resource allocation, and long-term goals. Develop and implement strategies to achieve financial and structural performance goals throughout the organization.

Building Coalitions: Work closely in a cross-functional environment to leverage communication partnerships and build consensus. Negotiate policy, structure, and strategic implementation for obtaining desired results.

PROFESSIONAL EXPERIENCE

MAGIC JOHNSON ENTERPRISES ♦ 6/06 to present ♦ Gaithersburg, MD
Senior Vice President of Human Resources, Corporate Services 6/07–present
Market Senior Director, Diversity 6/06–6/07

➢ Aggressively recruited to lead diversity and inclusion (D&I) efforts for the corporate and government services division. Increased internal and external visibility of D&I efforts to position MJ Enterprises among one of the most recognized companies in North America. Enhanced corporation's diversity model by leading global diversity training initiatives and establishing benchmarking models.

➢ Rapidly advanced to Senior Vice President of Human Resources as a strategic leader to the Executive Leadership Team. Manage 36 member cross-functional team with an annual budget of $7,000,000 and report directly to the COO/Market President for Corporate Services.

Selected Accomplishments
➢ Propelled diversity and inclusion initiatives to the forefront of MJ Enterprises organizational/cultural philosophies through diversity-training initiatives, closely analyzing employee-engagement metrics, coordinating trendsetting mentoring programs, and emphasizing external communications.
➢ Spearheaded D&I branding efforts for corporate market division achieving recognition in *Diversity, Inc.'s* Top Ten Companies List.

MAGIC JOHNSON ENTERPRISES (continued)

➢ Implemented reorganization efforts to streamline talent base by shifting operational emphasis away from geographical alignment toward a market-need alignment. Aligned talent to coincide with business development forecasts to double revenue and triple EBIT (Earnings Before Interest and Tax) within 10 years.

➢ Increased engagement, performance, morale, and productivity of non-exempt employees through heightened communications, employee recognition, and service incentive programs.

➢ Established executive talent development and leadership management training structure, resulting in elevated executive talent, improved on-boarding of senior managers, and increased team engagement.

➢ Improved service delivery and performance of non-exempt employees by designing and implementing training programs in coordination with MJ Enterprise University. Improved bottom line and performance goals by minimizing talent gaps, improving recruiting objectives, and enhancing client relationships.

NATIONAL RAILROAD PASSENGER CORPORATION (Amtrak) ♦ 2/1997 to 5/2006 ♦ Washington, D.C.
Vice President, Business Diversity and Strategic Initiatives 2/2001–5/2006
Assistant Vice President, Human Resources 2/1999–2/2001
Senior Director, Human Resources 2/1997–2/1999

➢ Steadily progressed into positions of increasing responsibility and authority with direct responsibility to the President and CEO. Key player in developing/implementing corporate-wide D&I policies and steering cultural shift that transformed Amtrak to a performance-based, profit-driven organization.

Selected Accomplishments

➢ Restructured entire human resources department to include benchmark performance initiatives, professional training and development, and improved talent sourcing and recruiting methods.

➢ Eliminated outsourcing costs by including functional roles into the human resource department's responsibilities.

➢ Assisted with the design and implementation of a comprehensive performance management system that included 360 feedback. Expedited employee on-boarding while significantly improving efficiency.

➢ Streamlined HR and Finance functions with the purchase and implementation of a new payroll and Human Resource Information System (HRIS).

➢ Contributed legal and strategic counsel in negotiating settlement terms for class action lawsuits.

➢ Awarded highest corporate recognition for development and successful implementation of diversity recruitment plan.

ADDITIONAL EXPERIENCE

U.S. COMMISSION OF CIVIL RIGHTS
Acting Agency Director/Deputy Assistant Director for Management, Director of Personnel

U.S. OFFICE OF PERSONNEL MANAGEMENT
Counsel to the Deputy Director

D.C. OFFICE OF PERSONNEL
Acting Director, Deputy Director of Personnel, General Counsel

EDUCATION

Juris Doctor ♦ National Law Center, The George Washington University
Bachelor of Arts ♦ Vassar College

Douglas Z. Cety

8912 South Landmark Court • Boise, Idaho 83704
Cell: (208) 555-1234 • E-mail: bpianalyst@protypeltd.com

SUMMARY OF QUALIFICATIONS

- Experienced Home Inspector and Energy Auditor with diverse experience in residential and commercial HVAC systems.
- Detail oriented, precise worker who produces consistently excellent products.
- Effective team player with strong communication and interpersonal skills.

CERTIFICATIONS

- BPI Certified Building Analyst
- RESNET Certified Home Energy Survey Professional (HESP)
- ITA Certified Home Inspector

PROFESSIONAL EXPERIENCE

HOME INSPECTOR / ENERGY AUDITOR
A Closer Look Home Inspections, Boise, Idaho (2006–present)
Todd's Heating and Cooling, Boise, Idaho (2007–2010)

Energy Auditor: Analyze residential buildings to determine how much energy they use, discover inefficiencies, and provide opportunities to save energy. Conduct visual, on-site inspections of the energy features of homes, including insulation levels, window/door efficiency, wall-to-window ratios, heating/cooling system efficiency, air balance, solar orientation of the home, and the water heating system. Document the general condition of systems (including envelope features, equipment types, characteristics, and ages) and appliance and lighting characteristics. Review utility usage and billing histories for comprehensive energy audits. Use blower door, duct leakage test, infrared camera, infiltrometer, and other test equipment to conduct more in-depth evaluations and performance testing. Calculate energy and environmental savings and propose treatments for improvements to existing homes.

- Recommended solutions that increased the energy efficiency, comfort, and durability of homes while at the same time reducing waste/pollution and protecting the environment.
- Gained experience with:
  - Heat transfer concepts
  - Calculating gross and net areas
  - Envelope leakage/insulation
  - HVAC equipment efficiencies
  - Measuring building dimensions
  - Building orientations
  - Building performance testing
  - Energy terminology
  - Thermal bypass/bridging
  - Appliance efficiencies
  - Window and door efficiencies
  - Building shading characteristics
  - Air distribution leakage
  - Combustion appliances
  - Insulation quality
  - Energy units
  - Specifications
  - Thermal boundaries

Home Inspector: Conduct objective visual examinations of the physical structure and systems of a home, from the roof to the foundation. Evaluate the condition of the home's heating system; central air conditioning system; interior plumbing and electrical systems; the roof, attic and visible insulation; walls, ceilings, floors, windows and doors; as well as the foundation, basement and structural components. Prepare reports of those systems and components that are not functioning properly or are significantly deficient, unsafe, or are near the end of their service lives. Make recommendations for corrections.

- Help home buyers make the biggest financial decision of their lives by learning all they can about their potential homes before making their final buying decisions.

TECHNICAL TRAINING

- **Certified Building Analyst Course,** Building Performance Institute (2009)—studied buildings and their systems, measurement and verification of building performance, BPI standards and specifications, analyzing building systems, and professional ethics/conduct/communications.

- **Home Energy Survey Professional Training Program,** RESNET (2009)—completed a battery of software verification tests and passed the RESNET National Rater Test.

- **Home Inspection Training Program,** Kaplan Inspection Training Associates (2006)—how to set up and run a successful business, roofing, exterior, structural, electrical, heating, cooling, heat pumps, insulation, plumbing, interior, appliances, and final exam.

COMPUTER SKILLS

- Knowledge of Windows, MS Word, Excel, Outlook, Internet Explorer, e-Inspection, HOBO Data Logger, and Infiltrometer software.

Difficult Dates

Where should you place your dates? It all depends on how much importance you want to give them. If you have gaps in your employment history that you would rather explain in an interview, then the dates should be less obvious. You can even leave them off altogether and list totals instead (pages 114, 115), although your reader will automatically assume you have something to hide. You need to make the decision whether leaving the dates off will harm your chances of getting an interview more than putting the dates on your résumé.

Another reason to de-emphasize dates is your age. If you would rather not give your age away, then make the reader work to figure it out. Tuck dates against the text with parentheses (pages 109–111), create a functional style (pages 112–113), or bury them somewhere else in the résumé. You can selectively choose to leave dates off your education and show them only on your experience.

So, how far back should you go when listing your experience? The answer is simple. When your past experience stops being relevant to your job search, leave it off. The usual is 10 to 15 years in the past, unless there is something in your older experience that is critical to your qualifications. This will help to deflect interest from your age.

Accuracy and honesty are the most important considerations when it comes to dates. Don't lie! I had a client who chose to fudge on his dates and I didn't know about it. He was invited for an interview and then lost the job when previous employers were contacted and the dates didn't match. It wasn't worth it. Honesty is always the best policy.

There are many ways to make room for the dates. One is to establish a clear column of dates to the right of a résumé, which keeps the text lines short and makes the dates easy to find (pages 124–126). You should not use this clear column of dates on the right if you want to de-emphasize your dates.

Putting dates on the left gives them a great deal of importance, as well. Since people read from left to right, information on the left of the page is read first and carries greater weight. Make sure you really want your dates to be that important before placing them in the left-hand column (pages 118–121).

You may use months with years or years only. Some people feel more comfortable with a full accounting of their time and prefer the month/year method. Government job applications, especially through *www.usajobs.gov,* require a full accounting for your start and end dates of every job, so expect to know the month and year for each one.

Making room for all those words becomes a problem if you choose to spell out the months, however, as in January 2008 to February 2010. Abbreviations or numbers for months make designing your résumé a little easier:

Jan. 2008 – Feb. 2010
or
Jan 2008 – Feb 2010
or
1/08 – 2/10

It is possible to stack the dates in order to make more room. For example:

Jan. 2002   or   January 2002
to Feb. 2005   to February 2005

Dot leaders ....2008 – 2010 can help draw the eye to the dates on paragraph-style résumés where it is difficult to create a clear column for the dates (pages 116, 117, 122, 123). However, dot leaders call a lot of attention to the dates, so don't use them if you are worried about age discrimination or gaps in employment.

There is no single, preferred method for the positioning of dates on a résumé. The key is to create a sense of balance by placing the dates in a position that is complementary to the rest of your information, while keeping in mind how much importance you wish to give them and the scannability of your résumé.

Phillip K. Fjellman, JR

P.O. Box 1234 • Avon, Colorado 81620 • Cell: (970) 555-1234 • Email: pkfjellman@protypeltd.com

PROFILE

- Dedicated law enforcement professional with definitive leadership and problem-solving abilities.
- Natural leader who instills confidence and motivates colleagues to deliver exceptional results.
- Flexible, quick learner who brings a sense of calm to high-stress situations.
- Effective team player with strong interpersonal and communication skills.
- Proficient in Windows, MS Word, Excel, PowerPoint, Internet Explorer, Outlook, I/LEADS Police Records Management System, I/MOBILE, COPLINK Solution Suite, and links to NCIC and CCIC.

CERTIFICATIONS

- Colorado POST Certified as a Colorado Peace Officer #B-14185 (2008–2011).
- Certified Intoxilyzer 5000EN Instructor, Colorado Department of Public Health and Environment.
- Certified Crime Scene Technician, Avon Police Department.
- Certified Advanced Roadside Impaired Driving Enforcement (ARIDE).
- Certified by the American Red Cross for First Aid, Adult CPR, and Automatic External Defibrillator.

RELEVANT EXPERIENCE

POLICE / PATROL OFFICER (February 2008 – present)
City of Avon—A Vail Valley Community, Colorado

- Serve as patrol officer, incident commander, team leader, and shift senior officer with up to three direct reports.
- Proficient in weapons handling, Israeli-developed Krav Maga defensive tactics, and hostage/crisis intervention.
- Enforce laws, statutes, ordinances, and codes using community-oriented policing techniques.
- Patrol districts to detect illegal activities, answer calls, maintain law and order, make arrests, protect wildlife, and perform animal control.
- Conduct criminal investigations and process crime scenes, including fingerprinting, photography, and evidence identification, packaging, and processing.
- Initiate search warrants. Identify, seize, and process evidence relating to cases.
- Serve summons, complaints, and warrants. Testify in court on criminal, traffic, and civil offenses.
- Enforce traffic and DUI codes/regulations and write traffic summons. Investigate major traffic accidents. Construct detailed reports and diagrams of serious and fatal traffic accidents.
- Participate on the Gore Range DUI Task Force to saturate areas of the county with highly trained DUI officers.
- Track and arrest persons wanted on warrants. Handle out-of-state extraditions and in-state prisoner transport.
- Perform background investigations, fugitive identification, surveillance, and general intelligence gathering.
- Train new recruits in basic crime scene processing, morals/ethics, and department expectations.

Key Accomplishments:

- Earned a 2010 Teamwork Award from the Avon Police Department for playing a key role with the SWAT team on two simultaneous incidents, a barricaded suicide suspect and a high-profile shooting in a public venue.
- Selected for the SWAT team—Waiting for funding to begin formal training.
- Ranked second in Eagle County for DUI arrests in 2008 and in the top 10 for 2009.
- Managed an assigned section in the annual National Night Out to improve community relations and neighborhood safety.
- Served as an instructor for the annual Citizens' Police Academy. Educated the public about the Avon Police Department's role in the community, firearms safety, crime scene forensics, and community policing.
- Accountable for a police vehicle, handguns, rifles, shotguns, tasers, batons, and high-value safety, communications, surveillance, radar, and computer equipment.
- Gained expertise in dealing with complex, high-profile cases as a result of the Vail Valley's diverse demographics that include wealthy celebrities, Latino gangs, and a large number of illegal immigrants.
- *"Phillip is a very dedicated and committed member of the Avon Police Department. He takes great pride in his appearance and is always early for work. He saved the life of a victim in July of 2008 when he stopped a suspect from smashing the head of a victim with a rock." – Lt. Greg Daly*
- *"Phillip has a strong drive to succeed and to be the best officer. His drive motivates him to be constantly out on the street and it shows in his professional appearance. Phillip is a top producer in reports and citations, with consistently higher output than any other officer on the shift. His drive is motivating to other officers and even to me." – Chief Bill Kovak*

RELEVANT EXPERIENCE

LIEUTENANT, SECURITY OFFICER
Allied-Barton Security Services, Castle Rock, Colorado (July 2003 – February 2006)
Wackenhut, Castle Rock, Colorado (2002 – 2003)
- Managed swing shift employees in maintaining the security of three main facilities, seven detached buildings, grounds, and parking lots of the DirecTV Main Broadcasting Center, as well as seven remote sites in six states.
- Evaluated the performance of two security officers every three months.
- Watched company gates, controlled access, issued badges, provided directions, patrolled buildings and grounds, and monitored property removal.
- Took reasonable and prudent action to ensure the safety of employees, visiting personnel, and physical assets.
- Provided immediate response in emergency situations, including fires, medical emergencies, and hazardous materials incidents. Assisted in building safety inspections.
- Investigated security breaches and emergency events. Wrote incident and fire alarm reports, escort and access logs, and other reports.
- Operated the communications center, which received emergency communications and monitored security, fires, and maintenance alarms. Dispatched personnel as necessary.
- Screened all mail and packages for suspicious contents, postmarks, and recipients.

SPECIALIST (E-4), LIGHT CAVALRY SCOUT
United States Army, Fort Carson, Colorado (September 1998 – September 2001)
Army National Guard (full time), Swanton, Vermont (January 1996 – September 1998)
- Held a secret security clearance through the U.S. Army. Top Secret security clearance completed by the TSA.
- Guarded equipment, vehicles, personnel, and other military assets 24 hours a day, 7 days a week.
- Gathered and reported information collected during field operations, including terrain features, enemy strength, disposition, equipment, and targets. Requested and adjusted indirect and aerial fire during military exercises.
- Used maps, compasses, and GPS to navigate on the ground and to distinguish topographic features.
- Experienced as a combat lifesaver, including first aid, CPR, field medical support, and IV certification.
- Expert marksman—M-16 rifles, grenades, M-203 grenade launchers, M-60 machine gun, 240-bravo machine gun, 50 caliber automatic machine gun, and 9mm handguns. Ranked Top Gun for the MK-19 grenade launcher (500/500). Experienced in the use of C-4 and TNT explosives.
- Trained in tactical hand-to-hand combat, nuclear/biological/chemical contamination, and intelligence.

Management:
- Supervised, trained, scheduled, and mentored a team of five soldiers.
- Coordinated personnel, logistics, transportation, and communication requirements during exercises.
- Worked in the S-3 shop responsible for battalion operations, tasking, logistics, and preparation of overlays for enemy positions. Implemented orders, directives, and battle plans. Prepared to assume the duties of the commander.
- Developed and presented classes to as many as 25 personnel on such subjects as weapons, safety, Army procedures, and vehicle maintenance.

Key Accomplishments:
- Maintained 100% operational readiness rate on assigned HMMWVs (Highly Mobile Multi-Wheeled Vehicle) and personnel carriers, including communications and other sensitive equipment valued at more than $1.2 million.
- Ensured the safety of workers and equipment during major field training exercises, sustaining no accidents for a continuous five-year period.
- Awarded two Commendation Medals, three Achievement Medals, and a Good Conduct Medal for meritorious service above and beyond the call of duty. Achieved an outstanding physical fitness level of 279 out of 300.

OTHER EXPERIENCE

ASSET MANAGEMENT, MATERIALS HANDLER (February 2006 – January 2007)
DirecTV, Castle Rock, Colorado
- Recognized for exceptional work ethic by DirecTV executives while working for their contract security agencies.
- Recruited to work in the Asset Management Department responsible for hundreds of thousands of line items.
- Received new equipment, tagged them, and entered tracking data into the Cruizer MRP computer system.
- Shipped damaged equipment to remote offices for repair—selected to travel to the South Bend, Indiana, facility for a week to help engineers with their repair functions and to learn how to better support them from Colorado.
- Discovered unused storage space in the warehouse, which saved the cost of container rentals.

EDUCATION	**LEVEL 1 PEACE OFFICER CERTIFICATION COURSE / PUEBLO LAW ENFORCEMENT ACADEMY** (December 2007)

LEVEL 1 PEACE OFFICER CERTIFICATION COURSE / PUEBLO LAW ENFORCEMENT ACADEMY (December 2007)
Pueblo Community College / Pueblo County Sheriff Department, Pueblo, Colorado
- Completed a 37-semester-hour program certified by the Colorado Peace Officers Standards and Training (POST) Board, including Basic Police Academy I/II, Basic Law Enforcement Academy III, Basic Law, Arrest Control Techniques, Law Enforcement Driving, and 67 hours of Firearms Training.

BACHELORS OF SCIENCE, CRIMINAL JUSTICE (December 2007)
Colorado Technical University, Colorado Springs, Colorado
- Selected for the High Academic Achievement List with a GPA of 4.0.
- Relevant course work: Victimology, Homeland Security, Laws of Evidence, Crime Lab and Evidence Management, Corrections in America, Forensic Psychology, Introduction to Psychology, Social Psychology, Criminal Justice Capstone, Creative Leadership, Ethics, Human Resource Management, Public Administration, Project Management Theory and Techniques, Business Law, Organizational Behavior, Professional Speaking, Professional Writing.

ASSOCIATE OF APPLIED SCIENCE, CRIMINAL JUSTICE (May 2003)
Pikes Peak Community College, Colorado Springs, Colorado
- Selected for the President's Honor Roll with a GPA of 4.0.
- Relevant course work: Constitutional Law, Law Enforcement Operations, Criminology I, Juvenile Law, Substantive Criminal Law, Procedural Criminal Law, Judicial Function, Police Report Writing, Police Supervision Techniques, Fingerprinting, Criminal Investigation I/II/III, Introduction to Criminal Justice, Police Photography, Police Investigative Internship, Human Relations/Social Conflicts, Psychology of Adjustment, General Psychology.

PROFESSIONAL DEVELOPMENT
- DNA Evidence Collection and Retention for all Colorado Peace Officers, Colorado POST (2010)
- Use and Deployment of the STOP STICK Tire-Deflation Devices, Avon Police Department (2009)
- Basic Crime Scene Investigation Class, Central Mountain Training Foundation (24 hours, 2009)
- Police Mountain Bike Familiarization, Avon Police Department (8 hours, 2009)
- Intoxilyzer 5000EN Instructor Certification, Colorado Department of Public Health and Environment (2009)
- Prescription Drug Crime, Colorado State Patrol (2009)
- Horizontal Gaze Nystagmus, Colorado State Patrol (2009)
- Standard Field Sobriety Test Refresher Course, Avon Police Department (4 hours, 2009)
- Reporting Writing Class, Colorado Law Enforcement Associations (8 hours, 2008)
- ICS For Single Resources and Initial Action Incidents, IS-00200, FEMA (2008)
- Precision Driving, CIRSA Loss Control Department (2008)
- Intoxilyzer 5000EN Operator Certification, Colorado Department of Public Health and Environment (2008)
- Colorado Crime Information Center Certification, Level E, Colorado Bureau of Investigation (2008)
- Introduction to the Incident Command System, IS-00100, FEMA (2007)
- National Incident Management System (NIMS), IS-00700, FEMA (2007)
- U.S. Army, Basic Training, Squad Leader (1997)
- U.S. Army, M-3 Bradley, CFV Cavalry Scout Specialist Training, 716 hours (1997)

CYD MARSTEN

15722 Arkansas Street
Newhall, California 91321

Residence: 661-253-1908
Cellular: 661-807-1171

CUSTOMER SERVICE / COLLECTIONS

Customer Service

Results-oriented, enthusiastic, creative client services professional with extensive experience in client relations **across broad industries** (medical, mortgage, insurance). Excellent problem-solving skills with a strong orientation in customer service/satisfaction. Able to work under pressure in fast-paced, time-sensitive environments. Demonstrated ability to assess problem areas and offer recommendations, resulting in increases in productivity and profitability. Background encompasses **strong leadership** as well as the ability to establish and build positive, solid relationships with clients and all levels of management. Outstanding listening and interpersonal skills. Energetic, with proven stamina. Computer literate.

Collections

- Expertise in re-energizing stagnant customer accounts.
- Superb negotiation skills with the ability to interact with clients, establish equitable payment policies, and resolve billing errors to maintain positive relations.
- Professional and articulate; ability to deal with clients at all levels.
- Conscientious application of policies, procedures, and systems.
- Quick and effective problem-solver while dealing with new concepts, systems, and procedures.
- Knowledge of how to deal with difficult people.

SYNOPSIS OF ACHIEVEMENTS

- Captured **$160,000 within one week** by reinstating three loans.
- Collected **$112,000 within a one-month period,** the highest amount ever collected by anyone during entire history of Collection Bureau of Modesto.
- Developed program facilitating processing of **medical claims** which was implemented company-wide. Still in use today.
- Reorganized high-delinquency mortgage accounts unit to lower delinquency ratios to acceptable standards.
- Reactivated key accounts utilizing persuasion/mediation skills.
- **People's Choice Award,** Security Pacific Home Loans.

HIGHLIGHTS OF RELATED WORK EXPERIENCE

COLLECTIONS COUNSELOR ● Security Pacific Home Loans – Riverside, CA
Communicated regularly and effectively with mortgagors who were delinquent on their mortgage loans. Completed documentation of collection efforts, including communications, reason for default, payment plans, updated telephone numbers, and mailing addresses. Explored alternatives to foreclosures, which led to reinstatement of 25 loans in September and 10 in October. Types of loans were various conventional loans and B&C paper loans—**90% performing commitment** for September 2003.

CUSTOMER SERVICE / COLLECTIONS ● Archibald Enterprises – Santa Paula, CA
Consistently exceeded collection quotas (currently **ranked No. 1** by collecting more than 50%) through diplomatic and sensitive interaction with debtors. Resolved clients' advertising difficultties. Handled all correspondence pertaining to customer service.

COLLECTOR / SUPERVISOR ● Collection Bureau of Modesto – San Jose, CA
Resolved most billing problems on behalf of policyholders while maintaining an ongoing professional relationship with most insurance companies. **Ranked No. 1** collector. Created programs which streamlined productivity and increased efficiency.

CLAIMS SUPERVISOR ● Allstate Insurance – River Falls, CA
Proactive planning led to notable increase in morale in all departments and in re-establishing clients' trust and loyalty.

LOAN SERVICE / COLLECTION OFFICER ● Great Western Savings – Northridge, CA
Diplomacy and assertiveness allowed for adherence to payment schedules and resolution of tax problems. Dealt with insurance queries, lawsuits, and culture/communication barriers. Handled FHA, VA, and conventional types of loans.

NONRELATED EXPERIENCE

OWNER ● L.A. Rottweilers – Modesto, CA
Bred, raised, showed, and sold Rottweilers trained as pet therapy dogs to bring sunshine to patients in Children's Hospital and elderly homes. Handled all daily administrative affairs, including A/P, A/R, general ledger, and running credit checks.

WORK HISTORY

Collections Counselor	Security Pacific Home Loans	Riverside, CA	2009
Customer Service/Collections	Archibald Enterprises	Santa Paula, CA	2007–2009
Administrative Assistant	Personnel Plus	Santa Clarita, CA	2006–2007
Server / Trainer	Mimi's Café, Birks	Modesto, CA	2001–2006
Business Owner	L.A. Rottweilers	Modesto, CA	1998–2001
Collector / Supervisor	Collection Bureau of Modesto	Modesto, CA	1995–1998
Claims Supervisor	Allstate Insurance	River Falls, CA	1993–1995
Loan Service/Collection Officer	Great Western Savings	Northridge, CA	1992–1993

CONTINUAL TRAINING

B&C 101 New Hire Training Course
B&C 102 New Hire Training Course
B&C 102 On The Job Training Course
Seminar in Customer Service

KENNETH T. KIRKPATRICK

SUMMARY
- Seasoned expert witness with 18 years of experience in construction-related litigation.
- Proven technical expertise in all phases of residential and light commercial construction gained through 32 years of hands-on experience in the industry.
- Able to assess inferior workmanship, construction defects, malfeasance, and catastrophic losses.
- Skilled at applying a strong knowledge of the Uniform Building Code and industry standards to reach fair conclusions.
- Effective communicator who is adept at presenting technical subjects in a way that is easy to understand.

CREDENTIALS
- Class B-1 Contractor License, El Paso County (1990 – present)
- General Residential Class C License 2555C, Teller County (2006 – present)
- Contractors License C94-257, Douglas County (2004 – 2007, 2009 – present)
- Certified Trade and Industry Instructor, Postsecondary/Adult Level, Colorado State Board for Community Colleges and Occupational Education (1990 – 2003)
- Class C Contractor License, El Paso County (1988 – 1990)

EXPERIENCE

CONSULTANT AND EXPERT WITNESS (18 years)
- Provided expert testimony in more than 130 construction cases.
- Successfully mediated cases between construction companies and their customers.
- Hired by insurance companies to estimate the cost of reconstruction in large losses.
- Consulted for El Paso County in the Bear Creek Nature Center loss. Successfully proved to the insurance company that the cost of reconstruction would be higher than their original estimate, resulting in a larger award.

GENERAL CONTRACTOR (26 years)
K.T. Kirkpatrick Construction, Colorado Springs, Colorado
- Build custom homes valued at up to $3.2 million in El Paso, Douglas, and Teller Counties.
- Manage estimating, bid preparation, drafting of plans, and project scheduling.
- Supervise all phases of construction; hire and manage employees and subcontractors.
- Consult with clients regarding design modifications and change orders; ensure customer satisfaction throughout the project life cycle.
- Source suppliers, order construction materials, and coordinate on-time delivery.
- Taught clinics for local construction supply companies in residential construction and remodeling.
- Succeeded in maintaining a perfect record with the Regional Building Department and the Better Business Bureau of the Pikes Peak Region.

COLLEGE INSTRUCTOR (14 years)
Pikes Peak Community College, Colorado Springs, Colorado
- Taught classes in blueprint interpretation, cabinetry, framing, concrete foundations, interior and exterior finishing, estimating, and construction procedures for expansive soils.
- Coordinated remodeling projects for student work-study programs.

PRESIDENT (3 years)
Carpenter's Local 515, Colorado Springs, Colorado
- Qualified journeymen carpenters and taught qualification training classes.
- Hired by the City of Colorado Springs to teach blueprint reading to local fire fighters.
- Supervised commercial construction projects.

VIETNAM VETERAN, United States Army (3 years)

ADDRESS
123 Stonegate Court • Colorado Springs, Colorado 80919
Home: (719) 555-1234 • Cellular: (719) 555-5678 • Fax: (719) 555-9876

EDUCATION

CARPENTER'S APPRENTICESHIP (4 years)
Colorado Apprenticeship Council, Denver, Colorado
United Brotherhood of Carpenters and Joiners of America, Fort Carson, Colorado

PROFESSIONAL DEVELOPMENT
- Advanced Arbitrator Training, American Arbitration Association (2009)
- Advanced Construction Law in Colorado, National Building Institute (2009)
- Construction Law Conferences, CLE International (2001, 2003, 2010)
- Construction Industry Arbitration Training, American Arbitration Association (2007)
- International Conference of Building Officials, Colorado Chapter, Educational Institute (2001)

AFFILIATIONS

- Appointed by the Colorado Springs City Council to represent the residential builders in El Paso County on the Pikes Peak Regional Building Department's Board of Review, Board of Appeals, and Advisory Board (2003 – present)
- Appointed to the American Arbitration Association (1993 – present)
- Former member of the National Association of Homebuilders (1996)

REFERENCES

In a recent case involving the defense of an architect who was sued for breach of contract and negligence in the design of an apartment complex, my firm retained Kenneth Kirkpatrick as an expert consultant. It is my belief that Mr. Kirkpatrick's assistance in this matter was a primary factor in our ability to reach a satisfactory settlement for our client. I highly recommend Mr. Kirkpatrick as an effective and experienced consultant in construction-related litigation and intend to solicit his assistance in the future. (Gail Holt, Holt & Associates, Denver, Colorado)

We have engaged Mr. Kirkpatrick's expertise to address a wide variety of issues ranging from catastrophic losses caused by flooding and expansive soils to the assessment of construction defects. In each instance, I have found Mr. Kirkpatrick's services to be professional, timely, and responsive. His opinions have been considered and well reasoned. He is a valuable resource in serving clients with construction and structurally related concerns. (James J. Schutz, Hanes & Schutz, Colorado Springs, Colorado)

Kenneth Kirkpatrick's ability to analyze an existing construction job site, identify areas of inferior workmanship and/or malfeasance are remarkable. He has total command of the Uniformed Building Code and its many nuances and has great credibility before all of our district judges here in El Paso County. His sense of fairness is acute, which gives him credibility. (Timothy G. Felt, P.C., Colorado Springs, Colorado)

Ken Kirkpatrick simplifies the complexity by breaking the problem down into manageable elements; then he communicates with me and my clients in plain English. He does not try to overwhelm his listener with technical jargon. He is plain spoken and persuasive under cross-examination. In heated adversarial situations, Ken has held his tongue and his temper. I can count on Ken Kirkpatrick's reliability. (Edward M. Murphy, P.C., Colorado Springs, Colorado)

I used Ken Kirkpatrick as an expert witness in a residential construction case. Not only was his testimony and expert opinion valuable, but Mr. Kirkpatrick provided substantial help in preparing to cross-examine the opponent's witness, including their expert witness. Mr. Kirkpatrick was able to provide ideas and information that ultimately benefitted my client's case. (Barry W. Holmes, Denver, Colorado)

Steve Jones

4321 Gilroy Avenue •• San Ramon, CA 94582
Office: 925.555.4637 •• Mobile: 925.555.5889 •• Home: 925.555.7709 •• Email: SteveJones@protypeltd.com

Vice President / Group Vice President—Sales and Service
Industries: Technology ~ Management Consulting ~ Information Services

Expert in driving sales, expansion, and profitability in startup, turnaround, and growth environments. Consistent peak performer and visionary sales leader with advanced skills in strategic and tactical planning, resource allocation and management, change management, product development and launch. Solid business acumen combines with particularly strong relationship management and talent for revitalizing, building, and developing teams that achieve impressive revenue gains within highly competitive markets/industries. Full complement of executive leadership competencies in technology organizations.

- *"Steve has an extraordinary talent for sales management and simply getting things done."* – Senior VP of Sales
- *"Steve has a natural ability to bring out the very best in people. That ability has allowed me to be one of the top salesmen in the company."* – Director of Sales
- *"Steve displays all of the qualities of a great manager. His leadership, business acumen, and communication skills are second to none and have played an integral role in his professional success."* – Group VP of Sales and Service

Professional Experience and Achievements

SOUTHLAND CORPORATION, SAN RAMON, CA .... 6/06 to present
Multinational provider of web-based, database, and business intelligence solutions.
Vice President, Corporate Accounts

Rebuilt relationships with major national accounts, producing $18 million.

Recruited to provide strategic sales leadership to the Major Accounts Management team. Challenged to expand, launch new products, and ensure retention of industry-leading insurance company accounts.

- **On track to deliver 6% growth this fiscal year**, representing a 3% growth in mature accounts and despite a declining industry. **Achieved President's Club status each year since joining company.**

- Increased customer workflow mapping efficiency by introducing program management approach to the sales process.

HANIFORD, INC., SAN DIEGO, CA .... 11/01 to 5/06
Leading provider of information products, software, and e-business solutions.
Group Vice President, National Sales (9/02 to 5/06)

Revitalized a non-performing sales organization to beat annual sales by 5% in a declining market.

Promoted to provide turnaround leadership and jump start sales, which were completely flat. Rebuilt, trained, and energized the sales group to produce results—providing vision, strategy, and structure that the sales organization did not previously have. Overhauled and instituted new sales processes. Created Major and Regional Accounts groups, including a new incentive plan based on growth achieved. Hired top performers and managed sales team of 20. Developed and strengthened sales force through training program implementation (target account selling to senior-level executives).

- **Drove national sales from $35 million to $48.6 million in four years** by focusing team on larger opportunities while maintaining smaller growth accounts. Named to President's Club in 2003 and 2004.

- Led and launched a new product (database program), with **first-year sales generating $6 million in business.**

- **Developed the sales team to close multimillion-dollar accounts** while efficiently managing smaller accounts.

- **Tapped as the Six Sigma champion** for the sales organization and served on cross-functional team that developed, implemented, and trained personnel on a more efficient order-processing system.

- **Instituted budgeting and expense control processes that ensured accountability** and enabled more accurate forecasting based on sound metrics. **Cut overall sales expenses 21%** by hiring in geographical areas to reduce travel and other costs.

- **Initiated relationships with product development management team** that led the sales organization to become an instrumental part of the product development planning process—for the first time.

Vice President, Corporate Accounts (11/01 to 8/02)

Brought on board to rebuild and manage relationships with company's largest corporate accounts. Restored customer confidence while expanding account business through sale of new products. Tapped for promotion within nine months.

- **Achieved 10% YOY growth,** building sales from $10.8 million to $12 million.
- **Produced two new contracts,** each one generating $2 million annually for three years.
- **Instrumental in bringing to market a revolutionary new product**—web-based automobile estimating for an industry leader.

INTELL COMPANY, LIBERTYVILLE, IL. ....8/99 to 7/01
Leading U.S. provider of clinical software, connectivity, and information solutions for the healthcare industry.

Group Vice President, Sales

Recruited and led a regional sales team promoting product lines to small physician practices. Led new product launch in the region as company repositioned itself from a single-solution to an integrated, multiple-solution provider of innovative software and workflow solutions for the healthcare industry. Negotiated sales contracts ranging from $5,000 to $100,000 in new business.

- **Grew eastern sales region from zero sales to $10 million in only two years** as company transitioned from a pre- to post-IPO paradigm. **Exceeded plan and named Manager of the Year in 2000** out of five regions nationwide.

ORINN CORPORATION, CHICAGO, IL ....6/92 to 8/99
Provider of advanced software, communication systems, and Internet and wireless-enabled technology for automotive claims and collision repair industries.

Zone Vice President (9/96 to 8/99)

Promoted to direct team of five region managers and 32 account executives selling software and hardware solutions. Delivered 20% annual growth from $29 million to $45 million in just three years—while quickly adapting to changing market demands for new technology. Developed and implemented annual sales plans and completely revamped bonus plan for all personnel division-wide. Negotiated sales contracts ranging from $100,000 to $5 million each. Created account management teams for sales, service, and support.

- **Tapped to spearhead initiative to build new Windows-based workflow application** for the insurance industry that gave CCC a competitive market advantage. Succeeded in delivering company's top-selling product where others had previously failed. Ten years later, **product continues to be #1 in sales, producing $50 million to $60 million annually.**
- Led development of a tire database solution for auto appraisers, **yielding $600,000 to $700,000 in annual renewable business.**
- **Named to President's Club in 1996.**
- Instrumental in organizing the annual industry conference attended by 350 customers each year.

Senior Region Manager (9/93 to 9/96)
Led seven-member sales team to grow the Northeast Region from $4 million to $5 million. Subsequently selected to take charge of and turned around the struggling Midwest Region by initiating a region support and sales model. **Produced a combined $10 million in sales for both regions during three-year tenure.**

National Account Manager (6/92 to 9/93)
Managed portfolio of 200 accounts and drove new product sales from zero to $2 million annually. Trained and advanced the skills of sales force on solution-selling techniques. Led product definition and development for software enhancements and add-on databases to existing software.

Education

Bachelor of Arts, Political Science   UNIVERSITY OF KENTUCKY

Sierra L. Carpenter

2020 Lithonia Road
Lithonia, GA 30028
(770) 555-1234
carpenter@protypeltd.com

Profile

Professional and dedicated resource teacher. Committed to excellence and creating meaningful and stimulating lessons to improve students' ability, creativity, perception, concentration, confidence, and motivation. Methodologies used include cooperative learning strategies, modeling, and outcome-based approaches designed to enhance learning. Strong knowledge of county and state curriculums. Exceptional rapport with administration, staff, parents, and students. Effective at multi-tasking, meeting deadlines, and adapting to situations as they arise. Well known for the following qualities:

- Personable
- Organized
- Focused

- Positive attitude
- Team player
- Results oriented

- Strong work ethic
- Respected by others
- Strong leadership skills

Education and Certifications

2009	Certificate of Advanced Study in Education (CASE) program, anticipated completion in 2009—University of Georgia, Athens, Georgia
2007	Certificate of Professional Development in Gifted Education, 66 hours—Center of Gifted Education at the University of Georgia, Athens, Georgia
2003	M.S., Curriculum and Instruction—Kennesaw State University, Kennesaw, Georgia
1991	B.S., Elementary Education—Kennesaw State University, Kennesaw, Georgia

Professional Development

2009	Technology and Differentiated Instruction, University of Georgia
2009	Differentiating Instruction (webcast), Carol Ann Tomlinson, University of Georgia
2003–2006	Gifted and Talented Education, Georgia State Conferences, Lanier, GA
2003	Staff Development Strategies that Impact Student Achievement, Cindy Harrison, Consultant

Teaching Experience

Gwinnett County Public Schools, Lawrenceville, Georgia   2001–present
Gifted Education Resource Teacher (2001–present)
Work closely with instructional leadership teams and administration at Alford and Corley elementary schools to ensure compliance with instructional standards.

- Wrote essential curriculum for the county as part of a team and remain involved in on-going revisions.
- Collect and assess formative and summative data to monitor and support school instructional programs.

Gifted Education Resource Teacher (continued)

- Collaborate with classroom teachers to differentiate instruction to meet the needs of high-able students.

- Conduct staff development in differentiated instruction, as well as county-wide initiatives.

- Create at-home strategies, including curriculum and interventions.

- Write summer enrichment reading curriculum for the county.

- Successfully implemented gifted services model at each school for pre-K to fifth grade.

- Model best instructional practices.

Classroom Teacher (1991–2003)
Used creative and adaptable teaching methods to implement all aspects of the academic curriculum. Formulated appropriate performance objectives, selected and organized classroom content, designed diversified instructional strategies, and evaluated objectives.

Accomplishments

2009	Nominated for Great Books Foundation's 2008–2009 Great Books, Great Teachers celebration
2007–2009	Grant Recipient of *The Atlanta Constitution's* Educational Foundation's Grants in Education for your "Evening to R.E.A.D.–Read" project
2002–2003	Participated in John Hopkins' reading and math pilot programs, Success for All
2002	Agnes Meyer Outstanding Teacher Award Nominee
2002	Champion for Children Award, Center for Children, Gwinnett County, Georgia
2001	ARC Educator of the Year—Gwinnett County, Georgia

Professional Memberships

National Education Association/GSTA/EACC
National Association for Gifted Children

VICKY RICHARD

1234 Anderson Drive
Colorado Springs, Colorado 80909
(719) 555-1234 ▪ vrichard@protypeltd.com

OBJECTIVE

Challenging position that would best utilize my diversified skills and experience in office administration and customer service. Ideal position would allow various opportunities for personal interaction with the general public and business relations.

QUALIFICATIONS

- Dedicated to excellence and organization, both professionally and personally.
- Multi-task, detail-oriented with ability and foresight to prioritize tasks in fast-paced, demanding environments; work well under pressure, maintaining an emphasis on quality.
- Courteous and diplomatic professional, experienced in customer and vendor relations.
- Flexible, quickly adapting to changing needs and demands.
- Team player who recognizes the need to maintain good working relations with coworkers to achieve company goals.

WORK HISTORY

02-2003 thru 08-2010, *Administrative Assistant,* **Dee's RV, Colorado Springs, Colorado**
Primary duties included A/P and A/R, reconciling Billing Statements from floor-plan companies, paying curtailments, interest and insurance monthly. In addition, assisted Office Manager/Controller with various other duties she required. Worked closely with Finance Manager, organizing all documents for Retail Security Agreements for outside lenders, assuring all documents were accurate and met lender requirements for funding.

- Assisted Controller during two software changes by providing and entering beginning balances and setting up data for transition.
- Successfully paid approximately 100 vendors, procuring hundreds of dollars each month in early payment discounts. Developed good business relations with vendors that aided in timely resolution of discrepancies.
- Maintained accurate unit inventory details and sales listings for the Sales Department.
- Dealt with floor-plan auditors monthly to assure compliance with our Dealer Agreements, always receiving positive reports from such audits.
- Consistently developed and maintained excellent rapport with fellow employees in all departments to enhance proficiency and smooth operation in customer service-oriented business.
- Courteously answered and directed phone calls on a six-line system.
- Timely entered completed work orders into software system for unit delivery inspections that aided Controller in posting deals monthly. In addition, submitted warranty claims for these units.

07-1995 thru 09-2002, *Office Manager,* **Baughman's OPE, Colorado Springs, Colorado**
Hired for counter sales and to train in office support. Successfully managed busy phone lines and walk-in customers, writing service orders, sales of parts and whole goods, filing, record maintenance, daily books and bank deposits. Quickly learned software and demonstrated ability to excel at and become responsible for all office functions to include A/Ps and A/Rs. Later added Inventory Manager to my responsibilities.

- Provided detailed and accurate bookkeeping and cash-related functions for $250,000 business, including bank deposits, checkbook balancing, and some general ledger entries and period-end routines.

WORK HISTORY   **Baughman's OPE (continued)**

- Generated timely payments to over 20 vendors, procuring discounts and maintaining good vendor relations.
- Maintained positive cash flow in A/R with accurate invoicing, careful documentation and follow-up on late payments.
- Computed and paid 941s, printed all necessary reports and documentation for Colorado State and Federal filings, adhering to deadlines.
- Supervised 2–4 employees (shop and counter personnel), trained employees in company policies, procedures, and owner's philosophy and business standards. Also monitored time sheets, calculated payroll hours, and assured up-to-date W-2s and various employee records.
- Improved parts department efficiency by utilizing previously unused functions of software, allowing the analysis of parts traffic and stock accordingly. Conversely, adjusted stock of slow-moving parts. Reduced inventory by approximately 500 low sales parts and concentrated on improving the special order process to improve cash flow.
- Designed, constructed and maintained MS Works database to track sales and timely payment of floor-planned units, saving the company $1,000 in annual finance charges and 2–3 hours per week of valuable time.

04-2001 thru 08-2001, *Accounts Payable Clerk,* **Central States Group, Omaha, Nebraska**
Responsible for entry and payment of 75–100 invoices daily for three branches of a successful wholesale distribution corporation. Also computed and paid sales tax to multiple states.

- Excelled in learning new software program quickly.
- Reconciled numerous vendor statements, which involved researching many that were very aged invoices and carried outstanding credits.
- Quickly established rapport with vendors to ensure continuance of good business relations.
- Promptly followed up with vendors and coworkers to resolve pricing, billing and shipping errors and other discrepancies.
- Thoroughly cleaned and organized work station for my replacement before leaving company.

08-1994 thru 02-1999, *Sales Associate,* **Target Stores, Colorado Springs, Colorado**

- Provided cashier and customer service functions in a busy retail environment.
- Assured customer satisfaction by providing friendly and efficient checkout service.
- Accurately and safely handled cash; ensured that drawer balanced daily.

1993 thru 1994, *Licensed Home Daycare Provider,* **Peterson AFB, Colorado**

EDUCATION   **1997 thru 1998,** *Accounting, Business and Computer Courses*
Blair Business College, Colorado Springs, Colorado

SKILLS
- Typing, 55 wpm
- 10 Key with accuracy
- Microsoft Word, Intermediate
- Various accounting and business software systems

JOHN POWERS

111 Field Avenue, Stamford, CT 06905 • (203) 123-5555 • jpowers@protypeltd.com

ASSISTANT CONTROLLER / SENIOR ACCOUNTANT

Financial Analysis • Audits • Corporate Accounting

Highly analytical finance professional with diverse experience in small, medium, and large businesses across industries: Telecom, Hedge Fund, Healthcare, Food Products, Import/Export, Insurance, Nonprofit, and Professional Services. Proven abilities to steer on-time, month-end and year-end closes, satisfying customers, management, auditors, partners, and investors for firms with U.S., European, and Asian offices. Strong work ethic coupled with effective communication skills and problem-solving approaches.

EXPERTISE	*Qualifications Summary*
General Ledger	• Turnaround specialist expediting return of backlogged firms to current close status.
Accounts Payable and Receivable	• Interim Assistant Controller for fast-growth company with 200% increase in revenue.
	• Track record for E&Y audit passes for multibillion and multimillion dollar firms.
P&L Statements	• Solid performance across rapid-growth, acquisition, and start-up environments.
Internal/External Audits	• Billings for Fortune 500 clients including J&J, Merck, Roche-Genentech & Bayer.
	• Singlehanded leadership of A/P with 40% vendor increase to overall total of 30K.

Additional Competencies

EXPERTISE (continued): Month- and Year-End Closings, Credit and Collections

- ➢ Financial Analysis and Reporting
- ➢ Partnership Distribution
- ➢ Fixed Assets
- ➢ Bank Reconciliation
- ➢ Client and Services Billings
- ➢ Cash Flow and Budget Analysis
- ➢ Advanced Excel Models and Statistics
- ➢ Loan Valuations
- ➢ Prepaid Expenses
- ➢ Multicurrency Exchange

EXPERIENCE

CONSULTANT 2005–Present

LAMONT DIGITAL SYSTEMS, Greenwich, CT   *(2008–Present)*
Large cable provider building advanced telecommunications platforms for more than 200 residential gated communities, colleges, and universities across the country.

Contracted through search firm to relieve workload of Controller and Director of Account Management, who was charged with dual oversight role in both finance and national sales. Passed two audits successfully with Ernst &Young.

- Assumed assistant controller/senior accountant duties during period of rapid growth—revenue doubled from $15 million to $30 million to date during my tenure.
- Contributed to post-acquisition transfer of assets and liabilities of multi-million dollar cable provider in NY.
- Reinstituted timely month-end close, journal entries, payroll, and bank reconciliations—critical for investor relations and major strategic partnership with Direct TV.

CALDWELL FUNDING, Stamford, CT   *(2008)*
Life insurance settlement provider that acquires and administrates life settlement assets and serves policyholders.

Challenged to fill "interim controller" role in $200 million rapid-growth, startup environment. Replaced individual who left corporation with four months of "unreconciled" accounting for four separate companies. Brought aboard after unsuccessful attempts by four consecutive professionals to close the books.

- Served as turnaround catalyst, returning all companies to on-time month-end closes within 60 days (worked extensive hours) while maintaining current accounting cycle and daily financial operations.

CHANDLER and CHICCO, New York, NY   *(2007–2008)*
World's largest full-service public relations company serving pharmaceutical, consumer product, and healthcare technology firms. Acquired by the inVentiv Health family of companies for $65 million.

Provided immediate financial expertise (no ramp-up period) to in-progress external audit conducted by Ernst & Young for the New York and London offices. Passed audit with flying colors.
• Partnered with Controller for this 70-person firm. Managed billings for Fortune 500 accounts, including: Johnson & Johnson, Bayer, Roche-Genentech, Merck, Schering-Plough, Novartis, and Philly Pharmaceuticals.

WOLFSON CASING, New Rochelle, NY   *(2007)*
Century-old industry leader that manufactures natural sausage casings on three continents with global customer sales.

Supported controller with day-to-day accounting activities for New York and California offices, including uncompleted journal entries, billing, accounts payables, and receivables.
• Assisted with sales tax filing and resolving discrepancy with the IRS.

D.B. ZWIRN & CO., New York, NY   *(2006)*
Privately owned multi-billion dollar hedge fund manager with offices in the U.S., Europe, and China.

Selected to assist controller and senior accountant of a high-growth corporation with 200+ clients through complex audits while maintaining daily financial operations.
• Created productivity initiative through new expense report coding system. Reduced expense entry time by 50% and subsequent billing preparation time by 20%.

WILDLIFE CONSERVATION SOCIETY, Bronx, NY   *(2005)*
Nonprofit organization that manages approximately 500 conservation projects in more than 60 countries and educates million at five living institutions/parks in New York City.

• Joined controller for the Society's "foreign sector" in complex audit of overseas offices in Africa and South America.

PRIOR EXPERIENCE:

THE WATCHTOWER & TRACT SOCIETY, Brooklyn, NY .... 2001 – 2007
Part-time missionary in the Peru branch teaching villages reading and writing skills, promoting a healthy living environment and assisting with medical attention.

HEALTHNET MEDICAL GROUP, Paramus, NJ .... 1998 – 2001
Accountant for seven hospital-owned urgent care centers in New York and New Jersey with staff of 40. Performed significant fixed assets capitalization scheduling, depreciation, and leasehold improvement activities.

LIVINGSTON INTERNATIONAL, Buffalo, NY .... 1996 – 1998
Accounts Payable Specialist for $90 million fast-growth customs and compliance brokerage firm with 30,000+ clients. Sole accounts payable department member orchestrating 40% vendor increase with thousands of monthly transactions.

EDUCATION

Pace University, New York, NY / Westchester College, White Plains, NY
Associate in Business Administration: Accounting Major

Certification: QuickBooks Pro 2008

ACCOUNTING SOFTWARE

NetSuite, Rebus, MAS 90, Advanced Excel, QuickBooks Pro

Susan Madigan

5511 West Main Street
Pittsburgh, PA 12345

(888) 555-1234
smadigan@protypeltd.com

EXECUTIVE MANAGEMENT—BANK OPERATIONS

Seasoned financial professional with extensive front- and back-end experience in the banking industry. Performance-driven manager, inspired by challenge to achieve and surpass goals. Analytical and detail-oriented; adept in identifying and resolving fraud, unethical practices and mismanagement. Effective in building, leading, and motivating strong teams of solid performers.

AREAS OF EXPERTISE

- Foreclosure/Bankruptcy
- Mortgage Loans
- Contract Underwriting
- Due Diligence
- Cost Control Measures

- Audit Supervision
- Default Services
- Loss Mitigation
- Quality Control
- REO Management

- Risk Management
- Appraisal Review
- Short Sales
- Problem Solving
- Team Building

PROFESSIONAL EXPERIENCE

STATE BANK, Pittsburgh, PA   2004–2007
Vice President, Due Diligence Manager
Administered and facilitated bulk-loan trade transactions through settlement. Finalized and reconciled investor trades. Supervised staff responsible for loan rebuttal issues related to credit, collateral, compliance, and property validation. Received rapid promotion from Assistant VP to VP in ten months.

- Recruited to streamline and improve personnel procedures. Hired 12 new employees; groomed one for a supervisory position. Established concrete job descriptions and evaluation procedures to promote teamwork and reduce inefficiencies.
- Reduced loan reject rate from 40% to 3% by locating missing documentation, facilitating document corrections, answering credit-risk questions, and ensuring regulatory compliance.
- Improved quality of individual trade results by establishing better lines of communication with operations managers, sales staff, and internal departments. Led monthly conference calls and onsite meetings to discuss trends, build rapport, and highlight key areas of concern.
- Increased productivity 50%, saved thousands of dollars, and eliminated duplication of effort by pioneering automated comprehensive mortgage risk database system to share loan status data among appraisal, valuation, and servicing departments.

ABC GROUP, Pittsburgh, PA   2002–2004
Mortgage Underwriter
Performed due diligence underwriting of prime and subprime mortgage loans to sell to secondary market. Produced average of 15 loans per day. Reviewed and analyzed credit, collateral, compliance, and appraisal loan files. Enforced quality control policy standards that ensured origination underwriting efforts met lender and investor guidelines. Conducted post-origination compliance audits.

- Protected investors from purchasing risky non-compliant loans by employing default service knowledge to identify fraud, credit risk, regulatory/state compliance, and data entry errors.

ABC CORPORATION, Pittsburgh, PA   2002
  Project Consultant, Corporate Operations
  Served as liaison between clients and vendors. Managed team of 67 coordinators and 2
  direct reports. Oversaw client off-site servicing of foreclosure and bankruptcy portfolios.
  - Brought on board to improve and streamline processes. Boosted production levels and
    met desired deadlines by replacing inadequate staff, analyzing staff strengths and
    providing training.

MNO INVESTMENT HOLDINGS LLC, Pittsburgh, PA   1999–2002
  Director, Default Services (7/01–4/02)
  Oversaw foreclosure, bankruptcy, REO, loss mitigation, FHA Title I claims, equity analysis,
  and default support for defaulted home loans. Managed divisional outsource vendor rela-
  tionships. Compiled monthly forecast and delinquency projections.
  - Tackled tremendous backlog of nonperforming portfolio subprime first and second lien
    loans within first 30 days of hire.
  - Reduced and maintained REO loss severity to 31%.
  - Improved delinquency modeling and scoring by developing electronic tracking system.

  Default Services Manager, Home Improvement Division (10/99–7/01)
  Inherited division with no reporting and a portfolio of loans unmonitored for months. Reorganized and restructured division, developed policies and procedures manuals and created
  employee training program. Hired and trained 15 additional employees for a total of 30
  associates and 2 direct reports. Created monthly employee score card to track success.
  - Achieved 55% overall delinquency reduction.
  - Facilitated transition of bankruptcy/foreclosure portfolio to Tempe location.

CONTIMORTGAGE CORPORATION, Horsham, PA   1998–1999
  Manager, Foreclosure/Bankruptcy
  Managed 40 coordinators responsible for legal process and monitored subprime portfolios
  nationwide.
  - Selected to facilitate start-up of West Coast Default Division.
  - Outperformed East Coast Operation while improving performance, production, timelines,
    and work quality of coordinators.

CENDANT MORTGAGE CORPORATION, Marlton, NJ   1993–1998
  Assistant Supervisor, Default Services
  Supervised team of 20 coordinators and monitored portfolio of 650 nationwide loans.
  Coordinated daily operations of foreclosure, bankruptcy, REO, and loss mitigation.
  - Ensured collection and loss mitigation efforts were exhausted before foreclosure.
    Curtailed future losses by providing leads to loss mitigation representatives.

———————————EDUCATION AND PROFESSIONAL DEVELOPMENT———————————

University of Texas, Arlington, TX
Bachelor of Science in Finance

Mortgage Banking Association
Real Estate Appraisal for Mortgage Lending
Legal Issues and Regulatory Compliance

Gordon Training International: Leadership Effectiveness Training (L.E.T.)
Franklin Covey: Focus Time Management

TAMMY RICHARDS

1234 Glenda Drive, Apt. 12 • Loveland, Colorado 80537
Home Phone: (970) 555-1234

SUMMARY OF QUALIFICATIONS

- Results-oriented self-starter with strong dedication to academic excellence and advanced studies
- Experienced in balancing personal and academic priorities
- Recognized as a creative and practical problem solver
- Proven record of creativity, flexibility, and adaptability to any assignment
- Outstanding credentials and motivation
- Excellent verbal and written communication skills

EDUCATION AND LICENSES

- Graduate Pikes Peak Community College LPN Program, Colorado Springs, Colorado
- Licensed Practical Nurse, State of Colorado
- Undergraduate college-level studies, core curricula, Portland Community College, Portland, Oregon
- Graduate Certified Nursing Assistant Program, New Care Directions, Portland, Oregon
- Licensed Certified Nursing Assistant, State of Colorado
- Graduate, East West School of Massage Therapy, Oregon
- Current certifications in CPR and Basic First Aid, American Heart Association

PROFESSIONAL EXPERIENCE

LICENSED PRACTICAL NURSE February 2008
Northern Colorado Hospice and Palliative Care, Greeley, CO to present
- Provided continuous care to terminally ill patients in their homes
- Responsible for assessments, direct patient and family care, and medication administration

CERTIFIED NURSING ASSISTANT October 2005
Pikes Peak Hospice, Colorado Springs, CO to December 2007
- Maintained patient care standards and supported families, nurses, physicians, and administrators
- Reviewed patient assessments and assisted in the planning of individualized patient care
- Provided instruction to patients in daily care
- Performed typical CNA responsibilities, including taking and recording vital signs; observing, reporting, and documenting patient activities; providing physical, emotional, and social needs to patients; and implementing appropriate emergency interventions

RESEARCH INTERVIEWER September 2000
National Opinion Research Center, Colorado Springs, CO to December 2007
- Performed research interviews in Colorado Springs and Pueblo for this Illinois firm
- Located and interviewed respondents for statistical studies
- Prepared detailed reports for the principal client (Department of Labor, Washington, DC)

CLINICAL NURSE February 2005
Long-term Care Facilities, Acute Care Settings, and Hospitals, Colorado Springs, CO to November 2007
- Responsible for all phases of patient care, medication administration

INDEPENDENT LICENSED MASSAGE THERAPIST June 1997
Richards Massage Therapy, Portland, OR to February 2005
- Provided massage therapy at various health clubs
- Completely responsible for all business development, marketing, and promotions

MEDICAL RECORDS CLERK May 1993
Good Samaritan Hospital, Portland, OR to June 1997
- Worked closely with physicians and staff nurses maintaining medical records
- Extensive computer data entry utilizing a state-of-the-art computer system

Personal Information

There are very few times when personal information is appropriate on a résumé. Usually such facts only take up valuable white space, especially details such as age, sex, race, health, or marital status, and other information that potential employers are not allowed to ask anyway. There are exceptions to every rule in the résumé business, however! Here are some of them:

1. International résumés in almost all cases require date of birth, place of birth, citizenship, marital status, sex, and a photograph.

2. Students, or those who have recently graduated, often have a difficult time coming up with enough paid experience to demonstrate their qualifications. But, if they have held leadership positions in campus organizations or have supervised groups of people and organized activities on a volunteer basis, then an "Activities" section could strengthen those qualifications.

3. A list of sporting interests would be helpful for a person looking for a sports marketing position.

4. If you are looking for a job in sales where you would need to travel a great deal, or overseas where relocating an entire family becomes expensive, showing that you are unmarried and willing to travel could be helpful.

5. Submitting a résumé to a U.S. company doing business in certain foreign countries could be another example. On such a résumé, an "Interests" section would show a prospective employer that your hobbies are compatible with the host country.

And the list goes on. It is important to use your judgment, since only you know best what qualifications are important in your field. Just remember this one rule: the information provided should be related directly to bona fide occupational qualifications for the job you are seeking.

PHOTOGRAPHS

Photographs on a résumé are required by foreign companies requesting a curriculum vitae. However, in the United States, photographs are discouraged in all but a few industries. For instance, if you are trying for a job as an actor, model, newscaster, or in some other field where your appearance is, again, a bona fide occupational qualification, then a photograph is appropriate. Remember, there is an exception to every rule in the résumé business, so use your judgment.

John P. Mission

123 Main Street
Saint Louis, MO 63115

jpmission@protypeltd.com

Home: 314-555-1234
Cell: 314-555-4321

Senior / Solo Pastor Candidate
Apologetic Evangelism • Leadership Vision • Firm Belief in the Power of Prayer

Preaching and Teaching

- Passionate and expressive preacher who relates equally well to nonbelievers, young converts, and mature Christians.
- Employ contextualization and vivid word pictures to explain ancient Biblical lessons, illustrations, and parables using 21st century terminology.
- Answer potential objections from nonbelievers in a loving but gentle way. Never take for granted what people know but challenge them with God's word to examine their beliefs.
- Ability to explain complex Biblical theology so that children, teens, adults and senior citizens comprehend meaning and application of scriptural texts.

Worship Leadership

- Create an atmosphere where believers and unbelievers feel welcome and accepted.
- Encourage congregants to participate fully in worship by often explaining the meaning, purpose, and placement of worship components such as communion, confession, offerings, and praise.
- Serve communion in a personal manner, reflecting on God's grace in Christ's atonement for sin.

> *"I can—without hesitation or reserve—attest to John's Christ-like character and gifts for ministry."*
> – Chris Jones, PhD.
>
> *"John will be an asset to any church, but he will thrive in a church that shares his passion for reaching the lost."* – Ed Johnson, Elder

EDUCATION AND ORDINATION

Ordained, MISSOURI PRESBYTERY PCA, 2006

Master of Divinity, COVENANT THEOLOGICAL SEMINARY, 2004

Bachelor of Science in Pharmacy, WAYNE STATE UNIVERSITY
College of Pharmacy and Allied Health Professions, 1995

MINISTRY EXPERIENCE

FIRST PRESBYTERIAN CHURCH   2002–present
Assistant Pastor of Youth and Family (2006–2010) , St. Louis, MO • **Intern** (2002–2005)
Provided stability to 150+ member church after untimely death of senior pastor in 2004, and during lengthy interim period when second pastor proved to be no longer a good fit for the church. Assumed leadership of youth group after former assistant pastor moved to missionary field.

Pastoral Ministry

- Received many opportunities to preach and lead worship both during traditional Sunday morning and contemporary Sunday evening worship services.
- Led weekly small adult Bible home study groups.
- Conducted weddings and funerals for church members and attendees.

Youth Ministry

- Planned weekly mid-week youth services, monthly and annual events, including retreats, social activities, evangelism outreach, and service projects for 10 to 50 youth, many who were non-Christian friends of youth group members.

FIRST PRESBYTERIAN CHURCH (continued)

- Developed student leader training programs; many students became active in church life as worship team members, ushers, nursery workers, VBS leaders, and short-term missionaries. Several students have continued in Christian leadership roles post-high school and college.
- Often partnered with other local Christian churches in youth outreach activities.
- Conducted one-on-one mentoring and led discipleship groups to help students grow in their faith.
- Counseled youth to work through simple-to-complex problems concerning relationships, family and spiritual issues with the goal of forgiveness and reconciliation.

Evangelism

- Initiated prayer meetings on front steps of public high school every Sunday evening where youth and parents prayed for God's influence. These meetings included prayer, singing, and preaching, and were endorsed and supported by the district superintendent.
- Penetrated local high school campus by volunteering to coach wrestling for two years. Developed encouraging relationships with students and prayed with Christian wrestlers to ask the Lord to reach non-Christian students. Invited wrestlers to church youth group meetings; many responded.

SECOND BAPTIST CHURCH, St. Louis, MO   1997–2005
Volunteer Youth Leader
Church with 100 attendees encompassing a large number of young people from broken homes in a low socio-economic area.

- Led team of four in building up youth group ranging in age from age 9–21, providing stability and structure to struggling program. Despite initial drop in numbers after assuming leadership, group was stabilized to 40 to 50 committed attendees.
- Picked up kids on Sunday morning in church van and led activities until the evening program. Prepared meals, played games, counseled, and discipled youth during informal meetings.
- Grew to love each of the youth and was privileged to witness one of them come to faith in Christ.

THIRD BIBLE CHURCH, St. Louis, MO   1989–1997
Volunteer Youth Leader • Deacon • Choir Member

- Participated in adult ministry including teaching adult Sunday school classes, leading worship and preaching during Sunday evening services.
- Assumed leadership of small youth group which previously met only once a month. Planned and executed weekly mid-week youth meetings and events. Witnessed significant spiritual and numerical growth, which created excitement within the church.
- Organized and conducted door-to-door evangelism campaigns in area neighborhoods.
- Canvassed low-income housing project and picked up 5 to 15 children every Sunday morning for worship services. Distributed Bibles and engaged in spiritual conversations with children and parents. Witnessed at least two parents come to Christ.

PERSONAL AND FAMILY INFORMATION

I am 38 years old and have been married to my beautiful wife Mary for close to ten years. We have three wonderful children; Jennifer (adopted in 2002), Lisa (2003), and Joshua (2006). We enjoy spending time together, traveling the world, participating in mission trips, and visiting with friends and neighbors. Our travels have taken us to Peru, England, Spain, Italy, Mexico, Greece, and across the United States.

CHARLES BARKLEY

1234 East 20th Avenue • Denver, CO 80203 • (720) 555-1234 • barkley@protypeltd.com • www.linkedin.com/in/cbarkley/

EXPERIENCED MARKETING MANAGER

AREAS OF EXPERTISE

Marketing • Sales • Promotions
Strategic Planning • Product Development
Brand Management
Websites • Online Social Marketing
Event Planning and Coordination
Selling/Managing Event Sponsorships
Pro-Athlete/Team Handling
Collateral Materials • Trade Shows
Agency Partners • Co-op Marketing

EXECUTIVE SUMMARY

- Driven Marketing Manager with diverse experience in sports marketing, project management, event planning, and nightlife/hospitality marketing.
- More than 17 years of experience in the marketing and management of running, cycling, skiing, mountain biking, and other sporting events.
- Proven leader who works well in fast-paced, high-energy environments and enjoys challenges and new ideas.
- Effective communicator who has developed an extensive network of contacts in the Denver area, including key influencers in the community, charities, social organizations, and network marketing groups.

MARKETING EXPERIENCE

MARKETING DIRECTOR (2008 – 2009)
The Wine Loft, Denver, Colorado
Recruited by this two-year-old franchise to energize their marketing programs and establish The Wine Loft as one of Denver's finest wine bars. Researched similar businesses throughout the U.S., and developed/deployed an innovative marketing plan. Collaborated with graphic designers to create collateral materials, flyers, menus, posters, and promotional materials for themed events and in-store promotions. Ensured that all advertising materials maintained a consistent "look and feel" to build brand awareness. Developed and managed website content. Created drink specials, in-store promotions, gift cards, and sponsorships. Assisted the owner with booking special/private events. Distributed flyers and event posters.

- Developed and implemented a viral marketing campaign utilizing MySpace, Facebook, Linked-In, Mobile Storm, and the corporate website. Wrote profiles for various Web 2.0 accounts, keeping the same look and feel as the website. Grew Mobile Storm subscribers from 51 to 2,750 in only three months.
- Designed, scheduled, and deployed weekly email blast campaigns with double opt-in to retain customers and generate new subscribers.
- Created a unique "sign me up" card that was used as an employee incentive to increase e-lists.
- Initiated, planned, and coordinated a very successful grand opening party that generated 800 guests over the weekend.
- Conceived a New Year's Eve event, hired an event planner, and generated co-op advertising from a well-known Champagne brand.
- Succeeded in increasing store traffic and revenue by 30–40% per year.

CEO / DIRECTOR OF MARKETING (1988 – 2005)
Denver Marathon, LLC, Denver, Colorado
Founded and managed the operations of an events management company that developed innovative sporting and entertainment programs. Produced, staffed, and directed running, cycling, mountain biking, in-line skating, and singles events, as well as pool parties, social mixers, theatrical social events, themed bar nights, and promotional street team events. Managed marketing/media campaigns and promotional tours (retail sites, expos, trade shows). Collaborated with advertising agency sponsor (Ogilvy) on the development of content and artwork for signs, vehicle wraps, collateral materials, billboards, television and newspaper ads, press releases, and media kits. Developed content for and designed the overall layout of the organization's website.

Researched potential sponsors, pitched events, and secured deals. Managed strategic partnerships with sponsors, media, co-op advertisers, contractors, vendors, and civic/parks departments. Planned and directed event logistics, including acquiring permits from the City, designing race courses and barricade plans, and registering participants. Recruited/managed street teams with more than 300 police officers, 200 volunteers, and 30 staff members. Gave interviews and performed radio spots to generate free publicity for events. Made presentations at retail stores and ensured that registration forms were strategically designed and placed to ensure maximum exposure.

- Raised a $6 million sponsorship budget the very first year, and secured alliances with the Denver City Mayor's office to help launch the annual Denver Marathon.
- Signed major sponsorship deals with Volkswagen, Kinko's, Nike, 24 Hour Fitness, Noodles & Company, Gatorade, Coca-Cola, Go Fast Sports, GU, Six Flags, State Farm Insurance, Rudy Project eye wear, Colorado Athletic Club, Hyatt Hotels, Active.com, 96.5 Radio, ESPN Radio, Tanqueray, Chandon Champagne, Ricochet, American Airlines, Ogilvy Public Relations, Denver's WB2 Television, and Great Big Color.

MARKETING EXPERIENCE

Denver Marathon (continued)
- Received both hard dollars and in-kind donations, including new promotional vehicles every year that were wrapped and detailed to promote the sponsor.
- Generated 3,722,591+ media impressions from radio and television coverage.

REGIONAL MARKETING DIRECTOR (1998 – 1999)
Life O^2, Inc., Boulder, Colorado
Served as brand educator, spokesperson, and promotional tour coordinator for this new brand of sports drink. Scheduled street teams, promoted events, and developed/implemented effective marketing strategies for all regional event efforts. Attended events to provide on-site product sampling and to create exposure for the brand.
- Secured a wrapped and branded Yukon truck to distribute samples and collateral materials at events.

SPONSORSHIP MANAGER (1997 – 1998)
Team Chevrolet / Klein, Boulder, Colorado
Managed professional athletic teams and events. Developed and managed all aspects of sponsorships, including contacting potential sponsors, setting up meetings, negotiating and securing endorsement deals, and drafting agreements.
- Increased the team's budget by signing major sponsorships with Ray-Ban, Killer-Loop, Reebok, Kinko's, and XL-L Energy Drink.
- Team Chevrolet was ranked as the best women's professional cycling team in 1996.

SPORTS DIVISION MANAGER (1991 – 1997)
SportsStar USA, Inc., Niwot, Colorado
Handled sports management and athlete marketing efforts for worldwide Olympic sponsor, Bausch & Lomb. Traveled worldwide to find sports superstars and negotiate/sign athlete endorsement deals. Evaluated proposals to ensure they were the right match for the brand. Represented Bausch & Lomb at trade shows and regional, national, and international sporting events, including two Olympic Games. Managed a sponsorship budget of more than $1 million. Introduced new eye-wear products to well-known amateur, professional, and Olympic athletes. Focused on driving brand exposure and sales of Ray-Ban, Killer-Loop, and X-Ray sunglasses. Made sales presentations on site to high-profile athletes, and distributed swag and retainers to sponsored athletes to support brand advocacy.
- Developed and managed more than 200 athlete contracts in road racing, track and field, thriathlon, in-line skating, mountain biking, cycling, and major league baseball.
- Facilitated sponsorship support for several national and world-class sporting events, including professional beach volleyball, cycling, mountain biking, track and field, skiing, and the Olympic Games.
- Created brand awareness during the launch of the new Killer-Loop and X-ray eye wear brands.
- Won significant market share from Oakley and Bolla brands, which had captured 85% and 15%, respectively, of the sports eye wear market. Grew Bausch & Lomb's market share from zero to 58%.

EDUCATION

BACHELOR OF ARTS, COMMUNICATIONS (1989)
University of Colorado, Boulder
- Received a full athletic scholarship.

SPORTS INTERESTS

- Running, marathons, cycling, skiing, mountain biking, swimming (lifeguard), snowboarding, weight lifting, power hiking, yoga, salsa dancing, traveling, and cross-training.
- Hold a second-degree black belt in Karate.
- Competed in numerous running events worldwide.
- Served as track and field coach at the University of Colorado before racing six years professionally for Team Reebok. Joined two U.S. World Teams.
- Won three Big Eight titles at the University of Colorado and was awarded three NCAA, Division 1, All-American appointments.
- Set the Colorado state record in the two-mile race at Northglenn High School.

COMPUTERS

- Proficient in Windows, MS Word, Excel, PowerPoint, Outlook, Internet Explorer, Restaurant Manager, Aloha Point of Sale System, Facebook, MySpace, Linked-In, Mobile Storm, Animoto, Banner Maker, Slide.
- Understand what it takes to design a visually appealing website that is optimized for search engine optimization. Involved in creating websites for The Denver Marathon, Sutra, and The Wine Loft.

Richard Philips

10, rue du Fierney ● F-1630 St. Genis-Pouilly, France ● Home: +33 555 12 34 56 ● Cellular: +33 6 55 78 90 12
E-mail: RPB2@protypeltd.fr ● Website: www.philipsr.com

PROFILE

- Seasoned telecom/IT professional with diverse experience in:
  - Product development
  - Project management
  - Business planning
  - Training programmes
  - HR supervision
  - Software design
  - Network architecture
  - Capacity management
  - Interactive voice response
- Effective team leader with the proven ability to motivate staff to achieve goals.
- High achiever with a passion for training others to excel in highly technical fields.

EXPERIENCE

CONSULTANT (2008 – present)
Founded a successful consulting company dedicated to resolving cutting-edge technology challenges for clients throughout Europe. Developed innovative training programmes.

Phonexion SA, Geneva, Switzerland (7 months)
- Sold the Digitalk platform to this rapidly growing startup company and then was hired as a consultant to integrate and maintain it.
- Facilitated the doubling of business every two months in the first six months from zero to $4 million per month.
- Created calling card and other value-added services.
- Installed and maintained new carrier interconnects and provided customer service.

Digitalk, Limited, France and Switzerland (16 months)
- Developed business relationships with and sold Digitalk products to telecom companies in both France and Switzerland.

Digitalk, Limited, Milton Keynes, UK (17 months)
- Developed the concept for and designed the complete Digitalk training programme and delivered it to engineering and sales staff, as well as customers.
- Solicited customer feedback and integrated their requirements into the software design.

DIRECTOR, TEDS Sàrl, Geneva, Switzerland (2007 – 2008)
- Designed and implemented new calling card and 0900, premium-rate products.
- Wrote a comprehensive business plan with pro forma financial statements.
- Sold products and services through direct marketing.
- Responsible for full profit and loss, sales, customer service, and new product development.

ENGINEERING MANAGER, Interoute SA, Geneva, Switzerland (2002 – 2007)
- Managed all technical and help desk aspects of the Interoute Swiss Network, including network architecture, capacity management, and operational maintenance.
- Directed operations, hired technical staff, and allocated the training budget.
- Led the installation of a $2 million, 200m^2 switch in both Geneva and Zurich, as well as its associated network operations centre, then transferred all traffic and services to it. Determined project scope, budget, location, architecture, and time lines.
- Managed network quality and proactively monitored the network.
- Developed and implemented improved processes and working practices.
- Performed an in-depth market research study of potential teleconferencing platform suppliers and their product offerings.
- Gained experience with Ericsson Diax ANS switch, Digitalk Value-Added Platform with SQL server, ECI Digital Circuit Multiplication Equipment (DCME), ATM and SDH networks, and SS7 Carrier Interconnect.

MAINTENANCE MANAGER, Certacom, Ltd., Wooburn Green, High Wycombe, UK (2000 – 2002)
- Provided pre- and post-sales support of Certacom's signaling conversion equipment; produced designs for signaling converters; and organized dealerboard installations and expansions.
- Hired, trained, and supervised 3–4 wire persons, 2 test technicians, 1 storekeeper, and 2 engineers.
- Designed and delivered a speech-band training course for employees and customers.
- Maintained ISO 9002 (QAG 1) license.
- Oversaw non-contract maintenance of all products supplied by the company, including echo cancellers, analogue signaling converters, voice compression equipment, dealerboards, channel banks, and high-speed data modems.

EXPERIENCE

SR. TECHNICAL SUPPORT ENGINEER, Extel Systems Support, London, UK (1998 – 2000)
- Rapidly promoted from Engineer to Senior Engineer and then to Senior Technical Support Engineer responsible for on-site maintenance of city brokerage systems (dealerboards), videoconferencing system design, and VSAT satellite data broadcast installation and maintenance.
- Planned and developed quotes for dealerboard installation projects.
- Led a team of four engineers in the installation and maintenance of dealerboards to ISO 9002 (BS 5750/QAG 931) standards.
- Installed X.25 packet switching on the existing Extel network.
- Participated in the design of the Comms '90 show display for Extel and managed the technical side of its installation.

FIELD ENGINEER, Apricot Computers, Birmingham, London, UK (1990 – 1998)
- Performed field maintenance and repairs to Apricot desktop PCs, peripherals, and LANs.

EDUCATION

OPEN UNIVERSITY, Milton Keynes, UK
- **Technology**: Digital Telecommunications, Digital Transmission Systems, Digital Switching Systems.
- **Business**: Complexity, Management, and Change—Applying a Systems Approach, Level 3.
- **Liberal Arts**: Introduction to Psychology.
- **Special Projects**: Directed the installation of a large telecom switch (AXE 501) in Geneva, Switzerland.

BRITISH TELECOMMUNICATION, PLC, Barking, London, UK (1989 – 1994)
Telecommunications Technician Certificate, East Ham College of Technical Education
- Completed a three-year apprenticeship program that focused on data circuit and data transmission equipment provision and maintenance, as well as private data circuits and speech-band circuits.
- Served as a technician and technical officer assigned to the Data Telecommunications Unit.
- Installed and maintained a wide range of personal computers and peripherals.
- Received Best Student—Technical Studies Award.

PROFESSIONAL DEVELOPMENT
- SQL Server Administration, Moebius Business Training, 2 days (2008)
- SQL Programming—Transact, Moebius Business Training, 1 day (2008)
- Bespoke TCP/IP and Understanding ATM, The Knowledge Centre, 4 days (2007)
- Diax ANS Basic and General O&M, Ericsson Diax, 14 days (2006)
- Landmark Education Courses (2004 – 2006)
  - Self-Expression and Leadership Program
  - Communication, Access to Power
  - Communication, Performance and Power
  - Introduction to the Forum Leadership Program and subsequent coaching
- Nokia Transmission Products, Nokia, 4 days (2004)
- Apricot PC Range Training Course, Apricot Computers Limited, 5 weeks (2002)
- Provision and Maintenance of Speech-band Circuits, British Telecom, 15 days (2002)

COMPUTERS
- **Software Applications**: MS Word, Excel, PowerPoint, Outlook, Visio, Photosuite
- **Languages**: SQL, GW Basic, Assembly
- **Operating Systems**: Windows, MS-DOS
- **Networking**: LAN, WAN, TCP/IP, ATM, ISDN, networking protocols, Cisco CCNA Introduction, Ericsson DIAX ANS switching system, interactive voice transmission switching and signaling, SS7, CCITT 7

PERSONAL
- **Languages**: native English speaker, fluent in French, knowledge of German
- **International**: lived and worked four years in Switzerland, three years in France
- **Personal**: U.K. citizen, born 8/7/65, married, three children
- **Interests**: marathon running and swimming, skiing, digital photography, building kit cars, assembling computers and servers from scratch, British MENSA

Kelly A. Messerly

1234 Summernight Terrace • Colorado Springs, Colorado 80909
Home: (719) 555-1234 • Email: kamess@protypeltd.com

SUMMARY
- Demonstrated success in television and radio announcer positions for more than 15 years.
- Background in television reporting, weather forecasting, editing, production, and camera work.
- Confident camera presence and broadcasting voice.
- Definitive abilities in research, writing, production, and sales.
- Self-motivated professional who is comfortable working independently with little supervision.

EXPERIENCE
Television
- Completed KRDO and KKTV television internships as a weather forecaster, traffic anchor, editor, and reporter.
- Presented weekend weather forecasts, including research, writing, editing, prompter setup, and on-camera performances.
- As a reporter, investigated backgrounds, traveled to shoot on location, set up cameras, interviewed contacts, and filed stories.
- Served as traffic anchor during the weekdays for Metro Networks.
- Worked as a production assistant and cameraman for KOAA television.
- Assisted production company in the creation of commercials by setting up cameras and lighting, writing scripts, editing videotape, and performing voiceovers.
- Acted in commercials for Fountain Valley Mechanical, Sun Spot Tanning Salons, and Eagle Hardware.
- Two years of college training in producing, behind-the-scenes directing, floor design, lighting, camera operations, and journalism.
- Attended modeling school in 1991 to further develop camera presence.

Radio
- Sixteen years of experience as a radio announcer and on-air personality for contemporary radio stations.
- Owned and operated a successful DJ service; developed markets for performances at private parties, conventions, weddings, and military gatherings.
- Performed public service announcements and voiceovers.
- Wrote and performed commercials for Computer Edge.

Communications
- Top trainer at Peterson Air Force Base for four years; instructed all enlisted personnel in emergency action procedures.
- Briefed Margaret Thatcher, Dan Quayle, Ted Kennedy, visiting generals, and other distinguished visitors.
- Staff reporter for the University of Southern Colorado weekly newspaper.
- Member of Toastmasters International; spoken before groups as large as 800.

WORK HISTORY

WeekendWeather Anchor, KKTV Television, Colorado Springs	2003 – present
Reporter, KKTV Television, Colorado Springs	2000 – present
Radio Announcer, KKLI 106.3 and KSPZ 92.9, Colorado Springs	1998 – present
Owner, James L. Brown DJ Service, Colorado Springs	1990 – present
Radio Announcer, KKMG 98.9, Colorado Springs	1995 – 1998
Television Intern, KRDO Television, Colorado Springs	1999
Television Intern, KOAA Television, Colorado Springs	1999

EDUCATION

Meteorology Certificate, Mississippi State University, Mississippi	2003
Bachelor of Science, Mass Communications, University of Southern Colorado	1998
Associate of Applied Science, Broadcasting, Pikes Peak Community College	1996
Columbia School of Broadcasting, Hollywood, California	1992

Fonts & Bullets

Chapter 8

Fonts (aka type style or type face) set the tone for the entire résumé. What is a font? It is that little bit of magic that enables humans to communicate in print. It is the alphabet set to music. It is art. Actually, a font is a set of curved, straight, or slanted shapes that your brain decodes into letters and then words, but that sounds too boring for a subject as fascinating as type style.

Every font has its own designer and its own personality. Each font projects a certain "feel." For instance, serif fonts (the kind with the little "feet" like the Times New Roman font on the first bullet below) are considered more traditional. They are usually used as text fonts in books and magazines. Some samples include

- Times New Roman
- New Century Schoolbook
- Palatino
- Bookman
- See page 137 for more serif fonts

Sans (meaning "without" in French) serif fonts, on the other hand, have no "feet" and are considered more contemporary, as in

- Helvetica (Arial)
- Avant Garde
- Tahoma
- **Antique Olive**
- See page 138 for more sans serif fonts

Serif fonts are commonly used as text type for the main body of published works because they are more readable when there are masses of text. Because résumés use a lot of white space and bulleted sentences, there aren't masses of text, so you don't have to restrict yourself to serif fonts for résumés. Either serif or sans serif fonts produces equally impressive résumés.

Headline fonts and wild type faces have their place in design, but only in the headlines or names and only for very creative professions. Remember, you want your résumé to be easy to read. You will find many samples of headline fonts on pages 139–140.

There is one font you never want to use on a résumé in any way, shape, or form—Comic Sans. It's bad enough that the name of the font is funky and informal, but it has a reputation as the worst font to grace the computer screen. In the summer of 2010, the Cleveland

Cavaliers' owner, Dan Gilbert, published a rant using the cutesy Comic Sans font after losing his star basketball player, LeBron James. Gilbert was ridiculed nationwide. No one took his letter seriously because of the font. Don't let that happen to your résumé.

In all my many years of designing résumés, I have discovered that my clients don't have to understand the science behind fonts or the difference between serif and sans serif fonts, and neither do you. It is more important that you look at samples of good résumé fonts and then choose the one that makes your eyes "feel good." In other words, choose the one you like the best. Again, it comes down to personality. If you feel a bit tentative about choosing the right font, conduct a "focus group" by asking friends or family to look at the font you have chosen and tell you whether it is readable and looks like "you."

BULLETS

Bullets are special characters used at the beginning of indented short sentences to call attention to individual items on a résumé. Short, bulleted sentences are easier to read than long paragraphs of text, and they highlight the information you want the reader to see quickly. Bullets also add some variety to a résumé and make it just a touch more creative.

In both MS Word and Corel WordPerfect, clicking on "Insert" gives you access to a myriad of special characters that are not found on your keyboard. That is how the bullets in this section were created. Your printing capabilities might not allow you to have access to all of these dingbats, wingdings, or symbols, but you can still be creative.

Be careful of hollow bullets that have the shape of letters, especially in scannable resumes. I avoid those types of bullets as a rule, since they are a bit weak anyway. Here are some of my suggestions for bullets.

Serif Fonts

Sans Serif Fonts

Headline Fonts

SANJAY BHAGAT

12345 Rockwood Terrace, Boulder, CO 80302
(303) 555-1234 / bhagat@protypeltd.com

SUMMARY

Competent Organic Scientist with strong background in the research and development of molecular compounds for the pharmaceutical/biotech industry. Experience with protein extraction, analysis, and characterization of microbially expressed enzymes in a GLP environment. Willing to perform repetitive analyses to assure consistent outcomes. Dedicated team contributor, attentive to detail, and able to deliver high-quality data in set timelines.

INSTRUMENTATION and TECHNIQUES

~ ^{1}H, ^{13}C, NMR, FTIR, GC, and GCMS for sample characterizations
~ TLC and column chromatography
~ UV-Vis spectrophotometry
~ Quantitative protein analysis (animal extraction and ELISA)
~ Purification procedures for organic solvents

Book Antigua Font

KNOWLEDGE AND SKILLS

~ Set up and maintenance of small-scale photochemical reactions
~ Excellent documentation and laboratory organization
~ Adherence to health, safety, and environmental policies and procedures
~ Mechanical ability to troubleshoot, maintain, and repair gas chromatograph
~ Thorough literature searches of relevant scientific material
~ Computer literacy for test control and creation of graphic presentations

PROFESSIONAL EXPERIENCE

Staff Scientist, Clinical Genetics Services
Syntex Laboratories, Boulder, CO (2002–Present)
Biotech research and development facility

~ Assist in a 15-member team developing products for the treatment of HIV/AIDS.
~ Monitor numerous animal models, ranging from rodents to primates in induced stages of disease.
~ Review quality of reagents, calibrate equipment, and log specimen processes.
~ Transition R&D assays and platforms to clinical genetics.
  – *Identified process obstacles and contributed to workflow improvements.*
  – *Selected to revise and develop new standard operating procedures.*

Quality Control Technician
AMX Formulations, Boulder, CO (1999–2002)
Generic pharmaceutical manufacturer

~ To establish and meet quality standards for pharmaceutical products, performed a variety of ongoing laboratory procedures, including:
  – *Precision volumetrics.*
  – *Comparison of compound ingredients to perfect samples.*
  – *Friability, dissolution, and uniformity testing on tablet formulations.*
~ Entrusted with the safe handling and disposal of narcotics and teratogenic substances.

EDUCATION

M.S. in Organic Chemistry — Colorado State University (1999)
Broad coursework in organic, inorganic, analytical, physical, and biochemistry

B.S. (equivalent) in Biology — Government College of Science, Gujarat State, India (1995)

Crystal Alva

123-456 College Blvd. #78-9 • Selden, New York 11784 • Cell: (631) 555-1234

OBJECTIVE

- An opportunity to share my unique talents with other hairdressers as a trainer and platform artist with Redken.

PROFILE

- Creative master stylist with a reputation as a truly talented artist with skills in:
  - Precision cutting
  - French layering
  - Razor cutting
  - Dimensional color
  - Foil highlights
  - Corrective color
  - Formal hair dressing
  - Hair straightening
  - Fusion extensions
- Effective manager who works well under pressure and motivates employees to excel.
- Warm and caring professional with the proven ability to generate new business and increase profitability.
- Licensed Cosmetologist who is certified in hair straightening, hair extensions, and various coloring products.

Bookman Font

EXPERIENCE

MASTER STYLIST
New Beginnings, Selden, New York (2005 – present)
Diamond Cut Hair and Nail Salon, Selden, New York (1996 – 2005)
- Helped clients feel pretty by using proven talents in hair cutting, styling, and coloring.
- Developed a reputation for being in tune with clients—able to listen to the desires of clients, make them feel comfortable, and then give them what they want.
- Committed to doing whatever it takes to make the customer happy while putting a personal touch on each style.
- Grossed more than $60,000 in annual styling and retail sales, growing a loyal customer base of more than 150 regular clients.
- Averaged one product per client in retail sales, and maintained a client retention rate of 90%.

OWNER / MASTER STYLIST
Crystalyn's, Selden/Centereach, New York (1984 – 1996)
- Managed the operations of a large salon providing haircut, styling, color, nail, facial, and waxing services.
- Increased retail sales and reduced operating costs by implementing process efficiencies.
- Recruited stylists, growing the team to 10 cosmetologists. Trained hairdressers on cutting, coloring, customer service, and techniques to meet personal sales goals.
- Marketed the salon through direct mail, demos, excellence in customer service, and consistent follow-up.
- Accountable for business planning, profit and loss, product selection, inventory management, sales, staffing, training, and record keeping.
- Received money, balanced daily accounts, prepared bookkeeping records, and made deposits.
- Gained in-depth experience in color applications, including basic retouch, bleach, foil weave, and corrective color using a variety of brand-name products.

EDUCATION

LICENSED COSMETOLOGIST (1976)
Wilford Academy, Patchogue, New York
- Graduated as one of the youngest licensed cosmetologists in the state at only 16.

CONTINUING EDUCATION

- Annual International Hair Show, New York, New York (10 years)
- Ongoing training from product representatives, including Redken, Wella, Paul Brown, Framesi, Sebastian, and other manufacturers
- Certified by Diamond in hair straightening and hair extensions

SUMMARY

- Resourceful, high-energy administrative assistant with diverse creative and computer skills.
- Outgoing "people person" who works well with internal and external clients.
- Effective team player with a positive outlook and excellent written/verbal communication skills.
- Well-established professional with a large network of industry contacts.

Cambria Font

EXPERIENCE

PHOTOGRAPHER (2004 – present)
Burleson Studios, LLC, Annapolis, Maryland
Built a full-service photography studio from the ground up, based on a passion for capturing beauty, emotion, and art through the camera. Took high-end studio, portrait, family, and product photos. Specialized in setting clients at ease and capturing their natural beauty. Used numerous photo software programs to process raw images, retouch photos, produce slideshows, and lay out albums and ads. Accountable for all record keeping, correspondence, telephones, and customer service.

INDEPENDENT MEDIA SPECIALIST (2001 – present)
Created and produced a pilot for a half-hour children's television series. Developed the foundations for corresponding school curriculum and interactive Web site. Acquired Internet domains and designed Web site content. Wrote proposals and pitched the series to national television networks (Food Network, Discovery, HBO Kids, PBS).

PRODUCER / DIRECTOR / WRITER (1991 – 1992, 1996 – 2004)
Independent Contractor, Washington, DC, metro area
Interviewed public figures, celebrities, and news-makers both on camera and off. Directed original music productions, including set design and graphics. Prepared off-line and online edits, rough cuts, and B-rolls. Conducted extensive stock footage, copyright, union photography, and literary research. Kept records and provided exceptional customer service.

STAFF PRODUCER / DIRECTOR / WRITER (1986 – 1990, 1992 – 1994)
MCI Telecommunications, McLean, Virginia (4 years)
Ernst and Young, Reston, Virginia (2 years)
Developed project proposals, schedules, and scripts for large broadcast and non-broadcast programs in full-service video production facilities. Pitched project ideas to senior corporate executives. Developed and implemented production budgets. Cast and directed professional and non-professional talent. Hired and supervised staff and free-lancers

VIDEO COORDINATOR (1983 – 1990)
The White House, Washington, DC
Worked with Presidents and First Ladies, celebrities, White House staff, Secret Service, and multi-camera crews in the production of videos used by national media.

ASSOCIATE PRODUCER / COORDINATOR / PRODUCTION MANAGER (1983 – 1986)
Independent Contractor, Washington, DC
Contracted for various long-term, free-lance video production projects for local film companies.

EDUCATION

BACHELOR OF ARTS, MEDIA AND JOURNALISM (1980)
University of South Carolina, Columbia, South Carolina

TECHNOLOGY

- Business Applications: Windows, MS Word, Excel, Outlook, QuickBooks, Quicken
- Desktop Publishing Applications: Pro-Show Producer, Photoshop, Adobe Bridge, Avid Video Editing, Adobe Premier, Corel Painter, Lumapix, Bludomain, Movie Budgeting, FrontPage, *Macintosh* Editing Software

1234 Burley Road • Annapolis, Maryland 21409

CAROLINE KAZYNSKI

12345 LINCOLN AVENUE, MILWAUKEE, WISCONSIN 53203
414-555-1234 / kazynski@protypeltd.com

PROFILE

Award-winning **Kitchen and Bath Designer**, offering solid, well-rounded experience to sell and manage clients' projects from concept to final details, positively influencing company performance, profitability, and operations. Areas of expertise include:

- Creative interior design
- Sales agreement negotiations/closings
- Space planning with precise measurements
- Architectural and construction knowledge
- Computer and hand drafting
- Budget development and monitoring

QUALIFICATIONS

- Totally committed to exceptional service and quality work for both new home construction and remodeling projects.
- Thoroughly handle the entire process of sales, design, construction, and follow-through of projects.
- Collaborate effectively with individuals at all levels, including with trade professionals.
- Enjoy extensive one-on-one contact with clients throughout all project stages, proactively resolving issues to ensure timely completion and client satisfaction.
- Possess exceptional listening skills to assess customers' real needs and translate their vision into attractive completed designs beyond their expectations.
- Suggest design alternatives to maximize clients' functionality and aesthetic requirements while respecting their budgetary limitations.
- Acknowledged as a highly organized, articulate professional who maintains excellent relationships with clients, staff, and senior management.
- Stay current with the latest kitchen and bath design trends through industry publications and showroom visits.
- Proficient in AutoCAD R-12, 20/20 Graphic Design, National Estimator 2001, and MS Word.

PROFESSIONAL EXPERIENCE

HOME EXPO
Designer, Kitchens and Baths

Milwaukee, WI
2005–2009

- Met one-on-one with potential customers, determined those who were serious minded about moving forward with their projects, and created two-dimensional presentations of design ideas for remodeling their kitchens and bathrooms.
- Developed strong organizational and administrative skills in order to properly service the large number of information requests and projects per day.
- Instrumental in creating the location's first-ever, in-store appointment chart and design center class, allowing customers greater personal time with design professionals that resulted in higher closing ratios and improved overall satisfaction.
- Received Shining Star Award conferred by Kraft Maid Cabinet Company and Home Expo's Gold Sales Achievement in 2007.

PAVLIK ASSOCIATES, RESIDENTIAL ARCHITECTS
Draftsperson/AutoCAD Operator

Racine, WI
2002–2005

- Transferred freehand architectural drawings into AutoCAD for final presentation.
- Gained design experience, made on-site inspections, gathered information, and ultimately had full autonomy over design and layout of areas within projects.

EDUCATION & TRAINING

Associate's degree in Computer-Aided Interior Design
Milwaukee Community College
Kitchen and Bath Design courses through NKBA

2002

2006–Present

Portfolio of designs available on request

GERI YOUNG

12 S. Ogden Street #123, Denver, Colorado 80209

Email: gyoung@protypeltd.com

Cellular: (303) 555-1234

PROFILE
- Experienced property manager who understands the importance of quality service and an owner's investment.
- Proven background in operations management, negotiations, and employee motivation.
- Flexible professional who adjusts rapidly to new and challenging situations and works well under pressure to meet time-sensitive deadlines.
- Effective team leader who successfully motivates by example.

> Classic Typewriter Font

SUMMARY
- Accountable for full profit and loss of properties, including budgeting, forecasting, accounting, accounts payable/receivable, and business planning.
- Recruited, hired, and supervised staff members, including assistant managers, maintenance personnel, leasing agents, and clerical staff.
- Developed and implemented new management policies and procedures.
- Analyzed market conditions and recommended price increases and property enhancements that significantly increased revenue.
- Managed tenant relations. Planned and directed special events and grand openings. Coordinated special promotions to increase the perceived value of the properties.
- Created successful marketing campaigns that included magazine and apartment guide advertising, incentives, referral programs, and relocation specialists.
- Planned and supervised multiple capital improvement projects, including interiors, paint, carpeting, and common areas.
- Developed safety programs and coordinated fire drills with the local fire department.
- Experienced in the use of property management software, including Yardi.

EXPERIENCE
PROPERTY MANAGER (2005 – present)
Club Valencia, Denver, Colorado
- Oversee a complex of 330 condominiums with a homeowner's association.
- Manage accounts receivable, accounts payable, payroll, maintenance, security, and housekeeping.
- Hire, train, supervise, schedule, and mentor 12 employees.
- Served as the project manager for a complete remodel of all of communal property, including 54,000 sq of hallway carpeting, a community center (events space, billiards, weight room, saunas, jacuzzi), courtyard, bridges, fountains, tennis court, basketball court, and indoor and outdoor pools.
- Assumed responsibility for $69,000 in delinquent HOA fees; collected 100% within 13 months.
- Significantly increased property values, improved the work environment, and lowered employee turnover.

COMMUNITY MANAGER (2004 – 2005)
ARC / Affordable Residential Communities, Arvada, Colorado
- Recruited away from Manchester for a better opportunity to manage two properties (Inspiration Valley, Sheridan Estates) with 300 units.
- Succeeded in improving an 81% occupancy rate to 95% in less than a year.

RESIDENT MANAGER, STOKES & COMPANY (2004)
Manchester Apartments, Denver, Colorado
- Managed a luxury high-rise with 100 units renting from $1,000 to $4,000 per month.
- Improved occupancy rates from 75% to 99% through target marketing and proactive problem solving.

Barry Walters

12345 Phoenixville Road, Chaplin, CT 06235-2212
(860) 555-9876 Home • (508) 555-1234 Cell
bwalters@protypeltd.com

WAREHOUSE WORKER

Dedicated individual offering an excellent work ethic with a solid background in packaging and handling of various size materials. Offer excellent interpersonal and communication skills, and ability to maintain a positive attitude with all staff members. Quick learner who can rapidly acquire new skills to contribute to team efforts. Background also includes machine operations and assembly within a production environment.

CORE SKILLS

• Shrink Wrapping	• Hand Trucks	• Organizing/Prioritizing	• Training
• Maintenance	• Inventory	• Chemical Handling	• OSHA
• Blueprints	• Circuit Boards	• Machine Operations	• Soldering

---

EXPERIENCE

Clearface Font

Warehouse
• Prepared and packaged products for shipment. Prepared pallets for shipment.
• Maintained inventory of shipping supplies.
• Prioritized shipments for timely delivery.

Wave Solder Operator
• Oversaw overall production in the wave solder operation of printed circuit boards.
• Inspected soldered components for quality control.
• Operated Hollis and Electrovert wave solder machines, utilizing fixtures as required.
• Worked directly with engineering in the production of prototype PCBs to determine future standard manufacturing processes.
• Performed all standard preventative maintenance on wave solder machinery.
• Handled hazardous waste and chemicals, maintaining all OSHA standards.
• Traveled to Ponce, Puerto Rico, facility to train 10 wave solder operators in operating procedures.

Printed Circuit Board Assembler, Touch-Up
• Inspected PCBs for compliance with quality standards prior to final assembly processes.
• Hand soldered individual components onto PCBs.
• Manually assembled PCBs using engineering documentation and blueprints.

EMPLOYMENT

Caregiver	Self-employed Caretaker for Family Member	2001–2009
Warehouse	AC Technology Corporation, Uxbridge, MA	1993–2001
Production	Design Circuits, Inc., Southboro, MA	1992–1993
Machine Operator	Computervision, Inc., Bedford, MA	1980–1991

BENJAMIN BEAUPRE

1111 Crystal Park Road • Manitou Springs, Colorado 80829
Home: (719) 555-1234 • Cell: (719) 555-5678 • Email: benbeaupre@protypeltd.com

PROFILE

- Experienced manager with a strong work ethic and sense of vision for the company.
- Background includes operations management, staffing, supervision, cost control, and production.
- Effective team leader who listens to his employees and motivates them to excel.
- Avid reader with a dedication to lifelong learning.
- Proficient in Windows, Microsoft Word, QuickBooks, Datek Online, and Outlook.

EXPERIENCE

GENERAL MANAGER AND OWNER (1982–present)
The Original Mission Bell Inn, Manitou Springs, Colorado

Key Accomplishments
- Successfully managed a family restaurant, increasing sales by 40% over a five-year period in spite of a highly competitive marketplace.
- Expanded service into a new market of custom parties for large groups, increasing revenue over the previous year by 10%.
- Achieved a three-star rating from the Mobil Travel Guide.
- Won several "Best of the Springs" awards for the category.
- Maintained expenses below budget through accurate planning, waste reduction, purchasing, and cost-effective operating procedures.
- Planned and managed two significant remodeling projects that enhance the ambiance of the facility and patio.

Management/Administration
- Accountable for budgeting, cost control, sales analysis, and full profit and loss.
- Planned menus to maximize food freshness, estimated food and beverage costs, sourced suppliers, and purchased inventory (liquor, food, and supplies) valued at nearly $100,000 per year. Negotiated cost-effective contracts and bought in volume to save money.
- Inspected food upon delivery to ensure that only the highest quality products were used.
- Managed projects for large group events, including menus, entertainment, decorations, wait staff, and recruitment of celebrities.
- Developed marketing campaigns to increase visibility of the restaurant using coupons, newspapers, and other print media.
- Analyzed the effectiveness of advertising and reallocated the budget to improve response.
- Responsible for the entire kitchen, including menus, recipes, food preparation, and presentation of dinners, buffets, and private parties.
- Investigated and resolved food/beverage quality and service complaints, ensuring customer satisfaction and repeat business.

Supervision/Training
- Recruited, hired, supervised, scheduled, and motivated up to 28 employees.
- Achieved very low turnover rates in a tight labor market.
- Trained service staff to enhance customer service and increase profits through suggestive selling.

EDUCATION

PIKES PEAK COMMUNITY COLLEGE, Colorado Springs, Colorado
- Currently taking courses toward a undergraduate degree in business (2009–present)
- Completed a year of culinary arts studies

MARILYN NOLAN

45 Murray Road ▪ East Windsor, CT 06016 ▪ (860) 555-5555 ▪ MNolan@rds.com

▪ PROFILE

Conferences ▪ Fund-raising ▪ Trade Shows ▪ Meeting Planning ▪ Cultural Programs

Creative professional with expertise in all aspects of successful event/program planning, development, and management. Excel in managing multiple projects concurrently with detail, problem-solving, and follow-through strengths. Demonstrated ability to recruit, motivate, and build cohesive teams. Sourced vendors, negotiated contracts, and managed project budgets.

▪ SELECTED ACCOMPLISHMENTS

Garamand Font

Special Events Management:

Planned and coordinated conferences, meetings and events for companies, professional associations, arts/cultural, and other organizations. Developed program content and administered budgets. Arranged all on-site logistics, including transportation, accommodations, meals, guest speakers, entertainers, and audiovisual support. Coordinated participation and represented companies at industry trade shows. Recognized for creating and planning some of the most successful events ever held in the state.

- **Created cultural events for an arts organization that boosted membership enrollment.**
- **Organized five conferences for two national professional associations, surpassing all prior attendance records.**
- **Designed successful community educational campaigns promoting safety awareness.**

Fundraising and Public Relations:

Created, planned and managed all aspects of several major fund-raising campaigns resulting in a significant increase in contributions raised for each function over prior years. Recruited volunteers and developed corporate sponsorships. Generated extensive media coverage through effective promotional and public relations strategies. Created newsletters distributed to employees, customers, and others.

- **Co-chaired capital fund campaign that raised $3.5 million for a new facility.**
- **Coordinated three auctions raising more than $140,000 for an educational institution.**
- **Initiated a successful publication generating $25,000 to finance community programs.**

Sales and Marketing:

Selected by management to spearhead opening of a regional office, including all logistics, staff relocation, and business development efforts. Designed and implemented creative sales and marketing strategies to capitalize on consumer trends and penetrate new markets. Coordinated and conducted sales training.

- **Developed and managed 17 key accounts generating $10 million annually.**
- **Recognized for managing the company's top revenue-generating program.**
- **Consistently exceeded sales forecast, and led region to rank number one out of six in profitability nationwide.**

▪ EXPERIENCE

VOLUNTEER EVENT/PROGRAM COORDINATOR, Arts Council, Botanical Gardens and Culture Exchange, Chicago, IL (1998 to present).

FINANCIAL UNDERWRITER, Marcon Financial Services, Chicago, IL (1990 to 2003).

▪ EDUCATION

B.A. in Business Administration, Springfield College, Springfield, MA

Gail McCann

318 Lloyd Avenue • Latrobe, PA 15650   724-384-1579 • gailmccann@protypeltd.com

Top Performer in Event Planning and Marketing

Entrepreneurial professional with 18-year record of successful planning and seamless execution of large-scale conferences and training events. **Additional background** in growing start-ups to profit-generating entities and driving profitable marketing and performance initiatives in Fortune 1000. **High-energy,** well-respected performer who consistently juggles multiple tasks with a positive, can-do attitude. **Proven track record** of creating venues, planning agendas, balancing priorities, and meeting tight deadlines to produce exceptional results.

Career Highlights

Talent Discovery Network, Greensburg, PA (2006–Present)
EVENT MANAGER / SALES / OPERATIONS —TALENT SCOUT ORGANIZATION
Operations: Identified business opportunity in the competitive talent scout market and led start-up from concept to revenue generation. Built profitable business alliances with casting directors, advertising agencies, and talent agencies. Fostered relationships with convention centers, vendors, and management companies.

Event-Planning: Plan and execute events for up to 600 attendees. Coordinate logistics with vendors, hotels, and caterers. Arrange travel accommodations. Set up event rooms and stage productions. Identify and schedule speakers. Personally deliver high-impact presentations.
- Crafted strategic business and marketing plans that catapulted annual sales from zero to $1 million.
- Triggered 800% growth in clients—from 100 to 850.
- Consistently exceeded sales goals by 10%–20%.

> **Georgia Font**

Gail's Attic, Ligonier, PA (2003–2006)
DIRECTOR OF MARKETING—COLLECTIBLES BOUTIQUE
New Business Initiative: Leveraged existing relationships and capabilities to grow specialty retail start-up into highly successful enterprise. Planned and managed all marketing and purchasing operations.
- Drove annual sales from zero to $250,000 in three years.

Your Wellness Spa, Pittsburgh, PA (2001–2003)
DIRECTOR OF SALES & MARKETING—WELLNESS, FITNESS AND BEAUTY CENTER
Developed and coordinated promotional strategies, multimedia advertising, and marketing events for health and fitness products. Established new business and expanded existing customers through planning and hosting on-site corporate events, bridal promotions, and health and fitness programs.
- Grew sales 65% in one year.

Revlon, Lower Burrell, PA (1998–2003)
PRODUCT AND SALES TRAINER / MAKEUP ARTIST—GLOBAL COSMETICS
Coordinated product merchandising and public relations with 42 department stores throughout three-state region. Planned and orchestrated 60+ on-site product training events for up to 12 store associates. Developed and implemented marketing and merchandising business plans to grow customer base and market share.
- Key player in driving 44% sales growth in 65% of the stores.

Professional Development

Certified Yoga Instructor, 2007
Clayton College of Holistic Nutrition, 2007
Certified Personal Trainer, International Fitness Professionals Association (IFPA), 2001

Accolades

Woman to Watch in Business, *Cambridge Who's Who in America,* 2008
Company to Watch, *Pageantry Magazine,* 2007
Woman of the Year to Watch for Event Planning, *Convention South Magazine,* 2005

LARRY H. (HAL) BYRD, JR.

PROFILE
- Goal-oriented sales professional with successful experience in medical/surgical supply sales.
- Demonstrated ability to create client loyalty above and beyond the sales relationship.
- Strong background in building territories and using creative marketing approaches.
- Self-motivated and well-organized; comfortable working independently with little supervision.
- Personable with the ability to communicate well with people of diverse backgrounds and levels of authority.

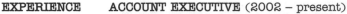

Memo Font

EXPERIENCE

ACCOUNT EXECUTIVE (2002 – present)
Henry Schein, Inc., Melville, New York
Aggressively sell medical and surgical supplies, equipment, pharmaceuticals, and specialty products in the Southern Colorado territory. Serve as an OSHA-certified field trainer for new sales representatives. Formulate, design, and conduct sales presentations to primary care physicians, hospitals, managed care facilities, rehabilitation centers, and retailers.
- Planned and organized the territory to increase market share of assigned products.
- Grew the territory from zero buying accounts to more than 100 active accounts.
- Sponsored the Pikes Peak Ascent numerous times.

ACCOUNT MANAGER (1997 – 2002)
Bergen Brunswig Medical Corporation, Denver, Colorado
Successfully sold medical/surgical supplies, home health care products and equipment, personal health products, pharmaceuticals, and specialty products for the second largest pharmaceuticals distributor in the United States.
- Grew the territory 300% in under two years, taking annual sales volume from $400,000 to $1.2 million.
- Used suggestive sales techniques to increase sales up to $180,000 per month.

DRIVING INSTRUCTOR (1990 – 1999)
Masterdrive, Inc., Colorado Springs, Colorado
Taught accident avoidance and driving skills to beginning and experienced drivers. Assisted senior drivers in finding solutions to age-related driving problems. Trained, coached, and evaluated new instructors.
- Implemented a driving rehabilitation program for head injury and stroke victims and those with phobic driving problems.

MEDICAL SALES REPRESENTATIVE (1992 – 1997)
Colorado Springs Surgical and Supply Company, Colorado Springs, Colorado
Sold medical supplies and maintained customer base through exceptional customer service.
- Increased territory sales from $200,000 to $750,000 per year with average monthly sales volumes of $45,000+.
- Added new accounts and expanded the Pueblo, Cañon City, and southern Colorado territories.

COURIER/SALES (1981 – 1992)
Federal Express, Colorado Springs, Colorado; Houston, Texas; and Memphis, Tennessee
Managed the operations of the Hunstville, Texas, station for two years. Coordinated the pickup and delivery of packages from hundreds of accounts. Initiated contact with potential new accounts through phone and personal contact, generating significant increases in account base and volume.
- Developed the account base from the ground up for this new location.
- Upgraded volume from existing accounts and placed drop boxes.

EDUCATION

CONTINUING EDUCATION
- Graduate of the Tony Robbins "Firewalker" course.
- Various advanced medical sales classes/designations.
- Graduate of the Dale Carnegie sales course.
- Completed courses and seminars in customer service, account retention, selling techniques, time management, and interpersonal skills.

BLAIR JUNIOR COLLEGE, Colorado Springs, Colorado (1989 – 1990)
MEMPHIS STATE UNIVERSITY, Memphis, Tennessee (1980 – 1982)
- Completed course work in business and marketing.

ADDRESS

1234 Mount Estes Drive • Colorado Springs, CO 80921 • (719) 123-9999 • lhbyrd@gmail.com

TIMOTHY M. SNELL

1234 Purcell Drive
Colorado Springs, CO 80922

E-mail: tsnell@protypeltd.com

Home: (719) 555-1234
Cellular: (719) 123-5555

PROFILE

- Well-trained, disciplined HVAC/Refrigeration Mechanic looking for an apprenticeship to hone skills learned in college.
- Proven problem-solver who has always had a talent for taking things apart and putting them back together again.
- Effective team player with strong communication and interpersonal skills.

EDUCATION

ASSOCIATE OF OCCUPATIONAL STUDIES (February 2008)
IntelliTec College, Colorado Springs, Colorado
Major in Refrigeration / HVAC.
Technology course work included:

- Advanced Controls—Electrical Servers and Wiring, Troubleshooting Control Circuits, Electrical Schematics, and Wiring Diagrams.
- Advanced Refrigeration I—Control Voltage, Line Voltage Controls, and Wiring for Commercial Refrigeration; Vaporization and Compression Components for Commercial Refrigeration; Specialized Refrigeration Components for Commercial Refrigeration.
- Advanced Refrigeration III—Service and Maintenance of Commercial Refrigeration, Ice Machines, Cooling Towers, Basic Operation of Chilled Water Systems.
- Domestic Refrigeration—Recovery, Evacuation, and Charging for Domestic Refrigeration; Recovery, Evacuation, and Charging for PTAC Air Conditioning; Line Voltage Wiring and Controls for PTACs, Domestic Refrigeration.
- Alternative Heating—Basic Fuel Oil Burner Operation and Diagnostics; Ignition Systems, Water Pump Characteristics, and Zone Controllers; Fundamentals of Hydronic Piping, Low Temperature Soldering.
- Service Technician Essentials—Sequence of Operation, Wiring, and Diagnostics for Gas Heating; Carbon Monoxide Safety and Combustible Leak Detection; Pikes Peak Regional Building Department Code Requirements.
- Gas Heating and Licensing, Electrical Controls, Fundamentals of Electronics, Basic Refrigeration, Specialized Commercial Applications, Air Conditioning/HVAC.
- Blueprint Reading, Professional Communications, MS Office.

Souvenir or Souvienne Font

UNDERGRADUATE COLLEGE STUDIES
Pikes Peak Community College, Colorado Springs, Colorado (2007 – present)

- Earned 12 credits of liberal arts study.

CERTIFICATIONS

- Commercial Refrigeration, HVAC Excellence (2007)
- Air Conditioning, HVAC Excellence (2007)
- Electrical Systems, HVAC Excellence (2007)
- Tiff 8800, Bacharach Informant and Bacharach Monoxor II Carbon Monoxide Detector (October 2006)
- Mechanic IV, HVAC Services Technician, Pikes Peak Regional Building Department (2007)
- EPA Certified Universal Technician, Esco Institute (2007)
- Section 609, Federal Clean Air Act, Esco Institute (2007)

COMPUTERS

- Proficient in Windows, MS Word, Excel, PowerPoint, Outlook, and Internet Explorer.

EXPERIENCE

Full-time College, Child Care Provider, Colorado Springs, Colorado (2001 – present)
Caregiver, Mary Haven Institute, Port Jefferson, New York (2000 – 2001)
Sales Associate, Garden Department, Home Depot, Comack, New York (1999 – 2000)
Area Captain / Cook, McDonald's, Port Jefferson, New York (1995 – 1998)

DAVID P. WECHSLER

1234 45th Avenue SW
Seattle, Washington 98136
Cell: (206) 555-1234

Email: dpwechsler@protypeltd.com

DRIVEN SALES MANAGER

"My customer's success is my success." – David Wechsler

Times New Roman Font

AREAS OF EXPERTISE

Sales Management
Customer Relationship Building
Strategic Planning • Scheduling
Workforce Management
Logistics Coordination

EXECUTIVE SUMMARY

Successful high achiever with in-depth knowledge of direct service delivery and a strong understanding of the sales process, including:
- Learning and communicating the features and benefits of a product / service.
- Quickly developing and maintaining profitable business relationships.
- Creating innovative sales programs that substantially increase revenue.

PROFESSIONAL EXPERIENCE

SALES MANAGER (2001 – present)
Schwartz Brothers Bakery, Seattle, Washington
Drive sales and profits for the Northwestern U.S. markets for this medium-sized bakery with more than $15 million in annual sales. Hire, train, and supervise a full-time merchandiser and a consultant for the bakery business. Provide direct customer service as the primary point of contact for bakery and deli managers.
- Grew the business year over year by expanding sales into retail outlets, including 30 Starbuck's licensed concepts and 110 grocery stores. Increased the product line consistently every year.
- Built profitable relationships with food service companies (Sodexo, Sysco, FSA, AAFES), grocery stores (Kroger and independent grocery stores), hotels, schools, hospitals, restaurants, retail stores, coffee shops, and membership warehouses (Costco).
- Successfully negotiated with bakery and deli directors for display space in a highly competitive market.
- Evaluated and revised delivery routes to increase efficiency and productivity.
- Improved relationships with drivers by increasing communication, empowering them to make decisions, and training them how to do their jobs better.
- Implemented safety training to minimize personal injuries, vehicle accidents, and workers' compensation claims.

CUSTOMER SERVICE MANAGER (1999 – 2001)
Schwartz Brothers Bakery, Seattle, Washington
Managed the order desk. Trained and supervised three clerks. Input payments into the accounting system. Oriented new customers to services and products. Served as the contact person for escalated customer service issues and the "face" of the bakery for a vast customer base.
- Developed a reputation for building long-term, profitable customer relations.

DRIVING SUPERVISOR (1991 – 1999), **DRIVER** (1990 – 1991)
Schwartz Brothers Bakery, Seattle, Washington
Supervised 10 route drivers in the western Washington market. Supervised loading of trucks, dispatched drivers, ensured accuracy of deliveries, and maintained documentation. Accounted for all products ordered on a daily basis. Conducted pre-trip inspections of route trucks.
- Maintained strong relationships with customers by providing exceptional customer service and resolving any problems quickly.

CONTINUING EDUCATION

- Dale Carnegie, Effective Communication and Human Relations
- Business Writing
- Microsoft Excel
- How to Correct Bad Behavior by Employees

COMPUTER SKILLS

Proficient in Windows, MS Word, Excel, Outlook, Internet Explorer, Monkey Bakery

SARAH WADDY

1234 Purcell Drive • Colorado Springs, Colorado 80922 • www.facebook.com/sarahwaddy
Home: (719) 555-1234 • Cell: (719) 123-4567 • E-mail: swaddy@protypeltd.com

PROFILE

- Certified Public Purchasing Buyer with experience in supply management, acquisition, shipping, receiving, and inventory control.
- Focused, reliable professional who works well under pressure and is able to multi-task.
- Effective team player with strong communication and interpersonal skills.
- Disciplined worker with proven skills in problem solving and attention to detail.

EXPERIENCE

UNIT SUPPLY CLERK
Active Duty, United States Army, Fort Carson, Colorado (2005 – 2010)

Candida Font

Managed unit assets. Requested, received, stored, issued, and preserved expendable supplies and equipment, including tents, cots, office supplies, food, and other necessities. Compared shipping documents to storage documents to ensure completeness and accuracy of information. Selected appropriate storage locations and ensured proper handling of classified materials. Prepared and maintained supply records and forms. Received, inspected, and counted physical inventories. Maintained the accounting system and used various computer applications. Performed general clerical duties. Served as the sole government purchase cardholder for the battalion's rear detachment. Ordered all supplies and maintained accountability with no discrepancies. Maintained the security of, organized, and administered the unit arms supply room, including small arms and ammunition. Scheduled and performed preventive maintenance on weapons.

- Maintained 100% accountability for installation property and hand-receipt holders.
- Ensured 100% completeness of CTA-50 and initial issue equipment needed during the pre-deployment phase in support of Operation Iraqi Freedom.
- Identified and turned in more than $150,000 worth of unserviceable equipment; ensured that the replacement equipment was ordered with minimal or no disruption.
- Recognized with an Army Achievement Medal for positive attitude, dedication to getting the job done, meticulous attention to detail, and selfless service.

HOSTESS
Boulder Creek Steakhouse, Riverhead, New York (2003 – 2005)
Phil's Restaurant, Wading River, New York (2001 – 2003)

Greeted guests, directed them to their tables, and notified servers. Trained and mentored new servers. Collected payments, processed credit cards, and balanced the cash register. Interacted professionally with patrons to provide high-quality service.

- Gained a strong customer service orientation and quick decision-making skills.

EDUCATION

U.S. ARMY TRAINING
- US Bank Corporate Payment System (2007)
- DoD Government Purchase Card, Defense Acquisition University (2006)
- Unit Supply Enhanced Training, Property Book Unit Supply Enhancement (2006)
- Unit Supply Specialist Training School (7 weeks, 3 days, 2006)
- Basic Combat Training (9 weeks, 2005)

COMPUTERS
- Proficient in Windows, MS Word, Excel, Outlook, Internet Explorer, PBUSE, and ULLS-S4 automated supply program.

Cameron Lasater

IT Technician | Network Technician

1234 Yellowwood Drive
Colorado Springs, Colorado 80920
Cellular: (719) 555-1234
Email: clasater@protypeltd.com

SUMMARY OF QUALIFICATIONS

- Self-motivated computer technician with more than five years of experience maintaining and servicing computers, networks, and peripherals.
- Dependable and hard working; able to troubleshoot complex problems and solve them logically.
- Effective team player with exceptional communication and interpersonal skills.

TECHNICAL SKILLS

- CompTIA A+ Hardware/Software Certified IT Technician (2007 – present)—Personal Computer Components, Laptops and Portable Devices, Operating Systems, Printers and Scanners, Networks, Security, Safety and Environmental Issues, Professionalism and Communication.
- Personally built and sold computers for countless clients, ranging from professionals to hobbyists.
- Installed, configured, maintained, and diagnosed software and hardware for networks, workstations, PCs, and laptops.
- Identified and resolved internal system and network conflicts, including conflicts between applications, hardware, devices, and operation systems.
- Removed and replaced hardware components, installed interface cards, upgraded memory, fixed storage, power supplies, sound cards, and IO/enhancement cards. Configured interfaces and device drivers.
- Installed and configured workstation and network operating systems and applications software
- Configured Microsoft Outlook and managed personal folders.
- Partitioned hard drives, set up Windows 2000/XP, and backed up computers using network storage media, external hard drives and flash memory, and optical media (DVD/CD).
- Installed, configured and service computer peripherals, including printers, scanners, modems, external hard drives, and other devices.
- Proficient in Microsoft Office (Word, Excel, PowerPoint, Outlook, Internet Explorer), Exchange, Netscape.
- Extensive experience with Windows operating systems, especially 2000 and XP. Knowledge of Linux.

EXPERIENCE

COMPUTER TECHNICIAN / CONTRACTOR (2006 – present)
Precision Repair Works, Inc., Colorado Springs, Colorado
- Service, maintain, and upgrade client computers, networks, and peripherals.
- Evaluate client problems and tailor solutions to the unique needs of each client.
- Developed an Internet work solution combining shared network resources and a printer subsystem.

COMPUTER TECHNICIAN / CONTRACTOR (2005 – present)
Karl Scheer, Colorado Springs, Colorado
- Sold and maintained PCs for this long-time client.

EDUCATION AND TRAINING

UNDERGRADUATE COLLEGE STUDIES (2007 – present)
Colorado Technical College, Colorado Springs, Colorado
- Accepted into their IT program.

HIGH SCHOOL DIPLOMA
Liberty High School, Colorado Springs, Colorado
- Completed two years of Cisco Network Academy course work (Levels 1, 2, 3, 4).
- President of the Gamers Club (Second Term 2006).
- Completed Level I and II Information Technology courses.
- Member of DECA Business Marketing Education Club (2004 – 2006).

Arial, Swiss, Helvetica Font

Gloria B. Swan

PROFILE

- *Experienced, hard-working flight attendant with a great customer service attitude.*
- *Able to foster cooperative relationships and generate enthusiasm.*
- *Skilled in taking the initiative—self-confident and conscientious.*
- *Traveled extensively in the United States, Hawaii, Mexico, and Europe.*

RELEVANT EXPERIENCE

FLIGHT ATTENDANT
Sky West Airlines, *Colorado Springs, Colorado (2009 – present)*
Virgin America Airlines, *San Francisco, California (2007)*
Frontier Airlines, *Denver, Colorado (1998 – 2007)*
Western Pacific Airlines, *Colorado Springs, Colorado (1997 – 1998)*
- *Provided top-of-the-line service to airline customers during flights.*
- *Assured the safety and comfort of passengers on domestic and international flights.*
- *Greeted passengers, verified tickets, recorded destinations, and directed passengers to their assigned seats.*
- *Explained the use of safety equipment, served meals and beverages, and performed other personal services.*
- *Evaluated passengers for those who might pose a possible security risk, and ensured the safety of the flight deck and pilots.*
- *Interviewed candidates for flight attendant positions and made hiring recommendations.*
- *Certified for CPR, first aid, automated external defibrillator, water ditching, and self-defense.*

FOOD AND COCKTAIL SERVER
Red Hawk Casino, *Placerville, California (2008 – 2009)*
Sizzler's Steakhouse, *Sacramento, California* | **Sheraton Maui,** *Hawaii (2007)*
Maggie Mae's Restaurant | **McKay's Restaurant**, *Colorado Springs, Colorado (1994 – 1997)*
- *Provided high-quality customer service in family-style restaurants.*
- *Awarded Employee of the Month at Red Hawk Casino for top-quality services and high performance ratings.*

PROFESSIONAL DEVELOPMENT

FLIGHT ATTENDANT TRAINING
Sky West Airlines, *Salt Lake City, Utah (2009)*
Virgin America Airlines, *San Francisco, California (2008)*
Frontier Airlines, *Denver, Colorado (1998)*
Western Pacific Airlines, *Colorado Springs, Colorado (1997)*
- *Completed three and a half weeks of intensive flight attendant training with each airline.*

GROUP EXERCISE LEADER BASIC TRAINING COURSE, *St. Louis, Missouri (1987, 1990)*

OTHER EXPERIENCE

STAFF ASSISTANT, DRUG COMMISSION OFFICER
United States Anti-Doping Agency, *Colorado Springs, Colorado (2000 – 2002)*
United States Olympic Committee, *Colorado Springs, Colorado (1997 – 2000)*
- *Assisted drug commission officers in the collection of samples to test for performance-enhancing substances in athletes who compete in Olympic, Paralympic, and Pan American games and/or train in the United States.*
- *Traveled throughout the U.S. to conduct doping controls both in competition and out of competition without notice.*

PHYSICAL AND HEALTH TRAINER
Straub Clinic and Hospital, Inc., *Wahiawa, Hawaii (1991 – 1993)*
Darmstadt Military Community, *Darmstadt, Germany (1987 – 1990)*
- *Taught aerobics and helped people to reach their health and fitness goals.*

1234 Ainakoa Avenue • Honolulu, Hawaii 96821 • gbswan@protypeltd.com • (720) 123-4567

JOHN K. BRYSON

1234 North Meade Avenue • Colorado Springs, Colorado 80907
Cellular: (719) 555-5555
Email: jbryson@protypeltd.com

SUMMARY OF QUALIFICATIONS

- Proven field experience in the framing to finish phases of residential home construction.
- Strong customer service skills in homeowner, contractor, manufacturer/supplier relationships.
- Qualified to market and sell a wide range of construction services and products.
- Experienced in bidding, permits, and quality control functions.
- Able to coordinate multiple projects with various time schedule constraints.
- Proven ability to adapt quickly to challenges and changing environments.
- Equally productive in individual or team environments.

Helvetica Condensed Font

EXPERIENCE

OWNER OPERATOR (January 2000 – present)
Vision Builders, Colorado Springs, Colorado
- Own and manage a construction company specializing in cabinetry and interior trim but also performing remodels, additions, siding/exterior trim, and window projects.
- Accountable for all business development and client retention services.
- Significant administrative and financial responsibilities.
- Always the final source for customer service satisfaction and problem resolution.

LEAD INSTALLER (August 1988 – November 2000)
The Cabinet Works, Colorado Springs, Colorado
- Interfaced with kitchen designers/store coordinators to complete cabinet installation projects.
- Responsible for cabinet inspection, site preparation, installation, customer approval, and sign-off.
- Trained and coordinated additional installers as scope of projects required.
- Communicated with business owners on the progress of projects.

KITCHEN DESIGNER (April 1997 – July 1998)
The Home Depot, Colorado Springs, Colorado
- Qualified customer projects in design, cabinet/countertop features, installation costs, and process.
- Coordinated project services with installation crews.
- Produced CAD 20/20 design drawings and specifications.
- Conducted site visits to verify project details and conditions.

OWNER/OPERATOR (March 1989 – April 1997)
Dovetail Custom Woodworking, Colorado Springs, Colorado
- Produced residential kitchen cabinets and various built-in systems.
- Managed procurement, receipt, storage, and distribution of materials and products.
- Responsible for daily operations management and customer service functions.

CARPENTER (June 1986 – February 1998)
Canaan Company/Nick Edelen Construction Company, Colorado Springs, Colorado
- Produced frame siding/exterior trim, window, and exterior door phases of residential structures.
- Developed blueprint reading skills.
- Served as crew leader on various projects.

EDUCATION

ASSOCIATE APPLIED SCIENCE, ELECTRONICS (1986)
Aims Community College, Greeley, Colorado
Major in Electronics Technology

Lance Smith

1234 Main Street ◆ Bozeman, Montana 59801 ◆ 406.555.1234 ◆ lance.smith@protypeltd.com ◆ www.facebook.com/lsmith

Electrical Telecommunications Engineer
B.S., Electrical Engineering, GPA 3.87/4.0
Montana State University, Bozeman, Montana, May 2009

Arial Narrow Font

Detail-oriented engineer specializing in microwave circuits and wireless and fiber-optic communications system design. Experienced in software conversion, application support, and troubleshooting in high-profile, multilingual environment. U.S. citizen fluent in Mandarin Chinese and Japanese complemented by conversational French. Member, Institute of Electrical and Electronics Engineers and Tau Beta Pi National Engineering Honor Society.

Core Competencies

- EIT Certification
- Laser Design Principles
- Project Cost Evaluation
- C Programming Language
- Digital Logic Circuit Design
- Technical Training Translation
- Electrical Schematic Design
- Spectrum Analyzer Operation
- Second Order Circuit Analysis
- Signal and System Analysis
- Planar Microwave Circuit Design
- Wireless Communication Code
- Vector Network Analyzer Operation
- Printed Circuit Board Layout
- Research Engineering Citations

Technical Competencies

MATLAB	OrCAD	HFSS	ADS	SILEX
PSpice	AutoCAD	PADS	SPSS	Excel

Work Experience

Simulation Researcher, *ABC Company*, Missoula, Montana, June 2007–May 2009
Member of four-person team charged with researching, authoring, and implementing feasibility studies of emergent telecommunications technology employing existing satellite-to-earth systems.

- Devised communication systems for remote regions, modeling and simulating successful satellite-to-earth optical communication links.
- Coded simulation in MATLAB, modeled satellite-to-earth communication in SILEX Experiment, and performed acceptance testing, documenting results in 20-page report and PowerPoint presentation.
- Planned and executed successful simulated communication system functionality testing.

Design Research Assistant, *Montana State University*, Bozeman, Montana, Summer 2006
Assisted with National Science Foundation grant-funded project designing, testing, troubleshooting, and implementing wave-guided combiner / divider communications system.

- Designed waveguide-based power combiner / divider for 8 GHz to 12 GHz x-band frequencies, patch antennas, and matching waveguides using HFSS, ADS, and Smith Charts.
- Created, assembled, and tested 3D divider / combiner structure model for machining.

Training Coordinator (Intern), *Dell Corporation*, Dalian, China, Summer 2005
Provided technical training and product support for innovative products and services offered by industry leader in personal computers.

- Translated more than 200 training and product support documents from English to Mandarin Chinese.
- Orchestrated and executed group orientations and one-on-one training sessions in English and Mandarin Chinese for 120 new sales support managers and staff.
- Trained and prepared 20 technical support teams and 36 lead staff trainers in the Asia-Pacific region on new software features, functionality, and implementation.

MARY ANN ZIMMER

1234 Fremont Street
Pascagoula, Mississippi 39567

mazimmer@protypeltd.com

Home: (228) 555-1234
Cellular: (228) 123-5555

PROFILE

- Flexible, hard worker with a positive attitude and the desire to bring diverse inventory management skills to a materials handler position.
- Proven problem solver who enjoys new challenges and works well in fast-paced environments. Driven to achieve goals and objectives.
- Effective team player with strong communication and interpersonal skills.
- *"Give me something to do and I'll get it done!"* –Mary Ann Zimmer

EXPERIENCE

HOME DEPOT, Mobile, Alabama (1992 – present)
Sales Associate, Department Supervisor, Cashier
Rapidly promoted from part-time cashier to full-time sales associate and then to supervisor for the Plumbing and Kitchen Cabinet Departments. Certified in hazardous material disposal. Completed a week-long department supervisor training program.

- Supervised, trained, scheduled, and evaluated up to four associates at a time. Participated in interviews and made hiring recommendations.
- Ensured the delivery of exceptional customer service, and handled complaints and other problems.
- Drove sales by focusing on exceeding the sales plan for the department.
- Trained other associates in computer use, safe lifting and moving, and hazardous material handling.
- Helped to open three stores throughout the state. Remodeled an old store using a Planogram to organize merchandise in the Garden Center. Led a team of 20 associates to taking down the department and rebuilding it from the ground up.
- Managed stocking and ensured that the Pack-out Crews filled all holes and merchandised inventory properly.
- Served as backup to the Receiving Department supervisor. Received merchandise at the docks, entered each item into the computerized inventory tracking system, and then delivered it to the floor for stocking. Shipped merchandise using UPS and FedEx. Served as the first point of contact when inventory counts were off.
- Selected multiple times as Employee of the Month.
- Developed a reputation as a good employee who could be counted on to be there on time and to know the business.

EDUCATION

BACHELOR OF SCIENCE, EDUCATION (1990)
University of South Alabama, Mobile, Alabama

- Minor in Physical Therapy
- Dean's List, Who's Who in American Junior Colleges

Antique
Olive Font

GRADUATE STUDIES
University of South Alabama, Mobile, Alabama

- Completed 12 credits of graduate courses in education

COMPUTERS

Proficient in Windows, MS Word, Outlook, Internet Explorer, Adobe Acrobat, and Home Depot Inventory Management Software

VOLUNTEER

- Red Cross—Completed disaster training and served as an administrative volunteer for blood drives.
- Salvation Army—Coordinated clothing drives, helped with indigent care, and served as a bell ringer during the holidays.
- Habitat for Humanity—Participated in the 100 Days, 100 Homes Program following Hurricane Katrina.
- Boys and Girls Club—Helped to reconstruct their damaged community center.
- Food Bank—Volunteered to collect food and help organize the warehouse.

Scott T. Fitzpatrick

1234 Oak Hills Drive • Colorado Springs, Colorado 80919 • Email: stfitz@protypeltd.com
Cellular: (501) 555-1234 • Home: (719) 123-5555 • www.linkedin.com/in/stfitz/

PROFILE
- Entry-level graphic designer with a natural talent and passion for the industry.
- Adept at listening to the client and developing a concrete concept that is true to their ideas.
- Able to bounce ideas off others and take criticism without being overly sensitive.
- Effective team player with strong communication and interpersonal skills.

COMPUTER SKILLS
- Skilled in both Macintosh and Windows environments.
- Proficient in Adobe Illustrator, Photoshop, InDesign, Autodesk 3ds Max, GoLive design.
- Experience with MS Word, PowerPoint, Internet Explorer, and other business applications.

EDUCATION

BACHELOR OF SCIENCE, ART (Fall 2007)
Harding University, Searcy, Arkansas

> Avant Garde Font

- Completing last six credits this summer via distance learning.
- Studied for a semester abroad in Florence, Italy.
- Design: Advanced Graphic Design I/II, Graphic Design I/II, Visual Aesthetics, 2D Design, Computer Graphics Design, Multimedia Drawing, Human Anatomy and Design, Composition I/II.
- Physical Art: Painting I/II, Drawing and Composition, Photography, Printmaking I/II, Basic Type Design, Metal Work and Jewelry.
- Theory: History of Graphic Design, Color Theory, Art Survey: Ancient/Medieval, Art Survey: Renaissance/Present.

DESIGN EXPERIENCE

FREELANCE GRAPHIC DESIGNER (2004 – present)
- Designed a logo, letterhead, business cards, billboards, calling cards, direct mail pieces, and bulletins for a church branding project. Talked to the elders and tailored the concept based on the organization's culture and goals.
- Created a logo, display and shipping boxes, letterhead, and business cards for Custom Gems Colorado.

SCHOOL PROJECTS, Harding University, Searcy, Arkansas (1999 – 2007)
- Designed and produced an annual report for Rockwell Automotive, including concept development, paper selection, and binding options. Developed a new look for the letter to shareholders, financial statements, financial highlights, and new project descriptions.
- Developed the concept and design for a children's museum program, a joint project with interior design majors. Created a music program and tickets for the Sillie Strings Concert Hall.
- Developed the concept for and designed the Jake's BBQ Sauce logo and product labels.
- Designed a science poster using scripture and words reflecting Christian concepts in the shape of an aspen leaf.
- Developed a luxury soap and bath salts line, including logo, boxes, definition of ingredients, and labels with descriptions and bar codes.
- Completed a type project with a rock music poster reflecting a New York Times Square feel.

INTERNSHIP, Harding Press, Searcy, Arkansas (June – July 2005)
- Converted logos to various formats using Adobe Illustrator.
- Assembled books and printed materials; delivered finished products.

EXHIBITS
- Senior Art Show, Harding University Art Gallery (2006)
- Juried Competition, PUSH Conference, AIGA of Memphis (2005)

AFFILIATIONS
- Student Member of AIGA, Harding Chapter (2006 – present)
- Dallas Visual Community (DSVC) National Convention (2005 – 2006)—Lectures on design, 3D production films, and developing a company "look."

Jane M. Avalon

avalon@protypeltd.com

123 Mockingbird Lane, New York, NY 10112
718-555-5555 H / 888.944.0484 C

EXPERIENCED MERCHANDISING AND SALES PROFESSIONAL
Expert in contemporary and high fashion women's apparel and accessories

Creative and energetic professional offering more than 10 years of combined experience in the areas of fashion merchandising, account development, and customer service.

Summary of Qualifications

- ➢ **Fashion Professional:** Strong sense of fashion with a proven ability to combine color and style that excites customers and inspires repeat business. Skilled at creating a "buzz" and excitement around a new line, product, or venture.
- ➢ **Industry Expert:** More than eight years of experience in the areas of direct consumer sales and merchandising for new and expanding apparel retail operations.
- ➢ **Relationship Builder:** Excellent client relationship management skills. Able to instantly connect with consumers, distill value, overcome challenges, secure sales, and build/sustain a high client retention rate.
- ➢ **Leader:** Proven ability to drive consensus, motivate staff, clearly and concisely communicate directives, and work effectively with corporate and field leadership.
- ➢ **Core Competencies:** Visuals, styling, merchandising, in-store/field communications, strategy development, special event management, operations management, staff mentoring/training/supervision.

PROFESSIONAL EXPERIENCE

FASHION HOUSE, NEW YORK, NY   2007 – PRESENT
ASSISTANT MANAGER / KEY HOLDER / SALES ASSOCIATE

Deliver first-class customer service. Develop staff on successful selling techniques through coaching, mentoring, and training. Oversee store opening and closing operations for the Flagship store in SOHO.

- ➢ **Sales:** Within the first year on the job, secured personal sales in excess of $890,000 and by the second year $1.5MM. Consistently ranked among the top 1% of sale performers.
- ➢ **Client Relationship Development:** Responsible for driving the client experience by managing the generation of sales and supporting the GM in all sales floor operations. Developed a strong client referral rate and loyal base by providing quality image consulting and wardrobe redesign.
- ➢ **Branding:** Serve as a day-to-day driver of brand and sales strategies implementation. Constantly assess and adopt industry best practices. Leverage customer intelligence gained through the frontline touch-point level.
- ➢ **Visual Merchandising:** Work closely with the visual director, utilizing creativity coupled with strong business instinct to drive excitement about the brand while ensuring compliance within corporate branding philosophies and standards.
- ➢ **Leveraging Customer Feedback:** Consult with designers and buyers, provide key consumer and market based insight. Such insight has helped influence merchandise sold in the flagship store.

ACME RETAIL SOLUTIONS, NEW YORK, NY / TAMPA, FL   2004 – 2007
MERCHANDISE COORDINATOR

Traveled to retail apparel stores throughout assigned territories to develop merchandising strategies for each store based on consumer demographics, recent versus historical sales trends, and revenue targets. Trained in-store personnel on products and brands. Carried marquee brands, including Calvin Klein, Vintage Red, C&C California, Ralph Lauren, Levi & Strauss, Mavi Jeans, Court of Versailles, etc.

- ➢ **Visual Merchandising:** Elevated brand lifestyle through the visuals, styling, merchandising, and creative aspects of stores. Created displays (tables, mannequins and glass displays) for new products with consistent, high-impact presentations. Translated creative from an intangible thought to a tangible execution.
- ➢ **Report Management:** Maintained Excel spreadsheets with weekly reports and photos to build brand, drive sales, and track trends and profits.
- ➢ **Relationship Management:** Built relationships with management and brand specialist on the brand.
- ➢ **Trends Analysis:** Analyzed sale trends, identified brand items such as color, size and styles. Negotiated locations on selling floor to ensure key position for brand to drive sales.

EDUCATION

Bachelor of Science, Communications, 1996
University at Albany, Albany, NY

dara britton

555 Main Street, Moorestown, NJ 08002 ● (267) 555-1234 ● britton@protypeltd.com

Century
Gothic Font

marketing ▣ branding ▣ production

Offering creative approaches in rapid-paced, creative environments. Talent for innovative marketing and grassroots promotions that grow a brand. Passion for film production and the entertainment industry. Excel in technology, social media, and media writing. Multi-tasker who "juggles" well. Attended college full time while employed.

- ✓ Skyrocketed GeeWhiz visibility through guerrilla marketing and launched a subculture
- ✓ Broadcast writing skills with a fun attitude
- ✓ Production experience with new genre entertainment
- ✓ Online video content that gained a following

technical skills ▣ Microsoft Office—Word, Excel, Access, PowerPoint; Adobe CS3, FTP, Avid, Final Cut Pro HD, HD cameras, camera rigs and lighting kits; marketing through social media networks.

education

Bachelors Degree in Communications with focus on film and broadcast. Fine Arts Music minor, Trenton College
WXYZ – College Radio; produced a popular weekly radio show

career accomplishments

PROJECTS, PROFESSIONAL DEVELOPMENT (NY, PA) ▣ 2009–PRESENT

Project–Currently starting a going-green nonprofit. Handle budget and gain government funding. ▣ Founding Member / Board Member–scholarships and fund research at top name medical center via We Care foundation (since 2008) ▣ Coursework–University Alliance with Princeton ▣ Seasonal Work

TECHNICOM, CREATIVE COORDINATOR (PA) ▣ 2006–2008

Key Clients: Bank of America, Comcast, Barnes & Noble, Chrysler, Wall Street Journal, Fordham University, Verizon, Pharacia, H&R Block, Corning, Audi, Mercedes, PepsiCo. Developed polished, exciting marketing media for top-name clients, in collaboration with other departments. Participated in concept development and RFP responses. Managed media resources. Assisted with video shoots and postproduction. Researched vendors. Processed shipments. *Personally recruited by president.*

- Steered unique strategies for engaging clients in a competitive industry via extensive research.
- Selected as author of company start-up newsletter based on talent for creating client pitches.
- Generated new business summaries—company bragging rights with a "fun attitude"—that had high visibility.
- Created PowerPoint presentations, proposal and show books, dubs, show tapes, and DVDs. Maintain FTP site.
- Assisted with high-volume trade shows / event planning, including on-site event assistance.

GEEWHIZ, CAPTAIN TEAM WHIZ EAST COAST, TEAM CAPTAIN (PA) ▣ 2004–2007

Introduced diverse promotions of unique skate-shoe product. Created events with product demonstrations, lessons, and safety education. Rigorously tested and evaluated prototype products. Advised leaders on targeted niches.

- Produced and posted on the Internet an entertaining video displaying fun-loving, skillful sporting ability in Heely's skate-shoes. Subsequently selected to champion guerrilla marketing of the product.
- Launched a subculture and recruited team members with strong ability to perform the freestyle sport.
- Filmed team meetings and edited videos.
- Appeared on company website and in nationally broadcast commercials.

internships

FunTV, INTERN (NYC) ▣ 2004–2005

- Assisted in postproduction for *Wake Up,* a leader in the new genre of reality T.V. mixed with documentary. Compiled various elements required for production binders. Created dubs and logged and packaged episode tapes for shipment to the Discovery Channel.
- Assisted in production of a Discovery Channel program. Created prop inventories and contact /call sheets. Prepared set for shoots. Directed calls from production office. Served as prop runner.

FANCY PICTURES, INTERN (NYC) ▣ 2004 (ONE SEMESTER)

- Assisted in postproduction for National Geographic Special—dubs and complex patch-bay assemblies.

RONALD SMAALAND

1234 Bridgewater Drive ‣ Colorado Springs, Colorado 80916 ‣ (719) 555-1234 ‣ ron.smaal@protypeltd.com

SUMMARY

- Experienced facility manager who is willing to go the extra mile.
- Background in supervision, preventive maintenance, HVAC, electrical, plumbing, equipment repair, pool/sauna maintenance, kitchen equipment, and carpentry.
- Loyal team player with a strong commitment to providing exceptional guest service.
- Personable and self-motivated; able to relate well to both workers and management.

EXPERIENCE

MANAGEMENT and SUPERVISION

- Supervised all on-site maintenance operations for ten hotels in Colorado (McBride) and seven properties in four states (one office building and six hotels with a total of 1,000 rooms) (Hotel Management Systems).
- Supervised the maintenance of smaller hotels (200–250 rooms each) for eight years, including full-service restaurants, bars, and banquet rooms (8,000 sf).
- Proven track record of managing the maintenance of a large apartment complex for four years.
- Interviewed, hired, and supervised 25 maintenance technicians.
- Developed and implemented preventative maintenance programs that contributed to a significant reduction in equipment failures.
- Supervised grounds keeping and the maintenance of pools and saunas.
- Responsible for ensuring that apartment units, common areas, and grounds were properly maintained.
- Purchased and maintained a full inventory of tools, parts, and supplies.
- Created systems for monitoring and tracking service requests, preventive maintenance, safety and OSHA requirements, material safety data sheets (MSDS), inventories, and purchases.
- Developed and managed annual budgets up to $250,000.
- Worked closely with contractors in the supervision of renovations.

TECHNICAL and CONSTRUCTION

- Performed hands-on maintenance of HVAC, pools/saunas, electrical, plumbing, appliances, kitchen equipment, and other equipment for service requests and preventive maintenance.
- Licenses: HVAC Service Technician, Mechanic IV Gas Service Technician, Air Conditioning and Refrigeration Universal License.
- Experienced in the construction of building improvements and renovations.
- Oversaw carpet cleaning, linoleum replacement, painting, and interior repairs.
- Experienced in the installation of solar heat pumps and residential plumbing.
- Roughed in and wired government houses, including drywall, painting, and carpentry finish.

WORK HISTORY

Chief Engineer (2006 – 2009)
Embassy Suites, Colorado Springs, Colorado

District Maintenance Manager (2001 – 2006)
McBride Associates, Denver, Colorado

Corporate Facilities Manager (1997 – 2001)
Hotel Management Systems, Colorado Springs, Colorado

Facility Manager (1987 – 1997)
Le Baron Hotel, Quality Inn, and Balcor Property Management, Colorado Springs, Colorado

> **CG Omega or Optima Font**

EDUCATION

ASSOCIATE OF ARTS
Leeward Community College, Pearl City, Hawaii

AIR CONDITIONING AND REFRIGERATION CERTIFICATE
Ryder Technical Institute, Tampa, Florida

CONTINUING EDUCATION
- Refrigerant Recovery Universal Certification
- Certified Pool Technician
- Mechanic IV Gas Service Technician, Pikes Peak Regional Building Department
- Training in CPR and Sexual Harassment Prevention

LYNNETTE LAWRENCE

1234 Mandalay Grove • Colorado Springs, CO 80917
Home: (719) 555-4567 • Cellular: (719) 555-1234
Email: lclaw@protypeltd.com

SUMMARY

- Hard-working, energetic supervisor who takes pride in a job well done.
- Independent worker who takes the initiative and doesn't have to be told what to do.
- Effective team player with strong communication and customer service skills.
- Experienced Notary Public who pays close attention to detail.
- Knowledge of Windows, MS Word, Excel, Outlook, Internet Explorer, and QuickBooks.

EXPERIENCE

FRONT-END SUPERVISOR (2006 – 2010)
Hobby Lobby, Colorado Springs, Colorado
Managed front-of-the-house operations for this large store selling craft supplies, furniture, interior decor, fabric and sewing supplies, frames, art supplies, and seasonal merchandise. Supervised cashiers, customer service, returns, refunds, and over-rings. Balanced the registers at the end of each day. Managed the home accents and seasonal merchandise departments of the store with monthly display turnovers. Responsible for department planning, fixture setup, merchandising, display design, and inventory tracking. Supervised and evaluated the performance of up to 10 sales associates.
- Assisted customers with buying decisions when on the floor, using relationship-building skills and suggestive selling techniques to increase average sales.
- Consistently exceeded target goals for sales revenue in assigned departments.
- Provided value-added service to customers by meeting or exceeding their expectations.
- Coordinated cashiers to minimize the time customers had to wait in line.
- Trained staff to provide exceptional customer service with strong product knowledge and unparalleled service.
- Ensured that departments were clean and well organized to enhance the shopping experience.

CUSTOMER SERVICE REPRESENTATIVE (2006)
Flowers-Flower, Inc., Colorado Springs, Colorado
Took orders by phone and in person, which required exceptional customer service skills and personal contact with the public. Assisted customers who were under stress while preparing for weddings and funerals.
- Consistently increased sales by upselling orders with add-ons and more flowers.
- Developed a strong pattern of repeat sales and customer loyalty for the shop.
- Gained personal satisfaction from translating what customer's wanted into exceptional finished products.

CO-OWNER, MANAGER (1987 – 2005)
TGL Construction, Inc., Castle Rock, Colorado
Helped to develop and manage a construction company providing residential framing and trim services to major builders in the area. Sourced vendors, negotiated contracts, purchased supplies and equipment, ensured timely delivery of materials, and authorized payment of invoices. Pulled permits and coordinated inspections. Negotiated bids from subcontractors, ensured the quality of their work, and resolved problems. Accountable for business planning, profit and loss of operations, controlling costs, invoicing, record keeping, payroll, accounts payable, accounts receivable, collections, and monitoring financial performance. Interviewed, hired, supervised, evaluated, and counseled 15–20 construction workers. Developed and presented safety and quality meetings for supervisors and employees. Briefed visitors on site safety requirements to minimize risk.
- Consulted with clients regarding design modifications and change orders, ensuring customer satisfaction throughout the project life cycle.
- Coordinated deadlines for construction, ensuring on-time completion of projects.

CONTINUING EDUCATION

Professional development courses sponsored by Hobby Lobby, including:
- Customer Service
- OSHA Safety
- Supervision
- Inventory Management
- Ordering
- Merchandising

Humanist Font

BENJAMIN B. BATES

1234 Hazy Morning Drive ▪ Colorado Springs, Colorado 80925
Home: (719) 123-5555 ▪ bbbates@protypeltd.com ▪ www.facebook.com/bbbates

Myriad Pro Font

PROFILE
- Experienced computer operator with a background in secure communications.
- Detail-oriented professional dedicated to a quality product.
- Patient hard worker with the ability to train others effectively.
- Hold a current Secret security clearance (previously held a TS/SCI clearance).

COMPUTERS
- Hardware: IBM PCs, mainframe computers (IBM 4381, IBM ES-9000, IBM RISC 6000, Honeywell 6060, AST 220, UNISYS 2200/400, 1100/72, and MV 10000), Xerox 4050 Page Printer, Distributed Print Work Station, Air Force Automated Message Exchange System, and other peripherals.
- Software: Windows, MS Word, Outlook, Internet Explorer, WordPerfect, and Excel.

EXPERIENCE

COMPUTER OPERATOR III
Raytheon Corporation, Peterson AFB, Colorado, 2008 – present
Configure and operate mainframe computers, associated peripherals, ADPE, signal processing equipment, and communications equipment. Control output products from all computer suites and prepare monthly contract reports. Work in the magnetic media vault and perform other duties as assigned.
- Developed a reputation for not incurring a single security incident in more than ten years.

SHIFT SUPERVISOR
USAF Academy, Colorado Springs, Colorado, 2005 – 2006
Managed the base telecommunications center, servicing more than 100 customers, acting as Network Control Center operator, and performing quality assurance of input/output. Supervised, motivated, and evaluated ten communication-computer operators. Managed the COMSEC account and edited/delivered top secret messages. Accountable for equipment valued in the hundreds of thousands of dollars.
- Developed training standards, ensuring 100% of the operators were trained and qualified in base communications procedures.
- Coordinated communications and computer resources for a remote location with assigned equipment valued in the hundreds of thousands of dollars.
- Reduced annual operating budget by implementing new procedures and procuring new, more efficient communication equipment.

COMMUNICATIONS COMPUTER OPERATOR / COMPUTER OPERATION OFFICER
U.S. Air Force, 1983 – 2004
Managed the overall operations of the AFSPACECOM Telecommunications Center and ensured physical security. Managed message flow, precedence, classification, security, handling procedures, and priorities for each message level. Supervised encoding and decoding of messages to and from remote sites. Edited and delivered top secret messages. Managed the COMSEC account, ensuring that top secret cryptographic keying was loaded to the proper equipment at the right time. Monitored the communication systems, diagnosed problems, reset settings, and made minor mechanical adjustments to maintain and restore equipment operation. Performed backups and reconfigured the computers to operate on the backup systems. Prevented hard drive crashes by ensuring that contractors followed maintenance procedures.
- Trained, supervised, and evaluated as many as twenty personnel, significantly reducing the combined operator error rate by more than 25%.
- Coordinated the consolidation of telecommunication services for USSPACECOM and AFSPACECOM, including the installation of the message distribution terminal, software updates, and peripherals.
- Developed a system for transmitting and receiving messages on floppy disk, resulting in a 99% reduction in paper usage and a 20% decrease in center workload.
- Used knowledge of system control language and console command terms to direct work around troublesome equipment, and reconfigured the system to function with reduced resources.

EDUCATION
ASSOCIATE OF ARTS, GENERAL STUDIES (anticipate graduation before end of 2011)
Pikes Peak Community College, Colorado Springs, Colorado
Completed liberal arts studies, business, DOS, microcomputer applications, operating systems, databases, local area networks, computer information systems management, electronic spreadsheets, telecommunications, logic and program design, and COBOL programming, among others.

Esther Lee

12 Horatio Street #123 • New York, NY 10014
Home: (646) 555-1234 • Cell: (786) 555-1234
Email: estherlee@protypeltd.com

DYNAMIC ACCOUNT EXECUTIVE

KEY AREAS OF EXPERTISE

Sales and Marketing
Brand Management • Launches
Business Development
Public Relations • Promotions
Operations Management
Event Planning • Merchandising

QUALIFICATIONS SUMMARY

Creative account executive with the proven ability to develop and launch innovative and luxury products. Experienced at getting to decision-makers and negotiating deals. Demonstrated ability to create client loyalty above and beyond the sales relationship. Self-motivated and focused; comfortable working independently with little supervision. Team player with exceptional communication and interpersonal skills.

PROFESSIONAL EXPERIENCE

ACCOUNT EXECUTIVE / PARTNER (2004 – 2010)
Secrets of Charm, New York, NY
Co-founder of a successful women's contemporary clothing label. Part of the entire business development process from operations, shipping, accounting, staffing, product development, pricing, placement, sales, marketing, promotion, public relations, merchandising, and event planning (shopping events and fashion shows). Launched new products and developed markets with high-end boutiques throughout the U.S., Canada, and Japan. Met with buyers and traveled to evaluate new retail outlets. Created personal roadmaps to success and evaluated them monthly to gain momentum. Provided customer service to wholesale accounts.

- Grew the line to 50 specialty stores nationwide, with products available in Secrets of Charm showrooms in New York and Los Angeles, and on the corporate website (www.secretsofcharm.com).
- Built name recognition for the brand and developed a reputation for a beautiful blend of vintage, feminine pieces with a modern sensibility. Created pieces that were covetable and unique, yet still practical and wearable. The collection was a perfect marriage between the highest quality fabrications, exclusive prints (from Italy, Japan and Peru), and flawless fits.
- Maintained existing accounts and developed new customers by constantly building relationships.
- Increased annual revenue by a steady 20% in a challenging industry until the economy turned down in the past year.

SALES EXECUTIVE (2001 – 2004)
Barbara Bui Group, New York, NY
Sold Barbara Bui Group collections (Grande Ligne, initials, shoes, and handbags) and the Alain Tondowski shoe collection to wholesale accounts in Paris and New York. Planned and organized territories to increase market share and profitability. Managed new business development processes by compiling and mailing press kits, catalogs, and other promotional materials. Prepared for market by creating line sheets/sketches, mechandising the showroom, and hiring showroom models. Planned and executed trunk shows.

- Developed and managed 50 accounts, including responsibility for shipment of merchandise, customer returns, reorder processing, and accounts payable.
- Quickly grew the U.S. customer base by 50% per season, grossing $2 million per year.

SALES ASSISTANT (2000 – 2001)
Calvin Klein, New York, NY
Introduced the runway collection to buyers and coordinated the development of packages to best suit each retailer. Supported department store and national accounts by providing customer service and processing returns/exchanges. Processed bulk, trunk show, and celebrity orders. Created weekly comparison and sell-through reports.

EDUCATION

BACHELOR OF ARTS, International Business Administration (2000)
American University of Paris, France (1998 – 2000)
University of Miami, Florida (1996 – 1998)

SPECIAL SKILLS

Languages: Native in English, Conversational in French

Computers: Knowledge of Windows, Macintosh, MS Word, Excel, Outlook, Internet Explorer, Adobe Photoshop, InDesign, and Illustrator

ANNA WAREN

12345 Sparling Cresent, Bloomfield, MI 48388
333-222-1828 ▪ annawaren@protypeltd.com

HEALTHCARE ADMINISTRATOR

Trebuchet Font

EDUCATION

MASTERS, PUBLIC ADMINISTRATION
Current GPA 3.29
Oakland University
Auburn Hills, MI
2007-Present

BACHELOR, FAMILY COMMUNITY SERVICES EARLY CHILDHOOD EDUCATION ENDORSEMENT
Michigan State University
Lansing, MI
2002

RELEVANT COURSES

Healthcare Administration
▪
Healthcare Policies
▪
Quantitative Methods in Public Administration
▪
Human Resource Management in the Public Sector
▪
Public Sector Employee Relations
▪
Public Administration Theory
▪
Government Accounting
▪
Government Information Systems
▪
Public Budgeting

PROFILE

Accomplished, well-rounded college professional seeking an internship position in Healthcare Administration. Self-motivated, innovative, and hard-working individual. Dependable, with an ability to lead or be part of a team.

RELATED PROFESSIONAL EXPERIENCE

LAKELAND PHYSICIANS, WATERFORD, MI

Medical Receptionist   2006 – Present
- Learned the complexities of the health care system to effectively assist the patient population in understanding their benefits.
- Liaison between patients, doctors, insurance companies, and other healthcare associates.
- Coordinate patient care with other practices, hospitals, and insurance companies.
- Troubleshoot issues that arise with patients, doctors, hospitals, and other health organizations.
- Organize and manage patient confidential files.
- Maintain position while carrying full course load.

SLATER RESIDENCE, WEST BLOOMFIELD, MI

Nanny/Professional Child Care Provider   2003 – Present
- Manage care and happiness of two small children.
- Plan daily activities.

BETH EL NURSERY SCHOOL, BLOOMFIELD HILLS, MI

Administrative Assistant/Head Teacher   2002 – 2005
- Developed and planned curriculum themes and projects for teachers to utilize with students.
- Assisted director with daily operations.
- Prepared invoices, managed office, and phone lines.
- Fostered strong relationships with both parents and children.

COMPUTER SKILLS

Microsoft Word, Microsoft Excel, PowerPoint, Numbers, Keynote, CRT Medical Billing System

TERRY K. SMITH

1234 Ptarmigan Lane East ▪ **Colorado Springs, Colorado 80918** ▪ **Home: (719) 555-5555** ▪ **Cell: (719) 123-1234**

SUMMARY

- Experienced facility maintenance manager with the ability to coordinate multiple projects and meet deadlines under pressure.
- Background in supervision, preventive maintenance, HVAC, electrical, plumbing, equipment repair, landscaping, paving, and snow removal.
- Effective communicator who works well with people at all levels and roles.
- Self-motivated worker who can balance priorities for to reach goals.
- HVAC certified by the Environmental Protection Agency (EPA).

EXPERIENCE

GROUNDS AND NURSERY SUPERVISOR (2002 – present)
University of Colorado, Colorado Springs, Colorado
Supervised the maintenance and repair of more than 500 acres of grounds, streets, sidewalks, and parking lots during a period of rapid expansion. Interviewed, hired, trained, and evaluated a staff of four groundskeepers. Maintained Material Safety Data Sheets (MSDS) for hazardous products used in grounds maintenance. Monitored grounds inventory and purchased supplies and services; managed a budget of more than $470,000. Interviewed and negotiated with vendors and contractors.

- Implemented safety programs that resulted in no reportable incidents in nearly three years.
- Significantly improved the quality of landscaping through new plantings, consistent trimming, and irrigating that met strict water conservation codes.
- Evaluated training needs and developed training programs to improve the quality of work performed.
- Improved operational plans and maps of the campus, which made snow removal and ice control more consistent.
- Spearheaded the acquisition of a $10,000 piece of snow removal equipment and negotiated the cost down to $4,500.
- Increased the payback for recycling and advertised the locations of recycling bins throughout the campus, which expanded student and faculty use of the recycling program.
- Completed Rainbird-sponsored training in preparation for a complete overhaul of the campus irrigation system.

> *"Terry has an exceptional capability to provide outstanding customer satisfaction. He innately understands customer expectations and goes the extra mile to provide the kind of service they expect before even being asked."*
>
> *– Supervisor*

FACILITY MAINTENANCE TECHNICIAN / STRUCTURAL TRADES II (2000 – 2002)
Colorado School for the Deaf and the Blind, Colorado Springs, Colorado
Performed work in the construction, renovation, maintenance, repair, and alteration of campus structures, fixtures, and associated equipment. This includes using skills in carpentry, glazing, roofing, electrical, telephone wiring, tile, drywall, painting and finishing, locksmithing, and demolition, among others. Evaluated the requirements for each project, developed project schedules, estimated time and material requirements, and performed the required work.

- Earned a reputation for developing creative solutions to problems.
- Adapted quickly to challenges and changing work environments.
- Significantly improved the quality of the facilities with no safety violations.

MAINTENANCE SUPERVISOR (1993 – 2000)
Union Printers Homes, Colorado Springs, Colorado
Directed repairs to 110-year-old buildings, grounds, and sprinkler systems, maintaining the integrity of the historical structures and managing quality control. Troubleshot, tested, and repaired the fire alarm and fire sprinkler systems. Maintained the boiler and other HVAC equipment. Performed electrical, mechanical, carpentry, plumbing, welding, and other types of maintenance. Directly supervised, scheduled, trained, and motivated more than eight subordinates. Served as a member of the Safety, Infection Control, Quality Improvement, and Fire/Disaster Plans Committees.

LEAD TECHNICIAN (1988 – 1993)
City of Manitou Springs, Manitou Springs, Colorado
Supervised the maintenance of all grounds and buildings of the Park and Recreation Department, including eight parks, the City Hall, and Library building. Responsible for three employees performing lawn mowing, snow removal, sprinkler repairs, street and sidewalk maintenance, and general repairs.

TRAINING

TECHNICAL TRAINING PROGRAM (six months)
Wapaton State School of Science, Wapaton, North Dakota

Jason C. Butler

1234 Lakeview Circle
Canal Winchester, OH 43110

Cell: 614-555-6231
e-mail: jas.butler@protypeltd.com

Professional Profile

Skilled jewelry and watch repair professional with 18+ years of retail and trade experience encompassing small independent jewelry stores and large jewelry franchises. Offer technical training, hands-on experience, strong transferable experience, and a keen desire to reconnect with the industry and provide customers with exceptional service and quality products.

Verdana Font

Technical Expertise

- Gold soldering and stamping
- Machine engraving
- Metal work: gold, platinum, and silver
- Watch repair: mechanical and quartz, band repair, battery replacement
- Jewelry repair: ring sizing, chain repair, stone setting, re-pronging, replacing heads and shanks

Professional Experience

Kings Jewelers ▪ Greensboro, NC ▪ 2008 to 2010
An exclusive East Coast jewelry franchise with more than 100 store locations and a centrally located repair center.
Quartz Watch Repair Specialist: Repaired and replaced batteries on hundreds of quartz watches received from the various company retail stores.

Ross Jewelers/Carson Gemological Services ▪ Milton, PA and Hollidaysburg, PA ▪ 2006 to 2007
Small, independent jewelry stores that outsourced watch and jewelry repair.
Jewelry/ Watch Repair Tradesman: Built relationships with independent jewelry stores and provided various repair and maintenance services to help satisfy customer requests.

Littman Jewelers ▪ Brockway, PA ▪ 1989 to 2006
A small-town, family-owned and operated jewelry store providing full-service repair service and sales.
Jeweler/Watchmaker/Sales Associate: Developed broad scope of skills and experience in all aspects of retail operations with primary responsibility for cleaning and repairing customer watches and jewelry. Ordered, unpacked, and displayed merchandise. Assisted with routine store maintenance. Helped customers in making selections, and processed cash and credit card sales transactions.

Professional Training and Affiliations

- *Certificate of Completion*: Watch Making and Repairing, Jewelry Repairing, Stone Setting; *Bowman Technical School,* Lancaster, PA
- American Watch Maker's Institute Quartz Repair, *Watchmakers Association*
- Stone Setting, *Trenton Jewelry School*, Little Rock, AR
- *Former Member*: Keystone Watchmakers Guild, Watchmakers Association of Pennsylvania
- *Former Member*: Golden Triangle Watchmaker's Guild, Greensboro, NC

Transferable Skills and Experience

Roadway Express ▪ Winston-Salem, NC; Columbus, OH; Hagerstown, MD ▪ 2000 to Present
As driver and dockworker for this large trucking company, developed and consistently demonstrated the following value-added skills:

- ***Willingness to work non-traditional business hours:*** Currently work 12-hour shifts beginning at 8:30 in the evening, including some weekends and holidays.
- ***Ability to prioritize and effectively manage time in fast-paced environment***: Load and unload **freight received and shipped from any of the terminal's 100 docks with up to 600 load areas.**
- ***Perform precision work:*** Safely maneuver trucks to align and connect double trailers. Scan freight bar codes and follow bills of laden to ensure proper merchandise is delivered on time and damage free.
- ***Building and maintaining effective relationships with managers and peers***: Adapt well to diverse personalities, in both union and non-union work environments. Respond to challenges in a spirit of cooperation and teamwork.

Samantha Lang, CSW

12345 Second Street ❖ Baltimore, MD 21233
lang@protypeltd.com ❖ (410) 555-1234

PROFILE

Self-motivated and dependable Human Services Program Administrator with 17 years of experience providing leadership and support to a private non-profit social service agency, with 15 years as a program director. A creative problem solver and hard working contributor, respected by peers, community, and professional groups. Eager to accept new challenges. Extremely well organized, detail oriented, budget and deadline conscious in all reporting functions.

CAREER STRENGTHS

- ❖ Budgeting and fiscal record keeping
- ❖ Program planning and management
- ❖ Policy development/implementation
- ❖ Staff supervision and training
- ❖ State licensing compliance
- ❖ Contract administration

PROFESSIONAL EXPERIENCE

TRI-COUNTY YOUTH SERVICES, INC., BALTIMORE, MD, 2001–PRESENT

Program Director/Head Teacher (1998–Present)
RAINBOW KIDS DAY CARE CENTER, a state licensed program affiliated with the Baltimore Board of Education, providing full-time care for approximately 100 children in the city of Baltimore.

- ❖ Directed two programs for three- and four-year-olds, each with different licensing components, staffing, scheduling, curriculums, budgets, and record keeping accountabilities.
- ❖ Held fiscal responsibility for a yearly budget in excess of $1.2 million and all related reporting requirements.
- ❖ Administered components for three separate contracts and accounted for all funding sources from state and city subsidies and fund raising activities.
- ❖ Supervised and facilitated professional development of a multi-ethnic, multi-generational staff of 25 as well as oversaw activities of 5 volunteers.
- ❖ Upgraded and implemented administrative and staff procedures, including establishing linkages with community-based programs.
- ❖ Played a key role in securing state recognition of Rainbow Kids Day Care Center as a model program in providing quality child care.
- ❖ In earlier position as Director of Child Care Food Program (2001–2005), worked closely with the State of Maryland to reorganize the Child and Adult Nutrition Program.

EDUCATION AND CREDENTIALS

MARYLAND STATE UNIVERSITY, BALTIMORE, MD
M.A. Social Work, *summa cum laude*, 2003
Graduate Assistant, Office of Public Relations, 2000–2002
B.A. English, *magna cum laude*, 1997
Minor in Art Education

STATE OF MARYLAND CERTIFIED SOCIAL WORKER

MICRO TRAINING TECHNOLOGIES, BALTIMORE, MD
Basic skills course in Windows and MS Office applications, 2000

> Wiessach Font

"... Samantha has served in various positions in the agency, and in each area she provided insight, cost-effective management techniques, advocacy for her staff and her clients, and has developed innovative systems to ensure timely accountability, record keeping, and program evaluation ... received many verbal commendations from the State of Maryland specialists with whom she interacts ... elicited the cooperation of a multi-cultural staff of child care providers ... contributed much to the agency." — Gilbert Craswell
Executive Director

"... Samantha assumed responsibility of this [Children's Nutrition] Program when it was in dire need of organization and sound administration. It is now one of the best programs with a strong reputation in the community for providing quality services. Samantha's ability to manage this multi-faceted program and its staff is strong evidence of her dedication not only to the organization but also to the many families served by the agency." — Odette Martin
Grants Program Administrator

"... Ms. Lang continues to provide quality leadership in her area of responsibility ... made significant improvements in maintaining budget within projected estimates ... was instrumental in getting Rainbow Kids Day Care recognized as a model program in providing quality child care." — Roberta Benito,
Former Executive Director

" Samantha Lang is a person who sets high standards and encourages the staff she supervises to follow her lead. Her commitment to serve the CPS clients is exemplary." — Anita Rubinstein
Contract Administrator
MD Children's Protection Services

DENA S. LAWRENCE

Post Office Box 1234
Cascade, CO 80809

E-mail: dena.n2travel@protypeltd.com

Fax: (719) 555-1234
Cell: (719) 555-5678

OBJECTIVE

- A position as a Tour Manager that would integrate customer service experience, travel knowledge, and outdoor skills.

STRENGTHS

- Certified International Tour Manager with a passion for protecting nature and respecting other cultures.
- Enthusiastic team player with effective research, communication, and interpersonal skills.
- Effective problem solver who adapts quickly to new situations and loves a challenge.

OUTDOOR ADVENTURE EXPERIENCE

- **Outdoor Interests:** Hiking, Ice Climbing, Dragon Boating.
- **Related Skills:** Wilderness First Aid, CPR, Map and Compass Reading.
- **Mountain Treks and Climbs:** Exploradores Glacier and Torres del Paine (Patagonia, 2007), Everest Base Camp (Nepal, 2006), Mt. Adams (Washington, 2006), Tour du Mont Blanc (Switzerland, France, and Italy, 2005), Primavera Valley (Mexico, 2005), Mt. Kilimanjaro (Tanzania, 2004), Mt. Baker (Washington, 2004).

TRAVEL EXPERIENCE

- Traveled to 30 plus countries on six continents, including Croatia, Germany, Belgium, Austria, U.K., Ireland, Netherlands, Portugal, Spain, Morocco, Kenya, Canada, Peru, Brazil, Paraguay, Uruguay, and Colombia, among many others (see also Mountain Treks and Climbs).
- Visited 42 states in the United States.
- Acquired insight and knowledge into the history, geography, and culture of areas visited.
- Developed strong cross-cultural communication skills—able to adjust quickly to different cultures and ways of thinking.
- Languages: Native English speaker; working knowledge of Spanish.

> Franklin Gothic Font

EDUCATION & TRAINING

INTERNATIONAL TOUR MANAGER CERTIFICATION (2006)
International Guide Academy, Denver, Colorado
Relevant course work:
- Professional Conduct and Ethics, Professional Image of a Tour Manager.
- Airline/Airport Procedures, International Arrivals, Reconfirmations, Cancellations, Rerouting.
- Hotel Procedures, Logistics, Luggage Supervision, Room Problems, Group Departures.
- Public Speaking Techniques, Tour Welcome Presentation, Motorcoach Commentary.
- Cultural Practices and Differences, The Tour Manager as a Cultural Ambassador.
- Motorcoach Travel, Teamwork with Driver, Microphone Training, Tipping Practices.
- Safety Issues, Client Emergencies, Group Psychology and Behavioral Warning Signals.

VIDEO PRODUCTION, The Art Institute of Colorado, Denver (2002 – 2003)

DOCUMENTARY PRODUCTION CERTIFICATE, University of Washington, Seattle (2001)

BACHELOR OF ARTS, ENGLISH, The University of Houston, Texas (1978)

WORK HISTORY

PARTNER, Sky Lines, Houston, Texas, and Olympia, Washington (10 years)

SUPERVISOR, IN-FLIGHT SERVICE / RESERVATION SALES AGENT
Continental Airlines, Houston, Texas (14 years)

IN-FLIGHT HOSTESS / RESERVATION SALES AGENT
American Airlines, Chicago, Illinois (8 years)

VOLUNTEER EXPERIENCE

Benevolence: Houston Hospice (3 years), My Sister's House (2 years).
Fund-raising: Chris Hooyman Outdoor Education Fund (1 year), Team Survivor Northwest (2 years).
Leadership: American Airlines Kiwi Club (20 years, President 3 years), Girl Scout Leader (2 years).

Graphic Lines

All of the résumés in this book were typeset using common word processing software (MS Word and Corel WordPerfect). That means you can reproduce everything you see in these pages, including the graphic lines. These lines can be either horizontal, vertical, or full-page borders.

Lines at the top of the résumé can be used to create a letterhead that sets the name and address section apart from the text so the reader's eyes can be drawn to the most important information first.

Horizontal lines between sections allow the reader to focus on each section separately and draw the eye from section to section, especially when there is little room for extra white space (which can serve the same purpose). The creative use of horizontal or vertical lines adds pizzazz to the design of a résumé without appearing too overdone. Résumés created with such lines can be used in all but the most conservative of industries.

It is important, however, to avoid the use of too many lines with different thicknesses on the same page. The résumé can get "busy," which makes the reader work too hard. It is a good idea to use no more than two line widths per résumé. For instance:

This line is .02 inch thick.

And this one is .005 inch thick.

You might combine the two together.

The samples that follow will give you some ideas for ways to use lines in a résumé. There are lines on almost every résumé in this book, so look at other pages for even more unique ideas.

Karen M. Manross

1234 Privet Place
San Antonio, Texas 78259
Cellular: (210) 555-1234
Email:kmanross@protypeltd.com

STRENGTHS

- Results-driven leader with an entrepreneurial spirit and extensive leadership experience.
- Adept at approaching challenges with uncommon professional balance and maturity.
- Knowledgeable, persuasive sales executive with a strong service orientation and a real sense of pride when pleasing customers.
- Effective problem-solver who thrives in fast-paced environments and maintains grace under pressure.
- Proven team leader with exceptional communication, interpersonal, and analytical skills.

AREAS OF EXPERTISE

- Operations management
- Supervision and mentoring
- Profit and loss accountability
- Marketing and sales
- Budgeting
- Accounts receivable/payable
- Customer service
- Inventory management
- Purchasing

EDUCATION & TRAINING

BACHELOR OF BUSINESS ADMINISTRATION (2007)
University of the Incarnate Word, San Antonio, Texas

- Concentration in Management, Dean's List
- Relevant course work:
  - Integrated Business Analysis I/II
  - Organizational Change and Development
  - Entrepreneurship/Small Business Management
  - Organizational Behavior and Leadership
  - Analytical Decision Making/Business I/II/III
  - International Business Management
  - Management Theory and Practice
  - Principles of Financial Management
  - Human Resource Management
  - Personal Productivity
  - Business Law
  - Principles of Marketing
  - Project Management
  - Management Skills
  - Introduction to Information Systems
  - Microeconomics
  - Macroeconomics
  - Principles of Accounting I/II

RELEVANT EXPERIENCE

SALES MANAGER (2001–present), **SALES REPRESENTATIVE** (2000–2001)
T-Mobile USA, San Antonio, Texas
Manage the merchandising and sale of T-Mobile's line of cutting-edge telecommunications products and services in a retail environment. Translate high-level, corporate marketing strategies into day-to-day actions. Accountable for full profit and loss of operations. Plan and implement local events and promotions. Manage all operations and human resource functions. Drive the store team to achieve sales goals for the region and to celebrate team successes. Recruit, screen, hire, train, and schedule staff. Coach five sales representatives on the latest, most-successful sales techniques, customer service skills, and product knowledge. Greet customers, listen carefully and actively, and match their needs with the right combination of products and services. Reconcile all daily register summary reports and point-of-sale transactions. Manage cash-handling procedures and make daily deposits. Oversee physical inventory levels and minimize shrinkage. Audit daily reports to ensure compliance with policies and procedures. Assist other locations with audit compliance.

- Consistently met or exceeded monthly sales goals and met controllable expense goals.
- Built long-term relationships that ensured customer retention and return sales, with some customers following moves from one store to another in order to maintain a personal relationship.

Continued ...

RELEVANT EXPERIENCE

Sales Manager (continued)
* Demonstrated superior performance in the areas of net activations, earned revenue, cost per gross add, and revenue per subscriber.
* Won frequent vendor sales contests. Recognized in the San Antonio market for:
  – Highest customer service for the second quarter of 2007.
  – Highest percent to quota for the second quarter of 2007.
  – Top accessories sales for the third quarter of 2004.
* Selected to open a new location and managed four different stores. Turned around an underperforming Austin store, increasing new customers from 100 to 225 in only eight months through increased brand awareness in the market.
* Maintained performance scorecards to track operational compliance, team dynamics, store appearance, customer satisfaction, and a rolling list of improvement areas.
* Inspired employees to be passionate about customer satisfaction. Mentored three staff members to management positions, including a regional manager position.
* Personally handled all escalated customer service issues, tactfully resolving them as quickly as possible while remaining polite.
* Attended annual summits / business reviews to evaluate industry best practices and benchmarks.

ASSISTANT MANAGER (1995–2000)
River City Gymnastics, San Antonio, Texas
Managed sales and customer service for a gymnastics business with 600 active students. Accountable for $300,000+ of fitness equipment. Hired, trained, and supervised eight staff members. Accountable for full profit and loss of operations, including budgeting, billing, accounts receivable, collections, record keeping, and purchasing. Answered telephones and handled member and new customer inquiries. Assigned new students to age-appropriate classes, ensuring correct teacher-student ratios. Helped schedule, plan, and organize gymnastic and cheerleading competitions.
* Organized competitions, and selected and ordered uniforms.
* Part of a national cheerleading team that traveled throughout the country to teach summer cheerleading camps.
* Professionally coached both competitive cheerleading and gymnastics teams.
* Brought skills gained in many years as a gymnast and cheerleader to train students for competitions.

UNDERWRITER (1996)
Safeway Managing General Agency, San Antonio, Texas
Helped to fund college education by determining eligibility for and processing auto insurance applications.

COMPUTER SKILLS

Proficient in Windows, MS Word, Excel, PowerPoint, Outlook, Internet Explorer, SAP, Point-of-Sale Systems, Customer Account Management System, Watson, QuickView.

Travis Herrera

1234 Raindrop Circle South • Colorado Springs, Colorado 80917
Home: (719) 555-1234 • Cell: (719) 123-5555
Email: travherrera@protypeltd.com

PROFILE

- Experienced maintenance technician with a broad background in both general construction and specialty HVAC contracting.
- Dependable, loyal worker who can fix just about anything and learns quickly.
- Flexible professional who can improvise when needed and believes there is usually more than one way to do something.
- Personable and courteous; proven track record of exceptional customer service; skilled at conflict resolution and problem solving.

CERTIFICATIONS

- EPA Universal Certification, ESCO Institute (2007 – present)
- Mechanic 4, HVAC Service Technician, El Paso County Building Department (2007 – present)
- HVAC Certification, Electrical Portion, HVAC Excellence (2007 – present)
- Top Secret security clearance with access to Sensitive Compartmented Information (SCI)

TECHNICAL TRAINING

HVAC CERTIFICATE, IntelliTec College, Colorado Springs, Colorado (September 2007)
Associate of Occupational Studies, HVAC / Refrigeration

- Advanced Refrigeration
- Basic Refrigeration
- Domestic Refrigeration
- Blueprint Reading
- Gas Heating and Licensing
- Alternative Heating
- Air Conditioning / HVAC
- Fundamentals of Electronics
- Electrical Controls
- Advanced Controls
- Specialized Commercial Applications
- Personal Communications

MARINE CORP INSTITUTE

- Interior Wiring
- Basic Shop Mechanics
- Sheet Metal Forming
- Construction Planning
- Metal Working / Welding
- Arc and Gas Welding
- Hand Tool Usage and Safety
- Mechanical Equipment
- Fundamentals of Refrigeration
- Interior Wiring / Electrical Installation
- Construction Blueprint Reading
- Safety and Quality Control

EXPERIENCE

CARPENTER, John Bowman, Inc., Colorado Springs, Colorado (2007 – present)

- Part of the labor team responsible for construction of commercial buildings from the foundation to the roof—use expertise in framing, drywall, painting, and interior finishing.
- Ensure that all work is in compliance with local codes and ready for inspection.
- Participated on fast-track commercial contracts, including remodeling of the U.S. Air Force Academy hospital dining facility.
- Built barriers, entrances, and a guard shack as part of an anti-terrorism project at the main gate of the U.S. Air Force Academy.

PARTNER, Pinnacle Home Inspections, LLC, Colorado Springs, Colorado (2006 – 2007)

- Formed a business providing residential inspection services to home buyers on the Front Range.
- Built profitable relationships with mortgage companies and real estate agents who referred their clients.
- Accountable for business planning, marketing, customer service, and full profit and loss of the operation.
- Inspected the structural integrity and safety of single-family homes.
- Searched for hidden damage and problems with HVAC systems, roof, foundation, electrical wiring, plumbing, and other home systems.

HVAC TECHNICIAN, Joseph Refrigeration, Colorado Springs, Colorado (2006)
- Worked on the installation, preventive maintenance, and repair of HVAC systems for light commercial and residential projects.
- Inspected HVAC systems, restaurant equipment, and appliances as part of preventive maintenance contracts.
- Installed and serviced heating and air conditioning systems in new homes and remodels.

MILITARY EXPERIENCE

PRESIDENTIAL SUPPORT SPECIALIST, Active Duty Marine Corps, Quantico, Virginia (2002 – 2006)
- Provided physical and personal security for the Presidential helicopter carrying the President, First Lady, First Family, Cabinet members, and heads of state.
- Trained, supervised, mentored, counseled, and disciplined 12–20 Marines. Wrote monthly performance evaluations.
- Conducted inspections and vehicle/personal searches, made perimeter rounds, and ensured the safety of helicopters, facilities, and personnel.
- Awarded the Presidential Service Badge and Certificate in recognition of service to the President of the United States (2004).

EDUCATION

ASSOCIATE OF SCIENCE, SOCIAL PSYCHOLOGY (in process)
Park University, Parkville, Missouri
- Completed all but the final six credits toward an undergraduate degree.

MILITARY POLICE BASIC COURSE (2002)
- Recognized as an Academic Honor Graduate for academic and leadership achievements while undergoing an intense and demanding program of instruction.
- Received a meritorious promotion based on class ranking—promoted to E-5 in only four years when most Marines only reach E-3.

COMPUTERS

Proficient in Windows, MS Word, Excel, PowerPoint, email, and Internet research (use the Internet to find parts and accessories).

BACKGROUND

If there is a hand or power tool, I've had my hands on it. My grandfather was a carpenter for more than 30 years, and I worked by his side as a boy, learning every aspect of construction. Recently, I remodeled the entire upstairs of my home, combining two bedrooms into a master suite with office and walk-in closet. Now, I'm preparing to remodel the bathroom.

Bart N. Azar

1234 South Center Drive
Dexter, Michigan
Mobile: (734) 555-1234
Email: bnazar@protypeltd.com

*"My success has been achieved through the
successful integration of diverse people
into a team that uses their individual gifts
and talents for the good of the vision and
mission of the organization."* – Bart N. Azar

**EXECUTIVE
SUMMARY**

→ More than 18 years of innovative *nonprofit leadership* and *fund development* experience
with a proven track record of success that consistently exceeds expectations.
→ Accomplished, dynamic communicator who speaks to thousands of people throughout the
year, presenting at seminars, symposiums, and lectures.
→ Visionary leader with exceptional team-building skills—able to develop relationships with a
myriad of organizations while bringing together like-minded groups to form productive coalitions.

**AREAS OF
EXPERTISE**

→ Leadership	→ Needs analysis	→ Public relations
→ Staffing and training	→ Fund-raising	→ Brand management
→ Organizational development	→ Partnership development	→ Rebranding
→ Budgeting, resource allocation	→ Planned giving	→ Change management

**PROFESSIONAL
EXPERIENCE**

FOUNDATION DIRECTOR (2003 – present)
Education Foundation, Society of Manufacturing Engineers, Dearborn, Michigan
Direct the operations of a 27-year-old nonprofit foundation reporting to the board of directors
of one of the country's oldest engineering societies. Hired to revitalize the foundation and change
its direction from college and university grants to educational programs for youth (K–12). Create
new operating policies and procedures, hiring processes, and budgets based on accurate forecasts. Recruit, train, and remotely supervise three managers and three support staff, most of
which are based in other states.

Program Growth:
→ Developed and implemented a national youth program that has grown from 5 pilot sites in
2004 to more than 180 sites in 27 states during 2008, offering engineering education programs
and scholarships to middle school students.
→ Added eight new manufacturing education programs for grade/high school students in 2008.
→ Secured more than $1.5 million in donations to help grow K–12 education-related programs.
→ Built the foundation's endowment from $18 million to $28 million, and grew annual fund
income from $550,000 in 2003 to $1.8 million in 2007 when the goal was $1.0 million.
→ Recently solicited $34 million in software from Siemens Corporation to distribute to schools
nationwide, as well as a $160,000 gift from Haas Automation to establish a scholarship for
machining technology.

Organizational Development:
→ Mentored the staff to become more productive and created a team learning culture that
enables delegation with complete confidence, allowing time for extensive strategic travel to
build foundation relationships.
→ Created a nimble, cutting-edge organization that adapts quickly to changing market needs.
→ Hired a PR firm to increase visibility of the brand. Directed the development of new Web sites
and videos. Used an in-depth understanding of national and local market advances/ needs to
rebrand the foundation.
→ Partnered with the parent Society, involving their members in programs, combining resources,
and improving communication between the two boards.
→ Developed partnerships with government entities, academic organizations, corporations, and
other foundations across the country.
→ Used letters of endorsement from other societies to gain entrance to premier organizations,
like the National Defense Industries Association, National Association of Manufacturing, and
Society of Automotive Engineers.

ASSOCIATE VICE PRESIDENT (1999 – 2003)
Foundation at New Jersey Institute of Technology, Newark, New Jersey
Solicited major and planned gifts for the six college campuses of New Jersey Institute through
a 501(c)(3) nonprofit foundation with the goal of improving architectural and engineering ...

PROFESSIONAL EXPERIENCE

Foundation at New Jersey Institute of Technology (continued)
… education through scholarships, better equipment, and endowed chairs. Charged with the task of jump starting a dormant planned-giving program. Served on several foundation board committees as well as some university-related committees. Supervised and evaluated the performance of seven staff members.

- Collaborated with the university president and college deans to cultivate relationships with major donors; made 202 donor visits per year, securing $15 million in gifts.
- Revamped the planned giving program, increasing the charitable gift annuity pool by 105% while securing the two largest charitable gift annuities in the history of NJIT.
- Secured 33 new bequests for the university that totaled more than $13 million.
- Led a $20 million capital campaign for the university's Honors College; solicited $22.25 million to close the campaign nine months before it was scheduled to end.

ASSISTANT VICE PRESIDENT (1996 – 1999)
Saint Peter's College, Jersey City, New Jersey
Recruited to reorganize the Department of Institutional Advancement (DIA) by integrating the Alumni, Fund Development, and Public Relations Departments into the DIA. Led a $50 million capital campaign. Traveled nationwide to institute alumni clubs and recruit members.

- Formed seven alumni clubs and increased attendance at the annual alumni reunion by 22%.
- Solicited $9+ million in bequests and $2.75 in charitable gift annuities in the first year.
- Served as interim vice president twice during three years when the position was vacated.
- Took over the capital campaign, keeping it on track and increasing donations.

SENIOR DEVELOPMENT OFFICER, MAJOR AND PLANNED GIFTS (1993 – 1996)
The Seeing Eye, Morristown, New Jersey
Managed the donor acquisition and national planned giving programs for this nonprofit organization providing trained dogs for the blind. Developed and implemented four direct mail campaigns per year. Supervised and evaluated the performance of four support staff.

- Generated more than $15 million annually—$8 million in bequests, $5 million in charitable remainder trusts, and $2 million in charitable gift annuities.
- Personally solicited a $6 million gift to the organization.
- Originally hired to manage the annual fund drive, donor acquisition program, and grant program. Increased annual fund gifts by 33% and grant income by 27% before being promoted.

EDUCATION

PROFESSIONAL CERTIFICATE, MANAGEMENT AND LEADERSHIP (2008)
University of Notre Dame, Mendoza College of Business, South Bend, Indiana

MASTER OF DIVINITY (1988)
Mount Saint Mary's University, Emmitsburg, Maryland

BACHELOR OF ARTS, PHILOSOPHY (1985)
Mount Saint Mary's University, Emmitsburg, Maryland

PROFESSIONAL DEVELOPMENT
- Dedicated to continuing personal and professional growth.
- Continuously upgrade skills through reading, seminars, and continuing education.

AFFILIATIONS

- Association of Fund-Raising Professionals (1998 – present)
- American Society of Association Executives (2003 – present)

COMPUTERS

Proficient in Windows, MS Word, Excel, PowerPoint, Outlook, Internet Explorer, Adobe Acrobat, Corel WordPerfect, Black Baud, and Crescendo.

CAMDEN MICHAELS, MFA

1234 Main Street, Portland, OR 97201
503.555.1234 (cell) | michaels@protypeltd.com
www.linkedin.com/in/cmichaelsmfa/

Creative Direction | Project Management
In-House Marketing and Design Firm Environments – Digital and Print Media

---

Technically sophisticated and business-savvy creative project leader with 17 years expertise in multi-channel, cross-media retail brand development, launch, marketing, and PR. Offer integrated management experience across up to 300 project components annually, working with stakeholders, including CEOs, designers, and project managers.

Seasoned problem solver, able to diplomatically balance the dynamic needs of creative teams and corporate leaders in achieving deadline-driven productivity. Known for sharp attention to detail and pragmatic work style.

- **Staffing, management, and performance optimization** for matrixed teams of up to 40 internal and external art directors, copywriters, graphic designers, ad agencies, and vendors.

- **Cost-conscious production work-flow management, prioritization, and systems development** for projects with budgets up to $4.5 million.

- **Management and delivery oversight** ranging from copyrights, media usage rights, and content management to art direction, digital photography, photography, pre-press management, and graphic design.

EXPERIENCE

FOUNDER AND CREATIVE DIRECTOR, Design Works, Portland, OR (2000 – present)
Strategy and Workflow | Design and Photography | Budget and Contract Negotiation | Brand Development

---

Retained by high-end retail clients to lead teams and independently produce multichannel market branding and design across traditional / print and Web 2.0 platforms. Supporting work includes art direction, design, photography, and marketing scheduling. Project management samples from 25-client list:

- **Amazon.com, Inc:** Interim creative director for 15 staff, $5 million, nine-month multi-channel marketing project.
- **Pottery Barn:** Art director for 13-staff, $4 million, six-month catalog promotion.
- **iVillage:** Brand strategist and director for $500K, five-month product introduction.
- **Snapfish:** Marketing and promotional materials for $100K, three-month marketing initiative.
- **L.L. Bean:** Creative brief developer for $80K, 12-month online brand launch.
- **Bristol Farms:** Art director, photographer, and brand strategist for three-month marketing project.
- **Godiva Chocolates:** Art director and photographer for ongoing $75K marketing project.

CREATIVE DIRECTOR, Design Warehouse, Santa Fe, NM (2004 – 2005)
Multi-Channel Brand Development | Creative Development | Team Management | Art Direction

---

Recruited for 13-month engagement. Charged with directing 13-member design and copywrite team in creating brand aesthetic and print advertising, direct-mail campaign, catalog, and Web site, while assuring brand consistency across channels.

EXPERIENCE – *cont'd*

CREATIVE MANAGER, Bed Bath & Beyond, Union, NJ (1997 – 2000)
Art Direction | Photography | Production | Talent/Design Process Development | Production Management

Hired to build and execute catalog production, negotiate and manage vendors, and oversee project budgets ranging between $10,000 and $4.5 million. Brands included:

- **Home:** Fall 1998 brand launch. Recruited and directed in-house / freelance creative development team of up 25 stylists, photographers, copywriters / editors, and designers.
- **Chambers:** All-channel brand development. Streamlined brand look and cohesiveness in collaboration with PR and visual merchandising department teams of up to 30 contributors. Developed e-commerce content for bridal registrty.

CREATIVE DIRECTOR, Open Air Design Studio, New York, NY, and Seattle, WA (1993 – 1997)
Advertising and Editorial Image Production | Copyright and Image Usage Rights

Founded photography and design consultancy supporting budgets up to $225K and photographers. Focused on marketing, accounting, budgets, client relations, and photography shoots / production. Client projects included:

- **Ben Sherman** and **Armani:** Advertising campaigns. Managed photo shoots and digital production.
- **Vogue:** Editorial projects. Oversaw high-end retouching, production, and content management.

PROFILE

EDUCATION

Master of Fine Arts, New York University, New York, NY, 1993
Bachelor of Fine Arts, School of Visual Concepts, Seattle, WA, 1991

AWARDS

- National Foundation for the National Advancement in the Arts (A.R.T.S.)
- The Creative Generation Excellence Awards in Visual Art and Design
- Arts National Award, Final Adjudication

DESIGN and PROJECT MANAGEMENT TOOLS

- **Expert:** Photoshop, InDesign, QuickTime, QuarkXpress, and QuickBooks
- **Skilled:** Illustrator, FileMaker Pro, DreamWeaver, ImageReady, PageMaker, PowerPoint, Microsoft Project, Word, Excel, and most Mac graphics programs
- **Basic:** HTML and Web image preparation

SAL BROWN, PMP
DIRECTOR-LEVEL EXECUTIVE

EXECUTIVE SUMMARY

- Dynamic leader with the proven ability to develop new business and accomplish both long-term and short-term corporate objectives.
- Successful at directing multi-million-dollar projects and resources in fast-paced environments.
- Experienced in managing the design, development, testing, and marketing of high-tech products.
- Effective team player who works well with others and strives to create win-win relationships.
- Able to motivate management and technical personnel to achieve maximum results.

EXPERIENCE

PRINCIPAL PROJECT MANAGER (2007 – present)
Exelon Generation, Inc., Kennett Square, Pennsylvania
Manage large projects (>$500,000) throughout the Exelon Power Fleet (hydroelectric, coal, natural gas/oil). Accountable for the full project life cycle, including project planning, scheduling, cost, resource allocation, construction, implementation, and reporting. Significant projects included:

- Executed a significant boiler tube replacement project ($3.5 million) at the Eddystone Plant (critical path). Completed the project under budget and three days early, saving $600,000 by allowing the plant to restart and produce revenue.
- Managed construction of a FERC-mandated, ADA-accessible fisherman's wharf and trail at the Conowingo Dam ($4.5 million). Completed the project on time and within budget in spite of extremely difficult site conditions. Received very positive community feedback on finished project quality.
- Developed and implemented a hydroelectric automation plan for two plants, with the goal of reducing the number of staff required to run each plant by one-half. Received senior management approval for a $28 million budget, developed the project plan in only nine months, and hired/managed contractors.
- Managed a $2 million emissions sampling project at two coal-fired plants mandated by the Pennsylvania Department of Environmental Protection. Completed the project four months early and 8% under budget.

DIRECTOR, Commercial Energy Management, Energy Solutions Operation (2004 – 2007)
Science Applications International Corporation (SAIC), Jersey City, New Jersey
Developed a team of 10 engineers to oversee energy-efficiency, commercial and industrial programs, including facility audits, fuel hedging, risk management, and project implementation.

- Performed detailed energy analysis studies for Army National Guard facilities in seven states. Saved the Federal government more than 15% on their energy bills (electric, oil, and natural gas).
- Served as program manager for a $1.5 million HVAC controls project at Andrews Air Force Base, Maryland. Completed the project four weeks early and 20% under budget.

DIRECTOR, Customer Performance Engineering and Assurance (2000 – 2004)
Telcordia Technologies, Inc. (formerly Bellcore), Piscataway, New Jersey
Led a staff of up to 15 developers in performance engineering of telecommunications software. Established software performance goals, hardware capacity planning, CPU/response time benchmarking, engineering analysis, and performance tuning on client/server computing systems. Managed a $7 million budget, cost estimates, and staffing plans.

- Mastered the job within six months of hire in spite of entering the position with no knowledge of the industry or products. Brought a fresh perspective to the company that focused on results.
- Inherited six different products generating $100 million in annual revenue.
- Consistently improved CPU/response time performance of software products by up to 25%, which improved customer satisfaction and increased company profit margins from 30% to 70%.

TECHNOLOGY MANAGER, Research, Development and Demonstration Group (1999 – 2000)
New York Gas Group (NYGAS), New York, New York
Directed the research and development of new products for the investor-owned natural gas utilities in New York State. Performed strategic planning and product development based on technology projections. Supervised up to 20 natural gas research contractors and managed a $1 million development budget.

- Increased revenues, reduced operating and maintenance costs, and improved pipeline safety.

ADDRESS

345 Shinnecock Hills • Avondale, Pennsylvania 19311   E-mail: sbrown@protypeltd.com
Home: (610) 555-1122 • Mobile: (610) 555-8912

EXPERIENCE
(continued)

PROGRAM MANAGER, Energy Services and Technology Business Unit (1994 – 1999)
New York Power Authority, New York, New York
Developed and directed the implementation of the award-winning, turnkey High-Efficiency Lighting Program (HELP) that included the installation of energy management systems for large commercial customers. Supervised 10 staff members and 50+ contractors. Trained installers, ensured compliance with strict guidelines, and coordinated scheduling of installations.
- Consistently surpassed construction installation goals of $15 million by an average of 40%.
- Achieved net revenue of 40% for the group when the goal was 2%.
- Executed agreements with the City of New York in record time, working closely with internal legal, marketing, and contracts departments.
- Succeeded in obtaining customer signatures on construction documents in only two weeks, a major accomplishment when dealing with government bureaucracies.
- Developed a free flow of communication between the customer and installers, and perfected a system of installation that compressed the construction period without compromising customer expectations. Achieved customer satisfaction levels of 95% as measured by survey.

ECONOMIST, Demand Side Management, Power Sales and Rates Division (1990 – 1994)
New York Power Authority, New York, New York
As a project engineer, supervised turnkey services for more than 60 projects. Performed needs assessment and economic cost/benefit analyses in order to save the customer the most money. Reviewed and approved equipment and subcontractor labor bid documents. Directed 25 contractors in the installation of high-efficiency lighting equipment to reduce the company's electrical load capacity.
- Generated $20 million of construction project revenue.
- Developed successful marketing strategies that enlisted more than 75% of the customer base.
- Created win-win propositions that earned 15 cents on the dollar.

SENIOR POWER ANALYST, Demand Side Management (1988 – 1990)
New York Power Authority, New York, New York
Directed the residential WattBuster Program, including marketing, economic cost/benefit analyses, and contractor supervision. Developed a large database to track installations and energy savings.
- Utilized only 50% of budgeted funds and reduced installed cost per kilowatt by 33%.
- Achieved customer response rates that were five times the national average.

PLANT ENGINEER, SHIFT TECHNICAL ADVISOR, Technical Services Department (1980 – 1988)
Indian Point 3 Nuclear Generating Facility, Buchanan, New York
- Created space for new equipment by removing unused disposal/chemical equipment packages, eliminating new facility costs of approximately $750,000.
- Conceived, designed, and installed permanent platforms for use in testing critical plant components that improved worker safety and effectiveness while eliminating recurring scaffolding costs of $200,000.

EDUCATION

MASTER OF BUSINESS ADMINISTRATION, FINANCE (1988)
Manhattan College, Riverdale, New York
Graduated in the top five percent of the class

BACHELOR OF ENGINEERING, MECHANICAL ENGINEERING (1980)
Manhattan College, Riverdale, New York

PROJECT MANAGEMENT PROFESSIONAL (PMP #1217608)

COMPUTERS

Proficient in Windows, MS Word, Excel, PowerPoint, Outlook, and MS Project

ROBERT GAMBLE

12345 Elm Avenue, Arlington, VA 22201 ♦
Cell: 703.555.1234 ♦
gamble@protypeltd.com ♦

AIRCRAFT TEST AND EVALUATION ♦ SYSTEMS ENGINEERING ♦ PROGRAM MANAGEMENT

LEADERSHIP: *Operational excellence for 15+ years, coupled with:*

Expertise in management of flight test and systems engineering for highly sophisticated, state-of-the-art aircraft.
Consistently rapid delivery of time-sensitive projects/programs with high customer-satisfaction ratings.
1700+ flight hours in both fleet and test aircraft.
Top-level engineering, systems and test/evaluation certifications.
Top Secret Security Clearance/SCI eligible.

Core Competencies

Program Management … Human Resource Management … Operations Planning … Budget Management
Acquisition … Team-building … Test and Evaluation … Communications (all levels)

Technologies

Radio Communications … Networks … Simulations … Information Processing
Software … Identification Systems

HIGHLIGHTS OF EXPERIENCE AND ACCOMPLISHMENTS

UNITED STATES NAVY   1989–2009
Assistant Program Manager for Projects (2006–2009)

As **Integrated Test Team Leader,** directed a composite department of 100+ military, civil-service, and contract employees in hardware and software testing for five aircraft and $300 million inventory. Managed $55+ million operations budget. Oversight included creation and evaluation of specifications, development of test plans, and writing/distribution of test reports for science and technology, system functionality, and airworthiness testing.

Highlights:
♦ Managed all test projects on the most complex aircraft. Team executed 100+ ground/flight test plans, accruing 1,200 flight hours and 13,000+ ground test hours. Staff performed nearly 2,000 maintenance actions, 10,000+ labor hours, and more than 450 aircraft configuration changes in support of operations.
♦ Led composite team to *Test Team of the Quarter* three times in less than three years.
♦ Successfully gained buy-in for new-facility construction to replace outdated rental structures. Projected construction cost will save $10+ million over planned rental fees within the next five years.
♦ Earned top-tier Acquisition Career Field Certification in test and evaluation.

Assistant Program Manager for Systems Engineering (2002–2006)
Oversaw all development and in-service engineering efforts for fleet of 75 aircraft. Supervised several engineering teams in providing safe, flight-ready assets to superiors. Responded to myriad engineering challenges in both in-service and new-production aircraft.

Highlights:
♦ Led team in rapid implementation of 1000+ changes to Aircrew Operator's Manual. Team completed a (normally) nine-month project in six weeks.
♦ Achieved Level 3 Acquisition Career Field Certification in Systems, Planning, Research, Development, and Engineering (SPRDE).

703.555.1234 ♦ gamble@protypeltd.com

Assistant Program Manager for Systems Engineering (continued)
- ♦ Post-9/11, successfully fielded new aircraft configuration to fleet, from evaluation of specs, through all ground and flight tests, to post-release technical instructions. Challenged to spearhead urgent fixes to numerous engineering defects to meet critical operational commitments safely. Coordinated with federal and civilian entities, resolving defects well ahead of schedule and enabling the concurrent deployment of six squadrons during Operation Iraqi Freedom.

Department Head (2000–2002)

As **Operations Officer,** orchestrated operations (20 months) for a 145-person squadron. Led squadron in achieving 1,300 flight hours and 79 support missions while enforcing the No Fly Zone over Iraq.

As **Maintenance Officer** (six months), despite crippling parts shortages, led Maintenance Department to supply two fully mission-capable aircraft to meet critical operational commitments on schedule.

Naval Flight Officer (NFO) Instructor (1997–2000)

In addition to NFO instruction, served as Aviation Department Head School Coordinator. Taught a variety of tactical and mission systems courses as well as providing mentorship.

AFFILIATIONS

Boy Scout Leader
United States Naval Academy Alumni Association
Association of Naval Aviation

EDUCATION

Naval Postgraduate School
Master of Science: System Technologies

United States Naval Academy
Bachelor of Science

ERICA VELARDE

1234 Palm Drive, Colorado Springs, Colorado 80918
Cell: (719) 123-5555 • Email: evelarde@protypeltd.com

PROFILE

- Self-motivated healthcare professional with a desire to build on biology/chemistry education and pharmacy experience to transition into pharmaceutical sales.
- Extensive knowledge of drugs, how they work, and their side effects, interactions, and contraindications.
- Proven ability to develop profitable, long-term relationships and provide exceptional customer service.
- Effective team player with exceptional communication, presentation, and interpersonal skills.

EDUCATION

BACHELOR OF SCIENCE, MOLECULAR / CELLULAR BIOLOGY (May 2007)
Adams State College, Alamosa, Colorado
- Relevant Course Work: Human Anatomy and Physiology, Molecular Biology, Developmental Biology, Cellular Biology, Genetics with Lab, Microbiology, Physiological Zoology, Ecology, Evolution, General Biology with Lab, Biology Thesis (with a presentation every three weeks), Speech, Communication Arts I/II.

BACHELOR OF ARTS, CHEMISTRY / ALLIED HEALTH (May 2007)
Adams State College, Alamosa, Colorado
- Relevant Course Work: Introduction to Statistical Methods, Research in Chemistry, Chemistry Seminar, Analytical Chemistry with Lab, Biochemistry I/II with Lab, Physics, Calculus, Issues in Wellness, Organic Chemistry with Lab, Trigonometry and Analytic Geometry, General Chemistry with Lab.

INTERNSHIP

DR. CHRISTINA MILLER, Adams State College, Alamosa, Colorado (2006 – 2007)
- Selected for an internship with the Biology Department for two semesters.
- Spent 12 hours every week conducting research in the lab using a great deal of independence to create experiments.
- Researched the literature and wrote "The Effects of Spingomyelin on the Formation of Lipid Rafts" based on lab research; presented the findings to all science faculty.

PROFESSIONAL EXPERIENCE

CERTIFIED PHARMACY TECHNICIAN
Safeway Pharmacy, Monument, Colorado (2007 – present)
Safeway Pharmacy, Alamosa, Colorado (2003 – 2007)
Valley Wide Health Services, Alamosa, Colorado (2002 – 2003)
- Assisted pharmacists in preparing and dispensing medications in accordance with prescriptions.
- Mixed pharmaceutical preparations and filled bottles with prescribed tablets, capsules, and liquids.
- Entered data for each prescription into the computer and prepared labels for bottles.
- Received and stocked incoming inventory; counted merchandise and entered data into the computer to maintain inventory records.
- Recorded insurance information for each patient to ensure accurate billing.
- Communicated with doctors, customers, and insurance companies and ensured the delivery of exceptional customer service.
- Accepted payments and operated the cash register.

VOLUNTEER

- Member, Tri-Beta Biological Honor Society at Adams State College, 2002 – present —Vice President, 2006 – 2007.
- Selected by college professors to serve as a judge for regional science fairs, 2003 – 2007.
- Hot Line Volunteer, Sexual Assault Response Team 2006 – 2007—On call for two weeks per semester to advocate for victims and direct them to community resources.

PROFESSIONAL DEVELOPMENT

POWER-PAK CE
- Management of Xerostomia: A Pharmacist-Based Approach (2007)
- The Management of Depression and Anxiety in the Long-Term Care Setting (2007)
- Emergency Contraception: A Guide to Over-the-Counter Availability (2007)
- The Role of the Pharmacist in the Management of Parkinson's Disease: Its Symptoms and Co-morbidities (2006)
- Advances in the Treatment and Prevention of Herpes Zoster and Post-therapeutic Neuralgia (2006)
- Smoking Cessation Therapy (2006)
- Strategies for Preventing Medication Misadventures: Impact on Insulin Safety (2006)
- Fixed-Dose Combination Products in the Treatment of HIV Infection (2006)
- Options in the Treatment of Alcohol Dependence (2006)
- Prescription Errors: Legal Consequences and Patient Safeguards (2004, 2005)
- Turning Information into Knowledge Using the Internet (2005)
- Management of Stress Urinary Incontinence (2005)
- Use of Long-acting Opioids for Chronic Pain: An Update on Issues, Research, and Treatment Trends (2005)
- Opioid Pharmacotherapy for the Management of Moderate to Severe Pain: Balancing Clinical and Risk Management Considerations (2005)
- Issues in Chronic Pain Management (2005)
- Advances in the Treatment of Depression: Clinical Implications of Dual-acting Antidepressants (2005)
- New Options in Chronic Obstructive Pulmonary Disease (COPD) Management (2005)
- Newer Options in the Management of Hyperlipidemia (2005)
- Treatment of Erectile Dysfunction (2005)
- Treatment Strategies for Moderate to Severe Alzheimer's Disease (2004)
- Health Benefits of Folic Acid (2004)

COMPUTERS

- Proficient in Windows, MS Word, Excel, PowerPoint, Access, Outlook, Internet Explorer.

BRAD LAWRENCE

89776 Ellington Drive
San Ramon, CA 94582

(925) 555-5555

E-mail: Lawrence@protypeltd.com

INFORMATION TECHNOLOGY MANAGEMENT

10+ years of consistent achievements in providing vision, innovation, strategic planning, and leadership of IT organizations in high-growth global companies.

CORE COMPETENCIES AND STRENGTHS

✓ Business-oriented IT professional with hands-on experience who champions business process improvements/cost reductions and identifies the most cost-effective, value-added IT solutions.

✓ Full project life cycle experience as a developer, consultant, and manager of large-scale IT projects, consistently producing quality deliverables on schedule and well under budget.

✓ Excel in introducing organizational change and leveraging existing technology and knowledge base with internal resources to facilitate business excellence and competitive advantage.

✓ Supervisory and budget experience combines with excellent communication skills to build and continually drive focused IT/cross-functional teams involving different cultures to accomplish results.

✓ Proven effectiveness in consensus building, partnering with senior business leaders, and working collaboratively at all levels to assess, plan, and implement IT solutions.

PROFESSIONAL EXPERIENCE

ELMAK MANUFACTURING, Walnut Creek, CA   **1999 to Present**
Senior Director of Applications

Direct the development, maintenance, and support of all standardized business applications at 14 plants worldwide in a rapid growth environment (60% growth rate during 1999–2000). Diverse responsibilities encompass development of applications and e-commerce strategies, IT policies/procedures, partnering with senior executives company-wide.

Supervise seven-member team in three application groups: E-commerce, ERP Systems, and Supply Chain. Collaborate with site resources in the delivery of IT solutions. Develop and manage relationships with enterprise software vendors, including Baan, i2, Agile, Oracle, Hyperion, GE and Valor. Manage $1.7 million budget. Perform applications due diligence, and lead system installation teams for new acquisitions.

ACHIEVEMENTS

- **Baan ERP Implementation:** Envisioned, pioneered the design, and leveraged existing internal technology and resources to implement Baan ERP system at company's German plant in record time (five weeks) at a fraction of the cost ($100,000) of prior implementations. **Results:** Enabled company to retain $40 million account and provided foundation for rapid Baan implementation methodology.

- **Customer Portal Implementation:** Salvaged a failed e-commerce project and delivered results that restored confidence while retaining largest, $350 million a year account. Currently utilizing the solution as an enterprise standard to provide cost-effective web access for all customers.

- **MES Strategy/Solution:** Established consistent strategy throughout company for Manufacturing Execution System (MES) from requirements definition through vendor selection and successful implementation. Instrumental in capturing $100 million a year account by architecting a solution to service avionic, medical, and industrial customers that required advanced product-tracking capabilities.

- **Development Cost Reduction:** Reduced Baan development costs $200,000 a year by replacing outside consultants with internal developer.

DELMAR SOLUTIONS, Dallas, TX   1996 to 1999
Manager of Information Systems

Recruited to build and lead the IT organization in alignment with company's accelerated growth from $36 million to $60 million in just three years. Modernized division's IT infrastructure which was standardized on SAP, Microsoft, Oracle, Compaq and Cisco—all accomplished with a staff of two. Initiated and managed partnerships with key application and infrastructure vendors. Maintained IT costs under 2% of sales throughout tenure (well under parent company's 7% of sales average).

ACHIEVEMENTS

- **SAP/R3 Implementation:** Spearheaded the Accelerated SAP/R3 implementation project at two sites, including leadership of cross-functional management and technical teams. **Results:** Awarded for delivering project in just 5 months—on schedule and under budget—at a total cost of only $900,000.

- **Infrastructure Improvements:** Replaced Novell with Microsoft NT and CCmail with MS Exchange, as well as all switches and routers with new Cisco equipment. Planned and implemented IT infrastructure at new headquarters. **Results:** Complied with mandate without any adverse impact on the business.

- **E-commerce:** Initiated and launched delmar.com, product micro-sites, and surgeons forum (online discussion group focused on use of company products).

- **Sales Force Automation:** Deployed laptops, provided training and web-based CRM solution to over 100 remote sales reps. Created automated Sales Force Tool Kit, providing sales force with same-day research and delivery of technical articles to customers, quote development, and other tools.

HANOVER CORPORATION, Dallas, TX   1991 to 1996
Assistant Manager—Information Management   1992 to 1996

Promoted to provide divisional IT strategy and leadership in support of corporate procurement and accounts payable department systems, users, and re-engineering initiatives. Developed and managed annual $1.3 million budget. Directed a team of nine in a mixed technical environment, including MVS, VM, VMS, and client server.

ACHIEVEMENTS

- Re-engineered interface between central procurement system and ERP systems at the plants. **Results:** Streamlined manufacturing purchasing and receiving processes while averting production downtime.
- Implemented several integrated self-service requisition applications for MRO.
- Earned Total Quality Ownership Award for duty drawback audit that saved company $200,000.
- Promoted from **Senior Systems Analyst** (1991 to 1992).

EDUCATION

Bachelor of Science, Computer Systems, Texas University, Dallas, Texas, 1991

MARGARET R. KREITNER

SUMMARY OF QUALIFICATIONS

"Minds are like parachutes...They only work when they're OPEN!"

- Proven customer service professional with a desire to help others as a patient advocate.
- Persuasive communicator with strong listening, writing, and verbal skills.
- Proactive problem solver who is good at "what if" thinking and setting up win-win solutions.
- Effective instructor with the definitive ability to help others understand complex subjects.
- Proven team player who works well alone, with little or no supervision, or as part of a group.

EDUCATION

ASSOCIATE OF APPLIED SCIENCE, HEALTH INFORMATION TECHNOLOGY (Summer 2008)
Arapahoe Community College, Littleton, Colorado
- Completing an RHRT (Certified Health Information Management Program).
- Relevant course work completed: CPT Coding and Reimbursement, ICD-9-CM Clinical Classification System, Legal Aspects, Anatomy, Medical Terminology, Health Information Management, Health Data Management and Statistics, among others.

BACHELOR OF SCIENCE, PARALEGAL STUDIES (1993)
University of Maryland, College Park, Maryland
- Relevant course work included Advanced Legal Research and Writing, Litigation, Evidence, Consumer Protection Law (Insurance and Warranties), Torts, Constitutional Law, Ethics, and Technical Writing, among others.

BACHELOR OF ARTS, POLITICAL SCIENCE (1992)
University of Maryland, College Park, Maryland

RELEVANT EXPERIENCE

CUSTOMER SERVICE, COMMUNICATION
- Provided exceptional customer service, ensuring complete satisfaction with project results.
- Wrote and assembled detailed reports, proposals, brochures, and correspondence.
- Answered telephone inquiries, greeted customers, and answered all questions and concerns.
- Created and coordinated *Byline,* an innovative, article-based advertising campaign for small businesses in Washington, DC, which was featured in local community newspapers.
- Wrote a training manual for antique furniture restoration and conservation.
- Researched and authored *Political Anathemas: Will They Ever Have a Law-Based Society,* published in 1992. This book traces the history of the democratic movement and constitutionalism in the former Soviet Union from the 18th century through 1992.
- Researched and authored a report with Mr. Patrick Petit J.D. for the Catholic University Law Library. The report, *Role of DNA Testing in Criminal and Civil Cases,* explained PCR and RFLP testing, and examined and reviewed legislative intent, sessions laws, legislation, and court cases within the federal system and in the 50 United States and U.S. territories.

ADMINISTRATION
- Owned and operated Antiques on the Mend, a business specializing in antique furniture repair and restoration. It was an authorized repair center recognized by national clearinghouses (Restoration Center Hotline and Claims Prevention Procedure Council).
- Developed business plans, prepared bids for projects, and wrote detailed insurance claim reports.
- Accountable for business development, record keeping, sales, purchasing, and inventory.
- Recruited, hired, trained, and supervised assistants and various part-time temporary workers.

RELEVANT EXPERIENCE

MARKETING, SALES, PROMOTION

- Built business by advertising in local newspapers and targeted magazines, creating flyers and brochures, and networking through the Chamber of Commerce and Business Networking International.
- Researched demographic and labor market trends to identify new sources of business.
- Won major accounts with national moving and storage companies (United Van Lines, Graebel, Mayflower), as well as national furniture retailers (Boyles, Lane, Ethan Allen).
- Created an informational website (www.antiquesonthemend.com) to generate new business.
- Grew sales by a consistent 25% every year, earning new accounts through referrals from satisfied customers.
- As an active volunteer member of various business and professional groups, prepared press releases and participated in other community outreach programs to involve people on issues relating to the preservation of old buildings and furnishings.
- Successfully developed a client base that generated $1.5 million in annual sales volume as a CLU (Chartered Life Insurance Underwriter) in early career.
- Appeared on local public radio station WPFW in Washington, DC as a frequent guest speaker discussing the role of insurance for women within the broader framework of personal financial planning.
- Regular guest speaker during the federal government's "open season" (employee selection and enrollment in group insurance coverage).

TECHNICAL SKILLS

- Proficient in Windows, MS Word, Outlook, and Internet Explorer.
- Proficient in legal research using Lexus-Nexus and Westlaw.
- Trained in AC/DC circuitry for computers, math for electronics (Boolean Algebra), electronic drafting, and technical writing.

WORK HISTORY

SOLE PROPRIETOR (2000 to 2010)
Antiques on the Mend, Colorado Springs, Colorado

LEGAL RESEARCH/FREE-LANCE WRITER (1996 to 1999)
Catholic University Law Library, Washington, DC

MANAGER (1992 to 1996)
Bombay Company, Arlington, Virginia

CORRESPONDENT (1989 to 1992)
National Flood Insurance Program, Bethesda, Maryland

RICHARD L. FORSYTH

22 Rockridge Avenue ▪ Austin, TX 73301
Phone: 512.555.1234 ▪ Cellular: 512.375.0948 ▪ Email: forsyth@protypeltd.com

MARKETING / ADVERTISING / PROMOTIONS / PUBLIC RELATIONS

Designed and delivered a wide range of marketing, sales, production, and public relations projects for employers and clients in media, entertainment, publishing, and nonprofit sectors. These include **A&E Network**, *Wired* **and** *CEO World* **Magazines**, **Austin Film Festival**, *Film Journal* **Magazine**, **Comic Relief**, **MTV**, **VH1**, **Time-Life**, **Time Warner**, **Swatch Watch**, and **Saturday Night Live**. Effectively coordinated a diversity of resources to consistently deliver high impact projects on time with budgets of zero to $1 million.

Entrepreneurial / Innovative / Creative / High Energy / Self-Motivated / Business Savvy / Versatile / Resourceful

EDUCATION: COLUMBIA UNIVERSITY, School of the Arts, New York, NY
Bachelor of Fine Arts, Film, Television, and Radio Production (1988)

EXPERIENCE

⇨ Writing and Design

⇨ Film/Video and Audio Production

⇨ Advertising

⇨ Public Relations

⇨ Event Marketing

⇨ E-Marketing and E-Commerce

⇨ Co-Marketing/ Sponsorships

⇨ Sales Collateral Design

⇨ Strategic Development

⇨ Project/Program Management

⇨ Selecting/Guiding Freelance Writers and Designers

⇨ Budgeting

⇨ Word, Excel, PowerPoint, Quark Xpress, Photoshop, Illustrator, FileMaker, HTML

PROFESSIONAL BACKGROUND

FIRST RUN PUBLICITY, Austin, TX   2003 to Present
Marketing Consultant

Leveraged vast industry experience to co-found a marketing and public relations firm serving Austin area cultural and arts organizations. Develop and execute marketing and PR plans for clients such as Austin Symphony, Mexico Art Museum, and Austin Segway Tours. Select and coordinate freelance photographers and writers. Develop and distribute press releases and work with print, television, and radio media to gain preview coverage and event reviews. Produce wrap-up summary packages for each event.

⇨ **Consistently secured a higher level of media coverage for clients and higher attendance than previous firms had delivered.**

CEO WORLD AND WIRED MAGAZINES, New York, NY 2000 to 2003
Marketing Sales Manager (promoted from Content Innovator)

Hired based on knowledge of production and promotions in all media forms (film, video, audio, print, web) to drive revenue generation programs for two award-winning monthly business publications. Supported sales teams by designing effective, customized sales materials, including CDs, proposals, PowerPoint presentations, and video segments to gain sponsorships for live events. Directed the creation and implementation of brand marketing efforts, including strategy development, web presence, marketing tools (including editorial content marketing), and e-commerce (branded merchandise). Facilitated conceptualization and rollout of online consumer acquisition and retention strategies. Supervised two administrative assistants.

⇨ **Brought award-winning editorial and design consistency to all live-event sales and marketing materials while reducing turnaround time to complete customized sales presentations for 'key' prospects.**

⇨ **Increased online traffic and revenues by driving implementation of a more user-friendly online store and working with numerous vendors to expand branded merchandise selection.**

AUSTIN FILM FESTIVAL, Austin, TX

1998 to 2000

Publications Manager (promoted from Promotions Manager)

Created marketing materials and coordinated promotional activities for one of the largest and most prestigious film festival in the U.S. with an audience of 120,000+. Produced consumer print pieces such as flyers and event programs. Authored editorial content for newspapers and scripts for radio giveaways. Coordinated public service announcements on television and in local theaters. Orchestrated free-ticket distribution promotions. Supervised editorial and design assistants, and coordinated numerous volunteers for publications and promotions tasks.

⇨ **Produced 25th Anniversary Commemorative Guide in only three months with limited funds.**

⇨ **Saved thousands of dollars by bringing design and production of program guide in house. New program received excellent response from attendees, sponsors, and partner companies.**

FILM JOURNAL MAGAZINE, Los Angeles, CA

1995 to 1998

Managing Editor (promoted from Subscription Manager)

Hired by owner to improve quality of this national trade publication aimed at filmmakers. Performed and participated in all activities associated with publishing an entertainment industry magazine, including defining editorial content, working with writers to secure articles, coordinating artists and photographers for cover art, managing subscription department, and resolving customer service issues. Supervised dozens of freelance writers and designers.

⇨ **Transformed publication from a black and white "fanzine" to a polished, professional title that is still in publication with same design template.**

⇨ **Designed first direct mail campaign, which generated 2% response rate and hundreds of new subscribers.**

A&E NETWORK, New York, NY

1990 to 1995

Senior Marketing Associate (promoted from Assistant to Director of Consumer Promotion)

Led and expanded the Off-Channel Promotion division charged with producing programming for non-traditional channels, such as airline in-flight entertainment, amusement parks, and commuter hubs. Contributed to general consumer promotion projects for A&E original programming, including movies, documentaries, family programs, dramas, and special features. Worked with internal and external resources, including sponsors, to execute promotional concepts. Administered budgets of $600,000 to $1 million.

⇨ **Added new airline clients, including Delta, United, Continental, and US Airways to Off-Channel division. Wrote and produced 100+ in-flight video promotional segments for 10+ airlines.**

FURLONG PICTURES, New York, NY

1987 to 1990

Production Manager (promoted from Production Assistant)

Coordinated talent, crew, location, and equipment for short- and long-term film productions, including commercials, feature films, and music videos for clients such as MTV, VH1, Elektra Records, A&E Network, Time-Life, Swatch Watch, and Saturday Night Live.

DONNA L. GANES

5 Little Neck Road | Lindenhurst, NY 11757 | ganes@protypeltd.com | 516.555.1234

INTERIOR DESIGNER

AREAS OF EXPERTISE

Client Advisement and Meetings • Space Planning and Drawings • Proposals and Contracts
Budgets and Materials Costing • Review and Approval of Invoices
Project Management • Vendor Hiring and Relationship Management
Installation Oversight and Quality Control • Fine Art Selection

"Donna is a visionary interior designer. Countless times she has been instrumental in helping us transform challenging architectural spaces into jaw-dropping oases. She is the only designer we now recommend for both residential and commercial projects."
– John James, Principal, James & Madison Architects, LLC

EXPERIENCE—INTERIOR DESIGN FIRMS

Interior Designer	DONNA L. GANES INTERIOR DESIGN, Lindenhurst, NY	2005 – Present
Interior Designer	MAX ROGERS & COMPANY, Roslyn, NY	2002 – 2005

- Conduct consultations with clients and architects to define scope of project, requirements, design preferences, and budget allocation.
- Write proposals and deliver sophisticated, yet friendly presentations. Up-sell extent of project or materials selection as appropriate.
- Create detailed space and floor plans through hand drawings or the use of Visio. On the residential side, plans have included every room in the home as well as exterior spaces. On the commercial side, plans have included professional offices, a country club, and a car dealership.
- Source furnishings, fabrics, and accessories from "to the trade" and retail vendors.
- Function as a project manager, hiring and overseeing the work of carpenters, electricians, tile installers, upholsterers, painters, and wallpaper hangers. Troubleshoot problems with vendors, manufacturers, contractors, and tradespeople. Travel to local and distant work sites to oversee installations.
- Meet with vendors to peruse and select sample materials.
- Revamp and maintain an extensive library of material samples.
- Research costs and provide price quotes on merchandise, including customized pieces.
- Utilize computer spreadsheets, databases, and Intranet to check stock, track orders, and expedite deliveries.

EXPERIENCE—FINE ART INDUSTRY

Sales Assistant	STRUMM GALLERY, Farmingdale, NY	2000 – 2002
Archiving Intern	SOTHEBY'S NEW YORK, New York, NY	Summer 2000

- Designed and arranged displays of showroom artwork to maximize impact.
- Assisted in the development of promotional materials for artists and artwork.
- Researched the value of art objects and advised patrons regarding their relative worth.
- Organized and archived auction selling prices for all departments.
- Wrote copy for sales brochures highlighting upcoming auction pieces.

EDUCATION—TRAINING

Bachelor of Arts, Art History, 2000, Long Island University/C.W. Post Campus, Brookville, NY
Diploma, Interior Design, 2002, Metropolitan Institute of Interior Design, Plainview, NY

Pictures & Graphics

Chapter 10

The following résumés aren't extremely elaborate in their use of graphic design elements. They are still basically conservative résumés with just a little something added to make them stand out.

Keep in mind that the graphic or picture should be directly related to your industry. You wouldn't put a world globe on a waitress's résumé or drafting tools on a paramedic's. In some more conservative professions (banking, accounting, senior management, for example) graphics on a résumé are not recommended, even if they are small and conservative.

The résumé on pages 198–199 uses a graphic that reflects an international focus, whereas the graphics on pages 194–197 and 200–212 reflect the person's industry. For more examples using graphics, see pages 224, 225, 238, 272, 290, 291, 295, 296, and 300.

By becoming a little more inventive, you can incorporate scanned letters or figures that reflect your personality more than the industry (see pages 145, 161, 292, 301, 302).

The use of the graphics is fine on a scannable résumé, provided the picture doesn't touch any of the words on the page. The scanning software will ignore your graphics in most cases. However, using a graphic image as the first initial of your name (like the résumés on pages 145, 161, 292, 301) will cause your name to be spelled wrong in the electronic database after scanning. Avoid graphic images that are part of your name or are watermarks behind text if you know your résumé will be scanned, faxed, or copied once it leaves your hands.

Those in more creative industries—the arts, entertainment, advertising, graphic design—have a license to be even more creative. You could definitely get away with the résumés in this chapter, but you can be as creative as the résumés in Chapter 15.

Gary Taft

1234 Larrel Lane, West Milton, Ohio 45383
Email: garytaft@protypeltd.com
Cell: (937) 555-1234

"A man does not climb a mountain without bringing some of it away with him; and leaving something of himself upon it." — Sir Martin Conway

SUMMARY

- Passionate wildlife and forestry conservationist with a true love for the great outdoors.
- Skilled manager with a proven track record of leadership in high-pressure businesses.
- Honest, hard-working outdoorsman who learns quickly and enjoys new challenges.

TRAINING AND DEVELOPMENT

PENN FOSTER CAREER SCHOOL, Scranton, Pennsylvania (February 2010)
Wildlife and Forestry Conservation Certificate
- Completed this year-long program in only three months.
- Relevant course work included: Conservation—People, Animals, and Habitat; Wildlife Management—Upland Birds, Waterfowl, Small Mammals I/II, Large Mammals I/II, Predators; Forest Protection; Rangelands Management; Forest Management I/II; Forest Protection; Cold Water Fish Management; Warm Water Fish Management; Aquaculture; International Conservation Issues; Safety in the Field; Wildlife Law Enforcement.

COLORADO OUTDOOR ADVENTURE GUIDE SCHOOL, Colorado Springs (June 2009)
Professional Hunting Guide Program and Basic Outdoor Adventure Program
- Graduated with high grades from an intensive, six-week guide preparation program.
- Renewed Red Cross certification in first aid, CPR, and AED.
- Mastered essential outdoor skills, including guiding, horsemanship, hiking, backpacking, orienteering (map, compass, GPS), wilderness survival, camp cooking, outdoor photography, conservation, mountain biking, hunting, and fishing.
- Developed leadership skills and the ability to thrive in a positive atmosphere of teamwork.
- Recognized for marksmanship with the Top Gun Award—number one in the class.

SUMMARY OF EXPERIENCE

- Expert marksman with experience shooting and maintaining rifles, shotguns, muzzle loaders, and compound bows.
- Successfully hunted deer, antelope, elk, bear, bighorn sheep, wild boar, turkey, and game birds.
- Knowledge of wild animal habitats, food, behavior, calls, decoys, and other hunting techniques.
- Earned a Pope and Young archery score of 162" for a whitetail deer.
- Proficient horseman with experience keeping horses and mules in the back country/wilderness. Rode and cared for grandfather's horses and mules as a youth.
- Knowledge of saddles (Decker, Sawbuck, Western riding), tack repair, horse/mule behavior, breaking, healthcare, shots, worming, shoeing, trail rides, pack trips, barrel/basket/crowfoot hitches, and leading a string.
- Experienced camp cook with special skills in menu planning, recipe development, safe food storage, hardwood coals, Dutch ovens, and gas stoves.
- Volunteered for numerous Ohio Department of Wildlife youth hunter programs, introducing young people to the sport of hunting and wildlife conservation.

RELEVANT EXPERIENCE

HUNTING GUIDE / CAMP COOK (August – November 2009)
Bear Paw Outfitters, Colville, Washington
Completed 15 days of extensive training with owner/operator in preparation for black bear, elk, mule deer, and whitetail deer hunting seasons. Studies DNR hunting laws/regulations for Washington, Montana, Idaho, and Utah.
- Achieved 100% successful on-shot opportunities using game tracking skills while guiding clients on black bear, elk, and mule deer hunts in Washington, northwestern Utah, and public areas of the Cache National Forest of southern Idaho.

RELEVANT EXEPRIENCE

Bear Paw Outfitters (continued)
- Provided optimal hunting conditions for guests by scouting animal movements and patterns, setting feed stations, spotting, and placing tree stands and ground blinds.
- Set up wilderness drop camps with tents for clients, guide, and cooking. Prepared daily meals over camp stoves and open fires. Maintained cleanliness of the campsite.
- Ensured all clients were comfortable and happy during their stay by paying special attention to details and understanding their needs during camp stays and while hunting.

AFFILIATIONS

- Rocky Mountain Elk Foundation
- National Wild Turkey Federation
- North American Hunting Club
- Wildlife Forever Conservation Organization

MANAGEMENT EXPERIENCE

COX OHIO PUBLISHING
Night Operations Production Manager, Dayton, Ohio (2002 – 2008)
Pressroom Manager, Dayton, Ohio (1993 – 2002)
Directed the production of five daily newspapers—250,000 copies per night, seven days a week. Led a team of 5 foremen, 16 pressmen, and 50 mail-room workers in a high-pressure, deadline-oriented operation. Maintained high quality levels while lowering production waste, increasing efficiencies, and establishing new operating procedures. Developed process efficiencies in all production departments that improved on-time delivery from 90% to 98%. Established weekly communication meetings between all departments.

THOMSON NEWSPAPER GROUP
Press, Camera, and Imaging Manager, Hamilton, Ohio, and Waukesha, Wisconsin (1991 – 1993)
Pressroom Foreman, Piqua, Ohio (1989 – 1991)
Journeyman Pressman, Enid, Oklahoma (1980 – 1989)
Promoted through the ranks of this large corporation with 126 newspapers throughout the U.S. Managed operations, crew training, and maintenance of presses, folders, cameras, plate makers, film processes, and light tables. Selected to install and commission new presses at facilities in various states and to train crew members converting from lead presses to offset printing. Developed and managed operating and expense budgets.

8888 Rivers St.
Seattle WA 98187
(206) 555-1234
daniellesierra@protypeltd.com

Danielle Sierra, MBA
(ITIL Version 3 Foundation Certified)

IT Program Manager

Balancing business, customer, and employee needs to produce ongoing growth opportunities.

Equal blend of business manager and technologist focused on developing long-term, trust-based relationships that produce qualitative and quantitative results.

Management and Leadership Expertise: Deliver quality customer care that makes a real difference in:

Contract Negotiations and Contract Management
Customer Satisfaction, Retention and Brand Loyalty
Project Management and Program Management

Lab and Data Center Management
Process and Service Improvements
Consistent Business Value

Technical Expertise: Use technology to deliver rapid and correct results to business-critical activities in:

Video and Multimedia Systems
ITIL Standardization of Processes and Procedures

Server Support and Administration
Client and Desktop Systems

Professional Experience

STEWART IT SOLUTIONS, Information and Technology Consultancy, Seattle, WA   2000–Present
Program Manager

Profitably managed $3 million in IT service contracts with 30 employees. Oversaw daily operations with Microsoft managers and staff. Assumed P&L responsibility for the life cycle of the contract.

- Created a visual tool to balance and align customer, individual, and corporate needs. *Managed to the Triangle* to increase collaborative discussions and shared responsibilities.
- Negotiated numerous contracts with Microsoft that made Stewart a long-term service provider.
- Met or exceeded targets for Service Level Agreements (SLAs) and Key Performance Indicators (KPIs) despite increasing workload without corresponding increase in resources.
- Managed data centers and networking contractors, including a team that deployed VLAN and hardware builds on production network.
- Met one-on-one with customers to discuss and document new business requirements. Priced new engagements and developed detailed pricing models for submission and approval.

Delivered consistent financial results and business value:
- Eliminated duplicate work and improved ROI by sharing solutions and best practices across multiple independent departments.
- Grew the MSN contract billing from **$12K a month to $131K per month within six months**.
- Exceeded target Gross Profit (GP) and Earnings before Interest and Taxes (EBIT) **by 5% annually for three years running**.
- Generated leads for other Stewart services (staffing and managed services) by referring current customers when appropriate to satisfy a customer need.
- Consistently maintained employee and contract retention levels well above industry averages. **Increased retention rate to 95%** from a predecessor low of 50%.

Built strong and sustainable customer and employee relationships:
- Developed trust-based relationships by being responsive to customer needs. Increased revenue and customer share with current customers. Generated numerous referrals to other departments.
- Prevented problems before they occurred by proactively seeking customer feedback, with special attention to open dialog about any issues.
- Invested in long-term relationships, eliminating systemic causes of customer complaints rather than relying on symptom repairs.
- Created employee skill and certification plans that matched potential capabilities. Developed teams and focused efforts on improving individual and team performance.

AMERICAN BROADCASTING   2000–2006
Internal IT Support Manager

Continuously recognized for improving processes and providing reliable technology in a time-sensitive and busy environment. Efficiently managed the IT infrastructure, development, and operations by establishing and implementing ITIL standards.

Managed IT Operations:
- Maintained and supported all eight of MSNBC.com's remote sites, connectivity, budgeting, infrastructure, and equipment.
- Resolved time-sensitive, complex issues with multiple business giants, including MSNBC-cable, GE, NBC, CNBC, Microsoft, and Wall Street Journal.
- Streamlined process for switching out PCs, significantly reducing downtime for busy editors and writers. New backup plan **eliminated the need for 45+ computers.**
- Implemented and maintained internal tools for employees (Tools CD, Self-help Intranet).
- Designed and implemented knowledge management system using SharePoint to centralize access to workarounds, configurations, and known errors.

Implemented cost savings and efficiency measures that followed ITIL best practices:
- Reduced time loss from machine failure by **standardizing to one user platform**. Conducted functionality and value/cost comparison to make final purchase decisions.
- Changed user service-level expectations from reactive to preventative by conducting regular service checks. New program aligned with organization's critical need for uninterrupted business services.
- Significantly reduced deployment time by **standardizing 90% of desktop builds**. Developed process that built, tested, and deployed images with minimum impact on a time-critical environment.
- Eliminated silos with standard processes, procedures, and PC configurations on both coasts.
- Managed master copies of software, version controls, and related documentation in central location using ITIL best practice (Definitive Software Library).

Managed special projects with short planning cycles:
Personally thanked by ABC operations manager for **outstanding contributions made on 9/11**. Agility in the face of constantly changing priorities in a hectic newsroom ensured that all important technical issues were immediately resolved.
- Worked on and planned nationally and internationally viewed events. Rapid response to changing needs ensured uninterrupted coverage. (Connected coast to coast with Ron Reagan, elections, NABJ, and Olympic Games—2002 Salt Lake, 2004 Athens, and 2006 Torino).
- Developed **rapid-fire project management skills** in response to quickly changing event plans. Took charge of a highly visual broadcast kiosk at the last minute during the national elections.

HITACHI CORPORATION   2000
IT Manager
- Designed and implemented a phased migration from Netscape to Exchange (300 users) and provided on-site training for employees. Recognized by CEO for **increasing user satisfaction from "poor" to "very high."**

Education and Professional Development

ITIL Version 3 Foundation Certified	2009
ITIL and Management Training, Siemens	2000–2008
Masters in Business Administration, City University, Seattle, WA (Concentration in IT and Project Management)	2006
MSCE/MCP+I Certification Courses, Keane, Inc., Seattle, WA	1999
BS, Business Administration, University of Washington, Seattle, WA	1996

Stacy S. Thigpen

1234 Coloniale
Montreal, QC, Canada H2W 2C6

Phone: (514) 123-5555
Email: thigpen@protypeltd.com

PROFILE

- Creative public relations and marketing specialist with extensive experience promoting organizational messages and planning for events worldwide.
- Dedicated sports management professional with more than 14 years of relevant experience that includes five Olympic and four Paralympic Games
- Effective team player with strong interpersonal and communication skills.

INTERNATIONAL EXPERIENCE

- Cross-culturally sensitive professional who has lived abroad and traveled extensively around the world.
- Worked for the World Anti-Doping Agency in Lausanne, Switzerland, and Montreal, Canada.
- Promoted WADA's athlete outreach program at more than 30 major international events
- Worked for the Australian Olympic Committee in Sydney for nearly three years in preparation for the 2000 Summer Olympics.
- One of three Americans selected to attend the 1998 International Olympic Academy (IOA), Olympia, Greece; selected to serve as delegation leader.
- Drug testing team member at the Olympic Games and Paralympic Games in Atlanta, Georgia.
- Participated in an international exchange to Perth, Australia, to assist with drug testing at the Swimming World Championships.
- Working knowledge of Spanish (with continuing education).

PROFESSIONAL EXPERIENCE

WORLD ANTI-DOPING AGENCY (WADA), Montreal, Canada (2006 – present)
Manager, Outreach and Athlete Programs, Montreal, Canada
Project Manager, Lausanne, Switzerland (2006)

One of the first staff members hired during the founding of this organization in Switzerland to harmonize anti-doping rules worldwide. After the first year, moved with the organization to Montreal. Currently travel internationally and manage a recruited team of international experts to reach out to athletes during major competitions. Manage an operations budget of $300,000, in addition to event-specific budgets. Promote the program to athletes, international federations, media, and oversight organizations worldwide. Manage WADA's Athlete Committee, including athlete relations. Source and manage supplier relationships with printers, designers, promotional item providers, exhibition companies, freight forwarders, and photo services. Serve as a photographer at major events. Prepare reports and updates that highlight the program and present them to board members, stakeholders, and the public.

- Designed and developed WADA's athlete outreach program and athlete outreach model.
- Delivered WADA's athlete outreach program at more than 30 major events worldwide—Olympic, PanAm, Paralympic, Asian, Central American and Caribbean, South Pacific, Mediterranean, and Commonwealth Games, European Youth Festivals, and various World Championships.
- Wrote articles for the quarterly newsletter and managed the annual design, layout, and printing of the corporate brochure, list of prohibited substances, athlete guide, and other core documents.
- Produced two videos following the Athens and Turin Olympic Games that were used on the website and for promoting the program to the media and internal/external stakeholders.

AUSTRALIAN OLYMPIC COMMITTEE (AOC), Sydney, Australia (2003 – 2006)
Sport and Anti-Doping Coordinator

Developed and promoted the AOC's PURE 100% Drug Free brand. Recruited and empowered Australian Olympians to deliver the program to young athletes. Prepared press releases and managed press conferences. Maintained an archive of press clippings to support the program. Coordinated more than 350 volunteers to support the Australian Olympic Team in preparation for and during the Summer Olympic Games.

- Successfully implemented the first national anti-doping awareness program to promote clean sports.
- Sold the program to a sponsor, providing ongoing funds to underwrite future operations.
- Hit all targets and took the program to every corner of the country.

UNITED STATES OLYMPIC COMMITTEE (USOC), Colorado Springs, Colorado (1994 – 1998)
Drug Education Administrator

Administered the USOC Drug Education Program and managed a $250,000 budget. Interviewed, hired, supervised, and evaluated education program staff members. Provided input for and reviewed international agreements. Successfully managed the concept, content, production, and distribution of USOC drug education materials. Developed and implemented an educational material inventory and tracking system. Coordinated all aspects of international meetings, crew chief training seminars, committee meetings, etc., including site selection, hotel contracts, meeting agendas, transportation, correspondence, logistics, faculty appointments, entertainment, and evaluation. Created educational campaigns, including the coordination of poster designs, video productions, photo shoots, post-production processes, and resource development. Served as crew chief for drug testing operations at sporting events throughout the United States.

→ Coordinated yearly dissemination of more than 25,000 pieces of educational resources to National Governing Bodies, athletes, and others.
→ Worked with SGMA, MusiCares, and the U.S. Department of Education, among others, in developing alternative avenues for drug education.
→ Authored articles for *Olympic Coach* and write-ups for the World University Games, Pan American Games, USOC Fact Book, and the USOC Annual Report.
→ Appointed by the Human Resources Director to the USOC Employee Advisory Committee.
→ Member of the USOC Family Days Committee.

MEDIA SERVICES, DeKalb, Illinois (1992 – 1993)
Media Production Assistant

Wrote scripts and edited/produced videos. Hired and trained student assistants. Taught gripping, lighting, cameras, and microphone mixers for studio and remote productions.

SUEZ CANAL AUTHORITY, Suez, Egypt (1991 – 1992)
International Business Intern

Examined the operations and marketing strategies of the Suez Canal Authority. Studied private and public businesses throughout the country.

NORTHERN ILLINOIS UNIVERSITY, ATHLETIC DEPARTMENT, DeKalb, Illinois (1990 – 1991)
Promotions and Marketing Assistant

EDUCATION

MASTER OF SCIENCE IN EDUCATION, Northern Illinois University, DeKalb, Illinois (1994)
→ Emphasis in Sports Management; self-financed 100% of college expenses.

BACHELOR OF ARTS IN COMMUNICATIONS, Northern Illinois University, DeKalb, Illinois (1992)
→ Emphasis in Media Production.
→ Received Outstanding Major Award for the Communications Department.

SPORTING INTERESTS

→ Finisher, Chicago Marathon, 4:20 (2006)
→ Member, Illinois High School Association (IHSA) All-State Tennis Team (1988)
→ Member, IHSA All-State Badminton Team (1987, 1988)
→ Interests: tennis, table tennis, golf, running, skiing

COMPUTER SKILLS

→ Proficient in Windows, MS Word, PowerPoint, Outlook, and Internet Explorer.

BRUNO AZAR

1234 Crest Place • Vienna, Virginia 22181 • (703) 555-1234 • banderson@protypeltd.com

CompTIA.
A+® Certified

SYSTEM / NETWORK ADMINISTRATOR
"Success is a journey, not a destination."

Microsoft Certified
Professional

AREAS OF EXPERTISE

LAN / WAN Network Systems
Analysis • Troubleshooting
Optimization • Configuration
Documentation • Support
Information Security

SUMMARY

- Results-driven IT professional with extensive industry experience creating information system hardware and software solutions.
- Demonstrated ability to support business-critical operations in a variety of client-server environments.
- Expertise in network system configuration, repair, upgrade, and maintenance.

TECHNICAL SKILLS

Systems: Windows 2000/2003 Server, Novell Netware, IntranetWare 4.11, Windows 3.x/95/98/ME/XP/2000/Pro/Vista, MS-DOS 6.22, UNIX Solaris, HP-UX.

Hardware: Dell PowerEdge servers, IBM RS/6000, HP, Compaq, IBM-PC compatibles AT/ATX, PS/2, Dell laptops, HP network printers, wireless access points, security.

Networking: Active Directory, DNS, WINS, DHCP, TCP/IP, IPXSPX, NetBEUI, SUP, PPP, SNMP, Ethernet 802.3/802.5, switches, hubs, IP switches, repeaters, and print servers, Alcatel NMS 5620, CTI platforms, PC-Anywhere, DameWare, Telnet, FTP, Norton Symantec, McAfee Antivirus.

Tools: UNIX, HTML 4.0, Oracle Designer, NetMeeting, SMS remote tools, Symantec Ghost, Acronis imaging software.

Applications: MS Office (Word, Excel, PowerPoint, Access), MS Outlook, Lotus Notes, Norton Utilities, Internet applications, Nortel VPN, RSA security.

Certifications: CompTIA A+ Certification, CompTIA Network+ Certification, Microsoft Certified Professional (MCP), currently working toward Microsoft Certified Systems Engineer (MCSE).

SUMMARY OF EXPERIENCE

Network Administration
- Diagnosed, configured, implemented, deployed, and supported complex networks, desktop infrastructures, hardware, and software.
- Set up and configured workstations for new hires; deployed new hardware/software across the organization; configured PCs for global remote access and mobile technology.
- Managed accounts, network rights, and access to network systems, equipment, files, and folders.
- Created email accounts in MS Exchange and administered Microsoft Active Directory.
- Installed the latest anti-virus software, hot fixes, service packs, and updates to operating systems.
- Troubleshot network connectivity issues for local and terminal server users.
- Configured, optimized, and tested network servers, hubs, routers, and switches.
- Removed and replaced hardware components, installed interface cards, and upgraded memory, fixed storage, and IO/enhancement cards. Configured interfaces and device drivers.
- Identified and resolved internal system and network conflicts using diagnostic equipment and software, including conflicts between applications, hardware, devices, and operating systems.
- Ensured enterprise desktop standardization (ED R3) and vendor interoperability for Windows 2000 and applications.

Network Security
- Provided network security support, focusing on threats and vulnerabilities, as well as improving the security of systems.
- Paid special attention to intrusion detection, finding and fixing unprotected vulnerabilities, and ensuring that remote access points were well secured.
- Configured workstation security parameters, performed system backups, and archived network user profile data.
- Created and enforced security measures for large networks of remote users.

**SUMMARY OF
EXPERIENCE**

User Support
- Provided Tier II support for networks, operating systems, software applications, and hardware installations or conflicts.
- Assessed user's technical issues and recommend hardware/software solutions to improve business workflow and productivity.
- Used remote software to troubleshoot servers and desktops.
- Interacted with Tier 3 support for technical resolution of various cases.
- Provided postmortems to customers explaining outages and technical courses of action taken.
- Developed and presented on-site training on system preventive maintenance, business productivity applications, and Internet usage.

**PROFESSIONAL
WORK HISTORY**

IT SUPPORT ANALYST (2010)
Beers & Cutler, Vienna, Virginia
Provided second-level telephone and on-site support for 330 high-end network users, including operating systems, email, hardware, and software applications.

SENIOR DESKTOP SUPPORT TIER II ANALYST (Contract with Comsys) (2006 – 2008)
ExxonMobil Information Technology (EMIT), Fairfax, Virginia
Supported a 1,100-user network—handled 35–40 trouble tickets per day, closing 20–25 the same day.

DESKTOP SUPPORT TIER II ANALYST (Contract with Apex) (2005 – 2006)
Inter-American Development Bank (IADB), Information Technology Services, Washington, DC
Provided Tier 2 support for 3,500 users throughout the world. Deployed, troubleshot, and maintained the bank's network and desktop infrastructure.

DESKTOP SUPPORT TIER II ANALYST (Contract with Ciber) (2003 – 2005)
The World Bank Group, Information Solutions Group (ISG), Washington, DC
Deployed and supported the bank's network and the desktop infrastructure of 350 users in the Human Resources Department. Supported remote offices worldwide in a highly confidential environment.

INFORMATION ANALYST (Contract with Manpower) (2002 – 2003)
The World Bank Group, International Finance Corporation (IFC), Washington, DC
Demonstrated expertise by supporting 150 users in Microsoft XP/2000/NT environments. Maintained and optimized proprietary data repositories, including confidential employee profile and compensation information.

CTAC ENGINEER TIER II, NETWORK MANAGEMENT SYSTEMS (2000 – 2002)
Alcatel, Broadband Network Division, Chantilly, Virginia
Identified, isolated, and resolved network and data communication issues for strategic Latin American wide area network accounts using an expertise in Network Management Systems (NMS) 5620, UNIX Solaris-based platform. Maintained and upgraded NMS 5620 platform telecom and Internet-working technologies, including Telnet troubleshooting, diverse WAN topologies, multi-vendor interoperability, telecom metrics/statistics, and billing platforms.
- Minimized downtime for all interoperable WANs (X.25, T-1, E-1, TDM, ATM, frame relay).
- Delivered technical support in diverse, heterogeneous environments.
- Staged connectivity technical issues and software pre-deployment for strategic accounts in a live laboratory environment.
- Handled the largest, most intricate WAN in the Americas, maintained by Embratel in Brazil.

EDUCATION

BACHELOR OF SCIENCE, INFORMATION SYSTEMS MANAGEMENT (2000)
University of Maryland, University College, College Park, Maryland
- GPA in major 3.55/4.00; cumulative GPA 3.55/4.00.
- Achieved the Dean's List (1999 – 2000).
- Awarded a full MATA Scholarship during senior year.

**PERSONAL
INFORMATION**

Affiliations: Member of the IEEE Computer Society
Languages: Bilingual in English and Spanish

John Howard

john.howard128@protypeltd.com

(650) 555-1234

Information Systems Manager, Infrastructure

More than nine years of experience as a proven manager of IT infrastructure and services for geographically distributed, multi-location companies. Balanced the cost of infrastructure, quality of service, data security, reliability, and recoverability to provide critical technical infrastructure. Hands-on technical manager with credibility from the boardroom to the data center.

Strengths

- **Alignment:** Matched IT capabilities with business needs, building strong and trust-based relationships, and ensuring real value from IT investments.
- **Team Building:** Grew IT capabilities through recruiting, retention, leadership, mentoring, motivation, and measured results.
- **Systems Planning:** Integrated strategic, tactical, and operational systems, balancing risks, priorities, short-term needs, and long-term goals.
- **Technical Expertise:** Demonstrated leadership and technical qualities. Solid understanding of network administration, application support, telecommunication, and help desk operations.

Professional Experience

Comteris, Inc. (formerly Alleraton, Inc.), South San Francisco, CA — Biotech company   2006–Present
IT DIRECTOR

Selected for expertise in building and reorganizing IT departments from the ground-up using industry best practices. Transformed a 100% outsourced IT environment into an efficient and productive in-house IT team with full program components. Earned open door policy with upper management to discuss organizational goals and strategies. Relied upon to align IT planning in support of the business model.

- Oversaw daily IT operations across three physical locations—$800k budget, 5 + team members plus contractors, as needed.
- Rolled out multiple systems with tested audit trail in place. Successes were credited to the design and implementation of a *21 CFR Part 11* and *Sarbanes-Oxley (SOX)* compliance program. Established written IT controls, policies, and procedures building controls into growing infrastructure.
- Negotiated 35% decrease in ERP system purchase. Extensive research confirmed that vendor met the established criteria.
- Established and implemented multi-location backup and disaster recovery plan. Virtualized server image and acted as fail-over production server. Fault tolerance ensured uninterrupted business services.
- Designed and deployed help desk ticketing system that monitored ticket trends. Analysis of ticket issues increased monthly ticket completion rate from 55% to 100% in dci months.
- Recognized for growing teams and improving individual and team performance through mentorship and opportunities for the open exchange by team members of ideas, methods, and techniques.
- Decision-making authority for staff hires and performance evaluations, software, equipment, and capital expenditures. Made decisions using extensive research and detailed cost-benefit analyses.
- Delivered collaborative Internet environment using SharePoint. Became MCTS certified during the process. Project met deadline for major collaboration with a Japanese company. Established user-friendly methods for encouraging employees to use the Intranet for all business-related items.

> *"John came to our company at a time of rapid growth but weak internal processes and procedures. Our IT infrastructure was barely meeting our growing needs. He came in and was of immediate value. He relieved us of all of our IT worries and allowed us to focus on our jobs." – Yoko Tanaka, Former Senior Director of HR at Buckerman*

Buckerman Pharmaceuticals, Redwood City, CA—Pharmaceutical manufacturer   2005–2006
SENIOR IT MANAGER/IT CONSULTANT

Recruited to join the company after delivering a comprehensive IT assessment of current environment. Drove dramatic turnaround of chaotic IT department unable to provide necessary systems. Resolution of all issues and implementation of new services enabled organization to refocus on business goals. Created a supportive team environment of shared responsibilities, pitching in when necessary to meet needs.

- Led four-person team that provided 24/7 support for 120+ workstations and 15+ server network.
- Built a new IT infrastructure from the ground up in a highly visual role. Re-architected Active Directory from application, security, and back up operations levels.
- Resolved all escalated Tier 2 issues and demonstrated strong competencies in Tier 3 support.
- Entrusted to provide final sign-off for all network projects ensuring that all deliverables had been met.
- Received audit approval from PricewaterhouseCoopers after completing first-round SOX testing and delivering on all IT controls.
- Implemented and supported Microsoft ERP business solution for financial systems. Improved financial accountability and minimized risk by enabling *SOX* compliance.

Dorixalla Corporation, South San Francisco, CA—Biotech company   1999–2005
IT SITE MANAGER (2001–2005)
MANAGER OF DESKTOP OPERATIONS (2000–2001)
HELP DESK TECHNICIAN (1999–2000)

- Promoted through a series of increasingly responsible technology positions to a leadership role.
- Administered six-person 300+ workstation network across three physical locations. Managed Windows servers (2000/2003/2008), Cisco products, backup/file servers, and telecommunications.
- Designed a customized program to support 40-person sales force. Developed hardware/software standards and different methods of remote access. Met or exceeded expectations outlined in the Service Level Agreement (SLA). Transitioned sales people from manual processes to new system.
- Successfully standardized workstations across all sites in Active Directory. Advantages included scalability using OUs, trust management, DFS, GPO, and site replication.
- Delivered a unified help desk database that was used across WAN. Additional functionality included a working knowledge base, accountability and history tracking, asset management, and collaboration.

Sangerman Medical Corporation—Biotech company   1998–1999
MIS/TELECOM ADMINISTRATOR

University of California at San Francisco (UCSF)—Medical University   1995–1998
DESKTOP SUPPORT TECHNICIAN

Technology Profile

Operating Systems:	Windows XP, Vista; Windows Server 2003, 2008; Mac OSX, Liniux CentOS
Hardware:	IBM, Dell, Lenovo, HP, Cisco, F5, Avaya, Polycom
Software:	MS Office 2003-2007, All Microsoft OS, Server 2003 and 2008, Exchange 2003 and 2007, MS Project, Visio, SQL 2000 and 2005, IIS 6, SharePoint MOSS 2007, Microsoft Dynamics, Great Plains, Equity Edge, ADP, Vmware ESX, Hyper V, SAS, Blackberry Enterprise, Symantec applications, Trend Micro, Backup Exec, Track IT
Networking:	Active Directory, VPN, DNS, DHCP, TCP/IP, VPN, SMTP, FTP, IPSEC, SSL, HTTP, SNMP, VLAN, VoIP, WSUS
Data Center:	HVAC, electrical wiring, cabling, rack storage, rack and server alignment, UPS

Education and Qualifications

A.S., Computer Science, College of San Mateo, CA
MCSA (Windows 2003 Server), **MCTS** (SharePoint 2007) **CCNA** (pending)

john henderson, CEC

555-555-1234 • henderson@protypeltd.com
1000 green mountain lane • birmingham, alabama 35200

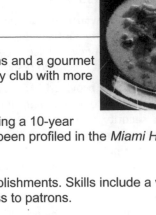

certified executive chef

- High-energy professional currently managing five kitchens and a gourmet bakery, supervising a 34-person staff for a private country club with more than 1,100 members.

- Award-winning chef with 20+ years of experience, including a 10-year tenure as Executive Chef. "Innovative culinary skill" has been profiled in the *Miami Herald*, *CulinaryTrends.net*, and *Southern Living.*

- Accomplished manager of multi-outlet million-dollar establishments. Skills include a vibrant, outgoing personality and a high degree of responsiveness to patrons.

- Graduate, with distinction, of the French Culinary Institute, New York City.

- Engaging training and development specialist with a track record of leveling costs while maintaining the highest standards of quality and presentation.

professional experience

executive chef   2007 to present
vestavia country club, birmingham, alabama

Direct all food service operations for a thriving private country club, coordinating four kitchens and a full-time bakery. Prepare an average of 350 meals daily, serving a wide variety of fare, from gourmet international cuisine to home-cooked meals and pizza. Coordinate workflow of a 26-person staff, leading quarterly staff meetings and working one-on-one to improve cooks' skills. Hold staff to the highest standards in hygiene and cleanliness. Negotiate favorable contracts with large vendors, locking in prices to reduce costs. Peak covers were 2,500 in one day.
- Opened successful upscale 40-seat spa cuisine restaurant and full-time bakery, adding them to the property's existing two restaurants.
- Direct catering events accommodating 1,000+ patrons.
- Improved efficiency by coordinating kitchen redesign and boosting adherence to time standards.
- Introduce approximately 300 new menu items annually to well-traveled, highly educated club members with distinctive tastes.

executive chef   2004 to 2007
the low country club, charleston, south carolina

Directed daily operations for the largest private club in the United States, overseeing three dining options, catering division, and full-time pastry department. Hired and trained all apprentices, and introduced exciting new events and theme nights. Budgeted food, labor, overhead and shrinkage costs and analyzed recipes to determine food, labor, and overhead costs and to assign prices to various dishes. Oversaw kitchen operations to ensure superior quality and presentation.
- Achieved a 20% increase in guest counts by training and developing a staff of 28, resulting in exceptional consistency of product off the line.
- Obtained feedback daily by listening to the wait staff and talking with club members about dining experience.
- Built community goodwill by initiating an American Culinary Foundation (ACF) approved apprenticeship program to enhance participants' skill sets and broaden opportunities for career advancement.
- During a multi-year period of cost increases, held banquet food costs at 31% and maintained club food costs at 36.5%.

professional experience (continued)

general manager / executive chef   2001 to 2004
carolina creek, charleston, south carolina

Directed a multi-outlet facility specializing in award-winning Southern cuisine. Increased customer base by introducing creative, innovative menu items and consistently maintaining high quality standards. Controlled food, labor, overhead, and shrinkage costs while enhancing presentation and improving kitchen techniques. Developed a new wine program. Supervised 31-person staff (kitchen staff of 14).
- Prepared an average of 250 à la carte dinners nightly during season.
- Completely restructured restaurant and earned recognition in local and national newspapers, including *Miami Herald* review complimenting outstanding food and service.

executive chef   1998 to 2001
tapas, charleston, south carolina

Revitalized a struggling, 35-year-old family restaurant, tripling menu size, adding fun dining items and creating a true success story. The consistently delectable food and inviting ambience remedied the restaurant's former struggles.
- Served an average of 175–200 from-scratch covers a day, supervising an 8-person kitchen staff.
- Business became so lucrative that during second year, owner retired debt on building.

awards and activities

- President, Charleston Chefs and Cooks Association
- Best Local Cuisine, Charleston, South Carolina, 2005 and 2006
- American Culinary Federation (ACF) Demonstrator, How to Do a Wine/Beer Dinner at Your Club
- Chef / Host, Chef's Table Fundraiser, Savannah, Georgia
- Chef / Host, Magnolia Culinary Challenge, Savannah, Georgia

education and certifications

- Honors graduate, French Culinary Institute, New York City, New York
- Certified Executive Chef (CEC)
- Member, American Culinary Federation
- Attended the acclaimed Club Chef's Institute at the Greenbrier in the Alleghenies (West Virginia), 2006
- Serve Safe Certified Certificates in Ice Carving, Nutrition, Management, and Sanitation

Robert C. Stanton

21864 Larimer Drive ★ Denver, CO 20653
719–888–3232 (M) ★ stanton@protypeltd.com

QUALIFICATION STATEMENT

Senior Criminal Investigator with multi–year experiences, personal reputation for integrity, high moral standards, and strong work ethic offering:

◇ Extensive professional development in law enforcement procedures and techniques.

◇ Cognizance of constitutional protection conducting search/seizure and arrest/detention methodologies.

◇ Competency to distinguish between relevant and irrelevant, and admissible and inadmissible information/evidence when collecting and preserving physical evidence.

◇ Capacities to communicate in writing in order to prepare, review, evaluate, and issue investigative reports.

AREAS OF PROFESSIONAL RESPONSIBILITY

Emergency Preparedness/Response ★ Infrastructure/Asset Protection★ Surveillance Observations
Operational Readiness/Mobilization Plans ★ Investigative Techniques/Methodologies ★ Search and Seizure
Conflict Resolution ★ Crisis Intervention Techniques ★ Security Administration ★ Risk Management

MILITARY PROFILE

U.S. NAVY   **Feb 1987–Mar 2009**

KEY POSITIONS

Anti-Terrorism/Physical Security Officer (Nov 2007–Mar 2009)
Military Investigator (Apr 2004–Mar 2009)
Chief of Detectives (Apr 2004–Nov 2007)
Law Enforcement Specialist (Jan 1995–Oct 2000)

INVESTIGATIVE ABILITY

Chief of Detectives—Managed police agency with a combined team of six civilian detectives and six military police investigators. Performed full range of investigative functions on assigned cases from planning through fact-finding to reporting investigation results. Partnered with Naval Criminal Investigative Service (NCIS) other federal and local law enforcement agencies

Investigating Crimes—Skillfully orchestrated hundreds of extensive investigations. Obtained facts or statements from complainants, witnesses, and accused persons and recorded interviews. Cases ranged from property and fund accountability, military offenses, soliciting, larceny, serious traffic offenses, narcotic transactions to robbery, grand theft/vehicle theft, and assault. Wrote case reports and submitted record of suspicion, statement of witnesses, and progress of investigation. Analyzed police reports to determine what additional information and investigative work was needed.

SURVEILLANCE EXPERTISE

Undercover Operations—Oversight management of officers conducting over 30 undercover operations ranging from car thefts, drugs, and retail theft. Continually evaluated investigations and determined at what stage to initiate major actions after obtaining appropriate clearances for purchasing of evidence, conducting searches and seizures, expansion or curtailment of cases, and apprehension and arrest of persons suspected of violating provisions of the law.

Conducting Surveillances—Maintained discretion in the observation and collection of facts related to investigations. Identified/obtained information and data necessary to assess situation accurately and quickly. Independently produced professional and fully detailed reports outlining activity. Testified to the collected facts obtained in hearings or court of law.

PROFESSIONAL PROFILE

DEPARTMENT OF CORRECTIONS, Raleigh, NC   **Jun 1980–Jan 1987**

EMERGENCY RESPONSE/SECURITY OPERATIONS

First Responder—Provided force security on high profile detainees involved in assaults, theft, destruction of property, gang violence, drugs, arson, death, murder in the facility, bombs, fire, hostage situations, suicides, and medical emergencies. Examined crime scenes to obtain clues and gather evidence. Established protected perimeter to aid evidence preservation for investigators of crime scenes. Performed tactical operations required securing areas or people based on situational necessity. Assessed situation, directed tactical responses, and provided immediate assistance as mandated by policies of The American Correctional Association, Bureau of Prisons, and facility, state, and federal government guidance.

ACADEMIC SHOWCASE / PROFESSIONAL DEVELOPMENT

BA DEGREE, CRIMINAL JUSTICE, Essex College, Roundtable, IL

PROFESSIONAL DEVELOPMENT
Incident Command: Capabilities, Planning and Response Actions, 2008
State and Local Anti-Terrorism Training, 2008
Leading Successful On-Site Teams, 2007
Understand and Investigating Street Gangs, 2007
Interviewing and Interrogation Techniques, 2004
Emergency Response Training, 2002

NETWORK CERTIFICATIONS / AFFILIATIONS

National Crime Information Center (NCIC)
National Integrated Ballistics Information Network (NIBIN)
Joint Personnel Adjudication System (JPAS)
Fraternal Order of Police; National Tactical Officer Association

Marty Jacobs

1234 Main Street • St. Louis, MO 63129
636-555-1234 • marty.jacobs@protypeltd.com

Restaurant Cook
"Only serve food fit for my mother"

Dependable, experienced cook with more than 18 years of experience in restaurant food preparation and management. Quick to learn new procedures and recipes; take pride in quality and attractiveness of plated meals. Follow recipes with meticulous accuracy, and receive excellent feedback when asked to create new menu items. Excellent knife skills; adept in cooking steaks by "feel" and rarely have steaks returned. Strength in planning and multi-tasking; always ensure enough stock is on hand to handle daily needs. Reputation for strong organizational skills, high standards of kitchen cleanliness, and turnaround of poorly performing restaurants.

SAMPLE MENU ITEMS

- Chicken Florentine
- Veal Saltimbocca
- Tortellini
- Chicken Pomadoro
- Tilapia Moutarde
- Smoked Pork Ribs
- Baked Potato Soup

- Tutto Mare
- Pasta Con Broccoli
- Minestrone Soup
- Grilled Orange Roughy
- Grilled Beef Tenderloin
- Grilled Portabella Mushrooms
- Ham and Bean Soup

- Chicken Spiedini
- Pasta Cambertti
- Shrimp Scampi
- Oyster Rockefeller
- Rib Eye Steak Sandwich
- Grilled BBQ Chicken Pizza
- Béarnaise / Hollandaise Sauces

RELATED EXPERIENCE

First Prize Winner, JONES CHIROPRACTIC FIRST ANNUAL BAKING CONTEST, Arnold, MO, 2009
Featured judge: Mary Hostetter, owner of the Blue Owl Restaurant and author of nine cookbooks.
- Bested 25 entrants to win **first prize** for bacon-wrapped shrimp (stuffed with jalapeño and pepper cheese).

Caterer, LACHEF AND CO., St. Louis, MO, 1995–2000
Full-service caterer for parties, weddings, and holiday events for 10 to 500 guests.
Prepared and displayed menu items, served as bartender, set up portable kitchens, and did whatever was necessary to make party experiences enjoyable for hosts and guests.
- Catered international event at the St. Louis Arch serving 500+ people.

Cook • Assistant Manager, J PARRINO'S PASTA HOUSE & BAR, Springfield, MO, 1983–1986
Authentic Italian restaurant serving pasta, steak and seafood entrees.
Partnered with owner to design, build, and open a new restaurant still in operation today. Developed menu, selected vendors, designed kitchen layout to optimize workflow, participated in actual building of restaurant, trained cooks, and coordinated food preparation.
- Easily managed large dinner rushes before and after Blues hockey games.

Marty Jacobs

1234 Main Street • St. Louis, MO 63129
636-555-1234 • marty.jacobs@protypeltd.com

Cook ▪ Kitchen Manager • Bartender, RICH & CHARLIE'S; THE PASTA HOUSE, St. Louis, MO, 1974–1983
The Pasta House Company offers over 25 pasta varieties and nearly 15 specialty chicken items, beef and seafood entrees.

Began as dishwasher at age 15, progressed rapidly to cook in three months. Prepared pasta and steak, made sauces to order, and cut veal, fish, and steaks. Monitored food costs, hired and trained new staff and managers, worked with vendors to place food orders, and kept kitchen clean.

- Chosen to work on-site at other Pasta House locations to identify and resolve food cost and labor problems. Dismissed employees for theft and hired and trained new managers and employees.
- Assisted in opening two new locations, one which later became the training store (Northwest Plaza).Opened new restaurant in the Central West End called "The Flamingo Café" adding menu items such as oysters Rockefeller, casino clams, and barbecued shrimp. Ordered fresh seafood from New Orleans and scheduled airport deliveries.

ADDITIONAL EXPERIENCE

Home Remodeler • Repairman, M-J HOME REPAIR, St. Louis, MO   1999–Present
Manage multi-service remodeling and handyman business. Perform major and minor home remodeling projects such as bathrooms, kitchens, basements, decks, and painting. Repair garage door openers, install doors and windows, and replace faucets and toilets.

"Marty was a perfectionist when remodeling our basement and adding new bathrooms to our old house." G.M.

"Marty replaced my broken windows quickly, and left the house perfectly spotless." D.P.

Apartment Maintenance Worker, MILLS PROPERTIES, INC., Clayton, MO   1986–1995
Maintained apartments and commercial properties: made units ready for rental, installed and repaired electrical and plumbing issues, maintained air conditioning window units, and promptly handled all-hours service calls.

COMMUNITY INVOLVEMENT

GOOD SHEPHERD PRESBYTERIAN CHURCH, St. Louis, MO   2008–Present

- As **Volunteer Event Coordinator,** handled food and logistics for church picnic for 100+ guests as an outreach to the community. Coordinated with health inspector, county planning and zoning, and highway departments to obtain all permits. Prepared and served pork steaks, bratwurst, grilled chicken, hot dogs, baked beans, coleslaw, and potato salad. Charged nominal fees to cover costs; extra money raised was donated to food pantries.
- As **Food Pantry Coordinator,** oversee Meal-a-Month program. Develop menus and ask church members to donate canned goods and staples to assist the needy. Coordinate with director to identify and meet greatest areas of need.

STANLEY L. THOMAS, EMT-P, EMT-T

12345 Main Street ◆ Rocky Point, NC 28457 ◆ 910.555.1212 ◆ thomas@ protypeltd.com

PARAMEDIC
Delivering medical excellence and situational control in every circumstance.

**REMOTE ◆ SWIFTWATER ◆ OCEAN ◆ SEARCH AND RESCUE ◆ SCUBA ◆ WILDERNESS ◆ ADVANCE TRAUMA ◆ HazMat
SUPERVISION ◆ SITUATIONAL CONTROL ◆ COMMAND CENTER ◆ PROTOCOL ◆ AIR SUPPORT**

Highly trained and credentialed paramedic with more than fifteen years of experience administering emergency care and shoring up departmental infrastructure with sound leadership and targeted, up-to-date protocols. Strong ability to conceptualize and implement site-specific emergency plans and manage details required to execute effective operation. Able to maintain equipment and supplies in support of response readiness. Skilled practitioner.

Spanish for Emergency Medical Services ◆ Student Pilot

Available for domestic and overseas assignments.

CERTIFICATION AND CREDENTIALS

Advanced Cardiac Life Support
Advance Trauma Life Support
All-Terrain Vehicle Medical
Technician
Basic Life Support
Basic Trauma Life Support
Hazardous Material Operations
NC EMT-Paramedic–**EMT-P**

NC Emergency Management–**Type 1**
Pediatric Advance Life Support
Rope Rescue Technician
Rescue Tech–Vehicle and Machinery
Rescue–**RT-VMR**
SCUBA Diving Certification
Search and Rescue Certification-**SAR**
Swift Water Rescue Tech–**SRT-1**

State Medical Assistant Team
Tactical Emergency Medical Support
(TEMS)–EMT-T
Tactical Combat Casuality Care–**TCCC**
USDOL Journeyman Paramedic
Wilderness Rescue Certification

PROFESSIONAL EXPERIENCE

PRACTICAL:

➤ Provided emergency medical services as a remote medic in areas with more than 45-minute backup response time. Capable of maintaining self and critically injured patient for 24–72 hours in wilderness and other situations. Assessed injuries, stabilized patients, set up IVs, administered drugs, performed emergency field procedures, documented treatment, prepared for transport, and communicated status to medical personnel.

➤ Evaluated situations and determined proper response, care, and rescue required. Called in support as needed to stabilize patient, secure area, and protect evidence. Set up incident command center and documented actions.

➤ Trained new team members, selected individuals for special-event coverage, and nominated personnel for special team training—swiftwater, ocean, dive, wilderness, special event, tactical medical.

➤ Liaised emergency room communications—directed and diverted transport vehicles, considering existing hospital workloads and potential wait times while ensuring proper patient care for sustained injuries.

MANAGERIAL:

➤ Supervised an 18-person team assigned to eight stations serving Pender County, NC. Covered 871 square miles—oceanfront resort to wilderness areas—and 51,000+ full-time residents. Handled human resource, credentialing and uniform duties for team. Established 30-day schedule for 160 personnel. Monitored radio transmissions from four radios, concurrently, verifying response protocol adherence and ensuring countywide coverage.

➤ Acted as the voice and face of emergency management. Relayed patient location and status information to families, responded to news reporter questions, on camera, during large-scale incidents and interfaced with high-ranking government officials, giving firm recommendations, when making difficult decisions regarding public safety.

➤ Amended existing procedures for all functions as needed. Drafted new policies and operating procedures for swiftwater and ocean rescue teams, addressing local topography, worker safety, concealed hazards, hazardous spills, governmental agency and EPA clean-up up requirements and other potential circumstances.

PROFESSIONAL EXPERIENCE, CONTINUED

➤ Adapted staffing and assignments to seasonal population influx from area resorts and colleges concurrent with summer tourist season and academic calendars.

➤ Adhered to fleet maintenance protocol as directed by maintenance department. Ensured scheduled maintenance routing for almost 30 land and water vehicles assigned to jurisdiction, and saw to proper country distribution of response equipment based on daily emergency requirements.

➤ Deployed staff national disasters joining the National Response Team, and adjusted county assignments for territory coverage during team reduction periods.

➤ Coordinated public safety efforts and set up command centers for planned events with 15,000+ attendees.

EMPLOYMENT CHRONOLOGY

PENDER RESCUE AND EMERGENCY MEDICAL SERVICES, Hampstead, NC, 2003–Present
    Shift Captain, Ocean Rescue Team Coordinator, Swiftwater Rescue Team Director 2005–Present
        Accepted Swift-water and ocean rescue team leadership assignments ,retaining previously held duties in 2007 and 2008, respectively.
    Field Training Officer, 2003–2004
        Promoted from paramedic to FTO within two months after hire based on exemplary performance.
    Paramedic, 2003

Paramedic, Onslow County Emergency Medical Services, Jacksonville, NC, 2000–2003
    Honed urban rescue capabilities.

Quick Response Paramedic, Johnston County Emergency Medical Services, Smithfield, NC, 1999–2000
    Stabilized patients on scene and prepared them from transport. Served on chart audit and review, and new protocol and system planning committees.

Crew Chief Paramedic, Selma Emergency Medical Services and Rescue, Selma, NC, 1998–1999
    Chaired chart audit and review committee. Taught paramedic classes at Johnston Community College.

Paramedic, Mid-South Medical Transport, Smithfield, NC, 1997–1999

United States Navy
    Maintained physical fitness reports, weight management, and MSDS documents for both assignments.
    Navy Corpsman, 2nd Battalion, 9th Marines H&S Company, BAS, Camp Lejeune, NC, 1995–1997
        Provided patient care during deployment and special operations. Wrote mass casualty and patient transport plans. Performed triage, stabilization, and minor surgeries in a combat zone, optimizing care for long-term recovery.
    Navy Corpsman, Portsmouth Naval Hospital Emergency Department, Portsmouth, VA, 1994–1995
        Administered care in emergency rooms, in flight, and during ambulance transport. Documented protocols.

EDUCATION

Associate Degree, Fire Science, Coastal Carolina Community College, Jacksonville, NC
Associate Degree *(NOTE: Lacking only three courses toward completion of both Associate Degrees)*
Emergency Medical Services, Fayetteville Technical Community College, Fayetteville, NC

Paramedic Certification, Fayetteville Technical Community College, Fayetteville, NC
Naval Hospital Corpsman, Advance Combat Corpsman, Naval School of Health and Science, San Diego, CA

NOTABLES

North Carolina Coastal Region Paramedic Competition 2003
State competitor; Eatman-Edwards Award 1998
Recognition for outstanding performances as a paramedic in Johnston County, NC
Outstanding Young Men of America 1993

 **Harry R. Moore**

1200 Arroyo Chamisa ◇ Santa Fe, NM 87505
Office: (505) 555-1234 ◇ Mobile: (505) 555-5678

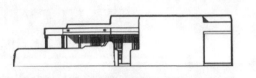

GENERAL CONTRACTOR / ARCHITECT / MASTER CRAFTSMAN
Specializing in Custom Designed/Built Adobe Homes that Capture the Spirit of Santa Fe

Award-winning, widely respected General Contractor specializing in designing and building unique, custom-made, energy-efficient *"Santa Fe Style"* adobe homes that incorporate the warmth, the spirituality, and the charm of the historical Santa Fe tradition by combining the best of both Native American and Hispanic cultures. Expert qualifications in merging modern technologies and new products with *"tried and true"* methods of building that have been around for centuries. Recognized for attention to detail and ability to create livable, high-quality homes.

Custom Aesthetic Specialties Include:
- ◇ Carved Corbels
- ◇ Plaster Ceilings with Vigas
- ◇ Latillas or Hand-Hewn Beams
- ◇ Ceramic Tile, Wood, or Flagstone Floors
- ◇ Hand-Trowelled Plaster Walls
- ◇ Arched and Curved Entryways, Doorways, and Walls
- ◇ Energy Efficient Passive Solar Designs

Home Builder's Association Awards:
Home Builder of the Year *(7 Awards)*
Winner – Best Custom Built Home
Winner – Best Custom Home Design

Professional Affiliations:
Member, National Home Builder's Association
Member, New Mexico Home Builder's Association
Member, Santa Fe Area Home Builder's Association

PROFESSIONAL BACKGROUND

Owner/General Contractor   *1995–present*
HARRY R. MOORE CONSTRUCTION COMPANY   *Santa Fe, New Mexico*

Oversee, direct, and coordinate custom-made home building projects ranging from $350K to $1.4 million. Manage all phases of project development from initial client contact, through contract negotiation and conceptual and architectural design, to the finished home. Recruit, hire, and manage 15 to 25 expert craftsmen; coordinate and direct carefully selected subcontractors. Demonstrated commitment to quality construction and exceptional client service.

EDUCATION

Bachelor of Business Administration
University of New Mexico, Albuquerque, New Mexico

Paragraph Style

Good advertisements are designed in such a way that the reader's eye is immediately drawn to important pieces of information using type and graphic elements, including bold, italics, and headline fonts, among others. Then the design must guide the reader's eye down the page from one piece of information to the next with the use of white space or graphic designs/lines between short paragraphs.

In this science of typography, very long lines of text (longer than five or six inches, depending on the font) and large blocks of text (more than seven typeset lines) are considered to be tiring to the reader's eye. If you look closely at textbooks, magazines, and newspapers, you will notice that the information is usually typeset in columns to reduce line lengths, and journalists intentionally write in short paragraphs because they are more reader friendly.

How does this science translate into the design of a résumé? As a general rule, you should keep your lines of text no longer than six inches—four to five inches is even better—and your paragraphs shorter than seven lines of text each. Many people find it difficult to cram the description of a job and its accomplishments into a single paragraph while following this rule. Therefore, you will often see bulleted sentences used on résumés instead of paragraphs or following an introductory paragraph.

If you prefer the paragraph style, there are some tricks of the trade that can help you make your résumé more readable:

1. List the job summary in paragraph form and then use bullets to highlight your achievements (pages 214–219).

2. Divide your experience into related information and use several shorter paragraphs under each job description (page 215).

3. Use left headings instead of centered headings (pages 216, 217, 222) to make the line lengths shorter. This won't work, however, when the shorter line length forces your information into very long paragraphs. It is better to have longer line lengths and shorter paragraphs.

Full justification—where all the lines end at the same place on the right margin (like the résumé on page 222)—makes paragraph-style résumés look more formal. Ragged right margins (like on this page and the rest of the résumés in this chapter) generally give a more informal appearance. Full justification creates a neater appearance any time the lines of text run all of the way to the right margin, even in bulleted résumés, but it can also cause "rivers" and "gutters" of white space that can be fixed with hyphenation. However, you can choose either style and not go wrong. Again, it is just a matter of your personal preference.

RICK NORTON

1234 Tuscarora Court ▪ Frederick, MD 21702
rick.norton@protypeltd.com ▪ 240.555.4321

TECHNICAL SALES SPECIALIST

Field Sales ▪ Business Development ▪ Territory Management ▪ Product Training

~ A trusted advisor who creates customized solutions ~

Competitive spirit, passion for setting and achieving performance-driven goals, consistent record of locking out the competition, and ability to quickly turn opportunities into orders—personal trademarks of a sales career spanning more than 15 years with a global provider of technology solutions for academic, research, and manufacturing sectors. Combine electrical engineering degree, prior hands-on experience, and exceptional interpersonal skills to intuitively facilitate the sales process, from the technician level to executive decision makers. Skilled at technical probing and qualifying customers; unwavering in overcoming obstacles and generating innovative ideas and solutions to close sales.

"Rick's ability to reach his overall annual quota year after year is a tribute to his ability to stay focused on results, a strong positive attitude, and strong work ethic to prospect for opportunities to fill his funnel and then convert these opportunities and close the business—amongst the strongest closers in the business." –District Sales Manager

★ **Surpassed aggressive sales quotas 13 out of 15 years. Overcame weak start in FY'04 and rallied 3rd and 4th quarters to secure $1.74 million in sales with 11.5% year-end gain.**

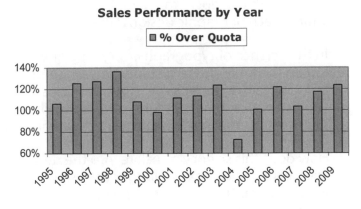

Sales Performance by Year

PROFESSIONAL EXPERIENCE

FIELD SALES ENGINEER, Ralston Technologies, Rockville, MD   1993–Present

Key contributor to Ralston's sustained reputation as the world's leading supplier of electronic test and measurement equipment. As outside sales representative, bring technical and product expertise to identifying potential business opportunities, implement strategies to capture competitors' market share, and grow existing accounts within assigned territories.

- Seamlessly transitioned through various business markets targeting telecommunications, manufacturing, research, and academic sectors. Use perceptive listening and questioning to analyze customer challenges and assimilate information pertaining to customer buying practices, budget cycles, funding sources, and procurement processes. Identify and connect with key decision makers, overcome obstacles and objections, and persist in pinpointing creative solutions to close sales.

- Collaborate with internal and external business partners (distributors, online sales organization, channel partners, field engineers, and program rental partners) to develop, refine, and execute well-thought-out reach plans that provide direction for forecasting monthly and quarterly sales performance, managing territories, and meeting quotas. Plan and facilitate various educational and promotional events aimed at improving customers' product knowledge and awareness of cutting-edge engineering design practices.

- A creative implementer of innovative company programs and sales tools, including customized financing, maintenance services and extended warranties, strategic and aggressive price discounts, direct mail and e-marketing campaigns, customer "lunch and learn" programs, and B2B promotional events.

"Rick is an excellent performer that I can always count on to exceed his goals, satisfy his customers, and use solid judgment in all aspects of his job … a hard worker … never satisfied with his own results and constantly searching for ways to improve." – District Sales Manager

RALSTON TECHNOLOGIES (*continued*)

Key Assignments and Outcomes

Target Account Organization (current)*: Territory*: Maryland and Virginia. *Targets*: Existing mix of high-volume, multimillion-dollar accounts and smaller strategic accounts with primary share-of-spend on competitors' products. *Challenge*: Strategically grow accounts and weaken competitors' hold.

Geographic and Target Account Organization (2005–2009): *Territory:* Large, geographically disperse territory encompassing parts of Maryland and Virginia. *Targets:* Competitive anchor accounts; existing key accounts with installed base and share-of-spend; current and potential distributors. *Challenge*: Overcome landmark economic recession while continuing to grow and sustain business.

Educational Institutions Rep (2000–2002): *Territory:* Maryland, Pennsylvania, and Virginia. *Targets:* Colleges and universities with engineering programs; key accounts included University of Maryland, Virginia Tech, Virginia Commonwealth University, Norfolk State University, Penn State, and Johns Hopkins University Applied Physics Lab. *Challenge:* Position Agilent products for inclusion in technical research proposals and permeate electrical, mechanical, and physics labs with test and measurement equipment.

New Business Team, Test and Measurement (1993–1999): *Territory:* Multimillion-dollar territory comprised of 150+ emerging accounts; largest geographic territory of any field-sales engineer in the district. *Targets:* Diverse market of wireless telecommunications, electronic manufacturing, fiber optics, and digital design firms. *Challenge:* Prospect and mine new business by focusing sales efforts on market sectors with strongest potential for growth.

- Aggressively penetrated Northern VA territory and shook competitors' stronghold. In eight months, secured sales approaching $700K.
- Persevered in hard-hitting battle with competitor that resulted in capturing key account and unleashing stream with projected FY '09 revenues approaching $1.5 million
- Triumphed over competitor's deep discounts and 40% lower price-point and prevailed throughout lengthy sales cycle to ultimately secure $400K sale and exclusive installation in 52 labs of a major university.
- Took immediate and collaborative action to salvage at-risk account by engaging national and regional sales managers in resolving purchasing agent's concerns about Agilent's transition to Oracle and the fall-out of problems and numerous obstacles impacting customers.
- Disrupted competitor's control of account and gained loyal customer by initiating collaborative cross-selling with internal business partner to offer customized product solution.
- Made significant contributions to Mid-Atlantic Mega Team's six-month success in producing $8.8 million in new business revenue.
- Trounced the competition and booked approximately $900K in business from a contract manufacturer aimed at expanding to a new market channel.
- Landed $280K deal with local division of a start-up wireless Internet provider that mushroomed to a sole-supplier national account.
- Pioneered operational restructuring models that shifted routine transactional sales activities to internal departments and administrative personnel, and equipped field sales engineers with more time for scouting complex "solution-oriented" opportunities.
- Recorded district's highest customer attendance for annual product road show by heavily marketing and promoting this one-week event through various repetitive outreach activities.

"Rick is exceptional at building and maintaining strong, positive working relationships resulting in unique competitive advantage because customers lose all interest in investigating other vendor options." – District Sales Manager

---

EDUCATION AND PROFESSIONAL DEVELOPMENT

Bachelor of Science, Electrical Engineering—Purdue University, Indianapolis, IN
Basho Strategies Sales Training
Hewlett-Packard Sales Training I / II Situational Sales Negotiations

VALERIE MCGOWAN, PMP

1234 East Old Stone Circle North • Chandler, Arizona 85249
Cell: (602) 555-5555 • Email: vmcgowan@protypeltd.com

DYNAMIC, PROJECT / PROGRAM MANAGER

AREAS OF EXPERTISE	EXECUTIVE SUMMARY
Program and Project Management Process Mapping and Improvement Strategic Planning Application of PM Methodologies Cross-Functional Team Leadership Proposal Development • RFP Response Budget Planning and Analysis Governance Compliance	• High-functioning *Project Management Professional (PMP)* with more than ten years of experience in retail services and information technology environments. • Broad background in full project life-cycle ownership using formalized process methodologies in network infrastructure and unified communications arenas. • Analytical thinker with the innate ability to see the entire picture of the challenges faced by organizations. • Effective communicator and team player who can build consensus and influence key decision-makers.

PROFESSIONAL EXPERIENCE

SENIOR PROJECT MANAGER / BUSINESS SOLUTIONS MANAGER (2003 – present)
Calence, LLC (a division of Insight Consulting), Tempe, Arizona
Direct complex projects (up to 20 per year) involving multiple vendors that deliver technical solutions to Fortune 500 clients in the financial, pharmaceutical, manufacturing, and global shipping industries, as well as the government sector. Manage the entire project life cycle for small to large projects, as well as for programs with multiple projects and project managers. Oversee a $6 million portfolio of projects, including core infrastructure initiatives and advanced technology deployment.

Key Accomplishments:

• *Currently managing a five-year program for a state government,* including such projects as an optical ring expansion, statewide end-of-life router replacement, voice/data infrastructure development, as well as large and small office IP telephony installations. Coach and lead geographically dispersed project and engineering teams. Manage third-party vendors and transport providers. Determine each project's scope, develop proposals, oversee project implementation, and periodically report the status of all projects

• *Managed the IP Contact Center project for a regional bank's 300-seat call center.* Implemented an IPCC infrastructure (including Cisco email manager and Web collaboration servers) for 19 contact center departments. Collaborated with call recording and workforce management integration teams to roll out services to select call center groups. Managed the work plan, budget, issue resolution, status reporting, and risks associated with the project.

• *Managed the deployment of a new infrastructure and IP telephony system at a regional bank,* migrating from a legacy system to decrease telephone expenses. The system consisted of 550 phones deployed centrally and to more than 45 regional locations. Coordinated training and planned a rollout schedule that relied on rotating resources to accommodate an aggressive deployment time frame.

• *Oversaw the end-to-end project life cycle of an enterprise network migration* that encompassed more than 3,000 users and 70 switches across 11 facilities of a community college district. Coordinated with project sponsors, individual site leaders, and support personnel. Managed all logistics related to product shipments in excess of $6 million, retirement of decommissioned equipment, and individual site and roll-up budget reporting and reconciliation.

• *Planned and coordinated a rolling national IPT deployment for a global beverage manufacturer.* Managed resource logistics, supported a centralized remote engineering deployment staff, drove field communication and data collection efforts, and assured adherence to deployment plans during implementations. Created the platform for greater access to network resources with significant cost savings.

• *Led a three-person security team in the migration of 140+ extranet clients* as the result of global merger of an international shipping company. Managed external client communications, project schedules, migration, status reporting, and change management. Achieved less than 2% outage during data center move.

• *Provided oversight for a portfolio of projects over an 18-month period for a global pharmaceutical company.* Supported internal client-service teams and served as the gatekeeper of information flowing to the customer. Managed the portfolio budget, forecasting, reporting, and staffing. Provided logistical and travel coordination for up to 20 consultants in five national locations.

PROFESSIONAL EXPERIENCE

Calence, LLC (continued)

- *Led a seven-person team that published more than 20 infrastructure, security, and advanced technology architectures for a financial services organization.* Partnered with individual architects to assist with the development of architectures. Coordinated organization-wide communications and processes related to gaining formal approval of architectures. Developed and presented documentation and diagrams. Planned regional meetings. Mapped and documented processes to support regulatory requirements.

MARKETING MANAGER, TRAVEL SERVICES (1994 – 1998, 2000 – 2003)
Arizona Automobile Association, Phoenix, Arizona

Developed and implemented annual cruise and tour marketing programs for the state's largest retail travel agency generating $40 million in annual revenue. Wrote the company's first-ever annual marketing plan. Managed vendor relations, created vendor-specific marketing plans, and negotiated co-op funding for advertising programs. Approved ongoing print and electronic media for 12–15 vendors annually. Coordinated creative services. Developed direct mail campaigns. Ensured compliance with a $1 million operating budget, managed financial transactions, and reported results directly to senior management.

Key Accomplishments:

- Ensured the timely, cost effective, and high-quality production of print and Web-based media, including bimonthly print advertising, quarterly (four-color, 32-page) product offering brochures, direct mail pieces, email newsletters, and Web content.

- Succeeded in negotiating vendor contributions to co-op advertising from 50¢ to 90¢ on the dollar.

- Grew sales 10% per year, with 20% growth in some years in spite of zero growth in support resources.

DIRECTOR OF SALES AND MARKETING / GROUP MANAGER (1999 – 2000)
Bon Voyage Travel, Tucson, Arizona

Recruited away from AAA to bring structure to the marketing department. Developed sales and marketing plans, quotas, and incentive programs. Completed the transition from an American Express affiliate to Virtuoso (API). Moved the agency to a demographics-driven, integrated marketing model.

Key Accomplishments:

- Ensured adequate return on investment in an environment with very narrow margins.

- Negotiated and executed a group contract for 3,000 people to travel to Disneyland. Coordinated logistics for the entire trip, including statewide motorcoach transportation, accommodations, group dining, and a private event at Disneyland. Generated more than $70,000 in bottom-line profit.

EDUCATION

PROJECT MANAGEMENT PROFESSIONAL (PMP 525303) (2008)
Project Management Institute, Newtown Square, Pennsylvania

CISCO CERTIFIED NETWORK ASSOCIATE (CCNA) CERTIFICATE PROGRAM (2003 – 2004)
Chandler Gilbert Community College, Chandler, Arizona

BACHELOR OF SCIENCE, BUSINESS ADMINISTRATION / MARKETING (1992)
Arizona State University, Tempe, Arizona

TECHNOLOGY EXPERIENCE

Business Applications: Proficient in Windows, MS Word, Excel, PowerPoint, Outlook, Visio, MS Project, SharePoint, HP Mercury for IT governance, and Remedy Action Request System for ticket management.

Unified Communications: Led Cisco nationwide IPT installations, Cisco IPCC enterprise and web collaboration deployment, and third-party applications, including call recording, fax servers, and paging systems.

Data Network Solutions: Managed Cisco multi-campus network refresh, Cisco statewide end-of-life router replacement, wireless LAN deployment, architecture development and documentation, and data center relocation/extranet consolidation.

RICHARD ROBERTSON, CPA, EA

Cellular: 205-555-1234 • Home: 205-555-1235 • Email: robertson@protypeltd.com
12345 Franklin Avenue • Nashville, TN 37066 • www.linkedin.com/in/rrobcpa/

CFO • VP FINANCE

Restructuring | Turnaround | Forensic Accounting | Acquisition | Cost Reduction

Accomplished financial executive with a history of eliminating inefficiencies, slashing expenses, and delivering rapid results. Enrolled agent and experienced forensic accountant who **cut corporate debt for current employer by $6.1 million in three years**. Decisive manager whose leadership positions in the health care industry included tenure as CFO for a regional medical center and as senior auditor for Blue Cross/Blue Shield of Tennessee. As director of reimbursement at a 550-bed hospital, **identified $300K in recoverable Medicare reimbursements—missed by external consultants—in only six months, and $2.5+ million over the next three years**. History of creating strong financial teams by developing clear performance objectives to promote quality work.

EXPERIENCE AND ACHIEVEMENTS

VP / CORPORATE CONTROLLER (January 2002 to present)
ALPHA INDUSTRIAL, INC. Nashville, TN
70-year-old provider of industrial products and services with over 500 employees in six states

Direct accounting functions for a regional industrial distributor with 550 employees. **Administer $110 million annual budget and manage all financial aspects of the holding company as well as three wholly owned subsidiaries**. Responsible for all internal controls, external audits, banking relationships, and financing issues. Promote cooperative working environment by managing a team who knows what is expected of them. Introduce new programs / strategies and continually improve the budget process.

Key Accomplishments:

❑ Instituted a productivity measurement tool that resulted in a **$450K increase in annual net income.**

❑ Decreased corporate debt by $6.1 million in a three-year period by identifying an unprofitable service center, improving cash flow, maximizing A/R collections, and increasing inventory turnover.

❑ Transformed a dysfunctional team within one year, improving operational accounting efficiencies, reducing accounting staff by 3.5 FTEs while increasing workload, and converting to a new accounting software program.

❑ Negotiated and facilitated the 2006 fiscal year purchase of U.S. Electronics, a $10 million company whose acquisition increased Alpha's sales by 11.7% to $95 million; subsequently, U.S. Electronics has led other divisions in sales growth.

❑ Exposed a $250K instance of employee theft by reviewing internal controls at a branch office.

CHIEF FINANCIAL OFFICER (April 1997 to December 2002)
Global Trucking Company, Memphis, TN
40-year-old motor vehicle wholesaler

Senior finance executive for trucking company, directing financial operations and administering a $25 million budget. Tasked with managing the company's emergence from Chapter 11, established new accounting controls, structured a 363 sale, and restored creditors' faith in the company's financial reporting. Installed new internal controls, dramatically improving employee morale and building positive relationships with vendors.

Key Accomplishments:

❑ Reduced operational expenses $278K by evaluating the necessity of administrative expenses and existing lease contracts.

CHIEF FINANCIAL OFFICER (April 1995 to April 1997)
Henderson Hardwood Flooring, Inc., Nashville, TN
Manufacturer / exporter of hardwood flooring with annual sales of $25 million

Directed and coordinated the organization's financial activities. Planned and implemented policies and objectives to increase efficiency and achieve financial reporting objectives. Managed a $30 million budget and improved the company's credibility in auditing and banking relationships. Provided strategic goals in order to grow the business by acquisition.

Key Accomplishments:

❑ Applying well-honed audit skills, identified overstated inventory and misclassified expenses, finally **uncovering a $2.4 million embezzlement scheme.**

❑ Having earned complete confidence of creditors due to high ethical standards, was tapped as trustee by creditors to preside over the company's liquidation; oversaw the dismantling of the company, fairly valued corporate assets for sale, and administered creditor claims.

PRIOR EXPERIENCE

Chief Financial Officer, General Hospital, Nashville, TN
Senior Auditor, Blue Cross/Blue Shield of Tennessee, Nashville, TN
Senior Reimbursement Consultant, HCA, Nashville, TN
Senior Auditor, Ernst & Young, Dallas, TX
Director of Budget & Reimbursement, Houston Medical Center, Houston, TX

EDUCATION AND PROFESSIONAL CERTIFICATION

CPA, State of Tennessee (active)
EA (Enrolled Agent)
BS in Accountancy, University of Mississippi

Experienced Sales and Marketing Professional
Project Management – Data Analysis – Sales Support

Market and Business Analysis – Program Development – Presentations
Copywriting – Training – Vendor Management – Database Marketing

► **Charlotte Johansen**
12345 Carmel Creek Rd.
San Diego, CA 92130

cjohansen@protypeltd.com
619.555.1234

Multi-talented business catalyst with a proven track record of accelerating growth by incorporating industry best practices, launching new organizations and programs, and identifying opportunities to streamline operations. Gifted consensus builder, cultivating meaningful relationships and rallying internal and external players behind win-win propositions. Thrive in fast-paced environments. Skilled presenter, seasoned in addressing individual decision-makers as well as large audiences.

► *Charlotte demonstrates a high degree of personal integrity and her work ethic is strong, embedded with a deep desire to succeed... She has strong communication skills and is solution-oriented in her approach... [she] is a high-achiever and ...likes to be challenged in her work assignments.* **–excerpt from performance review**

Experience and Accomplishments

► **Random House Retail Sales and Marketing**, San Diego, CA   2001–2003, 2005–Present
Largest publisher-owned magazine retail marketer and distribution services company. Handles 300+ magazine brands, including four of the top-five sellers in the U.S. and Canada.

Key Contributions: Conceived and executed many first-time programs including a cross-merchandising initiative that increased sales up to 300%, a sales support program that increased Account Manager productivity, and business intelligence strategies that built one of the top-performing territories in the country.

Regional Manager (2007–Present)
Establish and manage relationships across multiple channels, including retail managers, third-party brokers, and distributors. Train, develop, and lead retail sales force. Project manage complex retail initiatives, gather business intelligence, and perform detailed analysis under high-pressure time constraints. Accountable for 570 stores in San Diego, Riverside, and Orange Counties, collaborating with merchandisers and area managers to meet or exceed performance standards.

- ► Consistently ranked top regional manager, including being number one in the West for *Time* magazine, improving pocket penetration 9.7% in an already saturated market.
- ► Turned around region that was struggling following 12 months without an area manager and takeover by a wholesaler who was not compliant with merchandising standards. Rallied buyers, account managers, the new area manager, and major retailers to correct the problem.
- ► Compensated for field force reduction by training inexperienced third-party brokers to take over remote locations.
- ► Spurred top performance from in-house and third-party merchandising teams by condensing instructions and processes to the essential elements that impact performance.
- ► Enhanced territory management capabilities enterprise wide by culling industry best practices to create business intelligence reports that powered targeted improvement efforts. Trained colleagues in analytical protocol and in using vendor's data analysis tool.

Assistant to Regional Vice President (2005–2007)
Led sales support activities for key account managers and directors, including proposal creation and business analysis. Liaised between retail, wholesale, and corporate stakeholders, ensuring optimum performance across multiple channels. Streamlined inter-departmental interactions, coordinating efforts of marketing, brand, and account managers. Planned multiple events, including a meeting of 150 people in Las Vegas.

- ► Implemented company's first formal sales support program, and transformed the assistant RVP position from an administrative assistant role to one of proactive project management.
- ► Ensured receipt of full credit for retail sales by managing UPC changeover projects and verifying that new codes were entered into retail tracking systems.
- ► Bolstered magazine sales by preparing and delivering presentations on product positioning to account managers.

► **Random House Sales and Marketing,** continued

Assistant to Regional Vice President (continued)
- ► Leveraged Random House's business contacts, suggesting multiple improvements to database management that were implemented by the regional vice president.
- ► Increased account managers' productivity by taking over production and customization of spreadsheets for client presentations and board meetings.

Sales Representative (2001–2003)
Hired into newly created position to manage merchandising team in San Diego County, ensuring adherence to company strategies and standards. Trained and supported merchandising associates. Designed solutions for evolving customer needs. Managed special projects, such as logo changes, special editions, and other mission-critical initiatives.

- ► Increased magazine sales as much as 300% by conceiving, developing, and implementing a cross-merchandising program that introduced magazine displays at Wal-Mart pharmacies in San Diego and Orange Counties.
- ► Trained colleagues in cross-merchandising techniques at annual meeting in Las Vegas.
- ► Achieved flawless execution of multiple complex planograms, up to three for each location.
- ► Assumed pivotal projects above and beyond scope of responsibility, including managing installation of new magazine brands at remote locations.
- ► Expanded in-store footprint by winning placement for special issue bins.

► **Acme Sales and Marketing,** San Diego, CA   2003–2004
Firm specializing in outsourced sales, merchandising, category management, and marketing services.

Area Manager (2003–2004)
Hired, trained, and managed magazine merchandising force covering Southern California, Nevada, and Northern Arizona. Created merchandising manuals and training materials. Built and managed relationships with clients and retail managers. Clients included Random House, M&M Mars, and Pfizer.

- ► Built a 16-member merchandising force from scratch for start-up division. Completed hiring across three states within one month, becoming part of the first fully staffed region and the only one to meet corporate staffing timeline.
- ► Met all in-store retail excellence goals of timely new-item retail placement and successful completion of special retail projects.
- ► Grew sales by launching promotional initiatives, winning retail space, designing effective displays, creating seasonal themes, and optimizing planograms.
- ► Boosted productivity and improved results by training clients to leverage Acme business intelligence software to be more efficient brokers.
- ► Enriched organizational intelligence, preparing and delivering multiple educational presentations for regional groups.

Education

BACHELOR OF ARTS, SOCIOLOGY
San Diego State University, San Diego, CA, 2001

Amy Elkayam

PROFILE

- Hard-working office manager with more than fifteen years of experience in fast-paced environments, including customer service, staffing, health care, and marketing.
- Well organized and meticulous; willing to work long hours to get the job done.
- Able to make people feel comfortable using empathetic communication skills.
- Computers: Windows, MS Word, WordPerfect, FoxPro, Empac, CPAS, Versyss, Lotus Notes, E-mail.

RELEVANT EXPERIENCE

FRONT OFFICE MANAGER, PAYROLL ASSISTANT (1997 – present)
WSI Personnel, Colorado Springs, Colorado

- Manage the offices of a staffing firm that specializes in recruiting and placing medical and dental professionals, including doctors, dentists, nurses, physician assistants, medical assistants, front office, and other personnel.
- Schedule first interviews for applicants and take job orders from clients.
- Cold call on prospective clients to introduce WSI and its services.
- Manage client relationships to ensure their needs are met or exceeded.
- Effectively locate, screen, and qualify candidates who meet client requirements.
- Audit time cards, enter payroll into the Ceridian software, and generate sales and payroll reports.

FRONT OFFICE RECEPTIONIST (1995 – 1996)
HealthSouth, Colorado Springs, Colorado

- Scheduled appointments and screened clients in a busy minor emergency center.
- Created new patient charts and managed paperwork associated with worker's compensation and physical examinations.
- Called in prescription refills and transcribed medical test results during phone calls from laboratories.
- Assembled work hours, posted payroll, answered telephones, and performed routine office duties.

CO-OWNER/MANAGER (1996 – 1997)
Sweet Willys, Colorado Springs, Colorado

- Developed a new business from the ground up, including the concept for a mobile espresso bar and lunch catering business.
- Responsible for bookkeeping, inventory purchasing, and estimating of jobs.
- Developed new markets through effective advertising and cold calling.
- Created corporate identity, including logo, brochures, menus, and artwork.
- Planned and scheduled menus and food preparation to ensure contracts were met.

OFFICE MANAGER (1982 – 1993)
Dr. Steven Lokken, Capitola, California

- Managed the offices of a busy medical practice, including customer relations, medical records, staffing, and recertification of physician credentials.
- Recruited, interviewed, hired, and supervised three employees.
- Responsible for payroll, accounts receivable, accounts payable, patient billing, insurance submittals, and attorney contacts.
- Verified coverage with insurance providers, collected co-payments from patients, and made deposits.
- Scheduled appointments and referrals, took patient histories, prepared patients for examination, developed x-rays, and charted treatments.

EDUCATION

CABRILLO COLLEGE, Aptos, California (1983 – 1984)

- Completed two years of liberal arts and childhood development studies

CONTINUING EDUCATION

- New Horizon's training in Basic Windows 95
- Medical Office Skills from Pat Munsen

ADDRESS

P.O. Box 1234 ▸ Colorado Springs, Colorado 80932
Phone: (719) 234-6789 ▸ E-mail: amy.elkayam@protypeltd.com

Functional or Chronological

There are three basic types of résumés—reverse chronological, functional, and a combination of the two. The most common form is the reverse chronological, which arranges your experience and education in chronological order with the most recent dates first.

One of the most frequent questions I am asked as a résumé writer is, "Do I have to list all of my jobs? It makes me look so old!" My answer is always, "No, you don't have to list every single position you have ever held. The trick is to pick and choose the ones that are relevant to your objective." You can also eliminate low-level positions and positions that duplicate later experience. *Relevant* is the keyword here!

More than 90% of the résumés in this book are reverse chronological, but that doesn't mean that a functional résumé might not fit your needs better. A functional résumé organizes your work experience by the functions you performed regardless of date. The functional résumé highlights your skills and potential instead of your work history. It allows you to play down gaps in your experience and is especially good for those people entering the job market for the first time. If you are reentering the job market, for example, after raising children, this type of résumé also allows you to list volunteer experience and community or school activities.

List your functional paragraphs in their order of importance, with the items listed first that will help you get the particular job you are targeting. Refer to Step Ten in the twelve-step résumé writing process outlined in Chapter 2 of this book for ideas on how to rearrange your résumé sentences to better capture your reader's attention.

You should know that there are very rare times when I would recommend a purely functional résumé. In the 1980s, true functional résumés developed a bad reputation because applicants were not listing where they gained their experience. It made recruiters suspicious that the applicant was trying to hide something. According to the 2010 Orange County Résumé Survey, 88.2% of recruiters prefer either chronological or combination chronological/functional résumés. If you choose to use a functional format, always list a brief synopsis of your actual work experience at the bottom of your functional résumé with your title, employer, and the dates worked.

Outside of this chapter, you will find other functional/chronological résumés on pages 91, 112, 113, 134, 146, 148, 162, 188, 189, 200, 201, 269, 270, 272, 273, 292–295, 301, 302, 353–356. On pages 50, 96, 97, 215, 252–255, you will find true chronological résumés that have added functional subdivisions under each job. You can also create a strong functional beginning to a chronological resume to highlight select skills, as on pages 84, 170, 178, 194, 242, 244, 258, 261, 264, 296, 298.

 **Gina DiNardo**

12345 Pleasant Avenue, Newark, NJ 07102
dinardo@protypeltd.com

Home: (201) 555-1234
Cellular: (201) 555-5678

Summary

More than 15 years of experience in all aspects of restaurant operations, from dishwasher to manager. Exposed from a young age to the authentic traditions of Italian cooking. Entrepreneurial spirit with proven ability to make improvements, directly contributing to business growth and increased profitability. Particular strength in supervising people and controlling financial matters.

Areas of Expertise

Food Preparation

- Prepared pizzas, strombolis, and calzones (including dough), with gourmet as well as standard toppings/fillings.
- Assisted chef with sauces, salads, sandwiches, and broiled or grilled meats and seafood.
- Increased menu offerings with unique items that met with popular appeal.
- Accommodated customer requests for special orders.

Purchasing/Vendor Negotiations

- Dealt with purveyors of food, soft drinks, beer and wine, paper stock, and linen service.
- Negotiated for best pricing without compromising quality or reliability expected by patrons.
- Place weekly orders in quantities based on inventory needs and previous sales trends.
- Took advantage of special pricing for bulk amounts if storage space allowed and spoilage was not a factor.
- Planned food and accessory needs for outside catered events for up to 200 people.

Cost Control

- Kept food costs to 25–30% of budget, and payroll costs at approximately 20%.
- Closely monitored price increases and sought alternative vendors, price guarantees, or comparable products.
- Utilized staff productively during both peak and slow periods.
- Cut waste by communicating with prep cooks as to daily amounts of food to prepare in line with anticipated business.
- Reduced unnecessary service calls on kitchen equipment by correcting routine mechanical malfunctions.
- Implemented easy-to-use computer system, facilitating kitchen orders, sales tracking, menu planning, and inventory control.

Staffing

- Managed staff of up to 35, mainly part-time, for front and back of house, phone/take-out orders, and delivery.
- Hired confident, enthusiastic and service-oriented people.
- Encouraged team participation among culturally diverse workers and settled any conflicts in early stages.
- Created motivational incentives and career progression that inspired loyalty and reduced turnover.

Customer Relations

- Established a reputation for consistent quality.
- Maintained customer good will by immediately resolving any issues that caused dissatisfaction.
- Encouraged repeat business and word-of-mouth referrals by getting to know customers by name and learning their preferences.

Areas of Expertise

Promotions and Marketing

- Coordinated coupon offers in town newspaper and for inclusion in newcomer welcoming packets.
- Provided restaurant reviewer with input for favorable public relations article.
- Participated in a cable television commercial on a local network.
- Assisted with decor changes to enhance image and upgraded soft drink product line.

Relevant Work Experience

PAPA GIUSEPPE'S FAMILY RESTAURANT, NEWARK, NJ   2003–2010
High-volume Italian restaurant and pizzeria with annual gross revenues in excess of $2 million.
General Manager

- Initially hired as pizza maker. Advanced to management position quickly and entirely on own merit.
- Implemented an expanded, innovative menu and improved service quality.
- Contributed to 20% business growth from new customers by creating a more visible community presence.
- Assumed responsibilities beyond normal job duties, putting owners in better financial position to open a second restaurant.
- Helped train manager of newly opened location.

PIZZA EXPRESS, NEWARK, NJ   2000–2003
Pizza Chef and Kitchen Helper

- Employed part-time since high school, preparing pizza, sandwiches, and simple Italian entrees.
- Took phone orders accurately and dispatched delivery person.
- Observed and learned all aspects of how a small business operates. Entrusted by owners with management duties in their absence.

Other Experience

HERTZ RENT-A-CAR, LIBERTY INTERNATIONAL AIRPORT, NEWARK, NJ   2001–2003
Automobile Rental Clerk

- Handled a high daily volume, averaging 150 daily car rentals and returns at busy international airport.
- Determined type of car needed by customers, its availability or appropriate substitution at rental site.
- Quoted costs of desired cars in terms of daily rates, estimated mileage, and insurance coverage requested.
- Checked customers' driver licenses, IDs, and validity of credit cards.
- Inspected returned vehicles for damage, fuel usage, and odometer readings, adding on charges accordingly.
- Calculated normal rental charges along with any other expenses incurred.
- Tracked whereabouts of rented vehicles if return site differed from originating site, keeping inventory in balance.

Education

Gibbs Business School, Newark, NJ—Courses in accounting and marketing   2004–2005

Computer Learning Center, Elizabeth, NJ—Six-month course in computer operations (MS Office)   2001

Ingrid Hägglund, M.A.

Influential • Analytical • Pragmatic • Resourceful • Tenacious • Inspiring • Engaging

INTERNATIONAL COMMUNICATIONS PROFESSIONAL

Key Competencies

Program Management
Project Support
Data Sets / Entry
Training and Instruction
Community Relations
Constituent Scheduling
Record Keeping

Languages

German
Dutch
Swedish
French
Spanish

Technology

Microsoft Office
Windows XP / Mac
QuarkXPress

Education

Master of Arts, 2006
PR & Publicity, GPA: 4.0
Halmstad University
Halmstad, Sweden

Bachelor of Arts, 2001
Philosophy
University of Gothenburg
Gothenburg, Sweden

15th Communication
Program, IDA / ICCO
Gothenburg, Sweden

SUMMARY AND TARGET

Pursuing part-time position in preparation for graduate studies in counseling psychology.

Multilingual people and project connector offering 8+ years of cumulative multinational work and volunteer experience for institutions in Sweden and the U.S. Organization of up to 25 diverse student team members and projects with many moving parts.

EXPERIENCE HIGHLIGHTS

Programmatic and Academic Research, Advising and Organization

- Achieved 98% participation among 200 students in academic advising, setting the bar by which all advisors performed.
- Managed university department activity reports presenting activities of 23 faculty members to Sweden's Council for Higher Education. Documented 6 semester measurements including up to 10 major events, 125+ presentations / publications, and 80 course descriptions.
- Collected and entered 2005 Swedish electoral data from 81 precincts / 923 districts.
- Surveyed 372 Swedish students about voter / gender issues.
- Advised students on EUEA international exchange for study in Europe.

Public Relations / Outreach

- Managed or assisted with media relations and PR across 15 events for 5 clients.
- Led communications and PR consulting for Junior Achievement Sweden.
- Conducted 12-month PR research project, presented to EUPRERA Congress.
- Coordinated 120-page, 2,000 student recruiting magazine, sponsored by university president. Distributed to 100 Gothenburg agencies and prospective students.

Translation / Communication

- Translated 400+ monthly press releases, product rollouts, and reports for 7 clients, intended for 12 Swedish newspapers (two-way translation, Swedish/English).
- Translated 18 published philosophy book articles from French to Swedish, as well as ancillary summary translations and edits across numerous university documents.

PROFESSIONAL CHRONOLOGY   2001–present

Clarkson University, Potsdam, NY
Multilingual Data Entry and Analysis / Research Specialist *(08/07–09/09; 07/06–08/07)*

XY&Z Public Relations, Gothenburg, Sweden
Public Relations Consultant / Account Executive *(05/06–06/06)*

University of Gothenburg, Gothenburg, Sweden
Research Assistant *(09/03–04/06)*
Students' Assistant *(06/01–06/03)*

Total Public Relations, Gothenburg, Sweden   Publishing Company, Gothenburg, Sweden
Translator *(01/01–06/01)*   **Translator** *(10/00–6/01)*

1234 Grove Street, Milwaukee, WI 53208 • 414-555-1234 (mb) • hagglund@protypeltd.com • Green Card Holder

CAROL ANN LEWIS

- Experienced manager with a strong background in human resources and accounting.
- Self-motivated quick learner who enjoys new challenges.
- Effective team player with proven communication and interpersonal skills.
- Knowledge of Windows, MS Word, WordPerfect, Internet Explorer, and e-mail.

EXPERIENCE
Human Resources

- Hired, supervised, and evaluated a staff of up to 11 employees; created congenial working conditions that resulted in an average tenure of 12 years.
- Developed a benefits package for exempt and nonexempt employees, including health insurance, profit sharing, 401k programs, worker's compensation, etc.
- Established and implemented sound hiring, interviewing, and performance evaluation practices.
- Developed policies and procedures for exit interviews and ensured compliance with federal and state laws and regulations.
- Wrote employee procedure manuals and benefits handbooks.
- Shopped annually for competitive employee health insurance rates.

Management

- Owned and managed a 15-unit motel and 78-site campground; succeeded in increasing sales by 100 percent and selling the business at a profit after six years of upgrading the property's image.
- Responsible for long-range planning, budgeting, profit and loss, controlling costs, and monitoring financial performance.
- Remodeled the facilities, including a new telephone systems, furniture, and interior design.
- Served as office manager, officer of the corporation (Assistant Secretary-Treasurer), and member of the Board of Directors of a Pizza Hut franchisee with 62 stores in five states.

Accounting

- Worked closely with the corporate attorney and accountant to form an S Corporation.
- Prepared daily, weekly, monthly, and quarterly bookkeeping records and financial reports, biweekly payroll for up to 1,500 employees, and monthly profit and loss statements for 62 stores.
- Balanced the ledgers, reconciled bank accounts, made daily deposits, and prepared budgets.
- Completed all state, federal, and county tax and health reports for both service and consumer product businesses. Responsible for sales tax, payroll tax, property tax, and worker's compensation reporting in five states.
- Increased the efficiency of inputting data so profit and loss statements were available to management by the third of the month instead of the 15th or 20th, allowing problems to be detected earlier and corrective measures taken.
- Transitioned the company from double-entry bookkeeping by hand through numerous computer upgrades, including customized accounting systems that tied all 62 store cash registers to the mainframe and polled daily sales information into the office every night.

WORK HISTORY

CO-OWNER AND OPERATOR (2008 – present)
Rocky Top Motel and Campground, Green Mountain Falls, Colorado

OFFICE MANAGER (2004 – 2008)
High Plains Pizza, Inc., Liberal, Kansas

EDUCATION

UNDERGRADUATE STUDIES
Seward County Community College, Liberal, Kansas
- Completed courses in business management and computers

PROFESSIONAL DEVELOPMENT
- Training Skills for Team Leaders
- Fairness in the Workplace (Equal Employment Opportunity)
- Managing and Appraising Employee Performance
- Eliminating Violence in the Workplace (Physical and Verbal)
- Dealing with Unacceptable Employee Behavior
- How to Be a Better Trainer
- Managing for Success
- Managing Time and Tasks
- Delegation
- Improving Memory Skills

CONTACT   1234-A Parkmoor Village Drive, Colorado Springs, Colorado 80917, (719) 555-1234

James Ben Thurman

1234 Bienville Boulevard #11 • Ocean Springs, Mississippi 39564
Cell: (228) 555-5555 • Email: benthurman@protypeltd.com

HIGHLIGHTS OF QUALIFICATIONS

- Experienced hospitality manager with a strong work ethic and passion for fine dining.
- Proven leader who is able to unify a diverse staff and maximize individual strengths.
- Creative, artistic chef with a finely tuned appreciation for good food and wine.
- Driven, results-oriented culinary professional who focuses on profitability and the bottom line.
- Effective problem solver who is able to resolve issues before they become major roadblocks.

AREAS OF EXPERTISE

- Food and beverage management
- Hiring, supervision, and training
- Purchasing and inventory management
- Budgeting and effective cost control

- Policy and procedure development
- Strategic planning
- Quality assurance, customer service
- New restaurant openings

SUMMARY OF EXPERIENCE

KEY ACCOMPLISHMENTS

- History of successfully managing the kitchens of fine-dining, casual, buffet, banquet, catering, and healthcare food service operations.
- Turned around unprofitable operations by developing and implementing new processes, upgrading food service, and improving customer service.
- Built operations from scratch, including menu development, staffing, training, and operating policies and procedures.
- Opened Captain's Quarters at Treasurer Bay and Torgy's at Casino Magic—staffed and furnished the entire operations, developed the menus and kitchen flow, set timing standards for chefs and servers, and created relationships with new purveyors.

OPERATIONS MANAGEMENT

- Maintained expenses at or below budget through accurate planning, purchasing, waste reduction, and cost-effective operating procedures.
- Recruited, hired, supervised, motivated, and trained kitchen staff.
- Developed innovative training programs that emphasized safety, organization, and the importance of exceptional customer service.
- Initiated systems of accountability, and perpetuated a firm, fair, and consistent management style that improved productivity and lowered turnover.
- Selected by senior management to serve as a consultant to underperforming Ocean Springs facilities in other states. Instituted a new chef's program with fewer premade foods, developed new menus, and located vendors for healthier food at a lower cost. Succeeded in reducing daily food costs from $8.00 to $5.00 per person. *"Ben's culinary skills exceed any chef I have ever worked with. Under his leadership, our company changed the way we look at food."*

PURCHASING

- Estimated food and beverage costs, sourced suppliers, and purchased inventory, equipment, china, glass, and silver.
- Set product standards and ingredient specifications; structured purchasing and receiving processes and procedures.
- Solicited competitive bids and negotiated cost-effective contracts with major wholesale suppliers and boutique vendors.
- Developed spreadsheets to manage purchasing budgets, ordering, receiving, and inventory.

CULINARY EXPERIENCE

- Managed the kitchens of fine-dining and casual restaurants, including menu and recipe development, food preparation, and presentation.
- Planned and coordinated banquets, buffets, private parties, and off-site catering.
- Focused on the highest quality ingredients and preparation, impeccable food appearance, and exquisite service.

SUMMARY OF EXPERIENCE

CULINARY EXPERIENCE (continued)

- Participated in regional ACF (American Culinary Federation) competitions—Won two silver medals for soup and salad, as well as four bronze medals in beef, seafood, classic, and salad divisions.
- Amateur Ice Carver—Won the Bronze Medal at a local ACF competition.
- Working toward the Certified Executive Chef (CEC) credential from the American Culinary Federation—Have completed all but the final exam.
- Beginning study toward certification as a sommelier.
- Certified Culinarian (CC), American Culinary Federation (1997).

EMPLOYMENT HISTORY

CHEF DE CUISINE

Delta Health Care, Ocean Springs, Mississippi (2004 – present)

Manage food service operations of five healthcare facilities, and provide consulting services at some of the 47 other corporate-owned nursing homes in the Southeast. Develop à la carte menus with the goal of better food quality at a lower cost. Hire, supervise, and evaluate the performance of 12–15 employees. Reduce food costs through competitive buying and zero-based inventory management.

CHEF DE CUISINE

Treasure Bay Casino, Biloxi, Mississippi (1998 – 2004)

Directed operations of the Captain's Quarter restaurant specializing in Gulf Coast cuisine and upscale steaks and seafood. Opened the restaurant as the first chef hired. Set standards for quality, creativity, menu development, food production, and presentation. Hired, mentored, and supervised eight employees. Participated in radio advertisements and television news spots. Developed a strong local following and a reputation for quality food.

SOUS CHEF / CHEF DE CUISINE

New Palace Casino, Biloxi, Mississippi (1996 – 1998)

Helped to manage Lawana's Restaurant, a fine-dining establishment serving Gulf Coast regional cuisine. Recruited, hired, and supervised a staff of eight. Estimated consumption, purchased food-stuffs, and inspected them upon delivery to ensure that only the highest quality products were used. Won several awards from local newspapers and magazines.

TOURNANT / BUFFET / BANQUET

Casino Magic, Bay St. Louis, Mississippi (1992 – 1995)

Opened Torgy's restaurant, an upscale steakhouse seating 220 guests. Gained experience in all stations of the kitchen, and managed the preparation of buffets and banquets.

LINE COOK / PREP COOK

Biloxi Beach Resort, Bixoli, Mississippi (1991 – 1992)
Diamond Head Country Club, Diamond Head, Mississippi (1990 – 1991)
Wind Dance Country Club, Lyman, Mississippi (1989 – 1990)

Gained experience in some of the finest local kitchens, including a resort created by Pat Boone. Menus were often rotated every night of the week, and the venues included extensive buffets, banquets, and catering events.

EDUCATION & TRAINING

DIPLOMA, FOOD PRODUCTION AND MANAGEMENT TECHNOLOGY (1996)

Mississippi Gulf Coast Community College, Gulfport, Mississippi

- President's List Scholar

PROFESSIONAL DEVELOPMENT

- SAFE SERV, Food Handling Certification (1997)
- The Chef's and Food Service Operator's Guide to Beef, ACF (1996)
- Certified ACF Lambassador, American Lamb Board (1996)

Marlene Hartwell

79 Somerset Drive
Wells, ME 04090

207-555-1212
mhartwell@protypeltd.com

Accomplished Marketing Manager ♦ Skilled Negotiator ♦ Respected Sales Team Leader

---

Highly self-motivated marketing manager who earned the respect of clients, colleagues, sales team, and upper management. Successfully increased overall revenue and market share by conceptualizing and implementing creative marketing programs. Extensive knowledge of broadcasting, pricing inventory, ratings, promotions, marketing, and sales principles and practices.

EXPERTISE

Inventory Management	Collections	Active Listener
Forecasting Activities	Revenue Generator	Sales Team Motivator
Strategic Prospecting	Innovative Thinker	Client Focused
Market Trend Analysis	Creative Problem Solver	Top Performer

HIGHLIGHTS OF SKILLS AND ACCOMPLISHMENTS

♦ Managed a team of senior sales representatives for the largest radio station in the state.
♦ Retained, maintained and grew company's largest account from $50,000 to $250,000 by earning a reputation as someone who consistently meets expectations.
♦ Partnered with largest client to bring them from the 272nd dealer to the 2nd dealer in the northeast by overseeing all aspects of promotions, from conceptualizing a theme to ensuring that all details were implemented completely, thoroughly, and in compliance with contractual obligations.
♦ Set and achieved performance goals that increased account base from $100,000 to $800,000.
♦ Recognized as top performer in company, billing with an 85% close ratio and a notably low accounts receivable balance.

PROFESSIONAL EXPERIENCE

♦ Developed and implemented profitable sales strategies by performing comparative market trend analysis that led to greater revenue generation.
♦ Researched, initiated, and executed promotional plans, schedules, and branding campaigns that met client-specific needs and earned repeat business.
♦ Trained and coached new sales professionals on successful practices and procedures.
♦ Collaborated effectively within the organization to motivate others and cultivate a positive and productive work environment.
♦ Forecasted, produced, and closed proposals by gaining a solid understanding of client needs, monitoring client activity, and effectively communicating options.

ADDITIONAL ACCOMPLISHMENTS

- Trusted by clients to organize and execute all details of open house activities to ensure successful implementation.
- Consolidated all marketing activities that resulted in creating greater buying power.
- Negotiated with vendors and clients to obtain the best agreement.
- Designed and created a product that was rated a "Top 10 Most Collectible" and was invited to be sold on QVC.
- Invited to co-chair the marketing committee as the result of spearheading a successful cost-saving initiative.

EMPLOYMENT HISTORY

Commonwealth Broadcasting, Kennebunk, ME
Senior Marketing Representative (2002 – Present)

Stillwater Communications, Saco, ME
Local Sales Manager (2007 – 2008)

WCSH TV, Scarborough, ME
Account Executive (2006)

Bradford Chanel, Freeport, ME
Assistant Marketing Manager (1999 – 2001)

Stewart and Stevens, Bethel, ME
Account Representative (1997 – 1999)

Brown Specialty Designs, Arundel, ME
President and Owner (1994 – 1997)

EDUCATION

University of New Hampshire, Durham, NH
Coursework in Business Administration

COMMUNITY INVOLVEMENT

Kennebunk Downtown Association, Kennebunk, ME
Co-chair of Marketing Committee

Sandi A. Michaels

54321 Robert Bost Rd ❖ Midland, NC 28107 ❖ Phone: 704-555-2456 ❖ E-mail: samich@protypeltd.com

---

Professional Profile

Personable and self-reliant professional eager to shift career in a new direction, while leveraging diverse employment experience and strong interpersonal skills to support customers, team members, and business operations. An active listener and good conversationalist, with excellent face-to-face and telephone communication skills. Patient and persistent; demonstrate natural talent for gaining trust and asking the right questions to identify needs and provide solutions. Excellent capacity for simultaneously managing multiple responsibilities and priorities without compromising on quality.

Summary of Skills and Experience

❖ **More than 10 years of experience as an Activities Director for various assisted-living facilities**
Robinwood Acres Retirement Living | Concord, NC | 2009 to present
Loyola Assisted Living of Richland | Richland, NC | 1999 to 2009
The Gables at Brighton | Brockport, NY | 1998

- *Planning and Scheduling:* Developed monthly calendar of activities for facilities with as many as 90 residents. Integrated crafts, games, social outings, and exercise programs aimed at enriching residents mental, physical, and spiritual needs. Scheduled and trained volunteers and facilitated small group and one-on-one activities.

- *Interviewing and Documentation:* Conducted initial interest and abilities assessments of residents to develop well-rounded program of activities for personal enrichment. Developed and maintained written records of each resident's participation and progress and presented documentation for social services inspectors' quarterly reviews. Credited for consistently presenting thorough and efficient documentation.

- *Interdisciplinary Coordination:* Participated in daily meetings with clinical and administrative teams to discuss resident, facility, and program issues. Stayed abreast of company-wide issues and policies through conference calls with corporate and local teams.

- *Interagency Collaboration:* Served for four years on the interagency planning committee for the *Annual Residents' Rights Celebration,* a nationally sponsored event celebrating and honoring residents of long-term communities. Assisted with selecting venue, planning meal and agenda, and facilitating program attended by approximately 130 long-term residents from 20 facilities in a three-county area.

- *Leadership and Professional Networking:* Member of North Carolina Activity Professionals Association; participated in annual conferences. Served as Vice President of Metrolina Activities Professionals Association. Charter member of Cabarrus County Association of Activity Professionals.

❖ **Three years of Corporate Food Service experience**
Sodexho Corporation | Brockport, NY | 1994 to 1998

- *Multi-tasking and Customer Service:* Employed under contract with Wegmans corporate cafeteria. Assisted with breakfast and lunch preparation for up to 300 employees and operated cash register.

❖ **Five years of experience providing administrative support in a university setting**
University of Rochester (dormitory and office complex) | Rochester, NY | 1989 to 1994

- *Office Assistance:* Provided comprehensive support to seven departments by serving as receptionist and first point of contact to callers and visitors, scheduling meeting rooms, and overseeing building maintenance.

Skills and Experience Summary *(continued)*

❖ **Twelve-plus years of self-employment / independent business experience.**

Residential Cleaning Services | Monroe County Area, NY | 1978 to 1990
The Creative Circle | Monroe County Area, NY | 1987 to 1989

- *Business Management:* Launched and independently managed small residential cleaning business. Built a diverse client base through networking and word of mouth. Planned and managed cleaning schedules, procured supplies and equipment, maintained client and financial records.
- *Sales and Instruction:* Booked, scheduled, and instructed in-home needlework classes and sold various needlework kits and accessories. Maintained inventories, collected payments, and reported sales revenues.

Education

State University of New York, Brockport, NY
Bachelor of Science, Recreation and Leisure Studies

- Completed internships at The Jewish Home of Rochester, The Gables at Brighton, and Friends at Westfall Adult Day Services.
- Inducted into Alpha Chi and Rho Phi Lambda Honor Societies. Graduated *Magna cum laude*.

Community Affiliations and Creative Talents

- Active member of Charlotte Community Singers. Previously performed with Piedmont Choral Society, Cabarrus Women's Chorale and the Cabarrus Vocal Ensemble.
- Award-winning creative nonfiction writer.
- Skilled craftswoman—practitioner and teacher of numerous needlecrafts, fabric creations, calligraphy, and beadwork.
- Participant in contra-dancing. Always receptive to learning new skills and meeting new people.
- Computer competent with MS Word and Publisher. Designed and distributed agency calendars and newsletters. Working knowledge of Excel.

1234 Zarzuela Avenue, NW • Albuquerque, New Mexico 87120
Cell: (505) 850-9813 • Email: dmilehighj@yahoo.com • www.twitter.com/dbschultz9

ELECTRICAL PROJECT MANAGER

Experienced Superintendent, Foreman, and Journeyman Electrician (New Mexico EE99-K #123456) with a comprehensive knowledge of construction and a strong work ethic. Effective team leader who is able to motivate workers to complete jobs on time with exceptional quality. Detail-oriented manager with the ability to see the entire project, find the root cause of problems, and develop cost-effective solutions. Offer extensive experience and skills in:

- Project management
- Supervision and scheduling
- Safety and quality control
- Estimating and takeoffs
- Materials and equipment
- Process efficiencies
- New construction
- Remodeling projects
- Electrical/mechanical systems

SUMMARY OF EXPERIENCE

Project Management

- Hired and supervised job foremen, journeymen electricians, and apprentices on multi-million-dollar commercial, industrial, and government electrical/mechanical construction projects.
- Met with clients to assess scope of work and to set project goals and objectives. Served as primary liaison with the prime client, architects, and engineers.
- Evaluated materials, time, labor, and overhead to accurately estimate project costs. Performed takeoffs from design drawings, specifications, blueprints, and schematics to prepare contract proposals.
- Developed project budgets, schedules, and milestones. Sourced vendors, ordered construction materials, and coordinated just-in-time delivery to the appropriate work site.
- Evaluated bids from subcontractors, selected vendors, negotiated agreements, and ensured the quality of work performed.
- Scheduled and managed personnel, budgets, materials, and equipment utilization to complete complex electrical and mechanical system installation contracts.
- Developed and implemented safety programs, policies, and procedures. Conducted mandatory weekly safety meetings. Achieved no reportable accidents in 20 years.
- Ensured completion of permits, construction documents, change order logs, and other records.
- Consulted with clients, architects, and engineers regarding designs and modifications. Prepared scope of work, material, and labor input for contract changes.
- Ensured quality control and customer satisfaction throughout the project life cycle.

Key Accomplishments

- Demonstrated track record of completing large projects on time and within or under budget, including:
  - Chujach Government Services (Department of Energy, Kirkland Air Force Base)—Electrical, grounding systems, fire alarm, computer and backup systems, and controls.
  - Los Alamos National Labs—High-security fuel station, warehouses, and office buildings. Electrical, grounding systems, fire alarm, computer and backup systems, and controls.
  - Public Schools (Albuquerque, Bernalillo)—New construction and remodeling projects that included electrical, security, fire alarm, and controls.
  - Commercial—New construction, tenant finish, and remodeling for stores (WalMart, Target, Victoria's Secret, Kmart), offices (H&R Block), and warehouses (Budweiser).
  - Residential—New homes, additions, and renovations.
- Continually evaluated margins to ensure profitability at project completion. Analyzed costs and instituted cost-cutting efficiencies. Developed shortcuts that made good business sense without compromising quality, schedule, or safety.
- Demonstrated success in motivating workers and coordinating with other trades.
- Consistently turned around under-bid and failing projects, returning them to schedule and profitability.
- Created documentation for all actions that validated work completed and facilitated payment.
- Taught classes for Electric Edge in basic electricity/electronics and troubleshooting techniques, including AC/DC circuitry, schematic reading, load calculations, the use of test equipment, transformers, and power supplies, among others.

Technical

- Designed, installed, troubleshot, and maintained electrical and mechanical systems to provide, cooling, heat, light, and power. Used thermal image testing to diagnose system problems. Provided customer service support and made emergency service calls. Performed scheduled inspections and preventive maintenance.
- Designed and engineered production control systems for industrial use.

SUMMARY OF EXPERIENCE

Technical (continued)

- Evaluated blueprints, wiring diagrams, and schematics—ensured compliance with local codes, standards, regulations, specifications, and National Electrical Codes (NEC).
- Developed expertise with major electrical systems, power distribution, transformers, controls, motors, instrumentation, security systems, fire alarm systems (including addressable), generators, temperature controls, lighting, communications/phone systems, computer systems, CATV, sound and light controls, and power for large commercial and government facilities.
- Installed backup power sources and manual/automatic transfer switches for secure and non-secured government operations.
- Designed, fabricated, and installed new electrical equipment, which required:
  - Source planning. Routing and location design. Calculations of service, conduit, and wire size. Design and fabrication of mounting structures.
  - Physically locating new equipment (starters, light fixtures, transformers, programmable logic controllers, conduit, circuit breakers, cable trays, motors, relays, and motor control centers, among others).
  - Installation of all types of industrial wiring, underground raceways (concrete-encased PVC and rigid, conduit up to 6"), above-ground conduit (EMT, rigid, IMC, cable trays, and NEMA 12 gutter), cable trays (up to 30"), direct burial and shielded cables, and duct banks of all configurations.
- Planned, laid out, and installed:
  - 15 kv, 480 volt power distribution systems.
  - 120 volt control systems, including PLC, relay logic, and variable frequency drives.
  - 120, 277, and 480 volt lighting systems.
- Terminated from 15 kv to 16 gauge 120 volt lines.
- Energized all systems and provided start-up assistance, including troubleshooting and megohm testing.
- Minimized waste of materials, provided access for future maintenance, and avoided hazardous and unsightly wiring.
- Prepared sketches showing location of wiring and equipment.

WORK HISTORY

PROJECT MANAGER / SUPERINTENDENT / ELECTRICIAN (Sep 2000 – Jan 2010)
Electric Edge, Inc., Albuquerque, New Mexico

PROJECT MANAGER / SUPERVISOR / SERVICE TECHNICIAN (Jul 1997 – Sep 2000)
National Electrical Contractors, Albuquerque, New Mexico

SUPERINTENDENT (Oct 1995 – Jul 1997)
Northridge Electric, Albuquerque, New Mexico

EDUCATION

MASTER CERTIFICATE IN APPLIED PROJECT MANAGEMENT (Mar 2010 – Nov 2010)
Villanova University, Tampa, Florida

- Completing 8-week certificate courses to prepare for PMI Project Management Professional (PMP) Certification, including Essentials of Project Management, Mastering Project Management, PMP Exam Preparation, Advanced Strategic Project Management.

PROFESSIONAL DEVELOPMENT: Dedicated to life-long learning through self-study, frequent formal professional development programs, and on-the-job training. Courses included:
- NEC 2008 Code Update Courses 1 and 2 (May 2008)
- CPR, American Red Cross Certification, Albuquerque, New Mexico (Jun 2005)
- OSHA 20 Certification, Albuquerque, New Mexico (Jun 2005)
- OSHA 10 Certification, Albuquerque, New Mexico (Apr 2001)
- Cat-5 Course, Los Alamos, New Mexico (Apr 1997)
- Fiber Optics Course, Los Alamos, New Mexico (Apr 1997)
- NEC Code Update, Fairfax, Virginia (Jun 1995)
- Load Calculation, Fairfax, Virginia (Apr 1995)
- IBEW Apprenticeship School, Washington, DC (May 1991)
- Biomedical Equipment Repairs, FAMC, Aurora, Colorado (1987)

OTHER SKILLS

- Bilingual in English and Spanish.
- Proficient in Windows, MS Word, Excel, Outlook, Internet Explorer.
- Knowledge of PowerPoint and AutoCAD.

sally ross

contact

1234 south roma road #5678 • scottsdale, arizona 85254 • www.facebook.com/sallyross
cell: 480.555.9123 • home/fax 480.555.4567 • email: sross@protyeltd.com

passion

Experienced event management professional who is passionate about educating through entertainment. Able to create a stage for causes and maximize opportunities on as many levels as possible. Developed a reputation for being able to create something from nothing.

strengths

- Entrepreneurial thinker
- Leader and motivator
- Effective communicator
- Resourceful
- Flexible
- Detail-oriented
- Innovative
- Self-starter
- Problem solver

summary of experience

Event Planning and Management

- Creative event planner with more than 15 years of relevant experience with designing, developing, and managing major special events that help drive sales and promote a brand's image by creating a visual and emotional impact.
- Proven ability to successfully manage multiple projects simultaneously.
- Experienced in the full project life cycle—visualized concepts, brain stormed ideas, researched resources, designed programs, and developed/implemented event proposals, budgets, and project execution strategies.
- Identified sponsors, co-branding opportunities, and corporate resources in noncompetitive markets for the purpose of increasing revenue.
- Arranged for product licensing, recruited spokespersons, negotiated contracts for facilities, catering, and entertainment, wrote press releases, and developed advertising campaigns to promote events.
- Led weekly team meetings to ensure consistent internal communication and on-time completion of projects.

Brand Management

- Developed three-dimensional marketing strategies that incorporated regional advertising campaigns, in-store presentations (personal appearances, demonstrations, fashion shows, etc.), public relations, and unique special events.
- Interpreted business plans for each brand, researched markets, created budgets, drove brand concepts, and reviewed assortment selections.
- Helped to develop and signed off on the creation of collateral materials, including in-store signage, displays, packaging, direct mail pieces, and newspaper/magazine advertising.
- Identified the optimal media mix for enhancing each brand strategy and evaluated the effectiveness of advertising.
- Managed relationships with PR agencies to ensure maximum exposure for brands, and developed unique programs to attract media attention.
- Developed and implemented public relations and publicity programs that identified the right press contacts, cultivated long-lasting relationships, and resulted in consistent trade press coverage.

event mgt. experience

CORPORATE SPECIAL EVENTS MANAGER, Macy's Southeast, Atlanta, Georgia (1996 – 2005)
- Produced and directed exciting promotional events for 78 stores in nine states that drove traffic and increased sales.
- Maximized return on investment by efficiently managing all financial elements of projects from budget projections and vendor negotiations to reconciliation of actuals to budget.
- Researched markets and other industries with similar demographics to uncover potential partners and best practices.
- Wrote detailed time-and-action plans, proposals, press releases, and collateral materials.
- Hired and supervised freelance contractors and vendors.
- Oversaw public relations, serving as a media liaison and spokesperson for the corporation.

event mgt. experience

CORPORATE SPECIAL EVENTS MANAGER (continued)
- Collaborated with buyers, store lines, advertising and legal departments, operations, security. visual merchandising, vendors, and other internal/external resources.
- Evaluated event effectiveness and impact on the bottom line.

Key Accomplishments:
- Created iconic events to drive traffic into the stores and to brand Macy's after the acquisition of Foley's, Rich's, and May's department stores.
- Restored some of the traditional mega-events for which Macy's had become famous, including the
  - Harvest Market: Reinstated the outdoor, summer market with fresh produce from local farmers. Used historical photographs to tie the event into modern marketing concepts.
  - Taste of Atlanta: Brought in major national celebrities like Emeril Lagasse for cooking shows, tastings, workshops, and radio/television shows.
  - Annual Flower Show: Installed live floral displays and water features throughout the store, and used models to launch the new spring fashions. Achieved 114% of goal.
  - Bridal Shows: Planned and managed the Duchess of York Bridal Show at Brookwood with 450 attendees, and the Vera Wang and Lord Wedgewood Bridal Show at Lenox with 550 participants.
- Created partnerships with nonprofit organizations to help them raise funds and increase awareness of their causes, while at the same time improving the image of Macy's in the community. Planned fashion shows, cocktail parties, tea parties, silent auctions, and other events.
- Developed the first mammography center in a retail store to honor Breast Cancer Month. Expanded the concept to seven mobile mammography units in nine markets.
- Selected as Home Style Specialist for the Home Store, the "Martha Stewart" for Macy's Southeast.

REGIONAL SPECIAL EVENTS MGR., Macy's South/Bullock's, Atlanta/Los Angeles (1991 – 1992)
- Planned and directed special events, store-wide promotions, designer appearances, major community tie-ins, public relations, and publicity for five stores in two states.

FASHION / PUBLICITY DIRECTOR, Saks Fifth Avenue, Los Angeles, California (1989 – 1991)
- Directed all fashion promotions, public relations, and special events.
- Built an effective cross-functional team between corporate divisional merchandisers, buyers, department managers, sales associates, and vendors.

EVENT PRODUCER / OWNER, Style Strategies, Los Angeles, California (1986 – 1989)
- Negotiated, sold, and orchestrated event packages for clients throughout Southern California, including fashion shows, fund-raisers, and seminars.
- Built a client base of major department stores (Bullock's, Robinson's, The Broadway, May Co., etc.) and national manufacturers (e.g., Speedo National Sales Convention).
- Closed more than 50% of contracts on the first sales call with prices ranging from $20,000 to $75,000.
- Planned and managed national magazine "on location" shows for *Vogue, Mademoiselle, Glamour, GQ,* and *New Woman* magazines.
- Helped to produce the 1989 AIDS Los Angeles Adrian Show.

FASHION EVENT COORDINATOR, California Mart, Los Angeles, California (1983 – 1986)
- Produced more than 100 shows per year, including "California Press Week."
- Conceived and coordinated 30 live shows in three days for 250 members of the national and international press for the FIDM Fashion Video Library.
- Created and implemented a national video retail program to distribute collections of California designers to major national retailers.
- Nominated for the "Best Runway Fashion Video Award" at the 1st Annual Fashion Video Awards in New York.

CORPORATE SPECIAL EVENTS MANAGER, May Company, Los Angeles, California (1980 – 1983)
- Produced fashion shows and special events for 34 stores with bottom-line results of increased traffic and relevant sales.
- Pioneered the Fashion Consultant Program co-funded by DuPont. Developed and sold the program, and trained incoming consultants.
- Negotiated contracts with noncompeting companies for promotional exchanges.

other experience

DESIGNER / OWNER, Designing Solutions, LLC, Scottsdale, Arizona (2005 – present)
- Professionally decorate and stage multi-million-dollar homes so they appeal to potential buyers and generate the highest price in the least amount of time on the market.
- Accountable for full business planning, marketing, sales, and profit and loss of operations.
- Design and manage installation projects. Purchase furnishings and negotiate discounts and contracts.

SOUTHEAST REGIONAL SALES MANAGER, Hindsgaul USA, Atlanta, Georgia (1994 – 1995)
- Sold mannequins to major department and specialty stores in 12 states and Puerto Rico.
- Built the territory from the ground up through aggressive networking, cold calling, and referrals.
- Consulted with clients by identifying their needs, recommending the right solutions, preparing proposals, negotiating prices, and closing deals.

SALES EXECUTIVE, Shepard Convention Services, Atlanta, Georgia (1993 – 1994)
- Successfully sold display systems and convention services to exhibiting companies.
- Prepared and presented sales proposals using complex formulas to price products and services. Developed design concepts based on each client's unique needs.

ADJUNCT INSTRUCTOR, University of California, Los Angeles (1990 – 1991)
- Taught fashion merchandising to undergraduate students.
- Developed course content, syllabi, examinations, and presentation materials.
- Used extensive network of contacts to create a special series on "A Day in the Life Of" various industry professionals.
- Received outstanding evaluations from a diverse student body by emphasizing experiential learning, interactive lectures and exercises, guest speakers, and participatory training.

ASSISTANT DIRECTOR OF ADVERTISING, Cole of California, Los Angeles, California (1979 – 1980)
- Coordinated publicity, national advertising campaigns, and cooperative advertising programs. Produced the national sales convention.
- Executed collateral materials, including brochures, sales catalogs, and newsletters.

education

UNIVERSITY OF CALIFORNIA, Los Angeles, California
- Completed 12 undergraduate courses on teaching philosophies and methods.

FASHION INSTITUTE OF DESIGN AND MERCHANDISING, Los Angeles, California
Associate of Arts, Fashion Merchandising

PROFESSIONAL DEVELOPMENT
- 8th International Conference on Science and Consciousness, Santa Fe.
- Certified Sales Athlete—completed an intensive sales training program that provides the tools needed to research, unearth, access, present, and cultivate profitable relationships that close out the competition.

affiliations

- International Association of Home Staging Professionals—Accredited Staging Professional.
- Phoenix Museum of Art—Sponsor of the Contemporary Forum.
- Make-a-Wish Foundation, Arizona—Member of the Sponsorship Committee for the 2007 Wish Ball.
- Careers for Women, Inc.—Presented seminars for the Dress for Success program. Received the Silver Award for volunteerism.
- Fashion Group International—Active member for more than 15 years. Served as chair of a 18-member committee responsible for producing "Look West", a multimedia extravaganza showcasing 196 designers in a live multimedia fashion extravaganza with a live simulcast in New York.

technology

Proficient with Windows, MS Word, Excel, PowerPoint, Outlook, Internet Explorer, Adobe Photoshop, and Lotus Notes.

Marian T. Parks

800 Arundel Drive • Crofton, MD 21047 • (410) 555-1234 • parks@protypeltd.com

Management • Customer Service • Human Resources • Operations

People- and results-oriented manager with more than 10 years of experience in consistently delivering results through collaboration, talent development, critical thinking, and good judgment. Effective leader, communicator, and problem solver with a proven record of exceeding sales projections, improving the bottom line through revenue growth, improving efficiency, and maximizing staff productivity. Areas of expertise include

Management and Leadership	Sales and Marketing	Human Resources Administration
Operations	Customer Service	Retail Management
Profit and Loss Management	Training and Development	Vendor Relations
Team Building	Safety/Sanitation	Sales and Shrink Inventory Control

Professional Experience

Pets R Us, Inc.   **March 1994—Present**

Steady progression from part-time cashier to store manager for the largest specialty retailer (over 1,000 stores in the U.S. and Canada) of services and solutions for pets.

POSITIONS HELD

Store Manager, Severn Park, MD
October 2004–Present

Operations Manager, Crofton, MD
March 2000–October 2004

Merchandising Manager,
Columbia, MD
May 1998–March 2000

Specialty Manager, Vienna, VA
March 1997–May 1998

Assistant Manager, Vienna, VA
November 1996–March 1997

Lead Cashier, Fairfax, VA
June 1995–October 1996

Cashier, Fairfax, VA
March 1994–June 1995

Operations Management—Promote operational excellence according to company vision and strategy. Manage all aspects of day-to-day store performance. Use inventory management tools to guarantee appropriate levels of in-stock merchandise. Audit store performance. Accountable for profit and loss. Ensure adherence to store, company, and government safety standards.

Supervision and Training—Manage staff of 40 employees, including vie managers. Experienced in personnel recruitment, selection, schedule preparation, and performance assessment. Open-style management includes respectful workplace training and continuous coaching for personal development and to promote team cohesiveness. Hold weekly manager meetings and monthly shrink and safety meetings.

Customer Relation—Develop and maintain customer relationships by offering superior service, personally addressing questions and concerns, and using effective interpersonal and communication skills.

Performance Highlights
- Consistently rated number one in customer service surveys out of 25 stores in district.
- Met and exceeded district sales objectives—10% over YTD sales plan.
- Improved safety conditions in store—25% under plan.
- Maintained low personnel turnover.

Computer Skills

MS Office Suite

Education

Associate of Liberal Arts, Northern Virginia Community College, Fairfax, VA

SARA COLLIER

123 E. Montreal Place, Phoenix, AZ 85032 → scollier@protypeltd.com → 480.555.1234 (H) → 602.555.5678 (C)

TARGET POSITION: <LOAN OFFICER—HOME MORTGAGE>

Go-getter and award-winning, multi-million-dollar producer in all types of market conditions.

Deliver the ultimate client experience through personable, responsive, consultative sales.

Multi-industry sales success with demonstrated talent proactively identifying and seizing opportunities. Generate leads, differentiate product / services from the competition, and forge beneficial relationships with referral partners and customers to capture new business and meet ambitious sales targets. Effective in territory development, coupled with expertise in all phases of the sales cycle. Familiar with residential mortgage types and structuring process. Well-versed in assessing clients' financial needs. Excel in demanding, high-volume, deadline-driven environments.

CAREER HIGHLIGHTS

SALES EXPERTISE

New Business Development / Partnership Building / Customer Relations

→ **Maintained high customer service scores based on post-sales surveys**, serving as an advisor to diverse client base, including first-time homebuyers, to ensure sound decision making.

→ **Cultivated and maintained extensive network of real estate agents** to create demand and generate new business and sales.

→ **Identified customer needs, educated clients on best options and features, referred them to financial institutions**, and provided updates throughout entire process to purchase their desired homes.

→ **Gained competitive advantage by researching market trends and competitors**.

SALES SUCCESSES

Goal Attainment / Awards

→ **Outperformed 66 colleagues to rank as #1 sales team** (two-person team) for two quarters.

→ **Surpassed sales goals each quarter for three consecutive years. Sold up to $13.5 million in one year** and consistently met/exceeded sales targets up to 24% during sales career.

→ **Earned *Lifetime Achievement Award, Sales Person of the Company,*** several *Sales Person of the Month,* and *Excellence in Negotiations Award.*

→ **Boosted market share significantly (18%)** through successful territory penetration.

→ **Executed diversified marketing plan** to generate interest in niche market.

ADMINISTRATIVE ACTIVITIES

Contract Preparation / Financial Assessment / Training

→ **Prepared high volume of administrative paperwork,** including extensive contract preparation, meeting specified deadlines, and ensuring compliance with industry guidelines.

→ **Calculated clients' financial creditworthiness,** assessing debt-to-income ratio and house payments.

→ **Trained less-seasoned professionals** to maximize sales effectiveness.

→ **Managed competing priorities/projects successfully** through detailed planning and prioritization.

PROFESSIONAL HISTORY	EDUCATION
NEW HOME SALESMAN	**Bachelor of Science (B.S.) in Finance**
TLM MORTGAGE, PHOENIX, AZ, 2005–2009	**Minor in Economics**
ST HOMES, Phoenix, AZ, 2002–2005	Michigan State University, Collegeville, MI
SBBE HOMES, Phoenix, AZ, 2000–2002	

Executive Résumés

Webster defines an executive as "a person whose function is to administer or manage affairs of a corporation, division, department, group of companies, etc." This can be the president, director, chief executive officer, chief financial officer, chief information officer, chief marketing officer, controller, executive director, vice president, general manager, treasurer, principal, owner, or any other C-level manager.

Generally, a person in such a position has strategically worked his/her way to the top echelons of management over a period of at least ten years. Executives tend to have many relevant past positions, credentials, achievements, published articles, speaking engagements, community service activities, and other important qualifications.

In order to reflect this experience, an executive résumé is almost always more than one page. In fact, an executive résumé can be as long as it needs to be in order to convince the reader that the candidate has what it takes to manage an organization effectively. The first page of the résumé, however, is the most important.

Just because an executive résumé is long doesn't mean it should be wordy. The same good writing described in Chapter 2 is even more important in an executive résumé. Because the number of applicants for an executive position is generally not as large as for lower-level positions, every word of an executive's résumé will be read many times before a decision is made. Make sure every word you write serves a purpose!

As a general rule, executive résumés should be conservative in style. Senior-level management is considered a rather sober position with considerable responsibility, so there is no room for frivolity or creativity. That doesn't mean, however, that the design of an executive résumé must be boring. The effective use of type style, white space, and discrete graphic lines can make your résumé stand out in the crowd.

Executives often need other types of career documents in addition to their résumés. When the résumé gets too long, a project list can handle some of the excess information. Corporate brochures and proposals usually include executive biographies. LinkedIn and other social networking sites can be used to manage your online brand with professionally written profiles. An executive should seriously consider having his or her own website and blog, and the list goes on. Refer to Chapter 18 for examples of these other career management documents.

Carolyn Sutter

c: 407-555-1234
csutter@protypeltd.com

SENIOR EXECUTIVE

MULTI-FAMILY PROPERTY MANAGEMENT | REDEVELOPMENT | ASSET MANAGEMENT

Growth-oriented real estate professional with more than 20 years of experience accelerating business goals via astute investment, lean operations, savvy supply chain management, inventive marketing, and progressive tenant relations. Deep understanding of full multi-family investment lifecycle, with the ability to manage HR, Finance, Business Development, and Marketing Departments, getting hands-on when needed.

Combine first-hand knowledge of materials sourcing in China with 10 years of focused hotel purchasing and management experience in the U.S., the Caribbean, and Mexico to deliver value-added redevelopment, high-occupancy management, and exceptional ROR on property investments.

ACADEMIC CREDENTIALS

MBA, Executive Level International Business Concentration
Crummer Graduate School of Business, Rollins College, Winter Park, FL

BS, Business Administration, Business Management Concentration
Elms College, Chicopee, MA

PROPERTY MANAGEMENT:
➢ Multifamily Operations
➢ Construction Management
➢ Redevelopment
➢ Real Estate Management
➢ Advertising/Marketing

PROCUREMENT:
➢ Contract Management
➢ Project Management
➢ RFP Development
➢ International Business
➢ Export Programs

HOSPITALITY MANAGEMENT:
➢ Hotel / Restaurant Operations
➢ Strategic Planning
➢ Budgeting
➢ Human Resources

PROFESSIONAL EXPERIENCE

PROGRESSIVE MANAGEMENT GROUP, LLC, Orlando, FL
COO / Vice President

1995–Present

Leveraged broker relationships and lean remodeling processes to yield double- and triple-digit returns on major property investments. Hired to lead formation of new company through post-merger integration and to manage assets in Florida, Georgia, Virginia, Connecticut, and Ohio. Created business systems and processes from scratch, cultivating redevelopment and brokerage/due diligence services revenue.

Directed full redevelopment lifecycle—including acquisition, construction, management, and disposition—for $35+ million in acquisitions. Supervise finance and accounting team in asset modeling, financial reporting, budget creation, and fiscal planning. Also accountable for HR and marketing departments. Manage up to 10K+ units and 58 properties at a time, $66 million operating budget, 200 direct and indirect reports.

➢ Consistently exceeded contractual ROR minimums (20%), yielding up to 100% profit by buying below market value, innovating materials sourcing for value-added construction, and creating dual exit strategy.

➢ Doubled redevelopment ROI, traveling to China and negotiating directly with suppliers to purchase high-value materials for the same price as mid- to low-tier materials from U.S. wholesalers. Avoided export fees leveraging loophole commonly missed by U.S. importers.

➢ Enhanced business agility, creating additional option of easy condo conversion for potential buyers by executing top-notch redevelopment.

➢ Increased occupancy by co-developing innovative quality guarantee that became an industry best practice. Superior service program translated hotel management concepts for application to multi-family properties, assuring best-in-class maintenance by implementing property manager penalties for poor performance.

➢ Exceeded service-level agreements and fostered profitability via Total Quality Management (TQM).

PROFESSIONAL EXPERIENCE, continued

RAMADA INVESTMENT CORPORATION (RIC), Orlando, FL 1985–1995
Regional Director; Florida, Georgia, Caribbean, and Mexico

Facilitated growth of Orlando office from startup to $50 million business unit, helming Purchasing Resource and Unifood divisions. Established all operations, including supply-chain strategy, vendor selection and negotiation, export agreements, and purchasing division (for products and foods). Sat on RIC World Purchasing Board and prepared annual budgets and strategic plans. Supervised all regional hotel staff and launched multiple locations.

➢ Negotiated favorable pricing by pooling purchases of all RIC hotels.
➢ Kept offshore operating costs low, performing detailed supply chain analysis weighing cost and logistics advantages of local, U.S., or alternate sourcing.
➢ Lowered materials costs by sourcing directly from China, gaining deep experience in Asian business practices.
➢ Played role in bringing new franchisees onboard, championing their success by creating robust buying support network.
➢ Delivered $1.3 million and $1.2 million in YOY savings (1992 and 1993).
➢ Negotiated $30 million annual supplies agreement for Southeast and Caribbean, chairing 25-member project team.

HONORS, CREDENTIALS, AND TECHNICAL REPERTOIRE

Honored with City of Orlando *Commissioners Award* for Crime Prevention Multifamily Redevelopment
Granted lifetime CPM by NAPM, 2004
Earned multiple awards and recognition

KNOWLEDGE OF

MS Office Suite

Yardi Property Management

AMSI

BJM Property Management

Rent Roll Property Management

Licensed Real Estate Broker, State of Florida

George Bergman

913-870-4678 ≈ 25 Park Orchard Street, Overland Park, KS 66209 ≈ gbergman@protypeltd.com

SENIOR HEALTHCARE EXECUTIVE
Capital Equipment | Business Development | Customer Operations

Growth, turnaround, and performance catalyst—Excel in creating, growing, and managing multi-million-dollar strategic business with exceptional focus on customer relationships, business efficiency, and service delivery. Hands-on leader with 20 years of industry experience, including 14 years of progressive leadership roles with Jillian & Rome and Fortune 15 Gravity Corporation. Strong network of key relationships and strategic partnerships across the industry. Change agent and consensus builder who champions aggressive advancements in products, services, and market approaches to maintain a competitive edge.

EXPERTISE

Sales Management: Field Sales Leadership / Team Building and Motivation / Consultative and Solutions Sales / Strategic Alliance Development / Territory Alignment and Optimization / Performance Incentives / Relationship Management

General Management: Strategic Planning and Leadership / Budgeting and Finance / Organizational Optimization / Revenue Growth and Bottom-Line Profit / Process Redesign / Contract Negotiations / Supply Chain Solutions

LEADERSHIP HIGHLIGHTS

- Improved region's sales margin performance nearly **500% in two years** to go from last place to number two in the region.
- Repeatedly build **strong and sustainable sales organizations** by implementing innovative training programs, redesigning work flow, and standardizing processes to transform lackluster performers into top producers.
- Leverage internal cross-divisional relationships to focus on **customer-driven sales,** strengthening value proposition to grow customer base and expand existing accounts.
- Successfully planned and pitched innovative new-hire training program that **doubled time to effectiveness.**

EXECUTIVE PERFORMANCE

FOLSOM MEDICATION, Pittsburgh, PA (corporate headquarters)   2003–2010

$410 million division of Fortune 15 Gravity Corporation (NYSE: GCO) providing comprehensive solutions that improve patient and medication care through bar-coding, robotics, software, and analytics.

▶ ***Vice President, Central Region***

Scope of Responsibility: 4–8-member sales team of medication safety consultants, pharmacists, and nurses in 9.5 states covering 300+ acute care hospitals with $75 million operating expenses each.

Recruited by president to breathe new life into declining, underperforming regional business. Oversaw aggressive strategic growth—improving operational procedures, establishing effective marketing messages, and motivating team members to strive for regional and company-wide recognition. Transformed territory to vibrant growth, building an exceptional sales organization and creating market-penetration strategies that **took the area from last place to second of nine regions in two years.** Full responsibility for true financial margins in contract negotiations and ensuring direct report expenses align with corporate T&L guidelines.

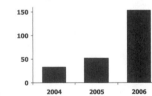

Margin Quota % to Goal

Operational Initiatives:
- **Member of leadership team** working with outside consulting group to develop and implement standard sales process focused on strategic and tactical overlay of sales consulting process with hospital buying process.
- **Forge solid, senior-level relationships** to gain sponsorship of medication/patient safety assessments for rapid approval.
- Use **Six Sigma** methodology to improve project process and workflow. Develop pro-forma and financing options with internal technical accounting and capital financing groups.
- Liaise with client accounts and gravity's drug distribution, hospital and advanced clinical information systems, and automated healthcare business units to **optimize value proposition** to the customer.
- Manage internal operational/financial/legal resources in **negotiating contracts** with customers.

Organizational Impact:
- **Improved margin quota 61%** and elevated region from **number six in 2007 to number 2 in 2008.**
- Averaged **106% of margin quota** in last four years amidst fluctuating personnel and regional alignments.
- **After six years of persistent lobbying, won approval for structured sales training program** that will reduce new-hire time to effectiveness from 1.5 to 2.0 years to **less than one year.**
- Achieved President's Club, 2006 and 2008.

JILLIAN & ROME, Rochester, NY (corporate headquarters)   1995–2003
A leading supplier of eye-care products, with $2.5 billion in annual sales.

▶ *Area Vice President, Central Region (2001–2003)*
Scope of responsibility: 84-member sales team and 8 regional directors in 14 states.

Appointed by president to confidential executive team to leverage expertise and relationships in realigning company-wide business units, strategic objectives, change management plans, and sales plans. Ensured that true financial margins were maintained in all customer contract negotiations.

Organizational Leadership:
- Structured a **highly talented new management team** from diverse backgrounds and specialties within the eye-care industry with mandate to build exceptional sales teams using the same criteria.
- Created cohesive environment and shared **best practices** area-wide in developing strategy and business opportunities.
- Led region to **top slot for five consecutive quarters,** exceeding all sales goals in three regions.

▶ *Director of Sales, Pharmaceutical Division (2000–2001)*
Scope of responsibility: 52-member sales team and six regional directors in U.S. and Puerto Rico.

Personally selected by exiting sales director and president of the business group to lead the sales group, stabilize employee turnover, and grow sales during the relocation of corporate headquarters from Tampa to Rochester.

Organizational Leadership:
- Triggered **$74 million** revenue growth (107% to national sales plan), working closely with director of marketing and corporate accounts to develop and implement quarterly sales objectives, plans, and programs.
- Successfully presented plan for budgeting and hiring **national training manager and a module-based training program** for new hires—reducing time-to-effectiveness and profitability from 12/8 months to nine months in territories afflicted with a high rate of attrition or promotion.

▶ *Senior Regional Director, Southeast and Central Regions (1996–2000)*

Established unprecedented record as the only regional director to reverse declining sales in two underperforming regions. Led southeast region from third to first place and last place central region to number one by restructuring sales teams, developing sound business plans, and monitoring resource allocation. Administered **$700K** operating budget.

Organizational Leadership:
- Mentored team of contract managers and marketing associates, building a **highly focused and cohesive team culture.**
- Instituted **new sales tracking methodologies** for consistent growth and improved accountability and performance.
- Established a **standardized contract management process,** including negotiations, fees, and terms.

▶ *Senior Pharmaceutical Representative (1995–1996)*

Pursued a field position even after elimination due to "over-qualification." Wrote to vice president of sales and vice president of marketing and offered to go at risk for one year in the territory. Determined to take territory from last place to first place nationwide.

Organizational Leadership:
- Moved territory from last place to sixth (48 territories). Promoted to regional director four months later.
- Rookie of the Year (of eight candidates).

▶ *Early Sales Career*
- Climax Labs, Inc., Palo Alto, CA | Runner-up Rookie of the Year (among 25 candidates)
- Omega Dental Plans of Kansas, Wichita | Top Producer (7.5 months) | #1 new account/employee enrollment (entire tenure)

EDUCATION | CAREER TRAINING | COMMUNITY

Certified Medical Representative, CMR Institute, Roanoke, VA, 1992
BBA in Marketing, Wichita State University, Wichita, KS, 1986
Six Sigma—How to Apply without Getting a Belt (Gravity)
Strategic Selling (Dale Miller)
Volunteer Leader, Trainer, and Advisor, Boy Scouts of America, 1991– Present

MEREDITH STRUNK, MGA

12345 Tunnel Road, Palo Alto, CA 94301 • 650-555-1234 (mb) • strunk@protypeltd.com

---

TECHNOLOGY | BUSINESS ANALYST | PROJECT MANAGER
Systems Development | Implementation | Technical and Operational Audits (Internal)

Financial Services | Education | Government | Retail | Healthcare

Technically sophisticated business management professional, offering 12+ years of in-house and client-based process improvement and systems implementation experience. Expertise leading teams of up to 22 people and budgets up to $4.3 million for Fortune 50 companies with managed assets up to $2.1 trillion.

End-to-end client delivery specialization focused on product strategy, risk reduction, and regulatory compliance as well as customer need and usage habits. Facilitate balance between project goals and gridlock, while translating business needs into requirements that achieve stakeholder trust and business-side buy-in.

PROFESSIONAL EXPERIENCE

CITIGROUP, INC, New York, NY ....2004 to present
One of the world's largest financial services firms. Custodied Assets: $3 trillion. Employees: 300,000

Business Analyst—Information Technology Services Group
Design and Functionality | User Experience | Business and Technical Requirements
Retained through Manpower, Inc., to support web development for Citigroup's Workforce Investment company. Presently drive projects, bridge communication, mitigate roadblocks, and balance product, legal and strategy priorities across seven internal groups. *Report to director, information technology services group.*

Principal roles on three proprietary, in-house, client-facing web technologies:

- **New Client Facing Application:** Multi-year, multi-million-dollar project to improve competitive offering and increase assets under management.
  - Increased participation adoption by 15% within three months of going live.
  - Reworked enrollment platform from rep-driven to consumer-directed online experience.
  - Streamlined enrollment methodology, decreasing intake questions from 18 to 4.
  - Retained post-go-live to prioritize and lead approximately $1 million in additional 2009/2010 work.

- **Existing Product Enhancement:** Multi-year, multi-million-dollar functionality enhancement designed to improve marketplace competitiveness and optimize participant and representative efficiencies.
  - Consolidated disparate transaction functionalities.
  - Decreased participant and representive interaction time 35–40%.
  - Increased rep-led and self-directed completed plans (KPI: 10% over five years).
  - Decreased representative costs to service customers (KPI: 6% over five years).

- **Web-Facing Tool Redesign:** Single-year, multi-million-dollar project targeting consumers 21–65 years old, prompting action by simplifying user experience.
  - Streamlined design, layout, charts, and content to maximize user experience, which clarified the participant action plan.
  - Increased completed plans and tool usage 20%.

BROMLEY COMMUNICATIONS, San Antonio, TX... 2002 to 2004
Direct marketing leader serving the international Latino segment. Revenues: $65.2 million (FY08). Employees: 400.

(continued on page 2)

Project Manager / Business Analyst – IT Division
Technology Implementation | Business Requirements | System Development Lifecycle | Vendor Selection
Recruited to clean up two previously failed attempts at integrating custom and third-party hardware / software applications. Charged with replacing antiquated technology supporting firm's core business. Managed $4.3 million budget, 17 external consultants, and 10 internal resources. *Reported to director of information technology.*

- Designed processes enabling four expansion opportunities including:
  - Single- to multi-product sales transaction conversion
  - Sales / media campaign tracking allocation
  - Incentive compensation and projection calculator automation
  - Discount promotions submission

- Automated and re-engineered business processes for order management and fulfillment, loan origination, and servicing and customer relations.

- Translated 200 functional requirements into technical requirements and use cases.

ERNST & YOUNG, Houston, TX .... 1998 to 2002
LLP: Big Four audit, tax, and advisory services. Revenues: $3.7 billion (FY02). Employees: 18,000 in 80 U.S. Offices. LLC: Technology consulting firm. Revenues: $680 million (FY01). Employees: 17,000.

Risk Management and Government Services Group
Senior Associate, Advisory Services, EY, LLP (2/01 – 6/02)

Public Works Practice
Senior Consultant, Ernst & Young Consulting, LLC (6/99 – 2/01)
Consultant, Ernst & Young Consulting, LLC (1/98 – 6/99)
Recruited to optimize third-party client business processes and technology systems. Retained and promoted to identify and make improvement recommendations to mitigate operational, compliance, and technology risks. *Reported to senior managers in all roles.*

Selected highlights from 16 client engagements:
- **Real Estate Conglomerate:** One of 10 auditors conducting functional / technology audits including IT Strategic Planning, Project Management, Systems Development Lifecycle, and Application.
- **Multi-channel Retail Group:** One of five-member team evaluating functional processes and technology operations to meet Sarbanes Oxley 404. Retained to develop IT policies and procedures.
- **State Commonwealth:** One of 11 conducting business processes re-engineering and change management on 55-member ERP team. One of four charged with assessing HIPAA compliance.
- **Statewide Information Technology Office:** One of three consultants building logical data model, framework, and management system, enabling data-sharing and improving access across state departments.

EDUCATION

Harvard University, Cambridge, MA
Master of Governmental Administration, 1998
Bachelor of Arts, 1996

THOMAS TANNER, MPA

12345 N. Wabash Lane
Chicago, Illinois 60001
Cellular: 773.555.1234 • Work: 312.555.1234
E-mail: tanner@protypeltd.com

HEALTHCARE OPERATIONS EXECUTIVE

Change manager with a proven history of increasing profitability, turning around underperforming organizations, and implementing innovative programs. Areas of strength include strategic planning, clinical operations, coding, billing, faculty affairs, facilities, clinical research, funds management, and philanthropy. **Expertise in:**

> **Financial Management**: Spearheaded programs to reduce expenditures and increase gross charges in emergency medicine department by 152%. Grew department reserves from $200,000 to $4 million over five years.

> **Research Program Development**: Grew clinical research program infrastructure from $50,000 in annual funding to more than $800,000.

> **Talent Management**: Implemented comprehensive process to acquire and retain top talent, resulting in low turnover.

"Thomas, you get a lot of points for doing a great job, working well with others, and exerting positive leadership."
– Brian M. Smith, MD, Professor and Chair, Department of Emergency Medicine, Hudson University

EXPERIENCE AND ACCOMPLISHMENTS

HUDSON MEDICAL FACULTY FOUNDATION AND HUDSON UNIVERSITY, Chicago Illinois   2001–present

Department Administrator Emergency Department (2004–present)
Division Administrator Emergency Department (2001–2004)

Direct practice affairs in support of 24 full-time and 15 part-time emergency medicine physicians staffing an urban Level-1 trauma center treating approximately 85,000 patients annually. Recruited to rebuild clinical and administrative operations department. Oversee annual practice budget of $40 million in clinical, residency, donor and endowment, and research and education areas. Supervise research administrator in stewardship of federal, state, local, and foundation grant submissions, and ongoing funding in excess of $2 million. Manage Profit and Loss and supervise staff of 16. Lead recruiting and hiring processes and appointments for faculty in hospital, medical school, and foundation. Collaborate with department chair to manage donor development program.

> **Increased clinical revenues by 90% in less than eight years and gross charges by more than 152%.**
> **Recruited 15+ emergency medicine physicians from across the United States.**
> **Created 23-hour short-stay observation unit in 2003.**
> **Acquired departmental status within Dermot School of Medicine in 2004.**
> **Spearheaded development of department Web site, now among the most comprehensive in this specialty.**
> **Oversaw entire construction process of 12,000 square foot department office space. Designed and constructed two-floor administrative suite for department.**

UNIVERSITY OF LAKEVIEW, Chicago, Illinois   1995–2001

Section Administrator Vascular and Dental Surgery (1998–2001)

Managed two clinical practices consisting of ten dental and five vascular surgeons, two dental clinics, two ultrasound procedure areas, and two research laboratories. Prepared hospital capital proposals and annual operating budgets of approximately $2.5 million. Coordinated annual vascular surgery fellowships, including case submission to American College of Surgeons. Organized functions of each section consisting of practice events, symposiums, and greeting visiting dignitaries. Supervised construction in laboratory, procedure area, and operating room.

> **Increased profit 25% by identifying new revenue strategies in international, technology, and satellite areas.**
> **Directed Joint Commission readiness task forces for vascular ambulatory clinic leading to outstanding assessment as part of overall institutional review.**

EXPERIENCE AND ACCOMPLISHMENTS, CONTINUED

Clinical Trial Contracts and Personnel Manager, Hematology / Oncology (1996–1998)

Led staff of 15 throughout 12 cancer programs to optimize data collection and sponsor reporting. Managed all aspects of more than 90 clinical trials.

> ➢ **Increased number of negotiated trials five-fold in 18 months, resulting in highest dollar amount ever achieved. Reduced turnaround time from months to weeks.**

Research Project Manager, Hematology / Oncology (1995–1996)

Supervised Phase-I cancer program and coordinated weekly review of program patients with research and clinical team. Screened patients to determine study eligibility.

UNIVERSITY OF INDIANA, School of Medicine, Hanover, Indiana   1993–1995
Department of Veterans' Affairs Medical Center

Research Coordinator, Cue-Response Conditioning Unit

Directed six employees in conducting polygraphic research studies using drug and alcohol dependent patients. Spearheaded strategic review (SWOT) of unit to turn around disorganized center. Presented findings to unit director prior to annual budget meeting.

EDUCATION

Master of Public Affairs (MPA) in Health Administration, 2002
Graduated magna cum laude
Illinois University, Chicago, Illinois

Bachelor of Arts (BA) in Biology, 1993
University of Indiana, Hanover, Indiana

PROFESSIONAL AFFILIATIONS

American College of Healthcare Executives (ACHE), Member, 2009–present
Healthcare Financial Management Association (HFMA), Member, 2009–present
Society for Academic Emergency Medicine (SAEM), Member, 2009–present

JUDITH S. WESTMORELAND

557 Broad Street, Chicago, IL 50607
Cell: (505) 555-1234
westmoreland@protypeltd.com

HEALTHCARE EXECUTIVE
CHIEF EXECUTIVE OFFICER / CHIEF OPERATING OFFICER

Healthcare CEO / COO whose leadership, communication, and physician relationship skills combined with executive ability have consistently enabled healthcare organizations to meet their strategic objectives, financial goals, and specific healthcare system outcomes. Experienced leading operations in complex organizations in competitive markets. Master of Healthcare Administration (MHA).

PROFESSIONAL HIGHLIGHTS

JOHNSON MEDICAL CENTER, Chicago, IL

A division of TRC, a leading provider of healthcare services with ~150 hospitals and 65 outpatient surgery centers in 24 states, England, and Switzerland. Johnson is a 275-bed adult acute care facility and a regional referral center for cardiac, stroke, orthopedics, and neurosurgery with projected gross revenues over $1 billion and net revenues over $175 million for FY 2008. Projected operating expenses are $164 million with 740 total FTEs. EBDITA reached over $29 million in FY 2007.

CHIEF EXECUTIVE OFFICER (2007 to present)

Full P&L responsibility for entire organization. Manage eight direct reports. Strategic planning and action plan development and implementation have resulted in **improvement across a number of key indices:**

New Revenue Contribution	$24.9M+
Cost Containment	$2M+
Total Staff Turnover	25% to 5%
RN Turnover	35% to 5.4%
RN Vacancy Rates	17% to 6%
EBDITA	38% from 2006–2007
Emergency Room Hold Hours	15K to <900 within six months
Satisfaction Scores	Patient, physician and employee increases
Quality Assurance	Every category of quality core measures increased
Ranking	Named "BEST" hospital in local area based on HCAHPS survey

Representative Leadership Highlights

Achievement #1. Inherited an underperforming emergency room with unacceptably high hold and diversion hours leading to poor service and consequently low volume and revenues. Rebuilt entire organization, including vision, culture, staffing, and vendor relationships. Improved processes and patient flow.

Results: Turned around ER performance: Slashed ER hold hours by 94%. Eliminated divert practices. Grew number of visits by 10%+. Produced an increase in net revenue of $10M+.

Achievement #2. Elevated the hospital's neuroscience service line into a regional referral center to improve patient care, revenues, and hospital reputation. Recruited a new neurosurgeon. Developed and implemented a strategic plan that encompassed a multidisciplinary spine counsel and an intake clinic.

Results: Neurosurgical and spine volumes have grown over 430% the past two years, leading to an increase in contribution margin of over $12 million.

Achievement #3. Addressed excessively high RN turnover and vacancy rates (reaching approximately 30%). Achieved buy-in among clinical leaders on patient-to-RN ratios. Raised salaries to be competitive locally. Made a commitment to candidate excellence in hiring. Eliminated lower-performing traveling nurses.

Results: Brought vacancy rates down 83% and turnover 76%, producing multimillion-dollar labor cost savings.

JOHNSON MEDICAL CENTER (continued)

Achievement #4. Took a low-profile, local Electrophysiology Program (EP) and worked with the local physicians to develop a strategic plan that encompassed regional/national strategies, improved operations and patient flow, as well as new advanced EP diagnostic/interventional equipment.

Results: Exceeded prior-year volumes by 33% and increased contribution margins by $2.5 million annually.

CENTER HOSPITAL, Chicago, IL   2003 to 2007

Center Hospital is a 110-bed adult acute care hospital with net revenues of $69 million and EBDITA of approximately $8.2 million. Center Hospital also has one freestanding, outpatient, diagnostic imaging facility. The hospital is located in a high-growth area and is currently approved to build a new hospital on 51 acres to expand its outpatient and acute-care services.

CHIEF EXECUTIVE OFFICER (2003 to 2007)

Held P&L, strategic, and operational responsibility for the hospital and satellite facility. Ensured that the financial performance, physician relations, and community image met community needs. Grasp of financial indicators essential with net revenues exceeding $69M. Managed eight direct reports. **Metrics demonstrating improvements include:**

Cost Savings	$1.1M
RN Turnover	32% to 8%
RN Vacancy Rates	36% to 6%
Satisfaction Scores	Patient, employee, and physician satisfaction climbed to all-time highs

Representative Leadership Highlights

Achievement #1. Assumed authority for an old hospital whose severe physical constraints and limited acreage curtailed growth. Developed a strategic plan that culminated in the purchase of 61 acres of land for $10 million. Won competitive bid for a Certificate of Need (CON) from the state of Florida to build a new $200 million hospital.

Results: Removed roadblocks to hospital growth by acquiring land strategically located in target market and planning a major building initiative.

Achievement #2: Replaced an underperforming legacy radiology group. Met the major challenge of communicating the best practices desired and how to implement them.

Results: Overcame resistance to plan by gaining support of the medical staff, enabling a successful transition toward a state-of-the-art radiology department that won accolades from satisfied customers, including physicians and patients.

Achievement #3: Addressed high RN turnover (32%) and vacancy (36%) rates. Developed a culture of "patient first" service, and used mentoring and personal influence to drive the culture to a higher standard of care.

Results: By stabilizing nursing staff and raising standards of care, was able to save the hospital ~$1.1 million.

EDUCATION

M.H.A. Health Administration Program, Johns Hopkins School of Medicine, Baltimore, MD
B.S. Healthcare Administration, Johns Hopkins School of Medicine, Baltimore, MD

COMMUNITY INVOLVEMENT

Board Memberships:
- American Heart Association 2008s
- American Heart Association, 2000–2008 (Vice Chair 2001)
- United Way 2000–2008

CHARLES CALHOUN

555 Elm Street
Seattle, WA
Mobile: 555-555-5555
Calhoun@protypeltd.com

BUILDING BEST-OF-BREED TREASURY FUNCTIONS
GLOBAL BANKING RELATIONSHIP MANAGEMENT
BALANCE SHEET AND LIQUIDITY MANAGEMENT
ADVANCED PENSION AND RISK MANAGEMENT
CORPORATE FINANCE DEAL EXECUTION
LEADING HIGH-PERFORMANCE TEAMS

SENIOR TREASURY / CORPORATE FINANCE PROFESSIONAL

Corporate Finance ▪ *Treasury* ▪ *Cash Management* ▪ *Liquidity Management* ▪ *Banking Relations*
Pension Management ▪ *Foreign Exchange (fx)* ▪ *Risk Management* ▪ *Corporate Governance*
Investor Relations ▪ *M&A* ▪ *Strategic Planning*

Senior-level treasury professional with 17+ years of experience planning, developing, and managing complex, global finance and treasury operations in multinational corporations. Broad experience base with strong record of making key contributions that increased shareholder value, reduced costs, and minimized risk. Expert at maintaining liquidity and optimizing the balance sheet during periods of fast growth as well as during times of rating downgrades and business downturns. Highly skilled at analyzing financial instruments/markets and creatively exploiting business opportunities.

- Successfully structured billions of dollars in 11 deals, with optimal pricing and distribution in challenging markets.
- Built relationships and managed two large, global banking syndicates lending $500 million and $2 billion.
- Managed $750 million swap portfolio, delivering $55 million revenue from interest rate swaps.

PROFESSIONAL EXPERIENCE AND SELECTED ACCOMPLISHMENTS

CHEMICALS CORPORATION   1999–Present
A $3 billion multinational commodity chemicals company with 19 locations in the U.S., Canada, Europe, and South America. Currently rated BB+ by the S&P rating agency. Shares trade on NYSE and Toronto exchanges.

Assistant Treasurer—Corporate Finance and Treasury Department
Broad-based corporate finance, treasury, pension, and risk management responsibilities in a multinational corporation with $3 billion in revenue and $2 billion in debt or debt-like instruments. Directed a team consisting of a Finance Specialist, Global Cash Manager, Pension Manager, and related staff. Managed global banking relationships, including a $500 million revolver facility, all short-term credit facilities, and long-term instruments. Managed a $200 million accounts receivable securitization program. Performed debt compliance analysis, forecasting, and reporting.

Liquidity Management and Balance Sheet Optimization
- Developed and achieved board approval for a debt management policy, focusing on limiting risk, maintaining liquidity, reducing interest costs, and maximizing profit through the optimization of the level of debt and mix of fixed/floating debt, currency, and term of debt.
- At a time when the company was losing money due to the 2001/2002 business downturn, produced $55 million in interest rate swap proceeds by developing an interest rate strategy and managing interest rate exposure in a $650 million swap portfolio.
- Proactively minimized the impact on debt agreements, share price, and investor groups of ratings downgrades in 2001/2002 (including a downgrade in rating to below investment grade).
- Managed $200 million accounts receivable securitization program through a severe business downturn and downgrade.

Corporate Finance and Issuance of New Debt
- Closed two major deals in the challenging lending environments of 2000–01, with optimal pricing and distribution:
  - Arranged a $250 million Canadian bond deal in September 2000—negotiated a ten-year deal (when achieving more than a five-year term was not deemed possible) in the company's first-ever Canadian deal.
  - Negotiated a $300 million U.S. bond deal in May 2001—completed the entire deal including road show over the phone in one day by moving swiftly and decisively to take advantage of a window of opportunity.

Global Banking Management
- Managed strong, long-term relationships with seven core global banks.
- Successfully renegotiated revolver and bridge facilities during credit downgrades and tight credit markets.
- Controlled and monitored the allocation of all ancillary business by bank.

CHEMICALS CORPORATION, CONTINUED

Global Cash Flow Management
- Managed an international Cash Management Group of five professionals in the U.S., U.K., and Switzerland:
  - Conceived, developed, and implemented a range of new systems and procedures designed to improve efficiencies, cut costs, and improve the quality of the reporting delivered to the board and executive team.
  - Introduced global cash flow forecasting by jurisdiction to facilitate strategic planning.
  - Implemented tax-advantaged pooling techniques and consolidation strategies, including converting cash held in 10 different countries and currencies.
  - Rescued a high-risk foreign exchange (fx) hedging program by designing fx hedging strategies and developing processes for analyzing fx portfolio and exposures.

Risk Management
- Minimized risk and ensured ethical, effective governance by preparing, recommending, and implementing a global enterprise risk management system through comprehensive review of governance structure. Set up an executive committee to ensure all decisions would be reviewed against established criteria before implementation.
- Maximized efficiencies and increased knowledge-sharing by instituting the first commodity price risk management policy to be approved by the executive since 1996.

Rating Agency Communications
- Enabled the corporation to optimize ratings through effective and timely communication with Canadian and U.S. rating agencies during an extended business trough.

Pension Management
- As manager of pension officer and member of the pension committees, reviewed and reorganized the pension committee structure for U.S., Canada, and Europe and elevated standards for members in order to help optimize the pension expense and assets (totaling $330 million in three jurisdictions).

Transition Management and New Office Opening
- Without a business interruption, achieved the seamless transition of the treasury department and all financial systems from Calgary to Pittsburgh (3Q/2000). Recruited, hired, and developed six staff, including two loyal, senior-level managers who changed companies and relocated countries in order to work on the team.

ENERGY COMPANY   **1985–1999**

A $6 billion multinational oil and gas exploration and production company with operations on five continents.

Assistant Treasurer, Treasury Department   (1997–1999)
Manager, Cash and Short Term Finance   (1996–1997)
Manager, Treasury   (1995–1996)
Advisor, Cash Management and Planning   (1991–1995)

Fast-track promotion through multiple treasury/corporate finance positions within a $6 billion global corporation. As assistant treasurer, managed $2 billion in debt and debt-like instruments and provided financial support for the acquisition of a $1.8 million oil and gas company. Hired, trained, managed, and led a leading-edge global cash management group of three and a global administration group of five professionals.

PROFESSIONAL AFFILIATIONS

Financial Executives Institute (FEI), since 1998
Association of Investment Management Research (AIMR), since 1987
Chartered Financial Analyst (CFA) Society, Calgary and Pittsburgh, since 1987
Treasury Management Association of Canada (TMAC), Executive, since 1991
Association for Financial Professionals (AFP), U.S.A., since 1996

EDUCATION AND CERTIFICATION

Bachelor of Arts, Washington University, St. Louis, MO
Double Major: Finance and Economics, Great Distinction

Chartered Financial Analyst (CFA), 1990
Association of Investment Management and Research, USA

James Nash

123 Life Place • West Palm Beach, FL 33333 • 561.555.1212 • JN12345@protypeltd.com

Director of Information Technology
Visionary Leadership for Global Business Solutions Impacting Infrastructure, Revenue, and Costs

"Achieving long-term architecture, while stripping out excess costs."–James Nash
Innovative Revenue Streams | Cost Containment | Technology Performance

Strategic executive with success in directing cross-functional teams of technical experts in multiple site locations across 15 countries, including China and India, to analyze systems/processes and implement infrastructure improvements. **Recognized for leadership in strategic planning, post-acquisition integration, RFPs/response, disaster recovery, cost control, budgeting, and definition of scope for enterprise information systems projects.** Demonstrated ability to focus on high-payoff improvements to achieve immediate bottom-line benefits. Proven track record of success in developing solutions that improve the efficiency of IT and business operations.

TEAM LEADERSHIP | VENDOR MANAGEMENT | NETWORK OPERATIONS | EXECUTIVE COMMUNICATIONS BUDGETING | FORECASTING | GLOBAL GROWTH STRATEGIES | SECURITY

"James has earned my respect and admiration for his leadership, technical accomplishment, and commitment to the highest possible standards." – G. Super, CEO, TTT Ads

"James is a great asset to any organization…person of vision and support for his team…leader…with James, I was able to perform at a higher standard to achieve our goals." – Bob Brumm, Author and Motivational Speaker

LEADERSHIP PERFORMANCE

JJJ Enterprise, West Palm Beach, FL • 2002 to Present
Global consumer products manufacturer/distributor with annual sales of $1.5B+.

INFORMATION TECHNOLOGY DIRECTOR OF GLOBAL NETWORK SERVICES AND OPERATIONS

Oversee all networks (including remote access), telecom (PBX, call centers), data centers, IT power/cooling systems, and $7 million budget. Lead direct team of 15 (nine engineers and six operations specialists) with four indirect reports for 32 site locations in 15 countries. Direct operations command center, data centers, and system deployments for new facilities. Establish design standards and oversee hosting and networking for multiple company divisions. Perform technical analysis of systems/requirements and advise business units on IT complexities.

PROVEN SUCCESS—$3,286,000 in Savings

Cost Containment Innovative Revenue Streams	2002	2003	2004	2005	2006	2007	2008	2009
Operations—Total $2,015,000	$80,000	$145,000	$145,000	$145,000	$125,000	$127,000	$625,000	$625,000
Voice—Total $813,000	$27,000	$46,000	$90,000	$110,000	$125,000	$130,000	$140,000	$145,000
Data—Total $458,000		$38,000	$50,000	$70,000	$75,000	$75,000	$75,000	$75,000

➢ **Cost Containment and Innovative Revenue Streams**
- **Identified and architected** a JJJ division. Out-sourced ERP system, to be hosted on systems in data centers, which reduced overall costs and returned $500,000 to the corporate family.
- **Decreased** costs $72,000 a year and tripled bandwidth by redesigning the WAN and utilizing regional carriers in the Far East.
- **Transitioned** networking from inter-site microwave links to WiFi bridges, saving $40,000 a year.

➢ **Technology Leadership**
- **Guided** the business team that selected a new disaster recovery/business continuity solution for the company. Directed the planning and implementation of the IT plan. Migrated to high-availability, redundant data centers, providing real-time synchronization of systems-based business prioritization.
- *Led the Global Architecture Review Committee and founding member of the Change Control Committee.*
- **Charged with** transitioning the computer operations team to expand their duties to encompass complete 24/7 operational monitoring globally and the coordination of on-call engineers to resolve issues.

➢ **Strategic Planning and Growth**
- **Developed** infrastructure change control process, project definition template, infrastructure project templates, contributed to defining architectural standards, and co-chair global architectural review committee.
- **Recruited** for the management team that in-sourced all IT functions, contributing through creating and executing a plan that delivered full infrastructure systems in six months, playing a vital role in saving $2 million.
- **Established and completed** a five-year telecommunication plan that migrated from traditional PBXs to a converged platform enabling the use of IP phones, both standard and soft phones, VoIP trunking across international sites, and the in-sourcing of audio conferencing. The last was a Six-Sigma project resulting in an annual savings that has grown to $170,000 a year.
- **Designed** a global plan to interconnect all divisions for data exchange and shared services and then worked with the separate IT departments to successfully implement the plan. Implemented a modular approach to building, upgrading, or renovating sites, which has resulted in reduced lead time for opening new sites, a shopping cart style project estimator, and enhanced centralized support.

Cap Money Financial, Tampa, FL and Richmond, VA • 1999 to 2002
International consumer financial services company with $14 billion in annual revenues.

INFORMATION TECHNOLOGY DIRECTOR OF EUS ENTERPRISE OPERATIONS

Directed processes for 207 EUS team members distributed across 45 locations and oversaw the PC repair/disposal unit (including 10 employees). Produced cost analyses and work flow forecasts. Enhanced alignment with performance standards by overseeing EUS projects, assessing project delivery/operations, and developing metrics. Substantially contributed to department's disaster recovery initiatives and testing. Created operational trainings with internal university.

- **Led** a team of senior support managers in the development of an operating plan for all service delivery tasks to define best practices for work processes and establish service level agreements for a staff of 167 that supported 24,000 users across 10 campuses.
- **Decreased** annual costs $600,000 while shortening PC repair cycle from 13 to 4 days by implementing repair programs at all locations to replace a centralized in-house facility.
- **Captured** an additional $400,000 in annual revenues by realizing gains on obsolete equipment through negotiation with a recycling vendor for collection and salvage sales (when possible).
- **Prevented** outsourcing of the EUS function and enabled an 18% cost savings by responding to the RFP and developing a proposal with SLAs, cost projections, and differentiators.
- **Saved** $3 million annually through improvement of technical staff to end-user ratio from 1:65 to 1:115 by leveraging root-cause analysis and minimization of repeating issues.

IMS Group, Tampa, FL • 1997 to 1999
Outsourced business processing solutions provider serving the flood insurance industry.

INFORMATION SYSTEMS DIRECTOR OF ENGINEERING AND OPERATIONS

Oversaw 14 employees and operations (six facilities) of the network, data center, MS servers, disaster recovery, and printing/e-mail. Enhanced functionality and managed maintenance.
- **Saved** $160,000 per year by establishing an AS/400 hierarchical storage management system.
- **Decreased** costs $250,000 by deploying an IVR solution and enabling 24/7 request verification.
- **Reduced** annual costs $200,000 by leveraging improvements including a centralized fax server.
- **Lowered** yearly costs $120,000 by transitioning from microfiche to AS/400 optical storage.

TECHNICAL PROFICIENCIES

IBM AS/400 | Dell | Avaya | Nortel | Cisco | Check Point | Juniper | Solarwinds Orion | APC
Microsoft (Project, Visio, Office) | JD Edwards | Showcase | Strohl LDRPS

EDUCATION/PROFESSIONAL DEVELOPMENT

Pinellas Vocational Technical Institute, Electronics, Clearwater, Florida
John Maxell Leadership Program, Achieve Global Leadership

SIMON SCHNELL, MBA

12345 Goddard Lane • Lexington, KY 40532
444-979-5452 • sschnell@protypeltd.com

Leader by example, analytical in approach, vision and foresight to manage complex technical and global systems.

PROGRAM MANAGER

Performance driven **Program Manager** with 12+ years of outstanding success developing teams that exceed corporate objectives. Consistent top 5% performer throughout career. Interface effortlessly with all levels of management and across all disciplines. Driven to establish the success of both team and corporation.

PROFESSIONAL EXPERIENCE

SENIOR GLOBAL COMMODITY MANAGER   TRADEMARK CORPORATION, Lexington, KY   2005–present

Recruited to merge all international commodity teams into a single global organization to meet corporate long-term procurement and supply-chain management goals.

Challenge............Pioneer development of a system to determine financially high-risk suppliers, which ultimately affect commodity supply and new product launches.

Result....................Developed a global supplier risk program providing a 95% forecast success rate. Predicted two critical suppliers' insolvencies, saving $1.1 million/day in potential shutdown costs.

Challenge..............Create a tracking system to determine suppliers' performance metrics and ability to develop plans, establish accountability, and improve performance.

Result..................Implemented first-ever corporate supplier quality improvement system and warranty reduction program, improving quality metrics by 175% and costs by 10% within six months.

Challenge............Tasked to improve corporate program management.

Result..................Implemented best practices, including commodity strategies, supplier development, negotiation strategies, sourcing for quality, and improving competitive market position. Within three months, recognized by senior management for increased staff performance due to higher levels of morale and cooperation.

SENIOR GLOBAL PURCHASING COMMODITY SPECIALIST   FORD MOTOR COMPANY, Dearborn, MI   2001–2005

Promoted to lead global cross-functional teams for procurement and supply of complex high-risk advanced vehicle technologies for all global vehicle programs.

Challenge............Define, implement, and manage new global direct injection strategy in less than 24 months, to support new Ford Motor Company Global Strategy which affected all global divisions and brands.

Result..................100% on-time launch of first 8 of 12 global direct injection programs worth $1.3 billion. Improved vehicle performance by 15% and reduced emissions by 10%. Lowered ED&T budget costs by 15%, and improved cost objectives by $120 million.

Challenge............Lead the development and execution of brand-new corporate emissions strategy for North America.

Result..................Led and managed cross-functional team, which initiated first North American vehicle strategy. Reduced vehicle system complexity by 75% and capital investment by $45 million. Saved $80 million in engineering costs and improved cost performance by $120 million within a three-year period.

Challenge ....Lead the creation and execution of the supplier risk evaluation management process.

Result..................Created and executed the first of a series of global commodity strategies, resulting in $65 million initial savings. Refined engineering specs, resulting in $20 million ED&T savings, reduced part complexity by 20%, resulting in $9 million logistic savings. Improved warranty performance by $85 million in two years, and improved global quality performance to <100PPM.

Challenge............Improve costs through analysis and optimization of critical manufacturing processes.

Result..................Collaborated with suppliers to design and develop flexible manufacturing to produce three parts on a single line instead of three production lines. Eliminated 60% estimated capital investment, reduced piece cost by 10%, and saved $2 million in tooling costs.

SUPPLY CHAIN MANAGEMENT　　　　FORD MOTOR COMPANY, Dearborn, MI　　　　1998–2001

Managed multiple global cross-functional teams to achieve critical milestones to support vehicle launch objectives and specifications.

Challenge:...........Manage critical supply base to support 10 new launches in 12 months. Supply base had systematic quality issues and poor performance, impacting customer satisfaction.

Result: ....100% on-time launch of all programs. Improved quality performance by 85%, warranty performance by 62%, and captured an additional 10% in cost savings.

Challenge: ....Achieve continuous supplier cost reduction and improve quality objectives.

Result: ....Exceeded performance objectives through implementation of Six Sigma projects to improve supplier costs by $350 million and quality by 182% within a three-year period.

Challenge:...........Manage supplier quality for 52 vehicle programs and 1,052 parts.

Result: ....Applied advanced program quality planning to achieve 100% flawless launch audits and supplier readiness reviews at a 95% success rate.

COMMODITY SPECIALIST　　　　DAIMLER-CHRYSLER, Auburn Hills, MI　　　　1994–1998

Promoted after 18 months to manage cross-functional teams including engineering, quality, manufacturing, development, and suppliers to ensure timing, cost, and quality objectives were met to support North American vehicle and engine program success.

Challenge............Manage and launch 12 vehicle programs within a three-year period.

Result..................Exceeded objectives through successful management of 120 suppliers and 970 components, achieving 92% delivery rate. Reduced capital investment by 15% and cost by $50 million.

Challenge............Transform underperforming commodity teams causing high-quality PPM, consistently late supplier deliverables, and federal government investigations.

Result..................Within 18 months, all commodity teams and suppliers were meeting corporate requirements.

Challenge ....Commodization of multiple commodities across global organization.

Result..................Exceeded objectives through commonization, resulting in synergy savings in technology of $80 million, quality improvements of 125%, and cost savings of $115 million within 15 months.

PROGRAM ENGINEER　　　　YAZAKI CORPORATION, Troy, MI　　　　1993–1994

Managed the electrical and software systems for Daimler-Chrysler vehicle programs. Led manufacturing and engineering teams to streamline designs and processes. Achieved 10% cost savings, increased quality by 24%, and reduced capital investment by 15% while meeting on-time delivery.

PROJECT ENGINEER　　　　CRUSADER ENGINES, Sterling Heights, MI　　　　1990–1993

Researched, developed, and released programs from conception to launch, maintaining timing, controlling budget, sourcing components, and continually evaluating program objectives. Achieved 100% on-time program launches and accomplishment of program requirements.

EDUCATION AND PROFESSIONAL DEVELOPMENT

MBA, Minor International Business, University of Michigan, Flint, MI　　　　2000
BS, Mechanical Engineering, Lawrence Technological University, Southfield, MI　　　　1993

- ✓ Green Belt Certified
- ✓ Negotiation Matrix Training
- ✓ Cost Model Development
- ✓ Government Policies / Procedures Training
- ✓ 8D Problem Solving
- ✓ Manufacturing SPC
- ✓ Currency Exchange
- ✓ Financial Risk Assessments
- ✓ FMEA / Control Plan Training
- ✓ Lean Manufacturing
- ✓ International Policies and Law
- ✓ Bankruptcy Laws and Procedures

Jaime Montal, MBA

2398 Palma Avenue
Honey Grove, Pennsylvania 17035   Cell: 680.756.5955

www.linkedin.com/in/jmontal
E-mail: jmontal@protypeltd.com

MANAGING DIRECTOR • GENERAL MANAGER
STRATEGIC PLANNING AND DEVELOPMENT

*Marketing strategist, innovator, and tactical leader of enterprise-wide initiatives
that build brand value and result in sustainable, profitable growth.*

Performance excellence, an unrelenting results focus, and aggressive implementation over two decades have become career hallmarks underscored by an indelible commitment toward ethical business practices and superior service. As an acknowledged change agent, expertise has been honed in delivering change that exceeds business objectives for cost containment and productivity while uniting teams to a common purpose. Expert in taking action and leading from the front through a rich blend of market insight, sharp-eyed pragmatism, financial acuity, and visionary leadership.

Driver and champion of transformational programs—able to gain executive sponsorship, build internal support at all levels, and create cross-functional project teams that deliver exceptional results. Expert in aligning strategy with organizational vision/goals and interpreting the voice of the customer through enhanced customer insight and knowledge management.

Met with State senators and representatives to discuss various issues affecting the restaurant industry and testified before the State Senate Labor Committee to oppose legislation which would negatively impact it.

AREAS OF EXPERTISE

- Finance and Operations Leadership
- Transformational Leadership
- Startups / New Ventures
- Strategic Alliances / Joint Ventures
- Organizational Infrastructure
- Business Process Redesign
- Competitive / Trend Analysis
- New Product Launches
- Human Resources Management
- CRM Tools

- P&L Management
- Investor / Vendor Relations
- Cash Conversion Cycle
- Evaluation of Key Financial Ratios
- Enterprise Risk Management
- Supply Chain Management
- Regulatory and Employment Law
- Micro / Macroeconomics and Global Business
- ROI Strategies
- Government Contracts and Regulations

BENCHMARKS AND MILESTONES

Exceeded budgeted profit by 1% against a backdrop of tumultuous cultural change that rejected unethical processes in favor of genuine competition. Despite major changes in corporate culture, vision, and marketing positioning, consistently increased sales over prior year and over plan in a down economy through introduction of exacting operational controls. Reduction of labor and food costs contributed to improved margin of over $90,000 annually.

Garnered **Mitsubishi Diamond Elite Award** for outstanding finance penetration and conversion. Provided the dealer group preferential consideration in discount consumer rates and inventory allocation.

Participate in **Honda / Acura** continuous improvement team. In response to consumer feedback, introduced process and technology improvements to expedite transaction completion. Improvements have contributed to a 10% increase in CSI index resulting in increased product allocation and consideration for premier finance rates.

In highly competitive markets devised retention programs to curtail employee and management turnover resulting in significant increases in operating profits and owner equity.

ACHIEVEMENTS

- Achieved highest profit ($4.9 million) on $19.4 million in sales; **profit increase of $94,359** from previous year.
- Reduced operating labor costs by lowering employee turnover by 22% and manager turnover by 3% below company average.
- Reduced regional food cost by approximately 1% and management turnover from 42% to 18%.
- Devised and implemented labor plan which reduced labor after minimum wage increase.
- Authored 1997/1998 business reviews.

PROFESSIONAL BUSINESS PERFORMANCE

THE POWER GROUP   2006–Present
FINANCE MANAGER – Honey Grove, PA

Promoted to accelerate growth of commercial portfolio. Direct 4 out of 15 divisions. Key brands include Mitsubishi, Mercedes, and Acura. Built high-impact client relationships and personally forged more than a dozen key relationships that have grown to become the dealer's most profitable accounts. Work collaboratively with banking community; applied risk evaluation techniques to secure financing. Acquired expertise in risk analysis and compliance.

Global management: evaluate company, provide analyses, and set up tactical strategy. Instrumental in adapting existing CRM software to optimize client relationships. Ensure state and federal compliance. Enforce privacy regulations. Design incentive program to improve penetration of after-market sales.

Constantly demonstrate and practice transformational leadership. Build and nurture extensive network. Invest in human capital development so that people are challenged, stimulated, rewarded, and experience growth opportunities.

Maximized shareholder wealth through following **achievements**:
- Expanded company's market share **7–9% across brand** in a sluggish automotive sales environment.
- **25% improvement** product index and income per retail unit.
- **10% improvement in CSI** which resulted in increased allocation and volume.

THE ROSADO GROUP   2004–2005
SALES CONSULTANT – Honey Grove, PA

Innovated sales and marketing techniques to create sustainable, long-term customer relationships for this new and used car sales and finance dealership. Transitioned into this previously unrelated industry in order to pursue advanced degree.

VALDEZ HOSPITALITY   2002–2004
VICE PRESIDENT, OPERATIONS – Honey Grove, PA

Completed marketing assessment: studied demographics and local economic development reports, provided detailed feasibility study, and wrote business plan. Performed all legwork to get project off the ground. Instrumental in sourcing funding. Evaluated franchises and effectuated agreement with Best Western. Compiled due diligence package. Worked in collaboration with environmental and tribal agencies as well as lending associations. Ensured local, state, and federal regulations.

Negotiated contracts with general contractor, excavators, and leasing company. Hands-on experience in design layout for restaurants led to sourcing alternate architect and consulting on building redesign. Designed commercial kitchen to handle volume of 85-seat full-serve restaurant and 450-seat banquet facility.

Coordinated FFE (Furniture, Fixtures, Equipment) package with interior designer. Conducted cost analysis on alarm and fire protection systems, laundry systems, technology systems (PMS and POS), workout equipment, and signage. Served as consultant on pool design.

Handled and obtained required license applications: PA-100, Department of Agriculture (Pool and Health), and PA liquor license. Compiled all necessary paperwork to comply with Pennsylvania's legal requirements for employers.

Authored management summary, *pro forma*, and employee handbook (policies and operational procedures as well as state regulations). Compared and set up benefit package. Bid insurance providers and negotiated proper coverage. Also negotiated credit card service agreement. Established preliminary rate structure.

Performed human resources management. Retained, trained, and motivated the proper people.

Acquired working knowledge of
- Phase I Environmental Study
- Commercial Appraisals
- Soil & Erosion Control Plans
- Site Utility Layouts
- Utility Will-Serve Documentation
- Township Zoning
- Township Sewer Authority
- Geotechnical Summary
- PA NPDES (National Pollutant Discharge Elimination System)

THE PORTOS RESTAURANT GROUP   1994–2002
REGIONAL MANAGER, Boston, MA (1997–2002); San Francisco, CA (1994–1997)

Challenged to identify and capitalize upon opportunities to build revenues, increase earnings, and outperform competition. Spearhead marketing and business development initiatives, recruited and trained professional staff, and built organizational infrastructure. Acted as liaison between food service reps, managers, and warehouse managers to coordinate deliveries and displays for special promotions, ensured timely and accurate deliveries, and facilitated communication with all parties involved. Successfully structured and negotiated marketing partnership with multiple vendors. Planned quarterly general manager meetings with vendor sponsoring.

Instituted regional trainer program. Developed and promoted five general managers. Recruited and trained 25 new managers. Staffed and operated new restaurant. Coordinated all capital improvements, repairs, and maintenance for five Connecticut properties.

EDUCATION AND PROFESSIONAL DEVELOPMENT

- **Master, Business Administration**, University of Phoenix
- Graduate course work in Philosophy and Economics, University of Arizona, Tucson, AZ
- **Bachelor of Arts**, **Philosophy**, Wilkes College, Wilkes Barre, PA
- **Diploma, Cultural Studies**, Institute of Balkan Studies, Thessaloniki, Greece

- Certificate of Completion in: County-sponsored **Leadership Wayne** 2003
- **Winery Training Seminar**, Beringer Winery, St. Helena, CA
- **Culinary Focus Training**, Culinary Institute of America, Poughkeepsie, NY

HONORS / ACTIVITIES / AFFILIATIONS

- **Member,** EXCELL (Business Continuous Improvement Plan, American Honda)
- **Board Member,** Texas Township Planning Board, PA
- **Board Member,** Texas Township Sewer Authority, PA
- Conducted statewide Bartender Championships, raising approximately $10,000 (**Children's Miracle Network**)
- Conducted T.G.I. Friday's Golf Tournament, raising approximately $12,000 (**Hartford Children's Hospital**)

HARRY PARADISO

1234 Crestview Blvd. • Mountain View, California 94040 • (612) 555-4567 • Email: hparadiso@protypeltd.com

VICE PRESIDENT / DIRECTOR • MANUFACTURING / OPERATIONS

"A proven executive and critical thinker, I am passionate about improving processes and developing people." – Harry Paradiso

AREAS OF EXPERTISE

High-performing, Innovative Solutions
Strategic Planning and Execution
Analysis and Problem Resolution
Team Performance Optimization
Productivity and Performance Improvement
Cost Reductions and Profit Growth
Process Analysis and Re-engineering
Change Management

EXECUTIVE SUMMARY

Strategic leader with 15+ years of hands-on experience revitalizing, accelerating growth, and maximizing ROI for *startup, turnaround, and multi-site* manufacturing operations in highly competitive environments. Consummate team builder who brings people and organizations to full productivity under tough conditions. Expertise in *profit-building and execution of successful business plans* with a creative approach that ensures rapid delivery of revenue. Committed to generating value for all stakeholders. Extensive *offshore outsourcing experience.* Multilingual/multicultural U.S. citizen with in-depth knowledge of *international business protocols.*

MANUFACTURING CORE COMPETENCIES

Production • Engineering • Prototyping
Roll-out • Facility Design • Process Design
Quality Assurance/Control
Lean Manufacturing Practices
Regulatory Compliance
Supply Chain Management
Vendor Selection and Negotiation

LEADERSHIP STRENGTHS

Cross-functional Leadership • Development of Key Alliances
Hiring, Training, and Motivating People to Achieve Peak Performance
Quick to Foster Team Confidence and Trust
Needs Analysis • Business Communications
P&L Responsibility • Budgeting • Cost Controls
Capital Investment Planning
Delivering Strong Results within Budgetary Constraints

PROFESSIONAL EXPERIENCE

EPICOR, Sunnyvale, California (2007 – 2010)
General Site Manager . . . Directed all design, manufacturing, regulatory, and administrative functions with full P&L accountability for this unit of a $3.3 billion medical technology company. Fostered a culture of continuous operational improvements and achievement of corporate goals.

- Led the worldwide launch of three new products with pioneering ultrasound technology, generating $18 million in annual sales.
- Reduced expenses by $925,000 per year in FY2008 and positioned the organization for $1.2 million savings in FY2009 through gradual, practical process improvements. Outsourced production of noncritical components off shore. Personally negotiated contracts and saved an additional $900,000 per year, bringing total FY2009 savings to $2.1 million.
- Drove successful FDA approval and CE mark, Health Canada, and ISO certification of three new products.
- Reduced customer complaints from 180 to 24, exceeding corporate target of 70.
- Engineered preliminary logistics for moving production to a new offshore plant. Identified facilities and developed startup protocols.

BIOMET, INC., Warsaw, Indiana (1995 – 2007)
Senior Manufacturing Operations Leader . . . Charged with driving corporate growth, improving operational performance, and enhancing the profitability of this $2.5 billion global medical technology company.

- Increased revenue for Lamar, Ltd., $3.6 million by setting up a new instrumentation manufacturing plant.
- Contributed to moving BiometMerck from number five to number three in its European sector.
- Enabled product support for EBI's explosive growth from $45 million to $80+ million.

Vice President, Operations (Lamar, Ltd., Romania) . . . Recruited internally by the division president to expand market penetration, improve operating efficiencies, and accelerate revenue for this Biomet distribution subsidiary.

- Personally acquired $600,000 in new sales. Augmented local revenue by $2 million per year and saved the European group more than $4.2 million by creating a new manufacturing and service operation from scratch.
- Delivered 12% growth in market share by fully restructuring the distribution network, launching targeted marketing campaigns, and negotiating better supplier agreements.
- Engineered countrywide exchange/loaner/refurbish program, reducing corporate up-front investment 36%.

PROFESSIONAL EXPERIENCE

BIOMET, INC. (continued)

Vice President and Director of European Manufacturing (BiometMerck, The Netherlands) . . . Developed and executed the strategic direction for this $350 million European division of Biomet. Managed growth, oversaw operations, and led a team of 1,200+ employees with 18 direct reports. Key executive responsible for traveling to eight manufacturing sites in seven countries to drive business development and roll out strategic priorities. Active member of Biomet's executive management board along with the CEO, CFO, and COO. Collaborated with the CFO to direct all manufacturing human resources activities. Hired managing directors for Germany, France, and Poland; the manufacturing director for Germany; and manufacturing engineers for France and the U.K.

- Established a trans-European "dream team" comprised of the manufacturing directors of all sites. Met routinely to brainstorm and benchmark ideas that solved what appeared to be insurmountable inter-site problems, saving considerable time and expenses for the company.
- Championed a "European corporate image" marketing concept and spearheaded the redesign of packaging for a new company brand, saving $1.7 million in packaging and subcontracting costs per year.
- Streamlined the supply chain infrastructure by moving to global suppliers, saving $2.8 million annually. Consolidated European and U.S. requirements and used U.S. suppliers with global presences, saving $3.4 million per year and improving supply chain performance by 60%. Negotiated with carriers to save $300,000 more a year.
- Championed the acquisition of a Synthes division. Performed full operational due diligence and integrated machinery, WIP, and inventory into other Biomet European locations without disruption of customer supply.

Select Savings:

- Implemented 12% cross-divisional cycle-time reductions and cost-cutting programs with average annual savings in COGS of 1.2%.
- Instituted lean manufacturing practices in two plants, resulting in 12% high productivity and reductions of 51% in work-in-process, 21% in floor space, and 42% in product travel distance.
- Converted one facility into a "center of excellence" for critical subcomponents. Saved $6.9 million per year by consolidating and processing in-house 95% of the group's forging requirements.
- Engineered a strategic plan for the creation of an independent instrument division that saved $4.2 million per year. Also created an alternative product division with an estimated additional profit of $1.2 million annually.
- Saved $450,000 by moving the manufacture of 80% of all plastic-molded components in house.
- Engineered the conversion of an underutilized 200m^2 clean room (Class 10,000, ISO 7) to avoid the prohibitive cost of acquiring a new production facility.
- Created a remote final packaging facility in Switzerland to avoid excessive tax burdens.

Director of Manufacturing (EBI LP, Parsippany, New Jersey) . . . Recruited externally by the president of EBI, a Biomet manufacturing division, to manage the integration of a newly acquired production facility. Accountable for all tactical/strategic aspects of manufacturing operations with five direct reports and a team of 126.

- Successfully led the team through post-acquisition adjustments and cultural changes, improving employee morale and integrating this once-privately-held company into a world-class manufacturing operation.
- Generated $9 million in new revenue by launching two new product lines into the market within six months of hiring. Also generated $500,000 per year in revenue by customizing products in house.
- Sourced, evaluated, and acquired $5.7 million in new equipment. Facilitated the explosive growth of the operations at a sustained 20% annual increase.
- Improved profitability by decreasing standard costs up to 6%. Reached positive budgetary variances of 8% annually. Maintained labor expenses at 9% below industry norm.
- Established concurrent design reviews, prototype analysis, and manufacturing engineering procedures to achieve peak performance for new product implementation, resulting in a 42% reduction in time-to-market.
- Achieved FDA QSR (cGMP) regulatory compliance within the first four months of tenure. Instrumental in obtaining facility CE mark and ISO certification.
- Established location-based quality assurance to ensure the uninterrupted flow of good parts to subsequent stations, which reduced rework 78% and cut the discrepant material rate to .0002% on 255 SKUs.

OMNITECH, LP, Englewood, New Jersey (1992 – 1995)

Managing Director . . . Primary driving force behind startup and growth of offshore operations for a U.S. investor group. Spearheaded transition from R&D to a multi-million-dollar, full-scale manufacturing plant in Europe for industrial and consumer condensation gas heating units. Authored and executed business plans, and built a modern manufacturing organization from scratch. Contributed vision and thought leadership.

- Created and staffed a high-quality production facility with complete business infrastructure.
- Acquired three large contracts with Spanish and British clients and achieved first-year profitability, boosting sales 42% over budget. Saved 72% of component costs by transferring technologies locally.
- Obtained ISO 9002 certification and facilitated highly profitable sale of the company.

PROFESSIONAL EXPERIENCE	**VMC / ARX,** Bloomingdale, New Jersey (1988 – 1992) **Manufacturing Director** . . . Recruited by the president to turn around and increase profitability of this ARX subsidiary that produced noise and vibration elimination systems. Negotiated with the union the implementation of the first employee operating manual.

- Boosted productivity 9%, shipments 21%, and cycle time 55% for all products.
- Delivered 97% inventory accuracy with 0.6% financial error. Decreased inventory by $700,000.
- Instituted the company's first performance-based training program, which improved plant quality 18% and slashed customer complaints 27% through rigorous technical analysis and corrective action.
- Enhanced plant safety 74% with implementation of a team-based safety committee.
- Cut insurance costs $350,000 per year with a comprehensive, companywide safety program.

IDI, Hackensack, New Jersey (1988 – 1989)
Production Plant Manager . . . Managed all production functions for this manufacturer of automotive cables with yearly sales of more than $25 million. Lead a team of 153 with four direct reports in production, planning, shipping, receiving, and warehouse operations.

- Reached the highest departmental efficiency level of 93% and lowest indirect labor ratio of 12% in the company's history.
- Reduced lead times by 18% and ensured near-perfect 96% on-time delivery record.
- Lowered customer complaints 27% with a full corrective action system and rigorous technical analysis.
- Instrumental in achieving TQM certification with Ford, Chrysler, AT&T, and Compaq.

MANUFACTURING PRODUCTION

Expertise in overseeing manufacturing facilities using:
- CNC mills—single, double, and multiple head
- Citizen and Citizen-type CNC screw machines—up to eight consecutive operations
- Mori-Seike lathes
- Wire EDM, welding, brazing, forging, sand blasting, heat treating, laser marking
- Injection and compression molding
- CMM test machines
- Electro-polishing, plasma spray finishing, electrostatic powder coating
- Forge presses, stamping presses, cold forming
- Assembly and packaging of complex electro-mechanical products
- Among many other processes

EDUCATION & TRAINING

MASTER OF SCIENCE, ELECTRO-MECHANICAL ENGINEERING
BACHELOR OF SCIENCE, MECHANICAL ENGINEERING
Polytechnic Institute, Bucharest, Romania
- Concentration in Electro-Mechanical Systems and Apparatus
- Completed the course work for a combined BS/MS degree in five years

THE MANAGEMENT COURSE (Mini-MBA)
American Management Association, New York, New York
- Completed 300+ hours of course work in leadership, management, quality, and communication

OTHER SKILLS

- **Multilingual**—Fluent in English, French, and Romanian. Working knowledge of Spanish and Italian. Basic knowledge of German. Hold dual U.S. and E.U. citizenship.
- **Computers**—Proficient in Windows, MS Word, Excel, PowerPoint, Access, Outlook, ERP/MRP MAPCS, BPCS, SAP, and proprietary applications.

MY PHILOSOPHY

"I drive an organization forward through action, using a bottom-line approach to operations, implementing new processes, creating new products, reducing costs, building skills and core competencies, and generating tangible added value for the entire organization. I am a strong, pragmatic leader who can excite and motivate a staff to success. I get the job done!" – Harry Paradiso

John E. Lindley, ABR

SENIOR REAL ESTATE EXECUTIVE

12345 Amberly Drive
Tampa, Florida 33647
Cell: (813) 555-1234
Email: jlindley@protypeltd.com

SUMMARY OF QUALIFICATIONS

- Dynamic real estate executive with proven sales success—sold more than 1,100 home in 11 years.
- Accomplished senior manager, visionary entrepreneur, and dexterous troubleshooter.
- Especially adept at uncovering the needs of salespeople/consumers and creating opportunities to address those needs.
- Skilled at motivating individuals to seek out their greatest desires and give them the tools to achieve them.

EXECUTIVE PHILOSOPHY

"As successful as I've been in the traditional real estate market, my true passion is to train, coach, and mentor sales professionals to become better than I ever was. I want to motivate salespeople, enhance their existing sales skills, and teach them new skills to dominate their market."

I talk the talk . . . better than that . . . I walk the walk.

KEY ACCOMPLISHMENTS

- Recognized as one of the premier real estate agents in the country. Selected by *The Wall Street Journal* as one of the "Top 200 Real Estate Professionals" in the nation out of 1.4 million for 2007.
- Chosen by *Real Trends Magazine* and *Lore Magazine* as 46th in the nation for closed transaction sides.
- Featured on the cover of *Savvy Executive,* Volume 5, Issue 1, 2006.

TRAINING / SPEAKING EXPERIENCE

- Trained tens of thousands of real estate agents throughout the United States and Canada. Constantly adapt training materials to ensure that corporate training keeps pace with industry changes.
- Certified Trainer, Instructor Training Institute (ITI)—completed course work in training engagement and curriculum writing.
- Auditioning with the Florida Association of Realtors in January 2008 to become a FAR Certified Instructor for GRI continuing education.
- Developed an aggressive training schedule for one of the most successful Exit Realty offices in the country, personally presenting 50 hours of training per month in all facets of the real estate business.
- Video Conference Trainer, Real Estate Training Institute (2005 – present). Developed course materials and curricula for the corporate FAStTRAC Video Conference Training Program.
- Guest Speaker, Tampa Bay Area Relocation Council (2007, 2008).
- Keynote Speaker, Exit Realty New England Annual Broker Retreat (2007).
- Keynote Speaker, Exit Realty 50G Event (2007)
- Emcee, Tampa Bay Realtor Builder Expo (2006, 2007).
- Guest Speaker, University of South Florida, Alumni Association (2006, 2007).
- Speaker, Exit International Annual Conventions (2005, 2006, 2007).
- Keynote Speaker, Moffitt Cancer Center, 20th Anniversary Celebration (2006).
- Keynote Speaker, Exit Realty Broker Retreat—Maryland, Delaware, Washington (2006).
- Keynote Speaker, Exit Realty Florida (2005).

REAL ESTATE EXPERIENCE

CEO / BROKER, Exit Extreme Realty, Tampa, Florida (2004 – present)
Own and manage one of the largest successful brokerages in the area, growing sales through aggressive agent training programs and one-on-one agent coaching while still maintaining a high level of personal production. Oversee all marketing to drive company growth. Plan and host events throughout the tri-county area to increase public awareness of the brand. Assist individual investors with the sale and purchase of investment properties. Facilitate bulk/discount purchases for individual and group investors. Successfully match buyers and sellers of single-family homes, helping sellers to achieve the best price for their homes and buyers to purchase the homes

EXIT EXTREME REALTY (continued)

of their choice. Provide the on-site sales and marketing team for Village Oaks Condominiums, listing 203 units for EB Developers. Review contracts for errors to minimize corporate liability and to ensure smooth transaction closings. Recruit new agents and assist Exit Realty International with franchise sales. Manage, coach, and mentor a rotating team of highly motivated buyer's agents in three offices to help them gain a better understanding of the real estate business while gaining experience in the field.

- Rapidly expanded the company from one office with three agents in 2004 to three real estate offices with nearly 250 agents in 2006.
- Handled on-site sales and marketing for nine condo conversion sites throughout Florida (2005 – 2006), listing 1,000+ units for sale and consistently exceeding monthly sales goals.

Exit International Awards:
- Owned and managed one of the Top 25 offices in the corporation out of 1,200 worldwide (2007).
- Named Fastest Growing Exit Franchise in the state out of 160 offices (2005), and third fastest in the entire corporation in 2005.
- Winner of the 2007 Esprit de Corps Award—one award given by Exit International per year.
- Honored for personally sponsoring agents (up to 29 per year) into Exit International (2005, 2006, 2007).
- Recognized as one of the top two real estate agents out of 40,000 worldwide in closed transaction sides (2007 Gold Award, 2006 Platinum Award).
- Winner of the Rising Star Broker of the Year Award in 2005.

Exit Florida Awards:
- Personally placed first in the state for sales volume in 2006 ($30+ million); won first place in sales volume again in 2007 and also placed first for closed transaction sides.
- Placed second in the state for listings taken in 2007 and placed third in 2006.
- Won fifth place for gross closed commissions in 2007.
- Led the office that ranked in the Top 5 statewide for closed transaction sides, gross closed commissions, and closed sales volume in 2007.

Greater Tampa Association of Realtors:
- Selected as the number one individual agent in closed transaction sides (2007).

SALES REPRESENTATIVE, Re/Max Realty Professionals, Tampa, Florida (2003 – 2004)
Managed a team of two buyer's agents successfully closing more than $20 million in production.

SALES REPRESENTATIVE, US Homes, Tampa, Florida (2003)
Successfully sold more than $7 million in new single-family homes located in a gated, country club environment.
- Sold out the town home community in less than three months, selling 150% more than the competing sales representative.

DIRECTOR OF MARKETING (2001 – 2003), **SALES REPRESENTATIVE** (2001)
Citrus Hills Development, Fernando, Florida
Hired and trained new lifestyle coordinators to entice potential customers via off-site marketing programs, then assisted them in transitioning to real estate sales. Sold full-custom homes valued from $200,000 to $3.1 million. Managed the Belmont Hills model home community in a country club environment with three golf courses, clubhouse, and related amenities. Worked closely with buyers by listening carefully to their needs, planning custom features, and making design suggestions.
- Successfully trained two lifestyle coordinators that ranked in the top three out of twelve salespeople.
- Succeeded in closing one out of four shoppers, exceeding quotas by 150% every month.

SALES REPRESENTATIVE, Creekstone Homes, Colorado Springs, Colorado (2000 – 2001)
Sold new homes ranging from $160,000 to $350,000 to prospective buyers in an upper-middle-class neighborhood. Shopped the competition monthly to compare incentives, pricing, and sales volume. Ensured that model homes were always in top condition and ready for customer traffic. Hired, trained, and provided constructive feedback to a new sales assistant.
- Sold more than $6 million in only five months, consistently achieving top salesperson every month.
- Created traffic through an innovative website, postcard mailings, signage, and sales flyers.

OWNER / BROKER, 1st Capital Realty Inc., Colorado Springs, Colorado (2000 – 2001)
Started a part-time independent real estate agency to resell homes in the Colorado Springs market.
- Succeeded in selling all listed homes within thirty days; managed more than 45 properties.

REGIONAL SALES MANAGER, Capital Pacific Homes, Westminster, Colorado (2000)
Managed new home sales ranging from $200,000 to $500,000 in six subdivisions across Colorado. Recruited, hired, trained, and supervised an assistant and 12 salespeople and provided constructive feedback.
- Achieved top salesperson statewide within 45 days of hire through aggressive sales techniques, positive energy, and effective follow-up.

COMMUNITY MANAGER, Rocky Mountain Homes, Colorado Springs, Colorado (1998 – 2000)
COMMUNITY MANAGER, Richmond American Homes, Colorado Springs, Colorado (1997 – 1998)
REALTOR, McGinnis Better Homes and Gardens, Colorado Springs, Colorado (1996 – 1997)
SALES SUPERVISOR, MCI Worldcom, Colorado Springs, Colorado (1994 – 1996)

PROFESSIONAL AFFILIATIONS

- Member, Florida Association of Realtors
- Member, National Association of Realtors
- Member, Greater Tampa Association of Realtors
- Member, Pinellas Realtor Organization
- Member, Hillsborough, Pasco, and Pinellas County Chambers of Commerce
- Member, Homebuilders Association

EDUCATION AND TRAINING

PROFESSIONAL DEVELOPMENT
- Personally trained by Charles Clark, III, on his BOLT personality selling system, and was recognized as a Master Closer with a one-in-four close ratio. Attended four three-day BOLT seminars.
- Course work in class engagement and curriculum writing, Instructor Training Institute (ITI).
- Maintain 14 hours of continuing education units every two years.
- Regularly attend industry training seminars and conventions.
- Currently working on becoming a certified pre-licensing instructor.

BOB HOGUE SCHOOL OF REAL ESTATE, Tampa, Florida
- Completed courses to prepare for the Florida real estate examination.

JONES REAL ESTATE SCHOOL, Colorado Springs, Colorado
- Licensed real estate agent (1996); completed course work in real estate law, Colorado contract law and practices, real estate practices, multi-state closings, escrows, etc.
- Certified Managing Broker; completed broker administration training in 1999.
- Earned the Effective Buyer Representation (ABR) designation in November 1999.

SUFFOLK COMMUNITY COLLEGE, Long Island, New York
- Completed one year of liberal arts studies (1989).

COMMUNITY SERVICE

- Volunteer weekly, Moffitt Cancer Center, Tampa, Florida (2004 – present)
- Volunteer, American Cancer Society (2004 – present)
- Volunteer, Joshua House—sponsor holiday parties and work with the children (2006 – present)

COMPUTER SKILLS

- Skilled in Windows, MS Word, Excel, PowerPoint, ACT 2000, MS Publisher, MLS, and the Internet.

Curricula Vitae

Remember when I said that there is an exception to every rule in the résumé business? Well, here's another one. In most cases, résumés should be concise and limited to one, two, or three pages at the most. You will carefully select your information to provide a synopsis. In the professions, however, a much longer résumé is expected, and the longer the résumé, the better your chances of getting an interview. Those industries generally include . . .

- Medicine
- Law
- Education
- Science
- Media (television, film, theater)

Such a professional résumé is called a curriculum vitae (CV) from the Latin meaning "course of one's life" (literally like running a race—and you just thought your life was a rat race!). For those of us who have trouble knowing how to spell the words, vitae is the "life" part (the spelling stays the same whether you are referring to one CV or multiple CVs), and the "course" part is either singular (curriculum) or plural (curricula). So, *curriculum vitae* is one CV and *curricula vitae* refers to multiple CVs.

A successful CV will include not only education and experience but also . . .

- Publications (books, magazines, journals, and other media)
- Certifications
- Licenses and other credentials
- Grants
- Research
- Professional affiliations
- Awards and honors
- Presentations
- Courses taught
- Relevant continuing education
- Among other sections

Anything relevant to your industry is appropriate to use on a CV, and the résumé can be as long as it needs to be to present the "course of your life."

A CV—or any résumé with multiple pages for that matter—must contain a header with your name and page number on each successive page. Should the pages become separated, the reader should be able to easily put your subsequent pages in their proper order and with *your* résumé!

If you are applying for a job in a foreign country, long CVs with more detail and a considerable amount of personal information are the norm (see Chapter 7). International employers want a lot of background, including personal characteristics, birth date (yes, even the year), place of birth, marital status, number of children, health status, and a photo in the upper right-hand corner. Employers in Asia want your educational background all the way to kindergarten. Now, aren't you glad you live in the United States?

For foreign job searches, your CV will also list any foreign languages you speak and/or write and your levels of proficiency. Include an "International" section on your résumé that lists your travel experience, including places you have lived and visited, even if it was just on vacation. Include a bullet that addresses your cross-cultural sensitivity and ability to think globally.

Foreign hiring managers are not accustomed to seeing strong accomplishment statements on a résumé, so be cautious when claiming credit for the results of a team project. Couch your results in the context of your role within the team. You need to be more subtle when choosing your wording for achievements, as well, even when you were solely responsible for the results. Make sure you use words appropriate to your experience and education; overly sophisticated language might put off a hiring manager. To be safe, it is better to be conservative in both the wording and design of your CV for international markets.

Unfortunately, international CV requirements vary from country to country and company to company. Some countries have requirements similar to those in the U.S., while others might ask for letters of recommendation and certificates of work to be sent with your CV. British employers expect to see your work history in reverse chronological order (like a U.S. résumé), but many international employers expect to see your work history in true chronological order (starting with your very first job and ending with your most recent).

Sometimes a company's website will list their CV requirements. If not, you can always pick up the telephone and call the company's human resources department or send an e-mail.

Janet Jones, RN, CMR

123 South Lemay Avenue, A-1 #123 ▪ Fort Collins, Colorado 80524
Cellular: (970) 555-1234 ▪ Home: (970) 123-5555
Email: jjones@protypeltd.com

PROFILE

- Innovative Registered Nurse with a reputation for astute clinical judgment and a broad background in emergency room and trauma care.
- Compassionate caregiver who is able to quickly establish and maintain rapport with patients.
- Established strong working relationships with doctors in multiple specialties, including cardiology, orthopedics, trauma, emergency, hematology, oncology, and general practitioners.
- Adept at working independently and in high-pressure situations that require quick thinking.
- Carry current professional liability insurance from CNA ($1 million each, $6 million aggregate).

CREDENTIALS

- Registered Nurse (RN), Colorado License #85167
- Advanced Cardiac Life Support (ACLS)
- Advanced Pediatric Life Support (APLS)
- Basic Life Support (BLS) and CPR
- Certified Medical Representative (CMR)

EDUCATION

CERTIFICATE, NURSE REFRESHER COURSE (2009 – 2010)
Central Colorado Area Health Education Center (AHEC), Aurora, Colorado
- Completed 120 hours of didactic training—Current Concepts in Nursing Theory, Therapeutic Advances, Systems Review and Current Trends, Contemporary Nursing Issues, including critical thinking exercises in adult health (all systems), med-surg problems, procedures and treatment, mathematical practice, acid base and electrolytes, infection control and wound care, and psychiatric fundamentals, procedures, and disorders and treatment.
- Completed a 120-hour clinical preceptorship in the critical care units of Exempla Lutheran Medical Center.

BACHELOR OF SCIENCE, NURSING
Montana State University, Bozeman, Montana

GRADUATE, THREE-YEAR DIPLOMA IN NURSING
Nebraska Methodist Hospital, School of Nursing, Omaha, Nebraska
- Completed both didactic and clinical nursing instruction.

CONTINUING EDUCATION

- 12th Annual Conference, Cardiovascular Institute of North Colorado (2010)
- Managing Patients with Metastatic Breast Cancer, Poudre Valley Health System (2010)
- Current Approaches to the Management of Venous Thromboembolism, Educational Review Systems (2010)
- An Overview of Immune Thrombocytopenic Purpura (2010)

SUMMARY OF EXPERIENCE

Nursing Experience
- Provided comprehensive nursing care in emergency departments and ambulatory care centers, ensuring appropriate assessment and trauma management.
- Collaborated with interdisciplinary teams to provide assessment and therapeutic management of patients in both hospital and clinic settings.
- Completed initial and episodic health histories and physical exams in order to identify existing and potential health problems.
- Created individualized nursing plans of care and initiated diagnostic, therapeutic, medical, and nursing actions at the request of physicians.
- Monitored and coordinated continuity of care and evaluated quality-of-life issues.
- Assessed progress, identified problems, initiated preventive measures, recognized and managed emergent problems, and initiated proper care. Documented information in patient charts.
- Started IVs, administered medication and blood products, and monitored patients for side effects and adverse events.
- Utilized basic life support skills in life-threatening crises and cardiopulmonary arrests.

SUMMARY OF EXPERIENCE

Nursing Administration Experience

- Served as a charge nurse responsible for providing leadership in the delivery of care and utilization of resources. Made staffing assignments that considered patient needs, staff competencies, and standards of care. Established priorities for patient care and bed management.
- Selected as head nurse of a free-standing minor emergency center. Hired and evaluated the performance of staff, and managed the facility's budget.
- As the house supervisor, represented hospital administration on weekends and after hours. Identified and solved problems throughout the hospital. Staffed units using the patient-acuity staffing model.
- Ensured that nursing performance met all regulatory agency requirements and hospital standards.
- Participated in the professional development of nurses through the preceptor program.
- Facilitated communication with patients, families, physicians, staff members, and other healthcare professionals to achieve desired patient outcomes.

NURSING EXPERIENCE

IN-SERVICE TRAINING (March 1989 – January 2010)
Sanofi-Aventis, Oncology Business Unit, Bridgewater, New Jersey
Sanofi-Aventis, Hospital Sales Unit, Bridgewater, New Jersey
Bayer Corporation, West Haven, Connecticut
Winthrop Pharmaceuticals, New York, New York
Developed and presented in-service training programs to doctors, nurses, and other healthcare providers. Trained them how to safely deliver chemotherapy instillations. Taught patients how to self-administer Lovenox injections. Supported local cancer meetings provided by hospitals. Established relationships with quality improvement staff to develop protocols for the prevention of deep-vein thrombosis in the hospital. Educated patients and families; provided counseling and supportive care. Collaborated with doctors and nurses to ensure proper wound care treatment.

REGISTERED NURSE / HOUSE SUPERVISOR (July 1991 – June 1993)
St. Joseph Hospital, Denver, Colorado
Provided quality nursing care to patients in the fast-paced Emergency Department of the largest nonprofit hospital in the region.

CHARGE NURSE / NURSING SUPERVISOR (June 1987 – March 1989)
Memorial Hospital, Colorado Springs, Colorado
Supervised the delivery of nursing services to patients in the Emergency Department of this Level II Trauma Center serving the Pikes Peak Region. Established the criteria for staffing of units based on patient acuity. Served as a liaison between staff and administration.

RELIEF NURSE SUPERVISOR (February 1984 – May 1987)
Irving Community Hospital, Irving, Texas
Served as house supervisor for this 275-bed community hospital.

HEAD NURSE (July 1984 – January 1986)
UCI Medical Affiliates, Dallas, Texas
Supervised nursing care for this freestanding ambulatory care center. Hired, trained, and supervised a staff of eight. Developed budgets and purchased capital equipment for the facility.

ASSISTANT CLINICAL MANAGER, EMERGENCY DEPARTMENT (July 1980 – January 1983)
Lutheran Medical Systems of North Texas, Carrollton Community Hospital, Carrollton, Texas
Helped manage the emergency department. Assisted in the development of departmental budget. Established a quality improvement program for nursing care provided to patients.

MEDICAL SALES EXPERIENCE

ONCOLOGY SALES SPECIALIST (April 2007 – January 2010)
Sanofi-Aventis, Oncology Business Unit, Bridgewater, New Jersey
Promoted Taxotere to oncologists specializing in lung, prostate, head, and neck tumors. Developed strategic sales plans with new tactics and best practices designed to drive long-term growth in a territory that includes northern Colorado, southern Wyoming, and western Nebraska. Used strong clinical background as a registered nurse to relate studies and research data to patient needs.

MEDICAL SALES EXPERIENCE	**Sanofi-Aventis, Oncology Business Unit (continued)**

- Won awards for sales achievements, including among others:
  - 2009 Power of One Award for excellent customer focus
  - 2009 Trailblazer Recognition for growing the Midtown account 141%
  - 2008 Drove 24.1% Taxotere growth over 2007 while the national average was 12.1%

SENIOR SPECIALITY REPRESENTATIVE (April 2000 – April 2007)
Sanofi-Aventis, Hospital Sales Unit, Bridgewater, New Jersey
Sold Lovenox to cardiologists, orthopedic specialists, hospitalists, and hematology/oncology physicians. Worked within the parameters of managed care guidelines, and supplied superior ethical service by ensuring compliance with FDA regulations.

- Recognized for high sales accomplishments with numerous awards, including among others:
  - 2007 4th Quarter Growth in Action contest for high percentage of growth over the prior year
  - 2004, 2002 Area Team of the Year for top sales in the region
  - 2003 Area Representative of the Year Award

PHARMACEUTICAL SALES REPRESENTATIVE (July 1993 – April 2000)
Bayer Corporation, West Haven, Connecticut
Successfully sold Cipro, Adalat CC, and Baycol to urologists, general practitioners, family practice physicians, and internal medicine specialist throughout the northern Colorado and southern Wyoming territory. Selected as a field trainer for Phase I training classes for new hires—provided real-life detailing opportunities, shared best practices, and served as a mentor.

- Maintained exclusive Cipro formulary status at Poudre Valley Hospital from 1995 through 1997. Convinced the Pharmacy and Therapeutics Committee of its efficacy and safety.
- Honored for sales growth with multiple awards and rewards.

TECHNICAL SALES REPRESENTATIVE (March 1989 – June 1991)
Winthrop Pharmaceuticals, New York, New York
Marketed Biobrane to burn units and burn/plastic surgeons in the western region. Designed and conducted sales presentations that demonstrated the most current product knowledge, including the physiology and therapeutics of each product. Educated users (doctors, nurses, and other healthcare providers) and provided technical support.

- Winner of the 1990 Team Leader Award (top sales); ranked second in the nation.
- Established product trials, resulting in a 12% increase in new account business.

PROFESSIONAL AFFILIATIONS	

- Member, National and Local Chapters, Oncology Nursing Society
- Member, Emergency Nurses Association
- Participant, PACE series to increase awareness of prostate cancer
- Served as alumni mentor for Pi Beta Phi, Colorado State University
- Volunteer, Breast Cancer Network of Strength
- Participant, Step for Life, Lung Cancer Walks
- Volunteer, Medical Support, National Figure Skating Association, Southwest Finals
- Volunteer Coordinator, Denver Children's Hospital Burn Camp

COMPUTERS	

- Proficient with Windows, MS Word, PowerPoint, Outlook, and Internet Explorer

PATRICIA SANDERS
1234 WESTERN DRIVE • SCOTCH PLAINS, NJ 07076
(908) 555-1234 • pat@protypeltd.com

HIGH SCHOOL SCIENCE TEACHER
Chemistry ➢ Biology ➢ Earth Science ➢ Physics ➢ General Science

Highly motivated, energetic educator with extensive and varied experience teaching science. Strong track record of fostering student motivation, creativity and enhanced learning. Committed to creating a classroom environment that is stimulating and encouraging. Demonstrated ability to individualize instruction as needed. Diplomatic approach to parent-teacher relationships, while actively soliciting and encouraging parental participation to ensure student development.

KEY SKILL AREAS

INSTRUCTIONAL STRATEGIES

- Utilize technology, cooperative learning, and hands-on experiences to align and meet core content and state standards.
- Evaluate instructional needs and ensure that all appropriate learning modalities for the given population are utilized.

STUDENT / PARENT RELATIONS

- Proactively and consistently correspond with parents via e-mail and phone to maintain open communication regarding student progress.
- Natural gift for getting students excited about learning.

EDUCATIONAL TECHNOLOGIES

- Utilize instructional media to enhance the scope and quality of education.
- Accomplished in the use of hands-on materials combined with technologies, such as PowerPoint presentations and overheads, to compliment lessons.

LEARNING STYLES / LEADERSHIP

- Establish a creative and inspiring learning environment by engaging student participation.
- Committed to motivating students, building self-esteem and encouraging a safety conscious classroom.

NOTEWORTHY ACCOMPLISHMENTS

- Continually and consistently achieved highest grade averages on final exams in the chemistry department.
- Spearheaded Basking Ridge Elementary School Science Fair through proactively recruiting and collaborating with volunteer high school students. Supervised all booths, operated an interactive demonstration, and handled all logistics for pre- and post-event.
- Taught SAT II after-school review classes for chemistry.
- Nominated by Flushing High School administrators for the Presidential Award for Excellence in Mathematics and Science Teaching, Washington, DC.
- Appointed and retained for seven years to oversee a peer-tutoring program in all aspects of development.
- Chosen by high school principal of a special education institution to design and present a two-day staff development workshop on how to teach Regents Biology to special education students.
- Selected to work on a committee of six to critique the Foundation of Science curriculum sponsored by the Brooklyn Union Gas Company implemented throughout the city. Further presented the curriculum to high school teachers for a staff development day at Stuyvesant High School.
- Awarded "Teacher of the Year" at Flushing High School.
- One of five borough representatives selected by the superintendent to be a planner and instructor for a televised student-teacher video lesson used for new teacher workshops and staff development throughout New York City (WNYE Television/Board of Education).
- Selected for Who's Who in America's Teachers.

LinkedIn: www.linkedin.com/in/patsanders/
Facebook: www.facebook.com/patsanders
YouTube: www.youtube.com/watch?v=AU7_3zF71yc

**PATRICIA
SANDERS**
Page 2

LICENSES, CERTIFICATIONS AND TRAINING

**NEW JERSEY STATE PERMANENT
CERTIFICATIONS/K–12**

Physical Science, Biological Science, Earth Science

**NEW YORK STATE PERMANENT
CERTIFICATIONS/K–12**

Chemistry, Biology, Earth Science, Physics

CONTINUING EDUCATION:

- Manhattan College, Riverdale, NY—Summer Institute for Teachers of AP Chemistry
- SUNY Purchase, Purchase, NY—Summer Institute for New Teachers of Regents Chemistry
- Stonybrook University, Stonybrook, NY—Science Education Seminars: Consumer Chemistry, Biotechnology, Microchemistry, Chemistry of Toys, and Electricity: Circuits and Resistors
- Madeline Hunter, Long Island, NY—Specialized training: Maximizing Teacher Effectiveness in the Classroom

CAREER HISTORY

Ridge High School, Science Teacher, Basking Ridge, NJ — 2006–2010

Millburn High School, Science Teacher, Millburn, NJ — 2004–2005
Courses: Physical Science

Great Neck South High School, Science Teacher, Great Neck, NY — 1998–2000
Courses: Regents Chemistry and Regents Biology

Flushing High School, Science Teacher/Supervisor, Peer Tutoring Program, Flushing, NY — 1988–1998
Courses: Regents Chemistry, Regents Earth Science, Regents Biology, General Chemistry, and Environmental Science

Clarke Junior/Senior High School, Student Teacher/Science Teacher, Westbury, NY — 1987–1988
Courses: Regents Chemistry, Honors Chemistry, Regents Physics, and Physical Science

COMPUTER SKILLS

Microsoft Word, Excel, PowerPoint, E-mail, Internet, YouTube, United Streaming.

EDUCATION

MASTER OF SCIENCE, SECONDARY EDUCATION, Hofstra University, Hempstead, NY
BACHELOR OF ARTS, BIOLOGY, Hofstra University, Hempstead, NY

Josephine N. Masias, PhD, RN

1234 Rolling Knolls Drive • Middletown, New Jersey 07748
Home: (732) 555-1234 • Cell: (732)555-5678 • JMasias@protypeltd.com

Profile

- Experienced educator with the proven ability to create innovative learning experiences.
- Astute clinician who brings real-world experience to the classroom and clinical training.
- Effective communicator with the proven ability to teach to the individual by adapting presentations to student learning styles and needs.

Teaching Philosophy

To be an effective nursing instructor, one must be sensitive to the students and their needs. Today's students come into nursing from more diverse backgrounds and life experiences than ever before. The student nurse today is not the traditional student who entered a nursing program 30 years ago from high school. Accelerated students present a challenge for instructors to provide clinical experiences that both motivate and instill a sense of meaning into the nursing role. It is vital that we teach these students to become professional nurses who can think critically using evidence-based practices. As instructors, we must provide a quality professional nursing education that enhances the standards of practice while at the same time meeting the needs of a diverse student body.

Education

Ph.D., New York University, Steinhardt School of Education, New York, New York (2005)
Dissertation: *"A study on the self-perceptions of parenting in adolescent mothers"*

Certificate in School Nursing, Seton Hall University, South Orange, New Jersey (1996)

MSN, Seton Hall University, College of Nursing, South Orange, New Jersey (1985)

BSN, Seton Hall University, College of Nursing, South Orange, New Jersey (1978)

Credentials

- Registered Professional Nurse, New Jersey
- Certificate in School Nursing, New Jersey

Teaching Experience

ASSISTANT PROFESSOR, MATERNAL CHILD NURSING (1992 – present)
Seton Hall University, South Orange, New Jersey
- Develop and teach courses in the traditional and accelerated undergraduate nursing programs, including
  - Obstetric Nursing Theory and Clinical
  - Introduction to Professional Nursing
  - Nursing Research
  - Gerontology Nursing
  - Dying with Dignity
  - Health Assessment
- Teach Obstetric Nursing Theory and Nursing Research to students in the accelerated BSN program at Georgian Court University, an off-campus program for Seton Hall University.
- Previously taught in the RN to BSN program at Seton Hall's off-campus location at Ocean County Medical Center in Brick, New Jersey.
- Utilize lecture, discussion, multimedia presentations, audiovisual materials, clinical training, interviews, and guest speakers to enrich the learning experience.

Teaching Experience (continued)

- Serve on the Doctoral Curriculum Committee, Undergraduate Curriculum Committee, Faculty Development Committee (Chair), and Doctoral Candidate Exam Committee.
- *"I enjoyed the whole semester, even though it was hard for me. You encouraged me despite my personal situation, and that made the difference."* – Michelle, 2006
- *"You were always willing to answer our questions and did not make us feel uncomfortable to express our opinions."* – Tara, 2004
- *"I thought our exams, assignments, and your grading system were very fair. I learned a lot. Thank you."* – Paul, 2003
- *"I appreciate your making my OB clinical experience 'male friendly'. I was not looking forward to this clinical rotation, but I learned a lot and enjoyed it."* – Jeff, 2003

DIRECTOR, VNG NURSING TRAINING AND EDUCATION (2007– present)
Private Investor, Shrewsbury, New Jersey
- Educate nurses on Video Nystagmography (VNG) diagnostic procedures used to evaluate dizziness, vertigo, and balance dysfunction in children and adults.
- Assess patients using oculomotor evaluation, positional testing, and caloric stimulation of the vestibular system.
- Collaborate with medical doctors, chiropractors, and neurologists in evaluating results.

MANAGER, STAFF DEVELOPMENT AND NURSING EDUCATION (2003)
Visiting Nurse Association of Central New Jersey, Red Bank, New Jersey
- Developed and implemented nursing training and continuing education programs using both didactic and clinical presentations.
- Evaluated assessment skills and documentation of outcomes using clinical competencies.

FACULTY MEMBER (1995 – 1997)
ANR Review Course, NCLEX Exam, New Jersey

FACULTY MEMBER (1983 – 1991)
Brookdale Community College, College of Nursing, Lincroft, New Jersey
- Developed and taught Maternal Child Nursing and Medical/Surgical Nursing.

Research

- Research Consultant, Nursing Research Committee, Trinitas Hospital (2004 – present)— Assist the Nursing Research Committee in the development and implementation of nursing research projects.
- Current research projects include:
  - The experience of parenting for adolescent mothers after the first year post-partum (funded by an SHU $6,000 grant awarded in 2007).
  - A study to investigate the OB clinical nursing experience for male nursing students.

Grants

- University Research Council Grant, Seton Hall University, $6,000 (April 2007)—Qualitative study of parenting for adolescent mothers after the first year postpartum.
- Pauline Greenidge Research Scholarship, New York University School of Education, Division of Nursing, $4,000 for dissertation research (2003).

Professional Nursing Experience

SCHOOL NURSE (part-time) (1996 – 2003)
St. James Grammar School, Red Bank, New Jersey
• Conducted healthcare screenings for K–8 classes.

STAFF NURSE—MEDICAL, SURGICAL, OBSTETRICS (1978 – 1980)
Monmouth Medical Center, Long Branch, New Jersey

STAFF NURSE—PERITONEAL DIALYSIS (1980)
St. Barnabas Medical Center, Livingston, New Jersey

International Presentations

• *Parenting as Experienced by Adolescent Mothers*, Sigma Theta Tau International Nursing Research Conference, Vienna, Austria (July 2007).
• *Self-perceptions of Parenting in Adolescent Mothers*, Sigma Theta Tau International Nursing Research Conference, Montreal, Canada (July 2006).
• *Advanced Nursing Education*, University of Rome, Jubilee Year 2000, Celebration for University Professors and Scholars at Vatican City (September 2000).

Selected Presentations

• *Preparing Clinical Experiences for Male Students in Obstetrical Nursing*, American Assembly of Men in Nursing, University of Pennsylvania (November 2007).
• *Keynote Speaker*, New Jersey City University, Nursing Research Day (April 2007).
• *Parenting as Experienced by Adolescent Mothers*, Eastern Nursing Research Society (April 2007).
• *An Educational Challenge: Strategies for Male Nursing Students in Obstetrical Nursing*, Midwest International Business Administration Conference, Chicago (March 2007).
• *Adolescent Parenting: A Nursing Management Challenge*, Midwest International Business Administration Conference, Chicago (May 2006).
• *Protection of Human Subjects in Research Studies and How to Develop a Nursing Research Study and Clinical Research Questions*, Trinitas Hospital, Nursing Research Committee (May 2006).
• *Factors Contributing to Self-perceptions of Parenting in Adolescent Mothers*, Eastern Research Society (April 2006).
• *Self-perceptions of Parenting in Adolescent Mothers*, Pacific Nursing Conference, Hawaii (February 2006).
• *Protection of Human Research Subjects*, St. Joseph's Regional Medical Center, Nursing Research (October 2005).
• *Panelist on Adolescent Mothers*, New York University, Alumni Weekend, Virginia Ferguson Second Annual Adolescent Research Day (May 2005).
• *A Study on the Self-perceptions of Parenting for Adolescent Mothers*, Sigma Theta Tau, Gamma Nu Chapter, Nursing Research Day (April 2005).
• *Factors Contributing to Self-perceptions of Parenting in Adolescent Mothers During the Four- to Six-Week Postpartum Period*, St. Joseph's Regional Medical Center, Nursing Research Day (October 2004).

Selected Publications

- Reviewer—Maternal Child Nursing Research Articles. (2007 – present). *Journal of Perinatal Education.* Washington, DC: Lamaze International Publishing.
- Masias, J. (2008). "Care of special populations during a disaster: Pregnant women." *Disaster Nursing Textbook.*
- Masias, J. (Submitted, 2007). "Stroke in the middle-aged adult: Implications for support and recovery." *Critical Care Nursing.* Aliso Viejo, CA: American Association of Critical-Care Nurses.
- Masias, J. (2007). "Self-perceptions of parenting among adolescent mothers." *The Journal of Perinatal Education, 16*(1).
- Reviewer. (2007). *Nursing Research Textbook.* Upper Saddle River, NJ: Prentice Hall Publishing.
- Masias, J. (2005, June). *Nursing education for future nurse educators attending master degree nursing programs* (video series). Orlando, FL: Laureate Nursing Education.

Professional Affiliations

- Seton Hall University (2004 – present)
  - Senator, Faculty Senate (2006 – 2008)
  - Faculty Development Committee Chairperson (2004 – 2007)
  - Alternate Senator, Faculty Senate (2005 – 2006)
- Charter Member, Gamma Nu Chapter, Sigma Theta Tau International Nursing Honor Society, Seton Hall University, College of Nursing (1977 – present)
  - President (2006 – present)
  - President Elect (2006)
  - Delegate, Baltimore National Convention (2007)
  - Vice President (1998)
  - Served as member or chair of various committees from 1978 to present, including the Fall Program, Spring Program, Nominating Committee, Induction Committee, Anniversary Committee, Gala Committee
  - Chair, Gamma Nu Annual Nursing Research Day (2006 – 2007)
- Member, Upsilon Chapter, Sigma Theta Tau International Nursing Honor Society, New York University, College of Nursing (2006 – present)
- American Nurses Association (1980 – present)
- New Jersey State Nurses Association (1996 – present)
- National League of Nursing (1978 – present
- Eastern Nursing Research Society (2005 – present)
- National Association of School Nurses (1996 – present)
- Monmouth County Association of School Nurses (1996 – present)

Recognitions

- Manchester Who's Who Registry of Executives and Professional Women (2005 – present)
- Recognized by Seton Hall University for 15 years of dedicated service as a faculty member (2007)
- Nominated for Sigma Theta Tau Excellence in Leadership, Excellence in Nursing Practice, and Excellence in Nursing Education (1995 – 1996)
- Professional Promise Award in Nursing, presented by the Seton Hall University College of Nursing Alumni Committee (1978)
- Selected for Seton Hall University's Iota Alpha Lamda Nursing Honor Society (1976 – 1977)

KATHLEEN WOJDYLA, N.D.

1234 Rain Dance Court
Colorado Springs, Colorado 80920

Cell Phone: (719) 555-1234
drkatwojdyla@protypeltd.com

PROFILE

- Licensed Naturopathic Doctor with 20+ years of experience in science-based medicine, research, and clinical practice.
- Experienced scientist with a strong background in pharmaceutical research and development, integrative and natural medicine, drug-herb interactions, patient relations, and caregiving.
- Proven leadership and verbal, written, and interpersonal communication skills.
- Effective presenter sought out by multiple organizations to provide educational and informative presentations to patients, students, medical providers, athletes, and the general public.

EDUCATION

RESIDENCY, NATUROPATHIC ONCOLOGY (October 2005 – June 2006)
Cancer Treatment Centers of America, Tulsa, Oklahoma
- Part of an Integrative hospital team providing quality care to cancer patients receiving cancer treatments.
- Rotations included surgery, interventional radiology, medical oncology, and radiation oncology.
- Participated in interdisciplinary team conferences, palliative care rounds, and case review meetings with treatment teams.

DOCTOR OF NATUROPATHIC MEDICINE (N.D.) (2005)
Bastyr University, Seattle, Washington
- Completed a 4,472-hour, full-time, accredited Ph.D. program of scientific and clinical training required for licensing in states that consider Naturopathic Doctors as primary care providers.
- Program included three years (1,100 hours) of supervised clinical hours in primary care, physical medicine, and counseling shifts.
- Extra training in IV therapy, pharmacology, and drug-herb interactions.
- *Basic and Clinical Science Courses:* Anatomy, Cell Biology, Physiology, Histology, Pathology, Biochemistry, Pharmacology, Lab Diagnosis, Neurosciences, Clinical Physical Diagnosis, Genetics, Pharmacognosy, Biostatistics, Epidemiology, Public Health, History and Philosophy, Ethics.
- *Clerkships and Allopathic Therapeutics* included lecture and clinical instruction in Dermatology, EENT, Gastroenterology, Cardiology, Rheumatology, Family Medicine, Psychiatry, Medicine, Pediatrics, Radiology, Obstetrics, Minor Surgery, Medical Procedures, Pharmacology, Orthopedics, Pulmonology, Gynecology, Neurology, Surgery Ophthalmology, and Naturopathic Oncology.
- *Naturopathic Therapeutics* included Therapeutic Nutrition, Botanical Medicine, Homeopathy, Oriental Medicine, Hydrotherapy, Naturopathic Manipulative Therapy, Ayurvedic Medicine, Naturopathic Case Analysis/Management, Naturopathic Philosophy, Advanced Naturopathic Therapeutics and Counseling.

BACHELOR OF SCIENCE, BIOCHEMISTRY (1988)
University of California, Davis, California
- Focus on Genetics, Biophysics, Analytical Chemistry, and Plant Biochemistry.
- Participated in Avidin-Biotin binding research studies under Dr. M. Ohto, 1988.

EXPERIENCE SUMMARY

STAFF NATUROPATHIC DOCTOR (June 2007 – present)
CLINIX Healing Center, Centennial, Colorado

PRIVATE PRACTICE, CONSULTANT (September 2006 – present)
Self-employed, Colorado Springs, Colorado

ASSOCIATE RESEARCH SCIENTIST (March 1995 – May 2000)
ZymoGenetics, Inc., Seattle, Washington

SENIOR DEVELOPMENT ASSOCIATE (August 1992 – March 1995)
ProCyte Corporation, Kirkland, Washington

ANALYTICAL CHEMIST / FORMULATION RESEARCHER (June 1988 – August 1992)
Syntex Research, Palo Alto, California

PATENTS

- United States Patent 6,790,439, *Thrombopoietin Compositions,* R. I. Senderoff, K. M. Kontor/Young, J. Heffernan, H. J. Clark, L. Garrison, L. Kreilgaard, and G. B. Rosenberg, September 2004.

LICENSES

- *Naturopathic Physician, License #1442*, State of Oregon (2005 – present)—Full formulary prescriptive rights and scope of practice similar to an M.D. Passed the Naturopathic Physicians Licensing Examination given by the North American Board of Naturopathic Examiners (NABNE), including Anatomy, Biochemistry, Botanical Medicine, Emergency Medicine, Lab Diagnosis, Jurisprudence, Microbiology, Nutrition, Oregon Formulary Boards, Psychology, Pathology and Immunology, Physical Clinical Diagnosis, Physical Medicine, and Physiology

RESEARCH
EXPERIENCE

ASSOCIATE RESEARCH SCIENTIST (March 1995 – May 2000)
ZymoGenetics, Inc., Seattle, Washington
Selected for this PhD-level position responsible for the investigation of novel drug delivery mechanisms and preformulation/formulation characterization for a small company owned by Novo Nordisk. Focused on protein structural characterization supporting bioprocessing, preformulation, and formulation of protein therapeutic candidates intended for clinical evaluations and commercial production. Specialized in working with diabetes, cancer, bone repair, and bleeding disorders.
- Gained advanced and independent research skills relating to spectrometry, HPLC, peptide mapping, GC, MS, lyophilization, light scattering calorimetry, electrophoresis, CE, cIEF, protein chemistry, and other analysis techniques.
- Special projects included thrombin, factor XIII, thrombopoietin, glucagon-like peptide, insulin, TACI (monoclonal antibody for multiple myeloma), and statin drugs.

SENIOR DEVELOPMENT ASSOCIATE (August 1992 – March 1995)
ProCyte Corporation, Kirkland, Washington
Designed and developed peptide formulations in support of preclinical and clinical projects. Characterized and optimized dosage delivery systems relating to drug release using in-vitro and in-vivo models. Worked specifically with wound healing, alopecia, and burn care. Supervised temporary employees. Served as health and safety chair.
- Ensured strict compliance with cGMP/cGLP standards.
- Assumed project planning responsibilities for investigational new drug application and biologic license filings for the flagship product.

ANALYTICAL CHEMIST / FORMULATION RESEARCH (June 1988 – August 1992)
Syntex Research, Palo Alto, California
Served as a research associate responsible for the research and development of novel parenteral formulations for the delivery of proteins in support of preclinical and clinical projects. This position required technology/methodology transfer from in-house, small-scale manufacturing to large-scale contract manufacturing.
- Gained extensive experience with formulation and drug delivery development of small molecules, peptides, and proteins, as well as lyophilization development for parenteral drug formulations.
- Worked with Alzheimer's disease, cancer, hormone replacement therapy, and pain management.
- Projects included Aleve, Toradol, birth control pills, Interleukin-1ß, and human nerve growth factor.

CLINICAL
EXPERIENCE

STAFF NATUROPATHIC DOCTOR (June 2007 – present)
CLINIX Healing Center, Centennial, Colorado
Key member of a medical team in an integrative healthcare clinic providing comprehensive, evidence-based healthcare to the general public, of which 90+% are covered by insurance. The core medical team is made up of physicians, physician assistants, and nurse practitioners. Adjunctive providers consist of naturopathic doctors, chiropractors, acupuncturists, exercise therapists, and massage therapists, who support total care for patients. Primarily treat the following conditions: hyperlipidemia, hypertension, diabetes, hormonal imbalance, thyroid disorders, obesity/weight management, migraines, asthma, cancer, chronic fatigue, fibromyalgia, and mood disorders. Interview, make hiring recommendations, and train physicians, nurse practitioners, and medical assistants. Develop training materials, sales tools, and operating policies/procedures.
- The clinic was recently chosen from among 12 clinics in Colorado as a "medical home" with associated grants and opportunities to provide input to future clinics on this unique format.
- Spearheading an effort to research food supplement formulations for possible addition to the newly founded retail store in the clinic, either under a private label or retail brand. Teach all employees how to sell the supplements, including appropriate uses for each supplement, how not to make claims, and how to answer questions. Successfully brought in an additional $240,000 of annual revenue.

CLINICAL
EXPERIENCE

Staff Naturopathic Doctor (continued)

- Develop evidence-based protocols for the use of nutritional and natural approaches. Write all contracts and criteria for standardized delegation of responsibility to practice providers. Maintain current knowledge of the Colorado Medical Practice Act.
- Recommend and treat a variety of medical conditions with evidence-based therapeutic lifestyle changes, including nutrition, lifestyle, and natural therapies. Give people the ideas and tools they need to make daily choices to modify their health conditions. Personally responsible for bringing in an additional $17,800 in new revenue per month.
- Provide bio-identical hormone replacement guidance, including thyroid and male/female hormones.
- Furnish medically supervised acute care for patients not able to see their primary care provider that same day, including colds, flu, skin rashes, eye infections, and other acute conditions. Responsible for case management, ensuring each patient receives appropriate care in compliance with insurance requirements.
- Frequently develop and present workshops on personal wellness and patient education subjects. Provide current, evidence-based nutritional and natural approaches to support topics. Address a variety of subjects, including
  - diabetes education relating to yearly foot exams
  - peak flow use for asthmatics
  - managing cholesterol through lifestyle changes
  - review of blood work
  - auto-immune disease
  - metabolic syndrome
  - bio-identical hormones
  - weight loss
  - chronic disease
  - cancer prevention

PRIVATE PRACTICE, CONSULTANT (September 2006 – present)

Self-employed, Colorado Springs, Colorado

Own and manage a private practice with a focus on fostering whole-person wellness, individualized to each patient with an emphasis on prevention and self-care. Provide nutritional and natural medicine support for a variety of disease states, overall health, and wellness. As a sub-focus, provide safe, effective recommendations to support cancer patients and cancer survivors.

- Selected to provide consulting services to Memorial Hospital and other N.D.s on the appropriate use of supplements with chemotherapy and radiation treatments.
- Make presentations to the employees of ENT Federal Credit Union, YMCA, Memorial Hospital, and Douglas County on such topics as nutrition, cancer prevention, heart health, chronic disease, detoxification, and wellness.

NATUROPATHIC ONCOLOGY RESIDENCY (October 2005 – June 2006)

Cancer Treatment Centers of America, Tulsa, Oklahoma

Provided complementary care to cancer patients as part of an integrative-medicine team. Made direct inpatient and outpatient contact with patients receiving concomitant chemotherapy, radiation, or other active form of cancer therapy. Recommended safe and effective natural therapies that did not interfere with active therapy, after reviewing and revising each patient's supplement regimens. Collaborated with research groups to initiate investigator-sponsored clinical trials; evaluated the concurrent effects of natural products with chemotherapy.

- Gained firm knowledge and understanding of current medical oncology treatment protocols, including chemotherapy, radiation therapy, and novel therapies.
- Obtained interactive clinical experience in the methods and tools used to evaluate the response to treatment and progression of cancer—blood work, CT, PET/CT, bone scans, x-rays, and MRIs.
- Specialized in drug-herb interactions, nutraceuticals, botanical medicine, physical medicine, nutrition, and counseling.
- Participated in bimonthly grand rounds and cancer conferences on clinical cases and new technology. Additional grand rounds at Tulsa Regional Medical Center on avian bird flu, management of diabetes, new research on hypertension/kidney disease, genetic counseling, and primary amoebic meningioencephalopathy.

PUBLICATIONS

- R. I. Senderoff, K. M. Kontor/Young, L. Kreilgaard, J. Krakover, J. K. Heffernan, L. B. Snell, and G. B. Rosenberg. (1998). Consideration of conformational transitions and racemization during process development of recombinant glucagon-like peptide-1, *Journal of Pharmaceutical Science, 87:(2)*, pp. 183–189.
- R. I. Senderoff, K. M. Kontor/Young, J. K. Heffernan, H. J. Clark, L. Garrison, L. Kreilgaard, and G. B. Rosenberg. (1996). Aqueous stability of recombinant human thrombopoietin as a function of processing schemes, *Journal of Pharmaceutical Science, 85:(3)*, pp. 83–85.

PUBLICATIONS
(continued)

- R. I. Senderoff, K. M. Kontor (Young), J K. Heffernan, H. J. Clark, L. Garrison, L. Kreilgaard, and G. B. Rosenberg. (1995). Degradation of ZG-976 in aqueous solutions as a function of processing schemes, *Pharmaceutical Research, 12:9.*

- K. M. Kontor (Young), T. S. Calderwood, R. Chan, T. R. Malefyt. (1990). A reversed phase method for the separation and quantitation of Interleukin-1ß, *Pharmaceutical Research, 7:S23.*

PRESENTATIONS

- K. M. Young. *Health and Wellness in the Workplace, Cancer, and Other Subjects,* workshops for such organizations as Douglas County, Colorado Housing Authority, Lupus Foundation, Comcast, Susan G. Komen Foundation, Memorial Hospital, YMCA, and ENT Federal Credit Union, among others, 2006 – present.

- R. I. Senderoff, K. M. Kontor/Young, J. F. Heffernan, J. Rosser, P. Shea, J. J. Chang, and G. B. Rosenbert. *Excipient-free Lyophilization of Recombinant Human Thrombin. Novo Nordisk Technology Symposium of Protein Stability,* Hvidore, Denmark, August 23–25, 1998.

- R. I. Senderoff, K. M. Kontor/Young, and G. B. Rosenberg. *Characterizing Proteins Using Multiangle Laser Light Scattering.* Novo Nordisk Technology Symposium of Protein Stability, Hvidore, Denmark, August 23–25, 1998.

- R. I. Senderoff, K. M. Kontor (Young), L. Kreilgaard, J. J. Chang, S. Patel, J. Krakover, J. K. Heffernan, L. B. Snell, and G. B. Rosenberg. *Physico-Chemical Consideration During Process Development of Recombinant Glucagon-like Peptide-I,* Conference of Formulations and Drug Delivery II, La Jolla, California, October 1997.

- R. I. Senderoff, K. M. Kontor/Young, J K. Heffernan, H. J. Clark, L. Garrison, L. Kreilgaard, and G. B. Rosenberg. *Degradation of ZG-976 in Aqueous Solutions as a Function of Processing Schemes,* AAPS Tenth Annual Meeting, Miami Beach, Florida, 1995.

- K. M. Kontor/Young, T. Calderwood, and T. Malefyt. *A Quantitative HPLC Method for the Analysis of Interleukin Iß,* AAPS, Las Vegas, Nevada, 1989.

CONTINUING EDUCATION

- *Testing and monitoring BHRT/Basics of Thyroid Endocrinology/Practical Applications of BHRT,* 2008
- *Rocky Mountain Metabolic Syndrome Symposium,* University of Colorado School of Medicine, 2008
- *The Emerging Therapeutic Treatment: Improving Therapeutic Outcomes,* University of Bridgeport Health Sciences, 2008
- *ZRT: Introduction / Clinical Approach to Bio-Identical Hormone Restoration Therapy,* 2008
- *Pain Management,* PharmCon, 2007
- *Level II BHRT Symposium,* Colorado Association for Medical Care, 2007
- *The Depression Pandemic,* University of Bridgeport Health Sciences, 2007
- *Oncology Perspectives,* American Society of Clinical Oncology, 2006
- *21st Annual Convention and Exposition,* American Association of Naturopathic Physicians, 2006
- *Integrated Oncology Seminar: Level 1 and 2,* Cancer Treatment Centers of America, 2005
- *Chemotherapy and Biotherapy Guidelines and Recommendations,* Oncology Nursing Society, 2005

AFFILIATIONS

- Colorado Association of Naturopathic Physicians, Active Member
- American Association of Naturopathic Physicians, Active Member
- American Cancer Society, Volunteer
- YMCA, Employee Wellness Program, Volunteer
- Oncology Association of Naturopathic Physicians, Previous Member (2005 – 2007)
- Society of Integrative Oncology, Previous Member (2005 – 2007)
- Oklahoma Association of Naturopathic Physicians, Secretary, Previous Member (2005 – 2006)
- Washington Association of Naturopathic Physicians, Previous Member (2000 – 2005)
- American Association of Pharmaceutical Scientists, Previous Member (1988 – 2000)

COMPUTER SKILLS

Proficient in Windows, MS Word, Excel, PowerPoint, Access, Outlook, Internet Explorer, MS Project, Electronic Medical Records (EMR) Systems, QuickBooks, Quicken.

MARY E. TUCKER, PhD

1234 Woodmen Mesa Circle • Colorado Springs, Colorado 80919 • (719) 555-1234 • marytucker@protypeltd.com

GOAL: SUPERINTENDENT OF SCHOOL DISTRICT 11

"People don't care how much you know until they know how much you care." – John C. Maxwell

AREAS OF EXPERTISE

Leadership with Integrity
Strategic Planning • Consensus Building
Operations Management
Student Achievement
Continuous Improvement Processes (CIP)
Budgeting • Funding
Human Resources • Staff Development
Community Involvement
Accreditation

ADMINISTRATIVE PHILOSOPHY

My responsibility as a superintendent is to provide vision, leadership, and support to district staff so students are prepared for the complex, ambiguous, and varied environments of the 21st century. Our students will live and work in diverse circumstances. It is our responsibility to prepare them to succeed in these environments by providing academically rich learning experiences that promote critical thinking, analysis of data, diversity tolerance, and the ability to learn and unlearn. We, as administrators, must give each student every opportunity to be successful, no matter the student's race, gender, or social economic status.

EDUCATION

DOCTOR OF PHILOSOPHY (2000)
University of Colorado, Denver, Colorado
Dissertation: *A Study of Self-esteem, Academic Self-concept, and Academic Achievement of African-American Students in Grades Five, Seven, and Ten in a Predominantly White Suburban School District*

MASTER OF SCIENCE, EDUCATIONAL ADMINISTRATION (1988)
Troy University, Troy, Alabama

BACHELOR OF SCIENCE, EDUCATION (1971)
Tuskegee University, Tuskegee, Alabama
Major: Physical Science • Minor: Mathematics

LICENSES

Professional Administrator License, Colorado #0398471

PROFESSIONAL EXPERIENCE

DEPUTY SUPERINTENDENT (Sep 2003 – present)
Colorado Springs School District 11, Colorado Springs, Colorado
The largest school district in the Pikes Peak Region with 28,600 students (47% free and reduced lunch), 2,092 teachers, 286 administrators, and 1,711 educational support professionals. The district is made up of 41 elementary schools, 9 middle schools, 5 high schools, 7 charter schools, and 6 alternative education programs.

Promoted to Deputy Superintendent after only one year to serve as second in command to the Superintendent. Represent the Superintendent in his absence. Currently supervise the Head of the Human Resources Division and Professional Development Director. Supervised the Executive Director for Student Achievement, Executive Director for Special Programs, Executive Director for Special Education, Gifted and Talented Facilitator, Curriculum and Instruction Director, Career and Technical Education, Adult and Continuing Education, Student Discipline/Athletics, and English Language Learner and Foreign Language Facilitator.

Manage district and school accreditation. As a member of the district leadership team, implement continuous improvement processes through the district, including deployment, training, and process management. Attend meetings of the Board of Education and its Executive Sessions— report on accreditation, CIP, and human resource issues. Represent the district in community organizations—help plan special events and make presentations on issues that affect the district.

- At the forefront of Response to Intervention (RTF) long before it was the "in" CIP. Implemented an RTF program to address the needs of students using a three-tiered approach. Designed and implemented a Comprehensive Academic Achievement Plan (CAAP) with schools receiving assistance weekly, twice a month, or monthly depending on their needs. Coaching included data analysis, classroom instructional strategies, development of action plans, and student progress monitoring, resulting in a dramatic change in the school's environment.

PROFESSIONAL EXPERIENCE

Deputy Superintendent (continued)

- Created a "no excuses" environment focusing on the three A's—attitude, alignment, and accountability—which inevitably leads to significantly increased student achievement.
- Key member of the team responsible for reviewing each school's improvement plan and then developing contracts for the district and all of the schools.
- Achieved full-day (tuition free) kindergarten in all 41 elementary schools in the district.
- Redesigned K–12 principal meetings to focus on professional development in order to create strong instructional leaders. Topics included balanced leadership, classroom walk throughs, creating culturally responsive learning environments, literacy, and the five components of reading.

Special Initiatives

- Planned and implemented a Leadership Development Program for aspiring school administrators in partnership with the University of Colorado at Colorado Springs. Developed the curriculum and served as an instructor for the 18-month program.
- Appointed to the Governor's Technical Assistance Panel to develop and implement a Colorado Growth Model to report and monitor students' annual growth on the Colorado Student Assessment Program (CSAP).
- Served on the Colorado Department of Education (CDE) Mathematics Content Standards Committee. Helped to develop the statewide K–12 mathematics contents standards.

EXECUTIVE DIRECTOR FOR SCHOOL LEADERSHIP (Sep 2002 – Sep 2003)
Colorado Springs School District 11, Colorado Springs, Colorado

Recruited back to Colorado Springs by the Superintendent who created an Executive Director position accountable for eight schools and their associated principals. Worked with principals to analyze student assessment data and developed action plans to improve student achievement. Trained district staff on continuous quality improvement processes/practices.

- Worked with the district's Advisory Accountability Committee to revise district and school accreditation contracts, and submitted them to the Board of Education for approval.
- Acquired tutoring funds to help schools offer before/during/after-school tutoring. Created an accountability structure for principals to report the effectiveness of tutoring services.
- Served on the district's Strategic Plan Development Committee charged with developing a strategic plan with five goal areas—student achievement, safety, high-quality workforce, parent/community involvement, and effective and efficient use of resources.

PRINCIPAL (Jan 2002 – Sep 2002)
Grace E. Metz Middle School, Manassas City Public Schools, Manassas, Virginia
An urban middle school with enrollment of 1,600 students (Grades 6–8) and a staff of 200.

Followed husband to Virginia for what turned out to be a poor opportunity for him. Provided the leadership this school needed to improve administration, school climate, and academic achievement for the second half of the school year. Managed all operations, including staffing, resource allocation, financial planning, budgeting, staff development, and accreditation. Served on the Superintendent's Cabinet, which had a laser focus on increasing student achievement.

- Succeeded in revitalizing the staff and building consensus and better morale among teachers, the community, staff, parents, and students. Promoted a collaborative working environment.
- Established an emphasis on instruction and ensured that all students were academically challenged and individually successful.
- Created before/after-school tutoring programs that were directly responsible for improved scores on Virginia Standards of Learning (SOL) assessment in spring 2002—100% of eighth grade algebra students passed the SOL, and SOL scores increased in all subject areas.
- Implemented initiatives that were responsible for the school's accreditation change from "provisionally accredited" to "fully accredited."
- Provided the structure to identify more students for the gifted and talented programs.

PROFESSIONAL EXPERIENCE

DEPUTY SUPERINTENDENT (Jul 1995 – Jan 2002)
Academy School District 20, Colorado Springs, Colorado
One of the most affluent school district in the region with 17,500 students (K–12).

Directly supervised 26 schools and their principals, ensuring their accountability. Interviewed all administrative candidates and made hiring recommendations. Second in command of all district operations. Supervised curriculum, instruction, student services, school technology, standards and assessments, school and district safety, and the talented and gifted program. Led numerous committees, including calendar, school start times, budget, sexuality, accountability, transition team, year-round schools, and graduation requirements, among others. Served as liaison to the District Accountability Committee, focusing on increasing the involvement of parents, the business community, and higher education.

- Led the district to a 10–20 percentile point increase on nationally normed assessments within a two-year period.
- Key member of the team responsible for developing Colorado's most extensive choice program for students, parents, and staff.
- Wrote the district's accreditation contract and gained approval from the Board of Education to submit it to the Colorado Department of Education.
- Collaborated with district staff, U.S. Air Force Academy personnel, Colorado Springs Police Department, and business leaders in the development of a comprehensive safety plan.
- Placed and coached a principal in a school where students were the lowest achievers on state and national assessments. Within a year the students were (and still are) among the highest achievers.
- *"Mary successfully demonstrated her skills in leading others in planning, developing, implementing, and supervising research-based instructional programs that led to dramatically improved student performance in conformance with Colorado's standards-based system."* – Donald J. Fielder, EdD

EXECUTIVE DIRECTOR (Jul 1992 – Jun 1995)
Academy School District 20, Colorado Springs, Colorado

Managed instruction and day-to-day operations of six schools, including supervision of building principals, curriculum development, and instruction. Coordinated efforts for vertical and horizontal articulation of student needs. Supervised the district's teachers on special assignment to language arts, technology, and science. Accountable for the Gifted and Talented Coordinator, Career and Technical Education, and the district's Library Cataloguer.

- Led a committee in developing district standards for reading, writing, mathematics, science, social studies, art, music, and physical education.
- Served on Colorado's Model Content Standards Committee—wrote mathematics standards for the state.
- Created a Volunteer Reading Tutors (VRT) program where district staff members became reading tutors in elementary schools. Trained volunteer tutors.
- *"Dr. Tucker is 100% dependable. When she says that something will get done, it will be completed and usually ahead of schedule. She is honest and candid while being supportive and helpful. She is the ultimate team player who will sacrifice for the good of the whole. Her integrity and ethical standards are beyond reproach."* – Donald J. Fielder, EdD

ASSISTANT PRINCIPAL (Jun 1989 – Jun 1992)
Timberview Middle School, Academy School District 20, Colorado Springs, Colorado

Assisted in the management of an urban middle school. Supervised and evaluated classroom teachers and school staff. Served as grade-level principal for a group of students as they progressed through middle school. Supervised various departments, including science, mathematics, exploratories, and special education. Developed and managed the school budget.

- Created a positive learning environment for students to succeed.
- Helped to establish a "learning community" approach to students instead of a "teaching community" approach.

PROFESSIONAL EXPERIENCE	**TEACHER** (14 years)

Taught chemistry, physics, physical science, algebra, and general mathematics in four states (Alabama, South Dakota, Colorado, Missouri) and a Department of Defense Dependent school in Bitburg, Germany. Designed mathematics and science curricula and taught these subjects for a summer school (Upward Bound Program) and for a nontraditional student program for military airmen who wanted to receive their high school diploma.

HONORS & AWARDS

- Educator of the Year, Martin Luther King Jr. Holiday Committee (2008).
- Educator of the Year, NAACP (2007).

SELECT PRESENTATIONS & WORKSHOPS

- "Using Response to Intervention in the Middle Years," National Middle School Association (NMSA) (2008, 2006).
- "Leadership Development," University of Colorado at Colorado Springs (2002 – 2008).
- "Making Math Fun," University of Colorado at Colorado Springs (1990).
- "The Principalship," University of Colorado at Colorado Springs (2001).
- "Educational Politics in a Democratic Society," University of Colorado at Colorado Springs (2003, 2006, 2008).
- "Creative Communication for School Leaders," University of Colorado at Colorado Springs (2001).
- "Using Response to Intervention in the Middle Years," Colorado Association of School Executives, Breckenridge, Colorado (August 2007).
- "Using a Response to Intervention Model to Meet Student Needs," Colorado Association of School Executives, Breckenridge, Colorado (August 2005).
- "Baldrige: Continuous Quality Improvement," Colorado Springs School District 11, Colorado Springs, Colorado (2002, 2003).
- "7 Habits of Highly Effective People," Colorado Springs School District 11, Colorado Springs, Colorado (2002 – 2004).
- "How to Find the Administrators You Need in Your Own Backyard," Colorado Association of School Executives, Breckenridge, Colorado (August 2001).
- "7 Habits of Highly Effective People," Academy School District 20, Colorado Springs, Colorado (1994 – 2001).
- "Consensus Building," Academy School District 20, Colorado Springs, Colorado (1993).
- "Managing Change," Academy School District 20, Colorado Springs, Colorado (1994).
- "Minority Student Achievement: Making the Gap Disappear," Colorado Association of School Executives, Breckenridge, Colorado (August 2000).
- "Accountability and Assessment," Association of Supervision and Curriculum Development (ASCD) (1998).
- "Choice Schools: It's Not Your Grandfather's School District Anymore," Colorado Association of School Executives, Breckenridge, Colorado (August 1997).
- "Diversity in the 21st Century," The Southern California Society of Certified Management Accountants (CMA) (1997).
- "Leadership in the Middle and Grant Writing," Colorado Association of Middle Level Education (CAMLE) (1991).

PROFESSIONAL DEVELOPMENT

- Leading at the Speed of Trust (facilitator)
- Bill Daggett's Model Schools
- Cognitive Coaching
- Dufour's Professional Learning Communities (PLC)
- Malcolm Baldrige's Leading Performance Excellence
- Superintendent's Endorsement
- Phil Schlechty's Schools for the 21st Century
- Certified Facilitator for Stephen Covey's "7 Habits of Highly Effective People"

PROFESSIONAL
DEVELOPMENT
- Consensus Building Facilitator Training with Bob Chadwick
- Bi/Polar Training: Understanding People Through Strengths
- Leadership Collaboration for Quality Education
- Unlimited Power Within Training with Anthony Robbins
- Total Quality Management Training

AFFILIATIONS
- American Association of School Administrators
- Association of Supervision and Curriculum Development
- Colorado Association of School Executives
- Colorado Association of Middle Level Educators
- National Middle School Association
- National Association of Secondary School Principals
- National Association of Elementary School Principals
- National Council of Teachers of Mathematics
- National Science Teachers Association
- Gamma Beta Phi Honor Society
- Delta Kappa Gamma Society
- Phi Delta Kappa

COMMUNITY
INVOLVEMENT
- Board of Directors, Home Health Care
- Board of Directors, Pikes Peak Hospice
- Youth Development Board, YMCA
- Board of Directors, YMCA/USO Metropolitan
- Board of Directors, Colorado Springs Children's Chorale
- Advisory Board, Colorado College Integrated Science Teachers Enhancement Program
- Board of Directors, The Women's Resource Agency
- Member, Colorado Springs Martin Luther King Holiday Committee
- Member, National Association for the Advancement of Colored People (NAACP)
- Priorities and Allocations Committee, United Way
- El Pomar Multicultural Youth Leadership Initiative
- El Pomar Leadership Institute
- Family and Committee Together (FACT)
- Colorado Springs Executive Association—represent the Superintendent in his absence
- Joint Initiatives—represent the Superintendent in his absence
- Colorado Springs Leadership Initiative—invited to participate April 2009

Creative Résumés

What fun to be in an industry where almost anything goes! In advertising, marketing, design, and the arts, you have a license to be creative with your résumé. After all, creativity is one of your strongest qualifications for the job. It is the need for this creativity that determines when résumés like the ones in this chapter are appropriate. Using a creative résumé takes a very special type of person. They are not for accountants, bankers, and executives.

No matter how creative you want to be, you must still keep readability in mind. If your audience can't read your résumé, what good is it?

In some career fields (artist or graphic designer, for instance), a creative résumé is the first page of a much larger portfolio, whether it is online or in a paper version that you take to an interview. The résumé doesn't replace the portfolio but summarizes it. The design must be a reflection of your "style" so it complements the entire package.

If you are working with a professional résumé writer, you might want to ask him or her to write the content for your résumé but leave the formatting generic so you can copy and paste the professional wording into your equally professional design. Many people in creative industries are much more comfortable with the design software than writers.

If you know that your résumé will be sent directly to an outside recruiting firm instead of to the company itself, you might want to consider having a "creative" résumé for paper purposes—like the one you will take to interviews or hand to networking contacts—and a more traditional style for e-mailing or mailing to recruiters. Large recruiting firms use computerized applicant tracking systems to manage their résumés, and creative style like those in this section won't import correctly into their databases.

According to a recent CareerBuilder survey of employers, nearly a quarter (22%) of hiring managers reported that they are seeing more job seekers trying unusual tactics to capture their attention. While these tactics may work occasionally, they still need to be done with professionalism. Hiring managers reported that the following tactics were effective:

- A DVD of a former boss giving a recommendation.
- A proposal explaining how to solve a technology issue the company was having.
- A prospective teacher brought in a box of props to demonstrate her teaching style.
- A complete business plan for one of the company's products.
- A full graphics portfolio of the company's brand.

Allison J. Dennison

RETAIL OPERATIONS EXECUTIVE

Experienced manager who looks for opportunities to turn inefficient operations into productive, profitable work environments. Results-oriented professional with exceptional problem-solving abilities. Effective team leader who is skilled at empowering staff to accomplish common business goals. Proven reputation as a "fixer" and creative thinker.

AREAS OF EXPERTISE

- Retail operations
- Wholesale markets
- Strategic planning
- Store openings
- Staffing / HR
- Team building
- Inventory management
- Market trends
- Technology solutions

PROFESSIONAL EXPERIENCE

DIRECTOR OF OPERATIONS (May 2007–present)
DIRECTOR OF RETAIL OPERATIONS (Apr 2006–May 2007)
Steven Alan, New York, New York
The Steven Alan (SA) brand of men's and women's apparel and accessories is known worldwide for its original, unique designs with edgy, new details. The brand has grown from one Manhattan boutique to nine stores throughout the U.S. with annual sales of $9 million.

Promoted through the ranks to this corporate position providing strategic direction for the wholesale, retail, and showroom operations of the SA brand. Develop retail infrastructures, open new stores, and strengthen the corporate culture. Maximize sales by developing sound business strategies and seasonal inventory plans that support sales, turnover, and margin goals. Analyze sales data, inventory, profitability performance, volume, and trends—use this knowledge to make recommendations that maximize business opportunities and limit liabilities. Recruit, hire, train, and mentor a staff of 15 direct reports, including operations managers, district managers, planners, buyers, inventory control specialist, and support personnel. Enforce trademarks and negotiate licensing deals. Manage special projects, including displays, merchandising, sample sales, photo shoots, grand opening events, and fashion night-outs. Assess distributor supply ordering processes and audit invoices.

- Managed the construction, staffing, and opening of seven new stores and a corporate office in New York City. Oversaw renovation and maintenance of two SA showrooms and expansion of the NYC Franklin Street store (integrated the design studio, main store, and stock areas).
- Upgraded the security systems of all stores, including cameras, DVR systems (Internet accessible), and cash-handling procedures, which prevented loss and expedited recovery.
- Implemented quarterly physical inventories and standard press and stylist pull/return processes.
- Negotiated cost-effective contracts for IT and point-of-sale (POS) systems, shipping/messenger services (saved 45% on UPS account), and insurance coverage.
- Created new collateral materials to standardize the brand identity at stores nationwide. Implemented Orbital gift card, birthday card, and dialogue card programs to increase customer loyalty.
- Developed store operations and employee manuals to standardize operating policies and procedures, forms, reports, employee hiring/training, and inventory ordering processes.
- Researched and implemented new healthcare benefits, dental insurance, and a 401k plan. Made benefits uniform throughout the company, created a positive work environment, reduced employee turnover, and decreased HR costs.
- Set up a website to make inventory information more accessible to all retail locations, which minimized out-of-stock situations.
- Integrated Shift 4 with Retail Pro and created custom reports and Excel spreadsheets to expedite financial analysis, compare year-to-year sales, and forecast payroll.
- Managed massive clearance sales generating $500,000 each. Selected inventory, located temporary locations, and staffed the events.

Continued . . .

1234 Bank Street, Apt. 9B
New York, New York 10014
Cell: (917) 555-1234
Email: adennison@protypeltd.com

PROFESSIONAL EXPERIENCE

STORE OPERATIONS MANAGER (Apr 2004–Apr 2006)
Diane von Furstenberg, New York, New York
Diane Von Furstenberg (DVF) is one of the leading names in American fashion. Founded by the designer in 1972, and re-launched in 1997, DVF has grown into a global luxury lifestyle brand with a complete collection of ready-to-wear, swimwear, accessories, footwear, and handbags.

Managed the operations of the flagship DVF store in New York City. Sourced, screened, hired, supervised, and evaluated sales and management staff. Identified and delivered business system and process improvements. Directed merchandising, floor moves, and promotional event setups. Trained staff in loss prevention policies, customer service, sales, and POS systems. Partnered with buyers to allocate/consolidate merchandise to outlet stores. Ensured a clean, professional working environment. Resolved escalated customer service issues.

- Selected to open four new stores, including construction, IT system selection/implementation, hiring, inventory, bank accounts, etc.
- Collaborated with Ronit Weinberg to create a strategic growth plan for the DVF brand, which helped to determine future store locations and financial growth models for existing and future stores.
- Created inventory standards for automatic ordering of year-round products based on predetermined minimums and maximums.
- Hired inventory control specialists and tightened the loss-prevention structure.
- Worked with the marketing director to create gift card and VIP programs.
- Consulted on the 2005 spring and fall clothing line, including merchandise selection—quantities, size breaks, performance, fabrication, etc.
- Integrated Blue Cherry warehousing system with Retail Pro to facilitate the import of style and codes.
- Created a standardized financial modeling system, custom reports, and sales analyses.
- Analyzed the profitability of various product lines and suggested new pricing to increase profitability.
- Created a systematic training program, and groomed a training assistant to train other employees.

FREELANCE WEB DESIGN / DEVELOPMENT (Feb 1998–Dec 2003)
Developed websites—wrote HTML code, created artwork and animation, and prepared images and page layouts. Held client meetings to determine preferences, needs, and content. Updated and maintained each site after going live. Used creative skills and training to gain experience in multiple industries.

- Served as production/wardrobe assistant for *Enter, Fleeing,* a movie produced by Goldheart Pictures.
- Collaborated with Smash Advertising house editor on editing, mixing, audio, and preparation of videos.
- Designed and managed SIM Broadcast Network biannual event to showcase student and alumni work.
- Taught web design at College Academy in Nashoba, Massachusetts. Formulated lesson plans and provided challenging learning experiences not commonly found in traditional schools.

EDUCATION

GRADUATE STUDIES (May 2004)
The Salt Institute for Documentary Studies, Portland, Maine
- One semester of documentary studies and photography courses toward an MFA degree.

BACHELOR OF FINE ARTS (2000)
Massachusetts College of Art, Boston, Massachusetts
- Major in Studio for Interrelated Media.
- Concentration in Video Editing and Digital Compositing.

UNDERGRADUATE STUDIES (1995–1998)
Western Michigan University, Kalamazoo, Michigan
- Major in Industrial Design, Imaging, and Digital Technology.
- Accepted to the Kalamazoo Institute of Art. Winner of the competitive WMU Medallion Scholarship.

TECHNOLOGY

Operating Systems: Macintosh and Windows.
Business Applications: MS Word, Excel, RetailPro, ASW Warehouse Management Application.
Publishing Applications: Adobe PhotoShop, Premier, AfterEffects, Illustrator, HTML.
Video/Audio Systems: Sound Edit 16, Sound Forge, Deck II, Avid Nonlinear Digital Video Editing Systems (1000/8000, Media Express), Edit DV, DVD Creation, Hi8 AB-Roll and SVHS Off-Line Analog Video Editing.
Photography, Etcetera: Black and White Developing and Printing, Silk Screening, and Lithography.

KENNETH F. JOHNSON
1234 Bridgewater Drive • Colorado Springs, CO 80916
Home: (719) 555-1234 • Cell: (719) 123-5555
Email: kenneth.johnson@.com

PROFILE
- Experienced engineer with a strong working knowledge of electronics and semiconductor devices.
- Hold graduate degrees in both electrical and mechanical engineering.
- Competent in the use of RF test equipment, Assembly language, and Visual C++ 2008.
- Extensive knowledge of electronic circuit behavior, embedded software programming languages, schematic entry, PCB layout, and RF embedded systems.

EXPERIENCE
Senior Application Engineer, Atmel, Colorado Springs, Colorado (2008 – present)
Collaborate with business development and other crypto solution team members to design Atmel products into systems, with particular emphasis on short time to market. Troubleshoot and solve hardware and software problems that customers report in their designs (relating to CryptoMemory and CryptoRF products). Use knowledge and ability to 1) analyze schematics and designs in hardware description languages, 2) work with several integrated development environments, and 3) design/code/analyze firmware systems, platform portability, and delivery strategies that safeguard sensitive intellectual property. Travel to customer sites and perform work on their systems. Assist marketing communications groups with product launches and promotions. Prepare and present training programs and customer seminars to assist the sale staff in their pre-sales efforts.
- Created tools to reduce customer design time. Drove the right product architecture/features for new products and support tools.
- Developed white papers, application notes, articles, presentations, boards, and related materials to aid in the customer's development process and reduce time to market.
- Drove customers to include other Atmel products in their designs using a deep understanding of embedded systems, including the inner workings of a variety of microcontrollers, system architectures, peripherals, and firmware.

Semiconductor Packaging Engineer, Atmel, Colorado Springs, Colorado (2002 – 2008)
Designed packages for integrated circuits using Advance Package Designer (APD). Collaborated with the Product Development Group and the offshore packaging subcontractor to determine appropriate packages for new products. Performed and interpreted thermal and electrical simulations/analyses for packages. Provided engineering support for the design of prototype packages.
- Recommended optimum packaging solutions for new products based on requirements, reliability requirements, and product cost targets.
- Procured new product packages, including procurement specifications, agreement on manufacturing flow and specifications, and reliability qualification.
- Stayed current with industry trends in advanced packaging technologies and materials, including thermal simulation and electrical characterization/simulation.

Associate Professor, University of Colorado, Colorado Springs, Colorado (2005 – present)
Develop and teach graduate-level college courses. Set learning goals and create effective curricula, syllabi, lesson plans, handouts, teaching aids, and audio-visual materials. Develop competency measurements, evaluations, and examinations to validate learning.
- Mechanical and Aerospace Engineering, Engineering Measurement Laboratory (MAE 3005 Lab).
- Automatic Control of Aerospace and Mechanical Systems (MAE 4421, Lecture and Lab).
- Created learning climates that facilitated learning and ensured that students were active participants in the learning process.

Test Engineer, Atmel, Colorado Springs, Colorado (2000 – 2002)
Tested integrated circuit products for the cellular, smart card, mobile communications, and consumer electronics industries in a high-volume production test environment. Matched test hardware to products, and developed diagnostic tools to troubleshoot problems. Created acceptable criteria for new products and programs, and evaluated new test hardware/software.
- Modified and improved production test programs; troubleshot and fixed product and test problems.
- Developed and maintained a system for hardware/product SPC in the test operation.
- Trained technicians and operators, and interacted with technical groups to remain abreast of new developments in the field.

EXPERIENCE (continued)

Process Technician, Atmel, Colorado Springs, Colorado (1997 – 2000)
Collaborated with engineers to determine materials, parts, dimensions, and tolerances necessary for operating wafer fabrication equipment. Initiated and implemented corrective action to resolve process and equipment problems. Troubleshot out-of-control SPC issues and performed routine equipment checks. Wrote and modified operating specifications, reports, and documentation of experiment results.
- Authorized to make decisions on production hold lots, stopped processes, and down equipment.
- Trained and certified operators; participated on preventative action and work area teams.

Photo Specialist, Atmel, Colorado Springs, Colorado (1996 – 1997)
Wafer Production Operator, Atmel, Colorado Springs, Colorado (1995 – 1996)
Manufactured 6-inch memory chip wafers and performed minor trouble shooting on the line. Trained peers in operations and protocols as a buddy trainer,
- Gained in-depth experienced in the use of Daninippon 60A Coater, UV Bake, OTI Vacuum Bake, DNS Developer, ASM 2500/5000 Stepper, and develop inspect.
- Perfect attendance; worked with minimal supervision.

Foreman/Mowing Crew (1992 – 1995)
Terranomics Landscape Management, Inc., Colorado Springs, Colorado
Supervised all aspects of mowing operations, including scheduling and training of workers. Ordered and maintained inventory of supplies and maintained a safe work environment. Performed preventive maintenance on all equipment.

Team Leader, Army National Guard, Fort Carson, Colorado (1992 – present)
Team Leader, United States Army, Fort Carson, Colorado (1987 – 1992)
Implemented orders and directives and ensured proper collection and reporting of intelligence data. Supervised training and activities of subordinates; evaluated performance and provided written and oral counseling; commended for outstanding leadership skills. Trained National Guard forces for Saudi Arabia.

EDUCATION

MASTER OF SCIENCE IN ELECTRICAL ENGINEERING (2008)
University of Colorado, Colorado Springs, Colorado
- Thesis: "Active Noise Control"

MASTER OF SCIENCE IN MECHANICAL ENGINEERING (2005)
University of Colorado, Colorado Springs, Colorado
- Thesis: "A Practical Approach to Modeling and Controlling a DC Motor"

BACHELOR OF SCIENCE IN ELECTRICAL ENGINEERING (2000)
University of Colorado, Colorado Springs, Colorado

PIKES PEAK COMMUNITY COLLEGE, Colorado Springs, Colorado (1993 – 1996)
- Completed 59 credit hours toward a degree in electrical engineering
- Computer programming classes in VAX, FORTRAN, Computer Science I & II, C++

CONTINUING EDUCATION

ATMEL
- Cadence Advanced Package Designer (APD) Software—trained by Cadence and AMKOR
- Visual C++ 6 and 2008
- Microcontroller Assembly Language
- RF Spectrum Analyzer
- RF Function Generator and Oscilloscope

UNITED STATES ARMY, Fort Carson, Colorado (1992)
Primary Leadership Development Course (PLDC)
- Selected for the Commandant's List for superior performance
- Scored 192 out of 200 on the E-5 promotions board

John Cooke, MA, ABD Voice

CONTACT
www.protypeltd.com
jcooke@protypeltd.com
(719) 555-1234

Teaching Philosophy

"I strive to instill in each student an understanding of the diversity of musical components and how they affect performance. Music is truly miraculous, and I believe it can change the lives of students. As a teacher, I validate each student as he or she reaches for success through music. I encourage singers to discover the most natural vocal emission, using speech, breath, and varying intensities of support."

Teaching Experience

- **Private Voice and Piano Instructor,** Colorado (1984 – present). Teach beginning to advanced students. Direct students in two recitals per year.
- **Public School Music Teacher** (K–12), various Colorado school districts (1991 – present). Develop vocal music programs and instruct children in choruses, general music theory, and musical arrangement.
- **Assistant Professor of Voice,** University of Northern Iowa, Cedar Falls, Iowa
- **Choral Director,** Prince George's Community College, Largo, Maryland
- **Adjunct Vocal Professor,** Glasborough College, Glasborough, New Jersey
- **Assistant Professor of Voice and Choral Activities,** Fort Lewis College, Durango, Colorado
- **Assistant Professor of Voice,** Northwestern State University, Nachitoches, Louisiana
- **Studio Voice Instructor,** West Texas A&M University, Canyon, Texas

Education

- **Doctoral Studies,** The Juilliard School, New York (full scholarship)
- **Master of Arts,** Vocal Performance, Catholic University, Washington, DC
- **Bachelor of Music Education,** Colorado State University, Pueblo, Colorado (state teaching certification)
- **Bachelor of Music, Vocal Performance,** University of Louisville, Kentucky

Professional Development

- Completed the Chicago Lyric Opera Apprentice Program.
- Coached by respected Metropolitan Opera professionals, including Joan Dornemann, Richard Woitach, Richard Marzollo (Assistant to Arturo Toscanini), Walter Taussig, Charles Kullman, Loretta di Franco, and Louise Sherman.
- Studied voice with some of the best teachers in the country, including:
  - Norman Phillips, former leading baritone with the Vienna State Opera (Wiener Staatsoper).
  - Todd Duncan, the original Porgy in *Porgy and Bess* by George Gershwin, lead in *Lost in the Stars* by Kurt Wilde.
  - As well as Fletcher Smith, Ed Baird, Armand Boyajian, and Vera Scammon.
- Studied piano with Dwight Anderson, then Dean of the Music School at the University of Louisville.
- Performed with renowned conductors, including James Levine, Richard Bonynge, Raymond Leppard, Erich Kunzel, and Joseph Rescigno.

Honors and Awards

- Winner of the Metropolitan Opera National Auditions with a 5-year contract as a principal artist.
- Winner of the Christopher Clark Award.
- Winner of the Richard Tucker Award.
- Winner of numerous competitions from the National Association of Teachers of Singing (NATS), including upper division and graduate division awards in two regions.
- Finalist in the WGN Auditions and the Chicago Lyric Opera Competition.

Compositions

- **Composed** *Now Thank We All, Our God,* for four-part mixed chorus and keyboard accompaniment.
- **Composed** *Latin Mass* for chorus, orchestra, and bell choir.

(continued)

Private Voice Teacher
Piano Teacher
Composer
Pianist
Recitalist

Reviews and Comments

▸ *"John Cooke's crisp diction and flawless vocal production were one of the highlights of the evening."*
  – Lawrence Sears, *Washington Star*
▸ *"As Cavaradossi, tenor John Cooke was a ravishing singer."* – Mark Arnest, *The Gazette*
▸ *"As Calaf, his 'Nessun dorma' was one of the evening's high points."* – Mark Arnest, *The Gazette*
▸ *"The last voice to be presented was the most exquisite of all, a tenor of rare beauty and tone."* – George
  Cromwell, *Washington Post*

Symphonies and Oratorio

▸ **Tenor soloist roles** Included:

– Dr. Marianus	*Symphony No. 8*, Mahler	New York Philharmonic
– First Wiseman	*Fiesta de la Posada*, Brubeck	Fifth Avenue Presbyterian Church, NYC
– Tenor Soloist	*Elijah*, Mendelssohn	Canterbury Choral Society
– Tenor Soloist	*Messiah*, Handel	New Jersey Symphony
– Tenor Soloist	*Opera Favorites*	Dallas Symphony
– Tenor Soloist	*Amahl and the Night Visitors*, Menotti	Minneapolis Symphony
– Tenor Soloist	*Gala Concert*	Guelph Festival Orchestra
– Tenor Soloist	*Requiem*, Verdi	Hamilton Symphony
– Tenor Soloist	*Symphony No. 9*, Beethoven	Amarillo Symphony
– Tenor Soloist	*Blue Monday*	Colorado Symphony
– Tenor Soloist	*Highlights from La Bohème*, Puccini	Arapahoe Symphony

Opera Roles

▸ **Major roles** included:

– Arturo	*Lucia di Lammermoor*, Donizetti	Metropolitan Opera
– Énéas	*Esclarmonde*, Massenet	Metropolitan Opera
– Ernesto	*Don Pasquale*, Donizetti	Metropolitan Opera (cover)
– Nemorino	*L'elisir d'amore*, Donizetti	Metropolitan Opera (cover)
– Alfredo	*La Traviata*, Verdi	Metropolitan Opera (cover)
– Faust	*Faust*, Gounod	Mostly Opera, New York
– B. F. Pinkerton	*Madama Butterfly*, Puccini	Mostly Opera, New York
– Alfredo	*La Traviata*, Verdi	New York Grand Opera
– Mario Cavaradossi	*Tosca*, Puccini	Opera in the Parks, New York
– Rodolfo	*La Bohème*, Puccini	Chicago Lyric Opera (apprentice program)
– Radames	*Aida*, Verdi	Toronto Symphony
– Rodolfo	*La Bohème*, Puccini	Miami Beach Symphony
– Edgardo	*Lucia di Lammermoor*, Donizetti	Manhasset Bay Opera
– Macduff	*Macbeth*, Verdi	New Orleans Opera
– Duke of Mantua	*Rigoletto*, Verdi	Manhasset Bay Opera, Shreveport Opera
– Martin	*The Tender Land*, Copland	Fort Worth Opera
– Manrico	*Il Trovatore*, Verdi	Jersey Lyric Opera
– Don José	*Carmen*, Bizet	Jersey Lyric Opera
– Riccardo	*Un Ballo in Maschera*, Verdi	Jersey Lyric Opera
– Mario Cavaradossi	*Tosca*, Puccini	Opera Theatre of the Rockies
– Alfred	*Die Fledermaus*, Strauss	Opera Theatre of Albuquerque
– Stiffelio	*Stiffelio*, Verdi	Amato Opera
– Dalibor (understudy)	*Dalibor*, Smetana	Eve Queler Concerts

Concerts, Recitals, Appearances

▸ **Church Soloist:** Fifth Avenue Presbyterian Church–New York City; Church of the Heavenly Rest–New York City; Canterbury Choral Society–New York City; Fort Meyer Chapel–Washington, DC; National Shrine–Washington, DC; First Church of Christ Scientist–Washington, DC; Church of the Holy Ghost–Denver; The Bach Society–Louisville, KY.
▸ **Recitals**—Operatic literature, chamber music, and works by Fauré, Debussy, Duparc, Schubert, Schumann, Strauss, Ralph Vaughan Williams, Benjamin Britten, Samuel Barber, David Diamond, Gian Carlo Menotti:
  - Columbia Artists Series
  - Featured Tenor with James Levine at Carnegie Hall, New York
  - Lamar University Concert Series
  - Stanley Hotel Concert Series
▸ **Concerts:** Performed excerpts from opera, operetta, Broadway, and requests as the duo, Singing Sweethearts, with Gail Allen in cabaret, concert, and on national tours (Ferragosto Festival in San Diego and in Italy).
▸ **Created a video** of *A Night at the Opera: Around the World in 120 Minutes with Music* for Fox Television.
▸ **Tenor soloist** for the U.S. Air Force Band and "Singing Sergeants" (national and international tours) for four years.

MAILING ADDRESS
1234 New London Way
Monument, CO 80132

Walt Rivers

"Commercial Property—Sales, Leasing, and Management—No Problem!"

Delivered $10M in gross sales per year...

Over 3 million square feet in Orlando alone...

Publix / Walgreens / Home Depot / Wal-Mart...and more!

New Approach to Business

Walt Rivers, Top-Performing Senior Executive with 15+ years of experience in Property Operations and Management for residential development, commercial, and investment/development property markets.

How many commercial property professionals do you know who:

- Are capable of managing portfolios in excess of $2.5 billion in assets.
- Delivered $30 million in revenue and profit growth through innovative hands-on operating leadership and high-profile property management.
- Are CPM and CAM certified.

Education and Training

Rivers is a graduate of the University of Miami, with a Bachelor of Business Administration in Business Management and Organization.

Expanding his knowledge with certifications and licenses:

- **Real Estate Brokers License**
- **Mortgage Brokers License**
- **Property Management Certification (CPM)**
- **Community Association Management Certification (CAM)**

Affiliations

AMO   IREM   CAI

ICSC   ULI

Steady Experience

Rivers has enjoyed a stellar career with more than 25 years experience in commercial property sales, leasing, and property management. He has been a Director of Leasing and Vice President of Dispositions with ABCDE Holdings and its subsidiaries since 1986 and is currently charged with the sales and disposition of commercial properties owned by ABCDE Properties, both for existing land and improved land sale, new development projects already built, totaling almost three million square feet in Orlando, Florida.

Rivers is a catalyst for property management, new tenant marketing and sales, leasing and renewals, new development, planning and budgeting, site selection, and market analysis.

Prior to joining ABCDE, Rivers was the CAM with Innsider Management Company. Continuing, as General Manager of The Hemispheres Condominium Association ...1,200 unit complex located on the Atlantic Ocean in Hallandale Beach, with amenities including two Olympic-size pools, a marina, 50,000 sq. ft. of retail/restaurants, health spa, and real estate office offering sales and rentals to the community. Later, Rivers went on to manage The Colonial House Apartments in Houston, Texas, a 1,300 unit complex and Delvista Towers, a 433-unit complex located in Aventura.

Rivers communicated with the president management team, and unit owners, including investment company syndicators, and the RTC and FDIC in some cases, he performed workouts on the Four Ambassadors Condominium in Miami and a portfolio of shopping centers foreclosed on by BHF Bank, New York.

Performance Excellence

SUCCESSFUL PROJECTS:

Avatar Poinciana Properties

- **Negotiations include**: Lowe's- 18.64 acre site, 117,000 sq. ft. of retail space, $18.5 million and 7,270 sq. ft. post office.
- Winner of two Best Master-Planned Community Awards.

SouthEast Centers, LLC, Village Shops at Bellalago- developed by Avatar

- $20 million shopping center on 13.9 acres
- Negotiations include: Publix, Sonoma Coffee, Buffalo Wings & Rings Restaurant, Citrus Garden Chinese Restaurant, Rita's Italian Ices, Collazzo Accounting, and more national chains being added.

Get In Touch

Walt A. Rivers, CPM

11111 Life Lane • Hall, FL 33333

• 954.666.6666 •

sellmyhouserivers@protypeltd.com

Glen Weston

12345 Deerfield Court
Burlington, VT 05401
(802) 555-1234
weston@protypeltd.com

career goal

To contribute innovative ideas and graphic design skills to a marketing organization with particular focus to outdoor sports enthusiasts

personal and professional qualifications

- Versatility to participate in all creative stages—conceptualization through production of advertising design. Expertise encompasses:
  - »» on-site photography as well as work from camera-ready art
  - »» graphic illustration in pencil, pen and ink, or watercolor
  - »» image scanning and computer manipulation in a combination of programs
  - »» four-color processing
  - »» typeface selection to convey client's message with style
- Well-read in design industry publications such as *HOW*, *Graphics News*, *Digital Arts*, and *Layers* magazines, especially attentive to aesthetics and ad layouts.
- Precise with details while conscious of project tracking and deadlines.
- Avid interest in seasonal sports that include skiing, snowboarding, surfing, rock climbing, and mountain biking.
- Relate easily to young adults in pursuit of outdoor activities; know what they look for when purchasing equipment and accessories.

education

Associate of Science in Graphic Design   August 2009
The Art Institute of Pittsburgh Online Division

mac computer skills

Illustrator	Photoshop	Freehand MX
Painter X	QuarkXPress	MS Word

related experience

Freelance graphic design and photography	ADVERTISING COMPS	Burton Snowboards *Outdoor Sports* magazine
Freelance graphic design and illustration	RETAIL LAYOUT CATALOG DESIGN	Slalom Ski Shops Sports Authority Empire Stores
	LOGO DESIGN	AllStar Tech Solutions

other experience

SALES ASSOCIATE at Slalom Ski Shop, Burlington, VT   2003–Present
- Advised customer on selections best suited to their needs.
- Met with sales representatives and evaluated new equipment for store inventory.
- Attended promotional demos, which afforded opportunities for photography.

ROBERT ROTH
1234 Havoo Drive • Colorado Springs, Colorado 80910
Cell: (719) 555-9999 • Email: rroth@protypeltd.com

CREATIVE TOY DESIGNER AND PRODUCT DEVELOPMENT MANAGER

"I'm a year-round Santa's elf . . . only bigger." — Robert Roth

AREAS OF EXPERTISE

Artist • Engineer • Sculptor
From Idea to "Ka-Ching!"
Project Management
Value Engineering
Brand Management • Licensing
Production and Quality Control

EXECUTIVE SUMMARY

- Strategic thinker who can see the vision for a project, break it down into manageable components, and develop an effective approach to success.
- Acclaimed designer and master model maker who brings 18 years of talent, enthusiasm, and know-how to toy design.
- High-energy, results-oriented professional with a passion for craftsmanship—skilled in three-dimensional design, tooling, and moldability of parts.

SUMMARY OF EXPERIENCE

DESIGN AND ENGINEERING

- Designed and engineered workable, sellable toys that were easily produced.
- Developed creative relationships with designers in jobs where design was not part of the job description.
- Took ideas and made them "happen"—interpreted the look of each idea, refined the design to ensure it was manufacturable, and created models that "nailed" the designer's vision.
- Incorporated new technologies into products, improved flight dynamics, and designed around existing parts, when they were available, to reduce cost of goods sold.
- Evaluated existing products to find areas where costs could be reduced, thereby increasing margins.

MODELING AND PROTOTYPE CREATION

- Acknowledged expert in all phases of model making from concept, aesthetics, and engineering to finished products.
- Recognized as a model aircraft design expert specializing in unusual aircraft configurations.
- Able to accurately and quickly translate ideas, sketches, and verbal descriptions into mock-up, bread board, tooling, engineering, and sales presentation models.
- Skilled at silicone mold making and the use of plastics, adhesives, and composites.

PROJECT / PRODUCTION MANAGEMENT

- Planned and managed the full life-cycle of projects (cradle to grave), ensuring adherence to budgets and deadlines.
- Traveled to China for up to 10 weeks at a time to evaluate preproduction samples and to ensure quality control. Had the authority to approve tooling and first shots. Gave permission to turn on production. Evaluated assembly line stations, debugged the production process, and designed fixtures to facilitate assembly.
- Searched for products that already existed in China, found new vendors, and developed strong relationships with factory owners. Selected the factory that would produce the best finished product for each toy.
- Inspired a sense of teamwork and mentored / motivated co-workers to excel at their crafts. Skilled at developing effective working relationships with creative people and getting the most out of them.
- Ensured the production of cost-effective, benchmarked, quality products while never missing a deadline.

MARKETING AND BRAND MANAGEMENT

- Created distinctive design themes, and ensured that designs stayed true to each brand's look and feel.
- Collaborated with marketing to determine price points, colors, and sellable designs to realize their placement.
- Provided expert technical support during television commercial shoots, at the New York Toy Fair, and the Nuremberg Toy Fair. Built quality, workable prototypes that raised product profiles.

RELEVANT ACCOMPLISHMENTS

PROJECT MANAGER / DESIGNER, Estes-Cox, Penrose, Colorado (2004 – present)

Direct the design and production of mass-market flying toys from cradle to grave. Travel to China for six to eight weeks per year to manage the production process. Search for competitors and new vendors at the annual New York and the Nuremberg Toy Fairs.

- Dramatically increased the sale of $20-price-point items from 68,000 to 380,000 pieces per year by making designs more exciting.
- Reduced returns by designing durability into products and making them more user friendly.
- Decreased the cost of production and increased margins by reducing the number of parts for each toy and making some toys end-user assembled.
- Changed the perception of the company's entire product line by creating a cohesive look that increased brand recognition.
- Designed and patented a helicopter rotor blade for the product that was selected as Wal-Mart's 2008 Toy of the Year.
- Reduced the product development life cycle by quickly moving from breadboard to engineering samples.

RELEVANT ACCOMPLISHMENTS	**FREELANCE DESIGNER AND MODEL MAKER** (1999 – present) Recognized as a master model maker. Consult with clients regarding product manufacturability. Sought out by toy manufacturers, inventors, and investors to create:

- Breadboard, mock-up, and looks-like / works-like models for the toy, computer peripheral, and die-cast model markets.
- Prototypes and sale sample models to match finished products.
- Engineering patterns for use in 3-D modeling to meet scanning requirements.

MASTER MODEL MAKER, Mattel / Tyco Toys, Inc., Mount Laurel, New Jersey (1996 – 2004)
Made patterns and models for the full range of Tyco/Mattel products, including Matchbox cars, Hot Wheels, the remote-controlled (Tyco RC) line, electric slot car racing sets, Barbie, and preschool, plush, and licensed items. Worked up through the ranks from pattern maker to master model maker.

- Created 85 master patterns for the Matchbox brand. Hold two design patents for Tyco RC products.
- Developed final patterns for all product lines, including vehicle bodies (car carving) and proof-of-concept models displaying mechanical and aesthetic changes to existing products as well as new ideas.
- Part of the product development team for Buzz Lightyear, Barbie playsets, M&M dispensers, and other major brands. Worked closely with designers to realize their vision as 3-D manufacturable products.
- Produced models for the New York Toy Fair, television commercials, and the Nuremberg Toy Fair. As a "Toy Tech," kept prototypes running right and looking great during demonstrations and television shoots.
- Re-sculpted rejected licensed products from outside vendors to make sure they would pass licensing inspections.
- Cut weeks out of the production process by eliminating a model stage without losing the details.
- Reduced the cost of production for Matchbox cars, saving hundreds of thousands of dollars in cost of goods sold.

DESIGNER / PROTOTYPE MODEL MAKER, Johnson Research & Development, Smyrna, Georgia (1996)
Recruited away from Professional Prototypes to modernize Johnson's model-making processes for patented, air-pressurized toys. Provided support for in-house concepts as well as development work for outside clients.

- Introduced silicon molding and casting, updated the model shop with digital equipment, and introduced other new technologies to bring Johnson R&D up to the level of a full-service prototyping facility.

PROTOTYPE MODEL MAKER, Professional Prototypes, Whitehouse, New Jersey (1990 – 1996)
Key team member for a company providing full-service product development (concept to working model) to clients specializing in mechanized toys, packaging for health and beauty aids, miniature tools, and other toys.

- Mentored by and learned the toy business from some of the best designers in the country.
- Developed new features for the company's SuperSoaker brand to keep the brand fresh from season to season. Played a key role in increasing sales of the brand, turning two initial water guns into an entire brand line that continues to fill the shelves of Wal-Mart every summer.

EDUCATION	**ASSOCIATE OF ARTS, STUDIO ARTS** (1992) **Raritan Valley Community College,** Raritan, New Jersey

- Dean's List
- Selected as the Finest Ceramic Artist in graduating class
- Juried to display ceramic works in several high-end galleries and shows

CONTINUING EDUCATION

- Independent study in ceramics
- Produced sculptural pottery under the guidance of the Raritan Valley Community College Art Department

AFFILIATIONS	

- President, East Coast Indoor Modelers—the oldest model aircraft club in the world (1997 – present)
- Member, Association of Professional Model Makers (1998 – present)
- Member, Academy of Model Aeronautics (1983 – present)—Contest Director (1993 – present)
- Contest Director, Indoor National Championships—Plan and direct the annual event (2003 – present)
- Team Manager, F1D World Championships, Belgrade, Serbia (2008), and Slonic, Romania (2002)
- Member, National Free Flight Society (1998 – present)
- Ranked among the Top Ten indoor model aircraft builders and flyers in the United States—hold four National Aircraft Endurance Records in aeronautical modeling

FRANKLIN G. BOOKMAN

12 Proclamation Way ♦ Decatur, IN 46733
(H) 260-555-1215 ♦ (C) 260-555-1062
Email: booker@protypeltd.com

EXECUTIVE PASTOR
Providing Leadership and Pastoral Care to All Members of the Congregation

Innovative executive pastor called to lead people and diverse ministry programs. Recognized for excellence in team-building, strategic planning, and vision casting / implementation. Able to positively impact the congregation and community, leverage talents and gifts to meet the needs of others, and fulfill the Great Commission through evangelism and outreach. Experienced in expanding the Kingdom of God through newcomer, celebrations, outreach, care, and small groups ministries.

GIFTED

Administrator—Seasoned decision-maker able to foster clear communications with staff and confer with senior pastor of all significant operations and personnel issues.

Visionary—Assist staff and ministry teams in development and execution of strategic plans for the church, staff, facility, and operations.

Evangelist—Called to preach the Gospel, teach Biblically sound doctrine, and reach out to others with the Good News of Salvation.

Missionary—Source opportunities to reach others for Christ and lead teams in providing care for the lost and hurting.

Marketer—Create community awareness of church services, programs, and events through website development and print advertisements.

EDUCATION

D.MIN – 2007
Theological Seminary, Dayton, OH

MASTER OF DIVINITY – 1997
Princeton Theological Seminary, Princeton, NJ

BACHELOR OF ARTS – 1995
IPFW University, Fort Wayne, IN

MINISTRY PATH

Mount of Olives Baptist Church, Romans, IN   12/2002 – present

PASTORAL ASSISTANT and CHIEF OF MINISTERIAL STAFF
Facilitate communications and supervise the ministerial staff and Associate Ministers while fostering the development of programs that meet the needs of those within the congregation and community. Fulfill the duties of Senior Pastor as needed.

Union Baptist Church, Christian County, NJ   5/1997 – 11/2002

PASTOR
Prayerfully established the vision and direction for ministry programs and activities offered by the church. Supervised staff members and volunteers, realized consistent financial growth, and ensured operations stayed within established yearly budget.

Metropolitan Baptist Church, Living Word, NJ   6/1995 – 5/1997

YOUTH MINISTER
Researched needs of the congregation and community. Established the vision, direction, goals and objectives for the youth ministry. Designed needs-based programs and activities, established policies and procedures, and maintained an effective ministry program. Built rapport with staff members and volunteers, and helped recruit and train leaders. Created program awareness. Coordinated and launched various marketing activities.

Shiloh Baptist Church, Jordan, MO   9/1994 – 6/1995

YOUTH MINISTER
Organized ministry schedules and programs for the youth ministry and ensured open communications between youth members, families, pastoral staff, and church ministries. Continually assessed needs of the youth and introduced appropriate ministry programs.

Mount of Olives Baptist Church, Romans, IN   7/1992 – 8/1994

ASSOCIATE MINISTER
Supervised the youth ministry, co-founded the prison ministry, and served as President of the Young Adult Auxiliary under the leadership and supervision of Dr. Levi Roman. Provided pastoral care to the grieving, sick, and shut-ins. Preached the Gospel and taught Bible study, VBS, and summer enrichment programs.

AFFILIATIONS

Member
Society of Biblical Literature
American Academy of Religion

PERSONAL

Married
To wife, Julie Anne, for 10 years

Children
John (8), Debra (6), and Micah (3)

Health
In good health with no major medical complications

Hobbies
Enjoy reading, playing basketball, and spending time with family

KIMBERLY SMITH

Internship:
Corporate Interior Design Firm

EDUCATION

B.A. INTERIOR DESIGN, 5/2010, GPA 3.5
TEXAS TECH UNIVERSITY, Lubbock, TX
Minor in Marketing

Relevant Coursework:
- Computer Aided Design (CAD)
- Construction and Building Systems
- Contract Design I
- Contract Design II
- Design I
- Design II
- History of Interior Design
- Interior Drawing
- Internship I
- Kitchen and Bath Design
- Professional Practices
- Rendering and Presentation
- Residential Design I
- Surface Materials

EXPERIENCE

Receptionist / Bookkeeper   **2004 – 2010**
SMITH & SMITH, Dallas, Texas

Worked summers full-time for family-owned
legal practice.
- Scheduled appointments
- Greeted clients
- Routed telephone calls
- Recorded messages
- Scheduled conference room
- Performed data entry
- Balanced books
- Recorded staff meeting minutes

AWARDS & HONORS

- President's List, Fall 2009, Spring 2010
- Dean's List, Fall 2006, Spring 2009
- National Honor Society, 2010
- Who's Who, 2010
- Study Abroad, Summer 2008
- Omega Pi Honor Society, 2006
- Merit Honor Scholarship, 2005

ORGANIZATIONS

Kappa Delta Sorority, TTU, 2000 – present
- Rush Chair, 2007
- President, 2009
The Marketing Association, TTU, 2004 – present
American Young Designer Association, 2010

1234 89th Street, #12
Lubbock, Texas 79414
Ksmith531@protypeltd.com

806.555.1234

JOHN DAVIS DESIGN GROUP
1234 Tannenbaum Road
Colorado Springs, CO 80908
(719) 555-1234 Home
(719) 555-5678 Mobile
(719) 555-4321 Office
jdavis@protypeltd.com

John R. Davis

EXECUTIVE SUMMARY

- Licensed Architect in Colorado, Arizona, and Nevada.
- Proven skills in design consulting, land planning, architectural document development, construction administration, and project management.
- Efficiently managed projects valued from $50,000 to $20,000,000 with a keen eye on the bottom line. Saved clients thousands of dollars on finished projects.
- True professional who is viewed as the foundation of a project's successful completion.

PROFESSIONAL WORK HISTORY

Principal, John Davis Design Group, Colorado Springs, CO (2005–present)
Partner, DCA Architects, Colorado Springs, CO (1998–2005)
Senior Associate, Christiansen, Reece & Partners, Colorado Springs, CO (1988–1998)

KEY STRENGTHS AND ACCOMPLISHMENTS

- Use a hands-on approach to project management, making the client the priority and ensuring that each project is completed on time and within budget.
- Understand the technology of construction from the ground up. Spent formative years building homes with a general contractor father.
- Survived as a solo practice in spite of a recession economy.
- Developed a reputation for creative designs, hard work, and being willing to do what it takes to get the job done.
- Used expertise in efficient planning and effective utilization of space to develop buildings with high net-to-gross ratio, which results in cost-effective buildings.

INPUT–ANALYSIS–ACTION PLAN–CONSTRUCTION–SERVICE

- **Input** = Data gathering and budget setting. Develop design criteria, schedules, goals, objectives, and cohesive teams.
- **Analysis** = Review data, define space relationship criteria, document architectural materials, and identify planning alternatives.
- **Action Plan** = Define the final concept and space criteria for the project in enough detail to establish probable costs and time lines. Finalize building elevations, space allocations, and floor plans. Minimize change orders by being responsive to each client's design needs and ensuring that final construction documents are clear.
- **Construction** = Make site visits, attend project progress meetings, and confront any problems at once. Communicate constantly with general contractor, project manager, and client. Document any changes, monitor delays, and prepare accurate punch lists.
- **Service** = Supply warranty information and instructions. Record drawings. Maintain contact with the client during the first year of occupancy. Conduct an eleventh-month walk-through before expiration of the one-year warranty.

EDUCATION

ASSOCIATE OF ARCHITECTURE
Pikes Peak Community College, Colorado Springs, CO
Selected to serve on the Architecture Department Advisory Committee (1998–present). Meet annually with the department head and other distinguished graduates to brainstorm industry trends and recommend new courses.

COMPUTER SKILLS

Proficient in Windows, AutoCAD, MS Word, Outlook, and Internet Explorer.

RUSS MILLS

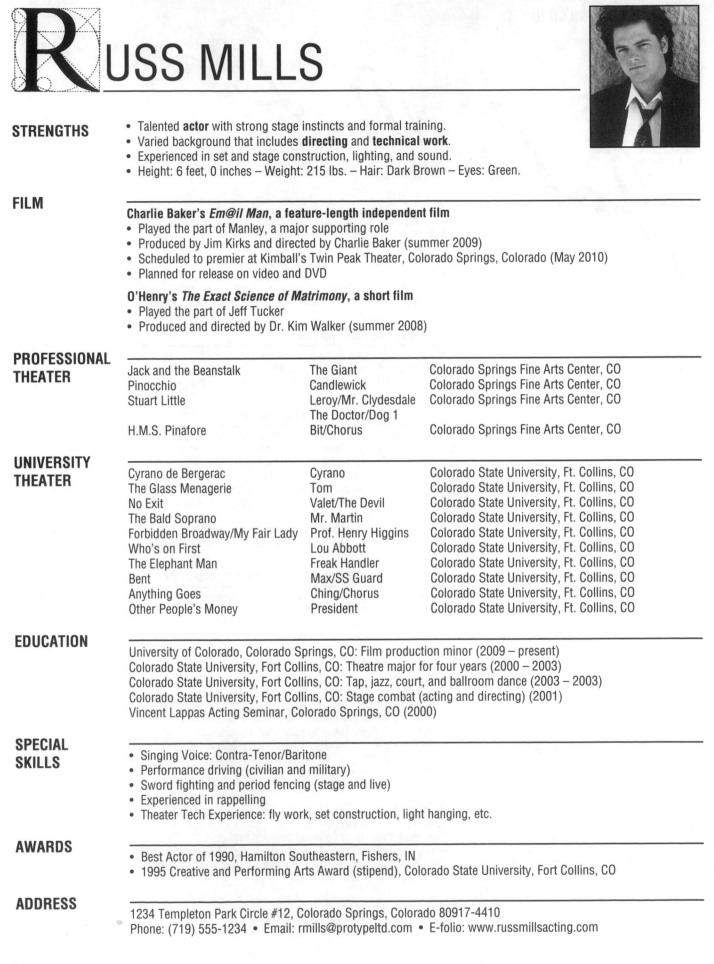

STRENGTHS
- Talented **actor** with strong stage instincts and formal training.
- Varied background that includes **directing** and **technical work**.
- Experienced in set and stage construction, lighting, and sound.
- Height: 6 feet, 0 inches – Weight: 215 lbs. – Hair: Dark Brown – Eyes: Green.

FILM

Charlie Baker's *Em@il Man*, a feature-length independent film
- Played the part of Manley, a major supporting role
- Produced by Jim Kirks and directed by Charlie Baker (summer 2009)
- Scheduled to premier at Kimball's Twin Peak Theater, Colorado Springs, Colorado (May 2010)
- Planned for release on video and DVD

O'Henry's *The Exact Science of Matrimony*, a short film
- Played the part of Jeff Tucker
- Produced and directed by Dr. Kim Walker (summer 2008)

PROFESSIONAL THEATER

Jack and the Beanstalk	The Giant	Colorado Springs Fine Arts Center, CO
Pinocchio	Candlewick	Colorado Springs Fine Arts Center, CO
Stuart Little	Leroy/Mr. Clydesdale	Colorado Springs Fine Arts Center, CO
	The Doctor/Dog 1	
H.M.S. Pinafore	Bit/Chorus	Colorado Springs Fine Arts Center, CO

UNIVERSITY THEATER

Cyrano de Bergerac	Cyrano	Colorado State University, Ft. Collins, CO
The Glass Menagerie	Tom	Colorado State University, Ft. Collins, CO
No Exit	Valet/The Devil	Colorado State University, Ft. Collins, CO
The Bald Soprano	Mr. Martin	Colorado State University, Ft. Collins, CO
Forbidden Broadway/My Fair Lady	Prof. Henry Higgins	Colorado State University, Ft. Collins, CO
Who's on First	Lou Abbott	Colorado State University, Ft. Collins, CO
The Elephant Man	Freak Handler	Colorado State University, Ft. Collins, CO
Bent	Max/SS Guard	Colorado State University, Ft. Collins, CO
Anything Goes	Ching/Chorus	Colorado State University, Ft. Collins, CO
Other People's Money	President	Colorado State University, Ft. Collins, CO

EDUCATION

University of Colorado, Colorado Springs, CO: Film production minor (2009 – present)
Colorado State University, Fort Collins, CO: Theatre major for four years (2000 – 2003)
Colorado State University, Fort Collins, CO: Tap, jazz, court, and ballroom dance (2003 – 2003)
Colorado State University, Fort Collins, CO: Stage combat (acting and directing) (2001)
Vincent Lappas Acting Seminar, Colorado Springs, CO (2000)

SPECIAL SKILLS
- Singing Voice: Contra-Tenor/Baritone
- Performance driving (civilian and military)
- Sword fighting and period fencing (stage and live)
- Experienced in rappelling
- Theater Tech Experience: fly work, set construction, light hanging, etc.

AWARDS
- Best Actor of 1990, Hamilton Southeastern, Fishers, IN
- 1995 Creative and Performing Arts Award (stipend), Colorado State University, Fort Collins, CO

ADDRESS

1234 Templeton Park Circle #12, Colorado Springs, Colorado 80917-4410
Phone: (719) 555-1234 • Email: rmills@protypeltd.com • E-folio: www.russmillsacting.com

302   *Creative Résumés*

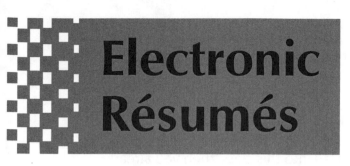

Electronic Résumés

Chapter 16

The Internet has changed the way the world does business, and job searching is no exception. On the Internet, you can find job openings anywhere in the world in a matter of seconds. According to The Conference Board, there were 4,150,000 unduplicated online job advertisements on 1,200 major Internet job boards at the beginning of 2010. The International Association of Employment websites *(www.employmentwebsites. org)* lists more than 60,000 premier job sites on the Internet that meet their strict membership requirements out of 100,000+ sites worldwide.

There have been massive changes in the recruiting industry over the past decade. Recruiting and job seeking transitioned from paper-based to electronic, and huge online job boards spurred a massive increase in online résumé submissions. Over the past few years, job boards have been contracting, consolidating, specializing, and evolving to the point where it's difficult to predict just how many will be left five years from now.

Web 2.0 has propelled hiring managers into real-time Googling of applicants, and applicants can now see job openings as soon as they hit the web. This real-time web makes it even easier to brand yourself and to keep the content you want employers to see on the first page of a Google search.

Résumés themselves have changed just as dramatically since 2000. Instead of paper résumés, digital résumés have become the main contact medium for more than 75% of the nation's employers. The only thing that hasn't changed is the purpose of a résumé. It is still an advertisement to promote your personal brand.

In order to make certain you have the right tools for today's job search, this chapter will cover three types of electronic résumés. The first type is a generic computer file that you create specifically to cut and paste your résumé into those little e-forms on the Internet—an ASCII text version. Sometimes these ASCII text files are what job sites expect you to "browse" for and upload.

The other two electronic résumés include your MS Word document and Adobe Acrobat PDF file, which you use to attach to e-mails or upload when a website allows you to "browse" for a résumé.

We will deal with a fourth type of electronic résumé in the next chapter, an HTML résumé that is posted on the Internet at your own website, e-folio, and/or blog.

Finally, I don't recommend a fifth type of electronic résumé—the digital video résumé—for the average job seeker, so this chapter won't even address the subject. Some recruiters are excited about the idea of screening candidates by video, but others are worried about the potential for discrimination based on race, age, and other factors, not to mention the time sink caused by viewing all of these files. In addition to these potential problems, the government requires that companies keep résumé data on file, and video résumés take up too much digital space.

I believe that video résumés cause more harm than good in most cases, since very few candidates are skilled in front of a camera. The exception might be a television broadcaster, news anchor, actor/actress, model, or musician. If you fall into this class, then you already know how to maximize the media, so you just need to find the technical help to create the kind of digital file you need and upload it to the Internet, either to your own personal website or to YouTube.

Video interviews, on the other hand, don't present the same potential and are used by recruiters to save travel costs of bringing a candidate to the company. To be successful on video, however, you need to feel comfortable with the medium, have a polished image, wear non-distractive clothing, watch what is in your background, sit close to the camera, speak slowly, keep your answers or comments brief, and don't yawn.

THE ASCII TEXT RÉSUMÉ

When you type words onto a computer screen in a word processing program (like MS Word), you are creating what is called a file or document. When you save that file, it is saved with special formatting codes like fonts, margins, tab settings, and so on, even if you didn't add these codes. Each word processing software saves its files in its own native format, making the file readable by anyone else with the same software version or with some other software that can convert that file to its own native format—think MS Word or Corel WordPerfect.

Only by choosing to save the document as a generic ASCII/Plain text file can your document be read by anyone, regardless of the word processing software he or she is using. This is the type of file you should create in order to send your résumé via e-mail.

An ASCII/Plain text file is simply words—no pictures, no fonts, no graphics, no tabs, no bold, no italics, etc.—just plain words. If you print this text, it looks very boring, but all the words that describe your life history are there, just as they are in the handsome paper résumé you created to mail to a potential employer or take to an interview. This computer file can be sent to a potential employer in one of two ways.

First, you can send the file directly to a company's recruiter via an e-mail address. Second, you can use this file to post your résumé onto the Internet at a company's website or to a job bank in answer to an online job posting (such as at *www.careerbuilder.com*). In any case, the file ends up in the same type of computerized database in which the e-mailed résumés have been stored.

There are many advantages to e-mailed résumés. First, they save you money over conventional mailing of a paper copy of your résumé with a cover letter. Second, they are faster, getting to a potential employer in only seconds instead of days. And, lastly, your résumé will be accessible every time time the hiring manager searches the résumé database using keywords. Your résumé will never again languish in a dusty filing cabinet.

A recent survey conducted by the Society of Human Resource Managers (SHRM) found that two-thirds of human resource professionals would prefer to receive résumés by e-mail—and your job is to make them happy.

STEPS FOR CREATING AN *ASCII* TEXT FILE OF YOUR RÉSUMÉ

To make sense of this topic, you must first understand the difference between a native word processing format and an ASCII text file. ASCII (pronounced "askee") is an abbreviation for American Standard Code for Information Interchange. It is a universal code that nearly all computers understand. ASCII text files (sometimes called Plain Text or MS-DOS Text) are very generic—they have no special fonts, margins, tabs, bold, italic, or other formatting codes added. When you create a file in a word processor (like Microsoft Word), on the other hand, the program automatically formats and saves its files in a "native" format. This native format includes codes that not all computers or software programs can read.

Don't use any special bells and whistles when you type your ASCII résumé in a word processing program. That means don't use boldface, underline, italics, fonts, font size, margin settings, and so on. Tabs will disappear when you convert your file to text, so use your spacebar to move words over instead of tabs. Rather than trying to force lines into bulleted phrases, I recommend using paragraphs and generous white space on an ASCII résumé.

Also be careful of the "smart quotes" that many word processing programs automatically place when you press the " key on your keyboard. These special characters will not translate when you save your file as ASCII text. That includes mathematical symbols, em-dashes, en-dashes, and any character that does not appear on your keyboard.

Your choices for bullets are also limited to the characters on your keyboard. Some of the better symbol choices to highlight lines of text are ~, *, +. You can use special characters from your keyboard to create dividers, like a series of ~~~~~ or ----------- or ===== or ********.

Do not set full justification on an ASCII résumé. Instead left justify all lines so the right margin is ragged.

You can't control how someone else's e-mail software will format your message at the other end. If you force lines in your e-mail message to end at 60 characters, they won't display properly on someone else's smaller screen (like a Blackberry, Palm Pre, or iPhone). When you type your résumé text, let your sentences "wrap" to a new line so the pasted text will adjust itself to the width of the e-mail message screen or electronic form on the Internet. Use the "enter" key to add extra white space between paragraphs and sections not at the end of lines within a paragraph. That way, you can be sure the lines will break correctly and your ASCII résumé will look neat on the screen.

Don't worry about the page breaks that your word processor shows you. They won't matter once the text is pasted into your e-mail or into an electronic form on the Internet, since the text adjusts itself to fit the available space.

An ASCII résumé can be longer than one page, but remember that you have one screen full of space (about 15 lines) to grab your reader's attention and motivate him or her to click down to the next screen. You should start with a summary of your qualifications and achievements at the top of your résumé and then list your chronology of experience.

If you have already created a neat, formatted paper résumé and have saved it on your computer, it is easy to strip it of all the codes by saving it as an ASCII text file. In most word processing software, you can select "Save As" from the "File" menu and choose "Plain Text" (or "MS DOS Text" in some versions). Remember to save the file under a new name with a ".txt" extension. You don't want to save over your formatted paper résumé and lose all that hard work! See the screen shot below for the process in Microsoft Word.

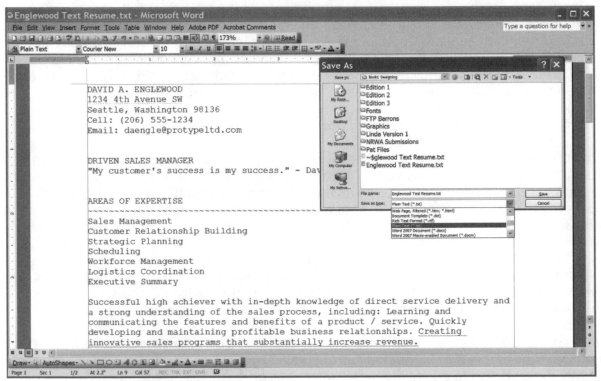

Screen shot of Microsoft Word used with permission of Microsoft Corporation.

In Corel WordPerfect, the best file type to select is "ASCII (DOS) Generic Word Processor," which maintains the wrap at the end of lines. If you choose "ASCII DOS Text" in WordPerfect, the file will be saved with hard returns at the end of every line of text and it won't wrap correctly when pasted into an e-mail or e-form on the Internet. Just as in Microsoft Word, after you have saved the file as a ".txt" file, you must then open it again and clean up the text.

Now that you have a generic file on your computer screen, you need to be careful how you save that file, or your word processor will still add hidden codes that will make your file jumbled on the Internet. You must always remember to "Save As" from the "File" menu or your word processor's default format will take over. Repeat the instructions above for saving the file as an "ASCII (DOS) Generic Word Processor" in Corel WordPerfect or "Plain Text" in Microsoft Word.

On the following pages are sample résumés created in word processing programs but saved as ASCII text files and then cleaned up. You will notice that they are nothing special to look at and are more than one page long, but hiring managers are accustomed to seeing these generic files and aren't expecting beauty. Their e-mail software will probably change the font (which you can't control), so your résumé won't look quite as bad as it does on your screen.

RENA D. SMITH
1234 Wild Trap Drive
Colorado Springs, Colorado 80925
Home: (719) 555-1234
Cell: (719) 555-5678
E-mail: rena.smith@protypeltd.com
LinkedIn: www.linkedin.com/in/rdsmith

PROFILE

Proven team leader with a strong background in telecommunications customer service. High-energy professional who enjoys the challenge of solving complex problems. Experienced supervisor with a reputation for team building, coaching, and mentoring. Strengths: detail oriented, flexible, analytical, self-motivated, and articulate. Experienced in Windows, MS Word, Excel, Netscape, Internet Explorer, and Vision software.

EXPERIENCE

QWEST (Formerly US WEST Communications), Denver, Colorado
Excelled in supervisory positions for this telecommunications leader over a 25+ year career. Awarded numerous certificates, stock options, and bonuses for excellence in service. Achieved President's Club twice, an honor reserved for the top 10 percent of employees nationwide.

LEAD PROCESS ANALYST
Federal Government Division, Colorado Springs, Colorado (2008 to present)
Provide tier-two technical support to sales personnel in all 50 states. Handle escalated and chronic problems for federal government customers, including missed deadlines, facility issues, and special projects. Required to respond within one hour of being contacted and to provide constant feedback to all parties involved. Collaborate with internal departments and nationwide customers to manage large projects. Serve as a member of the Emergency Response Team for 14 states in the Qwest network. On call 24/7. Received recognition for exceptional service. Fill in for supervisors and peers during absences. Assist in coaching customer relations managers in the Federal Government Customer Care Group. Received a Certificate of Appreciation for coordinating the NATO project in 2007.

PROCESS MANAGER
Construction/Engineering Staff, Denver, Colorado (2005 to 2008)
Evaluated whether the Perigon initiative (a legacy system upgrade) and its four component projects will improve productivity, cost effectiveness, contractor accountability, accuracy and quality of work, and the ability to interface with current systems. Created 30 user guides to provide standard methods and procedures for each type of user. Assisted in deploying the new systems in 14 states, including user demonstrations and training programs. Worked closely with creative services to develop a training video to educate users on new systems; responsible for scripting, editing, music and graphic selection, and content. Collaborated with field, construction, and engineering staff to ensure a smooth transition of work and to develop productivity measures for system users.

CONSTRUCTION MANAGEMENT CENTER SUPERVISOR
Colorado Springs, Colorado (2004 to 2005)
Supervised the Construction Management Center for the southern and western Colorado territories. Processed 400 to 500 construction jobs a month, including scheduling, monitoring, updating, tracking, and ordering of materials for the office and outside plant cable. Supervised 10 analytical associates, 2 clerical contractors, an administrative assistant, network technician, and job force manager. Worked closely with engineers, senior executives, and other internal/external customers to maintain work flow and certification

standards. Responsible for reports, held orders, designed services, and database maintenance. Served as management's representative to the union; responded to discrimination, performance, and attendance issues.

CENTRAL OFFICE MANAGER
Colorado Springs, Colorado (1997 to 2004)
Managed the daily operations of a 1,500 square-mile territory with 24 offices and 3 area codes that included Colorado Springs, Glenwood Springs, and Idaho Springs. Supervised, coached, and trained 17 technicians, ensuring safety, productivity, and quality performance. Coordinated the scheduling and completion of all central office jobs. Responsible for meeting design service and delayed order commitments. Managed several projects to convert switches from analog to digital and to upgrade, add, or remove central office and power equipment. Succeeded in reducing staff overtime by changing work schedules to better meet customer demand and by cross-training technicians.

NAC/MPAC MANAGER
Colorado Springs, Colorado (1996 to 1997)
Managed the Number Assignment Center (NAC) and the Machine Performance Assignment Center (MPAC). Supervised a system support group of 15 employees responsible for assigning telephone numbers and tracking central office equipment. Collaborated with engineers to add or replace central office equipment.

EDUCATION

REGIS UNIVERSITY, Colorado Springs, Colorado (2004 to 2008)
Courses in business management

CONTINUING EDUCATION
Computers: Microsoft Word, Excel, PowerPoint, Internet Explorer, Outlook
Leadership: Quality Team, Leadership Renewal, Team Problem Solving, Initial Management Course, Team Building, Project Management, Labor Relations
Training: Train the Trainer, Detailed Quality Engineering

AFFILIATIONS

Executive Women International, Vice President and various committees. Coordinated the national conference hosted by the Denver chapter. Selected the location, lodging, meals, hospitality room, and conference agenda.

Silver Key, Board of Directors, 7 years.

MATTHEW C. GELLER
1234 Knoll Lane, Apt. 123
Colorado Springs, Colorado 80917
Home: (719) 555-1234
Cellular: (719) 555-5678
E-mail: mcgeller@protypeltd.com

BACKGROUND
==
Experienced Engineer with a strong background in:
* Electromechanical systems
* Research and development
* Hydraulics and pneumatics
* Robots and robotic controllers
* Lasers
* Optics
* Servo systems
* Precision measuring instruments
* Extremely close tolerances
Eight years of experience servicing medical equipment in the field and
factory, including x-ray, mammography, hematology,and immunoassay sys-
tems. Experienced with FDA inspections and regulations for the inspec-
tion of prototype medical equipment. Extensive expertise in module inte-
gration at the system level. Collaborated with R&D engineers to build
and test prototyped enhancements to existing systems.

STRENGTHS
==
Adaptable engineer who can readily transfer skills and bring a fresh
perspective to any industry. Effective communicator with the ability to
provide exceptional customer service at all levels. Experienced trainer
with extensive hands-on and classroom technical experience. Proficient in
Windows, MS Word, Excel, PowerPoint, Outlook, and Internet Explorer.

MEDICAL EXPERIENCE
==
ENGINEERING SERVICE TECHNICIAN (2002 to 2005)
Lorad, Inc., Danbury, Connecticut
Directed a team of eight electromechanical technicians in the construction and testing of mammography and x-ray equipment. Spent 50 percent
of time providing field service to downed equipment in a large territory
with ten hospitals. Collaborated with R&D engineers on design improvements and prototype enhancements for new product lines. Met with customers to determine liability for warranty problems and negotiated settle-
ments. Trained new technicians, field engineers, and customers on equipment and tool repair. Helped write assembly and repair procedures for
factory and field service personnel. Installed and monitored systems at
hospital beta test sites. Provided technical phone assistance to service
engineers. Performed system upgrades in both field and factory settings.

SENIOR ENGINEERING SERVICE TECHNICIAN (1997 to 2002)
Miles, Inc., Tarrytown, New York
Led a team of 15 electromechanical, electrical, and test technicians
in the research and development of hematology and immunoassay systems.
Conducted quality control inspections of in-production and finished modules. Managed materials and production control for the entire product
line. Worked closely with design engineers on product improvements and
prototype development. Responsible for troubleshooting and repairing all
electromechanical, cable, hydraulic, and pneumatic problems. Wrote all
training manuals for new electromechanical assemblies. Trained domestic
and international field engineers on electromechanical systems and served
as an expert resource for field service engineers. Transferred systems
from an R&D environment to the production plant in Puerto Rico. Trained,
installed, and retrofit legacy systems. Accountable for controlling
inventory of parts and maintaining repair logs of systems. Installed
systems at beta testing sites for FDA approval; collaborated with FDA
inspectors on revisions to new systems before production release.

TECHNOLOGY EXPERIENCE
==
SENIOR FIELD SERVICE ENGINEER (2000 to 2008)
SVG Lithography, Wilton, Connecticut / ASML, Tempe, Arizona
Stationed at an Intel chip-manufacturing site in Colorado Springs in
order to troubleshoot and maintain SVG lithography equipment (valued
at $10 million) from component to system levels. Installed new tools
as they arrived at the site, and performed lithographic testing to
ensure tools meet customer specifications. Performed system upgrades
and modifications at the request of customer and/or factory. Provided
technical phone assistance to other sites and managed all warranty
issues. Diagnosed and repaired computerized electromechanical systems. Maintained and tracked precision-calibrated tools used for system
repairs. Trained new employees on all tool phases from module replacement to troubleshooting down to the component level. Interviewed, made
hiring recommendations, supervised, and evaluated 10 engineering technicians. Prepared daily and weekly site reports and part repair logs; met
with senior customer engineers daily. Wrote training manuals for certain
modules and documented repair procedures. Developed an automated journal
system that tracked weekly repair time using Excel.

Key Accomplishments: Helped identify a duct work error that was costing Intel $100,000 per shift because of contamination blowing up from
the sub-fab. Saved Intel $250,000 by changing motor coils in the
system rather than replacing the entire module. Cleaned vacuum ports,
which prevented replacement of the system, saving Intel an additional
$250,000. Received a Silicon Valley Group award in recognition of out-
standing contributions to the MSX and REA build process.

COMPUTER TECHNICIAN / ENGINEERING TECHNICIAN (1988 to 1992)
TAD Technical Services, Poughkeepsie, New York
Assigned to IBM to manage a team of five electromechanical technicians in
cabling and power supply installation on million-dollar mainframe computer systems. Served as a repair technician for all electromechanical,
cabling, and power supply issues. Collaborated with design engineers on

```
product improvements. Performed quality control inspections on cabling
with a 98 percent defect-free rate for the entire group. Rewrote assem-
bly procedures, enabling a reduction in build time from eight hours to
four hours or less. Responsible for materials management and production
control in designated area. Trained new employees on cabling and power
supply system installation and quality control.


EDUCATION
=========================================================
UNDERGRADUATE STUDIES (2005 to 2008)
Duchess Community College, Poughkeepsie, New York

PROFESSIONAL DEVELOPMENT
General Industry Safety and Health (10 hours, 2001)
* OSHA/SVG Safety
* Lockout/Tag Out
* Walking and Working Surfaces
* Physical Hazards
* Job Hazard Analysis
* Chemical Hazards
* Hazardous Energies
* Egress and Fire Protection
* Electrical Safety
* Personal Protection/PPE

Micrascan Training (2006)
* Computerized Electromechanical Systems
* Environmental Control Systems
```

HOW TO COMPOSE AND SEND AN E-MAILED RÉSUMÉ

You may be thinking, "I can do this. I'll just skip this section." Don't! Even though the pro-cess itself is pretty basic, there are a few tricks of the trade that you shouldn't miss, so please read this section completely.

You can type your entire résumé into an e-mail message from scratch, but why would you do that when you have already typed it, spell checked it, and used your word processor's grammar function? When you are composing a cover letter and/or résumé for e-mail, it is always much better to start with your word processor since you can use its power-ful grammar and spell check features to make certain your document is perfect before e-mailing it to a potential employer.

After you have created this perfect résumé in your word processor and saved it in ASCII text format, open the ASCII file again in your word processor. Click on "Edit" and choose "Select All." Then click on "Edit" and choose "Copy."

Open your e-mail software. After you have typed in the address where you will be send-ing your message and added your subject line, click on the message box so your cursor is active in the large white space. Then select "Edit" and choose "Paste." Your text will appear in the message box.

Now you are ready to attach your Word file and click on "Send." Most e-mail programs will automatically log on for you and send your message, or you can schedule it to send later. Here are some screen shots from MS Word and Outlook to walk you through the process.

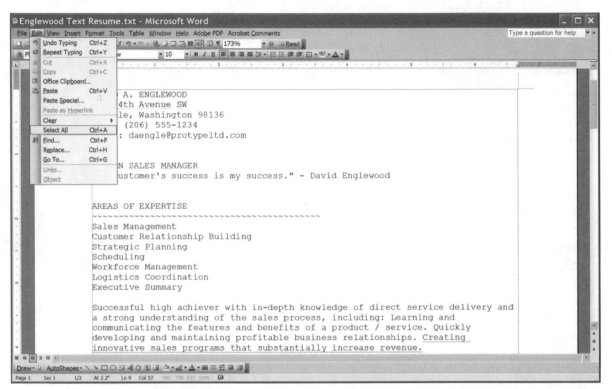

Screen shot of Microsoft Word used with permission of Microsoft Corporation.

Screen shot of Microsoft Word used with permission of Microsoft Corporation.

Screen shot of Microsoft Outlook used with permission of Microsoft Corporation.

Screen shot of Microsoft Outlook used with permission of Microsoft Corporation.

The subject line is a valuable tool for introducing who you are and what you do. Don't neglect this line. You can use it for your objective statement, to reference the job opening for which you are applying, or to show that you are updating a résumé you have sent previously. Never leave a subject line blank, since that is the hallmark of spam (junk mail). I know that I never open e-mail messages sent to me without a subject line, and I've heard the same comment from many recruiters.

What about a cover letter? Remember that e-mail is intended to be quick, so don't precede your pasted résumé with a long-winded cover letter. A simple paragraph or two that highlights your best qualifications and tells your reader where you heard about the position is all you need. I recommend that you limit your cover letter to no more than two paragraphs, although there are exceptions to every rule in the career business. Here's a sample cover letter that you can paste above your résumé in an e-mail:

> *I found your posting for a Customer Service Manager (Job #12343) on the Internet at Indeed.com and would appreciate your serious consideration of my qualifications. I have more than thirteen years of operations management experience that included budget analysis and tracking ($13 million), expense control, staffing, training, and customer service. I have succeeded in significantly controlling costs and maximizing productivity in all my jobs. I could also bring to this position my team spirit, ability to manage multiple priorities with time-sensitive deadlines, and strong communication skills.*
>
> *Pasted below is the text version of my résumé and attached is the MS Word document as your advertisement requested. I look forward to hearing from you soon.*
>
> *Sincerely, Jane Doe*

Now, experiment. Send the résumé to yourself or a friend, print it, and see what it looks like. Also look at it on your computer screen. If the text and spacing didn't translate correctly, this is the time to fix it. Save it again and then try the e-mail one more time. Once it is perfect, you are ready to use the file in e-mail and on the Internet.

MS WORD AND PDF RÉSUMÉS

You may be asking why you can't just attach a Microsoft Word file to the e-mail message and forget about this cut and paste thing. First of all, when you attach a file to an e-mail message, the recipient of your e-mail will see only what you have typed in the subject line and your brief cover letter in the message box saying that your résumé is attached. If he doesn't have time to double click the attached file to open it immediately, then he will click on "Download Now" to save your résumé on his hard drive. Later, he will have to remember that he has a file to view, recall where he saved it on the hard drive, and then open MS Word in order to view your résumé. Wouldn't you much rather have him begin reading the text of your résumé the minute he opens his e-mail? If he wants to see the formatted version, he can always download your PDF file or MS Word document and look at it later.

There is also the chance that the recipient won't have the right software to open your file, either. For many years, I have known a small, niche recruiter without a large office staff. He never invested in the Microsoft Office software, so every time he received an attached MS Word file, he would send it to me to print and then he would collect the paper printouts once a week or so. He didn't have Adobe Acrobat on his system until just last week, even though it's free at *www.adobe.com!*

Speaking of Adobe Acrobat (PDF) files, there was a time when applicant tracking software could not interpret PDF files, so résumés sent in that format were never added to the databases. That is changing now. The majority of these software systems have now become capable of importing PDF files and extracting the information into their applicant tracking systems. Résumés created using Adobe InDesign, Corel WordPerfect, Microsoft Works, or Microsoft Publisher should be printed to PDF or converted to MS Word before sending to a hiring company.

If you don't have Microsoft Word software, there are several free programs available online that can save your information in Word or PDF format. Try Google Docs (*docs.google.com*), ZoHo Writer *(writer.zoho.com),* Open Office Suite *(download.openoffice.org),* or Microsoft Office Web Apps *(www.officelive.com/en-us/).*

There was a time when recruiters were afraid of viruses in attached files, but nearly all companies have implemented antivirus software or realize that they can choose not to download an attached file if they are concerned. In the 2010 Orange County Résumé Survey, 62.70% of recruiters preferred receiving résumés in MS Word (.doc or docx) format and 36.10% preferred Adobe Acrobat (.pdf).

You should send only one attachment with any one e-mail, and that file should be your MS Word or PDF résumé. Some people still have difficulty with "zipped" (compressed) files. When you attach more than one file to any e-mail, it is automatically compressed into a single file for transmission over the Internet. At your recipient's end, you have to be confident that the person's e-mail software will automatically "unzip" the files. Although it is becoming more likely that the decompression will be automatic, I can't guarantee it in every case. For that reason, I recommend that you send only one file attached to your e-mail. It is better to be safe than sorry.

Sending ASCII text e-mail across the Internet is relatively painless, but attaching binary files can get complicated. First, both you and your recipient must have the same (or newer) version of the software used to create your "pretty" résumé. For instance, if you created a résumé in Microsoft Word 2010 and your recipient has Word 95, she won't be able to open the file at all.

What if you used a unique font to design your Word résumé, but your recipient's computer doesn't support that font? Then your résumé will adjust to a new default font, and your résumé will look different from how you created it. The newer versions of MS Word and Corel WordPerfect now allow you to embed TrueType and OpenType fonts (but not Adobe Type One fonts) in documents, which helps prevent this problem. However, you must set up each document in MS Word by clicking on "Tools," "Options," "Save," and "Embed True-Type Fonts." In WordPerfect, you check the "Embed Fonts" box on the "Save As" option.

There are many things you can't control when sending e-mail. You can't control whether the recipient's printer definition will reformat your MS Word file. And you can't control how your recipient's e-mail software decodes your MS Word file. In order to send files across the network of computers that make up the Internet, binary files must be encoded in a special way before they are sent and then decoded when they are received at the other end. Each file is broken into tiny packets of information and sent across various parts of the web. At the recipient's end, those packets must be put back together again . . . and in the right order!

Most e-mail software will automatically encode an attached file, so it is invisible to you. However, sending between different platforms (PCs, Macintosh, UNIX) can sometimes cause problems with decoding.

There are so many things you can't control when sending binary files across the Internet that you want to take the safest route possible. And that route is to cut and paste your ASCII text file into the e-mail message screen. Then it is okay to attach an MS Word document or PDF file to the e-mail. Your reader can choose to download it or not, but you haven't lost anything because your résumé is being read right on the screen.

Let's take a look at how you attach a file in Microsoft Outlook at the top of the next page. It is as simple as clicking on the paper clip and telling Outlook where to find the file you want to attach. That file can be stored on your hard drive, a CD-ROM, flash drive, or some other digital storage medium. Once you select the file, it is automatically attached to your e-mail message and is ready to be sent.

UPLOADING YOUR RÉSUMÉ TO THE INTERNET

Once you have the ASCII text, MS Word, and PDF versions of your résumé stored on your hard drive, you are ready to upload the appropriate one to job boards on the Internet, create profiles, and set up job alerts/agents.

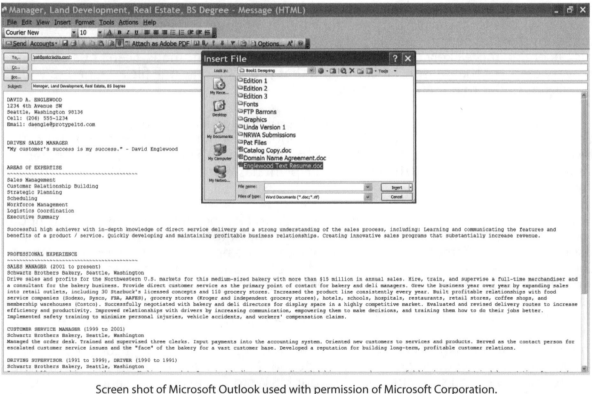

Screen shot of Microsoft Outlook used with permission of Microsoft Corporation.

First, upload your résumé to company websites that interest you. Then choose niche job sites that are specific to your industry or specialty. Find them with keyword searches on Google or Yahoo. Lastly, I recommend setting up accounts with one or two job aggregators—*like www.indeed.com, www.simplyhired.com, www.jobster.com*—and big job boards— like *www.careerbuilder.com* and *www.usajobs.opm.gov.* The big job boards—like *www. monster.com*—are so huge and so full of junk résumés and stale job openings that recruiters are turning to niche sites, free sites *(www.craigslist.com),* and social networking media to post their jobs. Instead of paying to post jobs on Monster or CareerBuilder, recruiters are gravitating toward career sites where they pay only when a candidate has pulled up their ad and either clicked through to the company's website or applied through the career site itself. It won't take long for the mega-career-sites to adapt to this pay-per-click format, but for now, you should cover all of your bases.

On job boards and company websites, you will have the option of filling out their online résumé builders or cutting and pasting your ASCII text résumé into e-forms on their websites. Open your ASCII text résumé in MS Word, highlight the portions of your résumé that you need for each block in the e-form, and then paste the text into the form. There is no reason to retype information that has already been spell checked.

CareerBuilder offers you the option to browse and upload your résumé, which most of us would assume would be an MS Word file. However, if you do upload a formatted, "pretty" résumé, it will look jumbled when you go to preview it. CareerBuilder is actually looking for an ASCII text file.

Regardless of where your résumé is saved on the Internet, refresh it every month by changing a word or two and re-saving it. Some sites have a "refresh" button so you don't have to change anything. Just click the button once per month and your résumé will be back on top of the heap.

While you are at it, create a profile at each site and set up job agents that send job openings to you every day or every week that match your keywords and geographic preferences. Don't just post your résumé and wait for employers to find you, which happens less than 7% of the time. Creating job agents allows you to take control of your search by responding to each job that interests you.

There are privacy issues to consider when setting up these accounts. The threat of identity theft, job scams, and exposure to spam are real issues on the web, although it happens much less often than you think. Use your common sense when you look for jobs online, including work-at-home offers. Job hunting scams rank fifth on the Better Business Bureau's top 10 scams and rip-offs for 2010, so you should evaluate each job advertisement with a healthy dose of skepticism. If it sounds too good to be true, it probably is.

Expect to get a lot of junk e-mail after setting up accounts with job boards. You will get spam, work-from-home offers, get-rich-quick schemes, and true scams, but they are easy to spot and sort out. If you have a favorite e-mail address that you want to keep forever, you might want to consider setting up a separate e-mail account just for your job search so you can trash it once you are done looking for a job. Then you won't continue to get inundated by spam and other junk e-mail.

So, what Internet resources should you use to reach the right recruiters and hiring managers? If you are an active job seeker who is either unemployed or actively looking for a new job, post your résumé on job boards, résumé databases, and social networking sites. Develop an e-folio and/or blog. Look for print advertising and job fairs.

Passive job seekers, on the other hand, are reached by recruiters through referrals, networking, blogs, e-folios, résumé databases, niche websites, professional associations, social networking sites, and even competitive intelligence. Passive job seekers are already working and are usually the star performers working for other companies.

If you have applied for a job online and are now sitting around waiting to hear from an employer, then you might want to consider a new CareerBuilder tool. HireINSIDER gives you insight into the jobs you've applied for by providing you with information about other people who have applied to the same job, including

- **Number of Applications**—How many people have applied? Were you first or last?
- **Years of Experience**—Are you competing against senior or entry level candidates?
- **Education Level**—What types of education are you up against? Masters? Bachelors?
- **Current Salary**—How much is your competition making now?
- **Top Majors**—What did your competition study in college?
- **Cover Letter Usage**—Is everyone submitting a cover letter? Should you submit one?

Katharine Hansen's Quintessential Careers 2010 Annual Report emphasizes that face-to-face job search techniques are more important than ever. She recommends stepping away from your computer to network with warm bodies. Deploy a combination of job boards, social media, and networking. You should remain vigilant about the downsides of job boards and learn how to use them most effectively. It's easy to spend too many hours trolling job sites instead of doing the harder work of calling and meeting people, so monitor yourself closely and cast as wide a net as possible.

Today, more than ever, job searching is about who you know and who knows you. It's also about identifying the needs of potential employers and demonstrating that you can fill these needs. The next chapter will address your online branding presence in the form of a personal website, e-folio, and/or a blog, which will allow you to connect your proven knowledge, skills, and abilities with the needs of those employers.

e-Folios & Blogs

Chapter

17

Imagine a musician playing her latest composition, a teacher incorporating a video of his teaching style, a poet reading clips from her poetry, or an entertainer demonstrating his latest dance steps. The creative juices are flowing! Web-based, HTML résumés and e-folios are the perfect places to showcase skills that are better seen (or heard) in all their glory, but that's not the limit.

If you are a C-level executive, self-employed consultant, computer programmer, website developer, politician, graphic designer, artist, sculptor, chef, actor, model, animator, cartoonist, poet, writer, or anyone who would benefit by the photographs, graphics, animation, sound, color, or movement inherent in a web-based portfolio, then you should definitely read this chapter.

If you don't fall into one of these categories, read the rest of this chapter anyway, because you will be surprised how an e-folio can enhance your job search and help you manage your career even while you are currently employed. If you want to control what a hiring manager sees when you are "Googled," then a well-designed and promoted e-folio and/or blog are your answer. They allow you to control your online image and differentiate yourself. Having an online presence should be a critical piece of your career management plan.

Before we get into the details, though, let's talk about the various names for these online forms of your résumé so you don't become confused. According to Webster, a portfolio is *"a hinged cover or flexible case for carrying loose papers, pictures, or pamphlets," "a set of pictures (as drawings or photographs) usually bound in book form or loose in a folder,"* or *"a selection of a student's work (as papers and tests) compiled over a period of time and used for assessing performance or progress."* Well, substitute the case or book for a website and the student's work for your work and you have an e-folio.

I held a contest among the nearly 500 members of the National Résumé Writers' Association to find the perfect name, but even though Cheryl Minnick (a career advisor at The University of Montana, Missoula) came close with CareerDocs, *e-folio* couldn't be beat, so I will use the word *e-folio*. You might find an e-folio called CareerDocs, Visual CV, CareerFolio, Portfolio, Personal Branding Portal, CareerDock, Professional Portal, Career Hub, and various versions of Web Resume (without the accents).

A Web Résumé or an e-Folio?

A web résumé is simply your paper résumé converted to a website using HTML codes. It is rather basic without a lot of extra information. Instead of having a single page on your website, however, a web résumé is usually divided into sections that are accessed through hyperlinks from an introductory page—Career Objective, Summary, Skills, Experience, Education, Affiliations, and so on. You can add information that you couldn't include in your paper résumé, but the more information you add, the more like an e-folio your web résumé will become.

If you have more information about your career than you can practically include in a résumé, then an e-folio is a great option for making this additional information available to a potential employer. An e-folio provides visible evidence of your knowledge, skills, abilities, and core competencies. It features links to proofs of performance that control how your target audience views your unique value proposition. Make sure your website looks professional, though. You want to establish a virtual rapport with your site visitors so you can emotionally connect with them.

You've heard the old saying, "A picture is worth a thousand words." That is the primary advantage of e-folios. They are more tangible with links to PDF files, scanned images, podcasts, and video downloads. You can talk about what you've accomplished in words (either on paper or verbally) from now until doomsday, but nothing makes an impression like tangible, visual backup, especially today when so many recruiters and hiring managers are skeptical of claims made on résumés.

Another advantage of an e-folio is the first impression it makes. Dr. John Sullivan, Head Professor of Human Resource Management in the College of Business at San Francisco State University, says that "because portfolios take some effort, they demonstrate a degree of commitment on the part of the candidate that is not required in a résumé . . . so it improves the quality of new hires."

Most of us think of artists, models, actors, and photographers when we think of a portfolio, but that's not the case today. Everyone should maintain a portfolio. More and more employers are asking to see concrete evidence of the experience, skills, education, and accomplishments shown on your résumé, especially during the interview.

An e-folio allows you to present additional details that expand on your résumé, like:

- Case studies
- Project lists
- Career highlights
- Consulting gigs
- Leadership initiatives
- Volunteer experience
- Photographs
- Professional affiliations
- Board positions
- Your blog and archives
- Links to your favorite blogs

- Credentials
- Education
- Certifications
- Achievements
- Skills and strengths
- Patents
- Honors and awards
- Endorsements
- Upcoming events
- Technical competencies
- Sales statistics

- Media interviews
- Presentations
- Demonstrations
- Speaking engagements
- Publications
- Book Reviews
- Newsletters
- Links to favorite blogs/sites
- Frequently asked questions
- A recommended reading list
- Writing samples

KEEP AN "I LOVE ME" FILE

For years, in my own practice, I've been advising my clients to keep an "I Love Me" file with performance evaluations, job descriptions, letters of recommendation, thank you notes from customers, vendors, or supervisors, sales statistics, growth charts, writing samples, awards, honors, scanned product images, photographs, or even three-dimensional items that expand on or support the outline that is inherent in their résumés. If you have collected this information during your entire career, then you have the foundation for an e-folio that will help you sell your special abilities and manage your entire career. If you haven't, then create an e-folio with whatever you do have or can get your hands on now. It's never too late to start collecting for your "I Love Me" file.

Your e-folio cannot take the place of your paper résumé, ASCII text résumé, and MS Word or PDF file. In today's busy world, most recruiters and hiring managers have so little time to read résumés that they are turning to applicant tracking systems to lighten their load. Unless they are highly motivated, they won't take the time to search for and then spend fifteen minutes clicking their way through a multimedia presentation of someone's qualifications.

The real purpose of an e-folio is to manage your online reputation and to provide extra information for when a potential employer is trying to narrow down his or her applicant pool. You can even direct the hiring manager to your website during an interview. You are more likely to be Googled at the weeding-out stage, which is either just before an interview offer or after the interview. That is when an e-folio becomes truly valuable. It might just tip the scales when a hiring manager is trying to choose between you and someone else.

You should always direct your reader to your e-folio by listing the URL on your résumé, letterhead, personal business card, and e-mail signature. Place your URL in the appropriate field on job boards and social networking profiles so recruiters can click on the link to get more information about you—information that you control. Just don't expect to get a job offer by simply creating an e-folio and waiting for a recruiter to find you. You must still be proactive in your job search by signing up for job agents on the major job boards, applying for each job that interests you, and networking in the real world like crazy.

E-FOLIOS FOR MORE THAN JOB HUNTING

Besides keeping your résumé in front of recruiters by being on the Internet all of the time, a well-planned e-folio is great for formal employment interviews, networking, informational interviews, performance assessments and evaluations on your current job, admission to colleges and universities, easily accessed information for your references, and an archive that lets you download your résumés from anywhere in the world (think Hurricane Katrina), among other functions. It is a professional self-marketing tool that can help you manage your entire career.

An e-folio is especially useful for entrepreneurs and consultants, since it can serve as a marketing tool for whatever products or services they sell. If you think about it, though, we should all be treating our careers as "entrepreneurial" ventures. When you take control of your career as a business owner controls his or her company, you make conscious choices about how to market your product—in the case of your career, that's you. Your résumé becomes your print advertising and your e-folio is your online brochure that convinces a "buyer" to call you instead of the "competition."

An e-folio is also a great career management tool that you don't have to save just for your job search. Imagine preparing for your annual performance evaluation with your current employer by reviewing the accomplishments you have collected in your "I Love Me" file and putting together either a paper-based or web-based portfolio. When it is time to sit down with your supervisor and talk about what you have achieved this year, you can take control of the discussion by making a "sales presentation" of your accomplishments and tangible examples of work samples. What an impression you will make! You've got a raise!

Don't wait for your annual evaluation to think about using this tool. Many companies have implemented performance assessment programs that are ongoing with periodic meetings throughout the year to assess goals, milestones, and incremental achievements toward objectives.

If your company isn't that progressive and barely uses annual performance evaluations, let alone performance goal setting, then make yourself stand out in the crowd of other employees by being proactive. Develop your e-folio or paper portfolio and set the meeting with your supervisor yourself. Take charge of your career path and show your entrepreneurial spirit. Remember that entrepreneurship is all about "ownership," and you can own your career whether or not you own the business for which you work. This kind of independent thinking is often rewarded with promotions and/or pay increases that reflect your value to the company. It also makes your job more secure, since you have proven value to your employer. With downsizing the norm in today's workforce, the more valuable you are, the less likely you will be laid off. Companies are in the business of making money. If you make your employer more money than you cost to keep around, it just makes business sense that you will be retained.

When developing an e-folio, avoid proprietary/confidential employer information, personal information, family photographs, or negative comments about previous employers. If your website developer recommends a design that includes automatic background music or a lot of Flash programming, think twice before agreeing. They tend to be irritating to site visitors.

It is easy to overdo an e-folio. It is sometimes hard to narrow down the items you want to include, so people have a tendency to make their e-folios much too long. Dr. Sullivan feels that a world-class portfolio has the following five characteristics:

1. It must be scannable in fifteen minutes or less.
2. It sells you with your work and your ideas.
3. It is customized for each job and each company.
4. It includes and highlights your accomplishments.
5. It excites the viewer.

PORTFOLIO IDEAS BY JOB TYPE

Everybody's e-folio will be different, especially across industries and job titles. Even when two people share the same position in the same company, they shouldn't expect the contents of their e-folios to be the same. We each have our own unique backgrounds, qualifications, and accomplishments. However, there are some basic items that will appear in all e-folios:

1. A home page that highlights your unique value proposition with a tagline and/or vision statement, executive summary, areas of expertise, contact information, your blog, and links to archives. If you use work samples or testimonials on your e-folio, get permission first. Integrate social media links, video, audio, or anything that enhances your professional image.

2. A résumé—Your résumé (or bio in some cases) generally serves as the foundation of your e-folio. If it is well written, your résumé determines the basic outline for your website and helps you decide what sections to include. Don't simply rehash your résumé verbatim in your e-folio, however, or there is no point to your website. Summarize and expand on your résumé with job descriptions, employer reviews, work samples, problem-solving examples, organizational charts, leadership examples, customer survey results, proposals, business plans, and so on.

3. Proofs of performance—These can be charts or graphs if your accomplishments are quantifiable (like in sales and positions with P&L responsibility where you can show your bottom line results), copies of publicity, articles you have written, photographs, videos, company newsletters, white papers, special projects, newspaper or magazine articles, thank you letters from supervisors/customers/vendors, performance evaluations with key accomplishments highlighted, honors, awards, archived blog articles, volunteer or community affiliations, and so on. If any of the information you want to use is copyrighted by someone else, you will need to get written permission to use it on your website first.

4. Credentials—This is where you back up your education, special training, licenses, certifications, and other credentials with scanned images of your diplomas, certificates, transcripts (for some positions), and other proof documents. Lists of major course work and select projects might be included if you are a recent graduate with little experience.

5. Recommendations—Scan your letters of reference from past employers, current supervisors, key customers or vendors, and other people who know your work well. Highlight key phrases or simply type a list of quotes with the person's name, job title, and company. These third-party recommendations validate what you say about yourself in your own documentation.

Once your e-folio has the five basics, you can add other things to make it unique. Rather than repeat the items above for every industry, the lists below are in addition to your résumé, credentials, recommendations, and proofs of accomplishments (although some items fall into this category just to give you more ideas). Use your imagination. These lists are just jumping off points for your own creativity, which is really what you are trying to display in your e-folio anyway.

Accounting & Finance

- Charts showing improvements in revenues, profits, ROI, EBITDA, etc.
- Special projects, i.e., automation projects, business performance optimization
- Mergers, acquisitions, joint ventures, and divestitures
- Client and/or industry specialties
- List of accounting software expertise

■ ■ ■ Administrative Assistant

- Lists of technical competencies
- Processes and procedures you improved
- Examples of various document preparation skills—correspondence, spreadsheets, PowerPoint presentations, forms, organizational charts, etc.
- Photos, agendas, budgets of events planned
- Letters of appreciation
- Certificates from classes, workshops, seminars, conferences

■ ■ ■ Antique & Art Dealer

- Areas of expertise
- Select finds and sources
- Valuation/appraisal experience
- Restoration experience with photos
- International travel
- Import/export
- Apprenticeships and other hands-on experience
- Education and credentials
- Letters or comments from clients

■ ■ ■ Apartment Manager

- Photos of properties
- Size and types of units (luxury, family, senior citizen)
- Amenities
- Construction or renovation
- Occupancy rates
- Special promotions, events, and open houses
- Activities for residents
- Graphics representing impact on the bottom line

■ ■ ■ Architect

- Drawings, photographs, blueprints
- Styles
- Honors and awards
- Media coverage
- Professional affiliations
- Presentations
- Letters from satisfied customers and builders
- Acknowledgments from peers
- Parade of Homes participation

■ ■ ■ Artist
(includes painters, sculptors, illustrators, designers, cartoonists, or anyone producing a visual art)

- Mediums
- Education and special training
- Photographs of artwork
- Published works
- Reviews in magazines, newspapers, and other publications
- Lists and photographs of exhibitions
- Representations

- Museum collections
- Descriptions of style and artist philosophy
- Hyperlinks to online displays of artwork

■ ■ ■ *Athlete*
- Sports
- Media coverage
- Records and times
- Competitions
- Honors, awards
- Coaches, trainers

■ ■ ■ *Attorney*
- Areas of specialty
- Credentials—diplomas, licenses, etc.
- Track record of success
- Client testimonials
- Lists of significant cases
- Legal precedents established
- Bar and court admissions
- Presentations
- Professional affiliations
- Pro bono work
- Volunteer board positions

■ ■ ■ *Chef*
- Menus
- Photographs of plated dinners and banquet presentations
- Thank you notes from customers
- Certificates of completion from special training programs
- Participation in stages and international programs
- Reviews in magazines, newspapers, and other publications
- Honors, awards, contests, chef's tables

■ ■ ■ *Computer Professional*
- Photographs of software packages or manuals
- Examples of a unique or difficult code and its result
- Screen shots of GUI interfaces
- Charts and graphs that show increases in productivity or profitability as a result of the finished product
- Technical skills divided into types
- Special projects
- Technical documents produced

■ ■ ■ *Construction*
- Areas of specialty
- Photos of completed projects
- Honors, awards, Parade of Homes, etc.
- Proof of licenses and bonding
- Letters from satisfied customers

- Community participation
- Professional affiliations

■ ■ ■ *Customer Service Representative*
- Letters from satisfied customers
- Awards for exceeding quotas
- Customer service scores
- Contributions to sales growth
- Personality tests (like Myers-Briggs) that show an aptitude for working with people

■ ■ ■ *Diplomat*
- Negotiations, conflict resolutions, treaties
- Languages, cultures
- Special events
- Media coverage
- White papers, publications
- Pictures with famous people
- Noteworthy speeches and other presentations

■ ■ ■ *Economist*
- Credentials are very important in this industry—education, degrees, training
- Areas of expertise—energy, inflation, imports, employment, monetary policy, consumer theory, markets, profits, costs, public policy
- Examples of research and analysis
- Expertise with statistical analysis software
- Sample spreadsheets, graphs, charts
- Publications
- Presentations
- Publicity

■ ■ ■ *Editor*
- Education and special training
- Writing samples
- List of own published works
- Types of editing—fiction, creative nonfiction, trade, nonfiction
- Editing samples—both hard copy and digital
- Titles of books edited

■ ■ ■ *Engineer*
- New products developed
- Drawings
- Schematics
- White papers
- Research
- Patents awarded or pending
- Products redesigned and their financial impact
- Project planning, management, results
- Integration of advanced technologies
- Education and credentials
- Media attention
- Honors and awards

■ ■ ■ *Event Planner*

- List of functions
- Venues
- Entertainment
- Menus
- Photos of decorations
- Thank you letters and other kudos
- Print promotions, invitations, newspaper coverage
- Video clips

■ ■ ■ *Executive*

- Executive summary
- Management philosophy
- Charts and graphs reflecting impact on the bottom line, performance improvement data, expansions
- List of business competencies showing levels of expertise
- Description of a major problem, your solution, and the result
- Leadership examples, recruitment and leadership of successful management teams
- Evidence of strategic planning and long-term business development
- Participation in joint ventures, mergers, acquisitions, divestitures, etc.
- Organizational charts showing subordinate personnel and areas of responsibility
- Affiliations and professional memberships with any leadership positions

■ ■ ■ *Firefighter*

- Certifications
- Areas of expertise
- Education and training
- Professional development
- Community involvement
- Special projects
- Professional affiliations
- Promotion record

■ ■ ■ *Flight Attendant*

- Photographs—head shot and full-body shot
- Special training
- Letters of appreciation from customers
- Recognition from supervisors
- Routes—domestic or international
- Languages and cross-cultural experience

■ ■ ■ *Florist*

- Lots of photographs that show quality of work
- Examples of different styles and types of arrangements
- Artistic designs using other media besides flowers
- Comments from satisfied customers

■ ■ ■ *Groomer*

- Photographs, photographs, photographs!
- Show dogs and champions

- Styles
- Humane treatment philosophy

■ ■ ■ *Healthcare*
- Impact on quality of care and outcome initiatives
- Expansion of healthcare services and programs
- Implementation of advanced healthcare support technologies
- Proof of accreditation
- Letters of appreciation
- Licenses, credentials, continuing education
- Teaching, in-services, workshops
- Professional affiliations

■ ■ ■ *Hospitality*
- Lists or photos of hotels or restaurants managed
- Growth charts showing proof of impact on the bottom line
- Occupancy rates
- Letters of appreciation from satisfied guests
- Property improvements/construction/renovation
- Operating improvements
- News coverage
- Grand openings

■ ■ ■ *Human Resources*
- Measurement of recruiting success
- Employee benefits packages, expand services, lower costs
- Interview worksheets
- Motivational and training programs
- Union negotiations
- Documentation of faster hiring or better retention
- Proof of lower costs for the hiring process
- Industry association participation
- Implementation of new technologies to manage the hiring process
- Measurable improvements in organizational performance/productivity

■ ■ ■ *Inventor or R&D*
- Areas of expertise
- Patents
- Photographs of inventions
- Professional associations
- Presentations and academic assignments
- Publications and white papers
- Media coverage

■ ■ ■ *Jeweler*
- Photos! Photos! Photos!
- Design specialties—rings, necklaces, bracelets
- Materials expertise—gold, silver, platinum, precious stones, stone cutting, jewelry repair
- Testimonials from customers

■ ■ ■ *Manufacturing*

- Proof of product development
- Charts and graphs showing process improvements
- Implementation of new technologies, robotics, and processes
- Safety improvement
- Improvements in quality; award of quality certifications
- Increases in production yield/output and worker productivity
- Reductions in operating costs and overhead expenses
- Schematics, blueprints, designs, technical drawings

■ ■ ■ *Marketing*

- Marketing plans
- Advertising programs (video, print, voice)
- New media productions (websites, CD-ROMs)
- Focus group design and results
- Proposals
- Photographs
- Results, results, results!

■ ■ ■ *Mechanic*

- Areas of specialty
- Photos of body work or design
- Certifications
- Testimonials from satisfied customers
- Location of shop with map

■ ■ ■ *Minister*

- Religious philosophies
- Family photos
- Personal information about children and spouse
- Sermon outlines
- List of topics
- Letters and comments from church members and leaders
- Presentations and special teaching assignments
- Media coverage
- Video clips or radio broadcasts

■ ■ ■ *Model*

- Photos, photos, photos!
- Copies of magazines or newspaper coverage
- Fashion show advertisements and runway shots
- Specialty areas
- Languages, singing, acting, musical instruments, sports, etc.
- Video tapes of commercial spots, movie appearances, etc.

■ ■ ■ *Museum Curator*

- Special events with invitations, photos, media coverage
- Lists and photos of special exhibits
- Fund-raising results
- Speakers acquired

- Permanent exhibits and acquisitions
- Capital improvements
- Advertising and promotions, including brochures, museum literature, television, radio, and print campaigns

■ ■ ■ *Musician*
- Recordings of performances and/or compositions made into sound files for the e-folio and CD-ROM
- Reviews in magazines, newspapers, and other publications
- Conservatory and special training programs
- Performances
- Honors, awards, contests

■ ■ ■ *Nonprofit Sector*
- Fund-raising
- Event planning
- Capital campaigns
- Volunteer management
- Areas of specialty
- Low turnover of employees and volunteers
- Publicity, media coverage

■ ■ ■ *Photographer*
- Photos! Photos! Photos!
- Genre specialties
- Recognitions, honors, awards
- Exhibits (both solo and group)
- Purchases—museum, gallery, business, individual
- Media reports and reviews

■ ■ ■ *Physician, Nurse, or Other Healthcare Practitioner*
- Licenses and other credentials
- Degrees
- Research projects
- Grants, awards, and honors
- Patient testimonials
- Philosophies
- Academic appointments and teaching assignments
- Publications
- Presentations
- Professional affiliations
- Community service

■ ■ ■ *Police Officer*
- Special projects and committees
- Community involvement
- Areas of expertise
- Education and special training
- Awards and honors

■ ■ ■ *Professor*

- Education and credentials are very important
- Courses developed and taught
- Research and development
- Professional presentations
- Publications—books, journals, and other periodicals
- Special committees and projects
- Student evaluations
- Administrative responsibilities
- Awards, honors, and other recognition
- Community involvement

■ ■ ■ *Project Manager*

- Lists of projects
- Outcomes
- Processes—needs analysis, resource allocation, project scheduling, product development, budgets, implementation
- Letters from satisfied customers (internal and external)

■ ■ ■ *Radio Broadcaster*

- Audio clips of shows, promos, jingles, etc.
- Expertise with digital editing equipment and other technology
- Examples of original scripts, journalism, and other writing
- Community outreach
- Promotions

■ ■ ■ *Real Estate Agent*

- Sales achievements—graphs, awards, honors
- Areas of specialty
- Success stories with photographs
- Client comments

■ ■ ■ *Recent Graduate*

- Diplomas
- Scholarships, grants, awards, honors
- Samples of class papers, projects, reports, videos
- Transcripts or lists of relevant courses
- Course descriptions to add keywords and depth
- Teacher evaluations
- Community service projects
- Clubs, honor societies, fraternities, and leadership positions

■ ■ ■ *Sales*

- Types of products sold, customers, and territories
- Documented achievements—increased revenue or profits
- Charts and graphs
- Significant account acquisition
- Number of leads generated and converted
- Closing ratio
- New territory or market development

- Sales honors, awards, trips, etc.
- Letters from customers
- Sale team-building exercises
- Training and motivation programs developed and presented
- Results, results, results!

Scientist
- Areas of specialty
- Special projects
- Inventions
- Patents
- Professional affiliations
- Honors, awards, or other special recognition
- News reports
- White papers
- Research
- Grants
- Presentations

Social Services
- Areas of specialty
- Credentials, licenses, diplomas
- Testimonials from clients helped
- Professional affiliations
- Volunteer work

Speaker
- Video of key presentations
- Areas of expertise
- Topics, prices, and schedules
- Honors, awards, accolades
- Future speaking engagements
- Past audiences
- Invitations to share your expertise
- Thank you letters
- Membership in speaker organizations
- Photographs of you in action
- Brochures from events

Teacher
- Teaching philosophy statement
- Lesson plans, syllabi, curricula
- Photographs of bulletin boards, classroom decorations, and learning aids
- Staff development projects, training other teachers
- Measurements of student achievement
- Examples of special challenges and how you overcame them
- Degrees, transcripts, continuing education—credentials are very important
- Examples of community partnerships, legislative or volunteer work, special committees
- Student portfolios or other proof of your legacy
- Affiliations and professional memberships

▨ ▨ ▨ Technology

- Lists of technical competencies
- Development of new technologies and their impact on the organization
- Financial benefits, including savings, cost reductions, revenue gains, etc.
- Patents awarded or pending
- Technology transfer programs
- Involvement in emerging technologies

▨ ▨ ▨ Television Newscaster

- Lists of major stories covered
- Writing examples
- Video clips
- Areas of specialty—hard news, breaking news, feature stories
- Professional head shots
- Promotional materials created by the station

▨ ▨ ▨ Translator

- Writing examples
- Lists of special projects
- Areas of specialty
- Languages and levels of proficiency
- Teaching or tutoring programs developed and presented
- Letters of appreciation

▨ ▨ ▨ Web Designer

- Examples of websites to show off your designs
- Link to pages to emphasize what makes them unique—Java scripts, flash graphics, e-commerce features
- Letters from satisfied clients
- List of technical competencies
- List of projects and clients with hyperlinks to their sites

▨ ▨ ▨ Writer

- Poems
- Excerpts from published works
- Media coverage
- Reviews
- Copies of articles in newspapers and magazines or hyperlinks to the online version of the article

▨ ▨ ▨ E-FOLIO SAMPLE

Kirsten Dixson, co-author of *Career Distinction: Stand Out by Building Your Brand,* develops unique, executive-level portfolios that she calls "personal brand portals." Kirsten agrees that "an e-folio is much more effective when it does more than just reiterate a person's paper résumé." She is also adamant that the design of the website doesn't detract from its message. Kirsten believes that a good e-folio will . . .

1. Position your unique value to your audience in a controllable way.

2. Feature links to proofs of performance/accomplishments.
3. Showcase thought leadership in the person's industry.
4. Integrate social media.

With Kirsten's permission, on the following pages you will find examples of two sophisti-cated e-folios, one with a blog and one without. For more samples, check her website at *www.kirstendixson.com*.

When you develop a website for the first time, deciding what message you are going to convey and then laying out the flow of the site to facilitate delivery of that message is the key to an effective finished product. Patricia Moriarty (the sample e-folio that follows) is a specialist in education and technology curriculum integration, so her website focuses on her knowledge, skills, and abilities in this arena. Her site is laid out using the outline begin-ning below.

INTRODUCTION

- A summary paragraph of history and qualifications.
- A list of areas of expertise.
- A keyword list of personal attributes or strengths.
- The introduction is the place for your personal branding statement, the unique value you bring to the job.

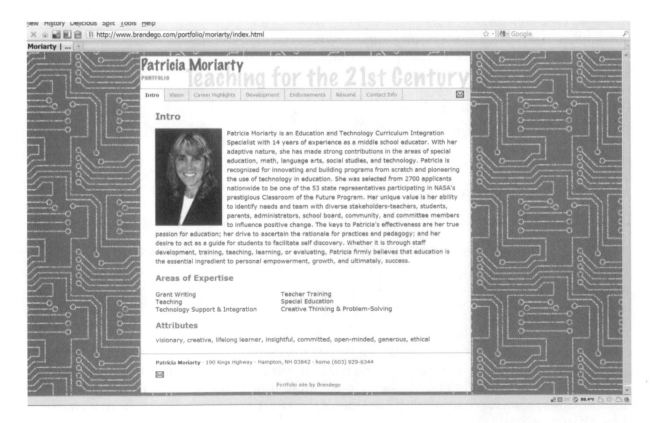

- A statement of personal philosophies about that work, which reveals values, vision, goal, purpose, etc.

- Notice that every page of the website contains:
    1. Full links to every other page of the site.
    2. Full contact information at the bottom of the page to make it easier for a potential employer to call.
    3. A little envelope that jumps directly to a contact form that the viewer can use to send an e-mail immediately.

- The point is to make the site easy to navigate.

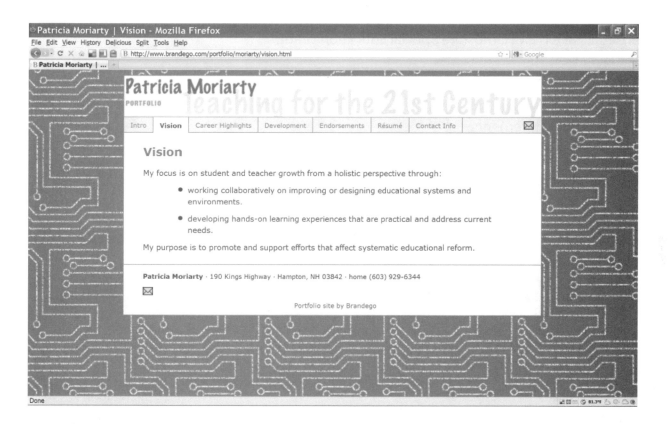

This section is not just a reiteration of the résumé. I especially like the fact that you don't have to use the "Back" button to return from the scanned images to the main page.

- Details of the NASA Classroom of the Future Program:
    – Challenge, Action, Results (CAR) statements
    – Scanned image of the citation
    – Scanned image of a newspaper article

- Details of the Technology Literacy Program:
    – CAR statements
    – Scanned image of a Compaq training certificate
    – Scanned image of a newspaper article

- Details of a New Hampshire Special Education Grant:
    – CAR statements
    – Quote from the parent of a former student

- Details of a State Work-to-School Grant:
    – CAR statements
    – Scanned image of a newspaper article

- Details of her study abroad:
    – CAR statements

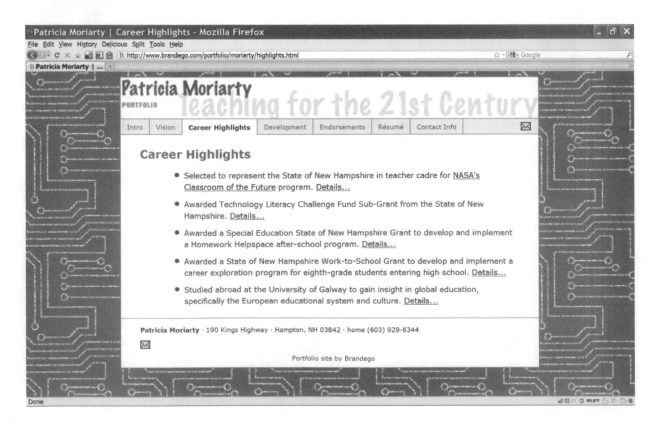

- Formal Education:
    - Scanned images of Master's degree
    - Scanned images of Bachelor's degrees

- Ongoing Professional Development:
    - Scanned images of various certificates

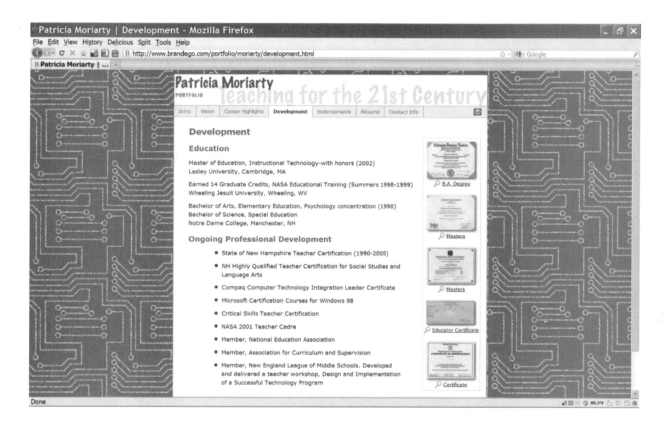

ENDORSEMENTS

- Quotes from former students.
- Quote from a parent of a former student.
- Quotes from colleagues.
- Quotes from an administrator.

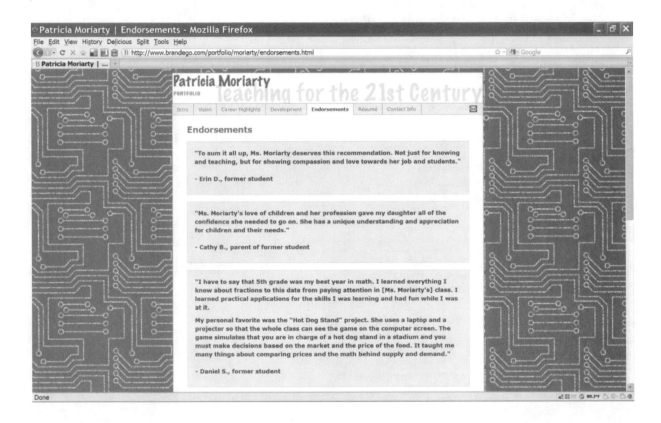

- The complete paper résumé is re-entered here using HTML formatting.

- The reader can choose to download either a PDF, ASCII text, or MS Word version of the résumé.

- The ASCII text file can be downloaded by the viewer for input into computerized applicant tracking systems.

- The MS Word file is for recruiters who like to customize résumés before submitting them to their clients.

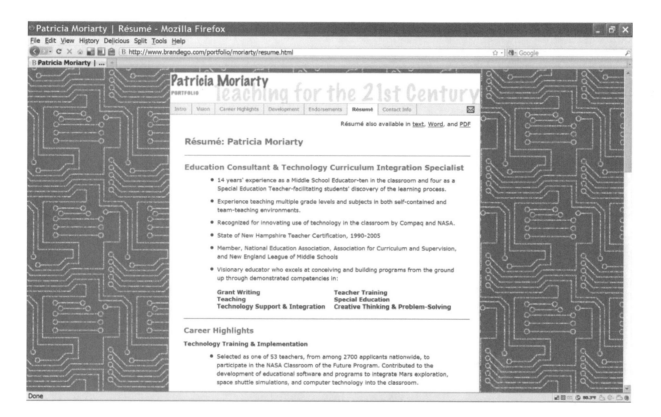

- In addition to the full mailing address and telephone numbers at the bottom of the page, this page provides a form that the viewer can complete and e-mail directly.
- If you have only a cellular number, always identify it as a cell phone so the viewer knows they can try to reach you during business hours.
- Add your website address, LinkedIn hyperlink, and any other web-based information about you.

BLOGS FOR PERSONAL BRANDING

The word *blog* is a rather new invention. It didn't exist before 1999. According to Webster, *blog* is short for *weblog,* which means "a website that contains an online personal journal with reflections, comments, and often hyperlinks provided by the writer".

Blogs are more revealing and authentic than résumés. Blogs are interactive spaces where you can see inside a prospect's head—their ability to think, write, communicate, and innovate. A blog gives an employer more of your essence and helps you to distinguish yourself. If your industry has a bazillion blogs, then it could hinder your job search if you don't have one, too.

As I mentioned earlier, the vast majority of potential employers will Google you either before issuing an interview invitation or after the interview to narrow down applicant choices. That means you need to Google yourself to see if there is anything negative about you on the web. If you do find something bad, you can try to get it removed, but it isn't always possible.

There are services on the Internet that will research your online reputation, help you repair it, and then manage your online brand for a fee. I have no personal experience with these services, but if you have a bad online reputation, it might be worth researching these companies by Googling the following terms: "online brand management" or "online reputation management." Your best bet, though, is to bury negative search results with more recent, positive links to an e-folio and/or a blog.

A blog is both an electronic business card and a tool for reinforcing the credentials on your résumé. A blog doesn't replace your résumé; it simply gives it credibility. Katharine Hansen, Ph.D., says in her Quintessential Careers website, "A good blog can establish you as a thought leader in your field by projecting confident expertise and current commentary about emerging trends." Dr. Hansen recommends "blogging with purpose" and "interviewing leading experts in your field and blogging about them to raise your profile."

Blogs may work best in certain fields, like high-tech, marketing, and C-level management. If you are a successful blogger, you will stand out from the crowd of bloggers in your industry, so be persistent.

Search engines love blogs because they are updated frequently and are often cross-linked to other blogs and websites. That means your e-folio with a blog can rank higher in organic searches than almost any other mention of your name when you are Googled. Bloggers often link to each other's postings, so there is the potential for viral publicity and exposure to audiences you never even considered.

You don't have to be a web designer to create a simple blog or website. Some of the applications available for blogs include TypePad, WordPress, Google Blogger, Movabletype, Posterous, Drupal, Joomla, Vignette, Blogger, and BlogHarbor. Some are more difficult to use than others, so take advantage of their free videos and trial periods to see which one works best for your level of technical experience.

If you create a blog, you must be a good writer. A blog should be engaging and perfect in grammar, spelling, and punctuation. If that is not one of your skills, then consider hiring a writer to help you fine tune your articles. If you aren't willing to commit to keeping up a blog, then create an e-folio, comment on other people's blogs whenever you can, subscribe to e-lists, and write articles or book reviews.

It's a good idea to outline your content and categories in advance. Write a week or two of posts before your website goes live. That way you won't feel pressured to write an article every day in the beginning. You should make a habit of posting an article to your blog once a week at the very least. Two or three times a week or daily are the best. Search for blogs in your industry by using *www.technorati.com*. Find subject-matter experts in your field and follow them for a while to get inspiration. But, stay away from controversial topics.

Be careful about writing blog posts about your current employer or you may find yourself unemployed. Check with your HR department about the company's blogging policies. Avoid writing something that might be construed as embarrassing or negative. Don't talk about specific projects, trade secrets, compensation, benefits, managers, colleagues, or proprietary, confidential, or competitively sensitive information about your employer.

Lastly, include the web address of your blog on your résumé, letterhead, business cards, e-mail signatures, and social networking profiles. Syndicate your blog using RSS software.

The better known you are, the more likely you will turn up on page one of a Google search. Christian Anscheutz's e-folio is a great example of using a blog as a career-management tool to raise visibility and credibility for one's personal brand. On this page and the next, you will notice how he built his e-folio around a blog that is very industry focused. There

are links to his LinkedIn account, his bio, highlights of leadership initiatives, and media contacts. At the bottom of the home page is a hyperlink to Christian's Gartner interview, and he has links to his archived blog articles along the left panel. Readers can download his PDF résumé or sign up for his blog feed.

Search Engine Optimization (SEO) is the use of keywords and other techniques designed to bring a website to the top of a search in Google, Yahoo, Bing, and other search engines. Optimizing the content of your website is about using keywords in such a way that you show up in the results when it matters.

SEO isn't just about your website content anymore. Twitter feeds, Facebook comments, blog posts, and more are now being picked up by search engines. Optimizing your social media channels and blog can increase the number of indexed pages. It is a fact that people who blog have 434% more indexed pages than those who don't.

So, what gets the attention of search engines? Fresh, well-written content that changes frequently. Search engines are primarily popularity contests. Google gives each web page a number called a "PageRank." The more sites that link to your page and the higher the PageRank of those sites, the higher your page will display in search engine results. The same goes for blogs. The more popular and "fresh" the blog, the higher it ranks, so add to your blog frequently and comment on other people's blogs. Including your full name in your website's titles and other meta tags will make it easier for search engines to rank you.

Peter Brown, an SEO expert and web traffic analyst, suggests five ways to draw traffic to your website and raise your SEO score:

1. **Article Marketing**—Write 300-word articles that explain your site and how it will benefit the visitor. Submit them to article directories, like *ezinearticles.com, goarticles.com,* or *articlesbase.com.* Write at least five articles initially, then follow up with an article a day or at least one a week.

2. **Backlink Building**—Search for websites similar to your own and propose a link exchange to their webmaster. Search engines judge a site's popularity by the number of links pointing to it. They assume that your site offers something worth linking to if other people want to link to your site.

3. **Search Engine Optimization**—Set up meta tags in the HTML coding of your website and use keywords in your page titles. Make sure that 5–7% of your site's content includes targeted keywords, which is known as your page's keyword density. To research what words people are searching for, go to *www.wordtracker.com* or *www.keyworddiscovery.com.* Enter a few sentences about the content of each page in the description field of the HTML code.

4. **Social Bookmarking**—When a visitor to your site likes your site's content and goes to a social bookmarking site (like *digg.com, del.icio.us,* etc.) and then tags your site's content with keywords, others can then find your site through that tag. Submit your site to a dozen or more social bookmarketing sites by using *onlywire.com.*

5. **Pay-Per-Click Advertising**—You can pay for web traffic, but it can be very expensive. Google AdWords is the leader in pay-per-click advertising. Extremely broad keywords can cost a lot, so make your keywords highly targeted if you decide to go this route.

To gauge your SEO efforts, go to *google.com/analytics* to measure how many people visit your site and how they got there. Visit *siteexplorer.search.yahoo.com/mysites* to monitor the number of outside links to your site and where they originated. Xinu *(xinureturns.com)* runs a battery of diagnostic tests on your site to evaluate your title tags and keywords.

Supporting Documents

Chapter 18

Your résumé isn't the only document you will need for your job search. At some point in the hiring process, you will be asked for a list of three to five references who know how you work and would be willing to speak with a potential employer about you. While you are currently employed, your company might ask for a bio. If your résumé is getting too long, you can create supporting documents that provide more information when needed. When you are invited back for a second interview, you might want to showcase your technology skills with a PowerPoint presentation of your résumé during a group or panel interview—just make sure you are well prepared with a presentation style that matches your audience. And let's not forget profiles on social networking sites like LinkedIn, Facebook, MySpace, YouTube, Flickr, and Twitter.

I will deal with cover letters, thank you notes, and resignation letters in Chapter 19. The previous chapter dealt with e-folios and blogs. This chapter is for everything else. One thing you will want to remember is that your brand must be consistent from one document to another. Make sure you are reflecting your unique value proposition in every word you write, regardless of which document you are creating.

REFERENCES

References are not usually presented on a résumé since most employers will not take the time to check references until after an interview. By then, they will have your completed application with a list of references. You also don't want to impose on your friends, coworkers, supervisors, mentors, college professors, customers, vendors, or former employers unnecessarily or too frequently. There is nothing wrong with taking a nicely printed list of professional references with you to an interview, however (page 359).

Here is one of those exceptions to the rule again. If an advertisement requests that a list of references be sent with the résumé and cover letter, then by all means supply the list. You don't want to be accused of not following directions.

Before deciding whom to include on your reference list, Google each person to get a feeling for their online reputation. You don't want a potential employer to find digital dirt on your references, since it could rub off on you.

Always get permission to use someone as a reference. Call the person and get their full contact information (company, title, mailing address, city, state, zip, e-mail address, work phone, cell phone). Provide all of your references with your most current résumé so they know your key accomplishments and skills. And don't forget to thank each reference after you win the job.

Another thing: Avoid that needless line at the bottom of the résumé that says, "References available upon request." It takes up valuable white space that you need to define the sections of your résumé in order to draw the reader's eyes logically down the page.

Pretend you are an interviewer. You ask, "Will you provide references?" The interviewee replies, "Sorry, no, I can't do that." Will you even think twice about continuing to consider this candidate? I think not. It is assumed that you will provide references when requested.

A new trend is to pull out some quotes from your reference letters or performance evaluations or customer satisfaction surveys and use them as "decorations" on your résumé (see pages 60, 118, 119, 167, 169). You can create a section at the bottom of your résumé for three or four quotes. I like to integrate select quotes here and there throughout the résumé as part of the bullets in the accomplishments sections (see page 214). That way, they relate directly to the bullets above them. Placing quotes inside text boxes in the margins or other white space of the résumé is also an option (see pages 41, 42, 60, 74, 75, 92, 116, 128, 214, 248, 254).

Another idea is more than a list of references. Reference dossiers are written testimonials from third parties that you can leave behind after an interview. You ask select employers, colleagues, vendors, or even someone from the volunteer work you do on the side to write short letters that you can copy and leave with an interviewer at the end of your meeting.

RÉSUMÉ EXTENDERS

As résumés get longer and longer, there are times when creating a shorter résumé and supplementing it with additional documents is the best option. Résumé extenders are great for expanding on your basic résumé with supporting credentials. They are often used in CVs and executive résumés to present philosophy statements (see pages 88, 263, 264, 274, 282, 292), KSAs (see page 360), and lists of presentations, publications, affiliations, professional development, technology expertise, projects, critical leadership initiatives (see pages 104, 250, 251, 256, 257, 272, 355, 357), and other qualifications that would make a résumé much too long. CAR statements are a great way to reflect the Challenge, Action, and Results (CAR) of key projects (see pages 250, 251, 256, 257, 355, 357) and their bottom-line results.

Deb Dib, president of Executive Power Brand, creates one-page precision résumés that are supplemented with a portfolio of documents that expand on the points made in the first page. She says, "Résumés are becoming more focused and results-oriented to show value and contribution, especially in a society where attention spans are becoming shorter with increasingly competing messages."

PROPOSALS

Proposals (see pages 358, 363) can be used to showcase your expertise with recommendations for long-range plans if you are hired (see page 362), business plans, marketing proposals, competitive analyses, case studies (see page 361), and technology solutions to problems the hiring company is facing. Use your imagination and build on these ideas to convince your dream company that you would be worth your salary.

A job proposal can convince hiring authorities that you are ready to hit the ground running. It proves that you have done your research, understand the challenges the company is facing, and have thought through your process for change. Each proposal will be unique and customized to the company, although you might be able to use your first proposal as a template for subsequent ones, so you don't have to start from scratch each time. A job proposal positions you as the company's solution to its key problems.

BIOGRAPHIES

Bios are often used by public speakers, consultants, public figures, writers, and executives. You might be asked for a biography when you apply for a board of director position or for internal publications, sales brochures, grant proposals, publishing opportunities, speaking engagements, book proposals, business plans, company websites, or networking contacts.

Bios are focused and short—one page long or even one paragraph long (see page 364). They are most often written in narrative, first-person format using personal pronouns (I, my, me), although they can also appear to have been written by someone else in third-person format. When writing your bio, lead off with your branding summary and what you bring to the "party" that makes you unique. Then provide a brief education and work history. Bios can also include some personal information that will help the reader connect with you.

KSAs

Federal government applications often ask for KSA statements (Knowledge, Skills, and Abilities) that are in addition to your résumé (see page 359). KSAs can also be called Supplemental Qualifications, Evaluation Factors, Quality Ranking Factors, Mandatory Technical Factors, and Core Qualification Statements, among other titles. The most popular government job site on the web, *usajobs.opm.gov*, asks for a version of KSAs on the majority of its job openings. Sometimes they are labeled KSAs or one of the other titles above. Other times they are hidden as essay questions among a plethora of selection-type questions.

You are the only person in the world who has your unique set of knowledge, skills, and abilities, which is what makes you special.

Knowledge is something you have learned from both your work and personal life, including your education, special training, and experience.

Skills are things you "do," like typing, computer programming, cooking, foreign languages, among many others. People possess skills in varying degrees.

Abilities are related to your unique talents and natural aptitudes. Abilities are the foundation of your passion, although your skills and knowledge play a part as well.

Kathryn Troutman, considered one of the most knowledgeable résumé writers on government applications, has developed a free online KSA builder, which you can access at *www.resume-place.com/ksa_builder/template*. She recommends using KSA statements to tell your story in an interesting and compelling way with two CAR examples for each KSA.

KSAs can repeat information from your résumé but also include what you learned in college, workshops, seminars, volunteer work, and any other experiential environment. If you do not provide KSAs with exactly what the hiring authority requests, your application will not be considered, so take KSAs seriously.

Social media sites (like LinkedIn, Facebook, MySpace, Twitter, and YouTube) are quickly growing as a recruiting method for passive candidates, particularly executives who aren't actively looking for a job but have specialized skills and experience that is difficult to find. Often, the most talented and sought-after recruits are those currently employed. One of the benefits of Internet social networking technology is that it can increase the diversity of the talent pool available to recruiters.

Oracle found CFO Jeff Epstein via LinkedIn in 2008. Since Home Depot started using social networking sites for recruiting, it has cut the time it takes to fill a job opening in half. Social networking sites are used by 47% of recruiters prior to actually contacting the applicant for the first time, and 41% use social networking sites before the first formal interview. Another 37% use these sites before making an offer.

Companies are increasingly using Twitter to broadcast their job openings. This might mean the death knell for job boards, but they are integrating social-media functions to create hybrid sites that take advantage of the best features of both. For instance, Jobster has joined forces with employers to enhance its career networking platform on Facebook. Recruiters can promote specific job openings and tap into referrals at Jobster.

The vast majority of recruiters conduct a Google search on applicants before interviewing them, and 60% of all online users are now members of a social network. That means recruiters are almost guaranteed to see your e-folio, as well as your LinkedIn, Facebook, MySpace, Twitter, and YouTube profiles. For that reason, your social media profiles should be customized to reflect your personal brand so they become billboards that showcase your talents.

Does your Facebook page have incriminating photos, dubious comments, and questionable friends? Then, remove them now and password protect the family and friends area to keep the public out. Don't let your children or other people use your computer to "favorite" videos and web pages or to Tweet others. If YouTube gets linked to your Facebook account, you could end up appearing to endorse things that could harm your personal brand.

Of all the social networking sites, LinkedIn is intended to be the most career oriented, so use it to the max. According to Jessi Hempel writing in *Fortune* magazine, "Facebook is for fun. Tweets have a short shelf life. If you're serious about managing your career, the only social site that really matters is LinkedIn. More than 60 million members have created [LinkedIn] profiles . . . and these include your customers, your colleagues, your competitors, your current boss, and possibly the person about to interview you."

One caveat. LinkedIn doesn't work for everyone. It isn't as effective for teachers, cashiers, administrative support, or seasonal workers as it is for corporate executives and hard-to-fill IT, engineering, supply chain, and global sourcing positions, ones usually filled by recruiters and not with simple classified ads.

LinkedIn also allows you to connect your online professional interactions in one place—join groups on the site (companies, school alumni, affiliations), offer advice, and link your e-folio, blog, and Twitter account to your LinkedIn profile.

Your LinkedIn profile is very important and should lead recruiters to your website/e-folio/blog. You can customize the URL of your public profile on LinkedIn to make it appropriate for your job search. Enter "customize my public profile URL" in the help menu for full instructions.

So, how can you make your profiles stronger? Think of your profile as an introduction and not a résumé. You can always embed a link to the PDF file of your résumé if someone wants more information. Use your own, unique voice when you write this "elevator pitch." Develop a tagline that reflects your "brand." The line of text under your name is the first thing people see, so make it count.

Take a look at the sample LinkedIn profile on the next page. It includes groups, résumé, shared connections, activities, recommendations, answers to questions, advertisements, contact information, and a status bar that can be linked to Twitter feeds.

The Specialties field of LinkedIn is a great place to list your industry buzzwords, passion, values, and even humor. This section is searchable, so think carefully about your career goals when you decide which words to include here. Explain your experience in the profile succinctly. In the Additional Information section, round out your profile with a few key interests. Make sure you link to your e-folio and/or blog.

All social networks can help you tap into your Six Degrees of Separation. You can search for people you know, and the people they know, and the people they know . . . until you reach someone in your dream company. Even if you aren't connected, you can research people who either worked there in the past or work there now to determine what sorts of background and education it took to be successful there. Then contact that person to pick his or her brain.

Don't forget to use all of the social networking sites to research the company before your interview. What's good for the goose is good for the gander.

On the following pages are examples of Twitter and LinkedIn profiles. The Twitter résumé below is from Ryon Harms, a social media consultant and creator of The Social Executive blog at *www.thesocialexe.com*. The sample LinkedIn profile is courtesy of Rosa Elizabeth Vargas of Creating Prints in Denver *(www.creatingprints.com)*.

SAMPLE TWITTER RÉSUMÉ

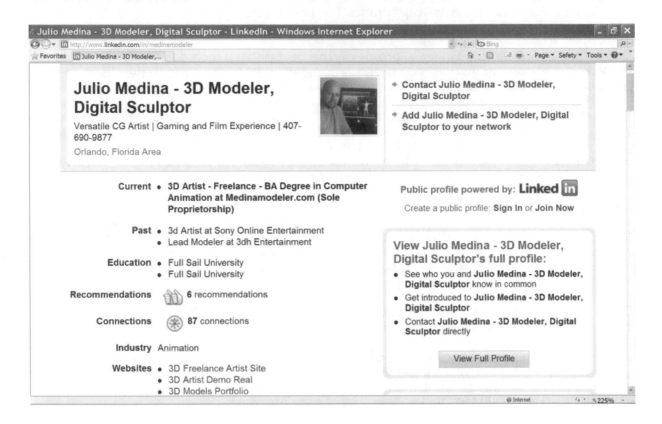

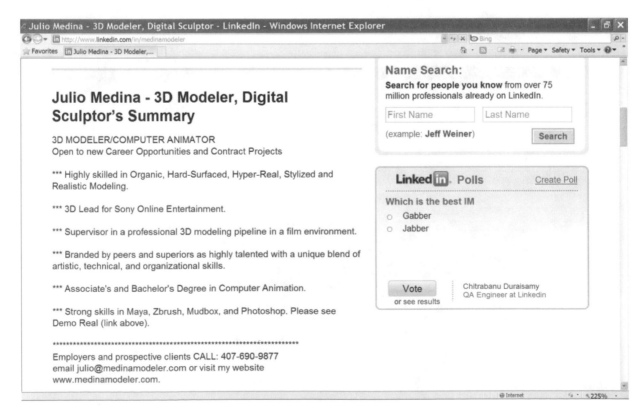

Link with me--I look forward to meeting you!

****

ARTIST BIO

Julio launched his 3d character modeling experience in a professional pipeline at 3dh Entertainment, working on stylized computer animation for film and television. Within a few months he was recognized for his unique talent in balancing artistic talent with technical aptitude and his high work ethic.

Superiors and colleagues referred to him as an artist who is a quick learner and reliable in meeting deadlines without compromising quality. He quickly earned the Lead Modeler position. As a Lead Modeler, Julio bridged the gap between departments, leveraging his versatility.

Julio later joined an industry-leader in entertainment, Sony SOE, as a 3d Artist. He continued to impress and exceed expectations in 3d character generation and as the Lead Setup Artist. He was key in developing the Sony Character Rigging Pipeline. He was involved from conceptualization to implementation. Julio embraced leading complex projects such as creating in-game effects and he became a major asset to the company.

Julio Medina - 3D Modeler, Digital Sculptor's Specialties:

Expertise in modeling Characters, Vehicles, Weapons/Props, Digital Sets/Environments, and Blendshapes with additional skills include Texturing, UV Mapping and Rigging. Proficient in Animation, Lighting and Rendering.

Internet   225%

Julio Medina - 3D Modeler, Digital Sculptor's Experience

3D Artist - Freelance - BA Degree in Computer Animation
Medinamodeler.com (Sole Proprietorship)

(Sole Proprietorship; Animation industry)

February 2007 — Present (3 years 7 months)

* Create high-end computer graphics, three-dimensional images depicting objects exactly, 3d modeling, texturing, rigging and digital sculpting.

* Excel in creating objects, environments, and characters to appear lifelike. Manipulate assets' lighting, color, texture to visually enhance.

* Provide comprehensive services which include rigging animation friendly characters, props, and vehicles.

* Remain abreast of industry trends.

Skill sets:

Organic/Character Modeling
Hard Surface/Prop Modeling
Environment/Digital Set Modeling
Blendshape Modeling
Digital Sculpting
UV Mapping
Rigging/Set-up
Texturing
3d Logo Creation

Internet   200%

http://www.linkedin.com/in/medinamodeler

Favorites   Julio Medina - 3D Modeler,...

Page ▼ Safety ▼ Tools ▼

Julio Medina - 3D Modeler, Digital Sculptor's Education

Full Sail University
Bachelor's Degree , Computer Animation , 2005 — 2006

Advanced Achievement Award
Modeling Team Leader
Course Directors Award for Software Technology
Course Directors Award for Advanced Gaming Techniques

Full Sail University
Associate's Degree , Computer Animation , 2003 — 2005

Course Director's Award for Object Perspective
Course Directors Award for Character Modeling

Additional Information

Julio Medina - 3D Modeler, Digital Sculptor's Websites:

3D Freelance Artist Site
3D Artist Demo Real
3D Models Portfolio

Julio Medina - 3D Modeler, Digital Sculptor's Interests:

Sculpt Clay Maquette's (Concept Character's). Build plastic models, and play videos games. Love good food and good wine!

Julio Medina - 3D Modeler, Digital Sculptor's Groups:

Graphic Design Freelancers

Freelance professionals

Internet   175%

---

http://www.linkedin.com/in/medinamodeler

Favorites   Julio Medina - 3D Modeler,...

Page ▼ Safety ▼ Tools ▼

Freelance Motion Graphics Designers & Animators

FOR ALL YOUR 3D ANIMATION, VFX, GRAPHICS & 3D GAME ART REQUIREMENTS

Animation and Film Jobs

3D Freelance Hub

Julio Medina - 3D Modeler, Digital Sculptor's Honors:

Advanced Achievement Award, December 2006, Bachelor's Degree

Julio Medina - 3D Modeler, Digital Sculptor's Contact Settings

Interested In:

career opportunities   consulting offers
new ventures   job inquiries
expertise requests   business deals
reference requests   getting back in touch

View Full Profile

Internet   200%

Janet Whitmore
Brookeville, MD 20833

Phone 301.555.1234
E-mail jwhitmore@protypeltd.com

Senior Manager / Project Manager—IT Industry

Senior-level IT Project Manager with 16 years of progressive experience in web application development, systems engineering, and software development. Highly skilled leader with proven expertise in PMBOK and SDLC life-cycle management, IT strategic plan development/implementation, and solutions design. Two-time award recipient: RGI Technologies NOVA Award for Team Work (2006) and RGII Technologies Pinnacle Award for Program Performance (2005).

PMP Certified, Implemented Lean Six Sigma Methodologies, Master's Degree

Operating Systems: UNIX, Windows XP, Windows Vista	
Program Languages: FoxPro, dBase, MS Access, COBOL, Easytrieve, JCL, Visual Basic, Omnis 7, SQL Server, Oracle, Perl, HTML, ColdFusion, JavaScript, Active Server Pages (ASP), Java, .NET, J2EE	
Software Applications: Microsoft Outlook, Excel, Word, PowerPoint, Publisher, Visio, Project, and SharePoint	
Hardware: SBS Server 2003, PowerEdge 840, Firebox Edge Firewall	

Highlights of Qualifications

Project Management
- Managed communication and follow-up on multiple projects ranging from $1,000,000-$20,000,000 varying in length from 1 to eight years.
- Assembled, trained, and managed teams of systems engineers, software designers, programmers, and technicians. Consistently met performance level guidelines, managed customer interface, and completed projects on time and within budget.

Systems Engineering
- Systems engineering management experience with oversight for up to 30 engineers.
- Led the impact analysis, insertion planning, and institutionalization of new COTS (Commercial off-the shelf) packages and technologies. Drove technological service oriented architecture initiatives/projects and delivered best value, standardized products and services solutions that met multiple strategic IT needs.

Software Development
- Emphasis on web application development with emerging technologies from early Perl technologies to current .Net and J2EE. Led projects utilizing ASP, ColdFusion, .NET, HTML, Java, JavaScript, VB Script, SQL Server, Oracle, commercial product / COTS integration, desktop, LAN, and WAN applications.

Professional Experience

Whitmore & Associates, LLC ♦ Information Technology Director ♦ 2008 to present
Manage all system design, systems engineering, network engineering, software implementation, and technical support for a small accounting firm.

RGI Technologies ♦ Progressive Career Culminating as Principal Systems Engineer ♦ 1993 to 2008
Steadily progressed from Software Engineer in 1993 to Principal Systems Engineer by 2007 with oversight of 30 Systems Engineers, Special Projects. Entrusted by the IT Director to oversee technical process excellence of 200 people. Reported directly to the IT Director.

Education and Certifications

M.S. Management of Technology ♦ Rensselear Polytechnic Institute
B.S. Math ♦ Mount St. Mary's College
PMP Certified ♦ Project Management Institute

RGI Technologies Career Progression

Principal Systems Engineer 12/07 to 9/08

♦ Reported directly to the IT Director. Managed directorate special projects.

♦ Project manager for the Corporate Headquarters Application Modernization Plan (CHAMP) application portfolio modernization and implementation, a $5,000,000 project over five years.

♦ Project manager for the Corporate Tax Reporting System (CorpTax) COTS implementation, $1,500,000 project over eight months.

♦ Supported IT Director by gathering the annual Service Level Agreements (SLA) and Statement of Works (SOW) for the Directorate.

♦ Provided day-to-day direction. Managed the tasks and activities by updating the MS Project schedule and conducting weekly status meetings.

♦ Managed extensive customer interface on multiple roadmap projects.

Senior Systems Engineering Manager 5/04 to 12/07

♦ Senior-level management position with direct accountability to the IT Director and management oversight of cost, schedule, quality, and delivery of Systems Engineering (SE) work products.

♦ Grew the engineering department by 70%. Managed annual direct budget of $1,000,000 and an overhead budget of $150,000.

♦ Managed SE pool deliverables such as concept of operations, technical solution proposals, systems requirements documents, requests for proposals (RFP), white papers, red team reviews, return-to-green plans, strategic plans, and software improvement teams.

♦ Five years of senior level IT management experience with oversight for recruiting, training, retention, skills integration, mentoring, and career development.

♦ Coordinated and facilitated Lean Six Sigma events as a key contributor to LM21/Lean thinking projects leading to cost avoidance of $2,000,000 to $3,000,000 in system retirements, application functionality improvements, and streamlining office internal processes.

Software Application Manager 7/01 to 5/04

♦ Oversaw a team of 18 software developers. Managed a direct budget of $3,000,000 and an overhead budget of $85,000.

♦ Delivered and managed COTS products, websites, and web applications to meet corporate headquarters' strategic IT goals.

♦ Participated on Integrated Product Teams (IPTs) with customer, account executives, and operations team manager.

PROJECT MANAGER 5/1997 to 7/2001

♦ Led the RFP, development, and maintenance of a $2,500,000 web application.

♦ Conducted system requirements review, systems design review, test readiness review, and operational readiness review.

♦ Led full scope of the SDLC life-cycle development project.

Software Engineer 06/93 to 5/97

Professional Training and Development

RGI Software Security Assurance for Leaders/Manager (2007)
RGI Security for System Engineers (2006)
RGI Management Training (2004)
RGI Project Management Qualification (2000)
RGI Information Systems Leadership Development Program (1996)
INROADS Career Development Organization (1993)

Notable Projects

Successfully led the Corporate Headquarters Application Modernization Plan (CHAMP) for 160 application portfolio roadmap development for a five-year plan budgeted at approximately $5 million.

Scope of Plan: Update, modernize, and streamline application technologies to make them consistent with the organization's strategy and technology architecture framework as part of a joint business/IT process improvement with the business partners and stakeholders.

Actions Taken:

♦ Collected application information via checklists and questionnaires, application, description, sponsor, user community, usage metrics, architecture, business processes supported, recurring and non-recurring labor, and non-labor operating costs.

♦ Conducted follow-on interviews with the project team.

♦ Established focus areas for identifying potential overlapping functionality, overlapping business processes, common technology, and common hosting requirements.

♦ Collaborated with technical leadership and the senior architect; produced a benefit-cost analysis as a guideline for recommended solutions.

♦ Produced monthly performance progress reports that were in line with application reviews led by the engineering department, senior management, technical leaders, and senior financial analyst.

♦ Coordinated the Service Oriented Architecture (SOA) with the directorate, consulted with technical leads, service delivery managers, project managers, and subject matter experts to develop the directorate roadmap.

Result: Ensured that the directorate met the milestone achievements including completing planned services, registering services in the UDDI, and establishing service-level agreements. Mitigated static HTML websites to SharePoint, and produced a savings of approximately $200,000 in recurring maintenance costs.

Successfully directed a team in the design, management, and delivery of a two-phase export/import web application.

Phase I—Scope of Plan: Replace a legacy FoxPro application within nine months.

Actions Taken:

♦ Analyzed project functions and requirements to assemble an RFP in accordance with State Department guidelines.

♦ Quickly realized that, due to high-level, application license requirements, the full project requirements could not be met within nine months.

♦ Proposed two parallel tracks that could meet the immediate customer need by delivering an interim solution that provided core requirements.

Result: Led the team to successful completion of both tracks within the nine-month schedule and under budget. Customer selected the same team to design, build, and implement the final product with a budget of $2,500,000.

Phase II—Actions Taken: Led the project team through developing the project management plan, including the work breakdown structure, estimates using the analogous and parametric approaches, resource planning, schedule development, and risk identification (positive and negative), and project dependencies.

Result: Successfully delivered the project on time and within budget, with this release running for a total of four years. Developed the final application using Active Server Pages with an Oracle database. Processed more than 100 change requests over four years that were processed against the baseline requirements. All audit reports where found to possess appropriate documentation and approvals for the change orders.

RICHE MELISSANDE

rmelissande@protypeltd.com

1837 Santorino Road • Cincinnati, Ohio 45207
Residence: 513-437-1057 • Cellular: 513-437-5551

OBJECTIVE: Docent Chair

Enthusiastic and passionate docent with **more than 8,350 volunteer hours** during 12-year tenure as docent at the Cincinnati Zoo. Tireless worker who serves as point person to anyone experiencing problems. Conduct thorough research through site inspection to reveal gaps and hidden obstacles to prevent hindrances and to ensure smooth flow of operation.

Delivered strong operating results in productivity and efficiency improvement. Excellent training, supervisory, leadership, and interpersonal skills. Expertise in dealing with difficult people. Organized and skillful project manager with attention to minute details. Knowledge and compliance of OSHA and HIPAA regulations.

Outstanding motivator who possesses a unique sense of innovation and resourcefulness with proven integrity and expertise in devising creative solutions to complex problems to overcome obstacles (encourage people to do what no one else wants to do), adapt to changing circumstances while achieving business goals. Hard-working and dependable with a **strong work ethic**. Decisive in implementation. Understanding of cultural diversity and art. Thorough knowledge of corporate zoo culture.

Provide positive, highly visible organizational presence. Constantly generate new ideas. Communicate well with business professionals, build and nurture strong business partnerships, easily establish rapport and gain client confidence; extremely sociable and articulate.

Effective communicator with excellent interpersonal and presentation skills. Interact with all levels of management and administration. Well-liked and respected above and beyond expected standards. Extensive network of contacts within the community. Partner with the community in support of high-profile community affairs, revitalization, and funding activities.

DOCENT HISTORY

Weekend Coordinator   July 2005–Present
Weekend Provisional Chair   December 2001–April 2005
Saturday C.O.D.   May 1997–May 2000

ACTIVE PARTICIPATION

- Member, Docent Chair Advisory Committee for former Docent Chair
- Member, Docent and Mentoring Committees
- Participant, Behavioral Research Projects for the Zoo's Research Department
- Participant, Animal Enrichment, Zoo Enrichment Department
- Completed Biology-Wild Animals in Captivity, UCLA Accredited Course

AWARD

President's Volunteer Service Award
(Issued by the President's Council on Service and Civic Participation)

PROFESSIONAL AFFILIATIONS

Member, Association of Zoo and Aquarium Docents
Member, Gibbon Conservation Center

DOCENT EMPLOYMENT CHRONICLE—HIGHLIGHTS

WEEKEND COORDINATOR   July 2005–Present

Acted as **interim weekday coordinator** for a six-month period—in addition to existing duties as weekend coordinator—upon former docent's death until a new weekday coordinator could be appointed. Scope of responsibility is expansive and includes the strategic planning, staffing, and management of all weekend docent affairs. Design and implement systems, processes, and procedures.

Executive liaison between docents and GZA to plan, schedule, and facilitate a broad range of GZA initiatives. Attend all meetings and prepare information. Design flexible administrative systems and processes to meet growth and expansion demands of docents.

Support GZA by staffing all V.I.P. tours for visiting dignitaries, trustees, and donors. Aid with all general docent weekend activities as well as with staffing all weekend tours and special events. Direct contact person for all colleges—as well as church groups, families, and members—in Cincinnati to schedule weekend tours.

Challenge: Provide the most appropriate docents for scheduled tours no matter what time or day.

Action 1:   Merge disparate personnel from membership, reservations, and admissions departments into a cohesive team-centered unit.

Results: Efficiently streamlined entrance into the zoo for weekend tour groups. Strengthened goodwill between staff, volunteers, and weekend guests.

Action 2:   Successfully pursued and booked tours for college professors who previously had not visited our zoo with their students.

Results: Booking of many more specialized tours providing more activities for our docents as well as additional revenue for the zoo.

Created a proactive employee communications campaign to link management expectations with employee incentives and performance goals.

Instrumental in building revenues by maintaining caliber, integrity, and strength of public affairs and public relations initiatives.

Serve as liaison among C.O.D.s, volunteer coordinators, and docent chair. Interact with each provisional chair to discover which student excels in which area and which student needs additional help or encourage. Evaluate and write performance reviews on docents six months after their graduation. Supervise, encourage, and mentor all weekend docents and student volunteers for all activities and special events. Implemented docent-on-duty program for weekend docents.

Achievements:
- Planned and participated in weekend volunteer fall and holiday parties for the past ten years.
- Farewell appreciation luncheons for outgoing docent chairs
- Provisional docent graduation ceremonies for the years 2001, 2002, and 2003.

PROPOSALS

- Increase docent presence and visibility throughout the zoo.

- Investigate the possibility of and devise new activities for weekday and weekend volunteers.

  Anticipated result: entice docents to extend their day once morning tours are completed and foster positive interaction between volunteers and zoo patrons.

- Devise incentives and rewards to increase docent morale and enthusiasm.

  Anticipated result: encourage greater attendance and participation in volunteer activities.

- Explore the possibility to revitalize and expand the animal encounters program which would include additional docents primarily on weekday and weekend afternoons (animals and weather permitting).

  Anticipated result: reach more of our zoo patrons and enhance their zoo experience.

- Encourage additional weekday "Docent on Duty" training and participation on weekdays. Strengthening a docent's willingness to extend his or her day, we can provide additional one-on-one interactions with zoo patrons.

  Anticipated result: greater patronage which would increase revenues.

- Inspire to build a more cohesive bond between weekday and weekend docent populations.

  Anticipated result: greater harmony by familiarizing weekend docents with weekday programs and vice versa, thereby fostering cross-functioning between docents.

Alice L. Brown, CPA

REFERENCES

John C. Brown
Herald, Haines & Brown, LLC
Certified Public Accountants
12 Beaver Ruin Road, Suite B
Lilburn, Georgia 30047-3401
Office: (770) 555-1234, ext. 100
Direct Line: (770) 555-5678
Fax: (770) 555-4321
jc@hhb.com

Rachel Speed
Speed & Associates
123 Echo Ridge Lane
Colorado Springs, Colorado 80918
Office: (719) 555-1234
rs@speed.com

Michelle Edwards
Attorney at Law
123 Fifth Avenue
Great Falls, Montana 59401
Office: (406) 555-1234
me@medwards.com

Michael Gonzales
123 Carlson Drive
Colorado Springs, Colorado 80919
Home: (719) 555-1234
mgonzales@protypeltd.com

Kathryn Stephens-Oakes
BiggsKofford
Certified Public Accountants
123 Southpointe Court
Colorado Springs, Colorado 80906
Office: (719) 555-1234
kso@biggs.com

RODNEY S. JACKSON

1234 Red Creek Springs Road #1 • Pueblo, Colorado 81005
Cell: (972) 555-1234 • E-mail: rodney.jackson@protypeltd.com
U.S. Citizen • Date of Birth: 1-23-45 • SSN 111-11-1111

KNOWLEDGE, SKILLS, AND ABILITIES
AVIATION TECHNICAL SYSTEMS SPECIALIST
(NAS PLANNING SPECIALIST)
ASW-ATO-10-258-122128 and ASW-ATO-10-257-122123

1. Knowledge of the National Airspace System (NAS). This includes the systems and facilities that interrelate for the control of aircraft movement.

For eight years, I worked on aircraft using the NAS, and for the past two and a half years, I have been maintaining the NAS itself. There are literally hundreds of thousands of components and processes that must be evaluated on numerous aircraft and ground communication and navigation systems, and it was my job to ensure that each one performed to design specifications.

As an Airway Transportation Systems Specialist, I currently support air traffic customers and other National Airspace System (NAS) users over a large geographic area with a focus on the availability and reliability of facilities, services, and equipment in southwestern Colorado (ATCT, ASR 11, TRACON, two MALSR, three PAPI, and two VORTAC, among others). I troubleshoot, repair, and maintain environmental control systems, visual/navigation aids, control and power distribution systems, and emergency power standby systems that support the NAS. My focus is on the overall system performance and causes of system degradation.

As a Line Maintenance Technician with both Delta Airlines and Atlantic Southeast Airlines, I gained expertise with diverse electronic systems, including VHF, HF, and ACARS communications systems, and Selcal, ELT, VOR, transponder, radar altimeter, GPS, EFIS, cockpit voice and flight data recorders, as well as environmental control and weather detection systems. I also installed, replaced, maintained, or repaired navigational equipment—ADC, ADI/HSI, VOR, ILS (localizer, glide slope, marker beacon), ADF, DME, TCAS, and onboard ATC transponders.

2. Ability to prioritize and accomplish assigned tasks independently and within established timeframes.

The Army trained me to organize and complete my work activities independently, efficiently, and in accordance with established priorities. After nine years of military service, I took those honed organizational skills into my career as an Airframe and Powerplant Mechanic and now as an Airway Transportation System Specialist. In my performance evaluations over the years, my supervisors have consistently rated my organizational abilities very highly. I have a proven track record of completing projects within established timeframes and within budget.

3. Ability to convey technical information to a variety of audiences in meetings, presentations, or briefings.

My annual performance reviews have always commented on my strong communication skills. I have supervised and trained teams that required the ability to communicate critical instructions in a clear, concise manner in English. I am able to customize my communication for the knowledge level of the target audience. Much of my nine years of Army training was directly related to leadership and communication. I often made presentations and gave briefing to senior management in the Army. I also gained extensive training experience. I established a comprehensive cross-training program and was recognized as the best trainer in the team.

4. Ability to direct, review the work of, and advise others to achieve technical objectives.

During my nine years in the Army, I led a team of up to 10 soldiers in the inspection, repair, maintenance, storage, and firing of Multiple Launch Rocket Systems (MLRS) and Pershing missiles. It was my responsibility as a supervisor to direct and review the work of these soldiers. When working on airplanes as a Line or Heavy Maintenance Mechanic, I directed the progress of the team working on each aircraft and ensured that they achieved technical objectives.

5. Ability to work collaboratively and constructively with others in a team environment.

My ability to work well with other team members has always been one of my strengths, and all of my supervisors have indicated such on my performance evaluations since my early Army days. The Army does a superior job of training soldiers in teamwork and how to use teams to ensure that goals are achieved. I led a team of soldiers to war in Kuwait and maintained a high level of motivation in spite of the difficult conditions we encountered in the Middle East. My Army career and the diversity training ingrained in every soldier prepared me to relate to individuals, consider differing views, needs, feelings, and capabilities, and manage conflict. In every supervisory position I have held, I provided constructive, positive feedback. I have a reputation for being easy to work with, and I get along well with others.

CASE STUDY
Weisberger, Ltd.

Weisberger, Ltd., a $14 billion oil and gas services company, has a plant in Charleston, South Carolina, that they can't seem to give away. Three attempts have been made to sell it, morale is in the trash, and sales are down from $35 million to around $21 million.

The Charleston plant manufactures the super-heavy-duty gas meters you see on the back of trucks delivering liquid propane around your neighborhood. The meters are extremely accurate and, even though they are mechanical devices (old technology), Weisberger has managed to capture 72% of the world market.

I was invited by a plant employee to see what my company might do to lower costs through outsourcing. Unfortunately, after getting a handle on the big picture, we began to suspect that the plant needed to focus its efforts on growing its business, not cutting costs. We immediately shifted from defense to offense and began digging.

Briefly, here is what we discovered:

1. Of the plant's $23 million in sales, spare parts account for a whopping $10.8 million.

2. If the meter is so rugged and lasts for 20 years on average, how could the company's sales possibly consist of almost 50% spare parts?

3. Weisberger's distributor network had built a significant business selling remanufactured meters outside the company's established sales channels.

4. Knowing that spare parts account for about 25% of the cost of a remanufactured meter, we concluded that the remanufactured market is $43.2 million ($10.8 million ÷ .25)!

So, my company proposed that:

1. Weisberger outsource 100% of its production to another local manufacturer with significant experience in re-manufacturing highly accurate fluid devices for Caterpillar.

2. Fully develop the $43 million market for remanufactured meters within its own sales channels.

3. Sell its plant and capital assets for approximately $7 million.

4. Focus on its core competencies, which are brand management, sales, and marketing.

If successfully executed, the net effect for Weisberger would be to grow sales from $23 million to $66.2 million, raise margins, reduce costs, reverse negative ROI, and pocket $7 million in cash from the sale of its capital assets.

MICHAEL ALLAN

12 East Dry Creek Place • Aurora, Colorado 80016
Home: (303) 555-1234 • Cell: (303) 555-5678 • Email: mallen@protypeltd.com

LONG-RANGE PLANS

- Work with the Superintendent to set up a process to review and possibly update the strategic plan.

- Work with the Superintendent and division heads to hold a summit with the central office to create or re-establish "core values" that will guide our work in serving the needs of the greater district and community.

- Ensure that the data retrieval on both state and district assessments are accessible to educators, reliable, and user friendly. These tools must also have the capability/potential to get data into the hands of our students on a monthly basis.

- Work with the Division of Instruction to begin or continue the process of "Smart Work"—teaching to CSAP Assessment Frameworks.

- Set up appointments to meet with every state legislator in El Paso County. These meetings will create an opportunity to discuss key educational issues and to share how the Board and the District look at the future.

- Develop professional development for principals and academic administrators that follows McRel's Balanced Leadership Model.

- Help prepare the Superintendent for opening day activities. The "Power of One" will be the main theme to continue moving the organization from "good" to "great."

- Provide leadership and direction to establish a tracking system for every high school student so that no individual falls through the cracks.

- Create a professional development plan that will impact every employee in the district. The plan must be created in collaboration with leaders of employee groups and with division heads.

PROPOSAL
THREE CRITICAL CHALLENGES FACING
PUBLIC EDUCATION IN THE NEXT DECADE

Public education is faced with many challenges during the next decade. Now more than ever we are being held accountable for increased student achievement and the responsibility of leaving no child behind. At a state and local level we are being asked to raise academic standards and demonstrate that our students are well prepared to enter college or seek further training. As a principal, I enthusiastically embrace these challenges and have been given an opportunity during my administrative career to implement strategies that make a difference in student achievement. Manitou High School has an excellent academic reputation. The high school has the additional benefit of an involved and caring community. This is exactly the strong foundation that I will utilize to assist Manitou Springs High School in meeting the following challenges that lie ahead.

Increasing Student Achievement

Increasing student achievement requires that we focus on the school's capacity and commitment to support all students in achieving their best. As an instructional leader at Manitou Springs High School, I will ensure that each student be given an opportunity to maximize their learning potential. Studies have shown that the quality and challenge of the high school curriculum has a direct correlation to success after high school. I am deeply committed to using research-based practices to close the achievement gap and to provide rigorous advanced curriculum opportunities for students. By accessing what is already in place and using existing energy and resources, we can create a learning community that will allow students to reach their highest potential.

Accountability

At every turn educators are being called upon to be accountable to the stakeholders they serve. Manitou Springs High School should be proud of its many accomplishments and the quality of education it provides students. CSAP testing and school report cards are important measures of accountability related to academic achievement. As principal, I will expand the scope of account-ability to ensure continued community trust and confidence in the school and district. I will accomplish this through a collaborative process of establishing goals that include school safety, expanded learning opportunities for all students, and community participation in school decision making. I will employ a variety of methods to ensure that the community is highly involved and well informed about how we are doing on meeting these goals.

Recruitment and Retention of Quality Teachers

A quality teacher is the single most important factor in whether students learn or whether they don't. I believe that developing leadership within the ranks of experienced teachers is an essential component of embedded staff development. This can be accomplished by creating a learning community where skilled, veteran teachers are provided opportunities to mentor new, less experienced teachers. It is critical that new teachers are provided with the strategies they need to be successful in the classroom and build the relationships needed to feel they are an integral part of the school and it's mission.

CHARLES TRUJILLO

1234 East 17th Avenue • Denver, Colorado 80203 • (720) 555-1234 • bocara@protypeltd.com • MySpace.com/sr8

BIOGRAPHY

Charles Trujillo, founder of the Denver Marathon, LLC, has made a career as a running athlete, event guru, and marketing maverick. With more than 21 years of development and operational experience, he has planned and managed a host of running, cycling, skiing, and mountain biking events in Colorado.

Trujillo began his running career by setting a 1984 Colorado state record at Northglenn High School in the two-mile event and was awarded a full running scholarship to the University of Colorado. At CU, he won three Big-Eight titles and was awarded three NCAA All-American appointments. Charles was a CU track and field coach before racing six years professionally for Team Reebok. He improved his running credentials by joining two U.S. World Teams, finishing 11th overall in the Junior World Cross-Country Championships.

In addition to his athletic career, Trujillo handled sports management and athlete marketing events for worldwide Olympic sponsor, Bausch & Lomb, from 1991 through 1995. He managed several professional teams and events for Reebok International, Ltd., and Team Chevrolet-Klein as an athlete manager and sponsorship manager, respectively, between 1995 and 1998.

Before founding the Denver Marathon, Trujillo created an events company that developed innovative sporting and entertaining events, primarily staffing, directing, and producing running, cycling, mountain biking, and inline skating events, as well as pool parties, singles affairs, social mixers, theatrical social gatherings, themed bar nights, and promotional street team events, among others.

Charles has managed strategic partnerships, sponsorships, media contacts, marketing, registration, and promotion during his 18 years as CEO of Denver Marathon. He raised a six-figure sponsorship budget the inaugural year and secured alliances with the Denver City Mayor's office to launch this successful event.

Currently, Charles has expanded his marketing knowledge by working in the nightlife Industry for the past three years as a general manager, managing partner, and marketing director for some of Denver's trendiest nightlife venues. This experience would be especially valuable to megahotels—like the Hard Rock in Las Vegas—who could exploit his strategic planning, brand building, and marketing expertise.

Trujillo's goals for the future include integrating his passion for sports with his experience marketing eyewear giants—like Bausch & Lomb, Ray-Ban, Killer-Loop, Von Zipper, Oakley, and Spy—through professional athletes and sponsorship deals. His expertise would also be valuable to clothing, shoe, or alcohol companies wishing to reach this rich market or to events companies that could use his experience selling sponsorships and creating/deploying events.

Cover Letters

Chapter 19

The first rule of cover letters: Never use a generic cover letter with only "To Whom It May Concern." With tons of work on your desk, would you be interested in such a mass mailing? You would probably consider it junk mail, right? You would be much more likely to read a letter that was directed to you personally, and so would human resources professionals.

The second rule: Every résumé sent by mail or fax needs a personalized cover letter even if the advertisement didn't request a cover letter.

The third rule: Résumés sent by e-mail don't need a true cover letter. Use only a quick paragraph with three to five sentences telling your reader where you heard about the position and why your qualifications are a perfect fit for the position's requirements. E-mail is intended to be short, sweet, and to the point. Then, cut and paste your ASCII text résumé into the e-mail message screen instead of just attaching your MS Word file (see Chapter 16 for an example of an ASCII text file and detailed instructions on how to create and use an electronic résumé).

This chapter will address several cover letter types. A letter to a recruiter requires different information than a letter in answer to an advertisement. A targeted cover letter that tells a story and captures your reader's attention is ideal when possible, but such letters aren't always practical. Not everyone has the writing skills to produce an effective story, and the time involved in researching and writing the story would be impractical for mass mailings. A hard-hitting salesperson can write a dynamic cover letter, but not everyone is comfortable with that style, and a good cover letter doesn't have to be "pushy."

Before we get into specific styles, let's cover some general rules that apply to most cover letters. The letters on pages 370, 373, 376–378, and 380 are general cover letters following these rules.

1. **Customize each cover letter** with an inside address (do not use "to whom it may concern").

2. **Personalize the greeting** (Dear Ms. Smith). Try to get the name of a person whenever possible. A blind advertisement makes that impossible, but in other cases a quick telephone call can often result in a name and sometimes a valuable

telephone conversation. When you can't get a name, use Dear Recruiter, Dear Hiring Manager, Dear Search Committee, or Dear Sir/Madam.

3. Mention where you heard about the position so your reader knows where to direct your résumé and letter. The first paragraph of your cover letter is a great place to state (or restate) your objective. Since you know the specific job being offered, you can tailor your objective to suit the position.

4. Keep the cover letter sounding positive and upbeat. You can open your cover letter with a strong accomplishments statement or emphasize why you want to work for that specific company. Kim Isaacs, one of *Monster.com's* résumé experts, has written the following example: *"Your company is truly a leader in healthcare information. You offer solutions that ultimately enhance the quality of healthcare delivery. I am excited about your mission and would be able to translate this excitement by providing top-notch administrative services to your team members."*

5. Be a name-dropper. In the first paragraph, mention the name of someone you know in the company. Hiring managers take unsolicited résumés more seriously when they assume you were referred by one of their employees or customers.

6. The second paragraph (or two) is your sales pitch. It is the perfect place to mention specific experience that is targeted to the job opening. This is your "I'm super great because" information. Here is where you summarize why you are absolutely perfect for the position. Really sell yourself and your passions. Your reader isn't interested in your life story. Hiring managers are inherently self-centered; they want to know what you can do for them. Show them that there is a direct match between their needs and what you can deliver. Focus on relevant accomplishments and proven performance to convince the reader that you are worthy of an interview.

   Pick and choose some of your experience and/or education that is specifically related to the company's requirements, or elaborate on qualifications that are not in your résumé but apply to this particular job. Research the company before writing your cover letter and become familiar with its mission, vision, and products or services. This will allow you to mention the specific needs of the company and your proposed solutions, which makes your letter more compelling to the reader.

   When your cover letter is targeted, it becomes immediately obvious that it is not generic. Don't make this section too long, though, or you will quickly lose the reader's interest. Entice the reader to find out more about you in your résumé.

7. The closing should be a concise "call to action." Reach out to the reader, letting him/her know what you want (an application, an interview, an opportunity to call). If you are planning to call the person on a certain day, you could close by saying, "I will contact you next Tuesday (or a more general "next week") to set up a mutually convenient time to meet." Don't call on Mondays or Fridays if you can help it. If you

aren't comfortable making these cold calls, then close your letter with something like: "I look forward to hearing from you soon." And remember to say, "Thank you for your consideration" or something to that effect (but don't be obsequious, please!).

STORY LETTERS

If you are planning a direct mail campaign to 50 or 100 or 400 companies, this type of letter is not for you. It just isn't practical. However, you will have to admit that the letter on page 375 is a great attention getter. For those dream jobs that require something special, this is the way to go. In a story cover letter, you must be able to tell a good story and write it well. If writing is not your forté, you can hire someone to write the letter, but you must still do the research and have a general outline of the story.

LETTERS TO RECRUITERS

There are two types of recruiters: retained and contingency. What is the difference between the two? Retained recruiters are hired by a company and are then paid by that company whether they ever find the right employee for the position or not. Contingency firms are also paid by the company but only when they find a good match and the job seeker is hired. Legitimate recruiting firms don't charge the job seeker a dime, which means they are working for their client companies and not *you*.

Because their mission is not to find the perfect job for you but to find the perfect employee for their client, they have little interest in communicating with you unless you are a prime candidate for a position they are seeking to fill *now*. Don't call recruiters; they will call you if they are interested. This affects both the beginning and ending of your cover letter. If you don't have a person's name, use Dear Recruiter. You should resign yourself to waiting for the recruiter to call you, so "I look forward to hearing from you soon" is an appropriate closing for a recruiter cover letter.

In addition to the "I'm super great because" paragraph(s), you need to add another paragraph just before the closing that tells the recruiter your ideal position title, industry, salary, and geographic preferences. Check the cover letter on page 384 for an example.

DYNAMIC LETTERS

Job openings that require a certain amount of dynamic spirit—like sales—deserve a more dynamic letter. This can be accomplished in the opening paragraph. The rest of the letter is written like a standard cover letter but with a little more energy than usual. The last paragraph can be a bit more aggressive—you call the hiring manager instead of waiting for him/her to call you. See pages 371, 372, 374, 379, 381–383, and 385 for examples of cover letters that exudes confidence and power.

According to a recent survey, less than 20% of applicants write a thank you note after an interview. Of the recruiters surveyed, 94% said that a thank you letter would increase the applicant's chances of getting the job, or at least help him/her stay in the running, provided the applicant is otherwise qualified. Fifteen minutes of your time and a first class postage stamp are very inexpensive investments in your career!

A good thank you letter continues the conversation you started during the interview. It simply thanks the interviewer for his or her time and reiterates some of the important things you learned about the company in the interview, which helps the interviewer remember who you are. Add some key qualifications that you forgot to mention in the interview, or emphasize some of the more important things you discussed. If the interviewer shared some information that gave you an insight into the company and its culture, build on it to prove you would be a good fit.

Your thank you letter should "connect" you to the interviewer. Put yourself in your interviewer's shoes and ask, "What would enlighten, delight, or inform me?" Find an article in a newspaper or magazine that would interest your interviewer and enclose it with your letter. It can be related to the industry or to your interviewer's hobbies and interests. Hopefully, you "connected" with the interviewer on a personal level by noticing things in his or her office that you can mention in your letter.

A thank you letter should be short—three paragraphs at the most. Don't try for the hard sell. You had your chance in the interview. The thank you letter just reinforces what you have already said and provides information you might have promised during the interview.

To be effective, your thank you letter should be mailed as soon as possible after the interview. I recommend no longer than seven days but preferably the day after the interview. Use the same letterhead as your résumé with a common business format and send it by snail mail. If the company and interviewer were very informal or you have received e-mail correspondence from the person before, then you can send a thank you letter by e-mail. E-mail might also be quicker if the candidate will be selected soon. Generally, a hard-copy letter is preferable. See the examples on pages 386 and 387.

LETTERHEADS

It is so easy to create a letterhead all your own and to make it match your résumé. Just copy into a new document the name and address you have already created for your résumé. It couldn't be simpler! It makes a very sharp impression when your cover letter and résumé match in every respect from paper color to font to letterhead.

PAPER COLOR

Color, like music, creates an atmosphere. Everyone knows that different colors evoke different feelings. Red can make a person feel warm, whereas blue does just the opposite.

Of course, you wouldn't want to use red in a résumé! . . . although an artist could get away with just about any color. As a general rule, résumé papers should be neutral or light in color. After 20 years in the résumé business, I have discovered that brilliant white linen paper is still the most popular, followed closely by a slightly off-white and then by shades of light gray.

Just make sure that the color of the paper you choose is representative of your personality and industry and that it doesn't detract from your message. For instance, a dark paper color makes your résumé hard to read.

In a scannable résumé, never use papers with a background (pictures, marble shades, or speckles). A scanner tries to interpret the patterns and dots as letters. This is a good rule to follow even for paper résumés that will never be scanned. Often companies will photocopy résumés for hiring managers, and dark colors or patterns will simply turn into dark masses that make your résumé difficult to read. If a company has multiple locations, the original résumé may even get faxed from one site to another and the same thing happens.

The type of paper (bond, linen, laid, cover stock, or coated) isn't as important, although it also projects an image. Uncoated paper (bond, linen, laid) makes a classic statement. It feels rich and makes people think of corporate stationery and important documents. Coated stock recalls memories of magazines, brochures, and annual reports. Heavy cover stock and laid paper can't be successfully folded and don't hold the ink from a laser printer or copier very well, so they must be handled gently. All of these factors play a part in your paper choice.

Regardless of the paper you choose, mail your résumé flat instead of folded. It costs a few extra cents in postage and a little more for the 9 × 12 envelope, but the impression it makes is well worth the extra cost. It also helps with the scannability of your résumé. Thank you letters and other follow-up letters can be folded in standard No. 10 business envelopes.

Experienced Sales and Marketing Professional
Project Management – Data Analysis – Sales Support

Market and Business Analysis – Project Management – High-Impact Presentations
Copywriting – Training – Vendor Management – Database Marketing

► **Charlotte Johansen**
12345 Carmel Creek Rd.
San Diego, CA 92130

cjohansen@protypeltd.com
619.555.1234

October 15, 2010

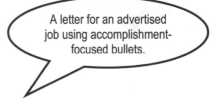

A letter for an advertised job using accomplishment-focused bullets.

Mr. Alan Robinson
National Aviation, Inc.
P.O. Box 456
Ft. Collins, Colorado 80522

Re: Manager of Vendor Performance

Dear Mr. Robinson:

Whether challenged to create a sales support program from scratch, hire and train a high-performance team in a matter of weeks, or create effective training programs and compelling presentations, I have repeatedly delivered stellar results. Examples include:

- ► Increasing sales up to 300% by conceiving and executing novel cross-merchandising strategy.
- ► Leading multiple top-performing internal and third-party teams.
- ► Improving management capabilities by adopting leading industry practices and innovating proprietary data analysis tools.
- ► Optimizing CRM by streamlining data management systems and practices.
- ► Defining and succeeding in newly defined positions and building specialized teams.

Your search for a **Manager of Vendor Performance** caught my eye because of your desire for a candidate who can launch a complex vendor quality program from scratch. Defining and implementing performance-oriented tools and processes involving multiple players is my expertise. I would welcome a personal meeting to learn more about your needs and discuss my potential contributions.

Thank you for taking the time to consider my candidacy.

Sincerely,

Charlotte Johansen

Charlotte Johansen

Enclosure

James Pitt
PRODUCTION MANAGER

Address: 12345 Park Way, Piedmont, CA 94611
Phone: (510) 555-1234
Email: pitt@protypeltd.com

July 22, 2010

Skill-focused, cold-calling letter with no job advertised.

Talent Acquisition
St. John Corporation
122 Armstrong Ave
Irvine, CA 92614

Dear Recruiter:

I am an exceptionally talented, award-winning, and self-directed production management professional who has made a mark in various facets of web-based project environments including team recruitment and management, user Interface direction, executive production, client relations, sales, and budgetary control. I am passionate and energetic and can quickly analyze complex projects in high-paced environments, establish priorities, and formulate effective solutions to consistently exceed expectations with timely and cost-effective results.

As an outstanding resource-builder, I will not rest until the project is completed to the highest possible standards. My technical understanding and hands-on abilities in the areas of web-based strategies will make me an invaluable member of your organization.

My experience supports this passion and I am proud to have delivered notable projects and solutions across a diverse, yet integrated landscape. My notable skills encompass workflow and process improvement, video production, web interactive production on usability design and improvement, 15 years Photoshop familiarity, experience in location photography in addition to color correction processes. I invite you to read more about my accomplishments in my attached resume.

Furthermore, I am recognized as an energetic motivator and communicator who is consistently acknowledged by colleagues, clients, and stakeholders alike as an intuitive problem-solver, excellent leader, and a dedicated professional with the talent and experience to deliver measurable results in high-volume web production platforms.

I will follow up with you in a few days to answer any questions you may have. In the meantime, you may reach me at the above phone number or via email. I look forward to learning more about your company's goals and how I can contribute to your continued success. Thank you for your time and consideration.

Sincerely,

James Pitt

James Pitt

Enc: Résumé

Eric T. Pryor

1015 Kent Street
Chicago, IL 88997

713-987-06543 or 713-687-5678
pryor@protypeltd.com

August 28, 2010

Ms. Michelle Stone
Chief, Human Resources Analyst
Sampson Human Resources Consulting Corporation, Inc
6655 Kumis Blvd
Chicago, IL 22665

SUBJECT: "Personnel Operations Manager" listed on your company website on Aug 27, 2010

Dear Ms. Stone:

 Based on each of our professional objectives today could ultimately prove to be both our lucky day!! In response to the employment opportunity listed on your web posting, I am submitting this cover letter and accompanying résumé for consideration. Evidenced by my employment history and career enhancement training are skills that demonstrate in-depth business acumen, industry specific intellect, distinctive qualifications, and accomplishments related to:

- ✓ **Performing special reviews and surveys in conjunction with manpower and management analysis surveys, to identify problems in alignment, supervisor/employee ratios, delineation of duties and responsibilities, career enhancing opportunities in the organization structure, employee retention, and delegations of authority.**
- ✓ **Making full use of special employment programs for students, youth, veterans, the handicapped, women, and minorities.**
- ✓ **Strategizing and executing quality assurance initiatives that define problems, analyze alternatives, and recommending solutions to assess effectiveness of programs.**

As requested, my previous positions commanded an average annual salary of $100K in addition to a full benefit package. I have no doubt that your company offers a salary that is both fair and competitive and therefore open for discussion.

I welcome being able to discuss my qualifications and this employment opportunity further. I will follow up with you early next week to discuss arranging a mutually agreeable time. Thank you in advance, for both your time and consideration.

Respectfully yours,

Eric T. Pryor

Eric T. Pryor

ATT: Résumé

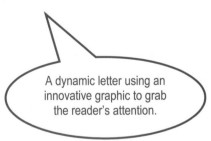

A dynamic letter using an innovative graphic to grab the reader's attention.

August 16, 2010

Unsolicited letter to create a job.

Ms. Nancy Waite
COO, Executive Vice President
Ports of Call
3333 Quebec Street, Suite 9100
Denver, Colorado 80207-2331

Dear Ms. Waite:

Carol Ingwersen recommended that I forward a copy of my résumé for your review. I am very interested in returning to the travel industry in a sales capacity and would appreciate an opportunity to sit down with you to talk about the unique ideas I could bring to your sales process.

As you can see in my résumé, I have extensive sales and customer service experience, but what you can't see is that I have worked for travel clubs twice in my career. I succeeded in selling 450 memberships in only three months for The Diplomats in Des Moines, Iowa, and I worked as the membership director for the Texas Air Travel Club during my early career. With its own private jet and 2,500 members, the Texas Air Travel Club was very similar to Ports of Call. I developed some innovative ways of increasing memberships that would be valuable to your company.

Even though you don't have any current openings, I think you will find my ideas worthy of a trial even if you have to create a position for me. I will give you a call next week to see if there is a mutually convenient time we can get together to talk about the possibilities. Thank you for your consideration.

Sincerely,

David Kovach

David F. Kovach

Enclosure

STEPHEN L. JOHNSON

ACCOUNT EXECUTIVE / SALES MANAGER

12345 Elizabeth Avenue, Pfafftown, NC 27040
Home: (336) 555-1234 • Cell: (336) 555-1234
johnson@protypeltd.com

November 15, 2009

Ms. Shelly Brockheimer
Human Resources Manager
Wachovia Bank
301 N. Main Street
Winston-Salem, NC 27101

A dynamic cover with a strong accomplishment focus.

Dear Ms. Brockheimer:

As a key account diplomat and sales manager, I am equipped with a commanding track record in finding and optimizing winning business ideas while driving solid company expansion within fast-paced, highly competitive landscapes.

You will notice one common thread throughout my career—I am a lateral-thinking negotiator and problem solver who knows how to identify new business opportunities, negotiate rewarding and mutually beneficial contracts based on detailed assessment of client requirements, and close the deal through masterful presentations and appropriate recommendations of products and services tailored to client business objectives. With this dynamic approach, I have successfully gained recognition for consistent first-ranking achievements in sales, superb management of the retail planning process for Hanesbrands, Inc. (a multi-billion dollar company), achievement of high-level product penetration percentages, facilitation of multi-million dollar sales results, and forging a multitude of referral client relationships from my devoted reputation for service delivery to the fullest.

Purposefully scrutinizing operational processes including inventory flows and shipment statistics, I dedicate all efforts to functional superiority. Emphasis on precision forecasting, troubleshooting, initiation of process, and planning improvements in addition to report preparation and presentation are all indicators of my unyielding follow-through and dedication.

Furthermore, I am a respected administrator, motivator, and mentor who has garnered trustworthiness and commitment across multi-talented groups of highly-skilled professionals from internal staff and client teams alike. I have trained staff in sales and marketing techniques as well as demonstrated appropriate product and service features to customers for assurance of business enrichment.

I encourage you to read more about my notable achievements in my attached résumé, as I am confident that I can deliver similar results for your company. My geographic preferences center on the southeastern United States, and I am quite willing to relocate for a mutually acceptable offer. I look forward to a discussion with you regarding your future goals and how I can contribute to their realization.

I will follow up with you in a few days to answer any questions you may have. Meanwhile, you may reach me at the above phone number or via email. I look forward to our conversation and thank you for your time and consideration.

Sincerely,

Stephen L. Johnson

Stephen L. Johnson

Enclosure: Résumé

"Steve's strong customer relationships have been instrumental in maintaining client satisfaction through some difficult operational challenges. He is extremely client-focused and is always in our clients' operating reality." **– John Truliant, Executive Vice President, Flexible Payroll Solutions**

CAROLINE KAZYNSKI
12345 LINCOLN AVENUE, MILWAUKEE, WISCONSIN 53203
414-555-1234 / kazynski@protypeltd.com

January 15, 2010

A letter to a former customer, explaining downsizing and asking for referrals.

Mr. and Mrs. Harvey Fredericks
12345 Sunnyside Lane
Milwaukee, WI 53203

Dear Mr. and Mrs. Fredericks:

It has always been my pleasure to work at Home Expo and to provide valuable design services for homeowners like yourself who made the decision to let us help with their remodeling plans. I trust that you are enjoying your new kitchen and receiving many compliments from visitors to your home. As you have probably heard by now, Home Expo has, unfortunately, closed all of its stores due to the downturn in the economy. However, I want to thank you for the confidence you had in me as your designer and to let you know that I am still available to answer any questions you may have.

I have now started my own business venture, representing many fine lines of stock and custom cabinetry. Together with my team of two talented design consultants, we have more than 30 years of combined experience as well as the services of skilled contractors I personally know would work hard to achieve a beautiful end result to any project. Enclosed is a copy of my current résumé that will provide a more comprehensive summary of my background and achievements. My major strengths include:

- Building relationships by listening carefully to clients' ideas and communicating through each step of design and installation to turn their visions into reality.

- Creativity and forward thinking in all project areas, with a special flair for creating eye-catching designs that meet customers' financial and aesthetic needs.

- Exceptional project management, budgeting, and organizational skills honed from a heavy workload and fast-paced, highly competitive environment that demands quality performance and timely completion.

- The ability to turn around adverse situations—including difficult building conditions both anticipated and previously unforeseen—to meet project demands without cost overruns.

Please take a few minutes to think about possible needs among your friends or acquaintances who may benefit from our design talents and pass along one of my enclosed business cards. I would be happy to arrange a meeting with them at no cost or obligation to discuss their kitchen and bath remodeling needs, no matter how large or small. Your continued support is greatly appreciated.

Sincerely,

Caroline Kazynski

Caroline Kazynski

Enclosures: Resume and business cards

MEREDITH STRUNK, MGA

12345 Tunnel Road, Palo Alto, CA 94301 • 650-555-1234 (mb) • strunk@protypeltd.com

January 1, 2010

A letter relating the writer's strengths to the hiring company's needs.

Human Resources
PricewaterhouseCoopers
1234 Avenue of the Americas
New York, NY 10013

Dear Hiring Team:

I am writing to express my considerable interest in the ***Senior Business and Technology Analyst*** position you announced on Monster.com. I believe I am uniquely qualified for the position, offering 12 years of experience as a trusted partner to senior managers and stakeholders on high-stakes technology consulting projects.

From my days at Ernst & Young to my current role at Citigroup, I have built a career hinged on the principles of information technology and web software development, centered on using analysis and improvement methodologies to efficiently execute business and user goals. My strengths include:

- **System Design and Revision Lifecycle Management:** Striking a balance between technical decisions and end-user experience, particularly relating to: problem solving / alternative solutions; user vs. business system requirements; testing, training and acceptance criteria; and information handling and reporting.

- **Constituent Relations and Project Leadership:** Building and managing relationships with internal and external stakeholders, including senior executives, IT managers and staff; vendors, consultants, and clients.

- **Technical Optimization and Efficiency Setting:** Analyzing core business objectives and technology solutions against multi-industry standards and best practices. Includes technology investment and feasibility advisement, system utilization, and documentation requirements facilitation.

Most importantly, I help organizations anticipate and confront roadblocks early in the project lifecycle, bringing to light weaknesses and potential risks while identifying areas for improvement. I thrive in ambiguous environments, with a practiced ability to align contributor and stakeholder expectations.

My résumé is enclosed for your review. Citigroup's IT division is moving out of state, and I am looking forward to exploring a new role with a company like yours. Please reach me any time at 650-555-1234 or strunk@protypeltd.com. I look forward to meeting you soon.

Sincerely,

Meredith Strunk

Meredith Strunk

Encl: Résumé

Ingrid Hägglund, M.A. ————————————

Influential • Analytical • Pragmatic • Resourceful • Tenacious • Inspiring • Engaging

August 14, 2009

> *"Ingrid was a valuable contributor to our department and we miss her ... exceptional interpersonal skills, determination, intellectual curiosity, ... upbeat outlook."*
> – Robyn Stone, Ph.D.
> Clarkson University

Roslyn Smith, M.S.
Community Programs Manager
Barrington, Inc.
2268 North Fountain Avenue
Milwaukee, WI 53201

Dear Ms. Smith:

I am writing to express my considerable interest in the **Program Specialist, Milwaukee** position announced by **Barrington, Inc.,** on TheLadders.com. With more than nine years of part-time and university-based professional experience, I believe I am uniquely qualified for the role.

As you may appreciate, I am searching for the right fit, which means returning to work in a team-oriented, part-time position after a family sabbatical that included U.S. relocation with my husband as he undertook a new assistant professorship at the University of Wisconsin.

Barrington's mission parallels my pursuit of a second master's degree in counseling psychology. Assisting the organization's staff would be an ideal environment to jumpstart my work and education in the world of family resource planning and assistance.

The enclosed résumé outlines the skills and experience I would bring to Barrington, Inc., in the areas of outreach and internal program support. Additionally, I offer a strong professional ethic; intellectual curiosity, warmth, and instinctive reasoning; and adaptability, critical thinking, and goal-directed diligence.

I am open to working during the times specified in Barrington's job description and look forward to having an opportunity to meet with you in person to discuss the position. Please contact me any time at 414-555-1234 (mobile) or hagglund@protypeltd.com.

Sincerely,

Ingrid Hägglund

Ingrid Hägglund

Encl: *Résumé*

A letter answering an online advertisement.

1234 Grove Street, Milwaukee, WI 53208 • 414-555-1234 (mb) • hagglund@protypeltd.com • Green Card Holder

JAMES D. KENT

222.777.7676 ★ jkent@protypeltd.com

October 12, 2010

Judy Benner, Chief
HR Department
Craddock Enterprise
1301 Fifth Avenue, Suite 4000
Seattle, Washington 98101

Dear Ms. Benner:

I was excited to learn of your need for a **Sales Representative** through your advertisement on Indeed.com. I believe my skills and unique background will be a tremendous benefit for you in developing, sustaining, and exceeding your sales targets.

My passion for servicing customers and strengthening my professional relationships has driven my success throughout my career. I savor the customer focus and contact, value each challenge, and thrive on exploiting new business opportunities, whether in additional sales or untapped niches.

Let me point out three good reasons to consider me for the position:

YOUR NEEDS	MY SKILLS
Driven, Self-Motivated Individual	In my most recent position as Sales Representative, I increased my company's market share and revenue 40% by developing a partnership with another firm.
Client Relationship Management	Throughout my career, clients have commented on the "special consideration" paid to them, which resulted in repeat business, referrals, and clients who requested my services and personal attention year over year.
New Business Development	In my most recent position, as well as in my personal businesses, I have multiplied the customer base anywhere from 25% to 50% in the first year.

I know I can deliver the same results for Craddock Enterprise, and I would welcome the opportunity to speak with you in more detail. I will call your office at 9:00 AM on Wednesday, October 22nd to speak with you further. Enclosed is my résumé for your review. Thank you for your time and consideration.

Sincerely,

James D. Kent

James D. Kent

Enclosure: Résumé

A letter answering an ad and associating the company's needs with the writer's qualifications.

Tamara Lynn Beckham
Certified Wedding Planner

~~~~~~~~~~~~~~~~~~~~~~~~~~~~~~~~~~~~

55 Westminster Avenue, London, W10 6LM
Tel: (020) 8072 9261 or (079) 4972 4323
tamara@protypeltd.com

~~~~~~~~~~~~~~~~~~~~~~~~~~~~~~~~~~~~

January 31, 2010

> A dynamic letter broadcast to all wedding shops in town to create a job.

Mrs. Valerie Davidson
Proprietor
The Wedding Shoppe
101 Chamberlain Road
London SW1 6RF

Dear Mrs. Davidson:

If you could delegate work to someone who would do it right the first time, would you increase your business, your profits, and your own free time?

As a recent graduate of The Wedding Planning Institute, I can effectively assist you—quickly and with a minimum of training—on a full-time, part-time, freelance, or short-notice basis.

I offer solid organizational and clerical skills gained from employment as a front-line customer service professional, office supervisor, bookkeeper, and administrator. Also, I have successfully planned and delivered two events. In addition, my referees will attest to my abilities to stay calm, cool, and collected during 'crisis' situations. Using well-honed customer service skills gained in the hotel industry, I'm able to defuse escalated customer complaints, act when others hesitate, and remain professionally polite under all circumstances.

Perhaps most importantly, I'm a cheerful and confident lady who wins the trust and confidence of clients. I deliver on my promises by being very well-organized, meticulously detail-orientated, and 100% serious about doing every job to the best of my abilities.

Thank you for taking the time to read this letter and enclosed résumé. If you could use a trusted and capable assistant, please call or email me at your convenience. I would especially appreciate the opportunity to meet with you so that we can discuss precisely how I could help you deliver a perfect wedding day to your clients.

Sincerely yours,

Tamara Beckham

Tamara Lynn Beckham
Certified Wedding Planner
Diploma, Event Management

Enclosure: Résumé

Susan Madigan

5511 West Main Street
Pittsburg, Pennsylvania 12345

(888) 555-1111
smadigan@protypeltd.com

October 6, 2010

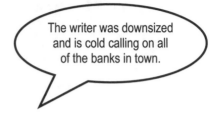

The writer was downsized
and is cold calling on all
of the banks in town.

Joan Baker, Vice President
ABC Mortgage Services
123 First Avenue
Pittsburg, PA 12345

Subject: Senior Risk Manager, Credit and Counterpart Risk, #22594

Dear Ms. Baker:

Given the country's current financial crisis, I have been compelled to offer my expertise in the banking industry, particularly in the area of risk management. During my 15+ years tenure in loss mitigation, quality control, and due diligence, I have acquired the reputation for increasing staff efficiency, establishing and maintaining project standards and compliance, and minimizing risk.

Some of my key accomplishments include:

- Reduced loan rejection rate from 40% to 3%.
- Established automated comprehensive mortgage risk database, increasing productivity by 50%.
- Revitalized, reorganized and trained staff to ensure regulatory compliance for 4 organizations.

After the unfortunate downsizing of Wachovia Bank, I would welcome the opportunity to speak with you about how I can help ABC Mortgage Services meet their current challenges head on. Please contact me at your earliest convenience to arrange an interview. Thank you in advance for your consideration.

Sincerely,

Susan Madigan

Susan Madigan

Enclosure: résumé

SARAH JOHNSON, R.N.
28549 Cloverfield Drive
Agua Dulce, California 91350
sarah5289@yahoo.com

Residence: 661-471-6501   Cellular: 661-295-8015

November 15, 2010

A dynamic letter for a career change.

Ms. Melanie Duff
Reliable Home Nurses
23589 Sue Drive, Suite 350
Studio City, California 91605

Dear Ms. Duff:

In this modern world, there is a new model for a successful career—a series of lateral moves that keeps a person involved in new tasks while using the same set of skills. The employee gets the satisfaction of variety and of doing something well, and the employer gets the benefit of a staff member with extensive related experience.

Having worked as both a registered nurse and an office manager in a dental practice, I find that my passion now lies in working as a clinical nurse.

Total commitment to the patients in my care and to the achievement of the objectives of the facility and medical staff is my primary focus. You will find me to be quick to learn and eager to initiate self-directed work when appropriate.

As my résumé details, I can ensure doctor's orders are implemented, that the patients have the needed supplies and meds, and evaluate nursing care. I excel at evaluating patient needs as they change such as physical therapy and nutritional evaluations. Equally strong is my aid with activities of daily living.

Unlike most clinical nurses, I have a strong background in business. You will find me unequalled in following up on appointments, willing to work for private duty shifts, being extremely flexible with days and hours, and being a valuable partner in your expansion to the Santa Clarita and Antelope Valleys. Of course, I would not neglect the San Fernando Valley.

A good fit seems to exist between your requirements and my experience. As such, a personal interview to further explore a mutually beneficial relationship would be greatly appreciated. Thank you for your time and consideration.

Sincerely,

Sarah Johnson

Sarah Johnson

Enclosure

Gerry-Ann Slater

Term Time: 120 Albert Sq., London E20 2MP
Home: 49 Hillside Ave., New York, NY 10034

Phone: (444) 208.716.2345
gerryann@protypeltd.com

May 19, 2009

As a potential intern, do I believe that the publishing industry is glamorous? Yes, I do!

But, I realize that it's also hard work and that the rewards and satisfaction make it all worthwhile.

Tanya Branning
Intern Program Manager
Fashion Market Magazine Group
617 West 46th Street, Second Floor
New York, NY 10036

Dear Ms. Branning:

If you are seeking a **Publishing Intern** who is truly committed to putting in the effort required to establish a career in publishing, please read on.

As outlined in the attached résumé, I bring the education and practical experience that you need. Next year, I will complete my Bachelor of Arts degree in magazine publishing from a prestigious university in London, UK. So far, I have studied design, print production, marketing, advertising sales, editorial skills, finance, and product development. Currently, I am a team member on a fashion magazine publishing project based on Grazia Italia.

Last summer, I gained "real world" publishing experience when I participated in an internship program at Haute Couture à Imprimer in Montréal, Canada. My work involved many of the processes behind magazine publishing, including editing, design, production, website maintenance, and client relationship management.

Before starting my studies, I worked in sales and office management at Rimmel London in New York. In this role, I used my multi-tasking skills to organize administrative and business functions and to ensure the smooth running of the office. I also liaised with international contacts on the phone, interacted with sales staff, and provided face-to-face customer service. I used various computer programs, including Adobe CS3 and an MS Access database.

All of my employers have praised my detail-oriented approach to administrative work and my self-assured manner when dealing with clients and contributing to team efforts. Whether at work or at university, I take a proactive approach to meeting deadlines under pressure and to resolving problems in challenging circumstances.

Perhaps most importantly, I am not just passionate about the magazine publishing business but also about your magazine's subject matter—fashion and beauty. Thank you for taking the time to consider my application, and I look forward to hearing from you.

With great interest,

Gerry-Ann Slater

Gerry-Ann Slater

Enclosure: Résumé

A dynamic letter to create an internship position.

HAROLD STEVENS

1325 Richards Road, #53 ▪ Seattle, WA 98117 ▪ (206) 555-1212 ▪ Email: harold.stevens@protypeltd.com

January 30, 2010

A dynamic letter graphically highlighting the applicant's strengths.

David Kosar
Network Manager
Qwest Communications
1256 Main Street
Seattle, WA 98118

Dear Mr. Kosar:

I take quite seriously my core responsibilities to identify and protect against security vulnerabilities and to provide best practice solutions that can be executed rapidly and reliably. My goal is to continuously refine my skills as a network security expert. I keep up to date on the latest techniques, policies, and practices in information security management. I enjoy my work and take great pride in the results that I produce.

My history of increasingly responsible roles is demonstrated by accomplishments in designing and maintaining secure systems. Highlights include:

Accountability—Monitor business and information management activities to ensure appropriate authentication of user accounts.

Integrity—Prevent unauthorized access by corrupted systems or individuals by maintaining the integrity of the data architecture and regularly conducting vulnerability assessments of critical systems.

Confidentiality—Foster good working relationships with business units. Conduct information sessions to discuss security policies and best practices for maintaining the organization's information assets.

Availability—React quickly to system anomalies; reduce downtime and unavailability due to overused or poorly configured security controls.

Thank you for your time and consideration. I would welcome the opportunity to interview for this position and I look forward to hearing from you.

Sincerely,

Harold Stevens

Harold Stevens

Enclosure

1234 Bridle Trail
Pueblo, Colorado 81005

Phone: (719) 555-1234
polacek@protypeltd.com

November 17, 2010

Letter to a recruiter. Note the third paragraph that is unique in letters to headhunters.

Mr. Stefan Smith
President
Management Search, Inc.
1234 S. Cook St., Suite 12
Barrington, IL 60010

Dear Mr. Smith:

Is one of your clients looking for a Human Resources or Labor Relations Manager with a proven track record of success in both manufacturing and high-tech services industries? Then you will want to review my qualifications.

As a successful human resource generalist with extensive labor relations experience, I have become well known for my ability to improve employee morale and increase trust between unions and management. I have negotiated and administered several collective bargaining agreements and was often called in to diffuse stalled bargaining processes. My dynamic leadership style motivates change within the corporate culture and builds support from within the ranks. These skills, plus many more, would be true assets to any company whether they are unionized or not.

My target job is at the middle-management level with an innovative company that could challenge my skills in human resource management, employee relations, and compensation and benefit administration. I have no geographic preferences and would be open to relocation. My salary requirements would of course depend on the city, but I would anticipate a base salary in the area of $60,000.

Should one of your clients have a current or emerging need for a member of their human resource management team, I would appreciate your serious consideration of my qualifications as outlined in the enclosed résumé. I am free to meet with you at your convenience and look forward to hearing from you soon.

Sincerely,

Tony Polacek

Tony Polacek

Enclosure

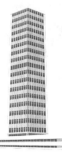

John G. Warren

1st Avenue #4C – Long Island City, New York 11106 – Cell: 407-555-1234 – Home: 212-555-5678 – E-mail: jgwarren@protypeltd.com

September 12, 2010

A dynamic letter for a senior management position.

Florida Hotel & Resort
3138 Terry Brook
Winter Park, Florida

Dear Employment Manager:

You need impeccable guest services, tenacious management, and a sincere desire to fulfill expectations to cement memorable experiences for customers in the hospitality industry. As an experienced General/Senior Manager with more than 10 years of experience ensuring excellent operations, propelling profits, and delivering superb service, I now offer you my assistance as your new General Resort Manager.

In order to annihilate your competition, retain your existing clientele, and win new ones, your hotel must service above the standards of your competitors and make an impression with competent and professional people. In addition, your facility must invite your existing and prospective guests with pleasing aesthetics and seductive comfort. Above all, every person in your team MUST exceed the expectations of every guest with which they interact. I offer to secure these essentials for your hotel and continue to uphold the professional image Florida Hotel & Resort exudes.

With an accomplished history under my current employer, I now seek an opportunity to contribute in the hotel industry with an upscale establishment like yours. Please review my attached résumé, and allow me to highlight the following. I have…

- ✓ Turned low-performing locations into profitable establishments that pleased directors, owners, and customers.
- ✓ Enhanced already successful establishments and produced in areas overlooked by other managers.
- ✓ Led large staffs by motivating them, infusing them with confidence, and leading them by example.
- ✓ Communicated with corporate and non-corporate personnel using language that is clear, sensible, intelligent, and persuasive.
- ✓ Developed a valuable reputation with a highly demanding clientele by delivering on promises and anticipating their comfort and service needs.
- ✓ Generated millions in annual gross by overhauling departments and decreasing expenditures.

The value I will bring to your hotel is not limited to the above. In me, you will gain a manager that can forecast financial, operational, and guest needs accurately, prioritize and manage intelligently, and own all responsibilities in your organization, which will lead to your continued success.

Thank you in advance for your time and consideration. I look forward to hearing from you.

Sincerely,

John Warren

John G. Warren

SALLY RENE STEWART

5000 West 5th Street
Lubbock, Texas 79400
(806) 555-1234
srs@protypeltd.com

September 20, 2010

Ms. Jane Young
The Design Center
Merimax Interiors, Inc.
234 Waukegan Road
Lubbock, Texas 79402

A thank you letter reiterating why she is perfect for the job.

Dear Ms. Young:

Thank you for the time you extended me during our interview last Tuesday. Our discussion was enlightening and enjoyable. I am sincerely interested in a designer position with Merimax Interiors, Inc., as I was impressed with your company's culture, growth options, and mission to provide creative yet functional interior designs to clients in the medical care industry.

As you may recall, my particular strength is a positive approach to my work and a commitment to excellence in any endeavor I attempt. The honors I attained during my college career at Texas Tech University reflect my quest for distinction. The prospect of putting my color and design knowledge to work in a business environment such as yours at Merimax Interiors, Inc., is thrilling.

If you have additional questions, please feel free to contact me at (806) 555-1234. I look forward to hearing again from you in the very near future.

Again, thank you for your interest in my qualifications for your designer vacancy.

Sincerely,

Sally Stewart

Sally Rene Stewart

David M. Hudson

4321 Oakmoore Avenue NE
Massillon, OH 44646
330-555-1234

February 10, 2010

An interview thank you letter.

Mr. Randall Killian
Manager, Prototype Operations
Topco Industries Inc.
4231 Seabrook Ave. NW
North Canton, OH 44720

Dear Mr. Killian:

I would like to take this opportunity to thank you for the interview Thursday afternoon at your office and to confirm my strong interest in the CNC Machinist position.

After we spoke, it became increasingly clear to me that the position we discussed would be a good fit for my skills and interest. I recognize that this is a busy department with a demanding schedule and a need for accuracy and the ability to meet deadlines. I believe my background, experience, and skills will allow me to make a positive contribution in this department. I hope you will consider me for this position.

In closing, I would like to again thank you for sharing your valuable time with me. I am excited about the possibilities of this position and remain even more convinced of the potential for a good match. I would consider it a privilege to be an employee of a company with an excellent reputation such as Topco. I look forward to a favorable outcome.

Sincerely,

David M. Hudson

David M. Hudson

MATT C. LINCOLN
8899 1st Place – Lubbock, Texas 79416
(806) 555-1234
mattlincoln89@protypeltd.com

August 26, 2010

The letter every job seeker can't wait to write.

Mr. Jack Preston
Vice President
Cox & Preston Advertising
9986 Avenue G
Lubbock, Texas 79401

Dear Jack:

It is with mixed emotions that I present this letter of resignation. As you know, my parents have been ailing for the last three years. Considering their poor health, I have secured a position with Braxton and Braxton in New York City to be near them. I will relocate to that area in two months. However, it is my intention to remain in the office for at least two to four weeks to ease the transition in filling my vacancy.

I want to express to you that my ten years with you and David have been rewarding and beneficial to my growth as a layout artist. You have both been great associates and mentors. I only hope my position with Braxton and Braxton will bring me as much job satisfaction.

Please let me know if there is anything else I must do to complete the resignation process.

Sincerely,

Matt Lincoln

Matt C. Lincoln

Résumé Worksheets

Chapter 20

I developed worksheets for my Barron's book *How to Write Better Résumés and Cover Letters* that have received rave reviews. Since they follow the twelve-step résumé writing process in Chapter 2 of this book, they can be useful for your résumé development. You can download free MS Word, Adobe Acrobat, or Corel WordPerfect files of the worksheets at *www.patcriscito.com* by selecting the "Pat's Books" link.

If you need more detail on how to use the worksheets than you find in Chapter 2, you might want to pick up a copy of *How to Write Better Résumés and Cover Letters* at your local library or bookstore.

You should copy as many of the Experience, College Education, Vocational/Technical Training, Professional Development, and Keyword worksheets as you need for your own experience.

■ ■ ■ CONTACT INFORMATION ■ ■ ■

This final stage of information gathering will provide you with all the information you need to begin your résumé. For the contact information, you can use your full name, first and last name only, or shortened names (Pat Criscito instead of Patricia K. Criscito). If you have a rather common name, you need to differentiate yourself or a Google search will result in pages of information that don't apply to you. Try using your legal name with middle initial or spelled out your middle name.

Do not use work telephone numbers or a work e-mail address on your résumé. Potential employers tend to consider that an abuse of company resources, which implies you might do the same if you are working for them. Listing a cell phone number on your résumé gives a hiring manager a way to reach you during working hours.

Avoid the use of "cutesy" e-mail addresses on a résumé. If you use *babycakes@aol.com* for your personal e-mail, create a second e-mail address under your account that will be more professional. If your only access to the Internet is at work, then create a free-mail account at *hotmail.com, aol.com, msn.com, juno.com, about.com, yahoo.com, excite.com, gmail.com, mail.com, gawab.com, inbox.com, fastmail.com, bigstream.com*, or any other free e-mail services.

If you have accounts with social networking sites, make sure they are "safe" for your career before listing them on your résumé. You don't want a potential employer to see photos of you at a drunken toga party. Even if you don't list your site addresses on your résumé, a potential employer could Google you and find them anyway.

NAME:

ADDRESS:

CITY / STATE / ZIP:

COUNTRY (if applying outside the country where you live):

HOME PHONE:	CELL PHONE:

E-MAIL ADDRESS:

WEBSITE / E-FOLIO URL:

LINKED IN:	FACEBOOK:
MY SPACE:	YOU TUBE:
TWITTER:	OTHER:

■ ■ ■ COLLEGE EDUCATION ■ ■ ■

Use this form to collect information on your formal college education. Write down everything you can think of, regardless of whether you use it on the final résumé. You will narrow the list later. Copy this page so you have a separate one for each degree.

DEGREE: _____

SCHOOL: _____

CITY AND STATE: _____

YEARS ATTENDED: _____

YEAR GRADUATED: _____ GPA: _____

MAJOR: _____

MINOR: _____

THESIS/DISSERTATION: _____

_____

_____

SIGNIFICANT PROJECTS: _____

_____

_____

_____

HONORS, AWARDS, SCHOLARSHIPS: _____

_____

_____

_____

ACTIVITIES (volunteer, leadership, sports, social groups, etc.): _____

_____

_____

_____

STUDY ABROAD (program, school, country, special areas of study): ___

_____

_____

_____

■ ■ ■ Vocational/Technical Training ■ ■ ■

Use this form to collect information on your vocational, technical, occupational, and military training. Write everything you can think of, regardless of whether it relates to your job goal. You will narrow the list later. Copy this page if you have more courses than you are able to list below.

NAME OF COURSE:

PRESENTED BY (company, school):

RESULT (certification, diploma):

DATES ATTENDED:

NAME OF COURSE:

PRESENTED BY (company, school):

RESULT (certification, diploma):

DATES ATTENDED:

NAME OF COURSE:

PRESENTED BY (company, school):

RESULT (certification, diploma):

DATES ATTENDED:

NAME OF COURSE:

PRESENTED BY (company, school):

RESULT (certification, diploma):

DATES ATTENDED:

NAME OF COURSE:

PRESENTED BY (company, school):

RESULT (certification, diploma):

DATES ATTENDED:

■ ■ ■ PROFESSIONAL DEVELOPMENT ■ ■ ■

Use this form to collect information on your professional development and continuing education, including in-services, workshops, seminars, corporate training programs, conferences, conventions, etc. Write down everything you can think of, regardless of whether it relates to your job goal. You will narrow the list later.

NAME OF COURSE: _____

PRESENTED BY (company, school): _____

DATES ATTENDED: _____

NAME OF COURSE: _____

PRESENTED BY (company, school): _____

DATES ATTENDED: _____

NAME OF COURSE: _____

PRESENTED BY (company, school): _____

DATES ATTENDED: _____

NAME OF COURSE: _____

PRESENTED BY (company, school): _____

DATES ATTENDED: _____

NAME OF COURSE: _____

PRESENTED BY (company, school): _____

DATES ATTENDED: _____

NAME OF COURSE: _____

PRESENTED BY (company, school): _____

DATES ATTENDED: _____

■ ■ ■ KEYWORDS ■ ■ ■

❑ Keyword:_____
   ❑ Synonym:_____
   ❑ Synonym:_____

❑ Keyword:_____
   ❑ Synonym:_____
   ❑ Synonym:_____

❑ Keyword:_____
   ❑ Synonym:_____
   ❑ Synonym:_____

❑ Keyword:_____
   ❑ Synonym:_____
   ❑ Synonym:_____

❑ Keyword:_____
   ❑ Synonym:_____
   ❑ Synonym:_____

❑ Keyword:_____
   ❑ Synonym:_____
   ❑ Synonym:_____

❑ Keyword:_____
   ❑ Synonym:_____
   ❑ Synonym:_____

❑ Keyword:_____
   ❑ Synonym:_____
   ❑ Synonym:_____

❑ Keyword:_____
   ❑ Synonym:_____
   ❑ Synonym:_____

❑ Keyword:_____
   ❑ Synonym:_____
   ❑ Synonym:_____

❑ Keyword:_____
   ❑ Synonym:_____
   ❑ Synonym:_____

❑ Keyword:_____
   ❑ Synonym:_____
   ❑ Synonym:_____

❑ Keyword:_____
   ❑ Synonym:_____
   ❑ Synonym:_____

❑ Keyword:_____
   ❑ Synonym:_____
   ❑ Synonym:_____

❑ Keyword:_____
   ❑ Synonym:_____
   ❑ Synonym:_____

❑ Keyword:_____
   ❑ Synonym:_____
   ❑ Synonym:_____

❑ Keyword:_____
   ❑ Synonym:_____
   ❑ Synonym:_____

❑ Keyword:_____
   ❑ Synonym:_____
   ❑ Synonym:_____

❑ Keyword:_____
   ❑ Synonym:_____
   ❑ Synonym:_____

❑ Keyword:_____
   ❑ Synonym:_____
   ❑ Synonym:_____

❑ Keyword:_____
   ❑ Synonym:_____
   ❑ Synonym:_____

❑ Keyword:_____
   ❑ Synonym:_____
   ❑ Synonym:_____

❑ Keyword:_____
   ❑ Synonym:_____
   ❑ Synonym:_____

❑ Keyword:_____
   ❑ Synonym:_____
   ❑ Synonym:_____

■ ■ ■ EXPERIENCE—JOB NO._____ ■ ■ ■
Print a copy of this page for each job you have held.

JOB TITLE:

NAME OF EMPLOYER:

CITY / STATE / COUNTRY:

DATE STARTED: | DATE ENDED:

SUMMARY SENTENCE (The overall scope of your responsibility, overview of your essential role in the company, kind of products or services for which you were responsible):

_____

_____

_____

NUMBER OF PEOPLE SUPERVISED AND THEIR TITLES OR FUNCTIONS:

_____

_____

DESCRIPTION OF RESPONSIBILITIES (Don't forget budget, hiring, training, operations, strategic planning, new business development, production, customer service, sales, marketing, advertising, etc.):

_____

_____

_____

_____

_____

_____

_____

_____

_____

_____

ACCOMPLISHMENTS (Leave this section blank until Step 6 in Chapter 2):

_____

_____

_____

_____

_____

_____

_____

_____

■ ■ ■ Related Qualifications ■ ■ ■

AFFILIATIONS (Professional Associations, Chambers of Commerce, Toastmasters, etc.):

_____

_____

_____

LANGUAGES—With levels of proficiency: **Fluent** (absolute ability, native), **Highly Proficient** (3 to 5 years of usage in the country), **Proficient** (able to understand the subtleties of the language), **Working Knowledge** (can conduct everyday business), **Knowledge** (exposure to the language, courtesy phases)

_____

_____

_____

LICENSES:

_____

_____

_____

CERTIFICATIONS:

_____

_____

_____

CREDENTIALS:

_____

_____

_____

PRESENTATIONS / SPEECHES (Title, Meeting, Sponsoring Organization, City, State, Year):

_____

_____

PUBLICATIONS (Authors, Article Title, Publication Title, Volume, Issue, Page Numbers, Date):

_____

_____

GRANTS:

_____

_____

_____

■ ■ ■ RELATED QUALIFICATIONS ■ ■ ■

SPECIAL PROJECTS:

_____

_____

RESEARCH:

_____

_____

UNIQUE SKILLS:

_____

_____

VOLUNTEER ACTIVITIES, COMMUNITY BOARDS, CIVIC CONTRIBUTIONS:

_____

_____

_____

HONORS, AWARDS, DISTINCTIONS, PROFESSIONAL RECOGNITION:

_____

_____

COMPUTERS:

Applications (MS Word, Excel, PowerPoint, Outlook, etc.)

Operating Systems (Windows, Macintosh, UNIX, etc.)

Databases (Access, Oracle, etc.)

Programming Languages

Software Tools

Computer Networking

Communications

Hardware

OTHER RELEVANT SKILLS:

Actors (singing, dancing, musical instruments, martial arts, etc.)

Administrative Assistants (typing speed, office equipment)

Welders (TIG, MIG, ARC, etc.)

INTERNATIONAL (travel, living, cross-cultural skills, etc.)

_____

_____

■ ■ ■ OTHER RELATED QUALIFICATIONS ■ ■ ■

_____
_____
_____
_____
_____
_____
_____
_____
_____
_____
_____
_____
_____
_____
_____
_____
_____
_____
_____
_____
_____
_____
_____
_____
_____
_____
_____
_____
_____
_____
_____
_____
_____
_____
_____
_____
_____
_____
_____
_____
_____

■ ■ ■ PROFILE / SUMMARY ■ ■ ■

Keep the qualifications profile short, sweet, and to the point. I tend to limit them to five or six bullets, although there are exceptions to this rule when creating a curriculum vitae or other types of professional résumés. I'll give you a few extra places to list that information if you need a longer profile, but try to use no more than six of the blanks.

You can title this section with any of the following headlines: Profile, Qualifications, Highlights of Qualifications, Expertise, Strengths, Summary, Synopsis, Background, Professional Background, Executive Summary, Highlights, Overview, Professional Overview, Capsule, or Keyword Profile.

OBJECTIVE / FOCUS (This can become the first sentence of your profile or stand alone as a section or title):

_____

_____

_____

SECOND SENTENCE (Areas of expertise):

_____

_____

_____

STRENGTHS:

_____

_____

_____

STRENGTHS:

_____

_____

_____

STRENGTHS:

_____

_____

_____

STRENGTHS:

_____

_____

_____

_____

■ ■ ■ REFERENCES ■ ■ ■

Unless an advertisement specifically requests references, don't send them with your résumé. Type a nice list of three to six references on the same letterhead as your résumé to take with you to the interview. Use this form to collect the information for your reference list. Choose people who know how you work and are not just personal friends or family members.

NAME
RELATIONSHIP TO YOU
COMPANY
MAILING ADDRESS
CITY / STATE / ZIP

WORK PHONE	CELL PHONE
HOME PHONE	E-MAIL

NAME
RELATIONSHIP TO YOU
COMPANY
MAILING ADDRESS
CITY / STATE / ZIP

WORK PHONE	CELL PHONE
HOME PHONE	E-MAIL

NAME
RELATIONSHIP TO YOU
COMPANY
MAILING ADDRESS
CITY / STATE / ZIP

WORK PHONE	CELL PHONE
HOME PHONE	E-MAIL

NAME
RELATIONSHIP TO YOU
COMPANY
MAILING ADDRESS
CITY / STATE / ZIP

WORK PHONE	CELL PHONE
HOME PHONE	E-MAIL

NAME
RELATIONSHIP TO YOU
COMPANY
MAILING ADDRESS
CITY / STATE / ZIP

WORK PHONE	CELL PHONE
HOME PHONE	E-MAIL

Index of
Job Titles

Chapter

21

How many times have you wished for a line or two to describe something you did in a job long ago or even just yesterday? If you are like me, it happens all the time. Unless you can get your hands on the actual job description for your position, finding the words to tell someone in a few short sentences what your duties were or what you accomplished is one of the hardest parts of writing a résumé.

That is what makes this index different from other résumé books. Instead of listing only the titles from the objectives of all the résumés in this book, it lists every job that every résumé mentions. That means you can turn to a page that has been referenced in the index and find wording somewhere in that résumé that applies to a specific job title. Sometimes it will be only one or two lines. Other times the entire résumé will be devoted to it. This should assist you in coming up with words to describe the various jobs you have performed in the past.

How to Write Better Résumés and Cover Letters, 2nd Edition

Pat Criscito, CPRW

Résumés that catch a prospective employer's eye are attractive to look at and easy to read. Author Pat Criscito presents a fail-safe 12-step process for producing that perfect résumé in both paper and electronic formats. Also important are the accompanying cover letters, and again, Criscito shows how to create a dynamic letter that stands out from the crowd. She includes scores of model résumés to inspire job seekers.

Paperback, ISBN 978-0-3917-8, $16.99, *Can$19.99*

100+ Winning Answers to the Toughest Interview Questions, 2nd Edition

Casey Hawley, M.A.

What do you tell a job interviewer when he asks about your background, and you know you have less experience than other job candidates? The author approaches this and other tough questions with solid advice. General tips that apply to all interview questions entail giving answers that ring true, answers that are direct and without hesitation, and answers that don't meander, but speak precisely to the questions the interviewer asks.

Paperback, ISBN 978-0-7641-3912-3, $8.99, *Can$10.99*

Interview Answers in a Flash

Pat Criscito, CPRW, and Dee Funkhouser

This book—each page in the form of a Q & A flashcard—offers ideal preparation for that big interview. Questions likely to be asked by an interviewer are printed on one side, with proven answers printed on the reverse. The book is designed so that pages can be pulled out, selected and shuffled according to need, and used as flashcards for practice. Category questions include:

- Work and Education questions (What have you done?)
- Skills and Competencies questions (What can you do?)
- Personality/Goals questions (Who are you?)
- Behavioral/Situational questions (Can you tell a story?)
- Job Fit questions (Are you a match?)
- Torture/Trick questions (Can you take the heat?)

The reverse side of each card tells why the question is asked, presents sample responses, and allows space to customize an answer.

Paperback, ISBN 978-0-7641-3331-2, $12.99, *Can$15.99*

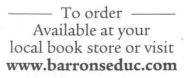